Choosing Yiddish

Choosing Yiddish

NEW FRONTIERS OF LANGUAGE AND CULTURE

Edited by

Lara Rabinovitch, Shiri Goren,
and Hannah S. Pressman

WAYNE STATE UNIVERSITY PRESS   DETROIT

17 16 15 14 13   5 4 3 2 1

Library of Congress Cataloging-in-Publication Data

Choosing Yiddish : new frontiers of language and culture / edited by Lara Rabinovitch, Shiri Goren, and Hannah S. Pressman.
    p. cm.
  Includes bibliographical references and index.
  ISBN 978-0-8143-3444-7 (pbk. : alk. paper) — ISBN 978-0-8143-3799-8 (ebook)
  1. Yiddish language—Social aspects.   2. Yiddish literature—History and criticism.   I. Rabinovitch, Lara, 1979–   II. Goren, Shiri, 1976–   III. Pressman, Hannah S., 1979–
  PJ5113.C46 2012
  439′.1—dc23
                                                                2012015788

♾

Designed by Angie Sheltz
Typeset by Newgen North America
Composed in Feijoa Medium and Whitney
Cover art by Joseph Remnant

CONTENTS

YIDDISH AND THE CITY

YIDDISH GOES POP

YIDDISH COMES TO AMERICA

ACKNOWLEDGMENTS

Befitting the nature of Yiddish studies today, *Choosing Yiddish: New Frontiers of Language and Culture* has evolved thanks to the work of numerous people from various disciplines, institutions, and locations around the world. Many have helped in small but instrumental ways.

Above all we are grateful to our home department at New York University, the Skirball Department of Hebrew and Judaic Studies, for providing us with much of the intellectual and financial means to see this project to fruition. Specifically, we thank Lawrence Schiffman, chair of the department during much of the period of this book's production, and his successor, David Engel, who also offered his support and wisdom as we undertook the tricky task of coediting a volume with so many contributors from diverse fields. We are also grateful to Gennady Estraikh, who not only was the impetus behind the Yiddish/Jewish Cultures symposium in 2006, which ultimately served as the inspiration for this book, but also served as a constant source of guidance on this project. Hasia Diner and two past Dorot faculty fellows in the department also directly helped shape this project: Tony Michels and Josh Lambert, both also contributors to *Choosing Yiddish*, shared their insight at crucial moments in the book's development. In addition, we thank Karolina Szymaniak for inspiring this book's title and Nancy Sinkoff, Judah Cohen, Ilana Szobel, Olga Gershenson, Ziv Eisenberg, Jeff Newelt, and Shayne Figueroa for their creative advice and support. We are grateful for the warm enthusiasm and judicious comments we received from them and others along the way.

Kathryn Wildfong, our editor at Wayne State University Press, has been a tireless supporter of this project. Her confidence in us, especially as we charted an unconventional approach, gave us the freedom to structure *Choosing Yiddish* in the way that we believe best reflects the scope of the field today. We owe our gratitude to her, not least of all for her insightful criticism, and to Maya Rhodes, Kristina Elizabeth Stonehill, Emily Nowak, Carrie Downes Teefey, and the rest of the staff at Wayne State for shepherding this book with such professionalism and grace.

We are also incredibly grateful for the careful work of our copyeditors Kelly Burch and Mimi Braverman, and we express our thanks to Anna Verschik for her assistance overseeing the Yiddish transliterations in our book.

Although we are often told not to judge a book by its cover, much thought went into visually conceptualizing what *Choosing Yiddish* has to offer. We are grateful to Oliver Noble for providing the initial inspiration for our cover art and to Joseph Remnant for creating it.

Lastly, though not least of all, *a hartsiken dank* to our respective families for their tremendous support throughout the various stages of this project and for their love and patience.

Lara Rabinovitch, Shiri Goren, and Hannah S. Pressman

FOREWORD

Yiddish Studies: Toward a Twenty-First-Century Mandate

BARBARA KIRSHENBLATT-GIMBLETT

It is now commonplace that as the number of native speakers of Yiddish declines, with the exception of the ultra-Orthodox, academic interest in Yiddish increases. As many have noted, this situation has profound implications for how Yiddish is taught and studied in the academy; most students now come to the subject with no connection to a Yiddish milieu or native speaker.

Two tropes persist: according to the first trope, Yiddish is dead. The rejoinders range from Isaac Bashevis Singer's quip "There's a big difference between 'dead' and 'dying'"[1] to Dov-Ber Kerler's comment that Yiddish may be waning as a mother tongue, but that is no reason to "bury it alive."[2] One of the first full responses to this trope is Jeffrey Shandler's 2005 book *Adventures in Yiddishland: Postvernacular Language and Culture*.[3] According to the second trope—whether Yiddish is dead or alive—Yiddish studies is ideological, or has been until very recently. Contrary to the second trope, we are now, to most everyone's relief, in the postideological period of Yiddish studies. That said, how does one envision a field whose language is said to be dead and the study of which has been damned for so long by fear of its ideological investments? During the past fifteen years, there has been considerable reflection on these questions. *Choosing Yiddish: New Frontiers of Language and Culture* is not only the latest contribution to these debates but also the first to offer in one volume the new and diverse approaches that now characterize the field, reconceptualized for a new generation.[4]

To study Yiddish is, it could be said, never neutral, notwithstanding the worthy goal of dispassionate study, because languages are by their very nature highly charged phenomena even after the best efforts to purge them of their politics.

Nowhere is this clearer than in the case of Yiddish studies, in which the language becomes a proxy for its absent speakers. More than a century after the first international Yiddish conference (Czernowitz [Cernauti], 1908) and more than sixty-five years after the world's largest Yiddish-speaking community was murdered, the politicization of Yiddish and Yiddish studies has reappeared as a burning issue. There is of course no field without its politics. Yiddish continues to be a language in contest, a legacy of the competing efforts to make the language an instrument of its own disappearance, on the one hand, and a national language in its own right, on the other.

Consider the political contexts of post-Holocaust Yiddish studies. For scholars in and from the former Soviet Union, their historical experience of ideologically overdetermined scholarship makes them particularly sensitive to anything that smacks of "ideology," which, in the case of Yiddish, is first and foremost Yiddishism. For scholars working in Israel, it was not until Yiddish as a first language was less of a threat to the project of making modern Hebrew the national language of the Jewish state that a chair in Yiddish studies could be established at the Hebrew University in 1947.[5] The first choice for that chair was Max Weinreich, who decided to stay in New York, the headquarters of the YIVO (Yidisher visnshaftlekher institut) Institute for Jewish Research after 1939. Yiddish studies at Oxford University, in Vilna, at Ohio State University, and elsewhere can be said to be animated by a passionate commitment to the language as a subject of study, a medium of scholarship, and an arena of contemporary literary and artistic creativity.[6] In the United States, where a higher proportion of Jewish students are attracted to the language than elsewhere, the fear is that Yiddish will not be taken seriously if it is seen as a variety of ethnic studies; the anxiety persists that students will come to Yiddish on a quest for their roots rather than as serious scholars and that the field will be partisan and parochial as a result.

What strikes me as I survey the Yiddish studies landscape of the past fifteen years is the intensity with which the politics of the language and the field has come not only into focus but also under attack. Even to advocate for the language is seen as making contestable claims for its importance. That said, there is palpable relief at the thought that the postideological period might bring with it the dispassionate study of Yiddish language, literature, and culture. Interestingly this development comes at a time in the academy when several other fields have put forward a model of engaged scholarship and actively pressed for recognition and resources.[7]

Nonetheless, the question persists: Why Yiddish? We do not ask, Why English? Why French? Why German? Nor do the departments devoted to these fields generally have to defend the worthiness of the languages and literatures they study, although they do have to defend themselves on other grounds, particularly in these times of scarce resources. Yes, Yiddish has gained ground in the academy, but the question remains: "Why does Yiddish continue to be marginal?"—to Jewish studies and to all the departmental nests in which this cuckoo's egg has been laid. Will this be the fate of Yiddish—a language on the defensive—for the foreseeable future?

A holistic approach to the subject of Yiddish studies would have the virtue of bringing work in disciplines historically marginal to Jewish studies into the center of the field. As Yiddish studies is configured today—and Jewish studies as well—fields such as anthropology, sociology, linguistics, theater studies, art history, and ethnomusicology are marginal to Yiddish and Jewish studies, while Jewish topics are at the same time marginal to those fields. Precisely because the disciplinary configuration of the field is not given in advance, Yiddish studies need not be driven by any one discipline but rather by their interaction. This is one of the potential strengths of area studies and indeed of *Choosing Yiddish*, even though most area studies fields are still dominated by language, literature, and history.

Similarly, a field organized around the idea of Ashkenaz would, by definition, be more holistic because it would encompass the totality of the languages (not only Yiddish) and cultural expressions of Jews within the historically defined Ashkenazi culture area and its diasporic extension. Ashkenaz as an organizing framework for the field in the twenty-first century would be less determined by language, though languages (and the history of their politics) are central to the endeavor, and the study of Yiddish might be differently configured were it not aligned with the institutionalization of national languages and literatures, which for Yiddish usually means German, Slavic, or Near Eastern languages. Interestingly, the literature fields, especially comparative literature, have been moving in a cultural studies direction that may be more or less interdisciplinary (if simply an extension of literary analysis to nonliterary phenomena). Ashkenaz as an organizing idea, as I envision it, is *not* an extension of Yiddish literary studies in a cultural studies direction but rather a way to broaden the domain of culture across a variety of media and hierarchies. An Ashkenazi culture area approach would provide contexts for Yiddish *in addition to* and *other than* Jewish studies proper and the various language departments in which the field is generally embedded. *Choosing Yiddish: New Frontiers of Language and Culture* signals an emerging conceptual reorganization of the field while building on the best tradition of Yiddish studies as a field.

Notes

1. "The Yiddish Voice/DOS YIDISHE KOL," WUNR 1600 AM/Brookline, MA, accessed June 22, 2012, http://www.yv.org.
2. Dov-Ber Kerler, "On the Politics of Yiddish," in *The Politics of Yiddish* (Lanham, MD: Alta-Mira, 1998), 1–8, 3.
3. Jeffrey Shandler, *Adventures in Yiddishland: Postvernacular Language and Culture* (Berkeley: University of California Press, 2005).

4. There are numerous surveys, guides, and assessments of the present state of the field, including Cecile Kuznitz's excellent article on Yiddish studies for *The Oxford Handbook for Jewish Studies* and autobiographical or personal accounts of a scholar's engagement with the field (Ruth Wisse, David Roskies, Anita Norich, and others), yet *Choosing Yiddish* pushes Yiddish studies into the twenty-first century. Anita Norich, "On the Yiddish Question," in *Mapping Jewish Identities*, ed. Laurence J. Silberstein (New York: New York University Press, 2000), 145–58; David G. Roskies, "Yiddish Studies and the Jewish Search for a Usable Past," in *Yiddish in the Contemporary World: Papers of the First Mendel Friedman International Conference on Yiddish* ed. Gennady Estraikh and Mikhail Krutikov (Oxford: Legenda, 1999); Ruth R. Wisse, "Yiddish: Past, Present, Imperfect," *Commentary* 104, no. 5 (1997): 32–39.

5. Avraham Novershtern, "Between Town and Gown: The Institutionalization of Yiddish at Israeli Universities," *Yiddish in the Contemporary World*, 2–10.

6. Kerler, "On the Politics of Yiddish," 5.

7. This tendency is clearest in such postdisciplinary formations as cultural studies, critical race studies, and gender studies but also occurs in area studies, in which postcolonial theory has played an especially important role. The social sciences have a long history of engaged scholarship. Anthropologists in particular have taken a serious look at their relationship to those they studied in the past and those to whom they are accountable today. Perhaps most applicable to Yiddish studies is the way in which language and literature departments have been reconfiguring the national language model.

A NOTE ON TRANSLITERATION

This book necessarily includes many transliterations of various foreign languages. We have attempted in all cases to provide clear, accessible, phonetically accurate renderings of non-English words. Transliterations of Yiddish have been rendered according to the YIVO Standard. Transliterations of Hebrew have followed a modified version of the Encyclopaedia Judaica rules. In Hebrew transliterations we have used ḥ for the Hebrew letter *ḥet,* kh for the Hebrew letter *khaf,* and *tz* for the Hebrew letter *tzadi.*

INTRODUCTION

LARA RABINOVITCH, SHIRI GOREN, AND HANNAH S. PRESSMAN

Someone choosing Yiddish today for a routine ATM transaction, as drawn on our cover, might strike you as incongruous, yet the real and metaphorical notions of Yiddish currency lie at the heart of our endeavor in this volume. In the sense of its circulation in academia and in the sense of its relevance and prevalence at this moment in time, the currency of Yiddish is undeniable. Early in the twenty-first century, Yiddish increasingly functions as an important form and forum of exchange in the marketplace of ideas, and the revived study of Yiddish language and culture represents one of the most innovative shifts in the academy today.

Choosing Yiddish: New Frontiers of Language and Culture highlights an international generation of scholars currently revitalizing the field of Yiddish studies. Scholars choosing Yiddish at the beginning of the twenty-first century take advantage of the latest interpretive paradigms and theoretical approaches and place Yiddish on the cutting edge of interdisciplinary innovation. This currency of Yiddish allows young academics to expand their research and teaching opportunities and traverse different disciplines and theoretical pursuits. Thus, the emerging scholars who come together in this book, as well as the subjects they have chosen, are all, in a sense, making transactions with and through Yiddish. It is precisely their choice of Yiddish that enables these new research directions to develop today, marking a new stage in the history of this field.

The academic study of Yiddish language and culture formally began soon after the turn of the twentieth century, most notably with the 1925 establishment of the YIVO Institute for Jewish Research. Its original impulse lay in modern Jewish nation building, and the founders of YIVO created a variety of projects and programs to suit this new endeavor. To a certain extent, the academic arm of this initiative, like today's, boasted a multidisciplinary approach, for its methodologies included linguistics, ethnography, history, literature, and folklore, even as they were driven by Yiddishist ideology. A similar ideologically driven approach characterized the rich development of Yiddish literary and cultural output in the Soviet Union, particularly during the 1920s and 1930s and, later, though to a lesser extent, under Nikita Khrushchev in the 1960s. Communist rule in Russia formalized Yiddish studies from an early age and inspired Internationalists around the world to partake in its development from afar.[1] These ideological impulses, whereby Yiddish was to serve as the language of the Jewish nation in the multinational world, continued to drive the field into the second half of the twentieth century, following the seismic shift of the center of world Jewry in the immediate years after the Holocaust.

In the preface to the watershed 1954 publication *The Field of Yiddish*, linguist Uriel Weinreich painted a vivid picture of the postwar Yiddish studies landscape. Announcing the volume as "a much needed fresh start," he invoked "the German massacre of the larger part of Yiddish-speaking Jewry," including the first generation of Yiddish studies scholars in Europe.[2] Following in the footsteps of his eminent father, Max, Weinreich envisioned the field's mandate as centered on linguistics and literature, adopting an ideology of "Yiddish for the sake of Yiddish." Although the world had been upturned, seminal Yiddishists such as Weinreich continued to view the language and culture, and the study thereof, as the means through which to revive the Jewish nation. Such rhetoric reflected this catastrophic historical moment as well as the original ideologies of the discipline that had taken root in prior decades, as Yiddishism took its place amid the rapidly acculturating, modernizing, nationalizing, and migrating European Jewry.

Dovetailing the growth of Jewish studies as an academic field of study, Yiddish studies, as it came to be known, developed in new directions when it began, slowly, to enter mainstream academia in the United States and, to a lesser extent, in other, smaller centers in Europe and the Americas.[3] This inspired projects such as the *Language and Culture Atlas of Ashkenazic Jewry*, initiated in 1959[4]; the 1961 establishment of *Sovietish Heimland*; and the creation of intensive Yiddish language courses and curricula such as those of YIVO's Max Weinreich Center for Advanced Jewish studies in 1968. However, Yiddish studies in these decades continued within the established prewar paradigm, favoring literary, ethnographic, and linguistic methodologies, even as the historical context changed and the ideological ramifications of this field of study diminished.

Choosing Yiddish: New Frontiers of Language and Culture comprises a renewed international engagement with Yiddish studies and expands on its originally innovative and interdisciplinary reach. One of our central contentions is that Yiddish, always a border-crossing language, has continually pushed the boundaries of vigorous disciplinary exchange.

Inspired by the vast reach of Yiddish as a historical lingua franca for millions and by its consequently rich areas for research, scholars today increasingly choose Yiddish. Their decision to study the Yiddish language and research its range of cultural and historical output from the perspective of multiple disciplines represents a new stage in the development of this field. With the exception of some ultra-Orthodox communities, the language is no longer a vernacular, no longer the "kitchen Yiddish" Anita Norich and Barbara Mann describe when they explain their relationships to the language.[5] The ability to consciously choose to learn this language and work with it, not as an ideological or nationally driven enterprise but as a subject of scholarly inquiry, is a recent phenomenon. Indeed the majority of the scholars who have contributed to this book are not native speakers of Yiddish but rather have embarked on studying it only as adults. In these ways, *Choosing Yiddish* emerges out of the "post-Golden Chain,"[6] "postvernacular"[7] moment in Yiddish studies and reflects on it simultaneously.

Whether the latest crop of Yiddish scholars represents a fully postideological endeavor, as some have claimed,[8] remains to be determined. However, the ideological spectrum of debates surrounding Yiddish has changed, and the field represents a different and evolving set of motivations, particularly as newer generations of scholars choose to engage with the language and further the revival of Yiddish as an instrument of academic research. Thus the essays gathered here help to reveal the issues at stake—ideological or otherwise—as the field continues to develop. No single book has yet captured the diverse reach of Yiddish studies today, or even more recently than half a century ago, and no book until *Choosing Yiddish* has commented on this self-reflexively, particularly from an academic perspective. This volume thereby captures a reinvigorated field at the turn of the twenty-first century by focusing on newer generations of scholars choosing Yiddish today.

In some ways Yiddish has always been a matter of choice, for it has rarely stood alone as a spoken or written tongue. Rather, it interacts with other languages, and the cultural output of Yiddish reflects that exchange. Several noteworthy scholars have described the ways in which the Yiddish language constitutes a borrowing, shifting, fusing, and "plurisignifying"[9] mix within its diasporic, multilingual settings.[10] Perhaps for this reason, Yiddish studies emerged out of the interstices of several disciplines.

Unlike some other fields—but like the language itself—Yiddish studies developed as a hybrid that depended on, and continues to affect, other fields. Arguably, the humanities have finally caught up to what was implicit in Yiddish studies from the beginning: the languages and cultures and histories we study are always, to quote Weinreich's title, "in contact."[11] The innovative structure of this book reflects the extent to which Yiddish scholarship today defies conventional disciplinary boundaries or even the traditional thematic divisions within Jewish studies.

The creative engagements with Yiddish in this volume, therefore, demand a division other than the standard demarcations into literature, history, and culture that might be expected in an edited collection. For this reason, we designed groupings, or rubrics, that we believe best allow the gathered authors to be "in contact" with each other. If *Choosing Yiddish* showcases the ways in which current research on Yiddish is creating a new conversation in both academic and popular settings, then our rubric arrangement most effectively accommodates the reach and possibilities of the field of Yiddish studies today.

Each rubric includes within its essays shared methodological approaches, thematics, or geographical concerns. Introductions by scholars who have elsewhere made significant contributions to the field foreground each rubric and foster a conversation between the research highlighted in each essay and the greater methodological questions raised by the rubric grouping.

Still, the rubric arrangement amounts only to a suggested order for clustered reading and not a stative structure. As readers will discover, several links exist between and among the different sections of this book. We only suggest certain ways to map the reading. That we could have organized the rubrics in many different ways attests to the multidisciplinary energy of the field of Yiddish studies.

The selected essays in *Choosing Yiddish* amount to some of the most exciting research directions in the marketplace of Yiddish studies today. At the same time, this volume does not claim to represent the field definitively or exclusively. To that end, there are certain subjects that do not, at first glance, find representation in the rubric headings. For example, although readers might expect a section on Yiddish and the Holocaust, we have chosen not to create such a rubric. This decision stems from our efforts to rethink the traditional thematic divisions of Jewish studies and, specifically, to avoid the teleological claim of citing the Holocaust for the end of Yiddish. Thus we have chosen not to pigeonhole this colossal event into an arbitrary category that would also not do justice to the historical trajectory of the language and culture of Yiddish. Instead numerous—if not most—essays throughout the collection address, both directly and indirectly, the impact of the Holocaust on the development and decline of Yiddish as a vernacular language. By the same token, this volume does not feature studies that focus on many of the so-called canonical Yiddish writers. Indeed, the most current scholarship in the field today often directly challenges canonical constructs.

In these ways *Choosing Yiddish* demonstrates in its very structure how Yiddish studies forces us to rethink not only the dimensions of this field, or Jewish studies more broadly, but also the greater divisions in our understanding of the humanities and social sciences. Thus although the number of native Yiddish speakers around the world continues to diminish, as a lingual and cultural field of study, Yiddish continues not only to grow but also to push academic scholarship in new directions.

Despite the diversity of approaches and topics, each essay considers the question of Yiddish within the context of its particular subject matter. The unifying theme—if there can be a unifying theme across such a diverse collection of essays—is that Yiddish has been and continues to be used to convey a wide array of expressions and emotions. As the essays in this volume demonstrate, Yiddish is an integral part of diverse cultural productions emerging from numerous arenas and geographies: from early twentieth-century Yiddish publications in Buenos Aires or Hasidic women's singing in New York City today to less known Yiddish literary works from European and Israeli writers or secular school textbooks in Montreal. A number of essays in this book focus on the decision by key individuals—political leaders, writers, educators—to choose Yiddish, even when some of them did not grow up speaking the language or possessed only rudimentary skills before actively pursuing the language as a means of cultural or social output. In that sense, the collective decision of this new generation of scholars to choose Yiddish may be understood as echoing their subject matter's choice to engage with this language.

The opening rubric, "Writing on the Edge," focuses on the realm of belles lettres. This grouping presents three cases of productive engagement with Yiddish to convey transgressed, emotionally charged, or suppressed content. The subjects illustrate the extent to which scholars are choosing to move beyond the canonical and popular writers of Yiddish literature in order to explore the more marginal writers and themes of the Yiddish world. Anita Norich's introduction considers the concept of "edginess" and contextualizes these essays within long-standing tensions in Yiddish culture.

Dara Horn's essay closely examines the consequences of storytelling in the work of the Berdychiv-born Yiddish writer Der Nister. Unpacking Der Nister's elaborate plot structures, Horn argues that the early twentieth-century writer developed what amounted to an entirely new self-contained mythology that destroyed the foundational idea of redemption that had motivated almost all of modern Yiddish prose before him.

Shiri Goren calls our attention to a powerful choice to write in Yiddish in a different historical context. Goren focuses on the singular Yiddish prose produced by the Hebrew writer David Vogel while in hiding in southeastern France during World War II. In her essay, Goren explores the significance of Vogel's decision to write this fictionalized autobiographical manuscript in his native tongue, even though he had only written and published in Hebrew and German until that momentous and ultimately catastrophic point.

As Jordan Finkin explores in his research on the underappreciated Yiddish genre of Sacco-Vanzetti poems, Yiddish writers could exist on the "edge" yet still use the language as a means of partaking in greater American political conversations. Accused and executed, despite shaky evidence, for supposed involvement in an armed robbery and murder, Nicola Sacco and Bartolomeo Vanzetti, Italian immigrants and anarchists, formed a cause célèbre in American society. Finkin argues that Yiddish poets staked their claim in the left-wing American political and cultural landscape writ large with a series of works inspired by the mishandled case. Taken together, the illuminating essays by Finkin, Goren, and Horn outline the transgressive function and impact of Yiddish in the works of these creative writers.

The rubric "Yiddish and the City" spans the urban centers of New York City, Paris, Buenos Aires, and Montreal to suggest some of the ways in which Yiddish language and culture developed in the urban context. As Gennady Estraikh argues in his introduction, the authors included in this rubric explore the ways in which Yiddish functioned as a vital part of the Jewish cultural and political life of the urban sphere, even as it reached temporally and geographically beyond the city.

Tony Michels calls attention to Jewish intellectuals in the United States of the early twentieth century who chose to learn and use Yiddish for the purposes of education, political agitation, or creative writing, reversing the trend of intellectuals moving away from the particularized language. Referring to this trend as "Yiddishization," Michels argues that politics and commerce played a central role in encouraging Jewish intellectuals to use Yiddish in America, altering the negative valence previously associated with the language in intellectual contexts.

By looking at the Polish-Jewish press in Paris, Gerben Zaagsma further develops the notion of Yiddish serving as a tool, in this case political and social, across boundaries. Zaagsma focuses on the Spanish Civil War as reported in Paris's *Naye Prese,* a communist newspaper mainly intended for Polish-Jewish immigrants in France. Through this case study Zaagsma uncovers some of the ways in which the Yiddish press functioned as a rich venue for political discourse on issues simultaneously close to home and abroad on the Spanish front.

Rebecca Kobrin also focuses on the Yiddish output of Polish immigrants, but in Buenos Aires and New York City. Using both transnational and comparative frameworks, Kobrin examines key *landsmanshaft* publications to suggest how Polish-Jewish immigrants articulated new conceptions of Polonia in the post–World War I era following the establishment of the new Polish state.

Finally, Rebecca Margolis taps into the similarly untraditional body of source material of school textbooks, curricula, and student literary endeavors to examine the unique Yiddish *shuln* of Montreal in the first half of the twentieth century. This divided French-English city demonstrated an unusual attachment to the Yiddish language and its cultural output, a connection nurtured in its long-lasting Yiddish school network.

In "Yiddish Goes Pop" three essays explore the role of Yiddish in mediating between artistic vision and popular culture in various media. Jeffrey Shandler provides a provocative introduction foregrounding the reading of the diverse essays in this rubric.

Through an analysis of the American Jewish critic and translator Isaac Goldberg, Josh Lambert addresses the idea of obscene Yiddish. Lambert argues that Yiddish in particular allowed a measure of freedom unknown to the English language because of the lax censorship guidelines surrounding its publication in the early twentieth century.

The transgressive function of Yiddish carried over into several forms of popular cultural consumption. Zehavit Stern illustrates the ways in which Yiddish film melodrama of the 1930s portrayed and subverted Jewish femininity through the figures of mothers and daughters. Stern focuses on the recurring plot of the reversed mother-daughter relationship on the silver screen to suggest how these films criticized ideologies surrounding Jewish womanhood.

Whereas the first two contributors to this rubric address Yiddish popular culture historically, Anna Shternshis examines recent and contemporary post-Soviet-Jewish culture. Shternshis points to the use of Yiddish in Russian performances today and argues that through this application of the language and culture, three mainstream Russian musicians evoke nostalgia for a romanticized Soviet and Jewish past.

"Yiddish Comes to America" focuses on the history and growth of Yiddish in the United States. As the lingua franca for an overwhelming number of immigrant Jews, Yiddish language and culture developed and transformed in the United States throughout the era of mass migration in particular, as Hasia Diner argues in her prelude to this rubric.

The Yiddish press helped develop and capture this journey, as Edward Portnoy shows by uncovering an 1876 Jewish murder case. Although it remains forgotten in much of American Jewish historiography, this sensationalized event represented, at the time, the most significant interface between Jews and the American media in the history of the country. Whereas the Yiddish and American non-Jewish press devoted great attention to the case, the English Jewish press chose to ignore it, suggesting the conflicting ways in which media outlets served as important vehicles of self-fashioning among differing and competing Jewish immigrant groups.

This idea of Yiddish migrating to America forms the subject of two essays in *Choosing Yiddish* on Max Weinreich, a central persona in the establishment of the academic field of Yiddish studies. Both essays focus on Weinreich's time in the United States to offer a reappraisal of his lifework. Jennifer Young examines Weinreich's 1932 trip to the Tuskegee Institute in Alabama, where he studied race relations. Young argues that this trip and Weinreich's time at Yale University's Institute of Human Relations that year helped him develop in 1935 a YIVO program in Europe directed toward Jewish youth with the hope of ensuring meaningful Jewish survival.

Five tumultuous years later, Weinreich arrived in New York City. Kalman Weiser focuses on this and YIVO's move during World War II and the years immediately following, when Weinreich and the institute's center migrated to New York City. This fraught development, Weiser argues, forced YIVO to reconsider its ideology, goals, and methods amid a changing world order.

Part of the changes in that world order included the rise of modern Hebrew amid the demise of spoken Yiddish throughout the twentieth century. From its inception as a language of literary output and political discourse, Yiddish (or Yiddishism) struggled with Hebrew (and Zionism) to serve as the national language of the Jewish people. The three pieces gathered in the rubric "Yiddish Encounters Hebrew" showcase the complex and intrinsic interactions between Yiddish and Hebrew during the late nineteenth century and the twentieth century.

As Ela Bauer's analysis shows, this clash played out earlier than is often perceived by looking at the early Hebrew newspapers of late nineteenth-century eastern Europe, *Hamelitz, Hatzefira,* and *Hamagid.* Bauer examines the ways in which Jewish intellectuals of the Russian Empire and Congress Poland argued, in Hebrew, over the place of *zhargon,* as Yiddish was known then, within the pages of these nationally oriented newspapers.

More than half a century later, the newly established State of Israel actively displaced Yiddish, even as it became a site for displaced Yiddish-speaking Holocaust survivors. Shachar Pinsker focuses on Yung Yisroel, a little-explored Yiddish literary group in Israel of the 1950s and 1960s. Through his examination of the lives and writings of its key players, Pinsker uncovers the ways in which Yung Yisroel prefigured later developments in Israeli literature, namely by engaging, even implicitly, with issues surrounding their own Holocaust experiences.

Adriana X. Jacobs also directs us to this theme in modern Hebrew writing by focusing on the twentieth-century Israeli poet Avot Yeshurun. Jacobs argues that Yeshurun employed Yiddish to engage questions of how Hebrew "fits" Yiddish through translation and other multilingual strategies. Ultimately, she suggests, Yeshurun's radical literary devices in relation to Yiddish subverted Israel's ethos of monolingualism and the rejection of the diaspora.

Bauer, Pinsker, and Jacobs engage centrally with the connection between language and space as it has played out in various Jewish political and cultural arenas during the recent past, as Barbara Mann points out in her prelude to this rubric. Impassioned debates on the function and status of Yiddish in the hierarchy of Jewish culture—regardless or in spite of geographic location—have always accompanied the language.

Traces of Yiddish appear in other unlikely places, some louder than others. The aural dimension of Yiddish in contemporary settings intrigued the scholars included in "Hear and Now." As Ari Y. Kelman stresses in his prelude to the rubric, in the postvernacular Yiddish world, listening becomes a premier form of interaction with Yiddish today. The three essays in this rubric point to the relationship between language and sound in cultural innovation at the start of the twenty-first century.

Sarah Bunin Benor focuses on contemporary linguistic practices of young American Jews and the way in which they exhibit significant new influences from Yiddish in their use of English, including words and grammatical constructions, with variations depending on religiosity and age. Using qualitative and quantitative research, Benor demonstrates how people today increasingly engage with Yiddish on mass levels, despite its demise as a spoken language.

Other forms of contemporary Yiddish studied in this volume include Ester-Basya (Asya) Vaisman's ethnographic research on Hasidic women's Yiddish songs. Vaisman argues not only that these songs have emerged within the past forty years but also that the styles and genres of the female song repertoire differ from the kinds of songs sung in previous generations, in contrast to male-centered *nigunim,* which remain largely unaltered by time.

Although the golden age of Yiddish cultural production has passed, Yiddish appears today in sites of creative cultural and geographic multilingualism. Perhaps it is no coincidence, then, that the internationally acclaimed hip-hop artist, SoCalled, is based in Montreal. SoCalled samples tracks from vintage Yiddish records, and, as Shayn E. Smulyan argues, his music probes the Jewish past even for audiences who, for the most part, neither understand the language nor share a common past. Smulyan explores the meaning of this artistic endeavor and its reception by closely analyzing Yiddish-dominant tracks within this artist's oeuvre.

By turning to Yiddish, by sampling its richness, all of the contributors in this volume call attention to previously overlooked areas and materials in order to gain a deeper understanding of Jewish cultural, political, and social life in the modern era. In some ways they continue the tradition of an innovative field ahead of its time, though without the ideological thrust of its forebears. Yet as we consider the choice to study Yiddish in the twenty-first century, it becomes clear that the range of scholarly approaches "in contact" throughout *Choosing Yiddish* reflects the breadth and diversity of an academic field still under construction. Furthermore, if Jeffrey Shandler has argued that the postvernacular mode "prompts us to rethink the possibilities of language,"[12] Yiddish studies in a postvernacular mode prompt us to consider not only the possibilities of this field but also the possibilities and potential of Yiddish studies as a paradigm for a language study field more broadly conceived.

We believe that the dynamic group of scholars gathered herein, along with many other voices emerging around the globe, will help shape the disciplinary debates about the Yiddish language and beyond for many years to come.

Notes

1. For more on the development of Yiddish studies in the Soviet Union, see Gennady Estraikh, *In Harness: Yiddish Writers' Romance with Communism* (Syracuse, NY: Syracuse University Press, 2005) and *Yiddish and the Cold War* (London: Legenda, 2008).
2. Uriel Weinreich, ed., *The Field of Yiddish: Studies in Yiddish Language, Folklore, and Literature* (New York: Linguistic Circle of New York, 1954), v.
3. See, for example, Ruth Wisse's preface to *The Modern Jewish Canon* (Chicago: Free Press, 2000), where she writes that, despite her great admiration of and exposure to Yiddish language and culture, when famed Yiddish poet Avrom Sutskever suggested in 1959 that she pursue Yiddish instead of English for her graduate studies, she laughed aloud.
4. Vera Baviskar, Marvin Herzog, and Uriel Weinreich, eds., *The Language and Culture Atlas of Ashkenazic Jewry* (New York: YIVO Institute for Jewish Research, 1992-1995).
5. Anita Norich, "On the Yiddish Question," in *Mapping Jewish Identities*, ed. Laurence Silberstein (New York: New York University Press, 2000), 145-58, 147; Barbara Mann, Prelude to "Yiddish Encounters Hebrew," in this volume, 253-54.
6. Gennady Estraikh, "Has the 'Golden Chain' Ended? Problems of Continuity in Yiddish Writing," in *Yiddish in the Contemporary World: Papers of the First Mendel Friedman International Conference on Yiddish*, ed. Gennady Estraikh and Mikhail Krutikov (Oxford: Legenda, 1999), 119-32, 129.
7. In using the term "postvernacular," we refer to the conception as put forth by Cecile Kuznitz and, soon after, Jeffrey Shandler. Cecile E. Kuznitz, "Yiddish Studies," in *The Oxford Handbook of Jewish Studies*, ed. Martin Goodman, Jeremy Cohen, and David Sorkin (New York: Oxford University Press, 2002), 541-71; Jeffrey Shandler, *Adventures in Yiddishland: Postvernacular Language and Culture* (Berkeley: University of California Press, 2005).
8. Kuznitz, "Yiddish Studies," 552.
9. Benjamin Harshav, *The Meaning of Yiddish* (Stanford: Stanford University Press, 1990), 36.
10. For more on this, see, for example, Joshua Fishman, ed., *Never Say Die! A Thousand Years of Yiddish in Jewish Life and Letters* (New York: Mouton de Gruyter, 1981); Harshav, *The Meaning of Yiddish*; Shandler, *Adventures in Yiddishland*; Weinreich, *The Field of Yiddish*.
11. Uriel Weinreich, *Languages in Contact: Findings and Problems* (New York, Linguistic Circle of New York, 1953).
12. Shandler, *Adventures in Yiddishland*, 31.

WRITING ON THE EDGE

Prelude

ANITA NORICH

These days, no one loves the edges and the edgy, the marginal and liminal, the modernist and the post- more than Yiddish scholars—and with good historical and cultural reason: given the current state of the publishing industry and academic job market, the stakes in claiming edginess are high. But the impulse is not only economic or self-serving. Scholars of Yiddish, like scholars and writers working *in* Yiddish, have long had a heightened sense of living and writing on the edge and of claiming newness. In the times and places in which Yiddish has flourished, Jewish history certainly gives us anguished justification for claiming to be always on the precipice, never fully at home, in a state of anxious waiting. Some of the major, if short-lived Yiddish literary movements of the twentieth century—Yung Vilne, Yung Yidish, Di khaliastre, Di yunge—lay claim to the vigor of youth, the intellectual excitement of the new, and the revolutionary potential in claiming no precedents or canon. In such claims, they keep excellent company with the concepts and declarations of European and American modernism. And yet, the opposite claim has been and still is made for Yiddish: in its texts, its cultural productions, its very syntax and grammar, it has been a home for the Jews who spoke it, a nation-within-a-nation, and a fully lived, fully experienced, fully rooted majority culture for the majority of its writers and readers, who were enriched by their synergistic connections to the languages and cultures among which they lived.

That synergy—the necessary exposure to a wide range of cultural forms and influences, including but not limited to traditional Jewish education; American, eastern, and western European literatures in their originals and in (abundant) translations; the cadences of Tanakh (the Jewish Bible); and *di yidishe gas* (the

Jewish street)—has meant that Yiddish cannot be considered in isolation. It seems, rather, to be the very definition of current discussions of multiculturalism and transnationalism. The case for Yiddish literature as being necessary to any understanding of American Jewish culture, ethnicity in America, Hebrew literary development, and eastern European history and culture is, by now, clear and largely uncontested, at least among Yiddishists and arguably well beyond. Inclusion and exclusion has, of course, both intellectual and quite pragmatic implications, and these certainly motivate current discussions about whether (or how) Yiddish might be included in postcolonial studies, minority discourse, feminism, media studies, and critical considerations of everything from exile to diaspora to emerging canons, to name but a few.

The quest for inclusion and equality, however, cannot erase the importance of difference as a political, social, or cultural category. Yiddish literary critics may like to think of ourselves as being vital to, and at the center of, all of the discussions cited above, but the dearth of publication in Yiddish, the number of tenure track positions in Yiddish, and the native speakers willing and able to read Yiddish literature are not encouraging. Still, I briefly thought of calling these comments "The Blessings of Marginality in Yiddish Literature." The title was a bow to Gerson Cohen's 1996 "The Blessings of Assimilation in Jewish History," a then still controversial but incontrovertible debunking of the myth that adherence to tradition somehow explains Jewish vitality through the ages. Pointing to Jewish adaptability, the various languages in which Jews lived, and the creative stimulus of the cultures within which they thrived, Gerson Cohen made a case for assimilation that we may now begin to make for marginality. I do not mean by this to enter into already-tired discussions of the culture of victimization or minority status but rather to acknowledge that being compelled by historical and material circumstances to embrace other languages, to come to terms with powerlessness, and to write without a room or nation or even intended audience of one's own may lead—indeed, *has led*—to incredibly creative literature.

Within my academic lifetime thus far, the methodological focus of Yiddish scholarship has shifted from linguistics to literary studies to social and cultural history. Not so long ago, one became a student of such traditional fields as Victorian literature, the German Enlightenment, or modernism first and then found one's way to Yiddish literature through circuitous paths of some biographical interest. Increasingly, Yiddish scholars are now trained to be Yiddish scholars from the beginning of their academic careers, which has come to mean that they are also trained to be comparatists–if they have any hope of speaking to the broader academic and cultural world. But this is not new. Yiddish scholars and writers were (to use an expression alien to them but no longer to most of us) always already comparatists. Indeed, as I have been suggesting, they had no more choice in this than do contemporary Yiddish speakers and writers.

Some other things also remain the same. Yiddishists continue to be concerned with the need for and status of translation, now from Yiddish rather than into it. There is a methodological focus on close readings, made more acute by the disappearance of the milieus in which Yiddish literature flourished. There continues to be a similar need for careful contextualization of the texts we read. Prominent, too, is the question of audience. Most of us write in a language foreign to the subjects of our study and study a language foreign to our readers. And, finally, there is both a difference between and an overlap of *yidn fun a gants yor* and *di hoykhe fentster*—between the common reader (or Jew) and the claims to high culture (and university positions). The latter may privilege complexity, ambiguity, and edginess, but the most memorable characters in Yiddish literature have been addressed to and modeled after the former.

The poet H. Leivick warned about the muteness that may result if the gap between reader and writer is not bridged. In "Yidishe poetn" ("Yiddish Poets"), he wrote,

> *Azoy meshunedik zeyen oys undzere lider.* . . .
> *az es kumt an eygener, a noenter*
> *fun a keler, tsi fun a shap aroys,—*
> *zayn shtume tsung nor in undz derkont er,*
> *un undzer fayerlekhkeyt maydt er oys.*
>
> Our poems look so strange. . . .
> that if one of our own, someone close comes out
> of a cellar, or a shop,—
> he recognizes in us only his own mute tongue
> and avoids our solemnity.[1]

Leivick was not lamenting the loss of Yiddish speakers or readers here; he was pointing to the sometimes enormous gap between the modernist verse written by Yiddish poets and the needs of the audience to whom they were presumably addressed. His poem stands as an accusation and a warning: if they do not find a way to address their audience, Yiddish writers will condemn themselves to silence. The essays that follow take up Leivick's daunting challenge in intriguing ways. Ultimately, this is the only edge that really matters—the edge on which we continue to try to find our balance.

Notes

1. My translation.

DER NISTER'S SYMBOLIST STORIES

Adventures in Yiddish Storytelling and Their Consequences

DARA HORN

The idea that Yiddish culture has a particular affinity for storytelling has exceeded its statute of limitations as a truism and has graduated to a cliché. Far more than other genres such as poetry, novels, and even drama, the short story form is the cornerstone of the modern Yiddish literary canon—and not the slice-of-life type of story but rather the plot-driven story, the kind of story that presents a morally fraught situation with a clear narrative arc, often following the patterns of religious tales while deliberately upending religious values. Even when writers of these tales tried to revolutionize Jewish life by casting new ideas into a traditional storytelling mode, there remained in their work a kind of faith in the power of the story itself. What remains pervasive, in both the stories themselves and even in the scholarship surrounding them, is the premise that literary stories offer their readers a kind of redemption—whether a substitute homeland, a moral commitment, a bridge between generations, a key to survival, or a promise of restitution in an otherwise unraveling world. But what if all of these writers and scholars, ultimately, were wrong? What if storytelling really cannot offer anyone redemption of any kind and the entire premise of Yiddish literature is in fact a horrifying lie? Here we will examine the work of the twentieth-century Soviet-Yiddish writer Der Nister, which suggests this very possibility—and therefore deserves our attention, because it has the potential to redefine the way we understand not only Yiddish storytelling but any kind of storytelling at all.

By the time Pinkhas Kahanovitch adopted his mystical pen name Der Nister, or "the Hidden One," the trajectory of the modern Yiddish writer was even more of a cliché than the idea of Yiddish storytelling. Born in 1884, Der Nister grew up in Berdychiv, Ukraine, received a traditional education as a child, and took on his pen name while dodging the czar's draft. Like many modern Yiddish writers, Der Nister found himself both incapable of remaining in the traditional world and incapable of completely abandoning it, and his route toward reconciling these two incompatible options led to his art. Der Nister published his first story collection at the age of twenty-three, and by 1929 he had established himself as a writer of short stories of astounding originality and imagination. Through a system of symbols drawn from both Jewish sources and European surrealism, Der Nister developed what amounted to an entirely new self-contained mythology through these extremely complex stories.[1] This symbolism has more or less been the only aspect of Der Nister's stories from this period that scholars have systematically studied. What few have examined, however, is what really captivates and startles the reader of these stories: not their symbolism, but their plots. Each of these stories features an elaborate, multiple-framed, madly interconnected, migraine-inducing plot structure. And this aspect of his symbolist stories demands our attention, because through this newly invented plot structure in his most developed symbolist stories, Der Nister ultimately destroys the foundational idea that had motivated almost all of modern Yiddish prose before him, which is that stories provide a path to redemption.

Of course, Der Nister was hardly the first Yiddish storyteller to use a bizarre plot structure to make a point. The tales of the Hasidic master Nakhman of Bratslav[2] were of particular importance to Der Nister's writing, and it is worth taking a moment here to briefly note Nakhman's approach to storytelling, which Nakhman himself quite explicitly saw as a redemptive act and which established this redemptive precedent for much of the Yiddish storytelling that followed it. Nakhman's brand of Hasidism drew heavily on Lurianic kabbalah, which, as befits a posttraumatic religious philosophy, is predicated on the idea of destruction and restitution. Its basic tenet is the idea of *tzimtzum*, or the "contraction" or retreat of the divine presence from the world, and the shattering of primordial vessels containing the divine presence. To greatly oversimplify this doctrine, the function of humankind's existence is to repair and rebuild these shattered vessels in a process called *tikkun*, or "restitution," of the divine and human world.[3] Derived from this doctrine, the stories of Nakhman of Bratslav are long and rather convoluted narratives usually structured around the idea of a quest, but also containing many complicated and somewhat surreal framing devices. In a typical Nakhman story, both symbol and plot structure direct the reader from an initial state of brokenness to a state of almost-completion, turning the entire storytelling experience into an extended metaphor for the idea of *tikkun* and raising the possibility that it is the reader's role to complete the restitution of the story and the world it represents. In Nakhman's vision, the narrative act itself serves as an essential part of the process of redemption.

Der Nister's early symbolist stories borrow the form of many of these tales. As was true for many modern Yiddish writers, Der Nister's appropriation of a traditional form did not mean appropriating traditional values but rather renegotiating them—and for Der Nister, the idea that stories could provide a kind of redemption became more and more fraught as his career progressed. His most mature symbolist stories draw on the doctrine of Nakhman's stories but then invert it. Considering Der Nister's writings with this background in mind, let us take a close look at an example of his work. To convey the level of complexity—or, perhaps, absurdity—of plot in a typical Der Nister story, we will attempt the nearly impossible task of summarizing "Fun mayne giter" ("From My Estates," 1929), a story that displays Der Nister's almost demented plot structure at its peak.[4]

"From My Estates" begins with an unnamed first-person narrator finding a piece of mud stuck to his forehead. Removing it, he discovers a gold coin, which he uses first to buy himself a meal. He then enters a raffle for a book, which he wins. The remainder of the story is the content of the book, titled *The Writings of a Madman,* by Der Nister. In this book, the internal author, Der Nister, relates how he lives with ten bears who literally eat him out of house and home, eventually even eating all of his fingers and threatening to murder him for food. While pleading for his life, Der Nister recounts for the bears how he arrived at this situation. Long ago, he describes, he climbed a ladder to the heavens and entered a town made of mud, where he quickly sickened from the filthy food and was hounded out of town for being unable to absorb the filth. Upon escaping to a neighboring town, however, he found that the mud that was covering him had turned into gold. He soon bought all of the property in the town, became astoundingly powerful, and hosted an unsurpassable feast to celebrate. At the feast, he demonstrated his power by ordering the constellation Ursa Major, the Great Bear, to come down from the sky and dance with him. Ursa Major came to the dance, but then a vast pit opened in the dance floor as Ursa Major chastised him for his greed, asking him whether he could even manage to feed a single family of "earthly bears." Der Nister was cast down into the pit, down the ladder he came from, landing with a bit of gold stuck to his forehead. When he tried to use his wealth in the world below, however—walking into stores and helping himself to merchandise on credit and so forth—he was considered insane and was sent to an asylum, where he recounted his experiences to his fellow inmates. Then, telling the reader that his "head was like a set of dark, empty rooms," he explains how he went for a walk through the empty rooms in his head, lighting candles in each of them, until he came across the room filled with the hungry bears. He pawns the candlesticks in the house to feed the bears, making the rooms darker and darker. The bears grow so hungry that they begin eating his fingers, but before they eat his heart, he manages to "buy them off with a tale"—the tale we have just read. The bears tell him to write down his story for the asylum doctor, which he does, using his own blood as ink. At the end of the story, he still awaits the doctor's reply.

Der Nister's stories are called "symbolist" for a reason, and any critic interested in interpreting a tale such as this one can have quite a field day. The symbols here are many, and some quite transparent—such as the bear, universal symbol of the Soviet Union, whom the writer initially courts but who then casts the writer down and demands that he literally sacrifice himself body and soul for the state's consumption. The ladder connecting heavenly and earthly realms, which makes an appearance in several of Der Nister's stories, echoes a legend from the Talmud claiming that one of the last things God created before the world's first Sabbath was a ladder connecting heaven and hell. One could interpret the constant back-and-forth between wealth and filth as what one critic, Delphine Bechtel, calls a "devaluation of all values," where it is not simply materialism that is denounced but also the idea that materialism can be replaced with a better system.[5] Khone Shmeruk interprets the conflicting aspects of the story as reflecting the conflict the artist faced in a world where there is "no place for doubt to rest."[6] The theme of madness, especially in its incarnation here in the *Writings of a Madman,* has an obvious precedent in Gogol's "Diary of a Madman." The list of cultural references and allusions in the story could be expanded almost endlessly.

Although interpreting the symbols in these stories may be an important or even essential element of understanding them, their symbolism is far from the most noteworthy effect of reading them. To truly appreciate the *experience* of reading these stories, one must, at least temporarily, set the question of symbolism aside. If Der Nister were interested in merely creating a set of allegorical symbols to make certain political or religious points, he surely could have created a more efficient way to showcase them. Instead, what startles (and captivates) the reader is not the symbolism in this whirlwind but rather the whirlwind itself: the unrelenting nature of this astoundingly convoluted plot that seems deliberately designed to confuse the reader. As soon as one thread is taken up, it seems, it is dropped; narrative contexts are switched with alarming frequency; settings change with no transition in sight; an apparent metaphor turns surprisingly literal and takes us into yet another tale-within-a-tale. The reader attempting to follow this bewildering string of events asks repeatedly, Where is this going, if anywhere? Is there any pattern here to what seems to be chaos? And, notably, is there any way out? Only by addressing these seemingly unanswerable questions can we begin to understand the rhetorical drive behind what appears to be a narrative run amok, and its disturbing implications for Yiddish storytelling as a whole.

Let us consider the structure of the plot. Despite its apparent rambling quality, the plot here is in fact not at all randomly composed. Rather, it is quite explicitly built out of a series of frames, each of which gives its own narrator a reason for reporting his own particular story. The framing device is used in modern Hebrew and Yiddish literature with rather astounding frequency. Some canonical examples include Joseph Hayyim Brenner's Hebrew novel *Shekhol vekhishalon* (*Breakdown and Bereavement*),[7] which begins with an introduction claiming that the text that follows has been compiled from the "found" journals of a disgruntled immigrant to Palestine; Sholem Aleichem's *Ayznbangeshikhtes* (*Railroad Stories*),[8] in which all the stories are related through conversations between the narrator and other passengers he meets while traveling by train; and Y. L. Peretz's story "Di toyte shtot" ("The Dead Town"),[9] in which the existence of the dead town is reported not through the narrator's direct experience but rather through a story told by a hitchhiker he picks up on the road. This approach to narrative is also a fundamental aspect of the work of the founding "grandfather" of both modern Hebrew and Yiddish literature, Mendele Mokher Seforim (Mendele the Book Peddler). The phenomenon of the frame story in modern Hebrew and Yiddish literature is even more prevalent than these few examples suggest—so prevalent, in fact, that it is worth asking why these authors so frequently choose to frame their stories within other stories.

The narratologist and literary critic Gerard Genette has described three potential purposes for narratives to feature embedded stories: First, narrative explanations, as in Odysseus's descriptions of his adventures to his listeners in Homer's *Odyssey*, which serve to explain where he was during previous months and years. Second, thematic contrast or analogy, as in a parable set into a text that serves to teach a lesson to those in the external story. Finally, distraction, as in Scheherazade's tales in *A Thousand and One Nights*, which serve to stay her execution. In all cases, Genette points out that the presence of the embedded narrative tends to foreground the act of narration itself, which becomes progressively more important through each of these three functions, while the embedded narrative itself becomes correspondingly less important.[10] Therefore frame stories offer a particular place of honor to the act of storytelling, infusing it with an importance that transcends even the story being told. Indeed, in many classic works of modern Yiddish literature, like Sholem Aleichem's *Railroad Stories*, the frame narrative does seem to lend a kind of sacred primacy to the narrative act.

In Der Nister's story, something quite different seems to be going on, and Genette offers a potential explanation for stories such as this one. As he describes the structure of frame stories, Genette offers a particularly intriguing description of what we might call a "broken frame" and what Genette terms a "narrative metalepsis," which is a moment when characters cross the boundaries dividing the frame stories or between the story and the reader.[11] Some examples Genette provides are Luigi Pirandello's *Six Characters in Search of an Author* and a story by Julio Cortazar in which a reader is murdered by a character in a novel he is reading.[12] One finds this phenomenon in "From My Estates" during the narrator Der Nister's stroll around in his own head, where he comes across his audience of bears, among other similar moments in the story. Genette gives a fascinating explanation of why narrative metalepsis, a kind of mathematical limit to framing devices, may be both compelling and disturbing: "All these games," Genette tells us, "by the intensity of their effects, demonstrate the importance of the boundary they . . . overstep." He quotes Jorge Luis Borges, who said, "Such inversions suggest that if the characters in a story can be readers or spectators, then we, *their* readers or spectators, might [also] be fictitious." "The most troubling thing about metalepsis," Genette says, "lies in this unacceptable and insistent hypothesis, that you and I . . . perhaps belong to some narrative."[13]

To most readers, this idea may seem much like the Chinese philosopher's conundrum about whether he is a person or merely a spider dreaming that he is a person: intriguing, but completely devoid of any practical consequences. Yet for Jewish readers and writers at the time of Der Nister's writing, a version of this "unacceptable hypothesis" was not only entirely real but also fraught with practical consequences that ranged from impaired personal integrity to bodily harm and death. In the social milieus from Ottoman Palestine to the Soviet Union, Jews frequently found themselves in situations in which their neighbors viewed them not as fellow human beings but as antagonistic characters in a vast and unrelenting narrative—religious or Nationalist in origin—in which these Jewish characters were very clearly slated to either die or otherwise surrender themselves at some point before the last page. The regime that ultimately put Der Nister into the gulag where he perished was no historical exception but was rather quite deliberately "performing," in the narratologist's parlance, a long-rehearsed script.

We might thus hypothesize that the appeal of the frame narratives so common in this literature lies in the way they create a kind of protective layer not only for the writer but also for the reader, keeping the events of the story or stories at arm's length so that he or she is free to absorb them as a genuine spectator, rather than as someone implicated in the story's action. Or perhaps the framing device does not merely protect the reader from being implicated in the events but also reminds the reader of the possibility that this privilege of being outside of the story is not always available to him or her. In both cases, we might conclude that the framing device creates a kind of narrative authority in situations in which the reader's trust of the narrator cannot be expected or assumed. When one considers this as the significance of a framing device, the narrative metalepsis, or broken frame, used in "From My Estates" produces a unique effect on the reader's expectations: it initially builds the reader's ostensible trust in the story's purpose and subsequently demolishes it, ultimately destroying Yiddish literature's time-honored faith in the redemptive act of storytelling.

Der Nister uses several frames (later broken) in "From My Estates." First, we begin with the outermost frame: a man whose face is hit by a patch of mud, which he discovers to contain the coin he uses to buy himself a meal just before acquiring the raffle ticket that wins him Der Nister's book. We are told relatively little about this outermost narrator, other than one very important fact: he is, first and foremost, a reader. Working inward, the second frame is the *Writings of a Madman,* in which the third-person author/narrator Der Nister currently resides in the company of ten hungry bears who first threaten his livelihood and then his life. The third frame is the story that this author/narrator Der Nister tells to the bears in order to stave off their aggression, a tale told in the first person and consisting of his travels in the realms of mud and gold and his subsequent fall from grace and into the insane asylum. The fourth frame, again in the first person, is the story Der Nister tells his fellow inmates at the asylum, consisting of his mental experiences walking around in his own head in which he encounters the ten bears and their unpleasant demands and attempts to provide for their needs by pawning imaginary items among his fellow inmates. The fifth and final frame is the letter that we are told Der Nister writes to his doctor about the bears' threat on his life, for which he is left at the end of the story awaiting the doctor's answer as he guards his heart.

Stories employing a frame device usually elicit two responses in the reader as she or he proceeds through the frames. The first is the acute awareness of the story as a performance or exchange.[14] The focus falls on the reader's relationship with the narrator, which becomes a relationship in which trust is not assumed but rather becomes a point of contention through which the reader is forced to constantly evaluate the narrator's motives for telling the story. The second response to the frame device, a direct consequence of the first, is the reader's feeling that the reliability or authenticity of the internal story or stories is also somehow in question. As a result of this feeling, despite one's doubts about the initial narrator, the outermost frame is considered the "real" story, which provides the reader with permission to suspend disbelief during the recounting of the internal tale or tales in order to continue reading. This suspension of disbelief, however, is a conditional one. The reader only suspends disbelief toward the internal story on the condition of returning to the "real" world of the outer frame, at which point an evaluation of both the narrator and the internal story will at last be possible. The reader's urge to complete the reading of the frame story, then, is motivated by the desire to see some justification for his or her suspended disbelief, that is, to discover the rhetorical value that has made participation in this exchange worthwhile. All of these readerly expectations are typically satisfied in a conventional frame narrative, in which one tale fits neatly into the next, returning the reader to the outermost frame by the story's conclusion without any paradoxical overlap.

These readerly expectations are utterly betrayed in Der Nister's "From My Estates." First of all, at least on initial consideration, the text apparently fails to return us to the outermost frame or even to some of the internal ones, denying us the opportunity to evaluate the worthiness of the storytelling enterprise. Moreover, the multiple frame narratives at work here, and their uncomfortable overlap, compel us to reevaluate our position on what is "real" each time the text plummets us into another tale-within-a-tale. The story's refusal to provide us with any consistent frame of authority gradually erodes any stable standpoint from which we may judge the story's events, leaving us with a series of shattered realities and forcing our own perspective on the content of reality to constantly dissolve. When the madman goes for a stroll inside his own head and happens on the bears to whom he is recounting his tale, we have passed the point of mere plot confusion and reached an unprecedented level of storytelling meltdown.

Second, our relationship with the narrator in "From My Estates" is a rocky one from the start: it seems that in the exchange of trust between reader and storyteller, we as readers have truly gotten a lousy deal. In a text using a framing device, the outermost narrator holds the privileged position of being the reader's stable point of reference. Yet from the opening lines of "From My Estates," this narrator does not seem even remotely capable of fulfilling that function. After all, this is a narrator who begins the story with these opening lines: "I don't know where it flew at me from, but suddenly in the middle of everything I had a wet patch of mud on my forehead. I looked around to see who could have thrown it. But I didn't notice anyone, and as soon as I wiped the patch off with my hand, I saw: a coin."[15] Until we make it further into the text, we can accept that this is going to be a surreal story, and we can suspend our disbelief for this highly fantastical introductory circumstance out of curiosity to see where it may be headed. Yet once this narrator introduces the first internal frame, thereby placing himself in the role of a port in a narrative storm, we know we are in trouble.

If that were not enough to betray the reader's trust in this "exchange," the very idea of storytelling as a meaningful enterprise is in fact parodied in the lines that follow the opening sentences. The narrator tells us, first, that he spends the coin on food for himself. Only afterward, having money left over from the coin and feeling pleased with his good fortune, does he stroll about the town and entirely accidentally happen across a book fair. At this book fair, however, books are being given away:

> Because throughout the country a cheap book week had been proclaimed, and people were raffling off books in the booths, and every raffle ticket, it was written, was required to win—so I went and drew a random ticket, and when the seller who was selling in the booth unfolded the ticket, he gave me a book.
>   The author—Der Nister!
>   The title—*Writings of a Madman*; and there was also an illustration on the cover flap: a pale lunatic standing in a long lunatic's shirt.[16]

Clearly books are not cherished objects of significance but rather cheap items that one gives away arbitrarily, a step below even the junk sold at yard sales, whose purchase at least requires a sense of selection and taste rather than a raffle. We therefore find ourselves reading a story in which the very idea of a story being worthwhile is subject to mockery from the start. Moreover, the authority of the Der Nister narrator figure is so obviously parodied here that the reader immediately knows that the faith she or he can no longer place in the outermost narrator cannot be placed in the subsequent one either. This damaged faith goes well beyond what Wayne Booth famously called the "unreliable narrator."[17] The reader's expectations of the narrator are jeopardized from the very beginning, and as the story progresses through the various frames, things do not appear to improve.

It would be quite simple to conclude here that the constant undermining of the reader's expectations, especially in its destruction of the conditions for suspension of disbelief, indicates that the story has no rhetorical drive at all—or, at best, that the story's purpose is to drive the reader toward the conclusion that stories are pointless. Indeed, one cannot deny that this possibility is vividly raised by the progress of the plot from the very first page. Nonetheless, if the text's goal really is to provide a kind of anti-story with no coherence or driving force at all, if "From My Estates" really is, in effect, the written equivalent of a five-year-old rambling at the breakfast table about his dream last night, then we would be hard-pressed to explain the many moments of overlap between the various frames. The more closely we examine them, the more these frames show themselves to be so delicately interrelated that it becomes impossible not to draw connections between them. Thus the experience of reading "From My Estates" is one not of narrative incoherence but, in fact, of the reader's *quest* for coherence.

At first the various frame stories seem unrelated to one another. But many similarities exist between them, and ultimately these similarities run deeper than mere symbolic ones, entering the level of fundamental plot structure. In fact, the trick here is even more complex than that: the story's frames are not really frames at all but rather echoes of the same figure again and again, as if in a doubled mirror.

The narrators of the various stories, on careful consideration, turn out to be not merely "parallel" but in fact the same individual, experiencing the same experiences. The overlap between the outermost narrator who finds a coin in the mud on his forehead and the narrator of the *Writings of a Madman* who journeys to the kingdom of mud that then turns into gold (and who later emerges with a piece of gold stuck to his forehead after the mud is rendered into gold) is not merely a similarity or a symbolic parallel but also an identical experience. In both cases, our narrator is not merely insane but also insane in such a way that his insanity is determined by how others perceive him, rather than how he perceives himself. The situation of the man who suddenly finds a patch of mud on his forehead containing a coin is not merely improbable but already irrational as well, apparently caused not by any understandable source but rather by the character's own perception—thereby identifying him with the protagonist of the innermost frame of the story, the asylum inmate.

The same may be said of the link between the second frame, the *Writings of a Madman,* in which the narrator faces down the bears, and the frame in which those same bears turn out to be a product of his own madness. Both narrators move through worlds where the question of sanity is determined not only by one's own mental state but also by the absurd circumstances that surround them, whether it be a kingdom of mud or a world where mud lands randomly on one's head. At first the reader is inclined to attribute the mud and coin landing on the man's head in the outermost frame to circumstances beyond the narrator's control, and only upon later reflection does the reader conclude that the narrator's account is irrational and insane. A similar process takes place in the second frame, where the other figures in the frame (first Ursa Major, who ejects him from her realm, and then the people in the kingdom below, who refuse to honor his claim to wealth) dismiss the narrator as acting irrationally and reject him as worthless.

Other overlaps between the various frames are even more obvious. Of all the constellations, the Der Nister narrator chooses to dance with Ursa Major, who then rejects him by demanding that he feed her "earthly bears," casting him down into the "real world," where he lands in the asylum, wanders around in his own head, and finds the predicted earthly bears. The letter the Der Nister narrator writes to the doctor is no different from the *Writings of a Madman* that the outermost narrator randomly "wins" in the raffle—and the word used for his raffle ticket, his *goyrl,* means not only "lot" but also "destiny," suggesting, along with everything else in the story, that the two narrators are one and the same. Furthermore, the author of the story itself is of course Der Nister, and the additional internal author whose name is also Der Nister is simply a double. In his analysis of Der Nister's work, Shmeruk has written about the figure of the "double," a common literary device consisting of a "temporary, pathological splitting of the ego," which in these stories by Der Nister "is represented by a real, live character" despite "never [being] brought to the point of physical separation from the character."[18] In "From My Estates," a large portion of the internal coherence comes from the strange fact that there is actually a single narrator, despite appearances to the contrary.

While reading "From My Estates," the reader senses that, although something has gone horribly wrong with the expected structure of the story, there is ample evidence that the story might have been, at one point, a coherent narrative, that is, it is not a haphazard story but rather a "broken" story, and one that the reader is charged with reconstructing. What compels the reader to continue reading is the unerring sense that the story's many internal frames are not simply arbitrary but have become interlocked with one another, with pieces of one frame story overlapping with pieces of another and shards of meaning scattered throughout the tale. Our drive to finish reading the story, despite its apparent incoherence, is a desperate act of trying to repair its brokenness.

Yet there is a dark side to the reader's quest for coherence in "From My Estates," which involves the question of whether a *tikkun*, or "restitution," of this broken story is possible at all. Even though the plot drives the reader to search for coherence, the reader is also driven by the story's suggestion of the impossibility of maintaining control over one's own destiny—and by the story's emphatic implication that storytelling cannot succeed as a redemptive act.

From the opening sentence of "From My Estates" ("I don't know where it flew at me from"), we as readers are ushered into a world where things happen not by accident but through causes and effects that cannot be explained and that are beyond the characters' control. Each detail of the story suggests, in a cumulative way, each of the various narrators'—or, one could claim, single narrator's—lack of control over his own destiny, along with an affirmation that such a destiny exists, from the *goyrl* (destiny/lot) drawn randomly for the book raffle to the sudden transformation of mud into gold to Ursa Major's unanticipated rage to the earthly bears' unanticipated aggression to the endless wait for the doctor's reply. Since the story began this way in a rather benign fashion, with fate literally throwing good things the narrator's way, the reader is lulled into believing that lack of control over one's fate is harmless or even profitable. We do not immediately fault the narrator for his apparently whimsical approach to his odd circumstances. As more negative events accumulate, however, our view of the narrator or narrators begins to dim. As we enter the story's first internal frame, we see the Der Nister narrator offering his own fingers to the aggressive bears, allowing them to eat them in a rather gory scene, and despite the illogic of the entire situation, we are horrified at his passive acceptance of his fate. When one of the bears reaches for his heart, asking, "And this, what is it?" the narrator Der Nister responds, "This? . . . It's nothing, it's a watch, of no significance, it's wrong and it already runs poorly."[19] This is a truly horrifying moment in the story, because here we see that the only defense mechanism of the passive narrator is to denigrate his own worth; he must outwardly claim that his own life is worthless in order to save it. When the narrator takes charge of the situation by at last pleading for his life, our relief is palpable, and thereafter we find ourselves hoping that he will continue taking the initiative needed to survive—because, through the story's rhetorical drive, we have become convinced that acceptance of the circumstances of fate is itself a fatal mistake.

And so we as readers have become engaged in a doubly doomed process of *tikkun*. First, as we read along with the torments of the story's arbitrarily tortured narrators, we begin to see the supreme necessity of assertiveness in battling against the insanity of an arbitrary and hostile world, that is, the absolute need to write one's own story rather than become a character in someone else's. Second, as we try to piece together the story's broken shards, we become acutely aware of our own weakness as readers, which is our debilitating need for the story to offer us some form of redemption. No matter how modern, secular, and sophisticated we believe ourselves to be, we refuse to accept the notion that arbitrary circumstances must define what happens next in a story's plot. We insist that there be some form of deliverance at the story's end, even if it is only a message of warning.

Yet the story does not provide us with the coherence or sense of a meaningful ending that would make *tikkun* possible. In fact, the implication of the story is that the narrative act can *never* serve the function of redemption that Nakhman set out for it and that we as readers ultimately want it to serve. The narrative act here—as it appears again and again in each broken frame, from the unfinished writings of the madman to the asylum inmate's unanswered letter to the doctor to the narrator's staving off of the bears with a tale—is not meaningful but rather a deferring of meaning, a postponing of the kind of purpose that comes from authorship of one's own life and choices. In Sholem Aleichem's canonical story "Der farkishefter shnayder," or "The Haunted Tailor"—subtitled in some versions as "A mayse on an ek," or "A Story without an Ending"—the narrator, after refusing to conclude a complicated plot, begs off with the wish that readers laugh more than they cry, concluding with the famous words, "Laughing is healthy. Doctors prescribe laughter."[20] These final lines suggest that redemption is possible, even if the author chooses not to provide it.

"From My Estates," in a devastating answer to Sholem Aleichem, offers no prescriptions at all, medical or otherwise—not even laughter. It concludes with a very different line: as the narrator waits for the doctor to answer his letter, which he has written in his own blood, the entire story ends with the narrator realizing that "for the doctor's answer, he will likely have to wait a long time."[21] This ending suggests that the idea of storytelling as a redemptive act, an idea that had sustained Yiddish storytelling for generations, is in fact a fantasy— and even a destructive fantasy, because it distracts from reality by pretending to offer the reader what only real actions can offer. It may be true, as Yiddish literature's metaplot has always taught, that storytelling is the key to cultural survival, the so-called paper bridge to the world to come. But what Der Nister suggests here is that although storytelling can stave off death, it can do so only at the price of rendering real life meaningless.

Der Nister stopped writing his unique stories in 1929. That year he returned from western Europe to the Soviet Union, a move he made presumably for reasons similar to many other Yiddish writers who made the same choice, out of a belief that the Soviet Union's state support of Yiddish cultural institutions would provide him with the best professional options as a Yiddish writer. Upon his return, Der Nister quickly discovered that the regime would not allow him to publish stories in the style he had so painstakingly developed, and thereafter he published only works of historical realism and reportage that show almost no trace of his previous style. During the Second World War, Der Nister, like many other Yiddish cultural luminaries in the Soviet Union, became affiliated with the Jewish Antifascist Committee, and after the war he shared the fate of many of these Yiddish cultural leaders. He was arrested in 1949 by the Soviet secret police, and for many years his exact fate was not known. With the opening of Soviet archives in the 1990s, however, documents of Der Nister's arrest, conviction, and incarceration in a labor camp are now available.[22] Records show that he perished in a prison hospital in 1950. The intervening decades were not kind to his reputation, since for many years his most imaginative work continued to be suppressed under Soviet rule. Only in recent years have more attempts been made to bring the work of this extremely complex artist to a wider audience. And with this rediscovery of the Hidden One's work, the clichés about Yiddish stories can be set aside, and the real debate on the purpose of storytelling can begin.

Notes

1. See Khone Shmeruk, "Der Nister: hayyav veyetzirato." Introduction to *Hanazir vehagdiyah*, by Der Nister, trans. Dov Sadan (Jerusalem: Mosad Bialik, 1963), 9-52, 17, 25.
2. Nakhman of Bratslav (1772-810), a grandson of Israel ben Eliezer, the Ba'al Shem Tov who founded the Hasidic movement, was an enigmatic rebbe (Hasidic leader) who became the founder of the Bratslaver or "dead" Hasidim, a sect so named because Nakhman, a mystic who believed himself to have messianic capabilities, appointed no successor. His most famous teachings took the form of cryptic stories that he recounted orally to his followers and that his scribe, Nathan of Nemirov, recorded in both Hebrew and Yiddish versions. The stories, often complex and with few resolutions to their plots, are symbolic expressions of kabbalistic teachings. Their apparent surrealism later inspired many modern Jewish writers.
3. For more detailed explanations of these doctrines, see Gershom Scholem's *On the Kabbalah and Its Symbolism*, trans. Ralph Manheim (New York: Schocken, 1965) and *Major Trends in Jewish Mysticism* (New York: Schocken, 1941).
4. Der Nister, "Fun mayne giter," in *Fun mayne giter* (Kharkiv, Ukraine: Melukhe-farlag fun Ukrayne, 1929), 7-40. A full English translation of this story is available in Joseph Leftwich, ed. and trans., *An Anthology of Modern Yiddish Literature* (The Hague: Mouton, 1974), 65-84. English translations of story excerpts within this essay are my own.
5. Delphine Bechtel, *Der Nister's Work, 1907-1929: A Study of a Yiddish Symbolist* (Berne: Peter Lang, 1990), 235.
6. Shmeruk, "Der Nister: ḥayav veyetzirato," 28.
7. Joseph Hayyim Brenner, *Shekhol vekhishalon* (1920; repr., Tel Aviv: Hakibbutz Hameuhad, 2006). Available in English as *Breakdown and Bereavement*, trans. Hillel Halkin (Ithaca: Cornell University Press, 1971).
8. Sholem Aleichem, *Ayznban-geshikhtes: ksovim fun a komi-voyazher*, vol. 5 of *Ale verk fun Sholem-Aleykhem* (New York: Forverts Association, 1942). Excerpts available in English translation in *Tevye the Dairyman and the Railroad Stories*, trans. Hillel Halkin (New York: Schocken, 1992).
9. Y. L. Peretz, "Di toyte shtot," in *Far kleyn un groys*, vol. 7 of *Ale verk fun Y. L. Perets* (Vilna, Lithuania: B. Kletskin, 1925-1929; repr., New York: Morgn-Frayhayt, n.d.), 104-17. Avail-

able in English as "The Dead Town," in *The Y. L. Peretz Reader*, ed. Ruth R. Wisse (New York: Schocken, 1990), 162-71.

10. Gerard Genette, *Narrative Discourse: An Essay in Method*, trans. Jane E. Lewin (Ithaca: Cornell University Press, 1980), 232-34.

11. Ibid.

12. Ibid., 234-35; Julio Cortazar, "Continuity of Parks," in *Blow-Up and Other Stories*, trans. Paul Blackburn (New York: Pantheon, 1967), 63-65.

13. Genette, *Narrative Discourse*, 236.

14. Barbara Herrnstein Smith, "Narrative Versions, Narrative Theories," in *On Narrative*, ed. W. J. T. Mitchell (Chicago: University of Chicago Press, 1981), 209-32, 227.

15. Der Nister, "Fun mayne giter," 7 (my translation).

16. Ibid.

17. Wayne Booth, *The Rhetoric of Fiction*, 2nd ed. (Chicago: University of Chicago Press, 1983).

18. Khone Shmeruk, "Der Nister's 'Under a Fence,'" in *The Field of Yiddish, Second Collection—Studies in Language, Folklore, and Literature*, ed. Uriel Weinreich (The Hague: Mouton, 1965), 263-87, 271.

19. Der Nister, "Fun mayne giter," 9.

20. Sholem Aleichem, "Der farkishefter shnayder," in *Ale verk fun Sholem-Aleykhem* (New York: Forverts Edition, 1942), 4:9-68, 68.

21. Der Nister, "Fun mayne giter," 40.

22. See Peter B. Maggs, *The Mandelstam and Der Nister Files: An Introduction to Stalin-Era Prison and Labor Camp Records* (Armonk, NY: M.E. Sharpe, 1995).

WRITING ON THE VERGE OF CATASTROPHE

David Vogel's Last Work of Prose

SHIRI GOREN

The last work of prose by the Hebrew poet and author David Vogel (1891-1944), posthumously titled *They All Went out to Battle,* depicts a fascinating testimonial narrative of a year of imprisonment in French prisoner of war camps during the Second World War. The manuscript was found after the war buried in a yard in the small town of Hauteville in southeastern France. Vogel buried it himself, together with the rest of his literary remains, shortly before the Lyon gestapo captured and transported him to Auschwitz, where he perished in March 1944.

Throughout his literary career, Vogel, a native Yiddish speaker, took it upon himself to write and publish only in Hebrew. Wandering through Europe's modernist centers and making a failed attempt to immigrate to Israel, Vogel managed to achieve this goal. Between the end of the First World War and the beginning of the Second, he published poems, a book of poetry, a novel, and two novellas—all, except for one, in Hebrew.[1] That exception appeared in the form of an unpublished manuscript of 127 large (8.3 by 11.7 inch) handwritten pages consisting of about 150,000 words composed entirely in Yiddish.

In the beginning of February 1944, the Lyon gestapo conducted an operation in the province of Ain in order to arrest several members of the French resistance as well as the few Jews who lived in the area, Vogel among them.[2] Shortly before that, he buried the manuscript of the novel along with two poems and the first pages of a comprehensive Hebrew novel he was rewriting.[3] He buried the texts in a yard of the house where he rented a room since his release from detainee camps in August of 1940. After the war, one of Vogel's friends, the painter Avraham Goldberg, dug in the ground of that house and discovered the literary remains.[4] Goldberg transferred the text to the Hebrew American author Shimon Halkin, then living in the United States, who delivered it to the

First page of Vogel's Yiddish manuscript. Photo by the author, courtesy of the Gnazim archive.

author Asher Barash in Israel.[5] In 1950, with the establishment of the Gnazim Institute for the Research of History of the Hebrew Literature in the New Era, Barash gave Vogel's Yiddish manuscript to the institute, where it remains in Tel Aviv to this day.[6]

The manuscript, as the image on page 30 shows, comprises a draft full of alternative words, erasures, and parentheses. Vogel's tiny handwriting makes some of the words difficult to decipher. Although the narrative is lucidly structured and has a beginning, middle, and end, Vogel never got a chance to finish it in terms of editing and preparing it for publication. This likely explains why, unlike the author's Hebrew works, this Yiddish text was never published in the original language, and it has received little scholarly attention. Only in 1990 did a heavily edited version become accessible to the Israeli public through a Hebrew translation by literary editor and scholar Menachem Perry.[7] For a title, Perry selected *They All Went out to Battle*—in Hebrew, *Kulam yatzu lakrav*—a line he took from one of two Hebrew poems by Vogel that survived the Second World War.[8]

Drawing on both Yiddish and Hebrew versions of the text and contextualizing Vogel's narrative within his biography, my analysis takes Vogel's work as a testimonial narrative created on the verge of catastrophe. By applying Maurice Blanchot's conceptualization of the writing of the disaster and Hans-Georg Gadamer's concept of the "fusion of horizons," this investigation offers a tentative explanation for Vogel's poetic decision to write this unique text in Yiddish.

The Geography of Vogel's Biography

Vogel's personal and literary histories seem related in several ways. Born in 1891 in Satanov, Podolia (now Ukraine), Vogel, as a teenager, decided to dedicate his life to becoming a Hebrew writer, even though his native tongue was Yiddish. Literary scholar Chana Kronfeld argues that "For Vogel, a famished, uprooted, perpetual wanderer through Europe's modernist centers, the very decision to become a Hebrew writer was an act of self-marginalization, and self-modernization."[9] In 1912 he migrated west, crossing the border to Austria and arriving in Vienna, where he stayed for thirteen years. By moving to Vienna not only did he change geographical locations within the continent, but Vogel also switched positions in the Jewish world: he attempted to abandon his *Ostjude* roots and reinvent himself as a west European man. In 1914, two weeks after the beginning of the world war, local police arrested him together with several other Russian citizens suspected of cooperating with the czar's troops. Vogel was imprisoned for two years, during which time he intermittently wrote a journal in Hebrew.[10] Although at first he viewed the incarceration as a convenient solution for his financial hardship, later on he suffered despair and loneliness. After his release in 1916 he went back to Vienna but could not find a place for himself there financially or existentially. Nevertheless he became an Austrian citizen, married his first wife, Ilka, in 1919,[11] and began publishing poems in various Hebrew journals toward the end of the First World War.[12] Undeniably, throughout his life, the more entrenched Vogel became in his individualism, the more world events chased him. The more he aimed at being particular, the more he unwillingly became a symbol for collective Jewish existence in interwar Europe.

Vogel's wandering among geographical locations is mirrored in his shifting of literary genres and styles. In fact, his poetics at that time, and throughout the rest of his life, reflected his biography in that he was a minor author whose writing evades any attempt at literary, political, or ideological categorization. Indeed, Dan Miron emphasizes that Vogel stubbornly adhered to a nonredemptive writing style: "bleak universal existentialism and introspective individualism which sees nothing but the absurd fate of the lonely individual progressing toward his end."[13]

Though writing in Hebrew, Vogel claimed no Zionist leanings, and he alienated himself from the linguistic and national Hebrew revival. In 1929 he immigrated to Palestine with his second wife, Adah. Their only daughter, Tamar,[14] was born there, but they returned to Europe after a year and settled in France. In 1939 when the Second World War broke out, Vogel lived in Paris with Tamar, then ten years old. At that time, his wife was hospitalized in a tuberculosis sanatorium in Hauteville, in the countryside of southeastern France. Vogel's train ride with his daughter from Paris to the countryside, a mere few hours before France declared war on Germany, forms the opening scene of the manuscript: "Dem tsveytn september [1939] hob ikh nokh uspeyet tsu khapn dem letstn tsug: paris-burg-shamberi" (On September 2nd I managed to catch the last train: Paris-Burg-Chambéry).[15]

A month after Vogel's arrival with his daughter in Hauteville, local police arrested him, together with other people whose origin was, as the manuscript stresses, "funem itstikn groysn daytshn raykh" (from the current large German Reich).[16] Ironically, twenty-five years after his arrest by the Habsburgian authorities as a Russian citizen, Vogel faced similar accusations by the French, this time as the carrier of an Austrian passport. He spent ten months (October 4, 1939–August 8, 1940) imprisoned in several French camps for citizens of enemy countries.[17]

Following his release, a few weeks after France surrendered to Germany and established the Vichy regime, Vogel decided to return to Hauteville to be near his wife's sanatorium.[18] He spent the next three years there, relatively safe, renting a room in the house of an elderly woman, and focused mainly on writing. As far as we know, during those years Vogel authored several poems in Hebrew,[19] revised a modernist Hebrew novel, and probably dedicated most of his creative time to writing the autobiographical novel in Yiddish.[20]

Vogel composed this highly uncharacteristic manuscript while on the verge of catastrophe in the midst of dramatic world events. Whether or not he suspected how the war would end for him toward the end of his time in Hauteville, the circumstances under which he wrote the manuscript were incredibly dramatic and fraught.[21] The care he took in ensuring the preservation of this manuscript requires us to read the narrative with particular attention to the circumstances under which he wrote and saved it. Vogel created in proximity to universal, national, and personal disasters. The phrase "verge of catastrophe," then, conveys here both the traumatic experience of Vogel's own imprisonment in 1939-1940 and the sense of temporality and indeterminacy that writing in the middle of a world war embodies.

Vogel's Last Work of Prose

Written in a first-person voice, Vogel's literary account is reminiscent of a journal or a diary. The main protagonist, however, is a fictional character named Rudolf—or in some cases, Ernest—Weichert, a Jewish painter with biographical and family circumstances very similar to Vogel's own. The different name and occupation of the main character seem to camouflage, in different degrees of displacement, the author's reworking of the trauma of his incarceration.

The narrative follows Weichert, together with a group of German and Austrian citizens, both Jewish and non-Jewish, through eight months of imprisonment. The prisoners are transferred from one camp to another, aiming to maintain their daily routine in the highly irregular and sometimes violent situations they encounter and continuously fighting French bureaucracy in failed attempts at release from the camps. This haunting Yiddish manuscript depicts the crisis of a sudden break from the outside world, the loss of freedom, and the ever increasing sense of vulnerability and helplessness that the prisoners experience.

The first paragraph of Vogel's manuscript, right before the scene at the train station, describes the French mandatory call, from September 3, 1939, for all foreign citizens of hostile countries to immediately report to the local police:

> Everyone whose origin is from the German Reich (with the handwritten addition: "from the current large German Reich") from the ages of seventeen to fifty years old (the day after, new posters announced: also from fifty to sixty-five years old) must report in the next twenty-four hours, at their own expense, to a concentration camp for foreigners. If not, they will be arrested by the police. One must bring food for two days, two small blankets (or one big one), underwear, clothes, shoes etc.[22]

The impersonal narration, which changes to first person in the second paragraph, provides the reader with the background and context for the entire narrative. By applying this impersonal voice and quoting the language in the posters announcing the call, Weichert distances himself from any personal ramifications the order must have entailed for him. The character of Weichert employs this technique of hiding behind formal language on other occasions throughout the novel, for example, when Captain Ledoux interrogates him in Camp Arandon[23] and when the authorities encourage the prisoners to volunteer for the French Foreign Legion.[24]

Weichert's detailed, matter-of-fact prose rarely contains expressed emotions. In fact, the narrator seldom reveals anything about his own feelings toward various situations he encounters, nor does he dwell on his life at any point. For example, although he introduces some of the other inmates by their professions (carpenter, judge, physician, lawyer, manufacturer of goods), he does not relate such information about himself. The reader vaguely learns about Weichert's occupation before the incarceration during two interviews with French captains in which he declares himself a painter in the first interview and a writer in the second.[25] The lack of details on Weichert's life before his arrest, the scarcity of his own emotional output in writing, and his overall passivity suggest a common representation of the incarceration experience, in which the individual is reduced to a mere number. Weichert and the group of prisoners, whom he meets in the first camp, Bourg, allude to this feeling in labeling their crowd with the number zero.[26] Here the group is composed of law-abiding citizens who become prisoners for an unspecified time for reasons beyond their control. This traumatic experience forms a sudden and complete break from their regular course of life. The prisoners' inability to do anything to amend the situation only strengthens their frustration, cynicism, and despair.

Vogel's narrative is a minor one, in that the events described in the text did not lead to the murder of the prisoners, who in the end were released from the camps. Rather, the occurrences appear as more links in the chain of dehumanization and deprivation of human rights. Moreover, Vogel does not structure the dichotomy of good and bad around the axis of Germans and Jews: whereas most of the inmates were Jewish, the oppressive personnel belonged, without exception, to the French nation. Weichert despises Hitler and the French administration equally for imprisoning him. He wishes a defeat for Hitler but at the same time hopes that the French, too, will learn their lesson. Writing in the middle of the war, Vogel seems painfully aware of the price it entails for all the parties involved yet nevertheless presents a humanistic worldview. The protagonist's fundamental resistance to the war derives not from pacifism or altruistic motives but from practical, perhaps even selfish, reasons—he does not want to die:

> I have only one life, limited in time, one and only, and it is dear to me. It is dearer to me than all the nations in the world and their stupid conflicts. It was given to me alone, to live in full, selfishly. I do not want to give my life to anyone

and nobody has the right to take it away from me. Had I been at fault, I would be willing to pay. But I haven't done a thing. It is not my fault that France wants to go to war. I would possibly be ready to sacrifice my life, but not to France alone. Never. But against Hitler, for the Jews. Yet I must make this decision for myself. Such a decision must be born in me, freely, without any outside coercion.[27]

Through the voice of his main character, Vogel therefore offers a subversive, universal critique of nationalism and its inevitable outcome, war.

Vogel's critique, however, is not limited to the big picture of the war but spans to the smallest details of the incarceration as well. The absurdities and inconsistencies that characterize the oppressive French regime in Vogel's narration are evocative of Kafka's depictions of the unidentified authority in his 1925 novel *The Trial*. Vogel, an avid reader and speaker of German who translated but failed to publish his own magnificent novel *Married Life* into this language, was surely familiar with Kafka's oeuvre. Although Weichert is not Joseph K., the bureaucratic process supposedly leading to the release of the prisoners is so obscure and unproductive that the reader is reminded of a Kafkaesque world. Ultimately, Vogel's narrative constitutes a literary meditation on the condition of the individual in the modern world, and in that respect, it certainly gestures toward Kafka's fable.

In more than one case, the author suggests a bitter irony toward the inherent impotency of the main character in various situations without Weichert's knowing. For example, depicting his visits to the local police station before the initial arrest, Weichert says,

> I immediately went to the city hall and then to the police. I did not believe that the announcements were directed to me as well. Me, a "former Austrian," a Jew who has been living in France for many years, who is certainly not a friend of Hitler (*may his name be forgotten!*) not at all, to the contrary: a friend of France that now will finally wipe him off the ground. I asked once and then many times over, as in such times, one has to know for sure. This is a war! They answered me, at the city hall and at the police, once and many times, that I do not have to go. Me, no. I am a former Austrian, I am a Jew, and Austrians are not Germans. We will free Austria, return its sovereignty. We'll free all the small countries. We fight for freedom and equality for all.[28]

The situation is ironic and even slightly amusing, particularly due to the reader's knowledge of Weichert's lengthy imprisonment shortly afterward. Weichert and the policemen's deep conviction that the French authorities did not target him becomes irrelevant a few paragraphs later when the same people come to arrest him. Moreover, the French policemen, speaking in first-person plural, quote empty slogans on freedom and equality. Similarly Weichert, in many ways like Vogel himself, has only limited interest in world politics. Therefore, his intentions to appear enthusiastic about the war and France's prospects of winning only stress his passivity throughout the actual incarceration. The narrator's wording ridicules—in a second reading—both the character and the agents of the state. By using literary devices of irony and comic relief, Vogel therefore creates the opposite effect and brings the reader to understand the ultimate gravity of the situation.

The text travels between a few literary genres: autobiography, testimony, personal journal, memoir, and fiction. Consequently, it does not fully follow the literary conventions of any of these genres. This hybrid form seems to be highly productive for the author and what he wishes to impart to his reader. Nevertheless, I read the manuscript as autobiographical fiction or, more precisely, a novel with autobiographical elements.[29] Such an interpretation views Vogel's manuscript as a literary creation with aesthetic values rather than a journal or a testimony, as scholars have referred to it thus far, and allows the application of tools from the field of literary theory in order to gain a better understanding of the text.[30]

Unlike a personal diary, Vogel's text does not contain separate daily or weekly entries, and although the manuscript occasionally mentions dates, the narrative progresses geographically. It starts with the train ride from Paris to Hauteville and continues with Weichert's arrest and transfer to the "concentration camp for foreigners" (*zaml-lager far oyslender*)[31] in Bourg-en-Bresse. From there the prisoners move to another camp in Arandon, and then to another one in Loriol.

The final scene, akin to the opening paragraphs, occurs on a train that takes the prisoners to an unknown destination. In both cases the setting symbolizes temporality, transition, and uncertainty, echoing the prisoners' emotional condition throughout their imprisonment. In the beginning of the novel, Weichert is a free man in a foreign crowd on the verge of becoming a prisoner. Although Vogel does not explain or intellectualize the final scene, by the story's end Weichert's release remains unknown and he stands in a familiar crowd of foreigners. In both images the train leaves at night and the travelers are unsure about the destination and whether or not the train will even reach it. Moreover, both situations present overcrowded train cars and mayhem—of people, limbs, and belongings. Despite the gloomy setting, in both instances Weichert, who in the first episode is accompanied by a child and in the second suffers from ill health, not only manages to get on each train but even locates places to sit each time.

The preparations for the train rides and then riding the trains quintessentially constitute, thus, Vogel's actual experience (disguised as Weichert) throughout the incarceration. The similarity between the two scenes represents a circular, repetitive motion that typifies the novel as a whole. Perry argues, for example, that the camps themselves serve as meticulous variations of one another, at times even parodied as such. There are several repetitive elements upon the arrival and settling down in each of the camps, from hammering nails into the walls to sorely missing the old camp to domesticating the new place.[32] The time spent in the camps is lost time, which Perry rightly labels "existence in parenthesis."[33] The recurrent temporality and the sense that the main character is stuck, both physically and emotionally, show the futility of the entire incarceration experience. The nine months that pass between the first and the last scenes—a period of time that according to literary conventions symbolizes a new beginning—only stress the feeling of stagnation and despair. The use of the pregnancy time period constitutes a cruel inversion of the typically blessed gestation time into a symbol of death and destruction. Vogel, it seems, made an informed decision to conclude the narrative with an open ending after nine months and chose to finalize Weichert's story fifty-nine days before the end of his own narrative. Here the author's poetic preferences overcome the authentic depiction of the events—an instance of the aesthetic prerogative overriding historical authenticity in Vogel's autobiographical fiction. The destination of the train he describes in the last scene is Le Camp d'étrangers des Milles, near Aix-en-Provence. Vogel spent almost two months there before his release in August 1940, but, again, this period of time remains absent from the manuscript.[34] Moreover, the decision not to provide the reader with closure to the narrative but rather to leave the fate of the prisoners unknown constitutes a powerful aesthetic choice, perhaps echoing the author's state of mind while writing the narrative in the middle of the Second World War.

The unjustified incarceration experience burned a permanent mark on Vogel, a scar that manifests itself in the way his text ends. Transformed and displaced, unhealthy, and deprived of basic rights, Weichert seems indifferent, even apathetic, to what may happen next. When some of the prisoners stand up to better view the direction of the train, Weichert only cares for his own comfort, stretching his legs and thinking, "Ven a teyl shteyen, ken ikh mikh beser oysshtrekkn, di fis gants grand."[35] Weichert remains apathetic, reflecting the trauma of his incarceration, with a diminished will to live, sensing that there is no place for him in the world. No place, perhaps, except for where he is located right now, in the text's present tense, on the train that carries him onward. This could explain why sitting comfortably means more to him at that moment then knowing, for example, the destination of the train. The narrative, thus, appropriately ends in transition, on a threshold, in between geographical spaces.

The transient metaphor and the train as a nonplace echo not only the emotional and physical experience of the imprisonment but also the type of world Vogel faced upon returning to Hauteville in 1940 in the middle of the war. The world he grew up in and left behind no longer existed, with circumstances that prevented him from returning to the Western metropolises, Paris and Vienna, where he previously resided. Vogel, then, lived in Hauteville and spent his time creating materials for his own time capsule. His Hebrew poem "Gallop of Troops around the World" ("She'atat tzeva'ot bimlo tevel"), written in December 1941, describes this period and the atmosphere of war lurking near him:

ru'aḥ ketel ba'olam titholel—
va'ani od rega nisharti po

wind of slaughter sprees around the world—
and I remained here [alone] for another moment

This image combines personal and international history. The speaker wants no part of the glory of death on the military battlefield and strives to maintain his individuality on the verge of an imminent disaster. Indeed, a present-day reading of the manuscript, with the knowledge of the catastrophe of the war in Europe and the Holocaust in particular occurring at the time of Vogel's writing, creates dramatic irony in the most classical sense of the term and greatly affects the experience of reading the novel.[36]

Yiddish on the Verge of Catastrophe

In his book *The Writing of the Disaster* (*L'Ecriture du désastre*), novelist and critic Maurice Blanchot discusses the possibility of writing about catastrophe and the ability of a text to register disaster. The Holocaust, he writes, "is the *absolute* event of history."[37] Blanchot conceptualizes disaster as unexperienced: "It is what escapes the very possibility of experience—it is the limit of writing. This must be repeated: the disaster de-scribes. Which does not mean that the disaster, as the force of writing, is excluded from it, is beyond the pale of writing or extratextual."[38]

The totality of the Holocaust catastrophe hovers above the reading experience of Vogel's last work of prose. The retrospective, extratextual knowledge about the tragic fate of the author in Auschwitz no doubt contributes to the shaping of this experience. Like the reader of other Holocaust diaries whose authors perished at the hands of the Nazis, Anne Frank being the most famous example, the reader of Vogel's work cannot help but be influenced by the historical knowledge of the author's untimely death.

The translator of Blanchot's work, Ann Smock, further explains,

> "The writing of the disaster" means not simply the process whereby something
> called the disaster is written—communicated, attested to, or prophesied. It also
> means the writing done by the disaster—by the disaster that ruins books and
> wrecks language. "The writing of the disaster" means the writing that the
> disaster—which liquidates writing—is, just as "knowledge of the disaster"
> means knowledge *as* disaster, and "the flight of thought" the loss of thought,
> which thinking is.[39]

The catastrophe in Vogel's narrative occurs only *after* the manuscript ends and is located outside the reality of the plot. At the same time, however, it forms an undeniable presence that already exists in the reader's collective past. In order to bridge these two levels of knowledge and experience—the text that describes traumatic events but does not contain "disaster" and the reader's retrospective contextualization of Vogel's death—I use Hans-Georg Gadamer's concept of the "fusion of horizons." Gadamer views understanding as a matter of negotiation between oneself and one's partner in a hermeneutical dialogue such that the process of understanding may be seen as a matter of coming to an "agreement" about a matter at issue. Coming to such an agreement means establishing a common framework or "horizon," which Gadamer takes to be a process involving the "fusion of horizons" (*Horizontverschmelzung*).[40] In his words, "A virtual horizon of interpretation and understanding must be opened in writing the text itself, one which the reader must fill out."[41] Although Vogel's narrative does not include the actual lingual encoding of the catastrophe that happens only after it has ended, the material surfacing of the text, after the war, already contains the knowledge of his personal catastrophe as well as the disaster of European Jewry. The very act of intimating the hiding place of his literary works to others proves that Vogel certainly considered the possibility that he would never return to Hauteville, perhaps even suspecting his own impending death. This historical intertext and the dramatic account of the preservation of the manuscript together create the fusion of horizons here.

This fusion of horizons between the reader and the text contributes to the effectiveness of the final scene of the novel. Delivered in the present tense, the scene depicts a train that carries the inmates to an unknown destination: "The clock passed eight, nine, and then ten o'clock. We started, we stopped, we rode further. We passed Marseille (some recognized the train station and the city from afar). We stayed there for about half an hour, then the train turned and drove a little bit backward. Then again forward. And now we travel farther, along the coast. The sea, smooth as a mirror without any wrinkle, spread to the horizon, deep-blue under the glowing southern sun, impartial."[42]

The narrative ends with a minor, anticlimatic tone similar to other prose works by Vogel.[43] The train could lead the prisoners to freedom or to another camp and a few more months of imprisonment. Historical knowledge attests that the inmates survived this ride and eventually returned to their homes and families.[44] As mentioned, the French authorities released Vogel in August 1940 and he joined his wife and daughter in Hauteville for the next three and a half years. However, knowledge of the Holocaust and Vogel's personal fate in Auschwitz force the reader today to interpret the open-ended plot as concluding in tragedy. The autobiographical component of the narrative, the similarities between Weichert and Vogel, thrust on the reader an understanding that even if after the train ride Weichert is released from the French detention camp, he will not be saved. The reader knows that this constitutes merely the first episode in the protagonist's war plight, and thus the possibly hopeful impact created by the open-ended narration is only temporal. In the mind of the reader

Last page of Vogel's Yiddish manuscript. Photo by the author, courtesy of the Gnazim archive.

today, a forced train ride to an unknown destination is a ubiquitous metaphor associated with the Holocaust, a prescient literary device of Vogel's. Therefore, the catastrophe that has already happened in the Jewish reader's collective past is bound to occur in the novel's future, beyond the pale of the text.

Still the questions remain: What does it mean to write such a narrative in Yiddish? Why choose Yiddish over Hebrew or German? In what ways does the personal biography relate to poetic decisions made by the author? Because Vogel did not have a chance to respond to these questions, scholars are left to provide their own explanations.

Vogel's choice to write in Yiddish contributes significantly to the shaping of the experience that the narrative portrays. For a native speaker who had never before applied the language creatively, such a decision entails a number of symbolic investments. First and foremost it derives from an attempt to make sense—in the form of a retelling—of a traumatic, disorienting experience. Vogel may have preferred Yiddish to Hebrew for describing daily life in the camps. A major part of the vocabulary needed for such a depiction in Hebrew did not yet exist at the time of his writing, and even if the colloquial Hebrew flourishing in Mandatory Palestine had already invented or renewed some of these terms, Vogel could not have had access to such information during wartime. In addition, according to the narrative, German was the most commonly spoken language in the French camps. It might have been easier to transfer dialogues and reenact situations in a language that semantically resembled the original tongue in which such conversations and experiences occurred. By switching the language in which the events took place from German to Yiddish, Vogel gained control over the depicted situation, perhaps even reducing the emotional risks involved in remembering and retelling. Crucially for a writer whose existence was synonymous with in-betweenness, Yiddish also metaphorically functioned here as a mediator between German and Hebrew, serving as a medium that allowed Vogel enough distance for distinct artistic creation.

Beyond the linguistic preferences, Vogel must have had other reasons for selecting Yiddish as the most suitable medium for the task of creating the narrative of his incarceration experience. Scholarly research also provides some clues beyond Vogel's own self-conscious motivation. Perry offers a stylistic explanation for Vogel's creative choice. According to him, the novel is written in Yiddish not as a result of a sense of Jewish companionship but rather as an attempt to echo grotesque forms of writing offered by Mendele and Gogol.[45] Laor connects the nature of Yiddish with Vogel's thematic intents and argues that "Yiddish was a reliable medium for representing the kind of world Vogel was interested in."[46] Viewing the novel as a testimonial narrative created on the verge of catastrophe may also assist in explaining the movement toward Yiddish.

Attempting to create an account of traumatic events involves a reconstruction and perhaps a reliving of the stressful experience. As Holocaust scholar James Young emphasizes, a parallel and contradictory impulse exists on the part of the writer to preserve in narrative form the very discontinuity that lends events their violent character. This same discontinuity is also effectively neutralized by its narrative rendering.[47] Vogel, negotiating between these two opposing processes, sought a way of constructing a narrative that would serve simultaneously as a testimony of events and a work of fiction. The experience he wanted to include in the narrative amounted to such unordinary circumstances that he may have wanted to move beyond his "regular" creative language, Hebrew, to relay those events. Although he could have picked German or even French, he consciously chose a language that by then was already in great decline, on the verge of its own vernacular death in western Europe particularly. Perhaps as an act of defiance, he decided against the Nationalist impulse he could now detect in both German and French.

Moreover, as a native speaker of Yiddish who mastered the language long before studying Hebrew, German, and other foreign languages, it might have been easier for Vogel to portray the experience of such displacement in his *mameloshn,* the language for which he possessed the most intimate knowledge. Vogel may have thus chosen Yiddish as the most adequate means to narrate his incarceration. Paradoxically, only through the application of his *mameloshn,* that most intimate and nurturing of languages, did Vogel find strength within himself to recount the disturbing events. Yiddish became for him a divider or a buffer zone between the traumatic experience and its poetic recreation. It also, paradoxically, formed a protective, intimate site from which he could create. In that way, Vogel's poetic decision to write in Yiddish and the proximity of the act of writing are directly and powerfully related to the author's own past trauma as well as the ongoing war around him.

Vogel's narrative depicts reality in dark, barely cloaked colors. His life experience led him to pessimism and despair. He no longer believed in the goodness of humankind. In one instance he writes, "And there will be no heaven. In a place where human beings are found, heaven cannot exist."[48] Writing on the verge of events that redefined the horizon for many, Vogel appeared to believe in nothing but artistic creation. He chose Yiddish, the language closest to him, despite or perhaps because of having avoided artistic creation in that language until that liminal point in his life. Like Vogel's earlier decision to become a Hebrew writer, his choice of Yiddish, a language that itself was on the verge of catastrophe both before and during the war, amounted to an act of defiance and self-marginalization. For him, the most rebellious act against the brutality he faced was to place it in a narrative structure using a familiar, intimate language suitable for what he had to say and tying, in the process, the survival of his account of events to the fate of his mother tongue.

Notes

I would like to thank Yael Feldman, Marion Kaplan, Hizky Shoham, Ziv Eisenberg, Lara Rabinovitch, and Hannah Pressman for their insightful comments and valuable suggestions. Unless otherwise noted, all English translations from the Yiddish are mine.

1. The collection of poetry *Lifney hasha'ar ha'afel* (*Before the Dark Gate*) appeared in 1923. The novella *Beveyt hamarpe* (*In the Sanatorium*) came out in 1928. In the following year, Vogel published the modernist novel *Ḥayey nisu'im* (*Married Life*). The novella *Facing the Sea* (*Nokhaḥ hayam*) appeared in 1932.
2. Literary historian Dan Laor traces this event to the night between February 5 and 6 in 1944. Laor located documents confirming the arrest of eighteen people in Hauteville-

Lompnes during these two days. According to him, Vogel was among them. See Dan Laor, "Le'an huvlu ha'atzurim: al haperek heḥaser bekhronikat hamilḥama shel David Fogel" [Where Were the Detainees Taken To: On the Missing Chapter of David Vogel's War Chronicle], in *Mimerkazim lemerkaz: sefer Nurit Govrin* [From Centers to Center: Festschrift in Honor of Nurit Govrin], ed. Avner Holzman, Michal Oron, and Ziva Shamir (Tel Aviv: Machon Katz, 2005), 385-411, 386.

3. A newly discovered Hebrew novel by Vogel was published in February 2012 by Am Oved. Literary scholar Lilach Netanel found the manuscript among drafts of the novella, "Facing the Sea," and gave it the title, *Roman Vina'i* [Viennese Romance]. Netanel and other scholars argue that Vogel wrote the majority of the manuscript circa 1937-1938. See Noa Limone, "The Vogel's Code," *Haaretz*, January 19, 2012, accessed January 27, 2012, http://www.haaretz.co.il/magazine/1.1620416. In all likelihood, the Hebrew pages in Vogel's buried literary remains are part of this novel.

4. Aharon Komem, "Introduction," in *Le'ever hadmama: shirim* [Towards Stillness: Poems], by David Vogel (Tel Aviv: Hakibbutz Hameuhad, 1983), 9-77, 11-12, 62.

5. Menachem Perry, "Eibed Fogel et Fogel—aḥarit davar" [Vogel Has Lost Vogel: An Afterword], in *Taḥanot kavot* [Extinguished Stations], by David Vogel, ed. Menachem Perry (Tel Aviv: Hakibbutz Hameuhad/Siman Kriah, 1990), 327-50, 328-29.

6. David Vogel archive, folder no. 231.29587 (handwritten manuscript) and 231.29587a (printed manuscript). My thanks to Hedva Rokhel, former director of the Gnazim Institute, and Dvora Stavi, director of the Gnazim archive, for their invaluable assistance in accessing and copying the original manuscript.

7. David Vogel, "Kulam yatzu lakrav" [They All Went out to Battle], *Extinguished Stations*, 65-197.

8. These poems are "Arey ne'uray" ["Cities of My Youth"] from September 1941 and "She'atat tzeva'ot bimlo tevel" ["Gallop of Troops around the World"] from December 1941. See Perry's afterword for Vogel's collection of prose *Extinguished Stations*, 328.

9. Chana Kronfeld, *On the Margins of Modernism: Decentering Literary Dynamics* (Berkeley: University of California Press, 1996), 160.

10. The diary (*yoman*), which spans from 1912 to 1922, contains no indication that Vogel meant to publish it. The full text appears in *Extinguished Stations*, 269-326, and is titled "Ketzot hayamim" ["Ends of Days"]. For an extensive discussion of this personal journal, see Robert Alter, "Fogel and the Forging of a Hebrew Self," *Prooftexts* 13 (1993): 3-13.

11. David Vogel, "Ends of Days," *Extinguished Stations*, 324-25. In this Hebrew entry in his journal from December 14, 1919, Vogel mentions briefly that he got married six months before and already buried a "six-month-old baby girl," whom he loved. "It was necessary to save the mother and we had to put the daughter to death," he writes. Despite this language it appears that Vogel meant that his wife Ilka, who was six months pregnant and suffered from tuberculosis, terminated the pregnancy in order to save her life. Such a practice was common in Europe in the first decades of the twentieth century.

12. Robert Alter, *The Invention of Hebrew Prose: Modern Fiction and the Language of Realism* (Seattle: University of Washington Press, 1988), 75-77; Aharon Komem, *Ha'ofel vehapele: iyunim beyetzirato shel David Fogel* [Darkness and Wonder: Studies in David Vogel's Work] (Jerusalem: Zemora Bitan, 2001), 205-12.

13. Dan Miron, "When Will We Cease to 'Discover' Vogel?" in *The Blind Library: Assorted Prose Pieces: 1980-2005* (Tel Aviv: Yediot Ahronot, Sifrey Hemed, 2005), 102-24, 105.

14. In a postcard Vogel sent to his wife from Camp des Milles dated June 18, 1940, he refers to his daughter as Tamara, which perhaps was her nickname. This is the only time he mentions her by name. See the full letter in Laor, "Where Were the Detainees," 391-92.

15. Vogel, 1 [unpublished manuscript]. The Yiddish quotations from Vogel's manuscript in this essay are based on both the original handwritten text and on a typed transcription made by Avram Nowersztern. Nowersztern's document, comprising 419 pages, formed

the basis of Perry's edited translation into Hebrew. Quotations from Nowersztern's document will henceforth be marked with "(N)." Notes or quotations that are based on the Hebrew translation will henceforth be marked with "(H)." My thanks to Zohar Weiman-Kelman of the University of California, Berkeley for sharing with me parts of Nowersztern's document as well as her ongoing work on Vogel's manuscript.

16. Vogel, 1 [unpublished manuscript].

17. French historiography of recent years refers to these camps as *les camps de la honte* (the camps of shame). See, for example, Anne Grynberg, *Les Camps de la honte: les internés juifs des camps français, 1939-1944* (Paris: La Découverte, 1991) or Patrick Coupechoux, *Mémoires de déportés: histoires singulières de la déportation* (Paris: La Découverte, 2003). See also Laor, "Where Were the Detainees," 386.

18. Komem, *Towards Stillness*, 12, 15; Laor, "Where Were the Detainees," 386-87.

19. Komem, *Towards Stillness*, 12-13.

20. Perry, "Vogel Has Lost Vogel," 328.

21. Although the sources we have are not sufficient to prove beyond doubt that Vogel knew about the fate of European Jewry, we know that confirmed information about the systematic mass murder of Jews arrived in Palestine and the United States (which were much farther away than Hauteville, France) as early as November 1942. In addition, Vogel must have felt at least some personal danger, for he decided to hide his literary production before the Lyon gestapo captured him in February 1944.

22. Vogel, 1 [unpublished manuscript].

23. Vogel (H), 122.

24. Vogel (H), 127-28.

25. The character appears to be lying to the interviewer on the second meeting. See Vogel (H), 165, 187. Reading Weichert as a painter is also in line with Vogel's attempt to distance himself—at least on the surface—from the main character of the novel. With that, literary scholars have used the trope of "painting" to describe Vogel's Hebrew writing style. For example, analyzing the novella *Facing the Sea*, which many consider Vogel's best prose writing, Robert Alter explains that the narrator has "painterly precision," which may easily depict Weichert as well. See Alter, *Invention of Hebrew Prose*, 79.

26. Vogel (H), 107.

27. Vogel (N), 262.

28. Vogel, 2 [unpublished manuscript].

29. For a good formulation of autobiographical fiction and its evolution in Hebrew literature, see Hannah Naveh, *Siperet haviduy: beḥinato shel janer* [Confessional Prose: Examination of the Genre] (Tel Aviv: Papirus, 1988). For "masked autobiography," see Yael Feldman, *No Room of Their Own: Israeli Women's Fiction* (New York: Columbia University Press, 1999), 22-28.

30. The one exception is the reading Perry has offered. However, although he views the manuscript as a novel, he does not apply theoretical tools other than close reading to analyze the text.

31. Vogel (N), 6.

32. Perry, "Vogel Has Lost Vogel," 341.

33. Perry, "Vogel Has Lost Vogel," 337-39.

34. For detailed information on Camp des Milles and the time Vogel spent there, see Laor, "Where Were the Detainees," 387-90.

35. Vogel (N), 419.

36. Dramatic irony arises when the words and actions of the characters of a work of literature have a different meaning for the reader than they do for the characters. This is the result of the reader having a greater knowledge than the characters themselves. See, for example, The Literary Encyclopedia, "Dramatic Irony," accessed October 2, 2009, http://www.litencyc.com/php/stopics.php?rec=true&UID=574.

37. Maurice Blanchot, *The Writing of the Disaster,* trans. Ann Smock (Lincoln: University of Nebraska Press, 1995), 47.

38. Ibid., 7.

39. Ibid., ix.

40. Stanford Encyclopedia of Philosophy, "Hans-Georg Gadamer," http://plato.stanford .edu/entries/gadamer.

41. Hans-Georg Gadamer, "Text and Interpretation," in *Hermeneutics and Modern Philosophy,* ed. Brice R. Wachterhauser (Albany: State University of New York Press, 1986), 377–400, 393.

42. Vogel, 127 [unpublished manuscript].

43. See, for example, the ending scene of the novella *Facing the Sea* from 1932, depicting the farewell of Barthes and Gina. David Vogel, *Nokhaḥ hayam* (Tel Aviv: Hasifria haketana, 2005), 93–96.

44. Laor, "Where Were the Detainees," 387–88.

45. Perry, "Vogel Has Lost Vogel," 331.

46. Laor, "Where Were the Detainees," 408.

47. James E. Young, "Interpreting Literary Testimonies: A Preface to Rereading Holocaust Diaries and Memoirs," in *New Literary History* 18, no. 2 (1987): 404–7.

48. Vogel (H), 171.

IN THE POT, HALF-MELTED

Sacco-Vanzetti Poems and Yiddish American Identity

JORDAN FINKIN

On April 15, 1920, in South Braintree, Massachusetts, two guards were murdered in a daring daylight payroll robbery. In the ensuing mishandled investigation, the police arrested two Italian immigrant workers—Nicola Sacco and Bartolomeo Vanzetti—on thin and largely circumstantial evidence, including their commitment to anarchism. In these waning days of the First Red Scare, the country was still reeling from the previous year's wave of anarchist-orchestrated bombings that had targeted major civic leaders, including the attorney general. Sacco, an accomplished shoe cutter and devoted family man, and Vanzetti, a fish peddler and lonely anarchist theoretician, had both immigrated in 1908 and became acquainted through their political activities. Their trial, lengthy seven-year imprisonment, and execution by electric chair on August 23, 1927 inextricably bound their lives and fateful ends, creating a cause célèbre of the age.

The Sacco-Vanzetti case provoked national and international outrage and inspired an impressive range of artistic productions, including Ben Shahn's famous drawings, an album of songs by Woody Guthrie, and a wide variety of literary responses. Alongside a number of plays, several acclaimed novels focused on the case, including the third book in John Dos Passos's *U.S.A. Trilogy, The Big Money* (1936); Upton Sinclair's *Boston* (1928), translated into Yiddish and published in Warsaw[1]; and the 1930 novel *Pay Day*, written by Nathan Asch, the son of the Yiddish writer Sholem Asch. However, by far the greatest number of literary responses came in the form of poetry. One reckoning is at least 144 poems published in American English and German alone.[2] The genre itself, which covered a wide variety of forms and thematic vocabulary, spanned the dizzying heights and pitying lows of quality, from important contributions by poets such as Edna St. Vincent Millay and Countee Cullen to mediocre flurries of anger or sentimentality.

A significant number of Sacco-Vanzetti poems also appeared in Yiddish, to the extent that, alongside the many examples in other languages, the "Sacco-Vanzetti poem" emerged as a distinctly American genre that reflected on the thematic constellation of race, class, and nation. Beginning during the trial and execution and continuing through the following decade, the writing of a "Sacco-Vanzetti" appeared routinely among Yiddish poets engaging the idea of "America." Although literary scholars often ignore or underestimate the role of this genre in the formation of the Jewish American canon,[3] the sheer breadth and cultural importance of the trial and the subsequent Jewish artistic output suggest the phenomenon of the Sacco-Vanzetti as a Jewish genre just as much as an American one. This applies not only for the writers of expressly engagé groups such as Proletpen[4]—who saw the miscarriage of justice perpetrated against two workingmen as almost made to order—but also for a romantic poet such as Naftoli Gros, the much harder to pigeonhole Moyshe-Leyb Halpern and H. Leivick, and all of the deans of Inzikhism: Yankev Glatshteyn, Aaron Glants-Leyeles, and Nokhum Borukh Minkov. The process of carving out creative and often very original poetic spaces within the landscape of this Sacco-Vanzetti genre constituted an important activity in their self-understanding as Yiddish American poets. The very act of writing a Sacco-Vanzetti not only declared one's participation in the American project, in particular on the American urban landscape, but also gives us a window on to the complicated anxieties particular to the community of Yiddish writers engaged in that project. Anxieties about politics and power, the relevance of poetry, and the role of Yiddish in American Jewish life and letters all surface as themes in the work of these writers.

The Sacco-Vanzetti poets emerged out of the context of the late nineteenth- and early twentieth-century "sweatshop poets," as they came to be known at the time. With their focus on social engagement and communal character, seen through the lens of the poor immigrant laborer, they turned out well-lathed lyrics that the poet Zishe Landoy would ultimately dismiss as "the rhyme department of the Jewish labor movement."[5] This, however, does not diminish the significance of the political taproot of this poetry. The political trajectory of American Yiddish poetry continued with Proletpen and other explicitly engagé groups, some of which kept writing through the 1930s and at least until World War II.

At the end of the first decade of the twentieth century a group of writers, appropriating the originally dismissive epithet applied to them, *di yunge* (the young ones), rejected this social function in favor of an aestheticist, pared-down, art for art's sake refinement of poetic voice and language. In turn, Moyshe-Leyb Halpern displaced this poetry with his sui generis approach, a displacement that also found willing participants among the poets clustered around the journal *In zikh* (*In the Self,* first published in 1920), who came to be known as Inzikhistn, or "introspectivists."[6] These poets embodied a kind of Americanness, seen particularly with their espousal of radical poetic individualism and a liberal dedication to the needs and demands of a poem. According to the Inzikhistn manifesto no poem *has* to be political; it *may* be political as long as it represents an authentic product of the poetic self.[7] Nevertheless, all of the manifesto's signers did write Sacco-Vanzetti poems, indicating their underlying or basic political sympathies.

The Sacco-Vanzetti Genre

Several overlapping tendencies and discrepancies exist between English-language thematology and the Yiddish poetry within the Sacco-Vanzetti genre. Scholars of the English-language poetry have isolated a number of prominent thematic features, including the mismatch between the crime and Sacco's and Vanzetti's characters; the Crucifixion of Jesus; "fatalism"; abstractions on the "death of justice"; ultimate comeuppance or retribution; and society's eventual realization of its own folly.[8] One of the subtextual concerns of these scholars rests in understanding Sacco-Vanzetti poetry as a gauge of contemporary social attitudes, predominantly a "cleavage in society."[9] Though they claim that this seldom appears as an overt theme, the almost universal stance of the poetry as some combination of hostility to the perpetrators, on the one hand, and sympathy for Sacco and Vanzetti, on the other, constitutes sufficient support for such a cleavage.

The Yiddish poetry in general conforms at least to the spirit of the latter analysis. For its part, the poetry of the Proletpen group—whose poets wore their political engagement fully on their sleeves—most closely matches the Joughin-Morgan model of boilerplate Sacco-Vanzetti themes and images. So, for example, despite the fact that in his poem "Sacco and Vanzetti" Ber Grin (1901–1989) apostrophizes both convicts, the initial stanza concludes,

> His red flowers were fresh greetings from a bleeding friend,
> Reminders of Dante, his son:
> The last today and the day's last end.[10]

Similar to the non-Yiddish poems Joughin and Morgan analyze, this work typifies the mismatch between crime and character as well as the strong tendency to focus on Sacco rather than Vanzetti.[11] In other words, such a mild-mannered and devoted family man as Nicola Sacco, with references to his son Dante as the icon of this attitude, could never have perpetrated this brutal and brazen crime. In turn, this sympathetic reading of Sacco made his portrayal more rhetorically useful for establishing the stark Manichean contrasts in the political poetry. This did not automatically entail Vanzetti's complete absence from this poetry.

Yosl Grinshpan's (1902–1934) "Vanzetti's Ghost" ("Vantsetis geshpenst"; 1929), for example, presents an almost Poeian macabre visitation of Vanzetti's ghost to the terrified and pathetic Judge Thayer.[12] However, by and large the loquacious and intellectual Vanzetti seems more elusive in these works or presents a more complicated aspect of the issues involved in the case.

Returning to Grin's poem, later on the ominous phrase "Fuller and Thayer lie in wait" (*fuler mit teyern loyern*), for example, which depicts Massachusetts Governor Alvan Fuller and the trial judge Webster Thayer lurking like beasts of prey, typifies the vilification of the prosecutors. Conversely, the following sentimental description shows again the equally typical sympathy for Sacco and Vanzetti:

> Childhood and their barefoot days,
> Grapevine and olive-tree, where they were raised,
> And Italian nights hang a dream on each long
> Branch. Morning rings with the sickle.[13]

The communist image of the sickle represents part of a broader co-opting of Sacco and Vanzetti as martyrs to their own ideology by many of the groups on the Left. The ideological pedestal on which these groups placed Sacco and Vanzetti serves ultimately to universalize both the alleged criminals and the Yiddish poets' participation in this American genre.

In literary scholar Rocco Marinaccio's account, anger over Sacco and Vanzetti's plight "instilled in many writers on the Left a sense of community that had been largely absent earlier in the decade and that was essential to their nascent identity as members of a distinct 'proletarian' literary movement."[14] This sense of a larger community beyond the factious fractures within the labor movement appears clearly in the Yiddish-speaking world as well.[15] Ultimately, Marinaccio seeks to describe, using John Dos Passos's *Facing the Chair* and Upton Sinclair's *Boston*—both of which focus on the image of Vanzetti—how the labor movement, the communists in particular, sought to "Americanize" and domesticate Sacco and Vanzetti. The goal involved countering xenophobia within the various components of the movement and demonstrating how the ideology of the labor movement resonated much more with "native" American ideals than the representatives of crass capitalism bent on executing Sacco and Vanzetti.

Despite the central position of the execution in both the English and Yiddish poetic iconography, Grin's poem demonstrates another thematic element present in the Yiddish poetics more than the English poems of this genre, namely, the period of Sacco and Vanzetti's imprisonment[16]:

> This barred-window sadness drinks the blood from hand and face,
> As the hangman kills every day for seven years in the deadened space.[17]

Excavating along the political seams, this focus on aging in prison reveals an anxiety about relevance: not only the relevance of labor ideology but also and more dramatically the relevance of the Yiddish-language poet to his community. Few poets gave voice to these anxieties with quite as much nuance as Moyshe-Leyb Halpern.

Moyshe-Leyb Halpern

Moyshe-Leyb Halpern (1886–1932), one of the most original voices of modern Yiddish letters, lived a life of penury. Just as his poetry charted its own unique course, so did the path of his ideological engagements bring him variously into and out of favor among those journals and publications from which a writer tried to eke out a living. Halpern's Sacco-Vanzetti poem, titled "Sacco-Vanzetti," represents one of the great achievements of the genre. Its opening line—"One can pull from one's head a gray hair" (*men ken zikh oysraysn a groye hor fun kop*)—presents a generalized image of growing old. The poem sets its anchor in reality by describing the noticeable graying of both of the inmates over their seven-year incarceration, especially Sacco, who fared poorly in his imprisonment and during his hunger strike. Unlike the poems of Glatshteyn, Leyeles, and Minkov, Halpern explicitly dated his poem to twelve days after the execution. Also unlike those other poems whose authors more often than not incorporated them into larger projects as part of more mature evaluations,[18] Halpern's poem relays an immediate response.[19] Not a poem of angry protest or incomprehension, it has more in common with Millay's simmering lament, "Justice Denied in Massachusetts," published the day of the execution.[20]

Halpern's "Sacco-Vanzetti" nevertheless remains the pinnacle of what Joughin and Morgan might call the fatalist response. In a subtle working out of small-paired images, Halpern conceives of the execution pessimistically as a "way out" (*oysveg*), accepting its inevitability:

> And if a child—the poorest,
> When you dress him up on a holiday,
> Will go wherever he is led;
> Then you too—no matter how old you are—
> May let them take you to the death-chair
> That is waiting.[21]

In its climactic assessment, the necessary compliance that the poem suggests to the condemned resembles that of the child done up in holiday clothes: sour-faced but innocent, even naïve. Halpern continues on this theme by focusing on the apparatus of execution:

And when the deadly copper gleams on your head,
What can be heavy then?
A king—even when the whole people weeps around his throne—
Must be still when they crown him.
And if the crown on the chosen one is made of fire,
It is a wonder-crown in this damn world.
And only the wolf, forever lurking, the wild animal,
And only the outlaw in the dark—
Fear the fire.[22]

The placing of the copper cap from the electric chair on the head appears as a grim coronation. Other poets also pay particular attention to both the metaphor of the coronation and the importance of electricity. Here Halpern focuses on the burning quality of the electricity; elsewhere others foreground different aspects of the electric current.[23] Second, Halpern presents the lurking (*loyert*) nature of the perpetrators, figured as beasts of prey and resembling a similar description in Grin's poem as part of the larger conversation about the miscarriage of justice.[24]

However, the end of the first stanza adds a sympathetic note:

Be still for a moment.
And, like a typhoid patient, bend your head
To him who shaves.
He is your brother.
You mustn't be mad at him
For not taking your skin along with your hair.
He only does what he's told and when he's paid.
And the death-clothes too—
These too—were tailored by your brother who was hungry.[25]

This passage offers yet another image of acquiescence at the heart of the poem, this time with a note of sympathy for the executioner and the functionaries of execution. They are "brothers," after all, not to be condemned by misdirected contempt or scorn. The poem describes them as part of a larger apparatus against which appeals are futile.

Although other scholars have suggested the contrary,[26] this poem is not an "apolitical" poem, especially since the very *writing* of a Sacco-Vanzetti itself constituted a political act. The deceptive simplicity of Halpern's description defies attempts to identify concretely the poem's depilating subject.[27] This could just as easily describe a mournful observer as one of the condemned. The visible and dramatic aging of Sacco and Vanzetti during their seven-year confinement, widely noted at the time, featured commonly in the Yiddish poetry. One need not, therefore, reject outright the poem's initial impression that it is the prisoner bloodying his head. Rather, one can *also* implicate the onlooker in the poem, which makes more sense if that onlooker is the *poet*, particularly given the anxieties implicit in the theme of premature senescence. Halpern's crucial insight establishes the fundamental *resemblance* of graying onlooker, or the poet, to an aging Sacco/Vanzetti. This mapping of subject and object onto one another adds dramatic power and fits into Halpern's fascination with the crafting and grafting of personae in his other poetry.[28] The dramatic thematic potential of the uses and abuses of Sacco and Vanzetti should come as no surprise nor should the attractiveness of the poetic image presenting the prisoner within mirrored in the prisoner without. Other poets make use of a different congeries of these thematic materials, most notably the Inzikhistn, whose intensely individualist poetics serve as an essential link in the discourse of identity at the heart of the Sacco-Vanzetti genre.

The Inzikhist Sacco-Vanzetti

Inzikhist Arn Leyeles's (1889-1966) deeply politicized depictions shared Halpern's thematics, particularly in Leyeles's poem "America 1927," which includes the rigged machinery of American justice and the futility of complaint. The fourth section of that poem presents a formalized dialogue between the warden and the executioner. The latter, rather plagued by guilt, asks the warden how he copes with those feelings. In the warden's words, no matter what we think or feel, "You have your money, I have my Office" (*du host dayn gelt, ikh hob mayn amt*); money and power make all else irrelevant.

This poem of Leyeles, from the 1937 collection *Fabius Lind*, represents the most Inzikhistically "kaleidoscopic"[29] account, with six separate points of view in the poem's six parts, each composed in a different poetic form. The opening sections present a negative history—"*No* parades are prepared for flying heroes. / *No* holiday banners are waved for returning victors," referring to Lindbergh's parade and the end of World War I—undermining American triumphalism. Indeed, with their avowed reliance on both Walt Whitman and the Anglo-American Imagists in crafting a self-consciously new poetics in Yiddish letters, the Inzikhistn also focused on American identity, expressing deep concerns simultaneously about the gains and losses of creating this American Yiddish art.

In the second section, we find a powerful combination of some of these themes:

> Light and life.
> Primeval eye [*ur-oyg*]. Universal eye [*al-oyg*]. Primeval and universal
>   [*ur un al*].
> In a parlor—no, in a room four by four.
> Behind a door that knows and conceals everything,
> A double coronation in the middle of the night.

(Heralds have announced the crowning
Weeks, months, years in advance.
In their bowels have seven years matured, pained
The royal ritual
Till they emptied it
Into the blackness of midnight.)
All of the eyes—one white, cold sight.
White, cold sight keeps watch.
Silence keeps watch.
The place of honor
The throne.
They're already putting on
The crown
Of cold metal.
A push.
1776 volts.
1789 volts.
1917 volts.
Yes. Yes. We've done what we wanted.[30]

The blatantly crude imagery mocks standard American proprieties. One should also note the combination of the image of the seven-year confinement, including its scatological reference to a seven-year injustice expelled by electrocuted bowels, the comic grotesque of the "urinal" pun, and the coronation metaphor, as in Halpern. Moreover, though linking the electrocution to the great revolutionary moments of America, France, and Russia, Leyeles nevertheless sarcastically casts the execution as a counterrevolutionary act. Leyeles deploys the "we" of the last line above as a repeated referent throughout the poem to those who control the country with legal and financial power. Leyeles calls them the "restlessly restless masters,"[31] who, though content in their power, grow uneasy at the thought of social and political unrest. His conclusion, "Yes. Yes. We've done what we wanted," echoes the assessment by these masters of the America they control.

The fifth section of this poem presents an unusual description in the form of a ballad:

A state among states is Massachusetts
In the land of the mountains and the lakes and the prairies.
Massachusetts has murdered Sacco and Vanzetti.
And a third—Celestino Madeiros.
The two have sanctified the third.
The murderer cried moronically with his silence:

Dull is my head and I only want to sleep,
But is there really no mercy?[32]

Celestino Madeiros, a murderer executed along with Sacco and Vanzetti, had confessed to the crime for which they were convicted. As Joughin and Morgan point out, in the English-language poetry generally little is made of "the presumably unpoetic Medeiros [*sic*]."[33] His appearance in several Yiddish poems is itself, therefore, noteworthy. Leyeles turns the scene into an inverted Golgotha, with two martyrs "sanctifying" the guilty man instead of the one Jesus's relation to the two thieves crucified with him. Among the sixty poems found in the English-language poetry anthology *America Arraigned!* (1928), and despite the rampant martyrological and Christological imagery (two of the three sections of the book are headed with explicit references to "the Crucifixion"), Madeiros hardly figures at all. To cite one noteworthy exception, which resonates with Leyeles's poem, Clement Wood's "Golgotha in Massachusetts" opens as follows:

Not even two thieves to grace this slow murder.
    Instead, two innocent dreamers, in place of one
Tortured for seven years, a hell harder
    Than the crude spitting and flogging of Mary's son.[34]

Yankev Glatshteyn (1896–1971) uses this sympathetic tone, which Leyeles reserves only for Sacco, Vanzetti, and Madeiros, for a very different character. Glatshteyn's "Sacco and Vanzetti's Monday" ("Sako un Vantsetis montik") centers on the mind of the governor of Massachusetts the day before the execution. Nearly unique in the Sacco-Vanzetti corpus, though not ultimately sympathetic, it turns the much vilified governor into a tragic figure. This long, twelve-page poem explores not only the contemporary urban American psyche but also the effect of power on those who possess it. After a prologue presenting the day before the execution as a day like any other in the alienating city[35]—an urban parallel to Millay's naturalism—the rest of the poem divides into two sections: the first presents the governor's ruminations on himself and the institutions of power, and the second gives his increasingly agonized thoughts on the martyrdom of Sacco and Vanzetti, couched in the dense and complicated Christian warp and weft of the poem's imagery. The governor's inner turmoil over the nature of power acts as a projection of a Yiddish poet's anxieties about his own relevance:

Do I then hold the seal in my hand?
I am not first and am not last,
Before me and after me a chain of men
Who have been cynically immortalized,

Stuck to the nape of a world of memory
And the waters will never wash away their names.
Woe is me. Woe and woe and woe.
In my ears sound two names
And together with them will sound my name.
And you who sing in the middle of the hard night
Sing me too into your song,
And weave me too into the thread of your poem
Hear me and my voice as it cuts through the world: Save![36]

The governor's desire to be included in the songs, thereby providing a poetic record of the event that will (in the governor's eyes) doubtless outlast all other accounts, constitutes a significant lyrical move for Yiddish Sacco-Vanzettis; for Glatshteyn daringly orchestrates that call to poeticize history as coming from the once scorned, now pitiable governor himself. Seeing his name lost in the stale lists of his fellow office holders, the governor sees his immortality in the poetry itself, linking him to these men who haunt him. Furthermore, Glatshteyn's deployment of the themes of ephemeralness and fungibility, in this case the ephemeral nature of power and the fungible character of the ones who wield it, effectively marginalizes the governor, displacing him as an individual from the center of the issue to the periphery of relevance. In this way the poem itself, presented as a "song" sung in Yiddish, is pulled into the vacuum.

Leyeles's poem also presents a similar image of poeticizing or lyricizing history, though in a much more problematic way:

Sing me a song of that which must come.
Sing me the song of payment.

How can I sing when every night I turn on and off electric lights,
When every day the names Sacco-Vanzetti burn me,
The silence of the unfortunate brother, Celestino Madeiros, burns me?[37]

In one construction, only immortalization and eternal consciousness brought about through art can repay the Sacco-Vanzetti debt. However, according to Leyeles, "flipping the switch," turning on a light, itself constitutes a commemorative (if inartistic) act that makes the artistic response nearly impossible.

One quickly discerns the image of electricity itself as an important thematic element in the Yiddish poetry. Nokhum Borukh Minkov's (1893–1958) "Electric Dead" ("Elektrishe meysim"), subtitled "Sacco-Vanzetti," offers a complicated meditation on their death. Using his recognizable dense and opaque intellectualized poetics, Minkov takes the particulate nature of electricity and turns Sacco and Vanzetti themselves into particles of electricity diffused into millions of homes and into the consciousness of the electric age itself. This presentation effectively isolates and concentrates the common depiction of the everyday realities observable in other poems—at the moment of the execution, for example:

> The two dead break open
> Their million light hands
>   Scattered to the most hidden
> Attics thresholds   cellars.[38]

The execution occurred at midnight, a quiet time for most Americans, or more precisely the urban masses—the main concern of these poets—figured here as Bostonians. Not only does the poem mean to jar domestic tranquility into momentary intranquility by the flickering of the lights at the execution, but that tranquility, or lack thereof, does not take place in public. It takes place neither at the hearth nor in the warm inner sanctums of the home but rather concealed in "attics" or "cellars." In other words this poem directs its attention to the peripheral corners of domestic existence, perhaps also a reference to the rooms for let in which workingmen like Sacco and Vanzetti might have otherwise slept. Minkov's poem also references "thresholds," the modernist emblem of liminal existence between two states of being. This construction situates Sacco and Vanzetti and the America that condemned and executed them and to which they belong on the margins—a key image and metaphor for immigrant communities as well as for their languages. The Yiddish poet's anxiety of relevance has to do in part with a concern over marginalization. The Inzikhistn had an especially prickly relationship to this idea. On the one hand, they wrote for themselves, or so they maintained. On the other hand, however, they grew irate not only over the relative lack of recognition of their achievements but also over specific slights taken against them. In an anonymous piece in a 1923 issue of their journal, *In zikh,* the author castigates the *English*-language American Jewish press and intellectuals either for ignoring Yiddish literature or for their ignorance of it. In averring that "no other immigrant group has built an original, independent, and in more than one aspect American literature in the course of some thirty years than we Jews,"[39] the Inzikhistn claimed the authentic "Americanness" both of their group and of American Yiddish literature more broadly. The author also excoriates *Poetry* magazine's stated incapacity to review *In zikh* due to their inability to read what they thought was "Chinese." "Making it" into the American literary world would take what the Inzikhistn considered a gallingly large amount of work.[40]

"Making it" in America, however, involved a complicated realization and adjustment. In the electric explosion, Minkov makes explicit what others left under the surface in their critiques:

> Lift them deep
> Lift them high
> Heart-windows   soul-doors
> Blood-stars of
> Race   nation   class.[41]

Race, nation, and class comprise categories of American identity politics running through the Sacco-Vanzetti genre writ large. In recognizing this prereq-
uisite to Americanness the poem articulates an important subtext to many of
these Sacco-Vanzetti poems, namely an anxiety about identity occasioned by an
empathic response to these two Italian immigrant workingmen.[42] Ultimately,
Minkov concludes his call to "lift them" as a call to memorialize them—"lift
them unforgettably."[43] Memorialization stands as a common theme in Sacco-
Vanzetti poetry. Minkov, however, makes his memorial the flick of a light
switch, a universal memorial in the modern age.

Sacco-Vanzetti and "Vespuccian" Identity

Taken together, the Yiddish Sacco-Vanzetti poets went beyond their English-
language contemporaries to develop a distinctive thematology, one that claims
a stake in American identity politics. This genre embraced the Yiddish language as a legitimate component of the American project and, from the specifically literary point of view, entailed the ability to write something unarguably
"American" *in* Yiddish. Glatshteyn's supposition that no other group had created a "more American" literature than Yiddish-speaking (and Yiddish-writing)
Jews gives voice to a real self-conception, no matter how nebulous, as Yiddish
American. Except for a few cases, such as Naftoli Gros's inclusion of the ballad
"The Song of Sacco and Vanzetti" in the second volume of his *Idn* (*Jews*),[44] little
if any Judaization of Sacco and Vanzetti appears in the Yiddish poetry. Instead
these poets see "Americanness" as something far more complicated than the
dryly descriptive construct "race—nation—class" per se, something greater
than the sum of these parts. They poetically construe a Yiddish American identity not as something stative but as something participatory. The themes, for
example, of Christianity, electricity, and fatalism, all relate to power and the
anxieties born of the conflict between an image of nationhood (the American
ideal) rooted in an *idea* and the exercise of power.

Indeed, power comes to the fore as a significant concern of early twentieth-
century American Yiddish literature's political understanding. This concern
with power adds issues of agency to the constellation of defining American
themes as well as pointing out the modernist Yiddish poet's anxieties about
having so little of it as a figure on the margins of a marginal community.[45] This
tension runs through Glatshteyn's poem, for instance, and its continuously
battling refrains: "something will happen" (*epes vet geshen*) and "nothing will

happen" (*gornit vet geshen*), the potential and the actual, the possible and the real. Sacco and Vanzetti represent, in Leyeles's words, "America 1927": epochal, on the cusp, on the threshold. "Outsidedness" and "marginality" stand at the center of Jewish American poetics, and that marginality "attests to the extent to which dominant accounts of literary culture depend on formulations of 'nation' (such as 'Americanness') or other stable models of identity (such as those based on ethnicity or race)."[46] The Sacco-Vanzetti forms part of a nondominant account, one that calls for further exploration.

Analyses of this idea of reconfigured identities often focus on English texts. Although English set the tone in American letters, the work of constructing American cultural identity, or identities, on precisely this pluralist platform was often undertaken with great dedication and sophistication in languages other than English. The poets of the Inzikh group, for example, clearly participated in this project. One finds it puzzling, therefore, that discussions of Jewish American writing do frequently elide mention of Sacco-Vanzetti.[47] Considering the status of the case at the time, this lacuna among Jewish English-language authors demands further investigation. Likely the nexus of Americanism in English lay elsewhere, such as in the preoccupation with contemporary prejudice toward and violence against African Americans, particularly in the South (a marked concern among Yiddish-language poets as well).

American Yiddish modernist letters, however, concentrated on a different set of complexities, not the least of which involved how to make Yiddish a language of American cultural productivity.[48] The process of both Americanization and nativization that this entailed proved central to the perception among its authors of writing within a Yiddish Sacco-Vanzetti genre. From the English-language—and politically hyperengaged—arena, Marinaccio asks programmatically, "How does a writer represent two persecuted immigrants, whose ethnicity is at the very heart of their tragedy, as suitable 'American' heroes?"[49] One can give an expressly political answer[50]; yet looking closely at these Yiddish poems reveals the contours of a specifically Yiddish poetic discourse about Americanness. This discourse involves a kind of hendiadys, a creation of a complex whole out of coordinated and not subordinated parts. One might call this model of Americanness, for lack of a better term, Vespuccian, which activates the foreign-sounding half of the name Amerigo Vespucci, the origin of "America." Using this term places the focus on another, different kind of Americanness, with the outsider as insider—the kind of Americanness that takes up the cause of two Italian immigrants and espouses a common cause with them as workers on the Left. This kind of Americanness reflexively assumes the place of Yiddish *language*—or for that matter any immigrant language other than English—in the American republic of letters. Though many poets made significant contributions to establishing a Sacco-Vanzetti genre, one cannot avoid examining this model particularly through the lens of Halpern and the writers of *In zikh* because of the unexpected direction of their discourse. So, for instance, taking just their use of Madeiros and Governor Fuller, these poets treat these figures not as peripheral but as central, not as objects of scorn or abuse but as objects of sympathy or at least subtlety. Artistically, culturally, and politically, then, the Yiddish Sacco-Vanzetti genre questions the position of the marginal and nondominant in American identity politics.

In the words of one critic, not only did these poets "see themselves as spokespeople for the American Idea" but "they were staking a claim for a politically progressive Yiddish literary culture in the America of the future"[51] as well. All of this points to that aspect of Vespuccian modernism, which brings the peripheral into focus. Through a Yiddish approach to a distinctly American genre, these poets move marginality—whether social, political, linguistic, or literary—front and center as a key aspect of Jewish American self-consciousness, and it in turn becomes part of the vocabulary of Americanness.

Notes

I would like to extend my sincerest thanks to Naomi Brenner for her keenly insightful comments and suggestions.

1. Upton Sinclair, *Boston: di tragedye fun Sako un Vantseti: roman* (Warsaw: Y. A. Tsuker, 1930).
2. Louis Joughin and Edmund M. Morgan, *The Legacy of Sacco and Vanzetti* (1948; Princeton: Princeton University Press, 1978), 576-80.
3. See, for example, Lawrence Rosenwald, "'Inclusions and Exclusions: The Shaping of an American Jewish Canon.' Rev. of *Jewish American Literature: A Norton Anthology,* ed. Jules Chametzky, John Felstiner, Hilene Flanzbaum, and Kathryn Hellerstein," *Prooftexts* 23 (2003): 407-17, 410.
4. Proletpen—shorthand for *proletarishe pen*, or "proletarian pen"—refers to the union of American Yiddish writers on the far Left (1929-1938). Dovid Katz, "Introduction: The Days of Proletpen in American Yiddish Poetry," in *Proletpen: America's Rebel Yiddish Poets*, ed. Amelia Glaser and David Weintraub (Madison: University of Wisconsin Press, 2005), 3-25. Though this was one of many such groups, its name had a kind of iconic status in the late 1920s and the 1930s.
5. Irving Howe, *World of Our Fathers* (New York: Harcourt Brace Jovanovich, 1976), 429.
6. See the significant analysis in Benjamin Harshav, *The Meaning of Yiddish* (Berkeley: University of California Press, 1990), 175-86.
7. Yankev Glatshteyn, Aaron Leyeles, and Nokhum Borukh Minkov, "Introspektivism" in *In zikh: a zamlung introspektive lider* (New York: M. N. Mayzel Farlag, 1920), 5-27, 16; the English translation is found in Benjamin Harshav and Barbara Harshav, eds., *American Yiddish Poetry: A Bilingual Anthology* (Berkeley: University of California Press, 1986), 779.
8. Joughin and Morgan, *Legacy,* 379-82, 384.
9. Joughin and Morgan, *Legacy,* 379, 384.
10. The text and translation are from Glaser and Weintraub, *Proletpen,* 74-75.
11. Joughin and Morgan, *Legacy,* 380: "In approaching this material it must be borne in mind that the majority of the poets had as an aid to knowing the men only the speeches at the sentencing and a few letters; most of the verse antedates the publication of the *Letters* of 1928. This paucity of source material may account for the fact that Sacco is treated more explicitly than Vanzetti."
12. Glaser and Weintraub, *Proletpen,* 76-79.

13. Ibid., 74–75.
14. Rocco Marinaccio, "Dago Christs or Hometown Heroes?: Proletarian Representations of Sacco and Vanzetti," *The Centennial Review* 41 (1997): 617–23, 617. Marinaccio's eye-catching title seems to be taken from Malcolm Cowley's poem "For St. Bartholomew's Day," published in *The Nation* on August 22, 1928, which includes the following lines:

> March on, O dago Christs, whilst we
> march on to spread your name abroad
> like ashes in the winds of God. (Cited in Joughin and Morgan, *Legacy*, 383)

15. As Ruth R. Wisse notes, "The moral strength of the radical Left reached something of a peak in the spring of 1927 with the execution in Massachusetts of Nicola Sacco and Bartolomeo Vanzetti. Among immigrant Jews, Sacco and Vanzetti were almost uniformly regarded as martyrs for their unpopular beliefs. . . . They [the communists] consolidated a protest movement that temporarily united most sectors of Yiddish political life and elicited from every kind of Yiddish writer an expression of outrage" (*A Little Love in Big Manhattan* [Cambridge: Harvard University Press, 1988], 184).
16. "Curiously, there are not many verses which consider the suffering of the men during their imprisonment" (Joughin and Morgan, *Legacy*, 383).
17. Glaser and Weintraub, *Proletpen*, 74–75.
18. It is worth noting that Yiddish Sacco-Vanzettis had by and large faded away by the end of the 1930s, when a new and troubling set of geopolitical concerns came to dominate Jewish literary consciousness.
19. I mean "immediate" in a chronological not a compositional sense. As Wisse notes, "Halpern's poem, dated September 4, 1927, two weeks after the execution, was the product of many painstaking drafts" (*A Little Love*, 184–85).
20. "Poem by Miss Millay on Sacco and Vanzetti," *New York Times*, August 22, 1927, 2. The Sacco-Vanzetti genre, and not only among the Yiddish poets, involved an almost exclusively urban poetics and urban imagery. Millay's poem, though outwardly focused on natural themes of decay and rot, still makes use of an urban intertext. Not only does its title in effect read as a newspaper headline, but the opening lines—"Let us abandon then our gardens and go home / And sit in the sitting room"—also respond almost antiphonically to T. S. Eliot's "The Love Song of J. Alfred Prufrock," a discernibly urban poem. Unlike the *New York Times* version, the version in *America Arraigned!* has "garden" in the singular. Lucia Trent and Ralph Cheyney, eds., *America Arraigned!* (New York: Dean, 1928), 79.
21. The text and translation are from Harshav and Harshav, *American Yiddish Poetry*, 438–39.
22. Ibid.
23. See, for example, Leyeles's focus on voltage or Minkov's interest in electricity's particulate nature.
24. See also H. Leivick's image of Governor Fuller's bared teeth—"the Fullerian bite" (*der fulerisher bis*)—in his poem "A Year of Sacco Vanzetti" ("A yor Sako Vantseti"; H. Leivick, *Ale verk fun H. Leyvik*, vol. 1, *Lider* [New York: H. Leivick yubiley-komitet, 1940], 290–91). H. Leivick's (1888–1962) collected works include two Sacco-Vanzetti poems—the above-mentioned poem and "Sacco and Vanzetti's Wednesday" ("Sako un Vantsetis mitvokh")—under the heading *Altmodish* (old-fashioned). Though contextualized as "old-fashioned," Leyvik clearly means this as neither a quaint nor a dismissive designation. Rather, Leyvik uses it to map the geography of his bitter experiences of his youth in eastern Europe (including mistreatment by a tyrannical father, years of forced labor for socialist activity, and exile to Siberia) onto the landmarks of his New York existence. He uses all of this as a critical framework to evaluate the Old World in the New, to un-

derstand how to refashion oneself in America when haunted both by the afterlives of one's European experiences *and* by the social problems of America. That he includes not one but two Sacco-Vanzetti poems within this framework gives some indication of the perceived power of this genre as a tool for calibrating identity.

25. Harshav and Harshav, *American Yiddish Poetry*, 438-39.
26. Wisse, *A Little Love*: "The Sacco-Vanzetti poem shows how out of joint Halpern was with the political atmosphere. Whether it was his humiliation at the hands of *Frayhayt* [NB: Halpern had been ostracized by this pro-Soviet newspaper, which had formerly supported him, for not towing the Party line] that turned him inward or the greater density of his art that precipitated his disengagement from politics, his poetry was losing the aggressive energy that radicalism had originally inspired in him" (186-87).
27. Ruth Wisse, for example, maintains, "The momentum of the poem sweeps Sacco and Vanzetti up into the forces of nature: they turn into a brilliant butterfly, two outspread wings of martyrdom, attracted to destruction as Jesus was to his cross. The person tearing his hair from his head and banging his head against stone walls in the opening lines of the poem is not the prisoner on death row, however, but the lamenting onlooker, wretched and uncomprehending" (*A Little Love*, 186).
28. See, for example, Marc Miller, "Modernism and Persona in the Works of Moyshe-Leyb Halpern," *Yiddish* 11 (1998): 48-71.
29. This kaleidoscopicness, as they called it, was an important quality of Inzikhist poetry; see their manifesto: Yankev Glatshteyn, Aaron Leyeles, and Nokhum Borukh Minkov, "Introspektivizm," 6.
30. Aaron Glants-Leyeles, *Fabyus lind* (New York: Farlag Inzikh, 1937), 87 (my translation).
31. "Umruik-ruik zenen di harn" (Glants-Leyeles, *Fabyus lind*, 86).
32. Ibid., 90 (my translation).
33. Joughin and Morgan, *Legacy*, 391. So, for example, one of the few explicit references to Madeiros in the contemporary anthology *America Arraigned!* is the prefatory remark in Josiah Titzell's poem "Harvest": "In the first few minutes of August 23rd, 1927 there were four executions in Boston, Massachusetts. Those murdered at this time were Madeiros, Sacco, Vanzetti, and a pathetic little hunchback, Justice" (Trent and Cheyney, *America Arraigned!*, 92).
34. Trent and Cheyney, *America Arraigned!*, 62.
35.   Each one made lonely in the togetherness,
         Each one together in the loneliness

         Yeder fareynzamt in der tsuzamenkayt,
         Yeder tsuzamen in der eynzamkayt (Yankev Glatshteyn, *Kredos* [New York: Farlag idish lebn, 1929], 53; my translation).

36. Glatshteyn, *Kredos*, 57-58 (my translation).
37. Glants-Leyeles, *Fabyus lind*, 91 (my translation).
38. Nokhum Borukh Minkov, *Masoes fun letstn shotn* (New York: Farlag bodn, 1936), 39 (my translation).
39. Harshav and Harshav, *American Yiddish Poetry*, 797.
40. Ibid., 797-98; see Norman Finkelstein, *Not One of Them in Place: Modern Poetry and Jewish American Identity* (Albany: State University of New York Press, 2001), 36-39. Citing Glatshteyn's bon mot to Irving Howe—"I have to be aware of Auden but Auden need never have heard of me"—the literary scholar Anita Norich notes inter alia his defiance: "Glatshteyn yokes his name to one of the most well-known, bold, and controversial poets then living in America.... Far from being self-effacing, Glatshteyn implies that Auden *should* have heard of him. In knowing Auden, in needing to know Auden, the Yiddish poet, he suggests, is more learned and well-read, with more expansive cultural sensibilities than his English-born colleague" (Anita Norich, *Discovering Exile:*

Yiddish and Jewish American Culture during the Holocaust [Stanford: Stanford University Press, 2007], 22).

41. Minkov, *Masoes*, 41 (my translation).

42. Walter Benn Michaels, in his book on what he calls American "nativist modernism," argues that in the 1920s there took place a reconfiguration of the terms used in the construction of collective and national identities (Walter Benn Michaels, *Our America: Nativism, Modernism, Pluralism* [Durham, NC: Duke University Press, 1995], 6). As a proving ground for this reconfiguration, one can consider the internally external groups, those in the pot but not yet melted, so to speak. What American *means* must include the presence, and contribution, of "marginal" groups. (Just as in the early nineteenth century—"an age obsessed with a search for American identity"—there was a sense that the presence of Native Americans was a necessary, though not sufficient, condition of "American" identity [Jill Lepore, *The Name of War: King Philip's War and the Origins of American Identity* (New York: Alfred A. Knopf, 1998), 199-200].) Put another way, *if* one takes Sacco-Vanzetti as a case of *American* identity, then in some sense they *had* to be Italians. Indeed, one of Michaels's goals is to show that one result of American literary modernism's "commit[ment] to the nativist project of racializing America" was "the perfection not of racial identity but of what would come to be called cultural identity." And therefore in an ironic way, "the commitment to pluralism—both racial and cultural—should probably be understood as nativism's most significant and distinctive contribution to the technology of racial identity in the United States" (Michaels, *Our America*, 13-14). This was a process that *began* in the 1920s, and, as Eric Foner points out, "Only the mobilization for World War II and the confrontation with Nazism, however, purged Americanism of the language of race. No longer identified as members of distinct 'races,' Italians, Poles, Jews, and the other new immigrants, became hyphenated ethnics" ("Who Is an American? The Imagined Community in American History," *The Centennial Review* 41 [1997]: 436-37).

43. *Heybt zey umfargeslekh* (Minkov, *Masoes*, 42).

44. Naftoli Gros, *Idn* (New York: Arbeter ring bildung-komitet, 1938), 2:29-31.

45. As a modernist poet among people of letters and as Yiddish-speaking Jews among American Jewry.

46. Maeera Y. Shreiber, "Jewish American Poetry," in *The Cambridge Companion to Jewish American Literature*, ed. Michael P. Kramer and Hana Wirth-Nesher (Cambridge: Cambridge University Press, 2003), 150-51.

47. For example, Alan Wald's article "Jewish American Writers on the Left" (Kramer and Wirth-Nesher, *Cambridge Companion*, 170-89), which uses only English-language sources, makes no mention of Sacco and Vanzetti; see also Finkelstein, *Not One of Them in Place*, for a similar elision.

48. In Rachel Rubinstein's analysis of the use simultaneously of Walt Whitman and Native American sources in the early twentieth-century journals of Di yunge, she asserts, "Yiddish interest in the Indian and in Whitman, would become acts of interpretation and transformation designed to assert the simultaneous modernism and Americanness of the Yiddish immigrant poet.... This reconstituting the Native American and Walt Whitman as, paradoxically, 'quintessentially' American and alien: that is, as both American and Jews." There is in her view "a particular matrix of Yiddish American modernism, one that sought to fuse the cosmopolitan and the local, the international and the American, the cultural and the countercultural" (Rubinstein, "Going Native, Becoming Modern: American Indians, Walt Whitman, and the Yiddish Poet," *American Quarterly* 58, no. 2 [2006]: 431-53, 438). See a similar assessment of an explicitly "Yiddish American identity" in Alan Trachtenberg, *Shades of Hiawatha: Staging Indians, Making Americans, 1880-1930* (New York: Hill and Wang, 2004), 169.

49. Marinaccio, "Dago Christs," 617.

50. "Both works [Dos Passos's *Facing the Chair* and Sinclair's *Boston*], I argue, attempt to assuage anxiety over the national identities of Sacco and Vanzetti and over the national identity of the proletarian movement itself by 'Americanizing' Sacco and Vanzetti and, thereby, assimilating into American culture both radical politics and the process of radicalization" (Marinaccio, "Dago Christs," 617).

51. Julian Levinson, *Exiles on Main Street: Jewish American Writers and American Literary Culture* (Bloomington: Indiana University Press, 2008), 141.

YIDDISH AND THE CITY
Prelude

GENNADY ESTRAIKH

Historians of Yiddish-related modernizing developments in the nineteenth and twentieth centuries have tended to gravitate to metropolitan environments, notably Warsaw and Vilna, paying much less attention to the *shtetl*, the main habitat for east European Jewish life. Indeed, until the beginning of World War II, Warsaw and Vilna played particularly significant roles as trendsetting centers whose influence was felt in all corners of the Yiddish-speaking *ecumene*.

Although it is problematic to give the definition for the *shtetl* (no doubt, it is not simply a translation of the Polish *miasteczko*, "small town"),[1] the term can be used for describing the traditional way of life, or *yidishkayt*. But it was the very objective of the modern ideology-driven Yiddish culture to establish alternative, non-*shtetl* (or even anti-*shtetl*) forms of Jewish life. Educated Jewish urbanites used the term *kleyn-shtetldikayt* (small-townness) also as a byword for "parasitic" existence, which they abhorred. *Productivization* of shopkeepers, trade agents, bungling artisans, and déclassé *luftmentshn*—by turning them into farmers, master artisans, factory workers, or professionals—was the metatheory for their conceptual approaches to solving Jewish-related problems. For Marxists, productivization also meant development of the proletariat, the avant-garde of a future just society.

To a considerable degree, Yiddishism emerged as an unwanted child in Jewish intellectuals' love affair with productivization, because initially the majority of them advocated rejection of Yiddish, the "jargon" of *kleyn-shtetldikayt*, in favor of "proper" languages, such as Russian, German, and Hebrew. The Russian state apparatus also regarded Yiddish as a stumbling block for their programs of "selective integration" of Jews into larger society.[2] Russian was the main language of those activists who promoted general and vocational schooling, credit associations, cultural organizations, and other forms of nascent Jewish civil society. Incipient Jewish political activism also preferred Russian. In all, Yiddish was deemed underdeveloped for any activity that transcended *kleyn-shtetldikayt*.

The expansion of the civil society network had altered the fabric of Jewish life and left a lasting mark on Jewish culture, particularly on the Jewish organizations' language politics. At the turn of the twentieth century, due to economic and social developments in eastern Europe, internal migration, and the emigration of hundreds of thousands of *shtetl* dwellers, masses of Yiddish speakers entered twentieth-century modernity and its associated civil society. For instance, in pre–World War I Russia, more than 600 Jewish cooperatives provided credits to more than 400,000 Jewish members.[3] Although the ideas about modernization could be formulated in "proper languages," the masses targeted by these ideas continued to speak and read Yiddish. As a result, the cooperatives, trade unions, and other mass organizations had to be supplied with literature written in Yiddish, their problems were discussed in the Yiddish press, and Yiddish writers portrayed in their works new economic and social forms of Jewish life.

The modernizers reacted in two ways. Some of them saw Yiddish as only a temporary and irksome obstacle on the high road to their ultimate (e.g., socialist, communist, or Zionist) objectives. Yet, many ideologists faced the reality and, as an illustration of the Hegelian negation of the negation, turned to or chose Yiddish, de-rusting the language of their childhood or even learning it from scratch. Ironically, the most successful Yiddish newspaper, the New York *Forverts*, was established and for many decades dominated by people with an "after-me-the-deluge" attitude to Yiddish. Vladimir Medem, the leading Bundist, wrote about the "psychological puzzle" of the *Forverts* editor Abraham Cahan, whose outlook combined flat dismissal of Yiddishism with momentous contribution to the development of Yiddish culture.[4]

On the other hand, thousands of activists began to feast their eyes on the emerging edifice of Yiddish-speaking civil society, dispersed all over the world in the form of political groupings, mutual aid associations, *landsmanshaftn* (hometown associations), cooperatives, and educational and cultural institutions. Such organizations as the Workmen's Circle in the United States and the Jewish Colonization Society in Imperial Russia formed, together with Jewish socialist and liberal political movements, the most important infrastructures for the development of Yiddish as the language used for a wide range of modern life functions. Significantly, such infrastructures also created numerous job opportunities for Yiddish-speaking literati, molding a whole stratum of functionaries, teachers, journalists, editors, proofreaders, typesetters, and secretaries.

Many Jewish Nationalists, who by the end of the 1900s became known as "Yiddishists," came to the conclusion that they were witnessing the emergence of the modern Jewish nation, united by high culture in Yiddish. They were convinced that culture could replace religion and cure secular Jews of the ills of assimilation. The pre–World War I decade can be seen as the crystallizing moment when Yiddishism attracted thousands of followers. The international Yiddish language conference, convened in the Austro-Hungarian city of Czernowitz (Cernauti) in August 1908, was one of many manifestations of the new direction.

Language planning and education were the most future-oriented directions in Yiddishist activities. Yiddish did not need to be standardized or learned if the next generation was supposed to acculturate somewhere in the diaspora or to morph into a Hebrew-speaking community. However, Ber Borokhov, who—in addition to being a founding father of Labor-Zionism—became the architect of modern Yiddish scholarship, suggested that the Yiddish spoken by Vilna intellectuals should be seen as the model for standard Yiddish pronunciation. As part of the new standard, he developed a new spelling code, which after World War I began to replace the quasi-German orthography.

It is no coincidence that Borokhov crowned Vilna the capital of modern Yiddish language and culture. Vilna was redolent of Yiddishism. Its circle of Yiddishists challenged the trend, associated with Warsaw commercial publishing, of the "after-me-the-deluge" attitude to Yiddish culture. To a considerable degree, the development of Yiddish literature, theater, and journalism in the twentieth century can be chronicled and analyzed as a history of coexistence of the two trends: the non-Yiddishist, Warsaw one and the Yiddishist, Vilna one.[5] Both trends had followers in various ideological camps. For instance, the *Forverts* had to fight on different Vilna fronts, including the two Yiddish dailies: the communist *Frayhayt* and the Liberal-Nationalist *Der tog*. In the Soviet Union, Minsk-based literati fought ideological battles against their counterparts in Kiev, which as early as 1900 became the main outpost of Vilna Yiddishism. Warsaw, too, housed numerous Yiddishist institutions, including the influential highbrow weekly *Literarishe bleter* (*Literary Pages*), whose 730 issues came out in 1924–1939. In the three essays of this section, Yiddish appears as an instrument for various political goals pursued by Jewish ideologists in such cities as New York, Paris, and Montreal.

Yiddishists have failed to develop an organized suprapolitical movement for the realization of their program of national survival in the diaspora. This does not mean that there were no attempts to launch such a movement. The *Kultur-lige,* one of the most notable projects, was established in Kiev in 1918 with scores of affiliations in Ukraine. Its concept was replicated in numerous sister organizations in such cities as Warsaw, Paris, Berlin, Amsterdam, and Detroit. However, the *Kultur-lige* was not destined to form a worldwide organization, and only a few of its outfits endured until World War II.[6] In 1937, an embryo of a similar network was established in Paris, in the form of the World Yiddish Cultural Association, or YKUF. Around the same time a term, *Yiddishland,* was coined for the Yiddish-speaking *ecumene*.[7] However, a decade later the YKUF organizations, most notably in the United States and Argentina, became parts of the ideological fortifications of the Cold War period rather than components of a pan-Yiddishist movement.

The struggle between the two trends continued until the beginning of the 1990s. By that time, Yiddishism had completely lost its initial meaning of a program for modern Jewish nation building. In the meantime, ideological divides also lost their relevance, especially after the collapse of communism. Nowadays, Yiddishists are driven by the ideas of maintaining Yiddish as a living language and celebrating Yiddish literature, theater, and klezmer culture. In contemporary Yiddishist circles, Vilna remains the symbolic capital of the vanished Yiddishland, though it would be wrong to interpret this fact as proof that the "Vilna trend" endures and, thus, has won a victory.

Notes

1. John D. Klier, "What Exactly Was a Shtetl?" in *The Shtetl: Image and Reality*, ed. Gennady Estraikh and Mikhail Krutikov (Oxford: Legenda, 2000), 23–35; Ben Cion Pinchuk, "Jewish Discourse and the Shtetl," *Jewish History* 15, no. 2 (2001): 169–79.
2. Cf. Benjamin Nathans, *Beyond the Pale: The Jewish Encounter with Late Imperial Russia* (Los Angeles: University of California Press, 2002), 83.
3. See also Gennady Estraikh, "Changing Ideologies of Artisanal 'Productivization': ORT in Late Imperial Russia," *East European Jewish Affairs* 39, no. 1 (2009): 3–18.
4. Vladimir Medem, "Di shtelung fun sotsialistn tsu tsionizm," *Forverts*, May 11, 1921, 4.
5. See also Gennady Estraikh, "The Vilna Yiddishist Quest for Modernity," in *Jüdische kultur(en) im Neuen Europa: Wilna 1918-1939*, ed. Marina Dmitrieva and Heidemarie Petersen (Wiesbaden, Germany: Harrassowitz Verlag, 2004), 101–16.
6. Hillel Kazovsky, *The Artists of the Kultur-Lige* (Jerusalem: Gesharim, 2003).
7. See, e.g., *Eshter alveltlekher yidisher kultur-kongres* (Paris: YKUF, 1937), 26, 33, 78; Matthew Hoffman, "From Czernowitz to Paris: The International Yiddish Culture Congress of 1937," in *Czernowitz at 100: The First Yiddish Language Conference in Historical Perspective*, ed. Kalman Weiser and Joshua Fogel (Lanham, MD: Lexington Books, 2010), 151–64.

THE LOWER EAST SIDE MEETS GREENWICH VILLAGE

Immigrant Jews, Yiddish, and the New York Intellectual Scene

TONY MICHELS

Starting in the 1880s, immigrant Jewish intellectuals fluent in various languages began to use Yiddish for journalistic, literary, educational, and political purposes. A similar turn to Yiddish occurred two decades earlier in Russia, when a small number of maskilim began writing fiction in Yiddish, thus laying the foundation of modern Yiddish literature.[1] However, the Yiddishization of Jewish intellectuals proceeded most rapidly and extensively in the United States, especially, but not only, in New York City. By the 1890s, dozens of intellectuals, based primarily in the Yiddish press and the Jewish labor movement, wrote and lectured in Yiddish on a regular basis.[2] Their numbers continued to grow until Congress drastically curtailed immigration from Europe in the mid-1920s. Before World War I, no other city in the world hosted a larger Yiddish-speaking intellectual community than New York.[3]

The turn to Yiddish did not lead to isolation from American intellectual life, as one might assume. All immigrant Jewish intellectuals sooner or later learned English, many wrote in the language, and some even achieved recognition among their English-speaking peers. Furthermore, immigrant Jewish intellectuals played an important role in the development of the English-speaking intelligentsia located primarily in Greenwich Village. European in orientation, politically radical, outsiders to "respectable society" yet highly regarded within the immigrant Jewish community, Yiddish-speaking intellectuals fascinated their American-born counterparts, who, as David Hollinger writes, "looked to a new intelligentsia to manifest a more diverse, more broadly based emotional and intellectual existence, and they were eager for this cause to be advanced by persons of any ethnic origin."[4] Jews constituted that new intelligentsia. American-born intellectuals, mostly of middle- to upper-class

Protestant backgrounds, sought out and interacted with immigrant Jews in cafés, left-wing political organizations, settlement houses, journals, and other institutions.[5] Immigrant Jews expanded the horizons of American intellectuals by serving as agents of radical thought, Russian politics and literature, and Yiddish culture.[6] As a result native-born intellectuals moved from "the more staid realms of reform into a bohemia open to different forms of radicalism," as Christine Stansell has argued.[7] In stressing the pivotal role played by Jews in the American intelligentsia, Stansell and Hollinger depart from the tendency of historians to treat immigrant Jewish intellectuals in near isolation from their American-born counterparts.[8] Still, further exploration is needed. Who interacted with whom? What were the points of contact? How did immigrant Jews influence English-speaking intellectual life?

The present essay attempts to draw out some of the extensive ties between two intellectual communities: one based in the Lower East Side, the other in nearby Greenwich Village. Two kinds of cultural crossings are charted here: the movement of immigrant Jewish intellectuals to the Yiddish language and their concurrent interactions with native-born, English-speaking intellectuals. Connections drawn between the two yield a picture of the American intelligentsia as more ethnically and culturally diverse than often supposed.

The immigrant Jewish intelligentsia took shape as a socially and culturally significant community through its use of Yiddish. Through the Jewish vernacular, intellectuals cohered as a distinct stratum of opinion shapers, producers of culture, political leaders, and labor activists within the immigrant Jewish population writ large. Ironically, their turn to Yiddish marked an abrupt departure from their original self-conception as intellectuals. At the beginning of their adult lives, few, if any, immigrant Jewish intellectuals would have considered *zhargon,* as they often referred to Yiddish with condescension if not derision, a natural or desirable choice. Many individuals did not know the language well, if at all, and in any case regarded it as inappropriate for formal or elevated discourse. The idea of using Yiddish in literary, educational, or political capacities would have struck virtually all of them as ridiculous had they considered it. That the turn to Yiddish should happen in the United States, thousands of miles from the Yiddish-speaking heartland of eastern Europe, would have seemed fantastic. What, then, explains the collective move to Yiddish? One may identify two main factors, neither unique to the American context but that nonetheless achieved fuller expression in the United States than anywhere in eastern Europe before World War I. Each may be distinguished conceptually, but they actually overlapped with and reinforced one another.

Ideology lay behind the first factor and was manifested mainly through commitment to either socialism (broadly defined here to include all ideological tendencies—anarchism, social democracy, communism, etc.—laying claim to that label) or Yiddish cultural nationalism (which overlapped with the political

Left to a great extent). Of the two, socialism appeared first. The socialist impetus became apparent in 1885–1886 amid the upsurge of labor protest known as the Great Upheaval. In response to the immense social and political unrest that occurred across the country and influenced by the example of German immigrants, a number of Jewish intellectuals in New York decided to use Yiddish to propagate socialism and organize Jewish workers.[9]

Composed of both men and women, these early intellectuals had been educated in Russian state schools but immigrated to the United States in the wake of the 1881–1882 pogroms. The most prominent figure to emerge from that first cohort was Abraham Cahan, who, before the Great Upheaval, had participated in Russian-speaking clubs and wrote for Russian periodicals overseas. Cahan saw no public use for Yiddish, despite the fact that he had given two lectures in the language shortly after his arrival in New York in 1882. At least one of Cahan's friends, Khayim Spivak, did not even realize Cahan could speak or write in Yiddish fluently. When publishers of a new Yiddish newspaper asked Spivak in 1886 if Cahan would make a suitable editor, he responded, "Cahan, of course not. He doesn't know *zhargon*." "I believed with full certitude," Spivak recalls in his memoir of 1910, "that Cahan could not count to two in Yiddish."[10] Spivak may have exaggerated his point, but he nonetheless underscored the basic truth that even someone as fluent in Yiddish as Cahan did not make that fact readily known.[11]

Intellectuals typically viewed Yiddish as a marker of cultural backwardness. Even if a given individual did not possess a well-formulated view of Yiddish, he or she usually looked down on it as the language of the marketplace, religion, family life, or the uneducated. Russian, on the other hand, signified educational attainment and worldliness. It was, in Cahan's words, the language of his "intellectual self."[12] Cahan never severed his connection to the Russian language and its literature, but with the outbreak of the Great Upheaval, he began writing and speaking in Yiddish as a full-time activity in the service of the Jewish labor movement. During the 1890s, he edited the socialist weekly *Di arbeter tsaytung* and the monthly *Di tsukunft* and regularly delivered speeches at rallies, parades, strikes, and all kinds of public events. His turn to Yiddish culminated in his editorship of the *Forverts*, the most widely circulated and financially profitable Yiddish newspaper in the world, from 1903 until his death in 1951.

Another Russian-speaking intellectual who turned to Yiddish during the Great Upheaval was Shoel Yanovsky. After immigrating to New York City in 1885, Yanovsky participated in Russian-speaking societies similar to those Cahan joined, but the events of 1886 galvanized Yanovsky and he soon moved to Yiddish. He delivered his first Yiddish lecture on Karl Marx's *Wage Labor and Capital* to members of the anarchist group Pioneers of Liberty. According to Yanovsky, other leaders of the group did not yet feel comfortable speaking in Yiddish, so the task fell to him, despite his own unease with the idea. As Yanovsky recalls in his memoirs, "When it came to speaking in Yiddish—my mother

tongue—I felt an inconceivable nervousness." To someone accustomed to using Russian for intellectual purposes, the idea of delivering a speech in Yiddish
seemed strange and inappropriate. Nonetheless, Yanovsky felt satisfied with
his first effort and continued to use Yiddish for the rest of his life, most notably
as the long-standing editor of the anarchist weekly *Di fraye arbeter shtime* and
the International Ladies' Garment Workers' weekly newspaper.[13]

For Cahan, Yanovsky, and many of their contemporaries, the newborn Jewish labor movement provided both an inducement and a justification for using
Yiddish. If *zhargon* previously seemed embarrassing, an increasing number of
intellectuals viewed it after 1886 as a useful, indeed, indispensable, tool.[14] It was
needed to advance the socialist cause among the ever growing masses of Jewish
workers. Recurrent strikes reinforced this new imperative as it became increasingly apparent to radical intellectuals that immigrant Jewry was highly restive,
open to socialist ideas, and in need of organization. "Thousands of enthusiastic
listeners" awaited those prepared to take up *zhargon*, Philip Krants stated in
an 1890 appeal to Russian-speaking intellectuals. Krants, the leading socialist
Yiddish editor next to Cahan, had himself learned Yiddish in London just five
years earlier. Now in New York, he called on his peers to follow his example if
they had any hope of social relevance.[15]

If socialism was the first ideological factor behind the turn to Yiddish, Jewish
nationalism intensified that trend. The most important figure in this regard
was Chaim Zhitlovsky, who came to the United States in 1904. Zhitlovsky pro-
pounded a theory of Yiddish cultural nationalism that challenged the regnant
(if poorly defined) belief in cultural assimilation among Jewish socialists. The
founders of the Jewish labor movement, figures such as Cahan and Yanovsky,
encouraged immigrants to learn English and shed their identification with
the Jewish people in favor of working-class solidarity. They justified the use
of Yiddish on instrumental grounds; it was needed only as long as immigrant
workers did not understand any other language. Zhitlovsky, on the other hand,
championed Yiddish as a goal in and of itself. He considered Yiddish the core
component of a new, secular Jewish culture in bloom and assigned intellectuals
the leading role in its creation.[16] Many socialists, Cahan and Yanovsky among
them, rejected Zhitlovsky's nationalism as a violation of socialist principles
and, anyway, inapplicable to American society, where Jews lived as equal citizens rather than a separate nation. Nonetheless, Zhitlovsky exercised considerable influence. One seemingly unlikely adherent was Liova Fradkin. A former
follower of Vladimir Lenin well-known for his opposition to all forms of Jewish
nationalism, Fradkin was a "devoted Russian speaker" and an "assimilation-
ist" at the time of his immigration in 1908. Yet he and a number of his friends
embraced Yiddish after hearing Zhitlovsky speak (presumably in Russian) in
Chicago. Fradkin started studying the Yiddish language, reading Yiddish books
and periodicals, and attending Yiddish lectures. Eventually he went so far as
to change his name to the more Jewish-sounding L. M. Shteyn. By the 1920s,

Shteyn became recognized as a leading Yiddish cultural activist in Chicago, a founder of the Sholem Aleichem Institute, and the proprietor of the L. M. Shteyn Farlag, a publisher of high quality art and literary books in Yiddish. The promise of a new, secular culture in Yiddish—rather than its mere utility—was what attracted Shteyn to the Jewish vernacular.[17]

If ideological motivations played an important role in steering intellectuals toward Yiddish, practical considerations also factored into the process. Yiddish provided a means to reach a large audience and opportunities to earn a living. In those respects, Yiddish possessed a distinct advantage over Russian, in which only a tiny number of immigrants were literate. The same may also be said of other languages, such as Hebrew, Polish, and Romanian, available to intellectuals. Thus the Romanian-born writer Konrad Bercovici "learned Yiddish rapidly" to participate in the "brouhaha of [public] discussions" in New York.[18] The weakness of the Russian American press—which was published, edited, and read mostly by Jews—reflected that reality. The first Russian-language newspaper in New York appeared in 1889, almost two decades after the first Yiddish newspaper, and it survived for less than a year. Five others followed over the next decade, all of them short lived.[19] Although the persistence of those efforts indicated an abiding preference among intellectuals for Russian, the Russian press showed itself to be highly unstable at a time when the Yiddish press flourished, affording intellectuals opportunities to earn a steady, if modest, income.

The journalist Louis Miller illustrates the pull of Yiddish from Russian. During his first four years in New York, in the late 1880s, Miller joined various Russian-speaking groups, none of which played a meaningful role in public life, and edited New York's first Russian newspaper, *Znamia*. After *Znamia* ceased publication in early 1890, amid the first strike wave in New York since the Great Upheaval, Miller abandoned Russian for Yiddish. A stranger to the language, Miller nonetheless became one of the Lower East Side's most popular Yiddish orators and journalists. In 1897, Miller helped found the *Forverts*, where he worked until he founded his own rival daily, *Di varhayt*, in 1905.[20] Miller's turn to Yiddish represents an early example of a long-term trend that continued even after the Russian American press achieved some stability in the 1910s.[21] Mark Khinoy, a former member of the Russian Social Democratic Workers' Party, is an example. According to Khinoy's own account, he had stopped reading and writing in Yiddish at the age of fourteen, when he left his parents' home. After Khinoy immigrated to Chicago in 1913, he wrote exclusively for Russian-language publications. Yet in 1921 Cahan convinced him to start writing for the *Forverts* and Khinoy soon joined the daily's editorial staff, where he remained for the rest of his career.[22] Others followed a similar path from Russian to Yiddish during the same time period.

Russian could not compete with the practical advantages of Yiddish, but the same did not hold true for English. The country's majority language offered a much larger audience than could Yiddish and therefore exerted a constant draw. Some of the most prominent Jewish intellectuals in late nineteenth-century New York, such as Emma Goldman and Morris Hillquit, moved primarily to English in the twentieth century as they gained in stature beyond the immigrant Jewish world. Even so, the relationship between Yiddish and English was not strictly unidirectional. The large number of Yiddish speakers, the vigor of the Yiddish press, and the organizational strength of the Jewish labor movement attracted even American-educated, English-speaking Jews.

William Edlin provides a case in point. Born in Russia, Edlin immigrated with his family to San Francisco in 1891 at the age of twelve. He became active in the Socialist Labor Party (predecessor of the much larger Socialist Party) as a journalist and organizer. In addition to his political activities, Edlin studied at the University of California and Stanford before he moved to New York City in 1897. The city's "great trade union and socialist movement drew me there like a magnet," Edlin recalls in his unpublished memoir. "Above all I was captivated by the stories of the great movement among Jews there."[23] Edlin's close friend, the writer Anna Strunsky, disapproved of his decision and urged him to finish his education in California. A Russian-Jewish immigrant herself, Strunsky believed Edlin's talents would be wasted in New York's immigrant Jewish scene, where there existed an "overproduction of such able, intelligent men as yourself."[24] But Edlin, ignoring Strunsky's advice, relocated and flourished on the Lower East Side, where he became a prominent activist in the Jewish labor movement, a writer for the *Forverts*, and, in 1914, the editor of *Der tog*, considered the most sophisticated Yiddish daily of the time. Strunsky eventually followed Edlin's path to New York, although she did not take up writing in Yiddish.

Edlin's choice of Yiddish was unusual for an Americanized, English-speaking immigrant, but it was not unique. A number of others, such as *Forverts* writers Adolph Held and Hillel Rogoff, made a similar move to Yiddish journalism and the Jewish labor movement. They were part of the larger trend that brought intellectuals to Yiddish, for either ideological or practical reasons, between the 1880s and 1920s.

While immigrant Jewish intellectuals embraced Yiddish and immersed themselves in the immigrant Jewish community, they concurrently developed ties to the English-speaking intelligentsia centered in Greenwich Village. Village intellectuals started to venture to the Lower East Side in the final years of the nineteenth century to witness firsthand the bustling activity in the Jewish quarter. They visited Jewish-run cafés, bookstores, and Yiddish theaters; observed the lively public squares; mingled with Yiddish writers; and returned deeply impressed by the cultural and political vibrancy they saw unfolding in the so-called Jewish ghetto. Christine Stansell describes the experience:

> It was an amazing place for young men whose intellects had been formed by
> the Ivy League of the 1890s, where a fashion for upper-class ennui tinted with

European decadence reigned. On the Lower East Side, they received another education entirely. Intellectually, some of the talk was almost certainly over their heads, turning upon fine points of revolutionary dogma, European literature or continental philosophy. Much of it was also linguistically incomprehensible. But by its very nature, bohemia invited this adoption of a transnational identity, one that piqued people's interests in one another.[25]

The critic, Van Wyck Brooks, was among those who had his interest piqued. As he writes in his autobiography, Brooks "relish[ed] the slums" and for a time frequented a café on East Houston Street where he "was surrounded ... by the real mysteries of the ghetto and by Yiddish actors and newspapermen playing chess and drinking tea like figures from the Russian novels I was greedily absorbing."[26] On the Lower East Side Brooks discovered a fascinating milieu more vital than the staid environs where he and his contemporaries had been raised and educated. Contrasting the Lower East Side's cafés with the gentlemen's clubs familiar to him, a resident of the University Settlement wrote, "Their convivial atmosphere and the lack of restraint such as the order and decorum of a club require, give more breadth to thought, more vividness to the imagination, more brilliancy to the expression." Max Eastman marveled at the passion of Russian Jews. "They burn with hot fire," he wrote in a review of a novel by Anna Strunsky. "Their being is self-justified. They live and are sources of life."[27]

In contradistinction to widespread anti-Semitic attitudes, some gentile intellectuals cultivated a philo-Semitic perception of Jews as idealists and lovers of education and culture who might revivify their adopted country. As the social reformer and journalist Ida Van Etten wrote in 1893, "Thousands of disciples of Karl Marx may be found among the organized Jewish workingmen. Their intense desire to study and discuss social questions I have never seen equalled [*sic*]."[28] Similarly, a journalist for the *New York Times* reported in 1910, "Any Jew has to struggle hard to keep from being a philosopher and for a Russian Jew the effort is impossible."[29] The *Times'* review of Arthur Bullard's 1913 novel, *Comrade Yetta*, described its heroine as a "dream-filled Russian Jew, lover alike of learning and of liberty."[30] And in his 1915 book *New Cosmopolis*, the arts critic James Huneker enthused, "The East Side is an omnivorous reader. Stupendous is the amount of books studied and digested; the books of solid worth, not 'best sellers' or other flimflam alleged 'literature.' As a nation we are becoming as superficial in our reading as we are in our taste for the theatre. ... We need the Jewish blood as spiritual leaven; the race is art-loving and will prove a barrier to the rapidly growing wave of fanatical puritanism."[31]

In the eyes of Huneker and his contemporaries Jews demonstrated a remarkable love of culture, a hunger for education, a passion for social justice, and a European outlook that might free American culture from its Anglo-Protestant confines. The radical essayist Randolph Bourne articulated perhaps the fullest expression of this perspective. In his 1916 essay "The Jew and Trans-National

America," Bourne argued that Jewish ideals (he was especially impressed by Zionism) promised to bring forth a new kind of cosmopolitan American identity, a "trans-national America." "The intellectual service [that Jews] are doing us with their clarity of expression, their radical philosophy, their masterly fibre of thought, can hardly be over-valued," Bourne declared. "Their contribution is so incomparably greater than that of any other American group of foreign cultural affiliations that one can scarcely get one's perspective." In "Jewish idealism" Bourne saw "our savior."[32]

Cahan probably played the most important role of linking Yiddish-speaking intellectuals with their gentile counterparts around the turn of the century. As a reporter for the *New York Commercial Adviser* between 1897 and 1902, Cahan came to know a host of important writers, such as William Dean Howells, Lincoln Steffens, Hutchins Hapgood, and Neath Boyce.[33] According to Steffens, Cahan animated the newspaper's editorial room with a passion for literature and politics said to be characteristic of immigrant Jewry. In Steffens's words, "He brought the spirit on the East Side into our shop."[34] Cahan also brought the *Commercial Advertiser*'s staff members to the Lower East Side, giving them tours of café life, introducing them to other Jewish intellectuals, and exposing them to the Yiddish theater, which in Steffens's opinion was "the best in New York at the time both in stuff and in acting."[35] Cahan's tours of the Lower East Side enabled Hapgood to write his classic portrait *The Spirit of the Ghetto* (1902), which, according to Moses Rischin, represented "a major cultural breakthrough" in its depiction of a "vital Jewish world working out its own destiny and oblivious to Christian categories or rhetoric." This was a community "too passionate and belligerent about politics, literature, and life, too redolent of the shadowy splendors of an ancient past and visions of an uncharted future, to be assigned to the lower depths."[36] Like Bourne and Huneker, Hapgood believed America had something profound to learn from immigrant Jews. "What we need at the present time more than anything else," Hapgood wrote, "is a spiritual unity such as, perhaps, will only be the distant result of our present special activities. We need something similar to the spirit underlying the national and religious unity of the Jewish culture." Hapgood did not elaborate on how Jews might fit into the spiritually unified American culture he wished for. Could they maintain their group distinctiveness or would they have to assimilate? He did not say. Hapgood's main point was that the Jews offered an example to the American nation as a whole.[37]

The marriage between Anna Strunsky and the "millionaire socialist" William English Walling further illustrates ties across the ethnic and linguistic divide. The son of a wealthy and politically prominent Kentucky family, Walling moved to New York City in 1902 after graduating from the University of Chicago. He took up residence as a writer and social worker at the University Settlement, an important meeting ground for native-born reformers and Jewish immigrants on the Lower East Side. Walling's encounter with Jews greatly affected him. "Make friends with these settlement people and listen, listen all the time," he counseled a new co-worker. "They've got a lot to teach us boys, so for the love of Jesus Christ don't let's be uplifters here."[38] While working at the settlement, Walling met Strunsky and the two married in Europe during a nearly two-year journey to Russia for the purpose of reporting on the 1905 revolution and its aftermath. Shortly after Walling returned to New York, he joined the Socialist Party, became a contributor to the Marxist theoretical journal *The New International Review*, and, with Strunsky and others, helped found the National Association for the Advancement of Colored People in 1910. His relationship with Strunsky, and other contacts with immigrant Jews, led directly to his conversion to socialism and causes associated with it, from the Russian Revolution to the nascent civil rights movement. It was a long journey from his home state of Kentucky.[39]

Based on available information and inference, we may reconstruct a web of personal contacts Walling likely developed through his marriage to Strunsky. Walling surely would have known Strunsky's old friend from California William Edlin, now a prominent Yiddish journalist, lecturer, and Socialist Party member, who, like Walling, served as a spokesman for the Socialist Party's prowar element during World War I.[40] Either through Edlin or on his own, Walling probably met Edlin's brother-in-law Louis Boudin, who in the 1890s wrote for Russian publications but soon thereafter switched to Yiddish, and eventually established himself as a prominent labor lawyer, legal scholar, and authority on Marxist thought. Like Walling, Boudin was a contributor to *The New International Review*.[41] Strunsky's dear friend and confidante Dr. Katherine Maryson connected Walling to leading figures in the Yiddish cultural movement. Maryson and her husband, Jacob, were well-known Yiddish writers, anarchists, and close friends and political associates of Chaim Zhitlovsky.[42] And, finally, Strunsky's own family members formed an intellectual cohort of their own. The Strunsky family circle included Anna's brother Hyman, a writer for the Socialist Party daily *The Call* and owner of a Russian café on Second Avenue, where, in early 1917, one could find Leon Trotsky arguing politics with other patrons.[43] There was Anna's sister Rose, a translator of Trotsky, Maxim Gorky, and Leo Tolstoy[44]; her cousin Simeon, the *New York Evening Post*'s literary editor and a widely published author; and Simeon's wife, Manya Gordon, a prominent member of the Russian Socialist Revolutionary Party and frequent writer in English on Russian affairs.[45] Thus Walling's marriage to Strunsky offers a window on to the larger cosmopolitan milieu fostered by interactions between Greenwich Village and the Lower East Side. A similarly wide web of personal connections might be possible to trace through other intermarried couples. One thinks of, for instance, the actress Fania Marinoff and her marriage to Carl Van Vechten, the well-known promoter of the Harlem renaissance. Marinoff's brother was the publisher of the Yiddish literary-political satirical magazine *Der groyser kundes*, which is to say that she stood on middle ground between the Lower East Side's Yiddish literati and their African American counterparts uptown.

Within New York's interethnic intelligentsia, immigrant Jews served as conduits of Russian culture and politics. They possessed knowledge of a country barely known to most Americans, yet of increasing interest after the outbreak of the 1905 revolution. Jewish intellectuals analyzed social, economic, and political developments in Russia; translated important books into English (and Yiddish); and brought recognition to Russian literature. It is telling that the "first extended notice in America of Chekhov's writings" came from the pen of Abraham Cahan.[46] Immigrant Jews not only possessed extensive knowledge of Russian literature and politics but also provided direct ties to Russian revolutionary parties of all tendencies. During the early 1900s, the Lower East Side had become a virtual outpost of the Russian revolutionary movement, as emissaries from rival parties traveled to the United States to raise funds.[47] Jewish intellectuals established headquarters for these parties on the Lower East Side, coordinated lecture tours, granted access to journalists, and promoted their cause to the larger American public. Such ties to the Russian revolutionary movement served to elevate the prestige and influence of immigrant Jewish intellectuals in the English-speaking world.[48]

The writer Moissaye Olgin illustrates the role Jewish intellectuals played as Russian experts. A former member of the Bund (General Alliance of Jewish Workers in Lithuania, Poland, and Russia), Olgin immigrated to the United States in 1914 and soon thereafter joined the staff of the *Forverts*, published in the Yiddish monthly *Di tsukunft*, and played a prominent role in immigrant Jewish politics. At the same time, Olgin moved beyond the immigrant Jewish community with apparent ease. In 1915, he enrolled in Columbia University, where he earned a PhD in literature two years later. In November 1917, he published his dissertation under the title *The Soul of the Russian Revolution*, a 400-page history of the Russian revolutionary movement up to March 1917.[49] As both a veteran revolutionary and a newly minted scholar, Olgin became a recognized expert in Russian affairs and his book received favorable reviews in important liberal magazines, such as *The Nation* and *The New Republic*, as well as the *New York Times*.[50] Olgin published a second book in early 1918, a translated collection of articles by Trotsky, whom Olgin had met several times in Europe and New York.[51] In the following year, Olgin joined the faculty of the New School for Social Research as a lecturer in Russian history.[52] In 1920, he published a third book, the highly regarded *A Guide to Russian Literature*.[53] Olgin also lectured frequently and authored articles on Russian politics and literature—including a lengthy series on the Bolshevik Revolution for *The New Republic*—for scholarly and popular publications.[54] Thus in a remarkably brief period, Olgin attained considerable recognition in English-speaking intellectual circles as an expert in Russian politics and literature, although without severing his ties to Yiddish, in which he continued to write for the remainder of his life.

In addition to serving as ambassadors of Russian revolutionary politics and culture, Jewish intellectuals brought Yiddish culture into English. Translations of Yiddish writers began appearing in the late 1890s and have continued ever since. The first and most famous example was the beloved poet Morris Rosenfeld. A tailor by trade, Rosenfeld started writing Yiddish verse during the Great Upheaval and soon became one of the most popular Yiddish poets in North America and Europe. Harvard University professor of Slavic studies Leo Weiner championed Rosenfeld and published a collection of his poems under the title *Songs from the Ghetto* (1898), which soon appeared in German, Polish, Hungarian, and Czech translations. The following year, Weiner published a 400-page survey of Yiddish literature in the nineteenth century, the first of its kind in English. Although Rosenfeld's fame proved short lived, and his reputation fared poorly among younger Yiddish poets, interest in Yiddish among English-speaking literati did not wane.[55]

The most concerted effort to bring Yiddish letters to the English-speaking public was the monthly magazine *East and West* (1915–1916). The magazine's founder and editor was *Forverts* staff member Hillel Rogoff, who came to the newspaper in 1906 after two friends introduced him to Cahan. Always eager to recruit American-educated Jews familiar with the country, Cahan invited Rogoff, then a student at the City College of New York, to join the newspaper. Rogoff had never written in the language but nonetheless accepted Cahan's offer and remained with the paper for the rest of his career, taking over as editor after Cahan's death in 1951.[56] With *East and West*, Rogoff aimed "to interpret in the common language the literature that has in it the power of unifying all classes of Jews, and to make known to a public that was excluded from firsthand knowledge of Yiddish literature, the fact that there were contemporary Yiddish writers—playwrights, poets, etc., whose talents were by no means negligent and the value of whose work was such that [it] had already found appreciation in at least one country—Russia."[57] *East and West* published translations of short stories, poems, essays, profiles, and, on two occasions, critical essays by literary scholars, who, it so happened, were unimpressed by the works they read.[58] *East and West* lasted only one year, presumably due to financial reasons, but the magazine may be understood as part of an ongoing process of cultural crossover characteristic of the period.

If *East and West* proved too specialized for English-language readers, general interest English-language magazines continued to publish articles on Yiddish literature, theater, and the periodical press. *The Nation*, for instance, reviewed English translations of Yiddish literature and Yiddish-language publications, such as Alexander Harkvay's *A Dictionary of the Yiddish Language* (1898) and Chaim Zhitlovsky's philosophical-political monthly *Dos naye lebn* (1908–1912).[59] Articles with titles such as "Yiddish Books and Their Readers," "Is Yiddish Literature Dying?," "Yiddish Literature: A Product of Revolt," and "America's Most Interesting Daily" (a profile of the *Forverts*) also ran in *The Nation*.[60]

The modernist literary monthly *The Pagan* (1916–1922) provides another example. Although largely forgotten today, *The Pagan* helped to "set the tone for the many Village magazines of the late-war and post-war period," according to a 1933 chronicle of bohemian life.[61] The magazine was edited and published by Joseph Kling, a poet, freethinker, and bookstore owner who mentored up-and-coming writers.[62] Ensconced in the Village literary scene, Kling was also well connected to the Yiddish literati through familial relations (the poet Berta Kling was his aunt) and friendships with members of Di yunge, the first cohort of Yiddish writers to declare a commitment to aestheticism.[63] Kling published a remarkable quantity of Yiddish literature in translation. At least one Yiddish poem or short story, and often more, appeared in every issue of *The Pagan* during its first four years. Kling, who translated all the works himself, gave special attention to Mani Leyb, Moyshe-Leyb Halpern, and, above all, Moyshe Nadir, but the novelists Sholem Aleichem, Joseph Opatoshu, Y. L. Peretz, and Sholem Asch were also well represented.[64] In addition, Kling published drawings, etchings, and monotypes of Yiddish writers by Jewish artists, such as Joseph Foshko, William Gropper, Louis Lozowick, Abraham Walkowitz, and William Auerbach-Levy. The most prominently displayed work of Jewish art appeared on the magazine's December 1917 cover: a design of interlocking menorahs reprinted from a Yiddish book published by the Socialist Zionist Party, Poale Zion.[65]

The above examples are not meant to suggest that *The Pagan* somehow presented itself as a Jewish magazine. Unlike *East and West*, *The Pagan* did not seek primarily to advance Yiddish literature, nor were most of its writers Jews, although a considerable number of Anglophone Jewish writers, such as Max Bodenheim, Alter Brody, and Louis Zukofsky appeared on its pages. *The Pagan* was "a magazine for Eudaemonists," believers in the idea that happiness is the chief good for humankind. The magazine's scope was insistently international, always featuring translations from major European languages. Still, for Kling it was altogether natural and valid that the best Yiddish writers should appear alongside the likes of Hart Crane and Eugene O'Neill, both associate editors at *The Pagan*. Yiddish literature, in Kling's opinion, stood "on a level with the finest in other modern languages" and should be appreciated as such.[66]

The personal interactions, linguistic crossings, and cultural transmissions traced in this essay do not amount to a complete picture. Needed, for instance, is research into how immigrant Jewish intellectuals viewed their gentile interlocutors. The role of affluent Jews of German family backgrounds also demands attention. The encounters discussed in this essay are intended to demonstrate some of the ways in which two seemingly disparate intellectual communities overlapped. On the one hand, immigrant Jewish intellectuals embraced Yiddish to propagate socialism, advance Yiddish culture, and participate in a vibrant, financially profitable Yiddish newspaper market. On the other, they developed ties to American-born intellectuals interested in and fascinated by the Jews' perceived emotional intensity, political idealism, love of learning, and cosmopolitanism. Personal interactions and cultural exchanges across linguistic boundaries ushered immigrant Jews into the center of New York intellectual life, bringing the cultural and political worlds of Russian and Yiddish with them.

Notes

The author wishes to thank Alisa Braun, Victoria Kingham, Cecile Kuznitz, Ken Moss, Eddy Portnoy, Jennifer Ratner-Rosenhagen, Sarah Abrevaya Stein, and the editors of this book for their comments.

1. Emmanuel Goldsmith, *Modern Yiddish Culture: The Story of the Modern Yiddish Language Movement* (New York: Fordham University Press, 1997), 45–69; Dan Miron, *A Traveler Disguised: The Rise of Modern Yiddish Fiction in the Nineteenth Century* (Syracuse, NY: Syracuse University Press, 1996), 1–33.

2. The term "intellectuals" was used in the immigrant Jewish context to refer to secularly educated, usually left-wing men and women engaged in the production and dissemination of ideas through nonacademic institutions, such as the labor movement and the popular press, from a politically/socially active standpoint. They fit Lewis Coser's definition of intellectuals as "gatekeepers of ideas and fountainheads of ideologies, but, unlike medieval churchmen or modern political propagandists and zealots, they tend at the same time to cultivate a critical attitude; they tend to scrutinize the received ideas and assumptions of their time and *milieu*. They are those who 'think otherwise,' the disturbers of intellectual peace." Coser, *Men of Ideas: A Sociologist's View* (New York: The Free Press, 1965), x.

3. Between the two world wars, however, Vilna and Warsaw surpassed New York as Yiddish cultural centers. Chone Shmeruk, "Aspects of the History of Warsaw as a Yiddish Literary Centre," *Polin* 3 (1988): 142–55, 151. However, Shmeruk's description of New York City as "no more than an admittedly very large offshoot of eastern Europe" (151) is mistaken.

4. David A. Hollinger, "Ethnic Diversity, Cosmopolitanism and the Emergence of the American Liberal Intelligentsia," *American Quarterly* 27, no. 2 (1975): 133–51, 138. Also, see Lewis S. Feuer, "The Political Linguistics of 'Intellectual,' 1898–1918," *Survey* 16 (winter 1971): 156–83.

5. A number of the early Greenwich Village intellectuals, such as Waldo Frank, Ludwig Lewisohn, and Paul Rosenfeld came from German-Jewish backgrounds. By World War I, Jews of eastern European Jewish backgrounds, such as Mike Gold, joined them. On Frank and Lewisohn, see Julian Levinson, *Exiles on Main Street: Jewish American Writers and American Literary Culture* (Bloomington: Indiana University Press, 2008), 56–92.

6. Evidence suggests that immigrant Jewish intellectuals played a similar role in cities outside of New York. See references to Haim Kantorovitch's influence on V. F. Calverton and the *Modern Quarterly* in Leonard Wilcox, *V. F. Calverton: Radical in the American Grain* (Philadelphia: Temple University Press, 1992), 36, 37–38, 45, 48, 73.

7. Christine Stansell, *American Moderns: Bohemian New York and the Creation of a New Century* (New York: Metropolitan Books, 2000), 64–65.

8. See, for example, Steven Biel, *Independent Intellectuals in the United States, 1910–1945* (New York: New York University Press, 1992) and Joanna Levin, *Bohemia in America, 1858–1920* (Stanford: Stanford University Press, 2010), 339–91. For an important exception in Yiddish literary studies, see Anita Norich, *Discovering Exile: Yiddish and Jewish American Culture during the Holocaust* (Stanford: Stanford University Press, 2007), 1–95.

The tendency to separate the two intellectual communities may be attributed, in part, to American-born "bohemians and avant-gardists" who, as Sara Blair argues, "sought to reframe their activities as sui generis, the creation of a distinctly modern stance and gestalt that obscured its indebtedness to the life-world that *Yiddishkeit* on the East Side was molding." Blair, "Whose Modernism Is It? Abraham Cahan, Fictions of Yiddish, and the Contest of Modernity," *Modern Fictions Studies* 51, no. 2 (2005): 258-84, 259. Even so, at least some American-born intellectuals did, in fact, acknowledge the influence of Jewish immigrants and Yiddish cultural life, as I argue in the present essay.

9. On the Great Upheaval's impact on immigrant Jews and the influence of immigrant German socialists, see Tony Michels, *A Fire in Their Hearts: Yiddish Socialists in New York* (Cambridge: Harvard University Press, 2005), 26-30, 50-68.

10. Khayim Spivak, "Erinerugen fun Kahan's grine tsaytn," in *Yubeleum-shrift tsu Ab. Kahan's 50stn geburtstog* (New York: Forverts Association, 1910), 30-35, 35.

11. Y. Lifshits and E. Tsherikover, "Di pionern-tkufe fun der yidisher arbeter bavegung," in *Geshikhte fun der yidisher arbeter-bavegung in di Fareynikte shtatn*, ed. E. Tsherikover (New York: YIVO Institute for Jewish Research, 1945), 2:263-65.

12. Abraham Cahan, *Bleter fun mayn lebn* (New York: Forverts Association, 1926), 2:193.

13. Shoel Yanovsky, *Ershte yorn fun yidishn frayhaytlekhn sotsyalizm* (New York: Fraye arbeter shtime, 1948), 86-87.

14. See, for instance, Morris Hillquit, *Loose Leaves from a Busy Life* (New York: Macmillan, 1934), 17.

15. Quoted in Robert A. Karlowich, *We Fall and Rise: Russian-Language Newspapers in New York City, 1889-1914* (Metuchen, NJ: Scarecrow Press, 1991), 108; Filip Krants, "Mit 25 yor tsurik," *Di fraye gezelshaft* (August 1910): 678, 680-81; M. Vintshevsky, "Der 'Arbeter fraynd,'" *Dos naye lebn* (July 1910): 37; Vintshevsky, "Filip Krants," *Di tsukunft* (January 1923): 12-13.

16. On Zhitlovsky in the United States, see Michels, *Fire in Their Hearts*, 125-52.

17. N. L. Horeker et al., "Liova Fradkin—L. M. Shteyn," in *Yoyvl bukh tsu L. M. Shteyns finf un tsvantsik yorikn yubiley fun kultur-gezelshaftlekhe tetikeyt*, ed. Y. Kh. Pomerants and A. Pravatiner (Chicago: Sholem Aleichem Folk Institute, 1938), 32-33, 36; Sarah Abrevaya Stein, "Illustrating Chicago's Jewish Left: The Cultural Aesthetics of Todros Geller and L. M. Shteyn Farlag," *Jewish Social Studies*, n.s., 3, no. 3 (1997): 74-77, 104-6.

18. "It was odd," Bercovici continues, "that the first language in which I learned to write in the United States should have been Yiddish, a language more alien to me than English was." Bercovici, *It's the Gypsy in Me: The Autobiography of Konrad Bercovici* (New York: Prentice-Hall, 1941), 51.

19. Steven Cassedy, *To the Other Shore: The Russian Jewish Intellectuals Who Came To America* (Princeton: Princeton University Press, 1997), 65-73; Karlowich, *We Fall and Rise*, 24-25.

20. Karlowich, *We Fall and Rise*, 102-10; Michels, *Fire in Their Hearts*, 84.

21. Karlowich, *We Fall and Rise*, 145-211; David Shub, "Bibliography: The Russian Press in the United States," *Russian Review* 3, no. 1 (1943): 120-28.

22. Mark Khinoy, *Fun tsarishn un sovetishn untergrunt* (New York: Farlag "Der veker," 1965), 23-25.

23. William Edlin, "Notitsn far an oytobiografye" (handwritten manuscript), p. G (RG 251, folder 11, YIVO archives); William Z. Spiegelman, "Molders of Jewish Public Opinion," *The Sentinel*, n.d. (RG 251, folder 45, YIVO archives). For a summary of Edlin's career, see Efraim Oyerbach and Moyshe Shtarkman, eds., *Leksikon fun der nayer yidisher literatur* (New York, 1965), 6:546-47.

24. Strunsky to Edlin, June 24, 1897 (RG 251, folder 229, YIVO archives).

25. Stansell, *American Moderns*, 22-23.

26. Van Wyck Brooks, *Autobiography* (New York: E. P. Dutton, 1963), 156.

27. Both quotations are in Stansell, *American Moderns*, 62, 165.

28. Ida Van Etten, "Russian Jews as Desirable Immigrants," *Forum* 15 (April 1893): 172–82, 173.

29. "Peripatetic Philosophers of This Many-Sided Town," *New York Times*, May 29, 1910, SM 11.

30. "On East Broadway," *New York Times*, March 16, 1913, 252.

31. James Huneker, *New Cosmopolis: A Book of Images* (New York: Charles Scribner's Sons, 1915), 69–70.

32. Randolph Bourne, "The Jew and Trans-National America," *The Menorah Journal* 2 (December 1916): 277–84, 284.

33. On Cahan's relationship with Howells, see Sarah Alisa Braun, "Jews, Writing, and the Dynamics of Literary Affiliation, 1880–1940" (PhD diss., University of Michigan, 2007), 27–71.

34. Lincoln Steffens, *The Autobiography of Lincoln Steffens* (New York: Harcourt, Brace, 1931), 317.

35. Ibid., 318. Referring to the debates about the Yiddish theater raging among the Jewish public, Steffens writes, "A remarkable phenomenon it was, a community of thousands of people fighting over an art question as savagely as other people had fought over political or religious questions, dividing families, setting brother against brother, breaking up business firms, and finally, actually forcing the organization of a rival theater" (Ibid., 317).

36. Moses Rischin, "Introduction" in *The Spirit of the Ghetto*, by Hutchins Hapgood (Cambridge: Harvard University Press, 1967), vii–xxxvi. Also, see Moses Rischin, "Abraham Cahan and the New York *Commercial Advertiser*: A Study in Acculturation," *Publications of the American Jewish Historical Society* 43, no. 1 (1953): 10–36.

37. Hapgood, *The Spirit of the Ghetto*, 37.

38. Quoted in Leon Fink, *Progressive Intellectuals and the Dilemmas of Democratic Commitment* (Cambridge: Harvard University Press, 1999), 123.

39. Ibid., 114–83; Richard Schneirov, "The Odyssey of William English Walling: Revisionism, Social Democracy, and Evolutionary Pragmatism," *The Journal of the Gilded Age and Progressive Era* 2, no. 4 (October 2003): 403–30. An extensive treatment of the romantic relationship between Walling and Strunsky can be found in James Boylan, *Revolutionary Lives: Anna Strunsky and William English Walling* (Amherst: University of Massachusetts Press, 1998). The book, however, does not explore Walling's connections to the immigrant Jewish intelligentsia.

40. Walling differed with Strunsky on the question of American involvement in the war, a disagreement that contributed to the demise of their marriage. Fink, *Progressive Intellectuals*, 168–81.

41. Susan Braudy, *Family Circle: The Boudins and the Aristocracy of the Left* (New York: Vintage/Anchor, 2004), 3–8.

42. Michels, *Fire in Their Hearts*, 140, 147, 148–49. Maryson is sometimes transliterated from the Yiddish as Merison.

43. Bercovici, *It's the Gypsy in Me*, 111.

44. Maxim Gorky, *The Confession*, trans. Rose Strunsky (New York: Frederick A. Stokes, 1916); Rose Strusnky, ed. and trans., *The Journal of Leo Tolstoi* (New York: Alfred A. Knopf, 1917); Leon Trotsky, *Literature and Revolution*, trans. Rose Strunsky (New York: International Publishers, 1925).

45. See, for instance, Manya Gordon, *Workers before and after Lenin* (New York: E. P. Dutton, 1941); Manya Gordon, *How to Tell Progress from Reaction* (New York: E. P. Dutton, 1944).

46. Charles W. Meister, "Chekhov's Reception in England and America," *American Slavic and East European Review* 12, no. 1 (1953): 109–121, 110. According to Moses Rischin, "Cahan

was also the first to introduce—prematurely as it proved—all the new Russian writers: Vladimir Korolenko, Ignaty Potapenko, Maxim Gorky, and others. At a time [1897-1902] when no American magazine editor was interested, Cahan translated some of the best contemporary Russian short stories for the *Advertiser*." Rischin, "Introduction," in *Grandma Never Lived in America: The New Journalism of Abraham Cahan*, ed. Abraham Cahan and Moses Rischin (Bloomington: Indiana University Press, 1985), xxxix.

47. Herts Burgin, *Di geshikhte fun der yidisher arbeter bavegung in Amerike, Rusland, un England* (New York: United Hebrew Trades, 1915), 667-77; Jonathan Frankel, *Prophecy and Politics: Socialism, Nationalism, and the Russian Jews, 1862-1917* (Cambridge: Cambridge University Press, 1981), 473-509; Michels, *Fire in Their Hearts*, 125-26; Ernest Poole, "Maxim Gorki in New York," *Slavonic and East European Review* 3, no. 1 (1944): 77-83; Arthur W. Thompson, "The Reception of Russian Revolutionary Leaders in America, 1904-1906," *American Quarterly* 18, no. 3 (1966): 452-76, 464; Louis Waldman, *Labor Lawyer* (New York: E. P. Dutton, 1944), 63-68.

48. See, for instance, "Strike for Freedom Is Bourtseff's Cry," *New York Times*, January 22, 1910, 9; "East Side Mourns Dr. Kaplan," *New York Times*, January 7, 1918, 11. It should be noted that Simeon Strunsky denies that Jews played an important role as promoters of Russian culture and politics, a role he attributes to the influence of the British intelligentsia. Without disregarding Strunsky's point altogether—Jewish immigrants were certainly not the only ones to bring attention to Russia in the United States—it should nonetheless be considered an overstatement. Strunsky's comments refer to the years after World War I, rather than the prewar period, when information about Russia was still quite limited and the role of Jews as Russian experts was all the more prominent. Furthermore, Strunsky's comments, written in the early 1940s, have the explicit apologetic intent of disproving accusations of a Jewish-led, international communist conspiracy as "formulated in the Protocols of Zion [sic] and enormously popularized by Adolph Hitler" (*No Mean City* [New York: E. P. Dutton, 1944], 95). In a period of murderous anti-Semitism, Strunsky understandably wanted to minimize the role of Jews as bearers of Russian culture and politics. Nonetheless, the literary, journalistic, and political activities of Strunsky's own extended family are enough to cast doubt on his contention.

49. Moissaye J. Olgin, *The Soul of the Russian Revolution* (New York: Henry Holt, 1917).

50. *The Nation*, December 6, 1917, 638-39; *The New Republic*, December 22, 1917, 220-21; *New York Times*, January 13, 1918, 14. According to the economist Isaac Hourwich, *The Soul of the Russian Revolution* was "surely the best" recent book to appear on the Russian Revolution. See Hourwich's review in *Di tsukunft* (August 1918), 494-95.

51. Leon Trotsky, *Our Revolution: Essays on Working-Class and International Revolution, 1904-1917*, collected and trans. Moissaye J. Olgin (New York: Henry Holt, 1918). See reviews in *New York Times*, February 17, 1918, 62 and *The Nation*, March 21, 1918, 327.

52. *New York Times*, September 30, 1919, 20.

53. Clarendon Ross, "A Handbook of Russian Literature," *The New Republic*, November 24, 1920, 334; Jacob Zeitlin, "A Guide to Russian Literature," *The Nation*, September 18, 1920, 327-28.

54. See, for instance, Moissaye J. Olgin, "The Intelligentzia and the People in the Russian Revolution," *Annals of the American Academy of Political and Social Science*, vol. 84, *International Reconstruction* (July 1919): 114-20; "Maxim Gorky," *The New Republic*, January 18, 1919, 333-34; "A Wounded Intellect: Leonid Andreyev (1871-1919)," *The New Republic*, December 24, 1919, 123-24; "A Sympathetic View of Russia," *The New Republic*, May 26, 1920, 426; "A Flashlight of the Russian Revolution," *The New Republic*, July 27, 1921, 250-51.

55. Braun, "Dynamics of Literary Affiliation," 72-121; Marc Miller, *Representing the Immigrant Experience: Morris Rosenfeld and the Emergence of Yiddish Literature in America* (Syracuse, NY: Syracuse University Press, 2007), 16-19.

Immigrant Jews, Yiddish, and the New York Intellectual Scene   85

56. Hillel Rogoff, *Der gayst fun "Forverts"* (New York: Forverts Association, 1954), 25-26.

57. Journal editor, "Our First Anniversary," *East and West* (March 1916): n.p.

58. John Erskine, "A Criticism," *East and West* (April 1915): 21-23; T. D. O'Bolger, "Jephthah's Daughter—A Criticism," *East and West* (August 1915): 129-30.

59. *The Nation*, October 27, 1898, 320-21; "The Minor Tongues," *The Nation*, April 22, 1909, 404.

60. A. A. Roback, "Yiddish Books and Their Readers," *The Nation*, October 12, 1918, 408-12; Oswald Garrison Villard, "America's Most Interesting Daily," *The Nation*, September 27, 1922, 301-2; Lewis Browne, "Is Yiddish Literature Dying?" *The Nation*, May 2, 1923, 513-14; L. Talmy, "Yiddish Literature: A Product of Revolt," *The Nation*, August 8, 1923, 137-39.

61. Albert Parry, *Garrets and Pretenders: A History of Bohemianism in America* (New York: Covici-Friede, 1933), 313. I thank Edward Portnoy for bringing this source to my attention.

62. On Kling and *The Pagan*, see Victoria Kingham, "Commerce and Modernism in Little Magazines, 1910-1922" (PhD diss., De Montfort University, United Kingdom, 2010), 136-79.

63. Kling's connections to the Yiddish literary scene are further indicated by his discussion of immigrant Jewish intellectuals in "In Re Judea Et Al.," *The Pagan*, July 1916, 43-45 and the fact that the Yiddish poet Zishe Vaynper placed an advertisement for his journal, *Der onheyb*, in *The Pagan*'s January 1918 issue, 45. On Di yunge, see Ruth Wisse, *A Little Love in Big Manhattan* (Cambridge: Harvard University Press, 1988), 1-104.

64. In 1920, Kling brought out a volume of Nadir's writings culled from *The Pagan*. Moishe Nadir, *Peh-el-peh* [Face-to-Face], trans. Joseph Kling (New York: Pagan, 1920). A. M. Dilon, Avrom Reyzin, and Yoysef Rolnik were also published in the magazine. Note that I transliterate the names of Yiddish writers and publications differently from Kling, whose own transliterations were inconsistent and, in any case, diverge considerably from current scholarly spelling.

65. The timing of the illustration was not incidental, following as it did the Balfour Declaration in the previous month and coinciding with Hanukkah.

66. Kling, "In Re Judea Et Al.," 44. Also, see Kling's defense of Yiddish literature in response to H. L. Mencken's statement that "Yiddish literature, in the main, is feeble and tawdry" and the Jews are a people "devoid of aesthetic sense." Kling, *The Pagan*, March 1918, 40-41. Mencken's comment serves as a reminder that not all American intellectuals held Jews or Yiddish in high regard.

PROPAGANDA OR FIGHTING THE MYTH OF *PAKHDONES*?

Naye Prese, *the Popular Front, and the Spanish Civil War*

GERBEN ZAAGSMA

On April 24, 1938, *Naye Prese,* the Paris-based Yiddish communist daily, published a greeting on its front page from Misha Reger, the political commissar of the Naftali Botwin Company. The Botwin Company, a small Jewish military unit within the International Brigades, was at that time fighting in Spain on the side of the Republican government against the military revolt by the so-called Nationalists headed by General Francisco Franco.[1] The lead article on that same front page announced a meeting of dozens of Jewish organizations in Paris, organized by the Initsiativ komitet far fareynikn demokratishe gezelshaftn (Committee to Unite the Democratic Organizations). The meeting arose as the result of an initiative of Jewish immigrant communists in Paris who wished to convene to create a new organizational platform among the Parisian Jewish immigrant population.[2]

This front-page configuration was not coincidental. Formed in December 1937 on the initiative of Jewish immigrant communists in Paris, the Botwin Company had since become an important tool to mobilize and maintain support for the Spanish cause as well as to promote the Popular Front on *der yidisher gas* (the Jewish street). Part of that effort included the April 24th meeting, and the Reger letter was aimed at reinforcing the specific message that only unity on the Jewish street could serve as an appropriate defense against the threats that immigrant Jews faced. Those threats consisted of economic hardship, a general rise of xenophobia and anti-Semitism in France, and, very concretely, restrictions on immigrant labor and the threat of expulsion faced by many paperless (Jewish) immigrants emanating from the decree laws that the new government of Edouard Daladier introduced in May 1938. Reger's article encouraged Jewish leaders in Paris to heed the example set by the many Jewish volunteers, the "best sons of the Jewish people," as *Naye Prese* often described them, who, according to the newspaper, fought united against fascism and anti-Semitism on the Spanish battlefields.

As this particular example shows, reports in *Naye Prese* closely tied the events in Spain, and particularly the participation of Jewish volunteers in the International Brigades, to the politics and strategies of Jewish communists on the Jewish street in Paris. Given the importance of Spain in the Popular Front strategy of the Communist International (or, Comintern) this should come as no surprise. Officially adopted at the Seventh Comintern Congress in July 1935, the Popular Front tactic entailed the formation of broad antifascist alliances, including nonworkers parties. In 1936 Popular Front coalitions won election victories in Spain (February) and France (April). When the military revolt that began in Spain in July received almost instant support from the main fascist leaders of the day, Hitler and Mussolini, a civil war deeply rooted in internal Spanish strife turned rapidly into a conflict with significant international dimensions. The Soviet Union and Comintern in turn actively supported the Republican government and decided on the formation of the International Brigades that saw deployment from October 1936 until their withdrawal in autumn 1938.

For the Comintern and its member parties, the Spanish cause subsequently served as a crucial propaganda tool to raise awareness about and maintain support for the Popular Front, and the brigades were presented as *the* example of united antifascist action in practice.[3] For Jewish communists in Paris the International Brigades were thus an important tool to promote what they called a "Jewish Popular Front" among the Jewish immigrant population. But representations of Jewish volunteers in *Naye Prese* did not merely propagate the Popular Front on the Jewish street. In the course of the war the subtext to that propaganda became increasingly Jewish as reports placed increasing emphasis on "Jewish heroism" in Spain. Many articles asserted that the participation of Jewish volunteers, symbolized most clearly by the Botwin Company, disproved prejudices and allegations of Jewish cowardice that had surfaced in the brigades as well as in the Polish immigrant press in Paris. Such representations of Jewish volunteers were related to Jewish communist concerns with relations between Polish and Jewish immigrants, as well as the position of Jewish workers in the French labor movement and France in general. As we will see, it was within this context that *Naye Prese* fashioned the participation of Jewish volunteers as a model of Jewish action to be emulated by Jewish immigrants in Paris.

From a broader historical-methodological perspective, the discursive construction of the struggle and experiences of Jewish volunteers in *Naye Prese* and the relation to Jewish communist politics and strategies on the Jewish street in Paris represent a prime example of an often overlooked historical phenomenon: the constitutive role of "the Jewish press" in shaping modern Jewish life.[4] Yiddish newspapers not only reflected Jewish social, cultural, and political life but also acted as agents in creating it. Ideological newspapers such as *Naye Prese* illustrate this particularly well, as their raison d'être was so clearly connected to the realization of a political program.

Although published for the Jewish immigrant population of France and Belgium, the majority of *Naye Prese*'s readership lived in Paris, the center of French Jewish life. In the late 1930s Jewish immigrants in the French capital numbered approximately 90,000 out of a total Jewish population of 150,000. Most of these Jewish immigrants originated from Poland (50,000) and non-Polish areas of the former Russian Empire (15,000), Hungary (11,000), and Romania (10,000), and most of them spoke Yiddish as a first language.[5] A majority worked in the clothing and textile industry, and many were so-called *façonniers*, or self-employed home workers.[6]

Jewish immigrants in France in the 1930s saw themselves confronted with a rising tide of xenophobia and anti-Semitism. Foreign Jews were traditionally seen as difficult to assimilate in the French nation due to their visibility and "otherness."[7] In addition they faced other problems. Unlike immigrants who worked in the mines in the north of France or in agriculture, they preferred to live in the cities, predominantly in Paris, where they were seen as competitors with French workers.[8] In contrast to non-Jewish Polish migrants, Jewish migrants conveyed an impression of not sharing (and being able to share) in "traditional" French values, such as manual labor and love for the land, that could make them more easily assimilable.[9] Because of their specific economic position, Jews were, more than other foreigners, separated from French workers who were prone to anti-Semitism.[10] After the Austrian *Anschluß* in March 1938 and the Munich crisis in November of that year, the fear of foreign Jews being "warmongers" surfaced more forcefully, resulting in several anti-Semitic incidents in France.

Yet Jewish immigrants faced hostility not only from French workers but also from other non-Jewish eastern European immigrants, especially Poles and Romanians. This is not to suggest that anti-Semitism was the sole determinant of Jewish immigrant life in France in this period.[11] Nevertheless, the activities of anti-Semitic groups in Paris are well documented and indicate that Jewish immigrants were confronted with anti-Jewish propaganda, and violence, on the city's streets.[12] And as will become clear, representations of Jewish volunteers in *Naye Prese* were significantly influenced by certain anti-Jewish stereotypes.

Within this urban immigrant context, Jewish communists stood as the most important leftist political force in the late 1930s. The Parti communiste français (PCF) organized them in the *sous-section juive*, one of several language sections of the Main d'oeuvre immigrée (MOI), an umbrella organization created by the PCF in the mid-1920s to accommodate foreign communists and to disseminate propaganda among various immigrant groups. The section numbered around 300 members but counted a greater number of sympathizers. The Fraynt fun

Naye Prese, for instance, had 2,000 to 3,000 members.[13] In March 1937 the PCF dissolved the language sections in an apparent bid to decrease the visibility of immigrants in the party and curb antiforeigner sentiment in its ranks within the context of increasing xenophobia in France.[14] The new focal point of Jewish communist activity now became *Naye Prese* and its support organization, the Fraynt.

The main political adversaries of the Jewish communists in Paris were the Jewish socialists of the Bund, with approximately 1,000 to 1,500 members in various affiliated organizations.[15] The journal of the Bundist Medem-Farband, *Undzer Shtime*, appeared highly irregularly in this period, making it rather unsuitable for a comparison with *Naye Prese*. More important in this respect was the main competitor of *Naye Prese*, Paris' other Yiddish daily, *Parizer Haynt*, created in 1926 by Shmuel Yatzkan, founder of the major Warsaw Yiddish newspaper *Haynt*.[16] Although *Parizer Haynt* lacked an official political affiliation, it had a Labor-Zionist character. Marc Jarblum, the leader of the moderate World Labor-Zionist Party Poale Zion Hitachduth in France, regularly published in *Parizer Haynt*. The newspaper also printed announcements of the Linke Poale Zion, which maintained a small branch in Paris, and occasionally published small reports on its meetings and other activities.[17]

Two umbrella organizations dominated Jewish immigrant life in the 1930s. The most important of these, the Fédération des sociétés juives founded in 1926, comprised several *landsmanshaftn* and mutual aid societies. The Fédération also operated a school system and a variety of cultural and sports organizations.[18] Many leftist Jews, often communists and usually of a younger generation of immigrants, regarded the Fédération as too apolitical and the *landsmanshaftn* and their activities as smacking of "old country," old-fashioned Jewish philanthropy. They set about to create their own, parallel, infrastructure of organizations. In 1938 many of the organizations not belonging to the Fédération, but not necessarily communist, created the Farband fun Yidishe Gezelshaftn.[19]

Following the aforementioned adoption by the Comintern of the Popular Front tactic in July 1935, Jewish communists, the Parisian Bundists organized in the Medem-Farband, and the Linke Poale Zion established the so-called Mouvement populaire juif, an initiative that ran parallel to PCF initiatives to create a French Popular Front. In May 1936 France saw the establishment of a Popular Front government, headed by socialist leader Leon Blum and supported by the PCF. Benefiting from the general popularity of the Popular Front, Jewish communists became an important force among immigrant Jews in this period. The Mouvement was a temporary alliance to defend the interests of Jewish workers, such as their legal status, and common activities were coordinated in a *koordinir-komitet*. After the dissolution of the MOI and the Jewish section, Jewish communists withdrew from the committee, a move that marked the beginning of the end of the Mouvement populaire juif.[20] Though a new *farshtendikungs-komitet* was formed in July 1937, relations between the various partners remained tense, as Jewish communists, who without their section were no longer an official *Jewish* political voice, had suffered a sensitive loss of credibility.[21]

In broad terms, the two Yiddish dailies fell along these organizational lines, with *Naye Prese* representing the younger generation of often more radically inclined immigrants and the Farband, and *Parizer Haynt* predominantly voicing the concerns of older immigrants, the Fédération, and the more moderate noncommunist Left. Both newspapers reported the main international events of the day while also focusing on Jewish communities and anti-Semitic incidents the world over but with an emphasis on Europe and in particular Poland and Romania, where most readers came from. *Parizer Haynt* concerned itself more with the Zionist struggle for independence and Arab-Jewish fighting in Mandate Palestine, whereas *Naye Prese* stressed, in accordance with communist propaganda, the "successful resolution of the Jewish question" in the Soviet Union as symbolized by Birobidzhan.[22] Above all, however, *Naye Prese* advertised itself as *the* newspaper that defended the interests of Jewish workers. Both newspapers also devoted space to Yiddish literature, theater, and movies with, in the case of *Naye Prese*, a particular emphasis on Soviet-Yiddish culture.

Against this backdrop, Jewish communists engaged with the Spanish conflict and the struggle of Jewish volunteers in the International Brigades. A couple of days after the start of the military revolt on July 17, 1936, Adam Rayski, editor of *Naye Prese* and the paper's liaison to PCF newspaper *L'Humanité*, published a first editorial on the events taking place in Spain. Rayski explained to his readers what lessons France could learn from the Spanish revolt and emphasized the importance of a united front against the fascist enemy.[23] When news of Hitler's support for the revolt reached the world two days later, he wrote in a second editorial that support for Republican Spain also implied fighting Franco's fascist sympathizers in France, following the party line as it had been set out by PCF leader Maurice Thorez in *L'Humanité*.[24]

But *Naye Prese* also added a "Jewish" layer to this general communist position. In an editorial on August 3, G. Kenig wrote that the Spanish conflict carried special relevance for Jews because it represented a struggle against the modern fascist *Torquemados*, a reference to the infamous fifteenth-century inquisitor Torquemada.[25] Two articles published later in August discussed the period when Jews were burned at the stake and the "times when Spain expelled all the Jews."[26] In this analysis of the revolt, Franco and his generals were cast as the heirs of the medieval inquisitors, an analogy confirmed by their rhetoric, as articles in *Naye Prese* underlined. Thus, volunteer reporter T. Elski cited a declaration stating the intention of the Nationalists to "expel all the Jews from Spain, just as our ancestors did hundreds of years ago."[27] Such references to the Spanish Inquisition, and the expulsion of the Jews from Spain in 1492, decreased significantly after the first two months of the uprising, but they did not vanish. Clearly, in these early stages of the conflict, the newspaper invoked a specific Jewish historical framework in order to explain the importance of the Spanish cause to its readers.

The Inquisition theme resurfaced a year later, in autumn 1937, when Jewish communists organized an exhibition in Paris about Jewish volunteers. This event deserves further analysis, for it illustrates the clever mix of Jewish symbolism and propaganda the Jewish communists employed. A headline about the exhibition in *Naye Prese* read, "From Rambam to Moritz Skalka," the latter a Jewish volunteer featured in the exhibition. The exhibition itself started with a photograph of the Rambam, acronym of the famous Spanish-Jewish philosopher Moshe ben Maimon or Maimonides (1135–1204). The article reported a discussion between several visitors to the exhibition in which one of them described Maimonides as "the first Jewish fighter who had fought in Spain against backwardness, darkness and barbarism." Thus, the writer cast Maimonides as a secular Jew *avant la lettre* who had dared to stand up against the same evil now confronting his Jewish "successors," the Jewish volunteers fighting in the brigades. For *Naye Prese* the historical analogies stood clear: the Nationalists originated from a long Spanish tradition dating back to the Middle Ages, and the same held true for their Jewish opponents who defended another, and very different, Spanish-Jewish tradition.[28]

In addition to invoking a particular Jewish historical framework, *Naye Prese* reported on anti-Jewish actions of the Nationalists in both Spanish Morocco and the Nationalist-occupied zones in Spain proper.[29] Furthermore, several articles highlighted anti-Semitic declarations by the generals and underlined that a Nationalist victory would mean a victory for fascism in Europe and thus by extension a victory for Hitlerite anti-Semitism. Importantly though, the editors of *Naye Prese* never put forward such assertions as the key arguments in explaining the importance of the Spanish conflict. And interestingly, it was *Parizer Haynt* that concerned itself much more with the actual fate of Jews in Spain and Spanish Morocco than did *Naye Prese*, resulting in a paradoxical situation; whereas the editors of *Naye Prese* were clearly more interested in arousing mass support for the Spanish Republic on the Jewish street than *Parizer Haynt*, the latter paid considerably more attention to the concrete consequences of the war for the Jews in Nationalist-occupied Spain and Spanish Morocco.

For Jewish communists, however, the real "Jewish" interest insofar as Spain was concerned lay not with fascist anti-Semitism nor with Francoist anti-Jewish oppression but with the position of Jewish volunteers within the International Brigades and relations with their non-Jewish, especially Polish, comrades. To be sure, stories about Jewish volunteers as they were printed on the pages of *Naye Prese* from the beginning of the conflict in Spain served clear propagandistic purposes. Following guidelines of the political commissariat of the International Brigades on how to propagate the fight of foreign volunteers, Jewish volunteers were presented by the editors of *Naye Prese* as heroes and the "best sons of the Jewish people," who fought united on the Spanish battlefield, irrespective of their political backgrounds.[30] They were also set as an example that should be followed by Jewish migrants and their organizations in France, whose unification Jewish communists were trying to bring about, as shown by the way in which the earlier mentioned April 24 meeting in Paris was endorsed by the Botwin Company's political commissar.

All this fit nicely with the Comintern's Popular Front strategy in which the International Brigades played such an important propagandistic role. Yet there was also a specific message in representations of Jewish volunteers in *Naye Prese* that was only relevant for Jews: the fight of Jewish volunteers in Spain proved allegations of Jewish cowardice wrong. The main reason for this Jewish communist concern with the classic stereotype of *pakhdones* was spelled out by *Parizer Haynt* when it published a small article headlined "Anti-Semitic Propaganda in Polish Communist Battalion" in August 1937.[31] But even before the formation of the brigades in October 1936, Jewish–non-Jewish relations among foreign volunteers were a matter of concern for Jewish communists in Paris. In the first months of the war, *Naye Prese* published many reports on early Jewish volunteers, many of whom had come from Paris and fought in the different militias hastily organized after the revolt had broken out. One of those militias was the so-called Telman group, which consisted mostly of Jewish men and was therefore described in *Naye Prese* as a "Jewish militia."[32] In an article about Jewish volunteers featuring one of the members of the group, *Naye Prese* editor Y. Lekhter underlined that their participation disproved prejudice about Jewish workers as cowards shying away from armed struggle.[33]

Such assertions that the participation of Jewish volunteers disproved allegations of Jewish cowardice became much more numerous after the formation of the International Brigades in October 1936, particularly the Botwin Company in December 1937.[34] In a special page devoted to the company on January 1, 1938, its first commander Karol Gutman explained in a letter addressed to a friend in Poland that a Jewish company had been created within the Polish Dombrowski Brigade. He wondered

> I am curious how the different parties in Poland will react to this. What will the Endek *Dziennik Narodowy* write? It will be hard for them to misrepresent. The anti-Semites will certainly not have the courage to write about Jewish cowardice.
>
> You should see what kind of friendship exists between Jews, Poles, Germans, Spaniards, between individuals of different peoples. Even Polish workers, who were convinced that one cannot fight with Jews and that they run away when they hear a shot, have altered their opinion here in Spain. When they hear news of a pogrom they are not less shocked than we, the Jewish fighters.[35]

Gutman thus first and foremost placed the participation of Jewish volunteers in the context of accusations of Jewish cowardice. Not much later the Polish-

Jewish communist Gershon Dua-Bogen, a member of the brigade staff who had been instrumental in the formation of the Botwin Company, wrote in an article that "seventeen months of common fighting against fascism [did] more in the struggle against racism, anti-Semitism and fascism than decades of propaganda and agitation through brochures and speeches."[36] To further illustrate this point, *Naye Prese* also paid consistent attention to the opinion of non-Jewish and specifically Polish officials about Jewish volunteers.[37] Moreover, the editors printed anecdotes about Polish volunteers who revised their negative opinions about the fighting capabilities of their Jewish comrades after having seen them in battle.

It has to be noted that, on the whole, Yiddish as a language did not play a significant role in reports on Jewish volunteers. Indeed, *Naye Prese* seems to have been an example of what Gennady Estraikh has called the "internationalist" view among Soviet-Jewish communists in which Yiddish was first and foremost a vehicle for spreading the communist message.[38] That is not to say that Yiddish, and particularly its status as a language, did not matter at all for the editors of *Naye Prese*. Just as the Botwin Company became the symbol of Jewish military emancipation on the Spanish battlefields, the Yiddish journals that were published in the course of the war became the symbol of Jewish linguistic emancipation. In August 1937 an issue of a journal called *Frayhaytskemfer* appeared and the Botwin Company published its own journal *Botvin*.[39]

Those publications served as a source of pride on the pages of *Naye Prese*; just as Jews as soldiers were emancipated on the Spanish battlefields, so was Yiddish, a point most clearly articulated by the writer Hanan Ayalti (real name Klenbort), who worked as a reporter in Spain during the Spanish Civil War for various Yiddish newspapers. After *Frayhaytskemfer* appeared, Ayalti related enthusiastically that Yiddish had become the ninth language in which the press service of the brigades published and commented, "Can a language receive a more prestigious recognition than by the fact that it expresses the struggle and will, the suffering and joys of a part of the international brigades, that are in the forefront of the struggle for human culture."[40] Ayalti's pride reflected that of a noncommunist, though engaged, Yiddish writer for whom Yiddish had an obvious and personal importance and should not be taken to imply a consistent glorification of Yiddish on the part of the editors of *Naye Prese*. Even if it was the language in which the myth of *pakhdones* was fought, and the struggle of Jewish volunteers propagated, it never appeared as a major concern in its coverage.

Notably, representations of Jewish volunteers as disproving stereotypes of Jewish cowardice in the brigades appeared only in Jewish communist discourse. Reports on Jewish volunteers in *Parizer Haynt* appeared much more sporadically and mainly referred to activists from the Linke Poale Zion or the LICA (Ligue internationale contre l'anti-sémitisme) who had come to join the fight in Spain. As a rule, they never mentioned communist volunteers. Moreover, *Parizer Haynt* writers attached no particular symbolism to their participation, as no link existed for them between the experiences of the Jewish volunteers and a political strategy. In fact, after the formation of the Botwin Company, Jewish volunteers effectively vanished from the pages of *Parizer Haynt* and hardly any references to the company appeared, an absence demonstrating the animosity that existed between the two Yiddish dailies.[41]

As Gutman's letter indicates, for the Jewish communists in Paris the importance of the participation of Jewish volunteers clearly went beyond Spain and Jewish–non-Jewish relations in the brigades. They were also concerned with the problematic aspects of Polish-Jewish relations in France, particularly anti-Semitic sentiments among Polish immigrants and anti-Jewish propaganda in the Polish immigrant press. Running the gamut from Catholic right-wing papers to various communist journals, some Polish periodicals published in France were not devoid of anti-Semitic content.[42] One example was the journal *Młot,* published in Metz, which was dubbed the Polish *Stürmer* by *Naye Prese.*[43] Another was the journal of the (devoutly Catholic) Union des commerçants et artisans polonais en France, which astutely defended the measures being taken in Poland to curtail Jewish commercial activity there.[44] Such publications illustrate how Polish anti-Jewish stereotypes and propaganda were transferred to France. Particularly worrying for Jewish communists, though, was the potential effect of these publications on the relations between Polish and Jewish workers there and, hence, the attention in *Naye Prese* to Polish-Jewish relations in the International Brigades and the effects the participation of Jewish volunteers had on these.

Certain Polish immigrant journals in fact specifically targeted Jewish communists and the presence of Jewish volunteers in the brigades. A small report in *Naye Prese* published in late May 1937 summarized the most recent donations to the exhibition for Jewish volunteers then in the making.[45] The report stated that editor Kenig had donated several items to the exhibition, including a number of "anti-Semitic outcries against Jewish volunteers, published by Polish anti-Semites in France." An article published in July gave more substance to this matter. Under the title "A Polish Anti-Semitic Newspaper Conducts a Smear Campaign against Parisian Jewish Workers," *Naye Prese* described a report that had appeared in the Polish newspaper *Siła* (published by the Société des ouvriers polonais en France) that alleged Jewish communist cowardice in relation to Spain.[46] In its reaction, *Naye Prese* underlined the joint struggle of Poles and Jews in the Dombrowski Battalion and emphasized the positive role that *Dziennik Ludowy,* the newspaper of the Polish section of the PCF, played in improving Polish-Jewish workers relations in France.

But the editors of *Naye Prese* were not just concerned about relations with other immigrant workers; the fight of Jewish volunteers was also linked to the position of Jewish workers in France and their relations with the French Main d'oeuvre. An example can be found in a letter from the Spanish front by a certain "Bernard," leader of the Parisian Jewish painters.[47] Bernard told his colleagues that, in his absence, they should continue his work in the union and reminded them that he was not the first painter to go and fight in Spain, adding that in so doing Jews played their part in the antifascist struggle. Reflecting on his work in the union and the position of Jews in its midst, he explained that all Jewish workers should become unionized to fight for better conditions and to show French workers that their Jewish comrades did not run away from their responsibility in the workers' struggle. Bernard, therefore, called on his colleagues to join the union and urged them to follow the decisions of "our French friends," a message that revealed the tensions between French and Jewish workers in the union. The analogies in his letter were clear: Jews did not shy away from the armed antifascist struggle in Spain, and so, too, they should not run away from actively participating in the unions with their French comrades.

Bernard's remarks reflected a broader concern with the position of Jewish immigrants in France. That concern was also very present in an editorial on the Botwin Company published by *Naye Prese*'s editor in chief Lerman, who similarly placed the participation of Jewish volunteers in the broader context of Jewish–non-Jewish relations in France, including both Poles and the French.[48] In doing so he also outlined a broader vision of how Jews should act in the face of hardship. According to Lerman the solution for Jewish suffering lay not in fleeing but rather in staying and jointly fighting with the masses of the countries where Jews lived. It was the duty of Jewish workers to support the Jewish volunteers who served as an example to inspire Jews to unite in the face of fascism. The final goal, wrote Lerman, was a better future for Jewish immigrants among the French population. Thus, he tied the fight of Jewish volunteers in Spain to the position of Jewish immigrants in France, a message he would repeat even more clearly during the annual outing organized by *Naye Prese* in June 1938 dedicated to the six-month anniversary of the Botwin Company.[49]

That message had acquired a particular urgency in spring 1938, as unrest among Jewish immigrants ran high following the introduction of the decree laws by the new Daladier government in May. Those laws introduced economic restrictions on foreigners on French soil and included prison sentences and expulsion for those without valid identity papers or work permits.[50] They affected immigrants and refugees in general, but for Jewish immigrants problems were compounded by the fact that many of them had been made stateless by their governments.[51] As Jewish immigrant organizations struggled to find an answer, negotiations between the Farband and the Fédération took place as part of renewed attempts to unify the Jewish street. The April 24 meeting was one of the results and illustrates how the fight of Jewish volunteers and the Botwin Company became all the more symbolic and important in the political activities and propaganda efforts of the Jewish communists.

Perhaps the most outspoken example of the multilayered message that was contained in representations of Jewish volunteers in *Naye Prese* came when on September 23, 1938, in the midst of the Munich crisis, *Naye Prese* published

"An Appeal from Jewish Fighters."[52] Addressed to "all Jewish organizations, po-litical movements and all of Jewish society in France," the article called for a unification to heal internal divisions. Pointing to the specific danger that fas-cism posed for Jews and emphasizing that they were part of a long tradition of Jewish struggle, the signatories wrote, "Enough expulsions! Enough inquisi-tions! Enough pogroms! Enough concentration camps!" Simultaneously refer-ring to the Jewish predicament in France, Spain, Poland, and Nazi Germany, they added it was better to be "eternal fighters" than "eternal wanderers." Fi-nally they presented their united struggle in Spain as an example for the Jewish masses in France and rhetorically asked why their readers had not understood the "unity lesson" they provided. Significantly, after nine months of virtually complete silence about the experiences of Jewish volunteers, *Parizer Haynt* also published this appeal.[53] It marked the only time during the existence of the International Brigades that *Parizer Haynt* printed a call so reminiscent of rep-resentations usually to be found only in *Naye Prese* and perhaps formed an indication of how the threat of war looming over Europe affected the mood among Jewish immigrants in France.

Representations of Jewish volunteers in *Naye Prese* and allusions to their hero-ism on the Spanish battlefields thus served different, though intertwined, pur-poses in Jewish communist strategies on the Jewish street. They were, in the first place, key to advancing the Spanish cause among Jewish immigrants; they helped establish the reputation of Jewish volunteers in Paris and by extension that of the Jewish communists, which facilitated the aid campaigns for Spain and for the volunteers of the brigades. Second, these reports also acted as tools to propagate the Popular Front strategy among Jewish immigrants and were part and parcel of Jewish communist campaigns for organizational unity and cooperation among the Jewish immigrant population.

But assertions to the effect that the participation of Jewish volunteers served to counter the myth of *pakhdones* also had a symbolic function that went be-yond propaganda. Jewish communists might have been faithful communists, but Spain also confronted them with the simple reality that the international vanguard of the Popular Front was itself not free from prejudice. The Inter-national Brigades thus became a place for Jewish communists to prove their worth and emancipate themselves. Being confronted with classic accusations of Jewish cowardice, they could not but tackle the problem, and they did so head-on. And within a context of growing Jewish communist concerns with the relations with Polish and French workers and the position of Jewish immi-grants in France, the image of heroic Jewish volunteers, symbolized by the Bot-win Company, also provided an emancipatory example and served as a means of empowering Jewish immigrants in France by instilling Jewish pride in them.

Indeed, this was the central message that was conveyed in *Naye Prese*: if Jew-ish volunteers in Spain could show that activism earned respect and equality,

so too could Jewish immigrants conquer their position in a society where xenophobia and anti-Semitism were on the rise and where Jewish immigrants
faced increasing pressure both politically and economically. Thus, the discursive construction of Jewish volunteers in *Naye Prese* ultimately provided a basis for Jewish communist activity among Jewish immigrants by proposing and
legitimizing a model of action. It is but one example of the complex performative role that was played by the Yiddish press in Jewish life as revealed through
the lens of one particular Yiddish immigrant newspaper in the late 1930s.

Notes

This essay is based on my work "'A Fresh Outburst of the Old Terror?' Jewish-Born Volunteers in the Spanish Civil War" (PhD diss., European University Institute, 2008), which
focuses on the symbolic significance of the participation of volunteers with a Jewish
background in the International Brigades during the Spanish Civil War (1936-1939).

1. "Polit. Komisar Misha Reger shikt a grus fun shpanishn front," *Naye Prese*, April 24,
   1938.
2. "Haynt-di konferents. 60 sosyetes un organisatsyes shikhn zeyere delegatn," *Naye Prese*,
   April 24, 1938.
3. For an elaborate discussion, see especially Dan R. Richardson, *Comintern Army: The International Brigades and the Spanish Civil War* (Lexington: University Press of Kentucky,
   1982).
4. See, for instance, Derek Penslar, "Introduction: The Press and the Jewish Public Sphere,"
   Jewish History 14, no. 1 (2000): 3–8, 4. Most recently, Susanne Marten-Finnis has argued
   that the Jewish press functioned not just to inform the reader but also to act as pedagogue and aimed to be a moral guide. The Jewish press thus not only reflected reality
   but also wanted to "contribute to its constitution and so create new reality." Marten-
   Finnis, "Die jüdische Presse in der osteuropäischen Diaspora: Eine Typologie," in *Die
   jüdische Presse: Forschungsmethoden, Erfahrungen, Ergebnisse*, ed. Susanne Marten-Finnis
   and Markus Bauer (Bremen, Germany: Edition Lumière, 2007), 75–86, 75–76. Marten-
   Finnis also argues for the use of critical discourse analysis in studying the Jewish press
   as it draws attention to how discourse helps to constitute reality: "Discourse is socially
   constitutive as well as socially shaped." Furthermore, in order to understand the relationship between a newspaper and its readership, it is also necessary to consider that
   the latter's "shared knowledge and beliefs" are constituted through discourse. Teun A.
   van Dijk, "Social Cognition and Discourse," in *Handbook of Language and Social Psychology*, ed. Howard Giles and W. P. Robinson (Chichester, UK: Wiley, 1990), 163–83, 165;
   Teun A. van Dijk, "Discourse and Cognition in Society," in *Communication Theory Today*,
   ed. D. Crowley and D. Mitchell (Oxford: Pergamon Press, 1993), 107–26, 110.
5. David H. Weinberg, *A Community on Trial. The Jews of Paris in the 1930s* (Chicago: University of Chicago Press, 1977), 4.
6. Ibid., 14; Paula Hyman, *From Dreyfus to Vichy. The Remaking of French Jewry, 1906-1939*
   (New York: Columbia University Press, 1979), 74–75.
7. See, for instance, Vicki Caron, "Prelude to Vichy: France and the Jewish Refugees in the
   Era of Appeasement," *Journal of Contemporary History* 20, no. 1 (1985): 157–76, 157–58;
   David H. Weinberg, "Heureux comme Dieu en France: Eastern European Jewish Im-
   migrants in France, 1881-1914," in *Studies in Contemporary Jewry*, ed. Jonathan Frankel
   (Bloomington: Indiana University Press, 1984), 1:26–54, 30; David H. Weinberg, "East
   European Jewish Immigrants in the Context of the General Migration of Europeans to

France, 1881–1939," in *Patterns of Migration*, ed. Aubrey Newman and Stephen W. Massil (London: Jewish Historical Society of England, 1996), 99–118, 112.

8. Hyman, *From Dreyfus to Vichy*, 66–67. For the differences between Jewish and non-Jewish Polish immigrants and their different occupational activities, see Janine Ponty, *Polonais méconnus: histoire des travailleurs immigrés en France dans l'entre-deux-guerres* (Paris: Publications de la Sorbonne, 1988); Janine Ponty, "L'Émigration des juifs de Pologne dans l'entre-deux-guerres," *Yod* 23 (1987): 21–40.

9. Vicki Caron, "The Antisemitic Revival in France in the 1930s: The Socioeconomic Dimension Reconsidered," *The Journal of Modern History* 70, no. 1 (1998): 24–73, 54.

10. Weinberg, *Community on Trial*, 130.

11. Indeed, as Paula Hyman has suggested, "It is difficult to measure the social and political impact of antisemitic ideas in periods when political groups proclaiming such ideas do not attain power." Hyman, *The Jews of Modern France* (Berkeley: University of California Press, 1998), 146.

12. See especially the files in the Archive de la préfecture de police de Paris, BA 1815-Antisémitisme, for propaganda. For anti-Semitic violence and Jewish counterreactions, see Michael G. Esch, "Appropriation of Urban Space and 'Integration': Immigrants from Eastern Europe in Paris, 1895–1940," paper presented at European Social Science History Conference (Amsterdam, March 22–25, 2006); Hyman, *From Dreyfus to Vichy*, 201.

13. Zosa Szajkowski, "Dos yidishe gezelshaftlekhe lebn in pariz tsum yor 1939 (loyt di enkete fun yivo)," in *Yidn in Frankraykh. Shtudyes Un Materialn I*, ed. E. Tcherikover (New York: Yidisher Visnshaftlekher Institut, Historishe Sektsye, 1942), 1:207–47, 213.

14. There is some debate about whether the MOI was really dissolved or merely reorganized. Courtois et al. suggest a more or less cosmetic reorganization. Stéphane Courtois et al., *Le'Sang de l'étranger. Les Immigrés de la M.O.I. dans la résistance* (Paris: Fayard, 1989), 46. Weinberg speaks of a dissolution. Weinberg, *A Community on Trial*, 134–36. An analysis of *Naye Prese*, *Parizer Haynt*, and *Undzer Shtime* in spring 1937 makes clear that Jewish communists themselves, and their opponents, spoke of a dissolution of the MOI and its *sous-section juive*, and the effects were more than cosmetic.

15. Szajkowski, "Dos Yidishe Gezelshaftlekhe Lebn," 212.

16. For a general overview, see Audrey Kichelewsky and Aline Benain, "*Parizer Haynt* et *Naïe Presse*, les itinéraires paradoxaux de deux quotidiens parisiens en langue yiddish," *Archives Juives. Revue d'histoire des juifs de France* 36, no. 1 (2003): 52–69. For an interesting inside account of a former editor, see Aaron Alperin, "The Yiddish Press in Paris," in *The Jewish Press That Was. Accounts, Evaluations and Memories of Jewish Papers in Pre-Holocaust Europe*, ed. David Finker (Tel Aviv: World Federation of Jewish Journalists, 1980), 370–77.

17. *Parizer Haynt* in fact provided the most comprehensive information on Linke Poale Zion activities in this period. The Linke Poale Zion published some issues of its journal *Arbeter Vort* in July and August 1936 but nothing afterward. See Zosa Szajkowski, "150 yor yidishe prese in frankraykh—bibliographye fun der yidisher prese in frankraykh un in di kolonyes," in *Yidn in frankraykh. shtudyes un materialn*, ed. A. Tcherikover (New York: Yidisher Visnshaftlekher Institut, 1942), 2:236–308, 250.

18. Weinberg, *A Community on Trial*, 29–30.

19. Ibid., 31–32.

20. The dissolution of the section and the withdrawal led to hefty reactions in both *Undzer Shtime* and *Parizer Haynt* that criticized what was seen as Jewish communist submissiveness in the face of pressures from the PCF. Historian Abraham Menes went so far as to describe it as a return to the era of *shtadlones* (intercession) during a special meeting. See "Farvos Iz Oyfgeleyzt Gevorn Di Idishe Komunistishe Su-Sektsye? Diskusye-Farzamlung Shabes Ovend," *Parizer Haynt*, March 11, 1937.

21. For an elaborate discussion of the dissolution and reactions to it in Jewish immigrant Paris, see Gerben Zaagsma, "The Local and the International—Jewish Communists in

Paris between the Wars," *Jahrbuch des Simon-Dubnow-Instituts/Simon Dubnow Institute Yearbook* 8 (2009): 345-63.

22. In 1928 the Soviet Union embarked on a project of Jewish settlement in the Soviet far east and created a "national territory" for Soviet Jews. From 1934 the region was officially known as the Jewish Autonomous Region or Birobidzhan. It was an important tool in Jewish communist anti-Zionist propaganda.

23. Adam Rayski, "Shpanye," *Naye Prese*, July 22, 1936.

24. Adam Rayski, "Di Natsis Viln an Intervents Kegn Shpanye," *Naye Prese*, July 24, 1936. For the general PCF attitude, see Carlos Serrano, *L'Enjeu espagnol: PCF et guerre d'Espagne* (Paris: Messidor/Editions sociales, 1987), 37-39.

25. G. Kenig, "A vagon mit shpayz farn shpanishn folk," *Naye Prese*, August 3, 1936.

26. Ts. Rubinstein. "In Shtet Fun Shayterhoyfns," *Naye Prese*, August 19, 1936; "In der tsayt ven shpanye hot aroysgetribn ale yidn," *Naye Prese*, August 25, 1936.

27. T. Elski, "Aroystraybn Ale Yidn Fun Shpanye," *Naye Prese*, August 5, 1936.

28. See "Fun Rambam biz Moris Skalka," *Naye Prese*, September 30, 1937.

29. See, for instance, "Sharfer teror kegn yidn in shpanishn maroke unter francos hershaft," *Naye Prese*, October 21, 1936.

30. The political commissariat of the International Brigades stressed that the fight of volunteers should be promoted as follows: "Every people, of every nation, must know who are their best sons, what heroic things they have done, how they fought, how they have died and in what manner they have finally won. All of you must communicate this to your people, from your lips they must know the truth about the fight and the heroism of your comrades." Quoted in Richardson, *Comintern Army*, 156.

31. It summarized a report that had appeared in the Dombrowski Battalion newspaper *Dombrowczak* in which the latter reported on "Francoist anti-Semitic propaganda" within the ranks of the Battalion, suggesting that some Polish volunteers had been susceptible. See "Anti-Semitishe propagande in poylishen komunistishen batalyon in shpanyen," *Parizer Haynt*, August 7, 1937.

32. For a list of its members based on information from Emmanuel Mink (the last commander of the Botwin Company), see Arno Lustiger, *Schalom libertad! Juden im spanischen Bürgerkrieg* (Berlin: Aufbau, 2001), 68-69.

33. Y. Lekhter, "Abrasha, yidisher arbeter fun brisl provyant-shef oyfn hueska-front," *Naye Prese*, October 17, 1936.

34. For a basic overview, see Joshua Rothenberg, "The Jewish Naftali Botwin Company," *Jewish Frontier* 47, no. 4 (1980): 14-19; Gerben Zaagsma, "'Red Devils': The Botwin Company in the Spanish Civil War," *East European Jewish Affairs* 33 (2003): 83-99.

35. Karol Gutman, "Mir veln vert zayn *Botvins* nomen," *Naye Prese*, January 1, 1938. The Endek was the Nationalist right-wing National Democratic Party of Poland; it strongly favored the "polonization" of the new post-WWI Polish state.

36. D. Bogen, "Di plats fun yidn in dem Shpanishn kamf," *Naye Prese*, January 20, 1938.

37. Y. Lekhter, "A bagegenish mit a yidishn militsioner komisar fun koylnvarfer-brigade," *Naye Prese*, November 16, 1936.

38. Gennady Estraikh, "The Yiddish-Language Communist Press," in *Dark Times, Dire Decisions. Jews and Communism*, ed. Jonathan Frankel (Oxford: Oxford University Press, 2004), 62-83, 64. Of course, the editors of *Naye Prese* engaged in discussions on Yiddish spelling, and the newspaper was printed using Soviet-Yiddish orthography. From June 19, 1937 onward, *Naye Prese* ran a series of articles titled "Emes oder emet" (spelled in Soviet-Yiddish and Hebrew orthography) dedicated to spelling issues.

39. Only one issue of *Frayhaytskemfer* seems to have appeared. David Diamant mentions that *Frayhaytskemfer* "a paru en plusieurs dizaines d'exemplaires, polycopié" (was published in several dozen copies, cyclostyled), which suggests several copies of a single issue. See David, *Combattan's juifs dans l'armée républicaine espagnole, 1936-1939* (Paris:

Éditions Renouveau, 1979), 192. Reports of the press service of the International Brigades do not yield more specific clues either. A letter from Luigi Longo to the press service on August 5, 1937 mentions a Yiddish publication. An overview of brigade press publications from November 12 also mentions this, but a similar overview from November 29 does not. See various reports in Comintern Archive, Russian State Archive of Socio-Political History (RGASPI), Fond 545 (International Brigades), opis 2, delo 88. Seven issues of *Botvin* were published, the last three after the formal dissolution of the brigades.

40. A. Yalti, "Di redaktsye in neyn sprakhn (tsum dershaynen fun 'Frayhayts kemfer'-organ fun internatsyonale brigades in yidish," *Naye Prese*, August 18, 1937. The article was published on page 3 but also advertised on the front page.

41. I should mention that in the print run used for this analysis, the issues for December 19, 21, 22, and 26 are missing.

42. For an overview, see Paczkowski, "La Presse des émigrés polonais en France, 1920-1940," *Revue du Nord* 60, no. 236 (1978): 151-63.

43. *Naye Prese*, February 24, 1937. See also Shmuel Bunim, "Les Pogromes de Pologne dans la presse yiddish de Paris de l'entre-deux-guerres," *Revue d'Histoire de la Shoah* 175 (2002): 176-95, 184.

44. The Union was also strongly anticommunist and targeted the Polish immigrant Left in France. See Edmond Gogolewski, "Le Kupiec polski we Francji, organe des commerçants et artisans polonais en France 1934-1969," in *La Presse polonaise en France. Prasa polska we Francij. 1918-1984*, ed. Daniel Beauvois (Villeneuve d'Ascq, France: Université de Lille III, 1988), 115-40, 130-32.

45. "Meldungen—Muzey fun yidishe militsionern i.n. Albert Vayts-Nakhumi," *Naye Prese*, May 29, 1937.

46. "A Poylishe anti-Semitishe tsaytung hetst kegn di Parizer yidishe arbeter," *Naye Prese*, July 23, 1937.

47. Bernard, "Tsu di idishe maler-a briv fun militsioner Bernard," *Naye Prese*, December 28, 1937.

48. Y. Lerman, "A historish gesheenish," *Naye Prese*, January 1, 1938.

49. For the speech he gave that day, see "Entuziastisher miting untern frayen himl far solidaritet mit di kemfer un zeyere familyes," *Naye Prese*, June 13, 1938.

50. Weinberg, *A Community on Trial*, 176; Timothy P. Maga, "Closing the Door: The French Government and Refugee Policy, 1933-1939," *French Historical Studies* 12, no. 3 (1982): 424-42; Vicki Caron, "The Politics of Frustration: French Jewry and the Refugee Crisis in the 1930s," *The Journal of Modern History* 65, no. 2 (1993): 311-56, 329; Rahma Harouni, "Le Debat autour du statut des étrangers dans les années 1930," *Le Mouvement social* 188 (1999): 61-75.

51. "Review of the Year 5699—France," in *American Jewish Year Book 1939-1940*, ed. American Jewish Committee (Philadelphia: Jewish Publication Society, 1940), 41:248-52, 251.

52. "Apel fun yidishe militsyonern," *Naye Prese*, September 23, 1938. The appeal is reproduced in David Diamant, *Yidn in shpanishn krig, 1936-1939* (Warsaw: Idish Bukh, 1967), 535-38 (not reprinted in the French edition that was published in 1979).

53. "A brif fun idishe kemfer in der Shpanisher folks-armey tsum 'Parizer Haynt,'" *Parizer Haynt*, September 21, 1938.

THE OTHER POLONIA

Yiddish Immigrant Writers in Buenos Aires and New York Respond to the New Polish State

REBECCA KOBRIN

"The Jewish emigrant (*oysvanderer*) from Poland who came to Argentina," lamented Avraham Hersch Fridman in Buenos Aires in 1924, is often confused with other Jewish emigrants from the Russian Empire. To be sure some shared an accent, literary inclinations, or food tastes, but Jews from Poland cared only for information about Poland and needed their "own organization (and publications) so that Jews from Poland in Argentina" could stand proud.[1] Emphasizing that Jews from Poland were not "Russians," the common moniker for Jews in early twentieth-century Argentina, but of Polish descent, Fridman explained that his new organization would only collect and distribute money to Jews in Poland or who hailed from that fine country.

Almost a decade later in New York, Benjamin Winter, president of the Federation of Polish Jews in America, similarly commented on the distinct nature and needs of Polish Jews in his celebration of the Federation of Polish Jews' twenty-fifth anniversary. He commented, "The Federation of Polish Jews in America . . . carries in its name the word 'Polish.' It means not only that it is composed of members who either were born or are descendents of Poles born Jewish but it certainly means something more, i.e., it is devoted and must be devoted to the cultivation of relations between the organization and Poland, the country of their birth and origin."[2] Although Fridman and Winter probably never encountered one another—living thousands of miles apart—they shared a desire to organize, inspire, and mobilize Yiddish-speaking Jews born in Poland who found themselves living scattered throughout the Americas by the interwar period. As Fridman emphasized, only through the "founding of this organization" can Polish Jews in Buenos Aires "erect a separation between those Jews of Polish-Jewish extraction and those Jews to which Jews from Poland feel no connection [*sheykhes*]."[3]

The Polish-Jewish émigré "reaction to the reappearance" of Poland in the international political realm, as Mieczysław Biskupski correctly points out, "is a topic without an historian."[4] With the founding of the Second Polish Republic in 1919, Jews in Poland were no longer subjects of an empire; they became citizens of the new democratic republic. Jewish immigrants in North and South America born in the lands of Congress Poland held dear their former hometowns but despised the czarist empire. They were thus forced to rethink their commitments, obligations, and activities from outside the renewed nation-state. Initially, like their coreligionists in Poland, Polish-Jewish immigrants expressed great enthusiasm over the establishment of the Second Polish Republic, particularly after Poland signed the minority rights treaty promising Jews in Poland the right to establish, manage, and control their own charitable, religious, and social institutions; schools; and other educational establishments.[5] This new entity transformed how Polish Jews living in the United States and Argentina conceptualized what it meant to be a Polish Jew living overseas.

Polish-Jewish immigrants articulated these new conceptualizations primarily within Yiddish journals in the genre of *landsmanshaft* writing. Thus the following cross-cultural comparative analysis of Yiddish journals has two main goals: first, to emphasize the importance of comparative analysis for Yiddish studies, a rare though vital methodological approach deployed in Jewish studies. Second, I hope to rescue from obscurity this genre of Yiddish literary creation. For much of the twentieth century, Yiddish intellectuals often disparaged immigrant *landsmanshaft* (hometown associational) journals despite their popularity within the larger Yiddish reading public. Originally formed as mutual aid societies, east European Jews' hometown associations, commonly known by their Yiddish name, *landsmanshaftn* (*landsmanshaft*, singular), had close to half a million members in New York in the interwar period and enjoyed similar popularity in Buenos Aires.[6] Their members contributed not only money to these organizations but also hundreds of pieces of poetry and prose published in organizational newsletters, magazines, and souvenir journals and read by thousands in the Yiddish immigrant community.[7] Scholars have often ignored the vast corpus of *landsmanshaft*-published materials, seeing these publications as possessing only limited aesthetic value. But as I have argued elsewhere, these naïve writers composed short stories, poems, and articles that vividly encapsulated the voice of the common people (*amkho*).[8] As a result, these journals specifically provide a lens through which to glimpse the inner thoughts of the Yiddish-speaking Polish immigrant community.

These journals conveyed a new type of Polish patriotism that sought to redefine what it meant to be a Pole and a Jew in the interwar world. How should Jews express their devotion to Poland, particularly as exiles? Should they merely associate with other Polish-Jewish immigrants (and their organizations)? Or should they engage with the new Polish state as well? Their ingenue immigrant contributors, by choosing Yiddish, the lingua franca of Polish Jewry, demonstrated that central to being a Polish Jew was the Yiddish language. Believing that the minority rights treaty signed by leaders of the Second Polish Republic in 1919 would establish Yiddish as a recognized official language of this new country, these immigrants implicitly engaged this new state and its policies through their use of Yiddish.[9] Whereas Polish Jews in Argentina steadfastly adhered to using only Yiddish in their publications (perhaps because they never felt as comfortable in Spanish), the Federation of Polish Jews incorporated English sections into its publications by the 1930s. When examined together, these journals bring into sharp focus the grappling of their immigrant contributors about whether they constituted a part of what had become known as Polonia. To be sure, Polonia, despite its Latin root that refers to anyone living dispersed from Poland, is deployed by historians to refer almost exclusively to the millions of Catholics who left Poland and founded organizations such as the Polish National Alliance in 1880 in Philadelphia and Chicago.[10] Jews from Poland may have not enlisted in the Polish Nationalist army, but as these two journals illustrate, these immigrant Jews saw themselves as central to Poland's reconstruction, even from abroad.

Comparative Analysis, Yiddish and the Study of Jewish Life

Scholars have much to gain by comparing the writings of Yiddish-speaking Jews across time and space, as this study aims to show by comparing Yiddish publications produced in New York and Buenos Aires. How would the dominant narrative of Yiddish studies or, even more broadly, modern Jewish history be revised when conceptualized and narrated within a comparative framework? Since 1963, when sociologist Martin Lipset wrote an eloquent plea for comparative research, scholars have lamented the absence of comparison in the field of Jewish studies.[11] Even three decades later in 1997, Todd Endelman commented that no full-scale monograph in Jewish studies has yet to deploy comparative analysis.[12] Although some historians have heard Endelman's clarion call for comparative work, in Yiddish studies, few systematically consider questions of comparative analysis even though the mass dispersal of Yiddish-speaking Jews in the late nineteenth and early twentieth centuries offers many productive arenas for such analysis.

Comparative scholarship of Jewish life undermines, as Sarah Stein argues, the notion that "the texture of Jewish life depended upon local laws, conditions, and economics, upon relationships between Jews and the state and between Jews and the minority and majority cultures they lived alongside."[13] Accordingly, we would expect Polish Jews in New York and Buenos Aires to have existed in discrete worlds, as the field has presumed this. In the absence of comparative scholarship, these suppositions have remained theoretical.[14] However, by exploring the linguistic forces that delineated immigrant Jewries from one another, Yiddish literary materials offer a rich venue for comparative study.

To assess the current state and future directions of comparative Yiddish and Jewish studies, one must start by considering the presuppositions inherent in making comparisons. Scholars of Jewish history have long employed comparative models in their studies to highlight that which is universal and that which is specific in the Jewish experience.[15] In the study of Jewish migration, Nancy Green has identified three types of comparative models—linear, convergent, and divergent—that have shaped the way scholars understand the impact of these mass population shifts in the modern Jewish experience. The linear comparative model, she notes, is the most commonly used and assesses the transformation of immigrants' identities and lifestyles during their transition from the Old World to life in the New World.[16] By examining the experiences of immigrants as they move from one point to another, this model compares the experiences of immigrants in different places—their country of departure and their country of arrival—and focuses on change over time.[17] Another popular mode of comparative analysis among those who study east European Jews in the United States assesses the experiences of Jews and different ethnic immigrant groups who settled in the same city in the early twentieth century.[18] With its focus on destination country, the convergent model highlights the centrality of *place* (or, more generally, *space*) to understanding the immigrant experience.[19] Whereas scholars using a convergent model see cultural origins as crucial in explaining immigrant adaptation, social scientists employing a divergent model "locate the explanation of difference at the point of arrival, not at the point of departure."[20] The divergent model, which compares the experiences of immigrants in many points of settlement, is rarely used but allows researchers to follow a specific group across time and space and evaluate how cultural origin, timing of migration, and socioeconomic factors intersected to shape the process of immigrant adaptation.[21]

Despite Yiddish-speaking Jews' dispersion throughout the world, few scholars have yet to evaluate their literary expressions through a divergent model.[22] The divergent model would push scholars to ponder why Jews in Mexico City succeeded in maintaining a Yiddish culture for several generations, whereas their compatriots in New York failed.[23] How did divergent social, political, and cultural trends in each country influence Yiddish cultural production? I employ such a divergent comparative model to examine the literary expressions of Polish Jews in the United States and Argentina because I believe it best illuminates how both structural constraints and individual choices shaped the lives of Polish Jews throughout the world during the interwar period.[24]

The two journals selected below shed light on larger questions shaping the study of Jewish migration: how did the adaptation of Jews from Poland in Argentina differ from that of their compatriots in the United States? What form did Polish-Jewish identity assume on foreign soils? The scholarly conflation of the religious and regional dimensions of east European Jewish immigrant identity has failed to analyze how regional and religious affiliations each acted in distinct, but not identical, ways to shape the adaptation of Jewish immigrants to life in their new homes.[25] By comparing how people from the same region of origin recast their identities in fundamentally different ways in their new homes, this study highlights the many variables that informed the multifaceted process of Jewish migration and adaptation in the late nineteenth and early twentieth centuries.[26]

Almanakh far Poylishe Yidn: Internal Jewish Communal Politics, Polish Pride, and Interwar Buenos Aires

The bulk of the Jewish community in Buenos Aires originates in the great wave of east European Jewish emigration to this region during the late nineteenth and early twentieth centuries. To be sure, Jews from locales as diverse as the Ottoman Empire and the Middle East had lived in this city since the mid-nineteenth century, but their numbers always hovered around several hundred; they maintained only small numbers of synagogues, charities, and organizations, which were nearly all quickly overwhelmed by the tens of thousands of east European Jews who arrived between 1892 and 1939.[27] The Jewish Colonization Association (JCA), founded in 1891 by Baron Maurice de Hirsch, initially fueled the attraction of most of these immigrant Jews to Argentina.[28] Hirsch believed that Jewish migration to Argentina would relieve population pressure and destitution in the Pale of Settlement and other neighboring regions. By settling east European Jews on farms in Argentina and training them to become farmers, Hirsch believed that the JCA could counter anti-Semitic claims that Jews were unproductive members of society.[29] Between 1891 and 1896, Hirsch contributed $10 million to purchase land in Argentina, pay for the transportation of east European Jews to Argentina, and facilitate their resettlement on collective farms.[30] In the history of modern Jewish migration, the JCA proved exceptional: in contrast to other Jewish organizations that provided aid to Jewish immigrants only after they arrived in their country of choice, the JCA actually recruited tens of thousands of east European Jews to settle in rural Argentina.[31]

Even with the JCA's instrumental aid, most immigrant Jews found it difficult to succeed on these collective farms or integrate into Argentina's distinct cultural and political environment. Argentina, one of the largest colonies of the Spanish empire, began its fight for independence in May 1810. Despite revolutionaries' efforts to overthrow the existing colonial power, they remained devoutly loyal to the Church. The new Argentine government's first manifesto pledged to make every effort "to preserve our [new nation's] holy faith," namely Catholicism.[32] Although the Argentine Constituent Assembly agreed unanimously in 1853 to encourage immigration, consensus vanished

once the question of the status of non-Catholic immigrants was raised. This
antagonism to non-Catholics grew over the next two decades, as evidenced by
the contentious debate that erupted after President Nicolás Avellaneda passed
the Immigration and Colonization Law in 1876. Whereas the president and his
advisors supported the law's establishment of new branches of government to
attract European immigrants to Argentina to bolster the country's developing
economy, others, such as members of the Constituent Assembly, championed
an explicit Catholic national code that would prohibit governmental support
of non-Catholic immigrants.[33]

In the end, however, Argentina's economic concerns outweighed its religious convictions. Beginning in 1876, the Argentine government began actively courting non-Catholic immigrants. The Argentine government even
sent dozens of consuls to eastern Europe to attract Jewish immigrants after the
1881 pogroms in Russia.[34] As these dynamic consuls traveled throughout eastern Europe, rumors began to spread about the endless economic opportunities
Argentina offered those who ventured to its hinterlands: in 1889 the Hebrew
newspaper *Hamelitz* reported the "Argentina fever" sweeping throughout the
Pale that pushed hundreds to flock to the JCA to inquire about immigrating to
Argentina.[35]

From the outset, despite the generous funding of Baron de Hirsch, most east
European Jewish settlers found their adjustment to agricultural life extremely
difficult. First and foremost, many were urban laborers who did not possess
many basic skills necessary for survival in a rural area.[36] Moreover, the JCA
failed to provide any classes on farming techniques before migration.[37] Floods,
locust plagues, and disagreements with the JCA over debt repayment exac-
erbated immigrant Jews' financial situation. Discouraged and disillusioned,
many decided to abandon the colonies.[38] As a 1907 JCA report described, approximately one out of every five east European Jewish settlers left their colonies and relocated to either Buenos Aires or new homes abroad.[39] By 1914, the
Jewish community of Buenos Aires grew into a vibrant immigrant community
of whom two thirds were foreign born.[40]

Although it is unclear in precisely which year Polish Jews decided to form
their own organization, by 1924, when Agudas-Akhim, the organization of Polish Jews in Buenos Aires, decided to publish its first magazine, approximately
100,000 Jews lived in Buenos Aires.[41] Despite "its *manias de superioridad*, it superior European airs," writes scholar Edna Aizenberg, the city of Buenos Aires
was painfully "Latin American, struggling with human rights, diversity and
equality for people of varying religious and ethnic backgrounds."[42] The majority Argentine Catholic population constantly reminded Jews in Buenos Aires
of their outsider status, with many political leaders often questioning whether
Jews could ever be incorporated into the nation.[43] To be sure, members of Argentina's government stressed in their rhetoric the centrality of immigration
and religious toleration to building up the new nation. But in fact, as Juan Bau-

tista Alberdi, the drafter of the 1853 Argentine constitution, argued, religious tolerance related only to Christian observance.[44] Indeed, the accepted maxim at the turn of the twentieth century was that "Argentina was a Catholic nation by virtue of its history, national identity and population."[45]

Such a rejection of the values of cultural and ethnic pluralism created a social milieu that demanded religious, political, and cultural conformity. Thus, Jews found themselves outsiders by faith even though they desperately tried to integrate themselves into their surroundings.[46] As Judith Elkin notes,

> One is struck over and over again by the reluctance of Latin Americans to make the changes necessary to integrate immigrants into their national societies. Despite demands that immigrants assimilate, the latter's efforts to integrate themselves met with suspicion, if not outright rejection ... [because the countries] of Latin America still were grounded in the pre-Enlightenment past ... [causing] the Jews of the Latin American republics [to still be associated with] the hateful religious and political stigmata [of the Old World].[47]

As seen through Yiddish publications such as *Almanakh far poylishe yidn*, Jewish immigrants from Poland originally sought to distinguish themselves from other east European Jews as part of a debate within the internal Jewish community to outline their place within Argentina. Non-Jews referred to most Jews from eastern Europe as *Rusos* (Russians), whether they were born in Romania, Russia, or Poland.[48] Governmental officials and immigrants hailing from countries such as Italy and Spain openly derided the despised *Rusos* for their political beliefs. Often depicted as revolutionaries, *Rusos* frequently found themselves targeted in political debates. During *la semana trágica* in 1919, when labor unrest led to violent attacks on Jewish workers and their families, Jews residing in Buenos Aires feared for their lives. After mobs ran the streets, shouting "death to the *Rusos*," ransacking the immigrant Jewish quarter, and dragging terrified Jews from their homes, many Jews in Argentina began to realize how fears of Russian radicalism had pushed Jews to the periphery of Argentine society.[49] By the end of *la semana trágica* not only had seventy-two people been killed, eighty gravely wounded, and more than eight hundred injured, but the entire Jewish community was also forced to realize that Argentina would never fully embrace the immigrant Jews who had settled there.[50]

This event triggered Polish Jews in Buenos Aires to create their own magazine with the goal of providing a forum for Polish Jews to demonstrate their differences. These differences surfaced vividly in the journal's rich depictions of Poland's divergent Jewish educational system, discussion of the distinct challenges facing Jews in interwar Poland, and poetry that nostalgically conjured up the landscapes of Warsaw.[51] They wrote that they needed to "voice" their concerns about the conditions in the newly independent Poland, their former home. Unlike Soviet Russia, the Second Polish Republic was a multieth-

nic democracy, embodying the ways in which they were not *Rusos* but a different entity all together.

From its inception *Almanakh far poylishe yidn* nurtured a reading public
that sought to navigate a new relationship to Poland and to other Polish Jews
scattered throughout the world. It is impossible to know precisely how many
people read this magazine that spanned more than 100 pages, but limited circulation numbers should not overshadow its influence. As Matthew Frye Jacobson emphasizes in his study of the immigrant vernacular press in the United
States, "Circulation figures for immigrant journals are notoriously unreliable"
because a single copy of an immigrant newspaper often reached "three, five or
ten readers ... [and] available figures understate the extent of a given journal's
reach."[52] This was equally true in Buenos Aires.

The world conveyed in the pages of the *Almanakh* had contours defined by
headlines such as "The Jews in Galicia: A Statistical Picture" and "Loan Kassas
in Poland" and feature stories discussing the new Polish constitution. Alongside these internationally focused pieces were articles describing very local
news such as "Activities of Our Dramatic Circle" and reports on "Activities of
Polish Jews in Buenos Aires during the Last Year."[53] In its front-page devotion to
Jews currently living in the historic lands of the Polish-Lithuanian commonwealth, the focus was on Poland, though the journal also included news on the
Polish-Jewish émigré enclave in Buenos Aires.

In these ways the *Almanakh* located its readers from the outset in an ideological universe with Greater Poland and its diaspora at its very center. Indeed, its
inclusion of regions such as Galicia, a region that was not fully included in the
borders of the Second Polish Republic, demonstrates how this publication was
distinct from, for example, Catholic immigrants' discussions of the new Poland
in its devotion to Greater Poland, which its authors continued to define according to eighteenth-century borders (in which Galicia, a region of dense Jewish
settlement, was considered part of the Polish-Lithuanian commonwealth) and
not the twentieth-century realities.

The *Almanakh* also contained amateur poetry that further sought to cultivate
the idea of cities in Poland as nurturing spaces for Jewish cultural output. Do
not all Jews long "to walk upon Warsaw's soil?" queried M. D. Giser in his ode to
his former home.[54] This was a common motif in many *landsmanshaft* publications throughout the world,[55] but one must bear in mind how such depictions
openly contradicted other portraits from the mainstream Yiddish immigrant
press in Buenos Aires, such as the socialist *Der avangard*.[56] *Der avangard* did not
pander to one local regional group, as the *Almanakh* did as it sought to mobilize
its readers for its socialist agenda. In its celebration of Poland and its rebirth,
the *Almanakh* created an almost false sense of historical continuity between its
readers and Poland, thus creating a fundamentally different portrait of Poland
from that of *Der avangard*. This striking difference served as a means to stress

that despite their origin in the Russian Empire, they were not *Rusos* but Poles, or *galitsianers*, of Jewish descent, even if they only claimed this title in exile.[57]

By identifying strongly with the newly established Polish state, the *Almanakh* used their depiction of Poland as a means to police the boundaries of group identity within the east European Jewish immigrant community of Buenos Aires. Rarely attempting to help Polish Jews in Buenos Aires politically engage the new entity that had been created in Europe, the *Almanakh* turned to discussing their distinct "Polish" identities as a means to carve out a new niche for themselves in Argentina: they were not *Rusos* but Poles who had been shaped by a distinct Polish-Jewish culture. Although writing in a Yiddish journal allowed their argument to be heard only in the east European Jewish immigrant community, despite its limited impact, the effort is still noteworthy. Seizing on the idea that Poland was a unique nation, separate from Russia, these exiled Jews who had left the lands of Congress Poland in the early twentieth century used their publications as a means to reflect on the ways in which they identified not with the despised *Rusos* and their supposed revolutionary inclinations but with a group who could easily integrate into the Argentine nation, like Italians and Spaniards, who also published their own newspapers but were quickly becoming the backbone of Argentine society.[58]

Poylishe yidn and the Politics of Polish Jewry in America, 1921–1939

> There are a million Polish Jews in the United States and they cherish a warm love for their old mother land. The evidence of it is to be found in the fact that wherever they have gone they have sought to retain at least a semblance of their old environment by organizing themselves into *landsmanshaftn* named after their old hometowns. There are an estimated eight thousand Polish *landmanshaftn* in the United States. . . . I go further and say, that I do not believe that any group of settlers in the United States, [such as] the German, French, or what not, can count so many societies retaining these old home ties. . . . [These] sympathetic bonds between Poland and Polish Jews who have settled here . . . constitutes a reservoir of potential force [for the Polish nation].[59]

When the Federation of Polish Jews was founded in 1908 by Henry Moskowitz in New York City, few would have imagined their organization would envision itself as a forceful reservoir for Poland when this statement appeared in 1933. Indeed, the idea of Polish independence remained a distant dream, and Jews who emigrated from Russian Poland had not united for political reasons but "to provide for the sick a hospital in case they cannot afford their treatment," which they achieved with the erection of the Beth David Hospital in New York City in 1912.[60] But not only did the end of the First World War see radical transformations take place in Europe with the formation of the Second

Polish Republic, it also witnessed the reorganization of the Federation of Polish Jews by Benjamin Winter, a New York real estate developer, and Zelig Tygel, a journalist who had worked at several Yiddish newspapers in Warsaw and immigrated to the United States in 1922. These two men expanded the organization's membership by inviting more than 100 *landsmanshaft* groups to join their ranks. More importantly, they also redirected this organization's activism away from the realm of social welfare, namely raising funds for hospitals, to political activism, focusing their energies on confronting the leaders of the Second Polish Republic and other Poles in America to address the concerns of Polish Jews.[61]

Although the Federation from the outset was supportive in theory of the new Second Polish Republic, it also, as historian Andrzej Kapiszewski notes, criticized "Polish attitudes towards Jews" and Polish officials, who they considered agents of the Polish state bent on "ruin[ing] and if possible, annihilat[ing] the Jews who live in Poland."[62] From the outset, its main publication, *Poylishe yidn*, devoted much space to chronicling the Federation's political entanglements. This publication came out annually, ran more than seventy pages, and included poetry and artwork from renowned artists such as Arthur Szyk, the Polish-born American famous for his political illustrations, caricatures, and cartoons during World War II.[63] As one can see from the cover shown below of *Poylishe yidn*, which sought to portray stereotypical *shtetl* Jews, Szyk's distinctive illustrations took the form of medieval miniaturists and illuminated manuscripts, serving as an illustrated counterpoint to the images presented by photographers, such as Roman Vishniac.

The journal's political activities took on many forms. In 1926, they reported when Jan Ciechanowski, Poland's envoy to the United States, spoke in honor of the Federation's twentieth anniversary, and in 1929, when Mieczysław Marchlewski, the Polish consul in New York, approached the American Federation of Polish Jews as part of his effort to expand Jewish relief efforts to increase commerce between the United States and Poland. The publication also reported when the Federation formed, together with other major Polish organizations in the United States, a goodwill committee in 1930 to address the political dilemmas of Poland and its Jews. Reports from Polish Jews from South America, Canada, and Germany appeared interspersed with these chronicles of the Federation's political endeavors, implicitly conveying how the United States functioned as the central arm of the Jewish "Polonia."[64]

President Woodrow Wilson may have failed to convince the American government to involve themselves diplomatically in the League of Nations and the politics of rebuilding in the region of eastern Europe, yet, as *Poylishe yidn* eloquently captured, individual nongovernmental organizations in America, such as the Polish Federation of Jews, saw themselves as assuming the mantle of Wilsonian idealism as they distributed money and intervened with Polish political figures in their own efforts to rebuild eastern Europe.

Cover of *Poylishe yidn*, 1935. Personal collection of the author.

Drawing on currents in American political culture, this publication argued in its reports for a new vision of Polish-Jewish identity that transcended traditional nation-state boundaries. Indeed, in contrast to those writing in Argentina, who merely used Poland and Polishness as a means to differentiate themselves within their small social world, the contributors to *Poylishe yidn* sought to build bridges, not only to other Poles in America but also to all those men and women still living in Poland. "American Jews of Polish stock," as they called themselves, saw themselves as integral to the rebuilding of Poland, and *Poylishe yidn* became the voice of this political mission.[65]

Economic power represented a central component to their understanding of this political mission. The Federation not only called for "strengthening of our relief activities for Polish Jewry" but also more importantly said, "American Jews of Polish stock . . . [must] endeavor to promote trade between the Republic of the United States and the Republic of Poland. If we could succeed in doing this, we could not only promote the mutual interests of the United States and Poland, but by benefitting Poland as whole, [we will help] Polish Jewry."[66] And what was the potential force that they hoped to deploy? As the pages of *Poylishe yidn* demonstrate, Tygel saw American Jews as the economic arm of the Greater Polonia. Whereas Catholic Poles may have returned to Poland following the fall of the czarist empire, Jews' patriotism, and power, lay in their ability to raise enormous sums. As Tygel opined in *Poylishe yidn,* "I want to submit for your consideration the thought whether this federation [of Polish Jews] cannot do something to strengthen the cords that tie our old homeland, Poland, with the land of our adoption, the United States. [We must do] something that will not only strengthen these bonds, but will [result] in mutual economic benefits."[67]

As the Polish government failed to protect Jews from the hostility and economic boycotts, the pages of *Poylishe yidn* diverged from its counterpart in Argentina. Unlike the *Almanakh*'s depiction of Poland as a nurturing motherland, *Poylishe yidn* focused on the country's attacks on Polish officials. As the attacks became more vitriolic, the portrait of Poland soured. "Deluged with letters requesting American Jews come to the aid of thousands of Jews in Poland," noted Tygel, he could no longer stand by as Marchlewski presented a "picture of Polish Jewry that is not entirely accurate."[68] The leaders of the Federation scheduled a meeting with Jerzy Potocki, the new Polish ambassador to the United States, to voice their concerns over the growing antagonism of the government to Jews' place in the Polish economy. As Tygel argued,

> The Jewish businessman and workingman is being displaced by monopolies of the government. . . . He is being refused employment in public works and in the civil service. The extent of the poverty is shown by the fact that on Pesach, 150,000 Jews were compelled to ask for charity at the Jewish Community Council. The number of suicides among Polish Jews was the largest at that time [in 1932] of any single group in the world.[69]

The distribution of money in interwar Poland, as the pages of this publication acknowledged, was an acutely political act through which American Jews exercised power.[70] Particularly in Poland, where poverty was rampant and the American dollar was, in 1921, worth more than 4,550 Polish marks—and would climb to be worth more than 23,000 Polish marks by 1923—American Jews and their dollars represented a formidable force.[71] If this "potential force" failed to convince Polish officials to make Jewish rights their top priority, it would be harnessed for another Jewish political goal: the erection of a new state for Jews.

Indeed, by the late 1930s, realizing the limited impact of their activism in changing the Polish government's treatment of Polish Jewry and the growing anti-Semitism in Poland among the general population, Benjamin Winter, president of the Federation of Polish Jews, decided to pursue a new agenda: financing Polish-Jewish migration to Palestine. Since it was already estimated that 2,000 Jews every month made the difficult decision to leave Poland, Winter "call[ed] upon the 1,000,000 Jews of Polish extraction in this country to assist and contribute to the fund being raised for the purpose" of facilitating migration to Palestine and, further, averred, "I would like to see the American Federation of Polish Jews sponsor a colony for Polish Jews in Palestine."[72]

This support for Polish-Jewish resettlement in Poland marks the dramatic turn of this organization away from identifying with Poland proper to viewing itself as a Jewish aid organization focused on the specific plight of Jews in Poland. Shifting from advocating the development of the Polish state to advancing a vision of Palestine as the panacea for Jews' problems in Poland, the pages of *Poylishe yidn* conveyed the complex matrix of motivations and beliefs that shaped interwar Jews' vision of themselves as Poles, Jews, and Americans. Even as the goal of this aid shifted to Palestine, it remained a project for Polish Jews that was financed and carried out with the direct help of Polish-Jewish émigrés, a testament to the continued strength of the Polish-Jewish diaspora and its identification through Greater Polonia.

Conclusion

The First World War not only fundamentally altered the map of eastern Europe but also formatively transformed how both Jews still living in this region and those who had immigrated abroad viewed and spoke about their identities as Jews from Poland. Polish-Jewish émigrés in Argentina and the United States saw the establishment of the Second Polish Republic as a critical juncture to redefine their conception of national identity and refine their relationship to Poland from the vantage point of their new homes in Buenos Aires or New York City. These discussions took place in large part within the pages of their *landsmanshaft* publications, internal venues for them to also comment on Jewish power at home and in Poland proper.

Jewish immigrants in New York, more than their compatriots and coreligionists in Buenos Aires, also used their publications to effect quantifiable change. Although others have noted the ways in which American Jewish immigrants used the formidable strength of their dollars to introduce revolutionary changes into Polish society, few have yet to discuss how these publications and organizations saw themselves as playing a direct role in overseas aid and action.

Further analysis of the Yiddish literary creations of interwar Polish-Jewish immigrants in Argentina and the United States would further demonstrate how fruitful a transnational turn may be for the field of Yiddish studies. Why, for example, were Polish Jews in Buenos Aires less interested in engaging the politics of the Polish state than their compatriots who immigrated in the same period to New York?[73] Although this short comparison of two journals only highlights some of the insights to be gained, it is clear that a comparative and transnational mode of analysis will bring to the fore subjects, questions, and types of sources previously ignored or marginalized in academic inquiry, such as the literary value of *landsmanshaft* publications for Yiddish studies, as well as the divergent experience of Yiddish-speaking Jews in South America. Can a scholar of Yiddish fully appreciate the impact migration had on the development of this language and its culture when she or he examines only the American component of their migration? I hope this essay at least suggests how different the field of Yiddish studies would look if a transnational approach stood at its center.

Notes

I would like to thank Columbia's Institute for Latin American Studies for providing a grant that made possible my trip to Buenos Aires and to the Idisher Visnshaftlejer Institut archives there. I would like to thank Silvia Hansman for all her help at the archives. All translations are mine unless otherwise noted.

1. Avraham Hersch Fridman, "Dr grindung fun Agudas-Akhim un veytere prespektivn," *Almanakh fun polisher yidn in boynes ayres 1929* (Funacion Idisher Visnshaftlejer Institut, Landmanshaft Collection, folder 22). This unpaginated journal can be found in the rich collections of YIVO in Buenos Aires.
2. Binyomin Vinter, *Poylishe yidn* 8 (July 1933): 3.
3. Fridman, "Dr grindung fun Agudas-Akhim un veytere prespektivn."
4. Mieczysław B. Biskupski, "Poles and Jews in America and the Polish Question, 1914–1918," in *Polish-Jewish Relations in North America*, vol. 19 of *Polin: Studies in Polish Jewry*, ed. Mieczysław B. Biskupski, Antony Polonsky, Littman Library of Jewish Civilization et al. (Oxford: Oxford University Press, 2007), 87–96.
5. For more on Jews and their understanding of minority rights in Europe, see Oscar I. Janowsky, *The Jews and Minority Rights, 1898-1919* (New York: Columbia University Press, 1933); Sholmo Netzer, *Ma'avak yehudei Polin al zekhuyoteihem ha'ezraḥiyot vehaleumiyot, 1918-1922* (Tel Aviv: Universitat Tel-Aviv, 1980); Mark Levene, *War, Jews and the New Europe: The Diplomacy of Lucien Wolf* (Oxford: Oxford University Press, 1992). The impetus to write the Minorities Rights Treaty grew out of the League of Nations' concern after the pogroms of 1918 and 1919 that minority rights would not be respected in the new states of eastern Europe. Poles, however, saw this treaty as evidence of Jews' power on the world stage. See David Engel, "Perceptions of Power—Poland and World Jewry," *Jahrbuch des Simon-Dubnow-Instituts/Simon Dubnow Institute Yearbook* 1 (2002): 17-28. The League of Nations required Poland to set up separate governing bodies and schools for

non-Polish nationals in order to maintain their independence. I. Lewin, *A History of Polish Jewry during the Revival of Poland, 1918-1919* (New York: Shengold, 1990), 167-205, 207-11. A copy of the treaty in its entirety can be found at *Australian Treaty Series*, accessed June 22, 2012, http://www.austlii.edu.au/au/other/dfat/treaties/1920/12.html.

6. Daniel Soyer, *Jewish Immigrant Associations and American Identity in New York, 1880-1939* (Cambridge: Harvard University Press, 1997), 1; Nathan Kaganoff, "The Jewish Landsmanshaftn in New York City before World War I," *American Jewish History* 76, no. 1 (1986): 56-60.

7. For additional information on *landsmanshaft* associations, see I. Rontoch, ed., *Di yidishe landsmanshaftn fun nyu york* (New York: WPA Yiddish Writers Group, 1938); Soyer, *Jewish Immigrant Associations*; Michael Weisser, *Brotherhood of Memory: Jewish Landsmanshaftn in the New World* (New York: Basic Books, 1985); Susan Milamed, "Proskurover landsmanshaftn: A Case Study in Jewish Communal Development," *American Jewish History* 76, no. 1 (1986): 40-55; Hannah Kliger, "Traditions of Grass-Roots Organization and Leadership: The Continuity of Landsmanshaftn in New York," *American Jewish History* 76, no. 1 (1986): 25-39.

8. Rebecca Kobrin, "The Shtetl by the Highway: The Literary Image of the East European City in New York's Yiddish Landsmanshaft Press, 1921-1939," *Prooftexts: A Journal of Jewish Literary History* 9, no. 4 (2006): 107-37.

9. The Minorities Rights Treaty required Poland to set up institutions to protect the rights of all minority groups living within its borders and allow these groups to use their native languages for official governmental purposes. The League of Nations was charged with overseeing Poland set up separate governing bodies and schools for non-Polish nationals in order to maintain their independence. Jews interpreted this treaty as supporting their use of Yiddish in the public sphere. For more on the Minorities Rights Treaty (including a translation of the treaty itself), see Lewin, *History of Polish Jewry*, 167-205, 207-11. For more general information on this treaty and its impact on Jews, see Carole Fink, *Defending the Rights of Others: The Great Powers, the Jews, and International Minority Protection, 1878-1939* (Cambridge: Cambridge University Press, 2004).

10. This organization ultimately sponsored the first Polish National Congress in Washington, D.C., to support the cause of Poland's independence. By 1924 the Polish National Alliance membership topped 200,000.

11. Seymour Martin Lipset, "The Study of Jewish Communities in a Comparative Context," *Jewish Journal of Sociology* 5, no. 2 (1963): 157-66.

12. Todd Endelman, "Introduction: Comparing Jewish Societies," in *Comparing Jewish Societies*, ed. T. Endelman (Ann Arbor: University of Michigan Press, 1997), 1-2.

13. Sarah Stein, *Making Jews Modern: The Yiddish and Ladino Press in the Russian and Ottoman Empires* (Bloomington: Indiana University Press, 2004), 212.

14. There is virtually no comparative work on Yiddish culture in the United States and Argentina. I have tried to address this lacuna in my examination of the *landsmanshaft* world. See Rebecca Kobrin, "'When a Jew Was a *Landsman*': Rethinking Jewish Regional Identity in the Age of Mass Migration," *Journal of Modern Jewish Studies* 7, no. 3 (2008): 357-76. But although there are dozens of articles and monographs that analyze, theorize about, and address Yiddish literary creativity in North America, few have paid close attention to similar trends in Argentina. With the exception of Ilán Stavans's thoughtful introduction to Alan Astro's *Yiddish South of the Border: An Anthology of Latin American Yiddish Writing* (Albuquerque: University of New Mexico Press, 2003), xii-xv, there are few recent studies of Yiddish literature created in Argentina. This is quite striking, since in the 1940s, Argentina emerged as a center for Yiddish publishing. Volumes such as Pinye Katz's *Antologye fun der yidisher literatur in Argentine* (Buenos Aires: Dovid Lerman, 1944) and Yankev Botoshanski's *Mame yidish: eseyen un lektsyes* (Buenos Aires: Dovid Lerman, 1949) suggest the rich insights these literary creations offered those

who devoted time to studying them. Two exciting models for future research can be found in Ilán Stavans, "Mexico: The Rise and Fall of Yiddish," in *The Jewish Diaspora in Latin America and the Caribbean: Fragments of Memory*, ed. Kristin Ruggiero (Portland, OR: Sussex Academic Press, 2005), 163-88 and Efraim Zadoff, "The Status of Yiddish in Jewish Educational Systems in Argentina and Mexico," in *Yiddish and the Left*, ed. Gennady Estraikh and Mikhail Krutikov (Oxford: Oxford University Press, 2001), 280-98.

15. Nancy L. Green, "The Comparative Method and Poststructural Structuralism—New Perspectives for Migration Studies," *Journal of American Ethnic History* 13, no. 4 (1994): 3-22, 4.

16. Ibid., 13-16. Also see Nancy Green, "L'Histoire comparative et le champ des etudes migratoires," *Annales: ESC* 45, no. 6 (1990): 1335-50.

17. General classical studies of Jewish immigrants in America, such as Moses Rischin's pioneering work *The Promised City: New York Jews, 1870-1914* (Cambridge: Harvard University Press, 1962) and Irving Howe's *World of Our Fathers* (New York: Harcourt Brace Jovanovich, 1976), have utilized a linear model of analysis. In addition, due to the influence of these works, studies of Jewish immigrant radicals and women—such as Gerald Sorin, *The Prophetic Minority: American Jewish Immigrant Radicals, 1880-1920* (Bloomington: Indiana University Press, 1985); Sydney Weinberg, *World of Our Mothers: The Lives of Jewish Immigrant Women* (Chapel Hill: University of North Carolina Press, 1988); and Susan Glenn, *Daughters of the Shtetl: Life and Labor in the Immigrant Generation* (Ithaca: Cornell University Press, 1990)—also employ a linear model for their analysis.

18. One of the seminal works in Jewish immigrant history to use the converging migration method is Thomas Kessner's *The Golden Door: Italian and Jewish Immigrant Mobility in New York City, 1880-1915* (New York: Oxford University Press, 1977). Another work that uses the converging migration model to structure its analysis is Judith Smith's *Family Connections: A History of Italian and Jewish Immigrant Lives in Providence, Rhode Island, 1900-1940* (Albany: State University of New York Press, 1985). In addition, see Thomas Kessner and Betty Caroli's "New Immigrant Women at Work: Italians and Jews in New York City, 1880-1915," *Journal of Ethnic Studies* 4 (winter 1978): 19-31 as well as Corianne Krause's "Urbanization without Breakdown: Italian, Jewish and Slavic Immigrant Women in Pittsburgh, 1900-1945," *Journal of Urban History* 4, no. 3 (1978): 291-306.

19. Green, "Comparative Method," 13-23.

20. Ibid., 15.

21. Preliminary work using the divergent comparative model concerning Italian and Irish immigration has demonstrated that region of origin also played a fundamental role in shaping divergent immigrant experiences and influenced even the choice of destination country. See Samuel Baily, *Italians in Lands of Promise: Italian Immigrants in Buenos Aires and New York, 1870-1914* (Ithaca: Cornell University Press, 1999); Malcolm Campbell, "The Other Immigrants: Comparing the Irish in Australia and the United States," *Journal of American Ethnic History* 14, no. 3 (1995): 3-22; Sandhya Shukla, *India Abroad: Diasporic Cultures of Postwar America and England* (Princeton: Princeton University Press, 2003); Margaret Byron and Stéphanie Condon, *Migration in Comparative Perspective: Caribbean Communities in Britain and France* (New York: Routledge, 2008); Rebecca Kobrin, *Jewish Bialystok and Its Diaspora* (Bloomington: Indiana University Press, 2010).

22. Dominique Schnapper, "Jewish Minorities and the State in the United States, France and Argentina," in *Center: Ideas and Institutions*, ed. Liah Greenfeld and Michel Martin (Chicago: University of Chicago Press, 1988), 186-209.

23. For how useful such a comparative type of examination can be, see a study on another ethnic group in Nancy Foner's "West Indians in New York City and London: A Comparative Analysis," *International Migration Review* 13 (summer 1979): 284-97.

24. Green, "Comparative Method," 3; Nancy Green, "The Modern Jewish Diaspora: Eastern European Jews in New York, London and Paris," in *European Migrants. Global and Local Perspectives*, ed. Dirk Hoerder and Leslie Page Moch (Boston: Northeastern University Press, 1996), 263–81. For a discussion of the theoretical implications of such a methodology, see Green, "Comparative Method," 16–18.

25. Religion has always been an important distinguishing characteristic in American history, particularly in studies of American immigration. Since Will Herberg's classic *Protestant, Catholic, Jew: An Essay in American Religious Sociology* (Garden City, NY: Doubleday, 1955), few have examined in detail the interrelationship between religious identifications and ethnic identifications. The recent literature has begun to reevaluate the political and social role that religion played in immigrant life but more in reference to issues of race than to issues of ethnicity. These new studies highlight how racial conflict often played itself out in religious arenas, but they deal primarily with the Christian context, and none has yet to fully explore how Jewish ethnic identity transformed and shaped Jewish religious identity. See John McGreevy, *Parish Boundaries: The Catholic Encounter with Race in Twentieth-Century America* (Chicago: University of Chicago Press, 1996); Brian Hayashi, *For the Sake of Our Japanese Brethren: Assimilation, Nationalism and Protestantism among the Japanese of Los Angeles* (Palo Alto: Stanford University Press, 1995); George Sanchez, *Becoming Mexican American: Ethnicity, Culture and Identity in Chicano Los Angeles, 1900–1945* (New York: Oxford University Press, 1993), 151–71; Robert Orsi, *The Madonna of 115th Street: Faith and Community in Italian Harlem, 1880–1950* (New Haven: Yale University Press, 1985).

26. Preliminary work using the divergent comparative model concerning Italian and Irish immigration has demonstrated how the different regional origins of immigrants in each of these countries also played a fundamental role in shaping divergent immigrant experiences and even choice of destination country in various countries throughout the world. See S. Baily, "The Adjustment of Italian Immigrants in Buenos Aires and New York, 1870–1914," *American Historical Review* 88, no. 2 (1983): 281–305; Malcolm Campbell, "The Other Immigrants: Comparing the Irish in Australia and the United States," *Journal of American Ethnic History* 14, no. 3 (1995): 3–22.

27. Victor Mirelman, *Jewish Buenos Aires, 1890–1930: In Search of an Identity* (Detroit: Wayne State University Press, 1990), 187.

28. Kurt Grumwald, *Turkenhirsch: A Study of Baron Maurice de Hirsch, Entrepreneur and Philanthropist* (Jerusalem: Israel Program for Scientific Translations, 1966); Theodore Norman, *An Outstretched Arm: A History of the Jewish Colonization Association* (London: Routledge and K. Paul, 1985).

29. Delagacion de Asociaciones Israelitas Argentinas, *50 años de colonizacion judia en la Argentina* (unpublished pamphlet, Buenos Aires, 1939).

30. Osias Shijman, *Colonizacion judia en la Argentina* (Buenos Aires: Germano Artes Gráficas, 1980); Haim Avni, *Argentina and the Jews: A History of Jewish Immigration* (Tuscaloosa: University of Alabama Press, 1991), 36.

31. For more on the JCA and the critical role it played in shaping the Jewish immigrant experience in Argentina, see Avni, *Argentina and the Jews*, 32–92.

32. Declaration of May 26, 1810 quoted in Avni, *Argentina and the Jews*, 2.

33. Ibid., 20.

34. Ibid., 22–23.

35. *Hamelitz* 275 (December 15, 1889): 3.

36. Moses Reisman noted that he felt totally unmoored by the rhythm of agricultural life. See Reisman, "Af di vegen fun 30 yor bialistoker mishpocha in Argentina," *Bialystoker Vegn* 5–6 (September 1950): 6.

37. Not only did the settlers arrive in Argentina before the JCA had purchased sufficient lands, but the JCA also had unrealistic expectations. For example, the JCA wanted the

colonists to produce for the world market some items that were impossible to grow in Argentina's climate. Avni, *Argentina and the Jews*, 34-38.

38. A similar phenomenon occurred in the JCA colonies in Canada. See, for example, Theodore H. Friedgut, "Jewish Pioneers on Canada's Prairies: The Lipton Jewish Agricultural Colony," *Jewish History* 21, no. 3-4 (2007): 385-411.

39. Avni, *Argentina and the Jews*, 54-62, 81.

40. Ira Rosenwaike, "The Jewish Population of Argentina: Census and Estimate, 1887-1947," *Jewish Social Studies* 22, no. 4 (1960): 193-221; Mirelman, *Jewish Buenos Aires*, 187.

41. Rosenwaike, "Jewish Population," 201; Mirelman, *Jewish Buenos Aires*, 26.

42. Edna Aizenberg, *Books and Bombs in Buenos Aires: Borges, Geruchoff and Argentine-Jewish Writing* (Waltham, MA: Brandeis University Press, 2002), 7.

43. Judith Elkin, *The Jews of Latin America* (New York: Holmes and Meier, 1998), 215.

44. Ibid., 16.

45. Ibid., 201.

46. Ibid., 215.

47. Ibid.

48. Ibid., 98-99.

49. Victor A. Mirelman, "The Semana Trágica of 1919 and the Jews in Argentina," *Jewish Social Studies* 37, no. 1 (1975): 61-73.

50. For more on this week of anti-Semitic violence and the poor response of the state, see Mirelman, "The Semana Trágica"; Edgardo Bilsky, *La semana trágica* (Buenos Aires: Centro Editor de América Latina, 1984); Federico Rivanera Carlés, *El judaísmo y la semana trágica: la verdadera historia de los sucesos de enero de 1919* (Buenos Aires: Instituto de Investigaciones sobre la Cuestión Judía, 1986); Daniel Lvovich, *Nacionalsimo y antisemitismo en la Argentina* (Buenos Aires: Javier Vergara, Grupo Zeta, 2003).

51. H. D. Nomberg, "In a poylishe yeshiva"; M. D. Giser, "Varshe"; Leybush Veisblat, "'Numerus cloysus' in Poylen"; S. K., "Di nes fun di yidishe shuln in poylen"; Leybush Veisblat, "Di konstitutsia fun di poylishe republic" all in Fridman, *Almanakh fun polisher yidn in boynes ayres 1929*.

52. Matthew Frye Jacobson, *Special Sorrows: The Diasporic Imagination of Irish, Polish and Jewish Immigrants in the United States* (Berkeley: University of California Press, 2002), 57.

53. Leybush Veisblat, "Di konstitutsia fun di poylishe republic," "Di yidn in galitze (a bisl statitik)," "Di tetinkayt fun farband in di letste yor," and "Di tetinkayt fun unzer dramatishn kreyz" all in Fridman, *Almanakh fun polisher yidn in boynes ayres 1929*.

54. Giser, "Varshe."

55. Rebecca Kobrin, "The Shtetl by the Highway: The Literary Image of the East European City in New York's Yiddish Landsmanshaft Press, 1921-1939."

56. *Der Avangard* was similar to mainstream Yiddish newspapers in the United States. See Ewa Morawska, "Changing Images of the Old Country in the Development of Ethnic Identity among East European Immigrants, 1880s-1930s: A Comparison of Jewish and Slavic Representations," *YIVO Annual* 21 (1993): 284-86. Popular immigrant literature in English by east European Jewish immigrants, such as Abraham Cahan's novel *The Rise of David Levinsky*, buttressed this idea that the United States was fundamentally different from eastern Europe. See Steven Zipperstein, *Imagining Russian Jewry: Memory, History, Identity* (Seattle: University of Washington Press, 1999), 21-23.

57. Morawska, "Changing Images of the Old Country," 284-86.

58. Jose Moya, *Cousins and Strangers: Spanish Immigrants in Buenos Aires, 1850-1930* (Berkeley: University of California Press, 1998), 277-332.

59. *Poylishe yidn* 8 (June 1933): 2.

60. *American Jewish Year Book 1922-1923*, ed. American Jewish Committee (Philadelphia: Jewish Publication Society, 1923), 24:227.

61. For a full discussion of this organization's activities, see Andrzej Kapiszewski, "Polish Jews in Polish-Jewish Relations, 1924-1939," *Polish-Jewish Relations in North America*, 97-116. See Kapiszewski's longer discussion in his *Conflicts across the Atlantic: Essays on Polish-Jewish Relations in the US during the First World War and the Inter-War Years* (Cracow: Ksieg Akademicka, 2004).

62. Kapiszewski, "American Federation of Polish Jews," 99, quoting from the Federation's newsletter, *Der Verband* 1-2 (October 1924): 1.

63. For more on Arthur Szyk, see Joseph P. Ansell, *Arthur Szyk: Artist, Jew, Pole* (Oxford: Littman Library of Jewish Civilization, 2004) as well as Ansell's article, "Arthur Szyk's Depiction of the 'New Jew': Art as a Weapon in the Campaign for an American Response to the Holocaust," *American Jewish History* 89, no. 1 (2001): 123-34. For images of his creations, see Katja Widmann and Johannes Zechner's exhibition catalog, *Arthur Szyk: Bilder gegen Nationalsozialismus und Terror/Drawing against National Socialism and Terror* (Berlin: Deutsche Historische Museum, 2008).

64. See *Poylishe yidn* 1 (June 1926); *Poylishe yidn* 4 (June 1929); *Poylishe yidn* 8 (June 1933).

65. *Poylishe yidn* 4 (1929): 3

66. *Poylishe yidn* 5 (1930): 3.

67. Ibid.

68. *Poylishe yidn* 7 (1932): 9.

69. Ibid.

70. Steven Zipperstein, "The Politics of Relief: The Transformation of Russian Jewish Communal Life during the First World War," in *Studies in Contemporary Jewry: The Jews and the European Crisis*, ed. Jonathan Frankel, Peter Y. Medding, and Ezra Mendelsohn (Oxford: Oxford University Press, 1988), 4:22-40; Ezra Mendelsohn, *Zionism in Poland: The Formative Years, 1915-1926* (New Haven: Yale University Press, 1981), 46-49.

71. Antony Polonsky, *Politics in Independent Poland* (Oxford: Clarendon Press, 1972), 108-9.

72. *Poylishe yidn* 8 (June 1933): 1-2.

73. For the ways a comparative type of examination may be useful, see a study on another ethnic group in Nancy Foner, "West Indians in New York City and London: A Comparative Analysis," *International Migration Review* 13, no. 2 (1979): 284-97.

CHOOSING YIDDISH IN THE CLASSROOM

Montreal's National Secular Schools, 1910–1950

REBECCA MARGOLIS

In an article about the Montreal *shuln*[1] authored in 1955, journalist Ben-Zion Goldberg (Waife) remarked in New York City's *Tog-morgn zhurnal*, "If there has ever been the possibility of Jewish/Yiddish autonomy (*yidishe oytonomye*) in English North America, it was in Montreal."[2] Goldberg was just one of many Jewish cultural activists with an eye on Montreal in the post-Holocaust period. When Yiddish culture was reeling from strong blows—acculturation, ideological shifts, and the losses of the Holocaust—Montreal represented a haven for Yiddish culture. The city boasted a community of Yiddish writers, a daily Yiddish newspaper, a public library with an extensive Yiddish collection as well as programming, and a strong Labor-Zionist movement that continued to promote Yiddish in its system of *shuln*. Because of its particular history, Montreal fostered a Jewish cultural autonomy that had formed part of the local fabric since the outset of Yiddish immigration at the turn of the twentieth century. This autonomy, which expressed itself most strongly in the development of the city's *shuln*, had acted as an anchor for Yiddish within a dominant tide away from the language across the Jewish world.

Under the aegis of the Labor-Zionist movement, the first *shuln* in North America were established in Montreal and Winnipeg in the 1910s.[3] In Montreal, these institutions—first in the form of supplementary schools and subsequently as full-day parochial schools—have continuously included Yiddish in their curricula and ensured exposure to the language and culture for successive generations. This longevity has not been a given: within a generation of their founding, the *shuln* found themselves fighting against the wider grain of linguistic acculturation away from Yiddish as a communicative language, and against wider ideological shifts away from the left-wing ideologies that spawned them.

Thus, Montreal's Morris Winchevsky Schools, a series of *shuln* that existed for a generation under the aegis of the communist movement, closed their doors in the 1950s due to state persecution of the far left wing. In addition, since the establishment of the State of Israel, modern Hebrew gradually supplanted Yiddish in the curricula of most Jewish day schools in Canada and throughout the diaspora. During the period between the world wars, the *shuln* in Montreal, as in other cities across Canada and internationally, actively perpetuated Yiddish as a living culture and carrier of Jewish identity among their students. However, most, including Winnipeg's, eventually amalgamated with other Jewish schools not offering Yiddish or closed their doors. Moreover, the neighboring United States, including its Yiddish immigrant center of New York City, never developed a day school model at all.

Today, Montreal stands out as home to one of the very few secular Jewish day school systems in the world that continues to teach Yiddish, with both the elementary and high school levels of the city's Jewish People's and Peretz School (JPPS) including Yiddish in their curricula. This study traces the roots of Montreal's *shuln* during their formative years, 1910 through 1950. It focuses on the ideological impetus behind their creation and the particular Montreal context, the challenges their founders and promoters faced, and the innovative mechanisms generated to counter them. It posits that virtually from the outset, these Montreal *shuln* brought together a group of dedicated ideologues, supporters, parents, and students who deliberately chose Yiddish—and that choice became more and more marginal on the world scene, in particular after the founding of the State of Israel. Montreal's *shuln* bucked dominant trends to produce a vibrant day school system, school clubs and publications, and a second generation of Yiddish writers. Although by the 1920s Yiddish was rapidly losing its status as the vernacular of Montreal's acculturating Jewish immigrant community, successive generations of Canadian-raised children received secular Jewish educations with a strong Yiddish component.

Among the factors that underlie Montreal's experience of Yiddish education is the particular history of Jews within a city historically sharply divided along religious and linguistic lines. In the province of Quebec during the period following Canadian confederation in 1867, each of the nation's two founding groups—French Catholic and Anglo-Celtic Protestant—maintained separate infrastructures dating to colonial roots, with an overriding Christian identity. With no separation of church and state, the governance and coordination of areas such as education and social services were left to religious communities. Before the late nineteenth century, the tiny Jewish population, which formed the province's first non-Christian group, integrated into the economically dominant English milieu while maintaining a collective Jewish identity. The mass immigration of eastern European Jews, most of which stemmed from the

Russian Empire, spoke Yiddish and were conspicuous in both their traditional religious observance and radical leftist and Nationalist inclinations, forming a "third solitude" sandwiched between the province's two charter groups.[4]

By 1931 the Jewish population of Montreal, which was Canada's primary immigrant destination, reached approximately 57,000 people—6 percent of the city's population—out of a total of some 155,000 Canadian Jews.[5] In an era before Canada's now deeply entrenched policies of multiculturalism, this mass immigration formed an "other" largely excluded from the dominant French and English mainstreams. The rapidly expanding Jewish immigrant community created a network of social, political, religious, and educational organizations in which Yiddish served as a Jewish lingua franca and the language of the community's institutions. Canada's first lasting Yiddish newspaper, Montreal's *Keneder adler* (*Canadian Jewish Eagle*), founded in 1907, broadcast daily on behalf of all segments of the Yiddish community, from anarchist to Orthodox. The city's Yidishe folksbiblyotek (Jewish Public Library), established in 1914 as a nonpartisan lending library, offered access to a variety of reading material as well as cultural and educational programming. The arrival of a sizable population of Yiddish-speaking Holocaust survivors in the late 1940s and 1950s bolstered this Yiddish framework. Although the Ashkenazi immigrant community eventually became English speaking, Yiddish maintained its hold on the community as an expression of Jewish identity in a province where language and ethnonational identity were inextricably linked, even though it largely ceased to be a communicative language.

Indeed, ideology represents another important factor behind Yiddish maintenance in Montreal. The city was home to a strong core of Labor-Zionist activists, with members of the local Poale Zion movement central to founding many of the city's lasting Yiddish institutions, notably its libraries and schools. For these Poale Zion activists, language—both Yiddish and Hebrew—was vital to Jewish national revitalization. For a local group of "lay revolutionaries," Yiddish assumed a primary role in what David Roskies has termed a forward-looking "utopian venture"[6] on Canadian soil whose implementation has outlasted the role of the language as a shared vernacular in the mainstream Jewish community.

This emphasis on language dovetailed broader trends. In the 1960s and 1970s, after Quebec's transformation into a secular state in what has become known as the "Quiet Revolution," language took the place of religion as the key marker of national identity in the province. Heightened concerns for the survival of French Canadian language and culture within the dominant English-language society translated into Nationalist and Separatist movements and, ultimately, into state legislation to promote French language use in the province of Quebec. In this new context, Yiddish education has benefited from state subsidies for parochial education as well as the province's wider preoccupation with issues of ethnolinguistic survival. The Jews' relative isolation in Montreal combined with the heightened role of language and culture within Quebecois consciousness encouraged a general awareness among the province's various ethnic groups that bolstered Yiddish in the long term.[7]

The *shul* system founded in Montreal before the First World War—the Natsyonale Radikale Shul/Peretz Shul (National Radical School/Peretz School) and the Yidishe Folksshul (Jewish People's School)—counted among the first institutions established by Canada's mass eastern European Jewish immigrant generation and filled practical needs for Jewish education in Montreal. The province of Quebec organized schooling along confessional lines, with two school boards divided according to the Christian affiliation of Canada's two charter groups: the Catholic School Commission used French language, and the Protestant School Commission, English language. Taxes paid by its religious adherents funded each commission, and like all non-Catholics, Jews were barred from the Catholic schools and funneled into the Protestant schools, with their taxes designated for the Protestant School Commission.

Until the turn of the twentieth century, Montreal's several hundred Jews were well integrated into the Anglo-Jewish milieu, supplementing their children's education in the Protestant schools with private Jewish education. On the eve of mass Jewish immigration, the Education Act of 1903 legally recognized Jews as Protestants for the purposes of formal education, although, as non-Protestants, it denied them equal representation.[8] However, the influx of Jewish immigrants after 1905 made the arrangement between the Protestant School Commission and the Jewish community increasingly problematic, with the existing system, which functioned to transmit Christian and British values and culture, suddenly accommodating a flood of Yiddish-speaking Jewish students, particularly in the immigrant core of the city. In 1903, Jews made up 23 percent of students in the Protestant schools, and the number reached 40 percent by 1919; however, the taxes contributed by the largely impoverished immigrant masses did not cover education costs for the Jewish students.[9]

The status of the Jews within the Protestant schools remained a matter of ongoing contention, coming to a head in the 1920s, when numerous efforts to secure Jewish representation in the Protestant School Commission culminated in an unsuccessful venture to establish a separate Jewish school board in Montreal at the end of the decade.[10] For their founders, the impetus behind the creation of Jewish schools—such as the *shuln* system—included combating their exclusion within the Quebec educational system as well as ideological motivations from within to promote a specific vision of Jewish identity. The infusion of political and religious movements that accompanied the Yiddish immigration translated into new options for Jewish schooling. By the First World War, the options available to parents included the *kheyder*, with its traditional focus on literacy in prayer and the Bible; the Talmud Torah, which provided a more modern religious education; and the *shuln*. In the absence of a non-Christian system of public schools, Jews devised their own educational institutions that eventually came to include full-day schooling.

For the reasons detailed above, Montreal's *shuln* stood at the forefront of a transnational movement to promote modern Yiddish culture in conjunction with leftist and Nationalist ideologies, where "the classroom became the venue par excellence for enacting a modernist transformation of traditional Ashkenazi culture."[11] In Europe, state suppression delayed the development of a comprehensive system of secular Yiddish education until the interwar period,[12] when a network of secular Yiddish and Hebrew schools flourished in the 1920s, only to decline in the precarious political and economic climate of the 1930s. In the United States, immigrant Jews encountered a national ethos that encouraged Americanization—and a public school system to enforce it. Moreover, the cosmopolitan ideology of the post-1880 mass immigration initially produced English-language socialist education for the Yiddish masses,[13] and although the American *shuln* movement expanded rapidly during the interwar years, the secular Yiddish schools in the United States remained a supplementary system to complement the public schools.[14] In this regard, Canadian Jews shared far more in common with other immigrant communities such as those in Argentina and Mexico, which also established long-term Yiddish educational institutions as part of a comprehensive communal infrastructure.[15]

Montreal's *shuln* were rooted in a strong Nationalist orientation that promoted Yiddish as a viable expression of Jewish national identity.[16] The catalyst for the new *shul* movement was the 1910 international Poale Zion convention held in Montreal. At that meeting, ideologue Chaim Zhitlowsky passed a resolution calling for a system of Yiddish-language Natsyonale Radikale Shuln (National Radical Schools) to transmit the movement's core Zionist and socialist values, defeating Nakhman Syrkin's rival resolution for schools based on Hebrew. The curricula of the Poale Zion *shuln* came to embody two streams of ideological Yiddishism: Chaim Zhitlowsky's creation of a Jewish nation through the production of a modern cultural life in Yiddish, and Y. L. Peretz's revitalization of Jewish culture that rendered the Jewish textual treasures into the language of the Jewish masses, Yiddish.[17] After repeated attempts beginning in 1911, a group of activists and parents established a supplementary school in the Jewish immigrant neighborhood of Mile End. Despite inadequate quarters, financial difficulties, and opposition from the more traditional sector of the Jewish community, the school expanded to more than 200 students by 1914. Renamed the Peretz Shul after the death of writer Y. L. Peretz in 1916, it purchased its first building in 1918, added a kindergarten in 1941, and added a full-day parochial school in 1942. With the motto *Di yidishe yugnt farn yidishn folk* (The Jewish youth for the Jewish people), Yiddish formed the core of the curriculum, which centered on the study of Jewish language, literature, and history.

This new *shuln* movement embodied the ongoing "language war" between Yiddish and Hebrew that pervaded the Jewish world in eastern Europe and its immigrant offshoots. Soon after the founding of Montreal's National Radical Schools, a group of activists broke away to found the Yidishe Folksshul (Jewish People's School), distinguished by its increased emphasis on Hebrew in the curriculum. Under the leadership of Zionist activist Yehuda Kaufman (later renowned lexicographer Even Shmuel Kaufman), the Folksshul was established in the summer of 1914. In contrast to the Natsyonale Radikale Shuln program, which did not introduce the study of Hebrew until the third grade, the Folksshul placed equal emphasis on Hebrew and Yiddish, with Hebrew conveyed as a modern, living language and taught in the *ivrit be'ivrit* (Hebrew in Hebrew) method. With steady expansion, the Folksshul purchased its first building in 1920, by which time the school had more than 200 students in thirteen classes. A high school was added in 1922 and full-day parochial education in 1927.[18] Despite efforts to unite beginning in the 1920s, ideological differences prevented the Peretz Shuln and Folksshuln from merging until 1971.[19]

The role of Yiddish in the Peretz Shuln and Folksshuln shifted with time. Many of the founders and early promoters of the schools were active in the local chapter of the Poale Zion and viewed the schools as carriers of the national spirit of the Jewish people. Initially, the school body was composed of children of Yiddish-speaking, working-class Jewish immigrants who lived in proximity to the schools. During the early years before the creation of day schools, these students frequented the English-language Protestant public schools during the day and attended the Peretz Shul or Folksshul in the afternoons, in the evenings, or on Sundays to receive a secular Jewish education of Labor-Zionist orientation. Although their parents had varying degrees of commitment to the ideology espoused by the *shuln*—oftentimes they sent their children to a given school because it was near their homes—they shared a common linguistic and cultural background as eastern European Jewish immigrants.

In the early years, virtually all of the students—like the schools' founders, teachers, and supporters—were native Yiddish speakers. However, by the 1920s, the makeup of the student body was changing, and the *shuln* with it. The expansion of the schools in the interwar period coincided with the two opposing global trends: the rapid expansion of modern Yiddish culture, and the onset of the attrition of Yiddish as the vernacular of the Jewish masses. Despite an explosion of ventures in Yiddish publishing, literature, theater, and education, upwardly mobile Jews worldwide began opting for languages other than Yiddish, whether in major centers in Poland, Russia, and the United States or minor centers such as Canada.[20] Moreover, with the country's increasing governmental limitations placed on Jewish immigration after the 1920s curtailing the replenishment of the community's Yiddish speakers, Canada's Jewish communities became increasingly English speaking. However, Yiddish was not jettisoned in favor of English as the language of instruction, and Yiddish instruction remained a core part of the curriculum in the Montreal *shuln*. In a cultural milieu with a close link between religious and ethnic identity and language, Yiddish shifted from an immigrant to an ethnic language even as its communicative functions declined. In this new model, Yiddish instruction increasingly came to function as a safeguard against wider cultural and linguistic assimilation.

For *shul* activists during the interwar period, Yiddish functioned as a means of fostering and perpetuating a particular vision of Jewish revitalization in the modern world, with Yiddish as a living language at the core of the schools' curricula—an approach common to secular Yiddish schools as a whole in the 1920s and 1930s. For example, Montreal's Peretz Shul offered Yiddish language and literature, instruction in Jewish and general history, composition, folklore, and singing, all in Yiddish. It stressed Yiddish over Hebrew and Jewish culture over religion, although eventually the schools introduced both Hebrew and the study of Jewish tradition. Similarly, the Folksshul educated students about the Jewish past and present, the former through Bible and history study, and the latter through modern Yiddish and Hebrew cultures. The teachers placed emphasis on speaking, reading, and writing in both languages, and students studied the works of Hebrew and Yiddish writers into advanced levels.[21] With the exception of Hebrew language, literature, and Bible classes, Yiddish served as the primary language in both the Peretz Shuln and the Folksshuln during the interwar period, including the language spoken between teacher and student and discussions of current events.

Folkshul principal Shloime Wiseman articulated the role of Yiddish and Yiddish literature in the *shuln* in 1934, twenty years after their founding:

> One of the first issues that confronted the schools over the years was the question of Yiddish. . . . The *shuln* have always regarded Yiddish as one of the most effective components in the national Jewish education of the Jewish child, and the study of Yiddish literature as the most reliable means of acquainting our children with Jewish folkways and with the social aspirations of our generation. As a result, Yiddish occupies a primary position in the program of our schools.[22]

Similarly, longtime Peretz Shul principal Yaacov Zipper expressed the early approach of the school: "The language of the masses, Yiddish, was the language of the new school and Yiddish literature was one of its primary tools."[23] In the Montreal *shuln*, teachers presented a variety of literary works as central texts in the development of Jewish national consciousness: Yiddish renditions of traditional Jewish literature from the Hebrew-Aramaic, in particular biblical passages and Jewish legends; Yiddish translations of world literature; and poetry, prose, and drama by classic Yiddish writers as well as contemporary Yiddish poets and authors. Teachers encouraged students to engage with Yiddish literary texts in classroom discussions, in recitations at public events, and through personal contact with local and international Yiddish writers. The curricula promoted Yiddish composition and actively encouraged students to develop their own skills as writers.

Along with the Yiddish press, the *shuln* promoted Yiddish literature horizontally among the Jewish masses as well as transmitting it vertically among the generations. Many writers became teachers in the *shuln* and maintained close associations with the teachers and students. In Montreal, these included M. M. Shaffir, Mordecai Hosid, and J. I. Segal. Both the Peretz Shul and the Folksshul came under the long-term leadership of writers committed to Jewish cultural continuity through Yiddish education: Shloime Wiseman as principal together with Shimshen Dunsky as vice-principal at the Folksshul, and Yaacov Zipper as principal at the Peretz Shul.

These teacher-writers instilled in their students a special appreciation for Yiddish language and literature. They also produced educational materials for use in the schools locally as well as abroad. For example, Wiseman's three-volume anthology titled *Dos vort* (*The Word*) featured poetry and prose by modern Yiddish writers as well as modern translations of Hebrew texts.[24] Moreover, the *shuln* deliberately fostered connections between their students and the wider Yiddish literary world, creating opportunities for the students to interact with Yiddish writers in a meaningful way. They invited Yiddish literary figures visiting Montreal into the classrooms and organized celebrations of milestones in the cultural world. Guests of the Peretz Shul during the 1920s and 1930s included poet Aaron Glants-Leyeles, novelist Sholem Asch, playwrights Peretz Hirschbein and David Pinski, literary critic Shmuel Niger, and Chaim Zhitlowsky.[25]

Writing in 1929 in the face of opposition to the secular schools by the city's more observant Jews, J. I. Segal characterized the *shul* movement as "one camp: poets, artists, writers, teachers, journalists, cultural activists and cultural builders (*klal-tuer*). I see us all as one edifice, one venture."[26] Given the relative isolation of the Montreal Jewish immigrant population and the exclusionary nature of its public school system, the *shuln* served as a magnet for the local Yiddish community of leftist, Zionist, and secular orientations. Members of Montreal's Jewish community attended public events such as plays, concerts, and graduation ceremonies presented by the schools. These programs, which featured poetry recitations by students or student productions of excerpts from Yiddish plays, routinely took place at the Monument National, the local home of the Yiddish theater.[27] Support organizations composed of members of the wider community devoted to the ideals of the schools helped to ensure their ongoing survival and success. For example, the Folksshul cultivated support within the community at large via its board of directors and a parents' association (*elter fareyn*) that managed and raised funds and popularized the ideals of the schools among the local Jewish population.[28]

The Folksshul established working relationships with mainstream Jewish organizations in the Montreal community, notably the Canadian Jewish

Congress (founded 1919) and the Vaad Ha-Ir (Montreal Jewish Community
Council, established 1922).[29] Moreover, in a city where Yiddish cultural activists occupied important community leadership positions, H. M. Caiserman,
the general secretary of the Canadian Jewish Congress and a local Yiddish literary critic, was very active in promoting the *shuln* as well as other ventures
such as amateur Yiddish theater. Looking back on the first twenty-five years of
the *shuln*, Folkshul principal Wiseman expressed the motivation behind these
wide-ranging efforts:

> We realize that the *shul* is only one of several agencies engaged in the educa-
> tion of the child. . . . We were also anxious to make the community realize that
> education is a community-wide duty and responsibility. . . . We take advantage
> of every occasion to bring together parents, children, teachers, and school work-
> ers for communal educational experiences. We have succeeded in educating
> and training a large group of Jewish men and women who are sensitive to the
> demands of our educational milieu. They are now fully qualified to carry the
> burden of modern Jewish education and are participating in social, cultural,
> and civic areas of activity.[30]

Montreal's solid school infrastructure and strong community-wide support
helped to alleviate the organizational crisis that struck the *shuln* in so many
American centers during the years of the Great Depression.[31]

Even so, in the 1920s, the *shuln* faced a growing problem head-on: the attrition of spoken Yiddish among the student body. With the decline of Yiddish as
the Canadian Jewish vernacular, promoting it as a living language and culture
became increasingly problematic. Although, in 1931, 99 percent of Quebec Jews
declared Yiddish as their mother tongue on the Canada census, only 3 percent
declared themselves unable to speak English. Between 1931 and 1951, the number of Jews declaring English as their mother tongue increased from 2 percent
to 51 percent.[32] Despite their ideological commitments to Yiddish as a language
of national and cultural revitalization, school pedagogues faced increasing
hurdles in creating a Yiddish-centered environment for an English-speaking
population. As Wiseman recalls in his memoirs, during the 1920s Folksshul
teachers struggled to teach Yiddish to a group of students who had basic knowledge of the language and could speak with relative ease but who hesitated to
speak it with each other. Although most spoke Yiddish at home, as students of
English-language Protestant day schools who received supplementary Jewish
educations at the Folksshul, English was the natural language of daily communication with their peers. The school administration took proactive steps to
remedy the preference for English over Yiddish among the student body: in
1924, a teachers' meeting initially determined that students should be strongly
encouraged to speak Yiddish at all times. However, as Wiseman recounts,

I recall going around in the hallways or in the yard at recess and telling the students, "redt yidish" (speak Yiddish). This went on for several years until we got sick of it and concluded that it was pointless. This did not, however, cause deterioration in the instruction of Yiddish in class; rather, the requirement that children speak Yiddish was limited to the classroom during interactions with the teacher, answering questions, or recounting the contents of a paragraph. Much emphasis was placed on writing. Composition class came to occupy an important place.[33]

Despite the development of increasingly sophisticated Yiddish pedagogical approaches, school educators were forced to acknowledge the alarming decline in the level of Yiddish among the student body due to the community's steady linguistic acculturation into English. Vice-principal Shimshen Dunsky remarked in his 1934 discussion of Yiddish language and literature study in the Folksshul,

True, the study of Yiddish in the *shuln* is becoming increasingly difficult as more and more native-born children are entering the schools. For many of them, Yiddish is almost a *seyfer-hakhosem* [difficult or impossible to decipher ancient Hebrew text], and the Yiddish that comes out of their mouths is far less natural and fluent than fifteen or twenty years earlier when the child was either himself an immigrant or lived in an immigrant environment. For this reason, greater and greater efforts must be made to make the Yiddish word come alive in the mouth of the child.[34]

To counteract Yiddish losing its hold as a communicative language among the younger generation, Montreal's *shuln*—with support from teachers, the student body, and the wider community—actively encouraged their students to engage with Yiddish culture beyond the classroom walls. Activities such as student clubs and publications served as a source of pride and validation for the schools and represented a conscious effort on the part of school educators to foster Yiddish literary activity among the students. The *shuln* sponsored student clubs whose activities included reading and discussion of Yiddish literature, the creation of original writing in Yiddish, and encounters with Yiddish cultural figures, with initiatives coming from both the *shul* leadership and the student body. In fact, the clubs expanded rapidly. The first Folksshul club, the Mendele Club, was founded in 1916 and was renamed the Sholem Aleichem Club in 1919.[35] In the 1920s the Peretz Shul sponsored a Yakov Dinezon Club, and students also founded a club for graduates under the name Undzer klub (Our Club) in 1930. By 1933, the Folksshul boasted six student clubs.[36] Yiddish club activities included discussions on current events, theater productions, and creative writing. The clubs also disseminated international Yiddish children's journals such as Vilna's *Grininke beymelekh* (*Green Trees*) and New York's *Kinder zhurnal* (*Children's Journal*). Moreover, the classroom and the clubs worked in tandem to promote direct contact between students and the wider Yiddish cultural milieu, with world-renowned Yiddish writers visiting the clubs and discussing their work with the students. For example, in 1927, a semiannual joint gathering of the Sholem Aleichem and Yakov Dinezon clubs cosponsored a guest appearance by David Pinski in which the playwright spoke with the students and read from his work.[37] These meetings reinforced and underscored the ongoing relevance of Yiddish in the cultural life of the local student body. In his 1926 diary, Yaacov Zipper described being invited to play an advisory role in the formation of a local Yiddish club:

> Last night [school and community activist] Mrs. (Sarah) Zucker called me to her home. A children's club has been organized, children from ten to twelve years old, a few attend Jewish schools. Interestingly, they have sworn to speak Yiddish amongst themselves. They want to help the Jewish schools in Poland. They asked me to come to their meeting and tell them about the situation there, help them choose a name, and advise them about future activities. So I sat with the children, told them stories, which seemed to please them. They sat with their mouths open, evidently quite happy. They said (following my suggestion): We are Jewish children, and therefore our club should be called simply "Jewish children" (*yidishe kinder*). Our aim is to speak and read Yiddish.[38]

Zipper's comments indicate that as early as the mid-1920s, members of the younger generation—increasingly Canadian raised and educated in the English-language Protestant schools—countered their own linguistic attrition by making a conscious choice to speak Yiddish and organizing themselves to do so.

A core activity of the *shul* clubs entailed the publication of journals spotlighting Yiddish student writing. Like the clubs, these journals encouraged active Yiddish use and creativity among the students that extended beyond the classroom walls. For a student body raised in Canada, this ensured that Yiddish remained a vital language in the lives of the younger generation and that the students had a concrete outlet for their Yiddish writing. In 1920, the Sholem Aleichem Club began to produce *Bliende tsvayglakh* (*Blooming Branches*), which appeared in honor of the Folksshuln graduation on an annual basis beginning in 1923. Alongside greetings from school leadership and members of the local and international Yiddish communities, the journal showcased student poetry and prose, with the majority of the contents in Yiddish and the final few pages devoted to Hebrew compositions. In 1929, the Sholem Aleichem Clubs published several issues of *Bay undz: khoydeshlekher buletin* (*Among Us: Monthly Bulletin*), a typewritten, mimeographed journal that offered club news as well as original Yiddish student writing and essays on literary topics. A journal titled *Shul klangen* (*School Sounds*), issued in honor of the 1935 Folksshul graduation, featured original writing in Yiddish and Hebrew penned by students in class or through the clubs. The Peretz Shul likewise sponsored *Yidishe kinder*, a journal published in honor of its graduating classes in the 1920s and 1930s. It featured poetry, prose, and essays on literary subjects from students in all grade levels and reflected the involvement of the *shuln* with the international Yiddish literary community.

The years of the Second World War marked a flowering of the *shuln*. In contrast to the many other *shuln* in Europe and the United States that closed their doors or ceased to teach the language, Montreal's Peretz Shul and Folksshul maintained the centrality of Yiddish in their educational program alongside Hebrew and, moreover, within a day school setting. In the shift from an immigrant to an ethnic language within an acculturating community, Yiddish took on a new role as a carrier of Jewish identity that linked it with the Poale Zion's particular brand of ideology where Yiddish and Hebrew coexisted.

By 1942, with the city's core of Labor-Zionist activists and supporters rallying behind them, both the Peretz Shul and Folksshul offered full-day parochial education, enrollment remained stable, and the schools had erected their own buildings. Shloime Wiseman's vision for a lasting school-sponsored Yiddish journal came to fruition: the Folksshul high school and *Grininke beymelekh* clubs produced a journal on a regular basis between 1941 and 1946 under the title *Kinder klangen* (*Children's Sounds*).[39] The typewritten, mimeographed, and hand-illustrated trilingual Yiddish-English-Hebrew journal featured editorials, world news, school news, sports, articles, stories, poems, and greetings. Readers and subscribers included *shul* students and activists as well as many members of the wider community who were committed to Yiddish. *Kinder klangen* fulfilled the hopes of local Yiddish cultural activists: "a regular school publication for the children and by the children." J. I. Segal called it "a true children's journal."[40]

Kinder klangen points to core characteristics of Yiddish within Montreal's *shuln* during the war years. First, it reflects the ongoing involvement of the schools with the international literary community. For example, the 1942 issue reproduced the lengthy greetings of a student to poet Avrom Reisen in honor of his visit to the school as well as student articles in Yiddish on Reisen and his works.[41] A subsequent "David Pinski number" contained several items dedicated to Pinski's writing, including an original student play based on his *Der eybiker yid* (*The Eternal Jew*).[42] As Anita Norich has pointed out in her study *Discovering Exile: Yiddish and Jewish American Culture during the Holocaust*, Yiddish culture remained vibrant in the United States during this period, even with far lower levels of Yiddish maintenance.[43] This was even more the case in Montreal, where Yiddish had long formed a primary component of local Jewish identity. Second, *Kinder klangen* also indicates that by the 1940s, Yiddish was a second language to a vast majority of the students, a majority of whom were second-generation immigrants raised in an English milieu.

The Yiddish writing was notably weaker and more anglicized than in the *shuln* publications of the 1920s and 1930s, when many of the students had themselves been immigrants or come from Yiddish-speaking immigrant homes. It also indicates that the students, nevertheless, opted to write in Yiddish: as a fifth grade student remarked in Yiddish, "The journal gives the children an opportunity to write their own stories and poems."[44] Those involved with the journal acknowledged the limitations of the publication: in a letter to the editor, Segal referred to the journal as a vital tribune for the children, regardless of their level.[45] Third, the local community and the international Labor-Zionist community celebrated the journal, as seen, for example, in a reprinted letter from an educational labor organization in Palestine that enthusiastically praised *Kinder klangen:* "The Yiddish is good, really good! And if there is no hidden trick behind the [journal], it indicates that the students are coming out of the school with very good Yiddish!"[46] With the Yiddish heartland in Europe in jeopardy, this reader perceived the appearance of a Yiddish journal by children as nothing less than a miracle. Indeed, the recognized decline of Yiddish worldwide made the appearance of *Kinder klangen* quite significant. Finally, the journal illustrated the wider shift from fostering Yiddish literary activity among the student body to the preservation of Yiddish itself.

These far-reaching efforts produced a handful of Yiddish writers who embodied the community's hopes for the future. These young writers represent some of the very few North American-raised Yiddish writers to emerge; even New York City did not produce a second generation of Yiddish writers. H. M. Caiserman's 1934 anthology *Yidishe dikhter in kanade (Jewish Poets in Canada)* included a handful of young Yiddish poets who were products of the schools, including two individuals who went on to literary careers as adults: Shulamis Borodensky (Shulamis Yelin) and Rivke Rosenblatt (Ruth Rubin). Both were native Yiddish speakers raised in Montreal, and like so many children of immigrants during the early period, both Borodensky and Rosenblatt attended the *shuln* to supplement their English-language daytime studies in the Protestant schools. As students in the *shuln,* both received several hours of Yiddish instruction a week and played an active role in the schools' extracurricular activities, including journals and clubs. Although Rosenblatt ceased to publish Yiddish verse after 1930, the influence of her secular Yiddish education expressed itself in her career as a world-renowned Yiddish folklorist. Shulamis Yelin's literary career was likewise deeply influenced by her *shul* experiences. In her book *Shulamis: Stories from a Montreal Childhood,* she offers a fictionalized account of growing up in the Montreal Jewish immigrant neighborhood in the 1910s and 1920s. Her education at the Peretz Shul appears as a recurring theme in her narrative, beginning with the following description of her first contact with the school:

> One wintry Sunday night I found myself with my parents and other members of the family in the Monument National Theatre on St. Lawrence Boulevard, The Main. We were attending the graduation exercises of the Jewish *Peretz*

shul, the afternoon Yiddish school then known as the Natsionale Radicale Shul [*sic*]. The auditorium was packed with parents, friends, and well-wishers, and an extravaganza had been mounted for the occasion—a musical rendition of Joseph and his Brethren. . . . From the thread that started spinning on that magical night at the Monument National Theatre, I began to weave a Coat of Many Colours of my own.[47]

In *Stories from a Montreal Childhood* Yelin later detailed how her Peretz School education helped form her as a poet.

In the end, the dream of Yiddish continuity that expressed itself in the production of a second generation of locally raised Yiddish writers was not for the long-term. For the most part, the graduates of the Peretz Shul and Folksshul did not continue to publish in Yiddish in their adult years and ultimately turned to English as their dominant language of expression. A lone exception is Peretz Shul graduate Leybl Botwinik, who became one of the estimated dozen secular writers in the world born after the Holocaust to publish books in Yiddish: he authored a novel titled *Geheyme shlikhes* (*Secret Mission*) in 1980 at age twenty-one.[48] Outside of the nurturing environment of the *shuln*, school graduates maintained a strong appreciation for Yiddish but could not sustain a Yiddish-centered cultural life. However, the *shuln* offered instruction in Yiddish language and literature to generations of students who maintained a connection to the culture.[49]

Although the remarkable and wide-ranging efforts of Montreal's *shuln* could not ultimately counteract the forces of attrition, they did bring sustained vitality to Yiddish language and culture for subsequent generations. As *shuln* across Canada were closing their doors, Montreal's Poale Zion *shuln* continued to grow. The influx of Yiddish-speaking Holocaust survivors who made Montreal their home in the late 1940s and early 1950s revitalized the schools. Montreal's survivor population, which was second only to New York City in numbers, played an active role in the vitality of the schools through their involvement as supporters, teachers, and parents. A generation later, with Quebec offering significant state subsidies to parochial schools that offered the required number of hours of French instruction, education in private Jewish day schools—be they Orthodox, traditional, or national secular in orientation—became, unlike much of the rest of the Jewish diaspora, an affordable option for parents. Today Montreal houses one of the world's few non-Orthodox Jewish day schools where Yiddish study remains a compulsory component of the curriculum, even if the curriculum now places Yiddish in a minor role as a heritage language of Ashkenazi culture and not a vernacular in any sense.[50]

Montreal's *shuln* have long been swimming against the tide in their ongoing promotion of Yiddish as a living, creative force. The particular historical context of twentieth-century Montreal combined with the zeal of devoted

Poale Zion activists produced lasting Yiddish educational institutions. Using innovative techniques, a core of ideologues and pedagogues engaged the wider community to perpetuate Yiddish as a living culture among generations for whom Yiddish represented less and less of a vernacular as the years progressed. They instilled an appreciation of the language and culture in generations of students, working in tandem with Yiddish activity offered through local institutions such as the Jewish Public Library and the Dora Wasserman Yiddish Theatre. Although in Montreal Yiddish has become a symbolic rather than a communicative language, the city continues to choose Yiddish.

Notes

I would like to thank Eiran Harris, Eddie Paul, and Janice Rosen for their assistance in accessing the archival material employed in this essay. Unless otherwise indicated, all translations from the Yiddish are mine.

1. The term *shul* (plural *shuln*) refers to the national secular Jewish schools founded by leftist movements in the twentieth century with a core Yiddish component.
2. Ben-Zion Goldberg, "In gang fun tog: ayndrukn—montreol," *Tog-morgn zhurnal*, April 19, 1955.
3. See Simon Belkin, *Di poyle-tsien bavegung in kanade, 1904-1920* (Montreal: Northern Printing, 1956); *Di poyle-tsien bavegung in kanade, 1904-1920/Le* Mouvement *ouvrier juif au Canada, 1904-1920*, trans. Pierre Anctil (Sillery, Canada: Septendrion Press, 1999).
4. For an overview of Jewish settlement in Montreal, see Gerald Tulchinsky, "The Third Solitude: A. M. Klein's Jewish Montreal, 1910-1950," *Journal of Canadian Jewish Studies* 19, no. 2 (1984): 96-112.
5. Louis Rosenberg, *Canada's Jews—A Social and Economic Study of the Jews in Canada* (Montreal: Canadian Jewish Congress, 1939), 12, 31-34.
6. David G. Roskies, *The Jewish Search for a Usable Past* (Bloomington: Indiana University Press, 1999), 148.
7. Grace Feuerverger, "Jewish Canadian Identity and Hebrew Language Learning: Belonging (or not Belonging)," in *Nation-Building, Identity and Citizenship Education*, ed. J. Zajda et al. (Dordrecht, Netherlands: Springer, 2008), 117-30, 126-27.
8. On Jewish education in Canada, see Joseph Kage, "Tsvey hundert yor yidishe dertsyung in kanade," in *Shloyme Vaysman bukh/Shloime Wiseman Book*, ed. Shimshon Dunsky (Montreal: Yidishe Folksshuln, 1961), 160-80.
9. B. G. Sack, *Canadian Jews: Early in This Century* (Montreal: Canadian Jewish Congress Archives, 1975), 15-16.
10. See David Rome, *On the Montreal Jewish School Question, 1903-31* (Montreal: Canadian Jewish Congress Archives, 1975); Simon Belkin, "Di bavegung far separate yidishe shuln in Montreal," *Shloyme Vaysman bukh/Shloime Wiseman Book*, 181-98; Arlette Corcos, *Montréal, les juifs et l'école* (Sillery, Canada: Éditions du Septendrion, 1997), 165-78.
11. Jeffrey Shandler, *Adventures in Yiddishland: Postvernacular Language and Culture* (Berkeley: University of California Press, 2005), 71.
12. David E. Fishman, *The Rise of Modern Yiddish Culture* (Pittsburgh: University of Pittsburgh Press, 2005).
13. For example, the children's educational program of the Arbeter Ring/Workmen's Circle did not introduce Yiddish content into the classroom until 1918. See Tony Michels, *A Fire in Their Hearts: Yiddish Socialists in New York* (Cambridge: Harvard University Press, 2005), 179-216.

14. See S. Yfroikin, "Yiddish Secular Schools in the United States," in *The Jewish People: Past and Present*, ed. R. Abramovitch (New York: Jewish Encyclopedia Handbooks, 1948), 2:44–50.

15. See Zevi Scharfstein, "Jewish Education in Latin America," *The Jewish People: Past and Present*, 2:172–77.

16. David Roskies, "Yiddish in Montreal: The Utopian Experiment," in *An Everyday Miracle: Yiddish Culture in Montreal*, ed. Ira Robinson, Pierre Anctil, and Mervin Butovsky (Montreal: Véhicule Press, 1990), 22–38.

17. See Fishman, *Modern Yiddish Culture*.

18. Shloime Wiseman, ed., *Folksshul bukh: fuftsn yor yubileyum* (Montreal: Jewish People's Schools, 1929), 6. By 1920, the smaller Jewish community in Winnipeg had established an all-day Peretz Shul.

19. When the schools did merge, it was due to financial necessity and only at the retirement of their two long-term principals. Yaacov Zipper led the Peretz Shul from 1934 to 1971, and Shloime Wiseman led the Folksshul from 1920 to 1971.

20. See Nathan Cohen, "The Jews of Independent Poland: Linguistic and Cultural Changes," in *Starting the Twenty-First Century: Sociological Reflections and Challenges*, ed. Ernest Krausz and Gitta Tulea (New Brunswick, NJ: Transaction Publishers, 2002), 161–75.

21. See "Yidishe-folksshuln montreol prospekt program un informatsye bukh/The Jewish People's Schools Montreal Prospectus" (September 1926, Jewish People's Schools [Folk Shule], Canadian Jewish Congress Charities Committee [CJCNA]).

22. Sh. Wiseman, "Dos lebn un dos shulnvezn," in *Folksshuln bukh, aroysgegebn tsum 20 yorikn yubileyum 1914–1934* (Montreal: Jewish People's Schools, 1934), 6–7.

23. Yaacov Zipper, "On the Occasion of the 50th Jubilee of the Jewish Peretz Schools." Playbill for the Peretz Shul production of the Folksbiene Playhouse of New York in H. Leivick's "The Sage of Rottenberg" (April 4, 1964, Jewish Peretz Schools, CJCNA).

24. Shloime Wiseman, ed., *Dos vort*, 3 vols. (New York: Tsentral komitet fun du yidishe folk shuln fun yidish-natsionaln arbeter farband un poale tsien-tsire tsien/Jewish Folk Schools of America, 1931). A second edition followed in 1938.

25. "Annual Campaign of the Peretz Shul" (Montreal: Jewish Peretz Schools, CJCNA, 193?).

26. J. I. Segal, "Akshones," *Folksshuln bukh: tsum 15-yorikn yubileyum* (1929): 45–47.

27. See Bluma Applebaum, "Reminiscences and After," in *Yoyvl bukh: 25 yeriker yubileyum/Jubilee Book*, ed. Farayn fun graduirte yidishe folks shuln/Graduates' Society, Jewish People's Schools (Montreal, 1947), 17.

28. *Finf un tsvantsik yeriker yubiley fun dem direktorn-rat bay di yidishe folksshuln, Montreal/ Twenty-Fifth Anniversary of the Founding of the Board of Directors, 1922–1947, at the Jewish People's Schools, Montreal* (Montreal: People's Schools, 1947).

29. *Yidishe folksshuln buletin*, December 1933.

30. *Yoyvl bukh: 25 yeriker yubileyum/Jubilee Book*, 4.

31. For example, in a 1928 article about the state of the secular Yiddish schools in the United States, pedagogue Sh. Hurvits complained extensively about the organizational crisis facing the schools. Hurvits, "Di yidishe veltlekhe shul in Amerike (vos zi iz un vos zi darf zayn)," *Tsukunft* 33, no. 1 (1928): 40–44.

32. Louis Rosenberg, "Jewish Population Characteristics," *Montreal Congress Bulletin*, September 1956, 3.

33. Shlime Wiseman, "A memuar fun mayn lebn vi a yidisher dertsyer," in *Kanader yidisher zamlbukh/Canadian Jewish Anthology/Anthologie Juive du Canada*, ed. Chaim Spilberg and Jacob Zipper (Montreal: National Committee on Yiddish, Canadian Jewish Congress, 1982), 380–415, 391.

34. Wiseman, "Dos lebn un dos shulnvezn," 6–7.

35. Jewish People's School, "Programme of Studies in the Jewish People's School" (unpublished pamphlet, September 1924), 2.

36. *Yidishe folksshuln buletin,* December 1933. Jewish People's Schools (Folk Shule), CJCNA.

37. "Shul khronik," *Bliende tsvayglakh,* May 1927, 12.

38. Yaacov Zipper, "The Journal of Yaacov Zipper 1925–1926," *An Everyday Miracle,* 63–64.

39. Between June 1943 and June 1944, only a single issue appeared, after which *Kinder klangen* appeared annually until 1946. The journal was available to subscribers at a cost of five (later ten) cents per issue.

40. *Kinder klangen* 1, no. 4 (1942): 2.

41. The students presented Reisen with a scrapbook and recited his work. *Kinder klangen* 2, no. 1 (1942): 5–6, 20.

42. *Kinder klangen* 2, no. 2 (1943).

43. Anita Norich, *Discovering Exile: Yiddish and Jewish American Culture during the Holocaust* (Stanford: Stanford University Press, 2007).

44. Leye Rottermund, *Kinder klangen* 1, no. 3 (1942): 5.

45. *Kinder klangen* 2, no. 2 (1943): 2.

46. Shalom Hektin, for the *Va'ad hamehankhim ha'ivrim lema'an eretz Yisra'el ha'ovedet,* in *Kinder klangen* 2, no. 4 (1943): 3–4.

47. Shulamis Yelin, *Shulamis: Stories from a Montreal Childhood* (Montreal: Shoreline, 1993), 34.

48. Dovid Katz, *Words on Fire: The Unfinished Story of Yiddish* (New York: Basic Books, 2004), 372.

49. See, for example, Eugene Orenstein, "Yiddish Culture in Canada Yesterday and Today," in *The Canadian Cultural Mosaic,* ed. M. Weinfeld, W. Shaffir, and I. Cotler (Rexdale, Canada: John Wiley and Sons, 1981), 293–314.

50. See Anna Fishman Gonshor and William Shaffir, "Commitment to a Language: Teaching Yiddish in a Hasidic and Secular School," in *Yiddish after the Holocaust,* ed. Joseph Sherman (Oxford: Boulevard Books, The Oxford Centre for Hebrew and Judaic Studies, 2004), 149–78; Grace Feuerverger, "'Jewish Canadian Identity and Hebrew Language Learning: Belonging (or not Belonging)' in Montreal and Toronto Diaspora: A Comparative Analysis," *Nation-Building,* 117–30. On wider trends in American pedagogy, see Jeffrey Shandler, "Beyond the Mother-Tongue: Learning the Meaning of Yiddish in America," *Jewish Social Studies* 6, no. 3 (2000): 97–123.

YIDDISH GOES POP
Prelude

JEFFREY SHANDLER

I have been asked to write a short essay on the theme "Yiddish Goes Pop," but I question the premise. Yiddish has not suddenly "gone pop"; it always has been "pop"—even in the efforts of avant-garde literati, secular scholars, and earnest *kultur-tuers* (cultural activists) to render the language highbrow. As Benjamin Harshav has observed,

> This "oral" and popular language has been successfully harnessed to impressionist prose, historiography, linguistic and statistical research, political propaganda, and "ivory tower" poetry. Nevertheless, in social perception, the language did carry a cluster of characteristic features, developed in its unique history and crystallized in its modern literature. The very fact that native speakers may assign such emotive qualities to the language, rather than seeing it as a neutral vehicle for communication, speaks for itself.[1]

In the semiotics of Jewish languages, Yiddish has long signified linguistic and cultural vernacularity. It is *di shprakh vos redt zikh* (the language that speaks by itself), the language that, as the linguist Max Weinreich observed, no one was ever flogged for not learning[2] (in contrast to Hebrew—not only the traditional *ivre* of Jewish worship or the rabbinic Hebrew of a religious elite but also the coercive teaching of *ivrit*, the exclusive official Jewish language of the State of Israel, where this was a matter not of corporal punishment but of browbeating). Yiddish is imagined as autochthonic, indigenous, a part of the Jewish soul—and, like the Jewish soul, part of the Jewish body. Associations of Yiddish with the corporeal and the vulgar (in its multiple meanings) are vital for much of the discourse on the language going back to the Enlightenment, both in disparaging Yiddish and in expressing its appeal.

Yiddish culture, increasingly realized in the mode I have termed "postvernacular," has developed a new dependence on the academy for its sustenance.[3] Therefore, it is a challenge (but also a delight) for scholars today to engage, sometimes to rediscover, Yiddish as vulgar. I'm reminded of an experience early in my career as a student of Yiddish: my first graduate course in Yiddish literature, which was taught in Yiddish by Avram Nowersztern during a guest stint at YIVO in the mid-1980s. I was still a struggling novice Yiddish reader, and Nowersztern kindly met with me individually to review some of the works we were reading in class. Once, we met to discuss "A Man from Buenos Aires," one of Sholem Aleichem's railroad stories. The story relates an encounter between the narrator, a traveling salesman, and the title character, who is very successful in a business that he never quite gets around to naming, despite the narrator's repeated efforts to ascertain what it is. "You know of course what the man's profession is," Nowersztern asked me, speaking in Yiddish. "No," I replied; it's never stated in the story, and I was just as bewildered as the narrator. In fact, the whole story didn't make sense to me; perhaps, being a less-than-fluent reader, I'd missed something? Blushing, Nowersztern explained: "*Er iz an alfonz*" (He's an *alfonz*—a Yiddish word I didn't know). "*Vos iz an alfonz?*" I asked. Nowersztern turned redder. "How do you say it in English? He's a pimp." "He is?!" I exclaimed—and Nowersztern reminded me that, at the time Sholem Aleichem wrote the story (it was published in 1909), Buenos Aires was a byword for white slavery among Yiddish-speaking Jews in eastern Europe and that Jews then figured prominently in running—and populating—the city's brothels.

What is now a largely forgotten (or deliberately ignored) episode of Jewish history was, a century ago, the subject of urgent, heated discussion among east European Jews contemplating immigration. Stories of Jewish women who had been duped into becoming prostitutes circulated orally and appeared in the Jewish press. The original readers of Sholem Aleichem's story, Nowersztern explained, would have recognized the profession of the man from Buenos Aires straightaway. The fact that the narrator could not figure it out would have been a source of growing amusement, as the story progresses and the hints become more and more telling (including how the man from Buenos Aires seems to be charming the narrator in much the way he would procure naïve young women).

Today, though, for someone as naïve as I was, Sholem Aleichem's story does not stand on its own. The joke that was originally on the narrator is now on the uninformed reader. But discovering the joke, under the guidance of a teacher, constitutes a new cultural encounter of significance in its own right. It is a discovery that I now replicate when I teach the story to undergraduates (who can be relied on not to read the translator's introduction explaining the story's original context). The fact that Sholem Aleichem's stories, read largely in translation, now require footnotes, may strike some as a symptom of cultural loss, but I argue that it is at least as much a sign of cultural tenacity. A disparity between the cultural literacy of the *folkmentshn* about whom Sholem Aleichem wrote and the knowledge base of his readership is not new; the author occasionally resorted to annotating his own work. Readers of his 1888 novel *Stempenyu* will recall that the author glosses the slang of *klezmorim,* signaling his expectation that readers of respectable, middle-class Yiddish literature would not understand the argot of such louche types.

Studying Jewish vulgarity within the academization of Yiddish is not a new cultural practice; it dates back at least to the Ansky expedition, in which collectors were instructed not to bowdlerize informants' crude stories. Today, this scholarly phenomenon takes place alongside the enduring popular practice of inheriting Yiddish as a fragmented signifier of Jewish vulgarity and carnivalesque.[4] (Consider, for example, the success of compendia of raucous Yiddish lore, from Ignacz Bernstein's *Erotica et Rustica* [1908] to Leo Rosten's *Joys of Yiddish* [1967] to Michael Wex's *Born to Kvetch* [2005].)

In the face of Yiddishists' long-standing commitment to vaunting Yiddish as a language of high culture, there is a special challenge for scholars to engage Yiddish vulgarity as a cultural practice of value in its own right. Beyond simply a matter of accepting the lowbrow, this entails a new kind of self-consciousness of the value of Yiddish as a signifier of the vulgar. It is generally a challenge for Jewish studies scholars to engage Jewish vulgarity—by dint of an overall conservative tendency in the field, perhaps, or a desire by many practitioners to show their subject in its best light—but it is one they should take on, and Yiddish can show the way. As the essays in this section demonstrate, Yiddish vulgarity demands that scholars think of Jewishness not only in idealized, elite forms but also as it has actually been lived by the full range of Jews, most of whom are never part of the intellectual leadership, either traditional or modern, and many of whom engage in practices, which they deem Jewish, that stand quite apart from—or sometimes fly in the face of—anything officially considered normative. Scholarly grappling with the vulgar does much to enhance the understanding of Jewish life, and not only in the academy. Given the growing importance of the academic study of Jews for the Jewish community, these studies have consequences for the lives Jews lead and for how they are understood by those who live among them.

Notes

1. Benjamin Harshav, *The Meaning of Yiddish* (Berkeley: University of California Press, 1990), 91.
2. Max Weinreich, *History of the Yiddish Language* (Chicago: University of Chicago Press, 1980), 270.

3. Jeffrey Shandler, *Adventures in Yiddishland: Postvernacular Language and Culture* (Berkeley: University of California Press, 2005). On the place of Yiddish in the academy, see Jeffrey Shandler, "The State of Yiddish Studies: Some Observations and Thoughts," *Conservative Judaism* 54, no. 4 (2002): 69-77.

4. I discuss this phenomenon in chapter 5 of *Adventures in Yiddishland*.

ISAAC GOLDBERG AND THE IDEA OF OBSCENE YIDDISH

JOSH LAMBERT

The Idea of Obscene Yiddish

By Lenny Bruce's second appearance on *The Steve Allen Show* on May 10, 1959, he had already begun to earn his reputation as, in Allen's words, "the most shocking comedian of our time . . . a comedian who will offend everybody." Building on this reputation, Bruce launched into his set by quoting two unsympathetic critics, holding up newspapers and reading aloud from their reviews of his last appearance: "'The bad taste award should be given to Lenny Bruce, who outshuddered every other comedian on television this year.' . . . But then," he continued, getting to the joke, "finally, a newspaper with some integrity came forth." Displaying a copy of the *Forverts*, America's best-known Yiddish newspaper, to a burst of laughter, he pretended to quote from it in English: "Last night, a star was born." The audience roared.[1]

Bruce's joke satirized Jewish chauvinism: the idea that a Yiddish newspaper always celebrates the work of a Jewish performer, whether he merits praise or not. But the other reason that Bruce's audience laughed so heartily at the sight of the *Forverts* was owing to their recognition that what English-language newspapers rejected as "bad taste," a Yiddish-language publication might celebrate as comic brilliance. Bruce's notoriety was due to his use of taboo words and to his frankness about sex, two forms of discourse then criminalized as "obscenity" by U.S. law.[2] The joke thus implied that a comedy routine offensive to English-speaking Americans and obscene by American legal standards would by contrast elicit praise, rather than scorn, from a Yiddish speaker. That this joke delighted a mainstream television show's studio audience reveals just how widely a view of Yiddish as a language unusually tolerant of such obscene discourse had spread by the late 1950s.

Sociolinguists note that languages frequently take on such associations. No language can sensibly be considered essentially or intractably dirtier, cleaner, uglier, or prettier than any other, but as Joshua A. Fishman has remarked apropos of language stereotypes, "The absence or presence of a 'kernel of truth' (or of verifiability itself) is entirely unrelated to the mobilizing power of such views."[3] In other words, whether Yiddish is essentially more obscene than other languages is beside the point. Why have its speakers and representatives characterized it as such?

Uriel Weinreich suggested one answer to this question in 1953, remarking that "an obsolescent language seems destined to acquire peculiar connotations."[4] Following through on Weinreich's observation, Jeffrey Shandler has shown that much "postvernacular" Yiddish culture—which developed as the number of the language's speakers declined in the years since World War II—has "fix[ed] the language as an emblem of the mock and the carnivalesque," as "inherently subversive, transgressive, emotive, and appetitive." Bruce's joke and general deployment of Yinglish accorded well with this observation.[5] Yet the idea of obscene Yiddish began to circulate long before WWII. In fact, as early as 1918, the American Jewish critic and translator Isaac Goldberg remarked that "the theme of sex … is treated by Yiddish writers with far greater freedom than would be permitted to their American confrères. . . . The Yiddish public will listen to and read, without hiding it, much of what the American public would affect not to care for, only to read it surreptitiously."[6]

A study of Goldberg's largely forgotten career as the most prolific translator of American Yiddish fiction and drama into English in the interwar United States elucidates another particular, concrete source for the idea of Yiddish obscenity. Goldberg's engagement with literary modernism positioned him well to understand that the unofficial status of Yiddish in America insulated it from the governmental censorships that constrained Yiddish literature in Russia and English literature in the United States and England in the early twentieth century. For Goldberg and other Americans, in other words, Yiddish possessed a major advantage over English: cops could not read it.[7] In America, unlike Europe, Yiddish functioned not simply as a landless language but also as a blissfully lawless one. This constituted a tremendous opportunity for literary expression.

Isaac Goldberg and Obscenity

Goldberg was born on November 1, 1887, in Boston to Yiddish-speaking Jewish parents. At the age of eleven he suffered from empyema, the filling of the pleural cavity with pus, and according to a biographical appreciation by an admiring reader named Allen Crandall, the surgery that saved the young boy's life transformed "a strong, athletic child" into "a delicate, introspective one."[8] Goldberg described his father as a man who "worshipped everything associated with education and made, together with my mother, great sacrifices that one of the family of six children … might go through college."[9] Like Ludwig Lewisohn, Goldberg achieved tremendous academic success despite the intense prejudice against Jews that dominated American academia in those years. He studied at Harvard University with esteemed professors including George Santayana, receiving his bachelor's degree in 1910, his master's in 1911, and his doctorate in 1912, at the age of twenty-five, in romance languages and literatures. His dissertation focused on the Spanish playwright Don José Echegaray, winner of the 1904 Nobel Prize in Literature.

Unlike Lewisohn, Goldberg never embraced Christianity in an attempt to avoid discrimination,[10] but, like him, Goldberg seems to have despaired when no university offered him a teaching position. The outline for an unpublished autobiographical novel in Goldberg's papers has its protagonist graduate summa cum laude from Harvard without election to Phi Beta Kappa, like Goldberg. After he receives his PhD "in philology, modern tongues," this character and his family feel "badly disillusioned as month after month goes by and no position is forthcoming" because of "his Jewish origin and his radicalism."[11] Crandall reports that after graduating Goldberg "suffered a nervous breakdown"—a reference, it seems, to the scholar's bitter disillusionment—and he quotes Goldberg as saying that "it knocked me out … for a couple of years, and has left permanent marks in my attitude toward life."[12]

Still, Goldberg managed to publish his first short book, "a handbook on Gilbert and the Gilbert-Sullivan operas," in 1913. By 1916 he founded a literary journal, *The Stratford Monthly*, and a publishing house, the Stratford Universal Library, with his childhood friend Henry T. Schnittkind. At the same time, Goldberg began to contribute theater reviews and essays about Spanish and Latin American literature to literary magazines and journals. By the latter half of the decade, he devoted much of his energy to translations of modern drama and fiction from Yiddish and other languages. According to a reminiscence of David Pinski, Goldberg "could barely read Yiddish" in 1916, when a newspaper sent him to interview Pinski.[13] If that was true, Goldberg learned quickly: within a few years, he translated a volume of plays by Pinski, Sholem Aleichem, Sholem Asch, and Peretz Hirschbein (1916); Asch's *Mottke the Vagabond* (1917); *Three Plays* by David Pinski (1918); Asch's *God of Vengeance* (1918); a second volume of plays by Pinski, Hirschbein, Leon Kobrin, and Z. Levin (1918); and a collection of Pinski's short stories, *Temptations* (1919). Though he translated from Yiddish enthusiastically, Goldberg does not seem to have written in that language. In one of his notebooks he scribbled, "My language is not Yiddish, not Hebrew, not Russian, but English."[14]

In the late 1910s, Goldberg also translated literature from Russian, Japanese, Portuguese, and Spanish into English, often in collaboration with Schnittkind.

Some evidence suggests that he garnered more respect, or at least better pay, for his Yiddish translations than for his translations from other languages. Lowell Brentano, a New York publisher who contracted Goldberg for translations both from Yiddish and from Latin American languages, remarked in one of their negotiations, "I presume that the translating of Spanish is considerably easier than translating from Yiddish," and added, "besides, good Spanish translators are not as rare as experts in Yiddish or Hebrew."[15]

Goldberg continued to translate in the 1920s—his complete list of translations from Yiddish to English would ultimately include Asch's *Uncle Moses* (1920), Leon Kobrin's *A Lithuanian Village* (1920), Yehoash's *The Feet of the Messenger* (1923), Pinski's *Arnold Levenberg* (1928), and Joseph Opatoshu's *In Polish Woods* (1938). In that decade, he also published a torrent of his own books, articles, and pamphlets in English. Notable titles include *Studies in Spanish-American Literature* (1920) and *Brazilian Literature* (1922), which established him as a leading scholar of Latin American literary history,[16] and *The Man Mencken* (1925), *Havelock Ellis* (1926), and *Major Noah: American-Jewish Pioneer* (1936), biographical studies of major cultural figures whom Goldberg admired. The book on Ellis, along with several pamphlets Goldberg published with Emanuel Haldeman-Julius's company, reflects one of his central interests: the debates raging at the time in the United States about censorship and the representation of sex.[17]

In those years, antivice organizations such as Boston's Watch and Ward Society and the New York Society for the Suppression of Vice (NYSSV) ramped up their campaigns against what they considered obscene literature as part of a general wave of reactionary politics following World War I. Targeting young Jewish publishers who favored the literary modernism that traditional American publishing houses disdained to print, the NYSSV, led by John Sumner, established itself as a major force in American literature in the early 1920s.[18] Sumner regularly raided the offices of publishers, including Thomas Seltzer and Horace Liveright, hauled them into court, and exerted his influence on others less eager to mount legal defenses, such as Alfred Knopf. Members of the literary old guard—critics William Lyon Phelps and Bliss Perry and authors Mary Austin and Hamlin Garland, for example—endorsed these efforts to suppress eroticism in contemporary writing, and their disapproval often implicitly or explicitly blamed Jews and foreigners for perverting American letters. Austin fumed in 1923 against contemporary "sex literature," averring that "neither the Russian nor the Jew has ever been able to understand . . . that not to have had any seriously upsetting sex adventures may be the end of an intelligently achieved life standard."[19] Such attacks in the sphere of literature evoked and built on the strain of turn-of-the-century populist anti-Semitism that represented Jewish men as hypersexual deviants.[20]

In this contentious atmosphere, Goldberg declared his staunch opposition to literary censorship, and he championed anticensorship activity. In *The*

Drama of Transition (1922), a survey of contemporary transnational theater, he asserted that he was "unequivocally opposed to any form of censorship what-soever" and opined that sex "is an eternal theme; it is at the center of life, and for the censor to govern its expression is ridiculously like letting the prison be run by the jail-birds." Recognizing that literary freedom might have negative consequences, too, Goldberg nonetheless proclaimed that he would rather see, "sex rampant than any form of censorship. . . . There is no compromise here; even thought of compromise is, on the artist's part, surrender."[21]

Despite Goldberg's absolutist rhetoric, a careful reading of his oeuvre sug-gests he believed in drawing a line between art and smut—leaving vague, of course, as so many critics, reformers, and judges have throughout the gener-ations, where or how precisely to draw that line between art and indecency. Tellingly, he personally eschewed libertinism and lived a remarkably quiet life. He abstained from alcohol, despite H. L. Mencken's suggestion that drinking would improve his writing,[22] and he reportedly ate mostly "dairy products, some vegetables, and lots of fruit."[23] He married his first cousin at the age of twenty-seven and never had children.[24]

Goldberg struck a pose of moderation, too, on the question of what linguists call "taboo words." Referring to himself in the third person in *Panorama,* a short-lived journal he edited, he noted that he "finds it difficult to endure, even from close friends, the type of humor that originates in digestion, elimination and their various functions, and even the common words that describe those functions. His habitual vocabulary, in fact, with only occasional expressions, is as pure as dreamless sleep."[25] The contradiction between this attitude and Goldberg's sincere opposition to censorship may be explained by the value he placed on the self-restraint of authors and cultural professionals. He argued that no law should restrict people from using taboo words—as American law has often done[26]—but that individuals should restrain themselves: "What we ourselves do not like, we can abstain from, without visiting our fears or our dislikes upon others," Goldberg proposed. "Printing [so-called obscene words] for their own sake is childish; they do not always belong. . . . Let us quit toying with obscenity for its own sake and relegate it to its proper, or improper, place in the artistic scheme of things."[27]

One observes this principle in action in Goldberg's two volumes of erotic short fiction, *Sexarians* (1931) and *Madame Sex* (1932).[28] Esar Levine's Panurge Press, a major dealer in mail-order erotica,[29] marketed Goldberg's collections as sexual literature. An advertisement inside *Sexarians* proclaimed that the book "probes the danger depths of sexuality" and listed Goldberg's work alongside books described as an "encyclopedia of venery, a kaleidoscope of perversions, a jungle of horrors," and "a wealthy rake's numerous gallantries with girls and women in Chicago, recorded with a freedom of expression invariably omitted from novels."[30] Levine printed Goldberg's collections beautifully on heavy pa-per, like all of Panurge Press's erotic publications, and prominent notes in the books indicated that only a limited number of copies (1,500 of *Sexarians*, 2,000 of *Madame Sex*) had "been printed and press-numbered for private collectors of erotica."[31] Levine found this a remarkably successful marketing tactic. In a 1930 letter, he remarked to a friend, "You have no idea . . . what a magic effect 'privately printed' on the title page of a book of snappy stories would have!"[32]

Although Goldberg's erotic stories narrated sexual relationships somewhat frankly, they did not resemble the most controversial works of the era, James Joyce's *Ulysses* and D. H. Lawrence's *Lady Chatterley's Lover*.[33] The most controversial English taboo words ("fuck," "shit," and "cunt") never appeared in Goldberg's stories, and in representing sex he employed the strategies typical of mainstream American fiction of the period, elision and florid imagery. One of his stories describes a young woman's first experience of sexual intercourse in the following terms: "She opened to him as a flower to the sun; drank him in as a flower drinks in the rain. . . . She strained him madly to her . . . they became one . . . fused in a heat that dissolved them into ecstasy."[34] With its gratuitous ellipses, broad metaphors, and vague verbs, this passage reproduces precisely the strategies and even some of the specific euphemisms that appeared in popular novels of the previous decade by such authors as Lewisohn and Anzia Yezierska.[35]

In another of Goldberg's stories, a hard-boiled Boston housewife attempts to cheat on her inattentive husband with his attractive business partner only to discover, to her dismay, that her husband has already cheated on her with that same partner. Although the story's language cannot be described as absolutely prim,[36] Goldberg consistently favored euphemism over graphic description. Consider, for instance, the following passage: "I let him touch me—all the places where men like to touch women; and that means every place there is to touch, doesn't it? . . . Then, naturally, I let him kiss me. And, when you get down to cases, that means almost every place, too."[37] The story implies manual and oral stimulation of the genitals here—the euphemistic "every place there is to touch" evokes most powerfully those "places" that one could not legally name—but Goldberg avoided explicitly mentioning these practices or using any of the taboo locutions that occasioned the censorships of *Lady Chatterley* and *Ulysses*. Exemplifying Goldberg's moderate position on the question of literary obscenity, his collections of stories engaged simultaneously in representational transgression and restraint.[38]

Goldberg's work as a critic and editor likewise reflected his belief that cultural professionals like him bear the responsibility for restraining the worst tendencies of artists. While abjuring theatrical censorship, he admitted that theater managers "are as businessmen justified in seeking to placate the powers" who seek to reform the stage—that is, the antivice crusaders—and he admits that "if a play is frankly and commercially indecent, that is a problem for the police; we are not interested in it."[39] Again, Goldberg believed neither in celebrating literary obscenity nor in giving it free rein. Rather, he relied on the efficacy of

authorial self-censorship and the restraints imposed within a creative field—
by editors, reviewers, and booksellers on published literature, and by theater
managers and critics on drama—rather than on the censorships imposed by
legal and governmental authorities. As he phrased the matter elsewhere,

> The Censor … may not always be wrong in wishing to do away with the object
> of his disapproval. The wrong lies in his method. He is a King who can do no
> wrong. His wish must be law. There is no argument; no discussion. There is only
> obedience.
>
> This is obviously preposterous.
>
> Let him believe what he pleases to believe; let him work in the interests of
> that belief. But why seek, by law and other compulsion, to tie his opponent
> hand and foot? Why deny to ideas different from his own the right to death—or
> life—in the open field?[40]

Goldberg's language emphasized his position: he rejected governmental and
legal censorship—foisted on the public by a "king," metaphorical or real, or the
"law"—in favor of self-regulation of creative industries by their practitioners
("work in the interests of that belief"). Goldberg's reasonable, if not unique,
position rejected free speech absolutism as an impossibly utopian ideal.[41] At
the same time, he refused to accept that anyone with a police badge, judicial
robe, or sense of righteous indignation should be entrusted with authority as
a literary or cultural übercritic. This background helps to explain Goldberg's
attraction to American Yiddish literature, his perspective on its toleration of
obscenity, and his approach to translating it.

Goldberg's Idea of Yiddish

Some critics of Yiddish literature have not shared Goldberg's sense that "the
theme of sex . . . is treated by Yiddish writers with far greater freedom than
would be permitted to their American confreres."[42] Yankev Glatshteyn argued,
in a 1964 essay on *grobe reyd* (vulgar speech) in literature and the recent flourishing of what he inventively labeled *nibl pen* (a punning coinage suggesting
"obscene writing"), that although "Yiddish possesses many 'healthy' vulgar expressions, with sexual insinuations [*grobe oysdrukn, mit geshlekhtlekher ontsuher-
enish*] . . . gradually Yiddish has become one of the most modest [*tsniesdikste*]
languages in world literature. It bears simply no coarse expressions—certainly
not in the literature—and no writer ventures to break this bridle, except those
who are sure that they write in the first place for the translation market."[43]

With this characteristic dig at Asch and Isaac Bashevis Singer, whose works
thrived in translation and scandalized audiences with their sexual frankness,
Glatshteyn dismissed the idea of Yiddish obscenity. Arguing for the essential
modesty of Jewish culture, Glatshteyn could have cited as evidence Y. L. Peretz's

statement in "Monish" (1888) that Yiddish contains no word for love, often quoted by Goldberg[44]; or, like Goldberg, he could have quoted Maimonides's prohibition of *nibl pe*, which has its source in the Talmudic dicta from which that traditional Jewish term for obscenity itself derives.[45]

Yet Glatshteyn neglected to mention that unlike the Hebrew writers in Israel and the English writers in America whom he discussed, and also unlike Yiddish writers in czarist Russia and the Soviet Union, who labored under pervasive, cruel, and sometimes fatal government censorships,[46] American Yiddish writers like him had virtually never suffered from censorships imposed by the courts, the police, or other governmental agencies.[47] If American Yiddish literature tended toward modesty, at least measured by the standards of the American 1960s, as Glatshteyn said[48]—a debatable but not unreasonable claim—that owed not to governmental censorship, but to the self-restraint of Yiddish authors, editors, readers, and literary critics. Goldberg, as we have seen, would have disapproved of "sex rampant" in literature, as Glatshteyn did in 1964. Given Goldberg's extensive dealings with censorship in English, he naturally found attractive the alternative model of literary control he perceived in American Yiddish. In the American Yiddish literary sphere, editors and critics like Glatshteyn—and not lawyers, custom officials, or politicians—brought charges of obscenity and prosecuted them not in the courts but in the pages of newspapers and literary journals.[49]

Several incidents might have dramatized this characteristic of modern Yiddish culture and particularly American Yiddish culture for Goldberg. He may have followed, for example, the extended debate about *grobe verter un sheyne literatur* (vulgar speech and belles lettres) in the *Freiheit* that centered on Moyshe-Leyb Halpern's poetry in the early 1920s.[50] He certainly would have noticed the starkly different receptions of Asch's *Got fun nekome*, which he translated in 1918, on the Yiddish and English stages: the play's Yiddish productions in 1907 sparked lively debates, but when it opened in English on Broadway in 1923, the producer and actors were arrested for immorality.[51] Goldberg and H. L. Mencken may also have noted that Winocur's Spanish-Yiddish dictionary (1931), which they both praised, included at least one word—*drek/mierda* (shit)—the translation of which did not appear in English dictionaries at that time.[52]

Sholem Aleichem's *Shomers mishpet* (1888), a classic work of literary critique presented in the form of a trial, furnishes a particularly resonant statement of the divergence between Yiddish and other national languages on the question of obscenity. Sholem Aleichem repeatedly castigated Shomer's prose as *nibl pe*, suggesting that Sholem Aleichem drew inspiration for his critique from the famous trials of Baudelaire's *Les Fleurs du mal*, Flaubert's *Madame Bovary*, and other belles lettres in mid-nineteenth-century France.[53] Unlike those cases, however, and many that Goldberg would witness and report on in the 1920s, *Shomers mishpet* was only a metaphorical trial. Although influential, Sholem

Aleichem, unlike Sumner and the NYSSV, had no authority to arrest booksellers, confiscate books, or deny mailing privileges to publishers.[54]

Whether or not Goldberg had read *Shomers mishpet*, another case, analogous
to the better known example of *Got fun nekome*, came to his attention on April 2,
1920 in a letter from Brentano. The publisher wrote,

> A week ago the N.Y. Society for the Suppression of Vice saw fit to suppress
> TEMPTATIONS, because of the alleged immorality of the first three stories. For
> the present we have taken the book off sale, and Pinski and we are talking over
> plans for further action. This news I repeat is between ourselves, but I mention
> it to you partly because it shows how careful we must be in these days of literary
> censorship; for instance they could send you to jail for five years for certain
> parts of [the Venezuelan author Rufino Blanco-Fombona's] THE MAN OF
> GOLD [of which Brentano published Goldberg's translation in 1920].[55]

Temptations never went to trial. Brentano, like Knopf and many other publishers of the period, placated Sumner by acceding to his demands to take the book
out of circulation.[56] Still, this event demonstrated to Goldberg that Yiddish
literature evaded the governmental regulations imposed on English literature. Although Yiddish critics in the United States may not have unanimously
lauded Pinski's "Beruriah" (1916), "The Temptations of Rabbi Akiva" (1917),
and "Johanan the High Priest" (1912), such critics had no power to jail Pinski or his publisher if they found the fiction offensive.[57] Goldberg, who rarely
left Boston—and who turned down a Guggenheim grant in 1932 because it
required him to leave the country for nine months[58]—would not, despite his
genuine opposition to censorship, have taken the prospect of a jail term lightly.
No wonder, then, his attraction to Yiddish literary modernism, in which the
most influential literary obscenity trial was Sholem Aleichem's fictional, metaphorical, nonbinding one.[59]

Goldberg's translations of Yiddish novels exemplified this difference between Yiddish and English writing in America, as he occasionally bowdlerized
their source material. Goldberg made this practice explicit. Regarding Asch's
Mottke the Scamp, he noted, "There are certain passages to which Comstockian
readers would certainly object strongly in an English version."[60] Thus, when introducing his translation of that novel, Goldberg indicated that he presented "a
close rendering of the original, with a few minor excisions (amounting scarcely
to a page in the whole work) agreed to in advance by the author."[61] Goldberg's
willingness to bowdlerize Asch's novel (and his attempt to interest a publisher
in later works by Asch by declaring them "free of Mottke-Vagabondish objectionable passages"[62]) seems at odds with his principled opposition to censorship and particularly with his pronouncement that "American squeamishness
and hyper-puritanism have much to profit from Yiddish fiction and Asch's
healthy elementalism in particular."[63] However, this contradiction may be ex-

plained by Goldberg's awareness of the risks attendant on provoking America's "Comstockian readers" as well as his belief in the legitimacy with which a literary professional like himself, as opposed to a judge or postmaster, could modify a work of art.

Goldberg bowdlerized while translating only minimally. Nevertheless, a couple of examples suggest Goldberg's awareness of the pressure imposed on English prose in America at that time by prudish vice crusaders. Take, for example, the small revisionary translations Goldberg imposed on Pinski's debut novel, *Arnold Levenberg*. Drafted from 1919 to 1925, serialized in *Der tog*, and published in 1928 in Goldberg's English translation,[64] the novel explicitly registered the censorious climate that suffused American culture during and after WWI. One of Pinski's ostensibly non-Yiddish-speaking American characters notes, for instance, that simply reporting her friends' speech would result in "a downright filthy book . . . a book that our pious, virtuous [*frume, tsniesdike*] postal system couldn't carry."[65] The post office comes up a second time, in a letter from an American soldier in France during WWI, to the titular protagonist in New York: "If I were to write down what I've seen with my own eyes," the soldier writes, ostensibly in English, "I'd be prosecuted as a most dangerous criminal by the American Post Office Department. . . . This much, I believe, our Post Office will be able to stand: in the town behind the lines the government maintains public houses. Women are on sale, the same as beer or boots."[66] Goldberg rendered this passage accurately, with one exception. The final line quoted above appeared in Pinski's Yiddish as "Froyen vern tsugeshtelt, vi es vern tsugeshtelt fleysh un shtivl." Although Goldberg's bowdlerization refrained from removing the most explicit and disturbing content of the sentence—the claim that American soldiers exploited the poverty of the French peasants and preyed sexually on their women—the substitution of the inoffensive "beer" for *fleysh* (flesh, meat) allowed Goldberg to avoid a term with particularly provocative sexual connotations at that time. In 1927, Goldberg proclaimed in a pamphlet that "'the flesh' is a metaphor, signifying not only materiality, but sex."[67]

At another point in the novel, one of Pinski's dissolute characters refers, in Goldberg's translation, to her own "impure language" and "cynicism."[68] In Pinski's Yiddish, the character references her *umreyne reyd* and *pornografiye*.[69] Translating "cynicism" for *pornografiye* makes as little sense as translating "beer" for *fleysh*.[70] Yet within its context, this emendation seems reasonable enough: why attract the attention of the censors by printing the one word that so unambiguously signaled the objectionability of literary texts? If Pinski's character refers to her own speech as pornography, might the NYSSV convince a judge to second that opinion? Although certainly minor, these modifications suggest how the tense and complex atmosphere around the question of obscenity influenced Goldberg's translations.

Goldberg understood such revisions not as translatorial hubris, nor as censorship-in-translation, but as a literary professional's prerogative to exercise thoughtful judgment about the form and content of a work of art. He may or may not have felt obliged to introduce these specific changes if he had not felt Sumner peering over his shoulder, so to speak, but he defended his right as translator and editor to determine the appropriate measure of representational restraint for a specific audience and piece of writing. He may also have recognized that if he had written or edited in Yiddish, he would have had the freedom, like Asch and Pinski, to determine for himself how best to represent sex.

This quality endeared contemporary American Yiddish fiction to Goldberg. He understood that American Yiddish literature had no essential approach to the representation of sex, but he recognized that Yiddish authors, editors, and reviewers could freely decide whether the representation of sex in a particular work merited praise or criticism. In a global literary marketplace that usually privileged major world languages such as French and English, as Pascale Casanova has argued, and in which writers "who 'choose' to write in a dominant language are able, in effect, to take a shortcut on the road to literary status,"[71] this characteristic of Yiddish offered multilingual writers and critics in America one reason to prefer it over "dominant" English. Indeed, precisely the nondominance of Yiddish allowed it to escape from Comstockery, from the policing of literary standards by lawyers and judges, vice crusaders, and politicians.

In one of his Little Blue Books, *The Spirit of Yiddish Literature* (1925), Goldberg wrote enthusiastically of "Yiddish sex in art," especially in the works of American writers: "It may flow deep and strong, as in Pinski; it may seethe and burst all bonds of social restraint, as in Ash; it may turn harsh and brutal, as in Kobrin; it may frisk about and tease, as in Hirschbein; it may blossom as an exotic, as in Opatoshu; but always it is there."[72] What more could Goldberg ask from a literature than that it treat, with this wide range of approaches, what he considered "an eternal theme ... at the center of life"?

Is Yiddish Obscene?

The idea that Yiddish tolerates or encourages more obscenity than other languages must be understood as one of the "language stereotypes" Fishman described. Yiddish possesses neither more nor less of an obscene essence than any other language. Yet in particular historical situations, laws constrain the words and modes of representation that circulate in a particular language and its textual and media culture. Broadcasting the word "goatshit" (*bobkes*) in 1965—or, for that matter, in 2012—might have cost an American television station hundreds of thousands of dollars in fines, whereas broadcasting the word *bobkes* just as widely, then or now, generally raises no eyebrows.[73] This fact reveals nothing about the essential modesty or obscenity of English or Yiddish but reflects the distinct positions those languages have occupied in relation to American law. The freedom from censorship that Yiddish speakers and writers

enjoyed in America owed not to the First Amendment, nor to any essential im-
modesty in Jewish culture, but to the peculiar situation of a language spoken
by millions, with a wide range of periodicals and broadcast programs that remained largely outside of the state's control.

Isaac Goldberg understood this, as did other figures poised, like him, between Yiddish and English in American culture.[74] Steve Allen's audience, on
the other hand, may not have understood why exactly the editors of the *Forverts* could have freely praised Lenny Bruce or approvingly quoted his routines
in 1959, if they so desired, whereas English-language newspaper editors felt
restrained from doing so. But like many Americans, Allen's audience associated obscenity with Yiddish, and they laughed at Bruce's joke. Such associations
have themselves provided the grounds for linguistic, literary, and cultural creativity, like Bruce's, even while contributing to a narrowing vision of Yiddish
that others have lamented.[75] Goldberg's career offers a vivid reminder that the
perceptions of Yiddish by non-Yiddish-speaking Americans owed in large part
to the efforts of Yiddish translators and critics and the degree to which the interventions of those figures depended not only on their personalities and pec-
cadilloes but also on the structures and institutions of the literary and cultural
marketplace.

Notes

1. This performance is replayed in the 1972 documentary *Lenny Bruce without Tears*, directed by Fred Baker (New York: First Run Features, 2005), DVD.
2. In 1959, US Postmaster General Arthur Summerfield effectively defined obscenity when
   he characterized a novel as not fit for transmission by mail because of its "descriptions
   in minute detail of sexual acts" and "filthy, offensive and degrading words and terms."
   Charles Rembar, *The End of Obscenity: The Trials of Lady Chatterley, Tropic of Cancer, and
   Fanny Hill* (New York: Bantam Books, 1969), 114. A concise survey of Bruce's career can
   be found in Gerald Nachman's *Seriously Funny: The Rebel Comedians of the 1950s and 1960s*
   (New York: Backstage Books, 2004), 389-435. For analysis of Bruce's obscenity trials by
   one of his lawyers, see Edward De Grazia, *Girls Lean Back Everywhere: The Law of Obscenity
   and the Assault on Genius* (New York: Random House, 1992), 444-79.
3. Joshua A. Fishman, "Language Maintenance and Language Shift as a Field of Inquiry,"
   Linguistics 9 (1964): 32-70, 60.
4. Uriel Weinreich, *Languages in Contact: Findings and Problems* (New York: Linguistic Circle of New York, 1953), 95.
5. Jeffrey Shandler, *Adventures in Yiddishland: Postvernacular Language and Culture* (Berkeley: University of California Press, 2005), 167, 169. Though Bruce is famous for his
   Yinglishisms, according to Albert Goldman he "had come to Broadway a veritable
   goy, without the slightest genuine knowledge of Jewish life, customs, beliefs, values,
   words, or mannerisms," and picked up his Yiddish from other performers; Bruce thus
   sharply represents postvernacular Yiddish culture. Quoted in Nachman, *Seriously
   Funny*, 396.
6. Isaac Goldberg, "New York's Yiddish Writers," *The Bookman* 46, no. 6 (1918): 684-89, 687.
7. There were, of course, occasional exceptions that proved the rule; some of these will be
   discussed below. Also, Bruce's biographers love to point out that one of the Los Ange-

les policemen who arrested Bruce translated his Yiddish profanities for the court. The policeman, Sherman Block—who, incidentally, later became the first Jewish sheriff of Los Angeles County—supposedly reported that Bruce "uttered obscene and offensive words including a reference to his ex-wife as being the type that became upset when he entered the bathroom while she was 'fressing' the maid. The term 'fressing' is Yiddish and means 'eating.' 'To eat' a person is to commit an act of oral copulation upon that person. Throughout his narration suspect interjected the terms 'shmuck' and 'putz,' which are Yiddish, and mean 'penis.' Suspect also used the word 'shtup,' a Yiddish word meaning sexual intercourse when used in the context that the suspect used it." Albert Goldman, from the journalism of Lawrence Schiller, *Ladies and Gentlemen, Lenny Bruce!!* (New York: Random House, 1974), 388. Although the use of these Yiddish words may not have helped Bruce's case, he would not likely have been targeted by the police if he had avoided English taboo words. See also Ronald Collins, *The Trials of Lenny Bruce* (Naperville, IL: Sourcebooks, 2002), 100-101.

8. Allen Crandall, *Isaac Goldberg: An Appreciation* (Sterling, CO: author, 1934), 26.

9. Goldberg quoted in Crandall, *Isaac Goldberg*, 28.

10. On Lewisohn, see Ralph Melnick, *The Life and Work of Ludwig Lewisohn*, vol. 1 (Detroit: Wayne State University Press, 1998). For Goldberg's account of his attitudes toward Jewish identity, Judaism, and socialist universalism, see "Non Credo: A Fragment of Spiritual Autobiography," *The Reflex* 1, no. 1 (1927): 26-31.

11. "Thematic Outline of a Proposed Novel Titled *Intellectual*," 13, 14. Isaac Goldberg Papers, Manuscripts, and Archives Division, New York Public Library, box 4.

12. Crandall, *Isaac Goldberg*, 30.

13. David Pinski, *Oysgeklibene shriftn: Ershter Bukh fun fir Yortsendling* (Haifa, Israel: National Yiddish Book Center, 1963), 1:85 (my translation). Thanks to Ben Furnish for pointing me to this source. Pinski seems to have enjoyed teasing Goldberg about his distance from traditional Jewish learning in general, which makes his memory of Goldberg's ignorance of Yiddish a little suspect, perhaps; responding to a query regarding a phrase in a story Goldberg was translating, Pinski explained that "the words which Jochanan murmurs are from the 104th psalm. It is the very famous psalm *barkhi nafshi* you goi!—." David Pinski to Isaac Goldberg, February 13, 1919. Isaac Goldberg Papers, box 1.

14. Notebook 4, Isaac Goldberg Papers, box 6.

15. Lowell Brentano to Isaac Goldberg, April 3, 1919. Isaac Goldberg Papers, box 1.

16. Goldberg seems to have been only slightly better remembered by Latin Americanists than by Yiddishists; see Frederick C. H. Garcia, "Critic Turned Author: Isaac Goldberg," *Luso-Brazilian Review* 9, no. 1 (1972): 21-27.

17. On Haldeman-Julius, see Jonathan Freedman, *The Temple of Culture: Assimilation and Anti-Semitism in Literary Anglo-America* (New York: Oxford University Press, 2000), 170-75.

18. Paul S. Boyer, *Purity in Print: The Vice-Society Movement and Book Censorship in America* (New York: Charles Scribner's Sons, 1968), 78-79; Boyer's is among the most useful of the many studies of literary suppression in this period. As for Sumner's targeting of Jews, it is revealing that in the years 1919, 1920, 1922, and 1923, of 105 obscenity arrests listed in the NYSSV ledgers for which the religion of the arrestee is recorded, at least fifty-six of the arrestees were Jewish. See Jay A. Gertzman, *Bookleggers and Smuthounds: The Trade in Erotica, 1920-1940* (Philadelphia: University of Pennsylvania Press, 1998), 29.

19. Quoted in Boyer, *Purity in Print*, 111.

20. On this strain of American anti-Semitism, see Jonathan Freedman, *Klezmer America: Jewishness, Ethnicity, Modernity* (New York: Columbia University Press, 2008), 45-48. Two fascinating, disturbing examples of how this trope played out in American propaganda and literary texts are, respectively, Telemachus Timayensis, "The Jew Lecher," in *The*

American Jew (New York: Minerva, 1888), 81–87 and Theodore Dreiser, *The Hand of the Potter* (New York: Boni and Liveright, 1918).

21. Isaac Goldberg, *The Drama of Transition: Native and Exotic Playcraft* (Cincinnati: Stewart Kidd, 1922), 52–54.

22. See Crandall, *Isaac Goldberg*, 34.

23. Charles Angoff, *The Tone of the Twenties* (South Brunswick, NJ: A. S. Barnes, 1966), 199.

24. Crandall, *Isaac Goldberg*, 34–35.

25. Isaac Goldberg, "Index Librorum Prohibitorum," *Panorama* (May 1934), 5. For an example of just how far Goldberg would go to avoid spelling out the taboo words, see "Index Librorum Prohibitorum," *Panorama* (April 1934), 5, in which he refers to them as "the plain Anglo-Saxon words indicative of micturition, eructation, breaking of wind, and other functions of the body beautiful … [and] bald reference[s] to phallic phenomena associated with tumescence, not to speak of the vulgar metaphor for testicles."

26. It was not until *Cohen v. California*, 403 U.S. 15 (1971) that the US Supreme Court clarified that the word "fuck," in and of itself, cannot render a statement criminally obscene. Recent Supreme Court treatments of indecency, *FCC v. Fox Television Stations, Inc.*, 556 U.S. 502 (2009) and *FCC v. Fox Television Stations, Inc.*, No. 10-1293 (Sup. Ct., Argued Jan. 10, 2012), consider the Federal Communication Commission's authority to punish the use of the "F-word" and the "S-word" during live television broadcasts with enormous penalties.

27. Goldberg, "Index Librorum Prohibitorum," 5. See also Goldberg, "Smut and Pornography," *Panorama* (January 1934), 4.

28. Isaac Goldberg, *Sexarians* (New York: Panurge Press, 1931); Isaac Goldberg, *Madame Sex* (New York: Panurge Press, 1932).

29. For a brief sketch of Levine's background, see Gertzman, *Bookleggers and Smuthounds*, 26–28.

30. Goldberg, *Sexarians*.

31. Ibid.

32. Quoted in Gertzman, *Bookleggers and Smuthounds*, 66.

33. Goldberg was, of course, familiar with these novels; one of the stories in his first collection, "Twilight" (*Sexarians*, 161–77), concerns a passionate collector of literary erotica, including these banned novels, who is—reflecting Goldberg's own ambivalence to some degree—too timid to have sex with a woman. For Goldberg's jubilation at the release of *Ulysses* from censorship in 1934, see Isaac Goldberg, "The Odyssey of James Joyce: 'Ulysses,' after Twelve Years, Returns from Ostracism," *Panorama* (March 1934): 1.

34. Goldberg, *Sexarians*, 157–58.

35. Compare this passage in Goldberg with Lewisohn, *The Island Within* (New York: Harper and Brothers, 1928), 213, and Yezierska, *Salome of the Tenements* (Urbana: University of Illinois Press, 1995), 107.

36. For instance, the narrator describes her "breasts" in some detail: "If I do say so myself they're small and tight and much more like an apple than like an over-ripe grapefruit." Goldberg, *Madame Sex*, 60.

37. Goldberg, *Madame Sex*, 56.

38. See Goldberg's comment that although he has written stories about sex, he is "not interested in smut." Goldberg, "My Recent Books," *Contempo*, January 15, 1932, 2.

39. Isaac Goldberg, *The Drama of Transition*, 53.

40. Isaac Goldberg, *The New Immorality: A Little Dictionary of Unorthodox Opinion*, Little Blue Book No. 1481 (Girard, KS: Haldeman-Julius, 1929), 25. I would like to thank Thomas M. Whitehead of the Special Collections Department at Temple University Libraries for providing me with a copy of this source.

41. Stanley Fish offers an apposite rejection of free speech absolutism in the title essay in *There's No Such Thing as Free Speech, and It's a Good Thing, Too* (New York: Oxford University Press, 1994), 102–19.

42. Isaac Goldberg, "New York's Yiddish Writers," 687.

43. Yankev Glatshteyn, "'*Grobe reyd*' *in literatur*" ["'Coarse Speech' in Literature"], *Yidisher kempfer* (December 4, 1964), reprinted in *Prost un poshet: Literarishe esayen* (New York: Knight Printing, 1978), 37-43 (my translation).

44. Goldberg quotes Peretz's line and Maimonides's prohibition in "Five Hundred Years of Yiddish Poetry," *Menorah Journal* 5, no. 1 (1919): 43-44, reprinted in Goldberg's *Great Yiddish Poetry*, Little Blue Book No. 488 (Girard, KS: Haldeman-Julius, 1923), 9-10; also see one of Goldberg's sources, Leo Weiner's *The History of Yiddish Literature in the Nineteenth Century* (New York: Charles Scribner's Sons, 1899), 57.

45. Maimonides's statement appears in *Moreh nevukhim* 3:8; for a relevant Talmudic prohibition of obscene speech, specifically relating to the description of sexual intercourse, see *B. Shabbos* 33a.

46. On the censorship of Yiddish under the czar, see David Fishman, "The Politics of Yiddish in Tsarist Russia," in *From Ancient Israel to Modern Judaism: Intellect in Quest of Understanding: Essays in Honor of Marvin Fox*, ed. Jacob Neusner, Ernest S. Frerichs, and Nahum M. Sarna (Atlanta: Scholars Press, 1989), 4:155-71. For an overview of Yiddish censorship under the Soviets, see David Shneer, *Yiddish and the Creation of Soviet Jewish Culture, 1918-1930* (Cambridge: Cambridge University Press, 2004), 125-31. On the law of obscenity in Mandate Palestine and Israel, see Nitsa Ben-Ari, *Suppression of the Erotic in Modern Hebrew Literature* (Ottawa, Ontario: University of Ottawa Press, 2006).

47. American authorities suppressed Yiddish political or informational texts on a few occasions but never, to my knowledge, Yiddish belles lettres. On the suppression of Benzion Liber's *Dos geshlekhts lebn* [The Sexual Life] (New York: Rational Living, 1927) by the US Postal Service in 1917 and later editorial impositions by that office, see "This Book and the Post Office" in the fourth edition of that book and B. Liber, "Dr. Liber and the Post Office," *The New Republic* 20, no. 249 (1919): 61. For a recent appraisal of Liber's work, see Eli Lederhendler, "Guides for the Perplexed: Sex, Manners, and Mores for the Yiddish Reader in America," *Modern Judaism* 11, no. 3 (1991): 321-41. It is probably just a coincidence that Goldberg published a pamphlet, *The Sexual Life of Man, Woman, and Child: Notes on a Changing Valuation of Behavior*, Big Blue Book, No. B-46 (Girard, KS: Haldeman-Julius, 1927), the title of which seems to allude to Liber's book. A crucial American free speech case, *Abrams v. United States* 250 U.S. 616 (1919)—in which Justices Holmes and Brandeis took a crucial step toward the modern legal argument for free speech as a right guaranteed by the US Constitution—concerned anarchist pamphlets published in Yiddish and English. The Yiddish pamphlet was translated for the court, but it is unclear whether the texts would have been as vulnerable to prosecution if they had been distributed in Yiddish only. On this case generally, see Richard Polenberg, *Fighting Faiths: The Abrams Case, the Supreme Court, and Free Speech* (New York: Viking, 1987) and, especially, on the belated and questionable translation of the Yiddish leaflet, pp. 51-55.

48. Glatshteyn noted that "Isaac Meir Weissenberg, with his 'Dvorele,'"—a one-act play, reprinted in Weissenberg's *Gezamelte shriftn* (New York: Literarisher Farlag, 1919), 8-22—"described a moment of sexual unfaithfulness [*geshlekhtlekher umtreyheyt*]. But the way he did it would be ridiculed by the contemporary American writers as modesty and restraint [*tsnies un tsurikgehaltnkeyt*]." Glatshteyn, *Grobe reyd*, 39.

49. Contrary to the facile suggestion of the editors of *Jewish American Literature: A Norton Anthology* (New York: Norton, 2001) that "the First Amendment assured the [Yiddish] press freedom from censorship" (115), the freedom of expression enjoyed by Yiddish writers and publishers in America cannot be ascribed to the First Amendment, which did little to protect politically and sexually radical publications in English in the late nineteenth and early twentieth centuries.

50. On this debate, see Ruth Wisse, *A Little Love in Big Manhattan: Two Yiddish Poets* (Cambridge: Harvard University Press, 1988), 125-28; Julian Levinson, "Modernism from

Below: Moyshe-Leyb Halpern and the Situation of Yiddish Poetry," *Jewish Social Studies* 10, no. 3 (2004): 143-60; and Glatshteyn, *Grobe reyd*, 39-40. Goldberg briefly mentions Halpern and other contemporary Yiddish poets in "Five Hundred Years," 43, and *Great Yiddish Poetry*, 8-9.

51. Detailing the earliest controversies, Nina Warnke remarks that "despite the fervent passions on both sides, their fight did not create the public spectacle that the 1923 production would later do, because performance and debate were kept largely within the linguistic realm of Yiddish and the geographical confines of the immigrant quarters—that is, on the periphery of American society." "*Got fun nekome*: The 1907 Controversy over Art and Morality," in *Sholem Asch Reconsidered*, ed. Nanette Stahl (New Haven, CT: Beinecke Rare Book and Manuscript Library, 2004), 63-77, 64. In the best article to date on the 1923 trial, Harley Erdman emphasizes that the controversy resulted from a "conflict between American Jewish communities in that transitional ground between the margins and the mainstream" and was not simply a case in which Jews were the "free-speakers [pitted] against the moralistic forces of censorship and status quo." What bears mentioning, in response to Erdman, is that the controversy in 1907-1908 was *also* largely contained within the Jewish community. The difference was that in the earlier, Yiddish controversy, those Jews who wished to see the play censored could not convince the state authorities—the police and courts—to act as their enforcers, whereas when the play was produced in English, state authorities cooperated. Harley Erdman, "Jewish Anxiety in 'Days of Judgment': Community Conflict, Anti-Semitism, and the *God of Vengeance* Obscenity Case," *Theatre Survey* 40, no. 1 (1999): 51-74. Decades later, in London, the government deputized a rabbi to decide which Yiddish plays could and could not be performed, again ending a Jewish community controversy by giving state support to one of the contesting parties. See Leonard Prager, "The Censorship of Sholem Asch's *Got fun nekome*, London, 1946," in *Yiddish Theater: New Approaches*, ed. Joel Berkowitz (Oxford: Littman Library of Jewish Civilization, 2003), 175-87. Of course, the promotion of a rabbi to the position of literary arbiter is about as ridiculous as the promotion of police officer or postmaster to the same role.

52. Mencken to Goldberg, March 4 and March 30, 1935. Isaac Goldberg Papers, box 1. See L. Winocur, *Diccionario español-idisch e idisch-español* (Buenos Aires: Libreria G. Kaplansky, 1931), 174. *Drek* also appeared in Alexander Harkavy's *Yiddish-English Dictionary* (New York: Hebrew Publishing, 1910), 122, though it is not included in Uriel Weinreich's standard *Modern English-Yiddish/Yiddish-English Dictionary* (New York: YIVO, 1968).

53. Sholem Aleichem, *Shomers mishpet* (Berdichev, Ukraine: Yakov Sheptil, 1888); Sholem Aleichem, "The Judgment of Shomer, or the Jury Trial of All of Shomer's Novels," trans. Justin Cammy, in *Arguing the Modern Jewish Canon: Essays on Literature and Culture in Honor of Ruth R. Wisse*, ed. Justin Cammy, Dara Horn, Alyssa Quint, and Rachel Rubinstein (Cambridge: Harvard University Center for Jewish Studies, 2008), 129-85. See pp. 8, 23, 24 in the Yiddish and 135, 142, 143 in the English. For a recent study of these French trials, see Elizabeth Ladenson, *Dirt for Art's Sake: Books on Trial from Madame Bovary to Lolita* (Ithaca: Cornell University Press, 2006), 1-77.

54. On the influence of *Shomers mishpet* and responses to it, see Justin Cammy, "Judging *The Judgment of Shomer*: Jewish Literature versus Jewish Reading," in *Arguing the Modern Jewish Canon*, 85-127. Shomer himself emphasized that Sholem Aleichem's verdict had absolutely no formal authority over Shomer or Shomer's publishers: as he wrote in response to *Shomers mishpet*, "You empty critics can say what you want, scream in the streets that my novels are foolish, pass verdicts against me as much as your hearts desire. I will do what I do, I will continue to write fairy tales for my readers which, thank God, are helpful to thousands of people and will continue to be more useful than the prattling of your foolish critics" (103).

55. Lowell Brentano to Isaac Goldberg, April 2, 1920. Goldberg papers, box 1.

56. Goldberg provides a brief account in "Anomalies of Censorship," *Reflex* 1, no. 2 (1927): 56-57.

57. For the composition dates and Yiddish texts, see *Beruriah un andere dertseylungen* (Warsaw: Farlag Ch. Brzoza, 1938). In Shmuel Niger's thoughtful overview of Pinski's fiction in *Dertseylers un romanistn* (New York: CYCO, 1946), 1:282-319, these stories do not even earn a mention. The story about Rabbi Akiva, which, according to Goldberg, was most offensive to readers, simply elaborates narratives from traditional texts; for Pinski's sources, see *The Fathers According to Rabbi Nathan*, trans. Judah Goldin (New Haven: Yale University Press, 1955), 84, and *B. Kuddishin* 81a.

58. See Crandall, *Isaac Goldberg*, 97.

59. For responses to *Shomers mishpet* by Yiddish critics, see Cammy, "Judging *The Judgment of Shomer*."

60. Goldberg, "New York's Yiddish Writers," 687. Anthony Comstock founded the NYSSV. His name became synonymous with philistine and reactionary book censorship.

61. Isaac Goldberg, "Translator's Notes," in *Mottke the Vagabond* by Sholem Asch, trans. Isaac Goldberg (Boston: John W. Luce, 1917), v. Among the striking changes from the 1916 Yiddish book edition (New York: Forverts Association, 1916) that Goldberg imposes are his translation of "skin" for *kerper* (body) (English 161; Yiddish 168) and his regular nontranslation of *mahmzer* (bastard) (e.g., pp. 102, 150). For a brief allusion to Goldberg's translation as deficient, see Ben Siegel, *The Controversial Sholem Asch: An Introduction to His Fiction* (Bowling Green, OH: Bowling Green University Popular Press, 1976), 58, 244-45n37.

62. Isaac Goldberg Papers, box 1.

63. Goldberg, "New York's Yiddish Writers," 687.

64. For the publication details, see Niger, *Dertseylers un romanistn*, 1:307.

65. David Pinski, *Arnold Levenberg: Der tserisener mentsh* (Warsaw: Dovid Pinski Bikher Komite, 1938), 93; Pinski, *Arnold Levenberg*, trans. Isaac Goldberg (New York: Simon and Schuster, 1928), 77.

66. Pinski, *Arnold Levenberg*, 251-52; Yiddish version: p. 93.

67. Isaac Goldberg, *The Sexual Life*, 12.

68. Pinski, *Arnold Levenberg* (English), 78.

69. Pinski, *Arnold Levenberg* (Yiddish), 94.

70. It seems possible, if unlikely, that Goldberg deliberately echoed Sholem Aleichem's *Shomers mishpet*, in which Shomer's *nibl pe mit tsinizm* (obscenity and cynicism) is critiqued (Yiddish: 8, English: 135).

71. Pascale Casanova, *The World Republic of Letters*, trans. M. DeBevoise (Cambridge: Harvard University Press, 2004), 264.

72. Isaac Goldberg, *The Spirit of Yiddish Literature*, Little Blue Book No. 732 (Girard, KS: Haldeman-Julius, 1925), 42-43.

73. As Michael Wex points out, a classic episode of *The Dick Van Dyke Show*, originally aired on March 10, 1965, featured a hit song titled "Bupkis." See Michael Wex, *Born to Kvetch: Yiddish Language and Culture in All of Its Moods* (New York: St. Martin's Press, 2005), 159-60. On the continuing censorship of the "S-Word" on American television, see *FCC v. Fox* (2009).

74. Aviva Taubenfeld has shown that Abraham Cahan included taboo English words in the Yiddish version of his first novel, *Yankl der Yankee* (serialized from October 18, 1895 to January 31, 1896), that do not appear in the English version, *Yekl* (1896). Cahan replaced the words "hell" and "damn" (which he rendered phonetically as English words in the Yiddish text) with dashes in the English version. This move demonstrates Cahan's canniness; he knew what to expect from the two different linguistic markets. Aviva Taubenfeld, "'Only an "L"': Linguistic Borders and the Immigrant Author in Abraham Cahan's *Yekl* and *Yankl der Yankee*," in *Multilingual America: Transnationalism, Ethnicity, and the*

Languages of American Literature, ed. Werner Sollors (New York: New York University Press, 1998), 144-65, 157-58.

75. On the place of "Yiddish obscenities" in American popular culture, see Irving Howe, *World of Our Fathers,* with the assistance of Kenneth Libo (New York: Harcourt Brace Jovanovich, 1976), 556-73. As Howe phrases it, the use of Yiddish by comedians "often grat[ed] on the ears of those who really knew and loved the language" and "spoke of cultural loss, not return" (570).

THE IDEALIZED MOTHER AND HER DISCONTENTS

Performing Maternity in Yiddish Film Melodrama

ZEHAVIT STERN

Upon discovering that her daughter Annie had become an accomplice of her gangster husband and stood behind bars accused of murder and armed robbery, Mrs. Waldman, the virtuous matriarch in the film *A Jewish Mother*, cries out, "My Annie—a thief! My daughter—a murderer! Woe is me, what I have lived to see!" Immediately thereafter she pulls herself together and expresses her readiness to venture out into the world to rescue her child gone awry. Determined to overcome all obstacles and willing to sacrifice her store (her means of living), she exclaims, "I'll go save her, I'm a mother!" Her zealous response positions her as taking on the mythic prototype of the mother, willing to go to extremes to fulfill her God-given maternal role. Powerful, self-sacrificing, and endlessly devoted to her children, Mrs. Waldman stands as the ultimate mother figure in Yiddish film melodrama.

Yiddish cinema of the 1930s constructed and promoted this martyrized mother ideal alongside the figure of her wayward child, often her sexually matured, eligible daughter on the threshold of marriage and motherhood herself. Yet several psychological and sociological struggles play out around the seemingly perfect and admired character of the mother and her relationship to her nubile daughter. The mother's egotistical urges underlying the self-abnegating façade, the heavy personal price paid for fulfilling the social ideal, and the performative quality of motherhood masquerading as a force of nature comprise the tensions of Yiddish film melodrama as embodied in this maternal figure.

Together the Jewish mother and her nubile daughter define the range of femininity in Yiddish film of the 1930s, with its two axes of motherhood and sexuality. These two key protagonists form fundamental symbolic figures while also embodying two respective forms of affection: agape—divine, selfless love, and eros—romantic, physical love. They also serve to construct a set of binary oppositions: the mother as asexual and selfless, her daughter as sexual and egotistical. Whereas the daughter is naïve and easily seduced by her cunning suitor, the mother is wise, strong willed, and experienced. And whereas the daughter embodies potential promise and the danger of the outside, modern world, the mother represents stability and the comfort of the domestic sphere ("Angel in the House"[1]) and the traditional values of an idealized "old country." However, despite the mother's propensity for traditionalism, she, rather than her child, represents the true subversive figure of Yiddish film. The daughter's typical track remains unidirectional in these films. After fatefully following a deceitful suitor, she returns home to the mother and to the groom chosen by the parents (der basherter).[2] The mother's story, on the other hand, follows a more complex trajectory. A heroic narrative of suffering and self-sacrifice, it nevertheless contains certain referential and discursive practices, including actions, monologues, gestures, and songs that implicitly or explicitly undermine this ideal. Moreover, the narrative structure in which a sudden turn of the plot presumably undoes years of suffering might in itself work against the film's main message, at least for those viewers who doubt that the happy ending justifies previous hardship.

Cases of inverted identity between the mother and her daughter also challenge social norms of womanhood. More than any of the mother figures, when daughters fulfill a mother's role, these substitute mothers subvert the idealized view of womanhood and motherhood advocated even within Yiddish melodrama. By donning the maternal role these characters challenge the view of maternity as a natural given, and by later rebelling against their own choice they defy the hardships and futility of maternal self-sacrifice. They thus express countervoices that accompany and even subvert the films' main message.[3] Whereas Judith Butler suggests drag performance as a model for gender formation, what I call "maternal drag" reveals the constructed and performative quality of this most fundamental and archetypal female role.[4] Therefore, while reinforcing an essentialist view of sacrificial motherhood as an ideal and as a force of nature, Yiddish melodrama inadvertently undercuts this very mission.

Inspired in large part by the Yiddish theater, Yiddish film melodramas served as the bread and butter of the Yiddish film industry of the 1930s, the brief golden age of Yiddish cinema. Typically aimed at audiences on both sides of the Atlantic, the small Yiddish film industry consisted of several dozen films produced in the interwar period in Poland and the United States and to a lesser extent in Austria and the Soviet Union.[5]

Both American immigrants and eastern European city dwellers favored sentimental family melodrama, often drawing from the common experiences of rapid urbanization and secularization. In the Unites States, these films often dramatized the social and moral concerns of the immigrants, such as the potential threat of American capitalism, the tension between the experienced immigrant (the *alrightnik*) and the greenhorn, and the gap between Jewish eastern European parents and their American-born children. Not surprisingly, plots typically took the conservative side of the parents, as audiences consisted mainly of the immigrant generation.

Though shaped according to views and values embedded in its specific cultural background, Yiddish film melodrama modeled itself also on the conventions of the cross-cultural genre of the melodrama.[6] According to literary scholar Peter Brooks, this infamous dramatic form fulfills a social task in that it strives to articulate a moral universe. The Manichaean world of melodrama, with its villains and victims punished and rewarded accordingly in the inevitable happy ending, offers not just an enjoyable formula but also the very raison d'être of this dramatic genre.[7] Furthermore, this quintessentially modern mode emerged in the context of the French Revolution and its aftermath: "Melodrama . . . comes into being in a world where the traditional imperatives of truth and ethics have been violently thrown into question." We should, therefore, understand the melodramatic form as "a desperate effort to renew contact with the scattered ethical and psychic fragments of the Sacred through the representation of fallen reality, insisting that behind reality . . . there is a realm where large moral forces are operative."[8] Brooks's hypothesis opens up the possibility to view Yiddish melodrama not merely as cheap entertainment but also as fulfilling an important social function. One could argue that just as theatrical melodrama evolved out of the loss of pre-Enlightenment values and symbolic forms, so did Yiddish melodrama develop from an erosion of traditional values. Jewish audiences of the interwar period in both eastern Europe and the United States experienced, in different forms and at different rates, relatively rapid secularization and urbanization by the early twentieth century. For them, as for theater spectators in post-Enlightenment France, the melodramatic form provided a way to reconnect to a realm of pure values. This constitutes, in Brooks's terms, the process of "resacralization," the effort to renew contact with the sacred through the creation of a moralistic universe conceived in personal terms.[9]

The strong emphasis on the family in Yiddish film melodrama thus relates not only to its prominence in Jewish discourse but perhaps also to its erosion and the symbolic meanings ascribed to it in times of rapid social change. In films such as *Where Is My Child* (*Vu iz mayn kind*, United States, 1937), *A Letter to the Mother* (*A brivele der mamen*, Poland, 1938), and *A Jewish Mother* (*A yidishe mame*, United States, 1939), the Jewish mother's struggle to maintain the tradition and unity of the family indicates an effort to retain the wholeness of the Jewish people, particularly in the face of mass migration. Filmmakers often amplified the mother's typical characteristics, endless devotion to and knowledge of what is best for her children, through allusions and analogies to the divine order. The resacralized mother, almost never named with her own individual identity, thus serves as a symbol and means of social coherence and values, the main bearer of the religious world's lost aura in the quasisacred realm of the family.[10]

The mother, however, achieves her immense power with a steep price: she is nothing but a mother, a pure agape with no hint of eros. Yiddish films typically portrayed the Jewish father/husband as a good-for-nothing gambler (as in *Mamele*) or a *luftmentsh* (impractical, dreamy person) unable to support his family (as in *A Letter to the Mother*), forcing his wife to take care of him like a child and thus erasing the sexual and romantic aspects of the husband-wife relationship. Widowed mothers in Yiddish film have close ties with the men who come to their aid, such as the neighbor in *A Jewish Mother* or the man from HIAS (Hebrew Immigrant Aid Society) in *A Letter to the Mother*, but the films make it clear that these men are married, thereby excluding the option that their intimate relationships involve a sexual component. Paradoxically, the only romantic overtones of the pure mother figure appear in her relation to her son, who often becomes the main bearer of her fantasies, passions, and hopes.[11]

The mother's special connection to her children borders not only on the romantic (in the case of the son) but also on the mystical. In *A Letter to the Mother* the mother dreams that her son dies in battle on the very same night when this actually occurs. The mother in *Where Is My Child* is certain, against all odds, that she will find her lost son, unknown since infancy. By the end of the narrative, she indeed finds her son and recognizes him immediately, thanks to her infallible maternal instincts. Yet the world of the Yiddish melodrama presents this not as a miraculous or even surprising event. In the moral world of melodrama, the power of motherhood appears as a self-evident truth.

The plotline of a mother separated from her young child only to reunite with him or her years later comprises a recurring narrative in *Where Is My Child*, *Love and Sacrifice* (*Libe un Laydnshaft*, United States, 1936), and *A Letter to the Mother*. Such narratives exemplify the mythical aura surrounding the archetypical figure of the mother, especially in the "larger-than-life" reunion scenes. The coming together of mother and child is often accompanied by the mother's reminiscences of her child's babyhood. Infancy, the time of total dependence of the child on the mother, symbolizes in a romanticist fashion a "paradise lost"—for the mother rather than for the child. Their ultimate reunion therefore signifies "paradise regained," not only a happy ending but also a return to the natural and just order of things. *Where Is My Child* ends with a triumphant reunification scene explicitly endowed with a cosmic and theological significance. The very last words, a joint exclamation by mother and son, summarize this best: "There's a God!" (*S'iz do a got!*). *A Letter to the Mother* emphasizes the transcendental import of the reunion by its occurrence on the mother's deathbed. By reuniting with her son, the mother accomplishes her life's mission and may then rest in peace, melodrama's predictable happy ending.

The return of rebellious, sinful children represents another typical myth-forming scene in the moralistic world of Yiddish melodrama. In *A Jewish Mother* the return of the two "birds" to the "nest" (as the mother describes the reunion with her children) is composed in a hyperdramatic manner, including gestures, exclamations, and a flat, picture-like arrangement (a tableau).[12] As if taking a bow, the various characters end the movie by forming a line and declaring their final resolutions. The evil characters instantly repent and turn to the mother—and simultaneously to the camera—for forgiveness. The break with the cinematic principle of the unnoticeable camera (and the fourth wall convention of realistic theater) marks a departure from the realistic mode in favor of the emblematic and helps shape melodrama's ethical universe. Laying bare the godlike manner of her merciful verdict, the mother responds, "Forgiving is divine. Let there be peace" (*Fargebn iz getlekh, zol zayn sholem*). All then move to find their rightful place in the final form, creating the tableau.

Similarly to other melodramas, the tableau operates here as a visual summary of emotions and moral states.[13] The scene ends when the son, a cantor who tries to renounce his profession to become an opera singer, declares his renewed faithfulness to Jewish melodies and recites a few words from the *Kol Nidre* prayer. Drawing on various conventions and intertexts, from theatrical tableaux to Yom Kippur's fateful signification (also known as the Day of Judgment, *yom hadin*), this melodrama constructs a black-and-white moral code with sacred overtones, a universe in which obedience to the mother is tied up with loyalty to the Jewish people and its traditions, and her sovereignty is analogous to God's rule.

Mrs. Waldman, the protagonist of *A Jewish Mother*, indeed serves as a prime example of the godlike matriarch. Her figure thus sheds light on the archetypal construction of mothers as bearers of the aura in the resacralized world of Yiddish film melodrama. One such archetype formation consists of referring to her almost exclusively in terms of her maternal role. Her first name is never mentioned and even her last name, Mrs. Waldman, appears only rarely. To most viewers of the film she is probably simply "a mother," as she repeatedly refers to herself, often in the third person, in utterances such as, "One bird has already returned to the mother, to the nest" (*Eyn foygl iz shoyn tsurikgekumen tsu der mamen, tsu der nest*) and "A mother shouldn't hate her children" (*A mame tor nisht trogn keyn has far ire kinder*).

Addressing oneself (and others) by social role is a typical practice in the melodramatic genre and is found even in nineteenth-century French melodrama. Brooks interprets this "rhetoric that names pure states of being and relationship" as part of melodrama's "interplay of emblems" and the characters' struggle to assert selfhood in "a universe of pure signs."[14] What matters for the characters, as for the viewers, is not deciphering the signs, which remain conventional and therefore obvious, but discovering the character's understanding of her own ethical position in society.[15] Like her viewers, the protagonist of

A Jewish Mother perceives herself as the exemplary mother figure and associates the maternal role with total devotion to the children. Her ubiquitous moralistic declarations, such as, "A mother doesn't take into consideration that her child is bad. A mother always fulfills her duty" (*A mame rekhnet nisht mit dem, vos ir kind iz shlekht. A mame filt ale mol ir flikht*) are both descriptive and normative in an essentialist view that combines (somewhat paradoxically) the natural with the ethical duty.[16]

Fusing the concrete and the symbolic, Mrs. Waldman brings the idealized mother of Yiddish film to tragic or even grotesque extremes. When the virtuous mother discovers that her daughter Annie is imprisoned and that her son Solomon sold the store, her means of living and thereby saving Annie, she instantly becomes blind. When the good-hearted neighbor suggests calling the doctor, she refuses: "My children were the apple of my eye and if they are gone, I'm better off blind" (*Mayne kinder zaynen geven bay mir di oygn in kop, un ven zey zaynen nishto, iz beser az ikh bin blind, beser*). In this melodramatic exclamation the Jewish mother literalizes the Yiddish idiom *an oyg in kop* ("the apple of one's eye," literally "an eye in head") and turns it into a melodramatic event. By expressing her reaction through a common idiom, she ascribes symbolic meaning to her fate and points to broader implications of her view of maternity. By declining help she turns her misfortune into an ethical self-made choice and, more generally, marks an acceptance of the suffering brought on any mother by her children. The usage of blindness, the handicap associated most of all with tragedy, supplements the scene's mythopoetic force and the mother's archetypal position.[17]

Although archetypal, the mother figure in Yiddish film melodrama appears far from a flat, perfect, and harmonious figure. Rather, a mechanism of resacralization is at work, with its dual nature of solidity hiding fragility and alleged eternal truths camouflaging deep crises. Whereas children act as explicit agents of social transformation in Yiddish film melodrama, the ostensibly stable mother figure provides the real site of conflict, less on the level of plot than in the very construction of her exemplary archetype. On a deeper level, the constant need to proclaim her social position and obligations signifies an ongoing performance of motherhood.

Furthermore, countervoices accompany mother figures of popular Yiddish film melodrama in the form of declarations of bitterness disturbing the mother's devotion and self-sacrifice. This falls in line with the work of Christian Gledhill and Laura Mulvey, who have argued that melodrama consists of a polyphone of voices. Refining Brooks's moralistic reading, Gledhill and Mulvey have argued that melodrama, indeed as a drama of morality, never expresses a sole voice or a single ideology.[18] Even as it aims to construct a clear-cut distinction between good and evil, melodrama ultimately undermines itself to disclose ambivalence, contradictions, and conflicts within its ethical universe. Whether we understand these countervoices as challenging patriarchal ideology or believe they ultimately reinforce it, manifestations of discontent in Yiddish cinema give voice to the usually repressed frustrations of the mother figures.[19]

Occasionally, articulated bitter feelings in Yiddish melodrama culminate in hostility directed at children, as in the 1939 film *Kol Nidre*. When Jennie, the protagonist, informs her parents of her pregnancy and marriage to Jack, the gangster (rather than her chosen one, Joseph, the rabbi), her father banishes her from the house. "She has ruined our dreams! Dance, mother, your daughter has just gotten married. Instead of a wedding we have a funeral!" he cries out bitterly, referring to a custom in traditional Jewish society, according to which, upon conversion, marriage to a gentile, or, at times, even deserting the religious way of life, parents declare their child dead and perform the mourning ritual of a *shive*. Although Jack is Jewish, her parents perceive his criminal behavior and secretive marriage to Jennie severely enough to cause them to react so extremely: "You are dead for us, dead!" exclaims the father. Immediately thereafter he has a stroke. Later on, the heartbroken mother, who now takes care of her paralyzed husband, sings a self-mourning lament that goes even further than the father's angry and sarcastic "Dance, mother!" reaction.

> We gave away our lives
> did not allow ourselves much. . . .
> She did not listen to her parents,
> she ruined our sweetest dreams. . . .
>
> Should you have children? they only bring trouble. . . .
> Children are good when they are young.
> As soon as they grow up
> they leave their parents behind.
> Should you have children?
> They bring us trouble, they bring pain.
> Oy, what do you need children for?
> You should strangle them when they are young.[20]

The song allows a greater freedom of speech that is otherwise unspeakable, as it enables the mother to express radical disappointment and self-pity transformed into a generalized lamentation on the destiny of parents. A song performed earlier in the film conveys similarly aggressive feelings, as it narrates the story of a father who, while trying to save his daughter from being raped by a Cossack, kills both perpetrator and victim. Sung by Joseph, the rabbi and cantor, this supposedly historical tale, performed as a public ritual in front of the whole community, may be understood as an insinuated threat against Jennie—and more generally, against any other potentially rebellious daughter. It implies that if she refuses to obey her parents, they might inflict violence and even death on her. Expressing hostile feelings toward one's children and casting doubt on the very worthiness of parenthood undermine the exemplary parental (and typically maternal) position of Yiddish film melodrama. By allowing such voices, melodrama enables the audience to identify with the idealized mother as well as her discontents.

Both the lighthearted musical comedy *Mamele* (*Mommy* or *Little Mother*) and the tragic melodrama *Two Sisters* (*Tsvey shvester*), created in 1938 in Poland and the United States, respectively, hinge on an inverted plot structure in which the protagonist daughter, in the absence of the real mother, takes care of her family members. Although these two narratives start with the daughter proudly undertaking the maternal role and displaying total dedication, the performance of exemplary motherhood ultimately shatters. Significantly, this break occurs once each daughter wishes to proceed to what the Yiddish films, following traditional Jewish social mores, describe as the fulfillment of her potential as a young, attractive woman: marriage.

This plotline offers an intriguing mixture of the two archetypal feminine roles that correlate with the two main functions assigned to women in the patriarchal order: mother and wife. American and European melodramas frequently juxtapose these two seemingly complementary functions with a third figure: the seductive fallen woman.[21] In Yiddish melodrama, perhaps due to strong social and religious taboos, the overtly sexual woman rarely appears, and thus, only the nubile daughter and the mother remain to occupy the two poles embodying eros and agape.[22] Filmmakers depict the sexual, self-centered daughter as the antithesis of the self-sacrificing and asexual mother. The Jewish daughter, as eros, represents an object of sexual desire and male courting. Even though traditionalist rules on the diegetic and extradiegetic levels regulate manifestations of her sexuality, she nevertheless serves as a potential source of danger, as she aims to realize her emotional and sexual desires. Her counterimage, the mother, figures in Yiddish film as agape, a selfless love, with unconditional devotion to her children (though accompanied, as we have seen, by undercurrents of narcissistic self-absorption).[23] Whereas sexuality remains an important characteristic of the daughter, within the conservative sexual ethics that regulated Yiddish cinema, the virtuous mother's sexuality, as we have seen, must never surface.

Whenever the daughter fulfills the role of the mother, this subversion suggests not a middle position between the two poles of eros and agape but an uncomfortable oscillation between them. Indeed, the restlessness of this in-between figure helps to clarify the opposition between the two polarized female figures. What is only implied in the case of the Jewish mother by means of exclusion or repression becomes explicit in the figure of the substitute mother. Moreover, the young heroines' failure to function as both attractive women and maternal figures emphasizes the contradiction between mother and lover, agape and eros, in the dichotomous moral universe of Yiddish film.

The oscillation between the two female roles entails, however, different consequences in the two maternal drag films, and what signifies a tragic downfall in *Two Sisters* serves as a source of endless pranks in *Mamele*. As its title suggests, the comedy *Mamele* engages humorously with the heroine's double nature as daughter and mother, adult and child. Played by the legendary actress Molly Picon, the protagonist of this film fulfills the mother role so terrifically—working hard and exuding generosity and self-abnegation—that hardly anyone calls her Khave anymore, only Mamele, suggesting not only her changed role but also her lack of individual identity. When her sister suggests that she buy herself a dress, she exclaims, "What for? For the pots?" (*Tsu vos? Tsu di teplekh?*). Beautiful dresses, parties, and suitors, in her opinion, are only meant for her sisters—still eligible, nubile daughters—not her.

Following the maternal ideal of self-sacrifice, she goes as far as surrendering to the will of her sister, Bertha, who fancies Khave's secret beloved. At the last moment, however, she changes her mind and decides to keep her lover for herself. For the first time Khave makes a selfish move and thus puts an end to her maternal self-abnegation, marking the beginning of her inverted metamorphosis from mother to bride and then, according to the appropriate order, from daughter to bride. Yet in order to become a bride, she must learn how to stop being a mother. This passage includes phases of separation and liminality, to follow Arnold van Gennep's rite of passage theory. No longer a mother, not yet a wife, Khave must leave the house for a few days, even though it falls into chaos without her.[24] The final stage in her transformation forms the typical happy ending of Yiddish melodrama, the wedding scene, signifying Khave's incorporation into society in the rightful female role. Dressed in her wedding gown, Khave still fixes her brother's outfit and gives milk (heavily laced with symbolism) to the cat.[25] No longer an unstable and unnatural mother-before-wife, Khave finally proceeds in the prescribed direction, from bride to wife—and then presumably to mother.

Betty, the older sister in *Two Sisters*, meets a more tragic end, and the clash between the two feminine roles in her case is more disastrous. From the age of twelve, when her mother dies, Betty, following her mother's deathbed request, serves as mother to her younger sister, Sally. Hard working and altruistic, she finances Sally's nursing school education as well as the medical studies of her fiancé, Max. In the end, however, even Max sees her as a mother figure. "Mama Betty, you love me with the tenderness of a mother" (*Mame Betty, du host mikh lib mit der tsertlekhkeyt fun a mame*), says Max, and Betty responds, "A mother? That is what I am for Sally, a mother, a sister. For you, however, I want to be a lover and a wife" (*A mame? Dos bin ikh far Sally, a mame, a shvester. Far dir, ober, vil ikh zayn a gelibte un a vayb*).

Yet by the time Betty finally realizes that the role of mother and potential wife are mutually exclusive, Max and Sally have fallen in love. When Betty discovers their romance, she deserts her maternal self-sacrifice for a moment.

"Mame" Betty (Jennie Goldstein) and her younger sister Sally (Sylvia Dell). Courtesy of the National Center for Jewish Film.

Enumerating all that she has done for her sister throughout the years, she begs Sally to give up Max. But when a desperate Sally threatens to throw herself out the window, Betty returns to her maternal role. "Don't worry," she says, and she hugs her. Following a flashback showing the oath to her dying mother, she declares her final decision: "I will fulfill my duties as a mother" (*Ikh vel derfiln mayne flikhtn vi a mame*). Like *Mamele* (and numerous other Yiddish films) this film ends with a wedding scene, sadly, though, Sally's wedding and not Betty's. While everyone dances, in another room Betty stands alone in front of the dead mother's picture. "Mazel tov, Mother," she says in a voice filled with bitterness.[26] Trapped as the metamorphosized *Mamele*, Betty has no way out.

Once again the melodrama demonstrates the contradictory roles of mother and wife. Is Betty punished, as Jim Hoberman suggests, for the hubris of acting as a mother without giving birth?[27] Although this idea appealingly lends the melodrama the overtones of a Greek tragedy, the film's internal logic calls for a different interpretation. Hoberman is partly correct: Betty's deep internalization of the mother figure indeed prevents her from transforming into a lover. This, however, signifies virtue rather than vice. Within the melodrama's ethical world we need not look for an original sin or tragic flaw. Rather, Betty's suffering provides the ultimate proof of her high morals and true maternal nature.

Both Betty and Mamele perform maternal devotion in fervent extremes typical of converts. Motivated by a sense of obligation, they present motherhood as a noble task and an honorable duty. At the same time, these in-between figures also reveal the flip side of the selfless mother ideal, namely the high price paid by young women who give up their youth for the sake of the children under their care. In keeping with Gledhill's and Mulvey's view of melodrama, these young liminal figures articulate the countervoices that undermine the very maternal ideal they embody and promote.

Both of these devout performers of motherhood break down at some point and express their frustration. They do so not within the framework of a song, as the biological mother figures do, but in long speeches in which they list all they have given up for their nonbiological children: "I was your servant, your cook . . . I gave my heart, my labor" (*Ikh bin geven ayer dinst, ayer kokh, gegebn mayn harts, mayn horevanye*), cries Mamele to her ungrateful sisters. Similarly, upon discovering the romance between Max and Sally, Betty screams desperately at her sister: "You owe me, you owe me a lot . . . you took away from me the best parts of my life, my labor, my youngest, most beautiful years. . . . My whole life was you and you and you" (*Du kumst mir, du kumst mir zeyer a sakh. . . . Du host mir tsugenumen di greste teyl fun mayn lebn, mayn horevanye, mayne yingste shenste yorn. . . . Mayn gants lebn iz geven du un du un du*). And when it comes to Max she reclaims all that she has given him through the years. Pointing at his office, furniture, and medical equipment, she cries out, "This is mine, and this is mine—everything here is mine!" (*Dos iz mayns, dos iz mayns, alts do iz mayns!*)

A significant difference exists, however, between Khave and Betty. Khave's attack on her sister's ungratefulness leads her to recognize that she ought to prioritize her own interests, and she consequently opts for her lover, leaving her siblings and domestic duties behind. Betty's outbursts of protest, on the other hand, result in an instant return to the maternal role. Following her attack on Sally, she hugs and comforts her, reassuring Sally of her maternal support. The assault on Max, who confesses his love to Betty's sister, ends with Betty declaring, "As long as it is one of us, as long as it's not a stranger" (*Abi an eygene, abi nisht keyn fremde*). Here, as in the "mazel tov" addressed to her mother's picture in the final scene, the apparent irony in Betty's tone marks her bitter acceptance of her fate and the suppression of her hurt, anger, and demand for due gratitude. Betty constantly oscillates between self-interested rebel and her selfless mission, yet she ultimately moves toward acceptance accompanied by sarcasm. This ironic tone enables her to simultaneously hold the two contradictory positions as text and its conflicting subtext.

Alternating between the two opposing feminine roles, Khave and Betty air their frustrations in ways that move beyond a protest against children's ingratitude, a common trope in other maternal melodramas. By emphasizing the mother's sacrifice, they reveal the underlying egotism behind the ostensibly altruistic act of self-sacrifice and bring to light the repressed personal needs of both biological and cross-dressed mothers. Their outbursts constitute the melodrama's countervoices, calling attention to the suffering that may occur when a woman follows the self-abnegating mother ideal.

By performing a maternal role and embodying the mother ideal, Khave and Betty also disclose its contingency. Ultimately, the maternal drag plots reveal the performative quality of motherhood as advocated in Yiddish film.[28] Along with Khave's maternal dress (a source of pride for her and scorn for others), she and Betty adopt a whole set of gestures and acts. In two scenes in *Mamele*, the protagonist wears her mother's dress. When people laugh at this "cross-dressing," a common reaction to gender drag, too, she replies, "If it was good enough for mother—it's good for me too." Motivated to prove themselves as legitimate mothers, these female characters imitate familiar, cinematic maternal figures, models that suggest an essentialized vision of natural motherhood. The maternal performance, however, runs against this naturalization process and indicates a break with the supposedly inherent connection between biological motherhood and the sacrificial model of maternal behavior.

Betty's and Khave's performance of motherhood may thus operate similarly to drag performance in Judith Butler's theory of gender, in which she argues that "in imitating gender, drag implicitly reveals the imitative structure of gender itself—as well as its contingency."[29] Gender attributes, she contends, "are not expressive but performative" and "constitute the identity they are said to express or reveal." Butler emphasizes the "three contingent dimensions of significant corporality: anatomical sex, gender identity, and gender," none of which necessitates the other.[30]

A triangulated dynamic operates in the case of the daughter-to-mother "cross-dressing" plots in which, in addition to the anatomical fact (young girls) and the maternal role performed, we have a third element: the young women's identities separate from their female-designated biological roles. This third dimension provides a site for Betty's and Khave's struggles as they align themselves first with one side then with the other, producing a comical effect in the case of Khave and a heartbreaking one in the case of Betty. Whereas Mamele ultimately reveals herself as the nubile daughter, proved by the concluding scene of her wedding, Betty remains first and foremost a mother, with Sally's wedding—once again the final scene—providing the ultimate proof. Betty's maternal nature is reaffirmed not only by her failure to marry but also by the noble gesture of giving her blessing to Sally and dancing at her wedding—an ironic take on the trope of the ultimate Jewish maternal joy.

The mother's picture on the wall, a trope found both in *Mamele* and in *Two Sisters*, paradoxically reminds viewers of the original figure behind the maternal imitation, with the young "mother" as a mere substitute. It also denotes the real mother as the moral authority behind these maternal drag acts, since in both cases the oath given to her on her deathbed obligates the daughter to take care of her siblings. At the same time, however, the real mother only appears in a photograph, a mere representation. The iconic nature of the references to the mother, as a lifeless framed image on the wall or as a traumatic, constantly replayed and reiterated deathbed scene (the scene opens the film *Two Sisters* and then reappears twice as Betty's flashbacks), emphasizes the symbolic quality of the dead mother, who embodies the exalted maternal ideal as well as the social demand to follow it. The imitated original thus reveals itself to be only a copy, an emblem. The imitation of motherhood, like the imitation of gender in Butler's theory, relies not on an original but rather always on an imitation of another imitation. The "Ur-mother" is inevitably a dead one: a memory, an internalized code of behavior, an ideal impossible to live up to. The godlike mother is ultimately a Moloch, to whom young women's desires must be surrendered. The maternal drag elucidates the meaning of motherhood in the ethical universe of Yiddish film, which ultimately entails partaking in an endless chain of ritualized sacrifice.

Why has sacrifice become such a key characteristic of these Jewish mothers? The question remains open, yet the answer relates not only to a stereotypical female position but also to the specific social function of mothers in Yiddish melodrama. In the resacralized world of Yiddish film melodrama the mythologized mother symbolizes strength, continuity, and unity and serves as metonymy for the Jewish family and for the Jewish people as a whole. Suffering and martyrdom may have even strengthened the connection between these powerful symbols. Whereas the father, typically symbolizing the religious tradition, shrinks to a helpless, tragic figure or disappears completely, the mother, who offers morality based on loyalty and sacrifice, flourishes. Yet countervoices often accompany the elevated ideal of martyrdom and self-abnegation, pointing to the personal price these female figures had to pay. The mother-to-daughter drag performances allow, on some level, an expression of these views and even present the mother ideal as an ethical choice rather than a natural given. Above all, the maternal performance opens up a space of masquerade—tragic or playful— on the margins of the grand maternal myth, or as a subversive companion to it.

Notes

1. The term "Angel in the House" refers to the Victorian image of the ideal wife or woman, devoted and submissive to her husband, self-sacrificing and chaste. It originated in the title of a popular poem by Coventry Patmore, published in 1854, in which he presents his angel-wife as a model for all women.

2. Three notable examples of this plotline are *A Letter to the Mother*, *Kol Nidre* (United States, 1939), and *A Jewish Mother*.

3. In using the term "countervoices" I follow neo-Marxian film scholars, who view domestic melodrama as a bourgeois form that reconfirms patriarchal and capitalist ideology while nevertheless pinpointing countervoices that contradict this moral lesson. For further discussion of countervoices and their social significance, see notes 18 and 19.

4. Judith Butler, *Gender Trouble: Feminism and the Subversion of Identity* (New York: Routledge, 2006), 186-92.

5. In fact, some of the most successful films, such as Joseph Green's movies, including *Yidl with the Fiddle* (*Yidl mitn fidl*, Poland, 1936), *Mamele* (Poland, 1938), and *A Letter to the Mother* (*A brivele der mamen*, Poland, 1939), were coproduced and filmed in Poland but involved American stars (such as Molly Picon and Miriam Kressyn), themes, and writers. Notwithstanding the highly different circumstances in these two centers of Yiddish culture, as far as Yiddish film is concerned American and European Yiddish speakers constituted a common audience. Moreover, from more than one hundred Yiddish films produced in this era, only about thirty are available today. Most Yiddish films produced in Poland were destroyed during the Second World War. This article, focusing on films rather than on their documentation, therefore suffers from a certain American bias. I do, however, believe that the strong interconnections between the Polish and the American Yiddish film industries along with the common experiences of secularization and urbanization allow us to discuss these films in the common context of interwar Yiddish culture.

6. For an overview of melodrama studies, see Christine Gledhill, "The Melodramatic Field: An Investigation," in *Home Is Where the Heart Is: Studies in Melodrama and the Woman's Film*, ed. Christine Gledhill (London: British Film Institute, 1987), 5-43, and other articles in this useful anthology. Another excellent collection of articles on the topic is Marcia Landy, ed., *Imitations of Life: A Reader of Film and Television Melodrama* (Detroit: Wayne State University Press, 1991). In addition, Peter Brooks's *The Melodramatic Imagination* (New Haven: Yale University Press, 1980) depicts key aspects of this ubiquitous form and has served as the foundation for a whole school of social interpretations of the melodrama that focuses on its ideological function.

7. Brooks, *Melodramatic Imagination*, 20.

8. Ibid., 15.

9. Ibid., 16.

10. The father is typically a tragic figure in Yiddish film and embodies the decline of the religious world and the parents' lost authority rather than any struggle or hope for a regained wholeness. See, for example, the father figures in *A Jewish Mother, Kol Nidre, A Letter to the Mother*, and *Tevye* (United States, 1939), based on Sholem Aleichem's novel *Gants Tevye der milkhiker*, vol. 5 of *Ale verk fun Sholem-Aleichem* (Vilnius: B. Kletskin, 1925).

11. Melodrama tends to present a son rather than a daughter in narratives of separation and belated reunion, and Yiddish film melodrama is no exception to this rule. In these narratives, the adult son reappears in the mother's world as a masculine, powerful savior. Ann Kaplan relates the emphasis on the mother-son relationship in Hollywood melodramas to the threat that an intense mother-daughter alliance (or any strong female bonding) poses to the patriarchal system. See E. Ann Kaplan, "Mothering, Feminism and Representation: The Maternal Melodrama and the Woman's Film 1910-1940," in Gledhill, *Home Is Where the Heart Is*, 113-38. This, however, can only be a partial explanation. In my view, the emphasis on cross-gendered parental relations (mother-son and father-daughter) in melodrama relates to the excessive dramatization of intense love, similar to the oedipal drama.

12. The tableau, a flat grouping of motionless figures, is a theatrical technique that played a central role in classical theatrical melodrama, used especially at the end of scenes and acts. See Brooks, *Melodramatic Imagination*, 61-62. In addition to the scene from *A Jewish Mother* discussed above, tableau-like scenes appear at the end of *Where Is My Child* and in *Love and Sacrifice* when the father informs his children of their mother's alleged death.

13. Brooks, *Melodramatic Imagination*, 62.

14. Ibid., 52-55.

15. Ibid.

16. Not only the mother but also other characters in Yiddish film melodrama refer to the social role as a sign of due or unfulfilled moral obligation. Thus, the regretful bad mother in *A Jewish Mother* addresses the good one: "Mrs. Waldman, I'm also a mother," and her husband complains to an unidentified audience, "Did you hear how a child speaks to a father?" Similarly, the father in *Kol Nidre* scolds his daughter: "A Jewish daughter must obey her parents."

17. According to Brooks, of all handicaps the loss of speech is the most typical of melodramatic form, which deals primarily with the problem of expression. Blindness, on the other hand, belongs above all to tragedy, a genre that deals mainly with knowledge and insight. See Brooks, *Melodramatic Imagination*, 58.

18. For Mulvey's and Gledhill's discussions of the melodrama, see Laura Mulvey, *Visual and Other Pleasures* (Bloomington: Indiana University Press, 1989) and Gledhill, "Melodramatic Field," 5-43. Mulvey criticizes neo-Marxist scholars for creating a distinction between the sophisticated director who implants subversive messages in the film and enlightened readers (e.g., film critics of the 1970s) who decode those messages, on the one hand, and the original naïve audiences of the 1950s, on the other hand. They argue that countervoices constituted inevitable companions to melodrama's hegemonic ideology and were understood by their original audiences. There is a significant gender aspect to this criticism, as the directors and scholars of women's melodrama are mostly men, whereas audiences are presumably mostly women. For neo-Marxian melodrama theory, see Thomas Elsaesser, "Tales of Sound and Fury: Observations on the Family Melodrama," *Imitations of Life*, 68-91; Geoffrey Nowell-Smith, "Minnelli and Melodrama," *Imitations of Life*, 267-74; and Robert Lang, *American Film Melodrama: Griffith, Vidor, Minnelli* (Princeton: Princeton University Press, 1989).

19. Although the existence of countervoices in melodrama seems to be a matter of general agreement among Brooksian scholars, the political significance of these undercurrents is under much debate. Following neo-Marxian film critics, Christian Gledhill argues that melodrama's typical features, such as exaggeration and extreme emotionality, offer an opposition to bourgeois realism and are ultimately subversive in nature. Laura Mulvey, on the other hand, emphasizes the repressed quality of the expressions of resistance found in the melodramatic form and ultimately views the genre as a safety valve, which reinforces rather than challenges the dominant ideology. Ann Kaplan holds a middle position between these two views. Although she believes that presenting female passivity and suffering works to reinforce the patriarchal order, she also claims that these plots and figures give expression to the fears and fantasies of women. In her view, even the most unsophisticated melodrama holds a certain subversive potential. See Kaplan, "Mothering, Feminism and Representation," 113-37.

20. *Undzer lebn avekgegebn*
keyn sakh nit fargint far zikh aleyn ...
Zi hot tsu di tate-mame nisht tsugehert,
zi hot di ziste khaloymes undzere tseshtert ...

Darf men hobn kinder? zey brengen tsores aleyn. ...
Kinder zaynen gut ven zey zaynen kleyn.
Vaksn zey nor oys,
lozn zey zeyer tate-mame aleyn.
Darf men hobn kinder?
Zey brengen undz tsores, zey brengen leyd.
Oy tsu vos darf men hobn kinder?
Dershtikn darf men zey kleynerheyt.

21. The fallen woman, a popular trope of Victorian literature and of theatrical melodrama, has also been a common figure in American and European films from their beginning. See, for example, *The Downward Path* (United States, 1900), *The Road to Ruin* (United States, 1928), and *Pandora's Box* (Germany, 1927). See Lea Jacobs, "Censorship and the Fallen Woman Cycle," in Gledhill, *Home Is Where the Heart Is*, 100–112; Christian Viviani, "Who Is without Sin: The Maternal Melodrama in American Film, 1930–1939," *Imitations of Life*, 168–82; and Russell Campbell, *Marked Women: Prostitutes and Prostitution in the Cinema* (Madison: University of Wisconsin Press, 2006).

22. A rare exception is the figure of the bad mother in *A Jewish Mother*, one of the "mothers of today" (*Hayntike mames*), the film's alternative title. Although not exactly a fallen or adulterous woman, the narrative views this sexy woman, who smokes, gambles, and goes out every night with her daughter, as directly responsible for her son's turn to organized crime.

23. In my opinion, the Christian tradition, in which agape has come to signify the kind of love God feels toward humanity, renders the term even more appropriately for the godlike portrayal of the mother in Yiddish film.

24. The terms "separation" and "liminality" are two of the central phases in Arnold van Gennep's famous rite of passage theory, the third being "incorporation." Khave's transition from mother to daughter operates similarly to a rite of passage, and her leaving the house constitutes an essential step toward her incorporation as a bride and then a wife. See Arnold van Gennep, *The Rites of Passage*, trans. Monika B. Vizedom and Gabrielle L. Caffe (Chicago: Chicago University Press, 1961).

25. Young women in early twentieth-century film often displayed maternal qualities before becoming literal mothers. A famous example is the scene in D. W. Griffith's *The Mothering Heart* in which a young woman picks up puppies and embraces them, which is aptly accompanied by the intertitle "The Mothering Spirit."

26. J. Hoberman claims that Betty speaks "without apparent irony," a view I find hard to accept. J. Hoberman, *Bridge of Light: Yiddish Film between Two Worlds* (New York: The Museum of Modern Art and Schocken Books, 1991), 215. In my view, Betty's irony is essential to the scene, as Betty finally expresses her protest against the social ideal she has tried so hard to fulfill.

27. Ibid.

28. Butler argues that the gendered body is performative, suggesting "that it has no ontological status apart from the various acts which constitute its reality" (Butler, *Gender Trouble*, 185). In this sense any behavior of a cinematic figure is, of course, performative. Yet a double faceted performance of maternity occurs in the daughter-to-mother plot both on the level of the fictional character and within the fictional world. The diegetic maternal performance sheds light on the naturalized mother image prevalent in Yiddish melodrama. Like drag performance, they also offer possibilities within what seems like a closed and deterministic ethical universe.

29. Butler, *Gender Trouble*, 187.

30. Ibid., 192. Consider Butler's challenging question: What is the truth of the drag performer, the masculine body or the feminine performance, sometimes perceived as correlating to a notion of an inner self or an identity? Butler's triangle of dimensions opens up a variety of possibilities and disrupts the common binaries of nature/culture, inner/outer, true/constructed, imitation/original.

RUSSIAN MILITIA SINGING IN YIDDISH

Jewish Nostalgia in Soviet and Post-Soviet Popular Culture

ANNA SHTERNSHIS

In 1997, Iosif Davidovich Kobzon (born in 1937) announced that he would say good-bye to his public by performing "a final concert" in 300 cities of the former Soviet Union. Kobzon, who likes to call himself the "Russian Frank Sinatra," was at the time one of the most popular and significant singers in the Soviet Union. The smallest concert hall on that tour hosted 2,000 viewers, the largest, 4,000. All shows sold out completely. The repertoire included Soviet oldies: Komsomol (Young Communist League) marches, romantic ballads about socialist construction, and songs from popular Soviet movies. The audience consisted largely of viewers born in or before the 1960s. For many, saying good-bye to Kobzon also meant saying good-bye to the Soviet Union.

Toward the end of each four-hour show, Kobzon invited a previously unknown group of male singers, called "Turetsky's Choir," to join him on stage. Backed by Turetsky's spectacularly arranged vocal octet and a full symphony orchestra, Kobzon sang the Yiddish folk classic "Tum balalaika." Written by an unknown author in the late 1930s, the song describes a "love that does not burn" and a "heart that cries without tears" and is a longtime favorite of Russian Jews. In perfect Yiddish, combined with Kobzon's patriotic voice, the song sounded to the audience who grew up in the Soviet Union as if it had arrived from a parallel universe. Next, he sang "A yiddishe mamma," a Yiddish hit written in the 1920s by Americans Jack Yellin and Lew Pollack. Kobzon sang it in both Russian and Yiddish, and he dedicated it to his own deceased mother. The audience, in awe after "Tum balalaika," was now in tears. Even for non-Jews, singing in Yiddish meant that Kobzon revealed an inner, sacred part of his soul and his most intimate memories. Performing Soviet patriotic music triggered nostalgia for the collective past, whereas performing Yiddish music made longing for one's youth personal.

Kobzon's performance of Yiddish songs at a nostalgic concert raises a number of questions. Performers rarely sang in Yiddish publicly in the Soviet Union between 1952 and 1987, thus "Tum balalaika" was usually heard behind closed doors, rather than in public concerts. Yet, Kobzon, who could not perform publicly in Yiddish before the late 1980s, chose to include Yiddish music in his concert devoted to nostalgia for Soviet culture. How did he pull it off? How can Soviet nostalgia include nostalgia for Yiddish in post-Soviet Russia, where many Jews have not spoken Yiddish in three generations? In the course of this essay, I will argue that one of the secrets of Kobzon's success is the fact that most of the audience associated Yiddish both with Soviet and pre-Soviet times. I will also demonstrate that Kobzon's Jewishness has more to do with Soviet nostalgia that developed in the post-Soviet times than with the revival of Jewish culture per se.

Svetlana Boym observed that outbursts of nostalgia (literally, "longing for home," or "longing for the past, often in idealized form") arise commonly after revolutions. A few years after the fall of the USSR, Russians began to view the Soviet age as the "golden age" of stability, strength, and normalcy.[1] In fact, most contemporary studies on post-Soviet nostalgia arrive to us from the field of business research, where researchers have discovered that Russian consumers are more likely to buy a product if its advertising uses Soviet symbols and allusions. More than 75 percent of Russian-produced products today are advertised using the sentiments and allegories related to the Soviet past.[2] Thus, the most successful Russian cultural products exploit the Soviet past and cleverly reinterpret it for Russian audiences.[3] Post-Soviet nostalgia developed in relation not only to the past but also to the place, as millions of former Soviet citizens moved to other countries at the end of the twentieth century.[4]

The development of nostalgia for the Soviet past and the Soviet space coincided with the largest migration of east European Jews to the Western Hemisphere since the turn of the twentieth century. It also coincided with the emergence of a new Russian-Jewish identity, which combined post-Soviet interest in religion, Soviet understanding of Jewish ethnicity, and the international nature of the Russian-Jewish experience. Although numerous studies have addressed this phenomenon, usually labeled "revival," scholars have yet to investigate Jewish participation in popular culture or specific Jewish motifs in this culture. Yet, the combination of longing for the Soviet past with post-Soviet possibilities created unique cultural products that combine languages and genres and appeal to large Jewish audiences across the globe.

During the 1920s and 1930s, the Soviet government conducted an intensive antireligious campaign, which attacked, among other religions, Judaism and successfully destroyed the meaningful connection between Judaism and Jewish identity among a majority of Soviet Jews. The Soviet government used the Yiddish language as a vernacular for delivering those ideas to the targeted audience; therefore, a large network of Yiddish schools, theaters, and cultural organizations developed in the early years after the Russian Revolution. By the end of the 1930s, when most Soviet Jews acquired Soviet values and largely abandoned the Yiddish language as their primary vernacular, this network was reduced to a few theaters that continued to stage plays and concerts of Yiddish songs. From the late 1940s until the 1980s, such public performances of Yiddish became very rare. However, affinity for Yiddish music remained quite strong, even among assimilated Jews. Moreover, this "soft spot for Yiddish music" often served as the sole manifestation of their ethnic identity. Throughout the Soviet period, some artists of Jewish origin managed to keep Yiddish music alive for the general audience by putting Russian lyrics to the tunes of Yiddish folksongs.[5]

In this essay, I will argue that the choice of Yiddish during the post-Soviet period development of Jewish culture is not accidental. I will demonstrate that because Yiddish alludes to Soviet and pre-Soviet periods equally effectively, it became the perfect vernacular for expressing nostalgia for the Soviet and pre-Soviet past among Jews. I propose to apply theoretical studies of nostalgia to the analysis of works by Jewish singers of three generations: Leonid Utesov (1895–1982), Iosif Kobzon (born 1937), and Mikhail Turetsky (born 1967). All three musicians and performers incorporated Jewish culture into their productions. Utesov did not live to see the collapse of the Soviet Union, Turetsky started his career only after the Soviet Union had ended, and Kobzon performed during both the Soviet and post-Soviet periods. All three enjoyed national recognition and tremendous popularity and received numerous awards, and all three have an obvious and unhidden Jewish agenda. To all three, nostalgia represents a fundamental concept that made and continues to make their performances appealing to the Russian-Jewish audiences. Although the works of these artists have never been studied together before, their use of the Yiddish language, and their allusions to it, constitutes a central aspect of post–Soviet-Jewish culture and identification.

Nostalgia: A Theoretical Concept

From the Middle Ages until the end of the nineteenth century, physicians understood nostalgia as a serious disease that needed treatment. For example, in the seventeenth century, a group of Swiss merchants was unable to conduct businesses in Italy and the south of France due to their homesickness. Johannes Hofer, the Swiss medical student who coined the term "nostalgia" in 1688, defined it as longing not just for a place but also for an experience.[6] Expanding Hofer's definition, Boym writes, "Modern nostalgia is a mourning for the impossibility of mythical return, the loss of an unchanged world with clear borders and values."[7] When eighteenth-century doctors failed to find a cure for nostalgia, they turned to poets and artists, who, in turn, after their own failures, focused on the quest for the old home itself. In the twentieth century, with its massive migrations, wars, and revolutions, almost every individual experienced nostalgia for many times and places.

One useful study proposed the following four-way classification of nostalgic experience: personal nostalgia, interpersonal nostalgia, cultural nostalgia, and virtual nostalgia.[8] "Personal nostalgia" refers to nostalgia based on a direct experience, which in turn comprises the subject of most psychological and sociological analysis.[9] "Interpersonal nostalgia" includes nostalgic experience based on interpersonal communication concerning the memories of others and combines the other person's experiences with the individual's own interaction with that person.[10] "Cultural nostalgia" involves direct experience in which members of the group share a similar response that helps to create cultural identity.[11] The fourth class, "virtual nostalgia," is the nostalgic equivalent of virtual reality, with the emotion based on shared indirect experience.

Many marketing uses of nostalgia emphasize cultural or virtual nostalgia due to the commonality of responses across members of a group or market segment.[12] Similarly, several works of popular culture, such as songs, often enjoy positive reception and popularity when they symbolize virtual nostalgia. In the early 1990s, first Russian historians and then filmmakers, writers, and composers began to express nostalgia for the early postrevolution period in the form of awe to the culture killed by the Russian Revolution and prohibited during Soviet times. At the same time, nostalgia for the prerevolutionary period also developed. It served as compensation of sorts, although the generation who lived through the revolutionary changes was almost entirely gone by the time the Soviets allowed that form of nostalgia to become public. Thus, nostalgic longing combined prerevolutionary idyllic life with the revolutionary past in an unlikely symbiosis, barely understood by outsiders, but making complete sense to Russians. For example, it can combine pre-Soviet images of heroic Jewish fighters and Hebrew biblical prophets with an awe for an honest Soviet grandfather from the *shtetl*, possibly a former commissar or a devoted communist (who probably fought against Hebrew and Jewish education).

In the 1920s and 1930s, millions of Jews left small and medium-sized towns in the former Pale of Settlement in Ukraine and Byelorussia and moved to Moscow, Leningrad, Kiev, and Minsk, where they took advantage of the unprecedented opportunities for economic and social mobility in exchange for abandoning their religious, and sometimes cultural, identities. These new Soviet-Jewish urban residents enthused over building their new lives, yet fondly remembered their parents and grandparents and their lives in the *shtetl*. However, they certainly chose not to pass on the values they considered "*shtetl*-like," such as Jewish religious observances, to their own children. Indeed for many the very word *shtetl*, a small town, the most widespread place of residence of Soviet Jews before the 1920s, quickly became a negative term associated with the lack of proper culture. Nevertheless, in memoirs and oral history interviews, a sustained longing for a "simple" *shtetl* life persists.[13]

In post-Soviet-Jewish culture, this longing translated into popular forms of Yiddish music. Many prominent Russian-Jewish artists used Yiddish, images of the *shtetl*, and references to the society that discouraged active Jewish observance to express their nostalgia for both Soviet and pre-Soviet periods. Those musicians and artists include Iosif Kobzon, Faina Ranevskaya, Mikhail Turetski, Yakov Yavne, Efim Aleksandrov, Ian Tabachnik, and, not least, Leonid Utesov.

Leonid Utesov and Soviet-Jewish Nostalgia

A central figure in Soviet popular culture, Leonid Utesov was born in Odessa, Ukraine in 1895 under the name Lazar Vaisbein. He changed his name to Leonid Utesov in 1912, when he began to perform in a local theater. Arguably the most accomplished Soviet performer from the 1920s until the 1970s, he first performed as a circus artist and then as a variety singer; he then founded the first Soviet jazz band in 1929. During the war, Utesov performed at the Soviet-German front and became famous for singing songs designed to remind soldiers of home, peace, and their families. After the war, Utesov's band was spared from the fate of many other Jewish artists thanks to a personal recommendation from Joseph Stalin, who loved Utesov's music. Utesov died at the age of eighty-seven in 1982, rich, famous, and loved by the Soviet public. He wrote three books of memoirs, starred in a handful of films, and gave thousands of concerts, and in Odessa a monument stands to commemorate his life.[14] Today, his songs have all been reissued on CDs and pirated on the Internet. Post-Soviets of all generations respect his work, including those born long after his death and after the collapse of the Soviet Union.

Although his songs are recognized by all, Jewish melodies form the basis of many of Utesov's early works, namely "Bublichki," "Uncle Elia," and "Samovar and Masha," which originate in Yiddish melodies yet include no specifically Jewish lyrics or content. Jewish audiences recognized these tunes with delight, and for many years considered these songs original "Jewish songs."[15] A native speaker of Yiddish, Utesov never publicly performed in this language, and only one recording of his "Jewish Rhapsody" exists, which he sings in Yiddish as well as Russian and Ukrainian. Moreover, rumors circulated throughout the 1960s that Utesov performed in Yiddish during a concert, but they remain unsubstantiated.[16] But even in Russian versions, these songs helped the audience to express their longing for the old way of life, their parents, their youth, and their childhood.

Though never officially (or even unofficially) acknowledged as a part of Jewish culture, the songs played a similar role for the Soviet-Jewish audience as did the Yiddish "Mayn shtetele belz" for their American counterparts in the 1920s[17]—they reminded them of their youth but did not encourage them to go back to the old country. Although most of the non-Jewish audience was not aware of the Jewish roots of these songs, the Jewish public certainly appreciated it, though subtly. Both his Russian and his more Jewishly oriented elements serve as vehicles for Soviet longing in the post-Soviet era among artists and the public alike, yet here we only focus on his Jewish bent and how it continues to influence post-Soviet-Jewish culture.

In fact, the last thing Utesov himself wanted was for audiences to see him as a Jewish singer or, worse, a *shtetl* singer. Though he recorded Russian songs based on Yiddish tunes early in his career, by the 1960s he resisted acknowledging them as part of his contribution to Soviet culture. In the 1960s, he publicly called these songs "vulgar" and of "low taste."[18] In a TV program called "In Utesov's Living Room," Rostislav Piatt (1908-1989), a renowned Soviet actor and filmmaker, staged a humorous dialogue with Utesov in which the musician explained that his "old repertoire" was not "the real Utesov"; rather Soviet patriotic songs, such as "Field, My Little Field" (1934) and "Two Comrades Served in One Regiment" (1936; Soviet-Jewish authors wrote the lyrics and tunes for many of these songs, but Yiddish music did not form their basis), comprised his true repertoire, for which he felt great pride.[19]

By the 1960s, these songs—written in the 1930s and 1940s—expressed nostalgia for a bygone era, albeit for military youth and war culture rather than for the prewar *shtetl*. However, no matter how Utesov felt about it, his Jewish audience refused to remember him solely as a patriotic singer.[20] During the post-Soviet period, his early songs were the first to be rereleased in a wave of increased interest in early Soviet culture. Even in the first decade of the twenty-first century, his works remain popular among various age groups as part of a virtual nostalgia for the early Soviet optimism, ideology, and spirit as expressed in popular culture.

Mikhail Krutikov has described the "token Jew" phenomenon in Soviet-Jewish literature, both in Yiddish and in Russian, where one can always find a figure of the "authentic Jew"—an old man from the *shtetl* who speaks Yiddish and has the eternal wisdom to help characters find universal truths.[21] Among artists, even Jewish artists, of the post-Soviet period, Utesov has become a sort of token Jew who serves, more than any other, as a focal point for creations of work that appeal to the public's virtual nostalgia for one's own ethnic culture, as opposed to the culture brought to them from the outside. Utesov, an artist still loved and remembered by the Russian public, managed to achieve the impossible: to remain a general Soviet artist but also a Jewish artist.

"Bublichki," Kupite "Bublichki": From Soviet New Economic Policy Cabaret to Post-Soviet Nostalgic Extravaganza

Russian composer Grigorii Bogomazov wrote the song "Bublichki," a song about bagels, in the 1920s, with lyrics by Yakov Davidov (known under his pen name as Yakov Yadov). With Utesov's performance, it quickly became a national hit. The song tells the story of a young girl who sells bagels in the streets of Odessa during the New Economic Policy (NEP) period from 1921 to 1927, when limited free trade was allowed by the revolutionary Russian government:

> *Noch' nadvigaetsia, mil'ton rugaetsia,*
> *Vse pogruzhaetsia v nochnuui mglu*
> *A ia zabytaia, triap'em prikrytaia,*
> *I neumytaia odna bredu . . .*
> *Kupite bubliki, gonite rubliki,*
> *Gonite rubliki vy mne skorei!*
> *I v noch' nenastnuiu menia neschastnuiu*
> *Torgovku chastnuiu ty pozhalei!*

> The night is approaching, the cop is yelling,
> Everything is sinking into night.
> I am forgotten, covered with rugs
> Not washed, I walk alone . . .
> Buy bagels, give me rubles,
> Give me rubles faster!
> This bad-weathered night, you have
> Pity on a miserable private seller!

Versions of this song spread across the country and abroad, and in 1927 a Yiddish version also appeared. The American artist Pesach Burstein (1896-1986) performed the song in Yiddish to American audience in 1929. By 1939, legendary swing and jazz bandleader Benny Goodman (1909-1986) recorded his version of the song, also in Yiddish, and after that it entered the repertoire of most Yiddish performers in North America. In the summer of 1959, the American duo Claire and Mina Bagelman, known as the Barry Sisters, performed this song in Yiddish to a large Moscow audience. Their Americanized, swing-inspired version of the song charmed the audience, who instantly recognized the 1920s hit, even though it had not been publicly performed in decades. Following that performance, homemade and smuggled recordings of the song made their way into Jewish homes.

A reissued version of Utesov's original appeared only following the collapse of the USSR. In 1989, the publishing house Melodiya (Melody) issued a cleaned-up version in CD format, and the song became one of the symbols of virtual nostalgia for generations of Russians who did not experience the 1920s firsthand yet learned about the era from books, movies, and stories.[22]

The Turetsky Choir (or Media Art Group) version of "Bublichki" proved one of the most popular adaptations of the song. The all-male band started in 1989 as a Jewish liturgical choir with the goal of promoting Jewish classical music.

Initially sponsored by the US-based Joint Distribution Committee, it became commercially independent in 1997 following its tour with Iosif Kobzon. The band then reduced the number of Yiddish and Hebrew tunes in its repertoire and began to include Soviet nostalgic music and light interpretations of opera in order to reach wider audiences. The Turetsky Choir has performed at stadiums and large theaters across Russia, Europe, and North America and remains among the most popular bands in post-Soviet Russia. Audiences vary in age, socioeconomic background, and ethnicity. With the exception of its founder Mikhail Turetsky, all current band members are ethnically non-Jewish. The choir performs Jewish songs as well as French, Spanish, Roma, Georgian, Ukrainian, and Latvian songs. They perform in foreign tongues as a tribute to these other cultures. However, in the case of Yiddish, Turetsky has acknowledged in several interviews that he continued to include Jewish music in his repertoire as a tribute to his deceased parents and grandparents, who understood Yiddish, not as a tribute to the Jewish contribution to civilization.[23]

Songs with Jewish content, such as "Bublichki," and other Yiddish and Hebrew tunes constitute about 10 percent of the repertoire of the Turetsky Choir. However, in order "not to antagonize" the Russian public, during concerts Turetsky does not call the language of these songs "Jewish."[24] He refers to Hebrew as the "language of prophets" and to Yiddish as the "language of my grandparents."[25] Thus, the audience conceivably associates Yiddish immediately with a private, family past, as opposed to a biblical or other, more global Jewish identity. "Bublichki" comprises an integral part of this intimate culture.

The choir's version of "Bublichki" is profoundly different from Utesov's subtle, intimate, and slightly ironic performance. Moreover, in the original there is no hint of the ethnicity of the main protagonist, "the private seller," yet Turetsky makes "Bublichki" into an elaborate large-scale overtly Jewish production complete with lights, dancing, complicated arrangements, and a combination of Russian and Yiddish languages. In addition, the choreography of the song includes elements taken from Yiddish dances that Turetsky learned from Mariya Kotliarova (1918–2008) and other surviving actors of the Moscow State Yiddish Theater (which functioned from 1918–1949). Finally, the Turetsky Choir stage performance of "Bublichki" includes a projection of black-and-white archival films depicting Jewish life in prewar Poland. In other words, though most of the song is performed in Russian, the musicians are unapologetic about including Jewish elements in this work, and Yiddish constitutes approximately 20 percent of the lyrics. Turetsky's stage performance of "Bublichki" exemplifies a clever use of both nostalgias: for the Soviet past and for Jewish collective identity, commonly expressed as resistance to the Soviet system.

The song appeals to different feelings and audiences, all with nostalgic overtones. First, it portrays the NEP era, when the Soviet government allowed limited free trade. The "woman private seller," who tries her best to earn some money and stands somewhere in between private enterprise and begging, refers to the instability, uncertainty, and risk of the NEP era. Anyone who lived through Sovietism knows that "the cop is yelling" meant nothing good for the protagonist and would lead to her arrest. Yet, her cheerfulness and persistence, and her desire to survive despite any circumstances, appealed to the audience, who probably listened to the song behind closed doors, either on old record players or performed by a friend with a guitar.

For a Jewish listener, the song also carried an ethnic meaning. Its reference to Odessa and to private business suggests the Jewish identity of the character (because Jews were heavily involved in private business during the NEP, and Odessa has long been known as the center for Russian-Jewish urban culture), and the Yiddish version helped to strengthen the Jewish nature of the song. Interestingly, for an American reader, the reference to *bublichkes* (bagels) did not make the song "Jewish," as bagels were not known as Jewish food in the Soviet Union or post-Soviet Russia.[26]

During the early post-Soviet period, and even during the final years of the USSR, the song became surprisingly relevant to daily life. In an atmosphere of emerging private enterprise and the shutdown of the socialist economy, private vendors, beggars, and street performers mushroomed in urban areas. The fear of militiamen, the uncertainty of business, and the bravery of the protagonist combined with her humiliation spoke not just to the nostalgic but also to the contemporary experiences of many engineers-turned-street-traders. The second factor that contributed to the return of the popularity of this song in the 1990s was, as mentioned, its allure of the semiforbidden during the Soviet period. Finally, in the twenty-first century, the performance of the song may be interpreted in the context of direct nostalgia for the 1990s, which appears widespread among the generation born in the 1970s and early 1980s.[27]

The lyrics alone, however, would not bring the song back into megapopularity. What was sufficient for a restaurant in the 1920s or an apartment concert in the 1970s did not fit the public culture of the 1990s, including the profiles of Jewish musical bands, such as the Turetsky Choir, who wanted to establish themselves as both educators and entertainers for the Jewish public while also providing entertainment for wider audiences. Professional musicians adapted the song but arranged it as a contemporary piece, albeit in retro style. The creators of "Bublichki" would never have dreamed of seeing this song performed in eight-level harmony accompanied by a sophisticated multimedia presentation.

For Turetsky, "Bublichki" and other Yiddish songs were intended to evoke sentiments similar to those that old Soviet songs evoked. These songs evoke a nostalgic gaze directed at different aspects of the Soviet period, even if ambivalent—a common characteristic of nostalgia. For example, attitudes toward the family often suggest ambivalent nostalgia in which the oppressive-

ness of the Soviet system and public culture led to a situation in which family stood as an island of independence and free thinking, the place to express
doubts and laugh at the inconsistencies and absurdities of the regime.[28] For
Jews, family culture included telling stories about Israel and jokes praising Jewish wit and wisdom, as well as quietly singing Yiddish songs. As the Soviet system ended, the role of the family as a safe haven began to diminish, and families found themselves dispersed around the globe. During post-Soviet times,
Yiddish music served as a nostalgic reminder of the times when home and
family life acted as a kind of protest against the official culture. It also refers
to the time when the entire family lived in the same city, or at least the same
country. The Turetsky Choir plays on that sentiment in building their Jewish
repertoire, which also includes a few Yiddish oldies such as "Papirosn" by Herman Yablokoff (with similar lyrics to "Bublichki"), "Tum balalaika," and "Bay
mir bistu sheyn." All these Yiddish songs come from the repertoire of the Barry
Sisters, and all have proved extremely popular among post-Soviet Jews.

Nevertheless, the Turetsky Choir's inclusion of Hebrew and Yiddish language pieces is not required for commercial success, at least for their concerts
in Russia. In addition, the choir performs all Yiddish and Hebrew songs bilin-
gually, in a similar style to "Bublichki," and a Russian translation always pre-
cedes the Yiddish or Hebrew text. However, numerous English-, French-, Ital-
ian-, and Spanish-language songs in the choir's repertoire are only performed
in their original, with a Russian synopsis provided orally as an introduction.
Turetsky explains the translation of these pieces in detail: "I explain Hebrew
so that the audience learns about Jewish religion, Jews get educated, non-Jews
find out that Jews do not put blood in matzo. I explain Yiddish because Yiddish
songs are not only part of a Jewish culture. They are also part of Russian culture.
The Russian audience should know that."[29]

The choir, then, not only demystifies Jewish culture for the Russian audience but also appropriates it as part of Russian culture and Russian nostalgia.
Similarly, the artists position themselves as part of Jewish culture, as well as
Russian culture, and "Bublichki" exemplifies this process. The song is popular among non-Jews and therefore provides universal appeal to both Jewish
and non-Jewish members of the audience. Including the Yiddish fragment
also allows the musicians to demonstrate, however subtly, that Jewish culture
belongs within Russian culture and to its nostalgic past, in addition to a specifically Jewish nostalgic past. The artists feel compelled to do this because expressing nostalgia for the Russian past asserts their claim to Russia as their
homeland.[30]

It is important for Turetsky to present the common appeal of the Yiddish
songs in order to emphasize the universalism of their content as well as the
Jewish contribution to Russian life, a widespread claim in Russian-Jewish identity politics. Performing Russian songs, which are often written by Jews, signi-

fies the participation of Jews in creating Soviet culture and asserts, once again, the integral role that Jews played and continue to play in Russian culture.

Post-Soviet Nostalgia for the Soviet Times

The amazing success of the Turetsky Choir is largely owed to the Jewish singer Iosif Kobzon—a megastar of Soviet culture and a favorite singer of Leonid Brezhnev. Kobzon's voice was heard in every Soviet household in the 1960s through the 1980s through radio and television. Unlike Utesov, who presented "socialism with a human face," Kobzon represented the official voice of the system, with its marches, slogans, and rituals. He performed at parades, official television concerts, and the nation's largest ceremonies. Giant orchestras accompanied his singing, including the most prestigious Orchestra of the Soviet Army. From the 1960s through the 1980s, his official repertoire never included any Jewish tunes or anything that even remotely hinted at his origins.[31] Yet, unlike Utesov, he never changed his name but kept it as the Jewish-sounding Iosif Davidovich Kobzon. The oppressive Soviet system did not seem to limit its arguably most successful Soviet singer.

Kobzon rose to an even more visible and prominent place immediately following the collapse of the Soviet system. Elected as a deputy in the Russian Duma, he also was one of the first stars of a caliber high enough to actively involve himself with the newly opened allowance of public Jewish culture. In 1998, he led the cantorial service at the Moscow Choral Synagogue. He also began to include Yiddish songs in his repertoire and performed them in his good-bye tour, discussed at the outset of this essay.

Kobzon's performance style of Yiddish music radically differs from that of Turetsky. Kobzon aims not to educate or to demystify Jewish culture, nor to bring art to the masses. Designed to serve as a purely nostalgic pleasure, Kobzon's Russian-language songs derive from the official Soviet repertoire, and as they are performed in the twenty-first century, they remind the audience of the Soviet past. The appearance of Yiddish songs in his repertoire brings out a different kind of nostalgia. In Kobzon's performance, "Tum balalaika" combines the intimacy of a favorite family tune performed around the table with the pathos of a Soviet march, probably heard in the same room from the TV set in the background. In his contemporary performances Kobzon does not make an effort to "Judaicize" himself by learning Yiddish intonations or Hebrew pronunciation. Rather, he sovietizes Jewish culture. For example, in his performance of "Hava nagila,"[32] the 100-member Orchestra of the Ministry of Internal Affairs accompanied Kobzon. All members, of course, were dressed in militia uniforms. The audience, which consisted of Jews and non-Jews, loved the show and demanded an encore.[33] The success of the show might be attributed to its absolute surrealism for anyone familiar with Soviet treatment of

Jewish culture. The performance triggers laughter as a response to the shock of observing new content in a familiar form, similarly to why one finds parodies funny.[34] Kobzon does not parody "Hava nagila," the most popular Jewish tune, in the former Soviet space. However, he performs it with the militia, the very group of people who would have persecuted him or anyone else for singing this song in the 1970s. Thus, essentially, he ridicules, however subtly, the militia itself by publicly making them perform in Hebrew and broadcasting the performance on national television.

The success of Kobzon as a performer of Jewish music may also be explained by the fact that such shows seem to uncover "the real Kobzon," with his Jewish soul hiding under the surface of the Soviet singer. It may seem to the viewers that behind the façade of the official, impersonal, and largely irrelevant marches lived a Jew, just like themselves, who practiced subtle Jewishness at home but not outside of it. Such sentiments trigger Soviet nostalgia as well. When Kobzon performs in Yiddish or Hebrew, he is subtly indicating that Soviet nostalgia may now include nostalgia for a time when being Jewish posed several difficulties. Similarly, "Bublichki" reminds the audience of the Soviet regime as well as their resistance against it.

Post–Soviet-Yiddish Nostalgia in the Rest of the World

In addition to playing on nostalgic feelings, both Kobzon and the Turetsky Choir emphasize that in today's Russia, the public performance of Jewish music is acceptable in central concert halls and even on central television. Kobzon, an iconic symbol himself, singing the Jewish hit "Hava nagila" on a mainstream stage represents a powerful image associated with the freedom of being Jewish in contemporary Russia. Turetsky Choir's performances of Yiddish songs on Russian television allude to this same new reality.[35]

Other genres of Yiddish music exist in Russia as well. They include intellectual, underground, bard-based, and klezmer-inspired music—with none immune to nostalgic sentiments. Wildly popular among intellectuals, musician Psoy Korolenko, for example, has a show based on Yiddish translations of Soviet patriotic songs. Igor Belyi created a program of Russian-Jewish and Yiddish songs, stylized as "bard" performances, and some klezmer bands find Yiddish songs from the early communist period and include them in their repertoire. All of these developments tie into and emerge from feelings of nostalgia: nostalgia for underground culture, ridicule of nostalgia for Soviet times, and even commemoration of nostalgic culture. Utesov's work and his popularity derived largely from nostalgic pleasures even during the Soviet period. Similarly, Turetsky and Kobzon pull on the same heartstrings and exist within the mainstream as widely known performers of contemporary Jewish music that sell out multithousand-seat concerts. Most importantly, the nostalgic overtones in their work are not hidden or subtle but rather are emphasized in order to sell tickets to their shows. Although Soviet-Jewish nostalgia uses Yiddish, it is no different from general post-Soviet nostalgia.

Soviet-Jewish nostalgia, however, is stunningly different from Jewish nostalgia everywhere else in the world. When Turetsky and Kobzon go on tours in the United States and Europe, they perform Yiddish music exclusively for Russian-speaking Jewish audiences. This suggests an even more striking phenomenon because their repertoire includes not intellectual Russian symphonic music but popular Yiddish hits performed at a professional level, something that North American Russian émigré and local English-speaking audiences crave. So why is there no English heard among the audience members at Turetsky Choir performances in the United States?

One reason stems from the fact that concert organizers do not advertise their tours in the mainstream press but rather only among Russian-speaking outlets. Thus, Western critics and viewers have limited access to such performances. In addition, American Klezmer musicians dismiss Turetsky Choir's innovative take on Jewish music, with its highly stylized performances, as vulgar partially because they see these performances as redundant versions of the American productions of the 1960s and therefore as not worthy of attention.[36] In addition, American klezmer today is more interested in innovation than in preserving the tradition.[37] The repertoire of mainstream post-Soviet performers contains no hidden jewels of Russian-Jewish culture but focuses, rather, on preserving the popular culture of the past. However, although such a repertoire explains the lack of interest from critics, it does not explain the lack of interest from the audience. The reason for this phenomenon might stem from the ways in which Jewish communities in the United States, Canada, and western Europe see Russian Jews, including Russian-Jewish performers, as possible carriers of authentic or innovative or even simply relevant Jewish culture. The lay opinion goes like this: how can Jews forbidden to practice Judaism or not literate in Jewish languages and traditions perform authentic Jewish music? In other words, how can post-Soviet Jews teach, as opposed to being taught? The lay opinion, as is often the case, is only partially wrong.

Audiences in the United States and Canada expect Yiddish music to evoke nostalgia as much for Yiddish culture as for some vision of bygone America. The Barry Sisters present "Bublichki" as a version of "The American Dream": the song features a poor and miserable seller waiting for a miracle—perhaps for a rich limo to pass by and take her to the wonderful world of opportunities, the *goldene medine* where everything is possible. Yet, the Turetsky Choir uses Yiddish songs for the expression of Soviet nostalgia, which is not only irrelevant but also incomprehensible to any audience but those born in the Soviet Union. Nevertheless, nostalgia for the American Jewish past and the Soviet period associated with anti-Semitism is musically expressed with the same handful of Yiddish songs, some of which were written in America and some in Russia.

Indeed, despite the great differences in Jewish cultural tastes between the United States and the USSR, from the 1930s to the 1980s both American and Russian-Jewish audiences listened to many of the same songs: "Tum balalaika," "Bay mir bistu sheyn," "A yiddishe mamma," "Papirosn," and a few others. Whereas in the United States artists performed these songs for small and large audiences and recorded them for commercial sales, in the Soviet Union the songs survived mainly in the context of home performances. In terms of public culture, their fate remained complicated. After public Soviet-Yiddish culture was suppressed in the late 1940s, Leonid Utesov managed to preserve some of the revolutionary Yiddish music by performing Soviet songs with their tunes. Although Utesov rejected many of these earlier works in the 1960s, he continued to perform the Soviet wartime songs set to Yiddish tunes. In the 1970s, these songs became part of general Soviet war nostalgia, and only a handful of Jews could recognize the tunes. However, the image of Utesov himself as a Soviet-Jewish performer became a focal point for nostalgia for the Soviet-Jewish culture that developed in the 1990s. When the public performance of Jewish music became allowed again, many Jewish artists chose precisely the songs from Utesov's repertoire to build their Yiddish repertoire.

In the late 1990s, many people, including musicians, combined nostalgia for Soviet culture with the nostalgia for the Jewish culture destroyed by the Soviet regime. The Turetsky Choir still performs Yiddish songs that survived despite their lack of public appearances. In their sophisticated performances, they affirm Yiddish songs as part of the Soviet experience and insist on including them in the Soviet past. Finally, Iosif Kobzon takes this idea to a new level and simply performs Jewish favorites as Soviet songs, even using a military orchestra, a symbol for Russian statehood, to accompany him in his performances. Kobzon performs his understanding of Yiddish culture, which combines his longing for both his deceased Yiddish-speaking mother and the Soviet system that suppressed the speaking of Yiddish. The popularity of Kobzon and Turetsky Choir signifies that many members of the post-Soviet-Jewish public share this sentiment. Paradoxically, then, the Yiddish language has become the best possible medium for expressing nostalgia for the country partially responsible for its worldwide disappearance as an everyday vernacular.

Notes

1. Svetlana Boym, *The Future of Nostalgia* (New York: Basic Books, 2002), xvi.
2. Susan Holak, Alexei V. Matveev, and William J. Havlena, "Nostalgia in Post-Socialist Russia: Exploring Applications to Advertising Strategies," *Journal of Business Research* 60, no. 6 (2007): 649–55.
3. Serguei Alex Oushakine, "'We're Nostalgic but We're Not Crazy': Retrofitting the Past in Russia," *Russian Review* 66, no. 3 (2007): 451–82.

4. Sheila Fitzpatrick, "The Soviet Union in the Twenty-First Century," *Journal of European Studies* 37, no. 1 (2007): 51-71.

5. For more on Yiddish and its treatment during the Soviet period, see Zvi Gitelman, *Century of Ambivalence* (Bloomington: Indiana University Press, 2002), 88-113 and David Sheer, *Yiddish and the Creation of Soviet Jewish Culture, 1918-1930* (New York: Cambridge University Press, 2004).

6. Johannes Hofer, *Dissertatio medica de nostalgia, oder Heimwehe* (Basel, Switzerland, 1688), translated in *The Bulletin of the Institute of the History of Medicine* 7 (1934): 379-91.

7. Boym, *Future of Nostalgia*, 8.

8. William Havlena and Susan Holak, "Exploring Nostalgia Imagery Using Consumer Collages," in *Advances in Consumer Research*, ed. K. P. Corfman and J. Lynch (Provo, UT: Association for Consumer Research, 1996), 23:35-42.

9. Fred Davis, *Yearning for Yesterday: A Sociology of Nostalgia* (New York: The Free Press, 1979).

10. Ibid.

11. Susan Holak and William Havlena, "Nostalgia: an Exploratory Study of Themes and Emotions in the Nostalgic Experience," in *Advances in Consumer Research*, ed. John F. Sherry, Jr. and Brian Sternthal (Provo, UT: Association for Consumer Research, 1992), 19:380-87; M. Wallendorf and E. J. Arnould, "'We Gather Today': Consumption Rituals of Thanksgiving Day," *Journal of Consumer Research* 18, no. 1 (1991): 13-31.

12. William Havlena and Susan Holak, "The Good Old Days: Observations on Nostalgia and Its Role in Consumer Behavior," in *Advances in Consumer Research* (Provo, UT: Association for Consumer Research, 1991), 18:323-29.

13. I base this assumption on more than 500 interviews that I conducted with the former residents of Soviet *shtetlekh*. The interviews were conducted in 1999-2008, and the participants included people born before 1930. Some of these interviews are available at sovietjewishculture.org. Selected memoirs include Grigorii Braziler, *Razbuzhennyie vospominaniya* [Awaken Dreams] (unpublished manuscript, 1998) and David Stavitsky, *Episody* [Episodes] (unpublished manuscript, 1997).

14. Leonid Utesov, *Spasibo, serdtse: vospominaniia, vstrechi, razdumia* [Thank You, Heart: Memories, Meetings, Thoughts] (Moscow: Vsesoyuznoe Teatralnoe Obschestvo, 1976), and Leonid Utesov, *S pesnei po zhizni* [Life with a Song] (Moscow: Iskusstvo, 1961).

15. Anna Shternshis, *Soviet and Kosher: Jewish Popular Culture in the Soviet Union, 1923-1939* (Bloomington: Indiana University Press, 2006), 173-78.

16. Ibid.

17. For a popular account of "Mayn shtetele belz," see Peter Applebome, "Nostalgia and Innovation in Yiddish Songs," *New York Times*, August 10, 1998, accessed May 24, 2009, http://www.nytimes.com/1998/08/10/arts/nostalgia-and-innovation-in-yiddish-songs .html?sec=&spon=&pagewanted=2. See also Ester-Basya Vaisman's and Shayn E. Smulyan's essays in this book. For more on Yiddish songs and nostalgia in Israel, see L. Silber, "The Return of Yiddish Music in Israel," *Journal of Jewish Music and Liturgy* 20 (1997): 11-22 and Abigail Wood, "Yiddish Song in Contemporary North America" (PhD diss., Cambridge University, 2004). For general studies on American Jewish nostalgia, see Hasia R. Diner, Jeffrey Shandler, Beth S. Wenger, eds., *Remembering the Lower East Side: American Jewish Reflections* (Bloomington: Indiana University Press, 2000); Daniel Soyer, *Jewish Immigrant Associations and American Identity in New York, 1880-1939* (Detroit: Wayne State University Press, 2002); Ben Furnish, *Nostalgia in Jewish-American Theatre and Film, 1979-2004* (New York: Peter Lang, 2005).

18. "Teatral'nye vstrechi. V gostiakh u Leonida Utesova" [Theatrical Meetings. Visiting Leonid Utesov]. First aired 1966, channel 1; last aired July 28, 2006, channel Kul'tura.

19. Ibid.

20. Shternshis, *Soviet and Kosher*, 173-78.

21. See Mikhail Krutikov, "Constructing Jewish Identity in Contemporary Russian Fiction," in *Jewish Life after the USSR*, ed. Zvi Gitelman, Musya Glants, and Marshall Goldman (Bloomington: Indiana University Press, 2001), 252–74, 254.

22. There are no data to prove or disprove that "Bublichki" was more popular among Jews in Yiddish than in Russian or that the Russian version was equally popular among non-Jews.

23. Mikhail Turetsky, interviewed by Marina Koroleva for radio station Ekho of Moscow, January 26, 2004, accessed September 16, 2008, http://www.echo.msk.ru/programs/beseda/24593.

24. Mikhail Turetsky, interviewed by Anna Shternshis, October 2008.

25. For example, see *Alleluya lyubvi* [Hallelujah to Love], a solo concert by the choir that aired on channel 5, last aired May 24, 2008.

26. Maria Balinksa, *The Bagel: The Surprising History of a Modest Bread* (New Haven: Yale University Press, 2008).

27. For example, Edna Lomsky-Feder and Tamar Rapoport, "Visit, Separation and Deconstructing Nostalgia: Russian Students Travel to Their Old Home," in *Homelands and Diasporas: Holy Lands and Other Places*, ed. Andre Levi and Alex Weingrod (Stanford: Stanford University Press, 2005), 296–320.

28. Vladimir Shlapentokh, *Love, Marriage and Friendship in the Soviet Union: Ideals and Practices* (New York: Praeger, 1984), 4.

29. Mikhail Turetsky, interviewed by Anna Shternshis, October 2008.

30. Yurii Slezkine, *The Jewish Century* (Princeton: Princeton University Press, 2004).

31. There is some anecdotal evidence that in the 1970s, Kobzon once sang in Yiddish during his concert in Czernowitz (Cernauti), knowing that Yiddish singer Sidy Tal was present in the audience (Iosif Vais, conversation with author, December 20, 2008).

32. "Hava nagila" is a Hebrew song written in 1911 by either Abraham Idelsohn (1882–1938) or Moshe Nathanson (1899–1981).

33. Iosif Kobzon performing "Hava nagila," accessed May 24, 2009, http://www.youtube.com/watch?v=n26uQOrNtlU.

34. Mary Douglas, "Jokes," in *Rethinking Popular Culture: Contemporary Perspectives in Cultural Studies*, ed. Chandra Mukerji and Michael Schudson (Berkeley: University of California Press, 1975), 291–310.

35. Between 2006 and 2009, the choir appeared thirty-one times on Russian TV broadcasts; three times Yiddish was included in the program.

36. Based on my conversation with several American klezmer performers. I have not sought their permission to quote them here; thus, I use the generic term as opposed to personal names.

37. Mark Slobin, *American Klezmer: Its Roots and Offshoots* (Berkeley: University of California Press, 2002).

YIDDISH COMES TO AMERICA

Prelude

HASIA DINER

Yiddish came to America in tandem with the Jews. At no point in the history of the Jewish people in America could the sounds of Yiddish not be heard. In fact, Yiddish provides an enduring thread that runs through the American Jewish experience and evolved as American Jewry evolved.

The history of the language and of those who spoke it in this particular spot in the "New World" can be traced back to the era before the American Revolution. As early as the middle of the eighteenth century, Jews from northern Europe, the former Polish lands in particular, outnumbered those whose forbears had left the Iberian Peninsula and in America founded "Spanish-Portuguese" synagogues. Although this formative period in American Jewish history has been dubbed the "Sephardic period" by virtue of the cultural hegemony of the Iberians, Ashkenazim—speakers of Yiddish—came early on to be the numerical majority.

Throughout the nineteenth century, predating the massive waves of Jews who hailed from east of the Elbe River, the great heartland of Yiddish speakers, Yiddish in one variant or another served as an American Jewish lingua franca. From the 1820s through the 1870s about 250,000 European Jews came to America. Many of those who came from the place that, after 1871, can properly be called "Germany" arrived in America not knowing German but speaking instead the forms of Yiddish distinctive of Bavaria, the Rhineland, Baden, and elsewhere. Like the sizable chunk who came from the Yiddish-speaking area of France, Alsace, and others from Bohemia and Moravia, they had lived in rural areas, making their living as peddlers, horse traders, and domestic servants. In the places they had abandoned in favor of America, the ungermanized Jewish masses in the middle decades of the nineteenth century spoke Yiddish. A major portion of the pre-1870 wave of "German" Jewish immigrants also came from Posen, the region that Prussia had swallowed up from the dismembered Polish nation. To the Jews from Posen, just as those from western Russia, particularly the province of Suwalk, who made their way to America before the 1870s, Yiddish functioned as their mother tongue, as the language in which they lived, worked, thought, and recreated.

In all of these places, to be sure, some Jews—especially the better educated, the city dwellers, and the economically better off—spoke German. But these more privileged Jews did not succumb to "America fever," having found opportunities opening up to them at home with emancipation, liberalization, and urbanization, and therefore they perceived no reason to leave. The Jewish flood that swept over central Europe instead engulfed precisely those most tied, because of their class position and residence, to Yiddish. For them Yiddish was a constant in their daily lives but carried no meaning beyond its quotidian utility. They did not celebrate it as authentic or as reflective of the "Jewish soul." They did not define it as inextricably bound up with the essence of Jewishness, nor did they see it as having a value beyond its ability to foster communication.

What made the history of Yiddish in America notable in the late nineteenth century and beyond involved not just the sheer number of its speakers who came to America, almost 3 million of them in those years, but also the fact that for many of them the language came to serve a range of political and ideological purposes and that it came to be seen as a bearer of cultural value beyond itself as merely a living language. Yiddish came to America in these years in the mouths of so many that they transformed it from something relatively unselfconscious into something that one faction or another hoped to utilize, preserve, foster, and advance.

In terms of numbers, Yiddish-speaking Jewish immigrants in the decades after the 1870s settled in ways that had a bearing on the history of Yiddish. Here in the cities of America, New York in particular, mass culture exploded. Every immigrant group and the working class in general developed venues in which to learn, to be entertained, to provide services, and to advance political agendas as they saw fit, without needing the permission of the state or the larger society. The millions of Yiddish-speaking immigrants of this era did so, too, and to a high degree. In the process they created and sustained a remarkable efflorescence of print and entertainment opportunities. Whatever their orientation—religious, atheist, socialist, capitalist, or one of many others—Jews saw Yiddish as a weapon in the battle to foster ideology; simultaneously, they used their ideologies to help foster Yiddish.

The post-1870 immigrants came to America from a European setting in which language in general had become politically charged and had emerged as a matter of intense public discussion. Groups of people in the ethnically and linguistically heterogeneous czarist and Austro-Hungarian empires started to demand not only political autonomy but linguistic rights as well. In Ireland,

Nationalists claimed that the British Empire had not only stripped them of their sovereignty but also alienated them from their authentic language. In all of these language battles, particular languages took on great valence beyond their "simple" power to foster communication. They came to be defined as the very soul of the people who spoke them.

Unlike the wave of Jewish immigrants who had come earlier in the century, those arriving in the late nineteenth century did so in large enough numbers to sustain an elaborate popular culture that made Yiddish more than just the language of life. They also came deeply divided among themselves by a much wider array of political and religious cleavages than that of those who had preceded them. Having emigrated from places in which language strife loomed large, they proceeded to enlist Yiddish as a weapon in their constant campaigns to win over the hearts and souls of the Jewish immigrant masses.

By the 1920s it became clear that Yiddish could not sustain itself in America. The children of the Yiddish-speaking immigrants, born and educated in America, may have known the language to some degree, but it did not function for them as a living language. No substantial pool of new Yiddish speakers would replenish the pool of the dying generation of previous immigrants. Immigration restriction saw to that, and in addition many of the east European Jews who did make their way to America had in fact also begun to shed Yiddish before immigration. They arrived primarily as speakers of Polish or Russian. This in the 1920s and 1930s, then, made the project of the advocates of Yiddish in America particularly salient and timely. Only they could save what time and the permanent move to America had begun to erode.

The three essays that follow span from the late nineteenth century with the start of the Yiddish press by recent immigrants in New York to the 1930s, when YIVO's founder, Max Weinreich, recognized the exigency to come to America, to bring YIVO with him, and in the process to make it—and Yiddish—adaptable to the American setting. The three essays share a conceptual interest in the portability of Yiddish, its utility to Jewish and American concerns, and the ways advocates of Yiddish and advocates of political causes converged around Yiddish. The assembled authors' perspectives on the historical contingency of Yiddish in America and the need to think of the language in terms of choice offer an agenda for future scholarship.

MY *YIDISHE* MURDER

The 1876 Case of Pesach Rubenstein, Hasidic Slasher

EDWARD PORTNOY

In December 1875, a Jewish immigrant from Russian-ruled Poland murdered his lover in a field in Brooklyn by slashing her throat with a cigar knife. The press had a field day and the explosion of articles that followed the story, from the discovery of the body through the trial and to the death in prison of the defendant, was eagerly provided by dozens of newspapers from New York to California. These hundreds of articles regaled their readers with the lurid details of the "Jew murderer," Pesach Rubenstein. Occurring as it did before the great wave of Jewish immigration in 1881, the episode eludes Jewish historiography, which has paid little attention to the life of Yiddish-speaking Jews in the United States before 1881, in spite of the huge press response it received at the time. Nonetheless, the case represented, at the time, the most significant interface between Jews and the American media in the history of the country.

The few English-language Jewish newspapers that existed in 1876 when the Rubenstein trial began made a serious effort to ignore a story that had been splashed over every front page of virtually every newspaper in the country. The Yiddish press, comprising only a few newspapers, acted quite differently. Understanding the trial's place as central to the Jews of the country, they dedicated entire issues to it. Why such a marked difference between the attitude of English-language Jewish editors and Yiddish editors?

The Yiddish press constituted a new phenomenon, not only in 1870s America but also in general.[1] The first Yiddish newspaper in the Russian Empire, which controlled the Pale of Settlement, the largest Jewish population in the world, had been permitted to publish only in 1862, and by 1868 it ceased to exist. As a newspaper, this publication provided few genuinely newsworthy items, yet it succeeded greatly as a birthplace for modern Yiddish literature. As a result, many of the Pale's Jews would end up seeing their first real Yiddish newspapers only after having emigrated to America.

In postbellum America, the number of Yiddish speakers was slowly increasing, but without a precedent for Yiddish periodicals, no attempts were made to publish any. As early as 1870, a need for a Yiddish newspaper in New York became apparent. Edited and published by Y. K. Bukhner, *Di yidishe tsaytung* was the first Yiddish newspaper in America. Whether Bukhner's idea or instigated by outside sources, its financing came from Tammany Hall in order to convince Yiddish-speaking immigrants to vote for them.[2] The advent of *Di yidishe tsaytung* represented the first indication that Yiddish culture would function in the United States on the basis of commercial interests, rather than intellectual and didactic.

Di yidishe tsaytung, ostensibly a weekly, was not particularly well run: extant issues indicate that approximately five years transpired between the publication of issue 1 and issue 15. A weekly, it was not. Moreover, Y. K. Bukhner, its publisher, editor, and writer, was too cheap to pay to have the newspaper typeset and, as a result, it was handwritten and lithographed instead. Newer Yiddish newspapers that appeared in its wake were professionally typeset and more closely resembled publications of the general press of the period.[3]

There was, however, something interesting and unusual about issue 15 of *Di yidishe tsaytung,* which appeared in March or April 1876. The use of engraved images dealing with the Rubenstein murder case marked this issue, and the case, as something different. Still a novelty in the nascent Yiddish press of the nineteenth century, these engravings had already been published in English-language periodicals dealing with the case. The four striking and somewhat lurid images in that issue, particularly one of a horrified man being shown the body of a half-naked and apparently dead woman by police, represented a new visual experience for Yiddish publications. Common in popular pulp magazines such as the *Police Gazette,* this type of imagery was very unusual for the Yiddish press of any place or any preceding period. It was the first known instance of the Yiddish press borrowing from "murder pamphlets," a type of popular pamphlet literature that described, in lurid language and image, the tales of well-known killers, victims, trials, and, more often than not, executions.[4]

The manner in which *Di yidishe tsaytung* dealt with the episode was also of interest: it offered a synopsis of a story in which a New York City resident named Pesach Rubenstein had murdered a maid working in his house who also happened to be his cousin. Not only did the newspaper editorialize against Rubenstein and bemoan the entire terrible situation, but it also made mention of similar attitudes in the one other Yiddish newspaper of the day, *Di yidishe gazetn,* the relevant issues of which are unfortunately not extant. Dedicating nearly the entire issue to the case, *Di yidishe tsaytung* gave the impression that the murder was a major news event. English-language Jewish newspapers, such as *The American Israelite* and *The Jewish Messenger,* on the other hand, published

Issue 15 of *Di yidishe tsaytung* (ed. Y. K. Bukhner). The images were taken from two different murder pamphlets, including Samuel Sterns's *Thrilling Mysteries of the Rubenstein Murder Never before Brought to Light* (New York: Stern & Cohn, 1876) and *The Murdered Jewess, Sarah Alexander: Life, Trial and Conviction of Rubenstein, the Polish Jew* (New York: Barclay & Co., 1876). Image courtesy of the Library of the Jewish Theological Seminary.

virtually nothing on the case. An obvious embarrassment to the community, writing about the case in English was akin to discussing it in a public forum. Yiddish, however, posed no problem whatsoever, since only Jews could read it.

Later historians apparently also had an issue with this case: material on the Pesach Rubenstein murder case in secondary American Jewish history texts remains minimal. Jacob Rader Marcus's *United States Jewry, 1776–1976*, contains two sentences on "the murderer Pesach Rubenstein" but offers no sources.[5] Moses Rischin's *Promised City* contains a bit more and gives Abraham Cahan's autobiography and *Manhattan Kaleidoscope,* a memoir of 1870s popular music, as sources.[6] In *Brownsville,* Alter Landesman devoted the most space of any historian. After consulting the trial transcript, he wrote two pages of text on the case.[7]

Considering that at the time the case caused the largest media frenzy involving Jews in the history of the United Sates, that so few historians have dealt with the case is remarkable. New York City and Brooklyn newspapers followed the case assiduously, as did dozens of newspapers across the country. It turned out that the Rubenstein episode constituted a media event of huge significance during the investigation, trial, and imprisonment of the accused. Moreover, in the wake of these events, multiple illustrated pamphlets appeared, and the entire trial transcript was published and sold in book form, something done, according to American legal historian Lawrence Friedman, only in the most high profile or sensational of trials.[8]

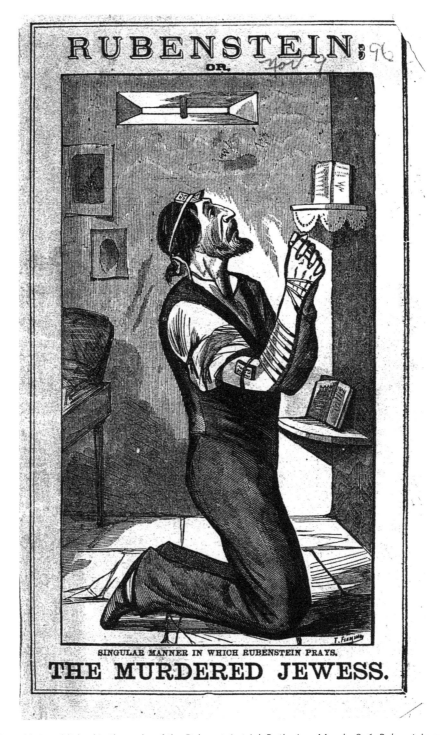

Pamphlets published in the wake of the Rubenstein trial. Both circa March 1876. *Rubenstein; or, The Murdered Jewess*, courtesy of Harvard University Law Library; and *The Murdered Jewess, Sara Alexander*, courtesy of the New York Historical Association.

'RUBENSTEIN;

OR,

The Murdered Jewess:

BEING A

FULL AND RELIABLE HISTORY OF THIS

TERRIBLE MYSTERY OF BLOOD.

————◆————

THE TRIAL IN FULL.

PUBLISHED BY

THE OLD FRANKLIN PUBLISHING HOUSE.

Entered according to Act of Congress, in the year 1876, by THE OLD FRANKLIN PUBLISHING
HOUSE, in the Office of the Librarian of Congress, Washington, D. C.

Cover of the Rubenstein Trial Transcript, 1876; *The Murdered Jewess* pamphlet folio, 1876. Images courtesy of the Harvard University Law Library.

THE
MURDERED JEWESS.

BEING

THE LIFE, TRIAL AND CONVICTION

OF

RUBENSTEIN,

THE POLISH JEW,

FOR THE

Murder of the Beautiful Sara Alexander,

HIS OWN COUSIN!

Startling Evidence! A Shocking Crime!

PHILADELPHIA:
BARCLAY & CO., PUBLISHERS,
No. 21 NORTH SEVENTH STREET.

Rubenstein, a Yiddish-speaking Hasid, represented an exotic mystery to journalists that for their readers elevated the sensation of the case. After all, in 1875 Jews comprised only a tiny one half of 1 percent of the population. Most Americans had little contact with the few hundred thousand Jews who had made their homes in the New World.[9] Even so, in the decade following the Civil War, the Jews had established a reputation for themselves as solid, upstanding citizens. In an 1867 editorial decrying the refusal of certain insurance companies to insure Jews, *The Philadelphia Sunday Dispatch* described Jews as being "fully the peers of any other religious sect in the country. We seldom or never hear of the failure of a Jewish merchant; Jews are very rarely accused or convicted of crimes, and the community is not charged with the support of Hebrew vagabonds and paupers in our almshouses and prisons. All of these facts speak very highly for the Jews, and show them to be orderly and well-behaved citizens."[10]

Compared to their existence as the European continent's most unloved minority, things looked reasonably good for the Jews in America during the 1870s. Even in 1871, when a Jew was discovered to be the culprit in a bizarre murder case known as "the great trunk mystery," the press seemed uninterested in the fact that the perpetrator was a Jew.[11] But the foreign exoticism of Rubenstein, his appearance, his language, his intense piety, among other factors, changed that perception. This time, the Jewishness of the perpetrator became a major factor in press reports of the case.

In order that the reader fully understand the context of the episode, a synopsis follows:[12]

On December 14, 1875, a woman's body was found in a cornfield in east New York City with her throat slashed and with multiple gashes on her hands and neck. She was frozen solid and covered with a dusting of snow. The farmhand who found her alerted the owner, who informed the Brooklyn police department. The police took the body to the morgue, put out a notice that a dead woman had been found, and asked people to attempt to identify her. No one was able to. The police concluded she must have come from Manhattan and began interviewing streetcar and ferry conductors. One of these drivers identified the girl and noted that two days previous he had seen her in his streetcar with "a swarthy Polish Jew of forbidding mien."[13]

Two days earlier, one Sarah Alexander, a recent immigrant from Russian-ruled Poland, did not return home from work. Her brother went to the home of her employer, Israel Rubenstein, who owned a dry goods store on Bayard Street, and asked of her whereabouts. She had last been seen there on Sunday afternoon, the twelfth. One of the Rubenstein sons, Pesach, went with Alexander to the police station to file a report. They were told to check the local brothels. Pesach Rubenstein casually mentioned that he had had a dream the previous night in which Sarah had been "abducted by loafers" and killed.[14] Her body was ten miles from the city, and she contacted him in the dream so he could come and bury her. The Rubensteins and the Alexanders, it should be noted, were also cousins.

Rubenstein and Alexander then placed a missing persons ad in a number of local newspapers. At the same time, the police contacted the press about a body that had been found in the east New York section of Brooklyn, and placed reports in some of the same newspapers. The two descriptions were nearly the same.

Israel Rubenstein, who employed Sarah Alexander as a maid, saw the found body notice, recognized it, and went to the police. Detectives from the Brooklyn police department were then dispatched to interview members of the Rubenstein household. When they interviewed Pesach, they were informed that Sarah Alexander had served as his nurse when he had consumption six months before and that they had a close, but not inappropriate relationship. When the police asked him to come to Brooklyn to identify the body, he blanched and adamantly refused. They took him by force.

In the Brooklyn morgue, where it had been discovered that the victim was five months pregnant, Sarah Alexander's body was shown to Rubenstein. Press reports indicate that his reaction was one of hysteria: he screamed and threw himself backward against a window. For Gilded Age Brooklyn police, that reaction was sufficient to arrest the suspect with murder charges.

As a major capital crime, the story made all of the city's newspapers—and many out of state newspapers as well. Even amid the frequent violence of 1870s New York City, a Jewish murderer of a Jewish girl was exotic enough to command the interest of editors and readers throughout the country. And with

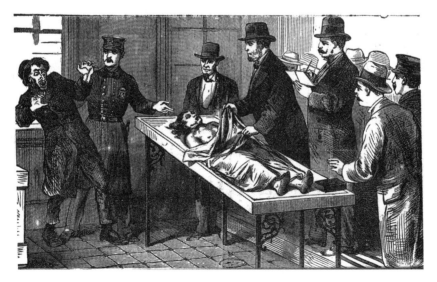

Pamphlet illustration of Rubenstein identifying Sara Alexander's body. Taken from *The Murdered Jewess, Sara Alexander: Life, Trial and Conviction of Rubenstein, the Polish Jew* (Philadelphia: 1876). Image courtesy of the New York Historical Association.

headlines like "The Hebrew Horror" and "Jewish Girl Murder," it would remain a popular story during the course of the trial and for months afterward.

Although Pesach Rubenstein claimed innocence, the Brooklyn police began to amass evidence against him, all of which would be brought out during the trial. Rubenstein's father, who was evidently comfortable financially, hired the well-known New York City attorneys William Beach and John Mott. This is no small matter when considering the expense the Rubenstein family demonstrated when defending their son. One chronicler of the American legal profession wrote in reference to Rubenstein's lead attorney, "When the history of American Jurisprudence is written . . . if the foremost advocates of the Nation's bar are marked on that scroll of fame, not the least one written there will be the name of William A. Beach." Mott was also considered one of New York City's top lawyers.[15] Moreover, one may also consider the notion that the Rubensteins, immigrants all, were not ignorant greenhorns but quite savvy regarding their son's legal defense. In regard to the financial aspect, a communal aspect was at play as well: various press reports indicated that the "Hebrews would spend a million dollars" to free the suspect, although no indication exists of any organized fundraising during the early stages of the trial.

Rubenstein's trial began on January 31, 1876. The Brooklyn courthouse was packed with spectators, many of whom had to be turned away for lack of space. Rubenstein pleaded not guilty. He concocted an alibi that he was out and about visiting clients and could not have been in east New York killing Sarah Alexander the night of her murder. The defense provided more than a dozen eyewitnesses who had seen Pesach in the *beys medresh* on Bayard Street, on Hester Street, or in shops on Maiden Lane during the time of the murder. The defense also suggested an alternate suspect, a local shoemaker named Nathan Levy who had been seen with the victim. Anonymous Rubenstein supporters also mailed letters to the Brooklyn police indicating that Sarah Alexander was a prostitute. They also claimed that Rubenstein was too consumptive and weak to have committed the murder. In all, the defense lawyers earned their keep.

Although the evidence was entirely circumstantial, it was strong. Streetcar and ferry conductors and passengers placed Rubenstein with the victim on the day of the murder. Furthermore, the murder weapon was a type of cigar knife made by a Division Street knife maker who used a distinctive three rivets instead of the usual two and was shown to have been sold to Rubenstein by the knife maker's daughter. Moreover, Rubenstein's boots were caked with mud and vegetation that matched that of the east New York cornfield, his boots matched the bootprints in the same field, and spots of blood were found on his boots and clothing. In a period that lacked DNA testing, and even fingerprinting, the Brooklyn police managed to build a solid case against Rubenstein.

What is more, the district attorney played the ever important race card. In his closing statement to the jury, he said,

Listen. This prisoner belongs to a class of people known as Polish Jews. They come from the conquered provinces of Russia; peculiar in their characteristics, they are ignorant, uncultivated, have no school education except what is obtained from their religious teachers; they are oppressed and despised by surrounding races … having their own customs, their own laws and their own faith; they discard from their minds as a natural result that broad fellowship which goes out to the whole human race. . . .

Comparatively a few years ago it was the boast of the Jews that while state prisons were filled with thousands of Protestants and Catholics and non-believers, no Jews were there. Gentlemen, when these people come to this country they bring the same characteristics which they possessed abroad; they live together, as it were, another people than ours, with different customs and different habits; in the extreme, clannish. And I have a right to argue to you my conclusion that the characteristics of this peculiar class of people are such that they would override other obligations for the protection of one of their own kind, to a degree to which more intelligent and more cultivated men, differently educated, would not assent.[16]

In short, he argued, the Jews are not like "us," a strategy that evidently worked. In spite of there not being one eyewitness or piece of evidence that directly connected the defendant to the crime, the jury convicted him of murder in just over an hour. Rubenstein was sentenced to hang.

In the wake of the decision, certain parties felt that Rubenstein had not received a fair trial. *The New York Sun*, for example, initiated an effort to help Rubenstein procure a new trial.[17] Discussion surrounding a retrial generally had to do with issues of anti-Jewish prejudice or the notion that such a religious person could never have committed so heinous a crime. But a major problem never mentioned, either at the time or in the few sources that later mention it, is that of translation and language difficulties. One police sergeant testified that he thought Rubenstein understood very little English.[18] George Zundt, the German-speaking detective instrumental in bringing Rubenstein to justice, admitted in courtroom testimony that when he interrogated the defendant, he could not completely understand him, and Zundt noted, "I would ask him a question, and he would ramble off for five or six minutes, and I would stop him; I do not remember what he said when he wandered off in this irregular conversation; he talked German and Polish mixed together; I understand the German only; I understood the German part of it, but not the Polish."[19] It is highly unlikely that Rubenstein was speaking Polish. It is much more likely that he spoke in Yiddish, and it was the Slavic and Hebraic admixtures that had rendered Rubenstein's testimony incomprehensible to Zundt. The fact that the language Rubenstein spoke was quite obviously Yiddish was noted by neither the defense nor the prosecution and perhaps played a role in his defense.

Because this was a case in which both the perpetrator and the victim were Jews, the exoticism of the defendant was emphasized to a significant degree. Although, the Brooklyn district attorney noted that few if any Jewish prisoners were imprisoned in US jails, he repeatedly claimed that there was something distinctly off kilter about Polish Jews. This notion was augmented by articles such as those that appeared in the *New York World* and elsewhere that focused on the unusual customs and nature of this type of Jew, which differentiated them from other types of Jews.[20]

None of this was aided by Rubenstein's behavior in court and in prison, about which the press wrote copiously. First, there was the issue of language that marked Rubenstein as glaringly different. Much of the testimony was given in Yiddish and translated by a German speaker. Second, Rubenstein's behavior at the trial, where he was described in the press as "repulsive," "pale, haggard, idiotic, corpse-like and filthy," with a "sallow, death-like face," stood him in poor stead with the press and public. Capping off the grueling twelve-day trial, Rubenstein stood up immediately after his sentence was pronounced, unfurled his long *peyes,* and shouted that he was innocent and that his *peyes* prevented him from committing sin.

While in prison awaiting his execution, Rubenstein was on constant suicide watch. He frequently refused food, and spent his days either curled up on the floor or in constant prayer. The drama he created made for compelling journalism and a remarkably poor portrayal of Jews.

Jewish prayer and ritual were evidently alien to the journalists of the New York press corps. Their portrayal of what they called the specifically Polish Jew, with his strange behavior and appearance, was very much of an exotic character, not unlike reportage of tribes of pygmies in *National Geographic.* This lack of knowledge and social distance from these Jews provided the public with reports such as the following in the *New York Sun*, which described the way in which Pesach Rubenstein prayed:

> On his forehead and on the inside of his arm, at the elbow, are firmly fastened two small cubes of wood about 2.5 inches thick, with a margin at the bottom of a half an inch, and a covering or case fitting over the cube and resting on the margin. On each of these cubes are written in Hebrew the Ten Commandments. The straps are bound so firmly as to interfere somewhat with the circulation of the blood, but the devoted Hebrew endures it as a duty. He says it is necessary to rid himself of a certain amount of animal force.[21]

Additionally, the press refers to his *arbe-kanfes* (a fringed ritual garment) variously as a "chest protector" or an "apron" with tassels. Reporters also taunted him about his religion, asking if he would become a Christian if freed. Little doubt exists that passages such as these were meant to mark Rubenstein as a freakish exotic.

Rubenstein, by pulling down his long curl, takes the most solemn oath known
by his race, and protests his innocence.

Rubenstein entwickelt seine lange Haarlocke. leistet einen Eid, der von seiner Race für den
heiligsten erachtet wird und betheuert seine Unschuld.

Pamphlet illustration showing Rubenstein unraveling his earlock and declaring his innocence.
From *The Murdered Jewess, Sara Alexander: Life, Trial and Conviction of Rubenstein, the Polish Jew*
(Philadelphia, 1876). Courtesy of the New York Historical Association.

The popular pamphlets that appeared in the wake of the trial worked in similar ways, one of them including an engraving of him praying on his knees, his hands clasped in front of him in the Christian manner, with his tefillin worn on his right arm.

This was captioned, "The singular manner in which Rubenstein prays." Whereas other images provided more accurate portrayals (see the tefillin image below), this also represented one of the first times that a mass American audience was introduced to images of Jewish prayer. That they were connected to a murderer certainly may have tainted their meaning.

The Rubenstein case, as mentioned, was reported on heavily in both the New York City and nationwide press. Articles on the case appeared in newspapers as far afield as Chicago; New Orleans; Macon, Georgia; and Idaho, among many other locales. What readers across the country thought of the case remains impossible to determine fully. However, the popular feeling in and around New York City was wholly negative. Effigies of Rubenstein hanging from trees appeared in and around Brooklyn. A song titled "My Name is Pesach Rubenstein" became quite popular, and the very name "Rubenstein" became a pejorative for Jews in general on New York City streets.[22] Reports in the weekly *Yidishe gazetn* indicate that young toughs were still yelling "Rubenstein" at Jews on the streets through the summer of 1876, half a year after the trial ended. Moreover, *Forverts* editor Abraham Cahan notes in his autobiography that when he arrived in the United States in 1882, people were still talking about the Rubenstein case six years after it closed.

The Jewish reaction to the episode is of particular interest here. The New York–based *Jewish Messenger* published nothing at all about the story, as if to say, "Ignore it and it will go away." The Cincinnati-based Reform movement's *American Israelite* managed to print two short "letters from New York," which bemoaned the widespread interest of press reportage on the case and, in a dig against Orthodoxy, noted that the murderer's in-depth knowledge of Jewish law was not an impediment to his crime. Mainly though, it appears as though the English-language Jewish newspapers wanted to avoid advertising this story any further. Its popularity was sufficiently mortifying.[23]

As is evident, this was not the case with New York's Yiddish newspapers. *Di yidishe tsaytung* had no problem printing the lurid images that had appeared in popular pamphlets, and *Di yidishe gazetn*, although not extant, was referenced in the former as having discussed the story extensively. Moreover, in an article discussing forty years of history of the Jewish settlement on the Lower East Side published in the *Forverts* in 1910, the Rubenstein case was noted in detail as a seminal event in the history of the area's Jews.[24]

The question still remains of why such a major convulsion in Jewish life has been ignored by historians. Was it just an anomalous criminal episode in American Jewish history, or was it an early major interface between Jews and American media? As it pertains to historiography, does this episode warrant

Rubenstein's singular manner of praying.
Rubenſtein's ſonderbare Manier beim Gebet.

From *Rubenstein; or, The Murdered Jewess: Being a Full and Reliable History of This Terrible Mystery of Blood—The Trial in Full* (Philadelphia: Old Franklin Publishing House 1876). Image courtesy of Harvard University Law Library.

Rubenstein at his very peculiar Religious Devotions.

Rubenſtein bei ſeinen eigenthümlichen religiöſen Andachten.

From *The Murdered Jewess, Sara Alexander: Life, Trial and Conviction of Rubenstein, the Polish Jew* (Philadelphia: 1876).

the few lines it has received in a few larger works? Or does it have no real bearing on the narrative that historians of American Jewry have crafted?

Commenting on these questions, historian Tony Michels noted that the lack of attention is probably related to research priorities and not to the fact that "historians have consciously ignored or suppressed Rubenstein, but they just don't understand why he would be important and are not inclined to give it any thought. I think ultimately the issue is how historians have conceived the scope of American Jewish history: who falls within, who falls beyond, and why?"[25]

Jonathan Sarna argued that many scholars believe American Jewish history begins with the great migration in 1881 and that, as a result, the 1870s remain a "black hole" in American Jewish history.[26] It may be added that Yiddish cultural production before the 1880s has not been of great interest to scholars. Although Yiddish documents in America date to the colonial period and the genesis of the Yiddish press occurred in the 1870s, very little of this material has interested twentieth-century academics, who have focused on the material created in the wake of the huge emigration that began in the 1880s.

In the end, the Rubenstein episode still raises more questions than answers. Whether it finds a place in American Jewish history will depend on the openness of current scholarship to differing conceptions of immigrants and their roles in American society. This forgotten case also suggests that further research might uncover more that has been avoided or neglected. The Rubenstein case, for example, forces us to consider the existence and significance of communities of Yiddish-speaking Jews in the often overlooked period preceding the 1880s. Although the Rubenstein case might present a glaring absence in American Jewish historiography, numerous other unmarked episodes in American Jewish life surely remain for the researcher to uncover.

The Yiddish press still stands as the chronicle of such unmarked episodes. The Rubenstein case demonstrates that the Yiddish press remains an unparalleled resource in recovering and researching the history of modern Jewry. Yiddish newspapers are pocked with thousands of stories enormously important to the localities in which they occurred but washed away in the wake of greater historical events. The Pesach Rubenstein episode is one of those events: disappeared or forgotten in part due to embarrassment and a desire to maintain a "proper" depiction of American Jewry, its recovery brings to light a transitional segment of immigrant Jewry thus far ignored.

Notes

1. For information on the origins of the Yiddish press in America, see Mordecai Soltes, *The Yiddish Press: An Americanizing Agency* (New York: Columbia University Press, 1925); Y. Chaikin, *Yidishe bleter in Amerike* (New York, 1946); and A. R. Malakhi, "Der baginen fun der yidisher prese," in *Pinkes far der forshung fun der yidisher prese un literatur un prese*, ed. Shloyme Bickel and Chaim Bez (New York: Alveltlechen Yidishen Kultur-Congres, 1972), 2:253–59.

2. See Chaikin, *Yidishe bleter in Amerike*, 53; Malakhi, "Der baginen fun der yidisher prese," 253-59.

3. See, for example, New York's *The Hebrew News*, 1871.

4. For more on the history of such publications, see Thomas M. McDade, *The Annals of Murder: A Bibliography of Books and Pamphlets on American Murders from Colonial Times to 1900* (Norman: University of Oklahoma Press, 1961).

5. Jacob Rader Marcus, *United States Jewry, 1776-1976* (Detroit: Wayne State University Press, 1989), 548.

6. Moses Rischin, *The Promised City: New York's Jews, 1870-1914* (Cambridge: Harvard University Press, 1962), 89.

7. Alter F. Landesman, *Brownsville: The Birth, Development and Passing of a Jewish Community in New York* (New York: Block Publishing, 1969), 31-33.

8. Lawrence Friedman, e-mail correspondence, December 12, 2007.

9. Marcus, *United States Jewry*, 548.

10. Morris Schappes, *A Documentary History of the Jews in the United States, 1654-1875* (New York: Schocken Books, 1971), 513.

11. For more on this episode, see Eddy Portnoy, "Jewish Abortion Technician," *Tablet Magazine*, August 20, 2009, accessed June 22, 2012, http://www.tabletmag.com/life-and-religion/13841/jewish-abortion-technician.

12. The synopsis of events was created using a number of sources, including *Rubenstein; or, the Murdered Jewess: Being a Full and Reliable History of This Terrible Mystery of Blood—The Trial in Full* (Philadelphia: Old Franklin Publishing House, 1876); *The Murdered Jewess: Life, Trial and Conviction of Rubenstein, the Polish Jew, for the Murder of the Beautiful Sara Alexander, His Own Cousin!* (Philadelphia: Barclay & Co., 1876); *The Murdered Jewess, Sara Alexander: Life, Trial and Conviction of Rubenstein, The Polish Jew* (Philadelphia, 1876); Samuel Stern, *Thrilling Mysteries of the Rubenstein Murder Never before Brought to Light* (New York: Stern & Cohn, 1876); *New York Times*, December 1875-May 1876; *New York Herald*, December 1875-May 1876; *Brooklyn Daily Eagle*, December 1875-May 1876; *Pomeroy's Democrat*, December 1875-May 1876.

13. *The Murdered Jewess, Sara Alexander*, 2.

14. Ibid.

15. Alvin Victor Sellers, *Classics of the Bar: Stories of the World's Great Legal Trials and a Compilation of Forensic Masterpieces*, vol. 4 (Baxley, GA: Classic Publishing, 1920), 148.

16. *Trial of Pesach N. Rubenstein for the Murder of Sarah Alexander, in the town of New Lots (near Brooklyn, New York), on the 12th day of December, 1875* (New York: Baker, Voorhis & Co., 1876), 309.

17. "The Hebrew Girl Murder," *New York Sun*, February 1, 1876, 1.

18. Ibid., 31.

19. Ibid., 22.

20. "Polish Jews," *New York World*, February 17, 1876, 1.

21. "Rubenstein's Devotions," *Chicago Daily Tribune*, February 26, 1876, 11 (Repr. *New York Sun*, February 24, 1876).

22. Frank Weitenkampf, *Manhattan Kaleidoscope* (New York: C. Scribners Sons, 1947), 82.

23. "New York Letter," *American Israelite* (Cincinnati), February 18 and 25, 1876, 5, 6.

24. "Dos 40te yor in dem idishn kvartal," *Forverts*, January 1, 1910, 4.

25. Tony Michels, e-mail communication, September 10, 2008.

26. Jonathan Sarna, e-mail communication, November 13, 2008.

RACE, CULTURE, AND THE CREATION OF YIDDISH SOCIAL SCIENCE

Max Weinreich's Trip to Tuskegee, 1932

JENNIFER YOUNG

In December 1932, the Yiddish scholar Max Weinreich took a trip to Booker T. Washington's Tuskegee Institute in Tuskegee, Alabama.[1] Taking leave from his duties at the Yiddish Research Institute (Yidisher visnshaftlekher institut, or YIVO), in Vilna, Poland, Weinreich had been invited to spend the 1932/33 academic year at Yale University as a fellow in a prestigious social science research seminar. Weinreich traveled to Tuskegee because he wanted to investigate first-hand the question of race in America, and he wished to apply his findings to his own work on Jewish cultural survival in eastern Europe. From his conversations with black students and teachers at the Tuskegee Institute, Weinreich expanded his notion of the role for national minorities within the nation-state. He saw the possibility of achieving economic integration into mainstream society while preserving a form of national autonomy and cultural integrity. Highly impressed by the success of the Tuskegee Institute, Weinreich returned to Poland, hoping to apply Washington's models of practical education and self-sufficiency through his work at YIVO.

Weinreich's later work cannot be fully understood without considering the role that his year at Yale played in his life's work as a Yiddish linguist, historian, and cultural advocate. His experiences in the United States in 1932-1933, both at Yale and in the South, especially his exposure to American racial, cultural, and linguistic diversity, firmly shaped his intellectual and political outlook. In his writings and speeches of the late 1930s, Weinreich praised the Tuskegee Institute and encouraged YIVO to follow its example. Far from seeing Yiddish culture and Jewish life in an eastern European bubble, Weinreich found comparisons across universal aspects of minority languages and cultures, and of oppression and discrimination, that transcended the contexts of particular peoples, regions, or nation-states. Weinreich's mission entailed raising Yiddish into a high culture, capable of uniting Jews by giving them a substantive sense of common history, identity, and destiny. Through his own scholarship, he demonstrated the importance of reaching outside of Jewish life in order to enrich it from within.

Max Weinreich did not speak Yiddish as a first language, yet through his scholarship and life experiences he came to the conviction that Yiddish constituted the most important aspect of Jewish life. Weinreich was born in the Russian imperial city of Kuldiga, Latvia, in 1894, into a German-speaking Jewish community. In his youth he joined the Bundist youth group SKIF (Sotsyalistisher kinder farband, or Socialist Children's Union), where he first learned Yiddish from his peers. After studying at Saint Petersburg University, Weinreich traveled to Germany, where he earned a doctorate in linguistics at Marburg University in 1923, writing his dissertation on the history of Yiddish linguistics. Weinreich then moved with his wife, Regina Shabad, to Vilna (Vilnius), Lithuania, her hometown.

With the financial support of his father-in-law, Dr. Tsemach Shabad, a wealthy physician and philanthropist, Weinreich became active in the new Yiddish Research Institute. Founded in Berlin in 1925 by a group of Yiddish scholars and intellectuals, YIVO's initial headquarters were located in the Weinreichs' Vilna apartment.[2] Weinreich proclaimed that the only way Jews could survive as a people was to embrace their own language and culture, Yiddish, and to build and support the Jewish communities of eastern Europe. YIVO, he and his colleagues believed, could serve as a proxy state administration for the Yiddish nation.[3] Scholars could serve as leaders, guiding Jews to develop their cultural awareness and to take pride in their language, literature, and folk customs. YIVO became Weinreich's passion, and he worked to make it the center of Jewish Vilna.

Despite the increasingly difficult circumstances for Jews in Poland in the 1930s, Weinreich's commitment to the continued presence and revitalization of Jewish culture in Poland remained steadfast. YIVO's founders considered the city of Vilna, with its large concentration of Yiddish speakers, the heartland of their Yiddish nation and thus the ideal location for their institute. They hoped that the newly reconstituted nation of Poland would live up to its promise to support ethnic minorities and thus provide Yiddish culture with a structural foundation. In order to be admitted to the League of Nations, Poland signed the Minority Treaties in Paris in 1919, which guaranteed protection of ethnic and religious minority rights. Jewish leaders in Poland promoted the concept of Poland as a multinational state, despite public opposition from ethnic Poles. Support for right-wing Nationalist parties such as the Endecja rose as faith in the European liberal political tradition plummeted, especially after the onset of the Great Depression. The Endecja launched a systematic anti-Jewish economic boycott and attempted to introduce official quotas in universities. The worsening economic crisis affected Jews disproportionately, especially the struggling middle class. Their increasingly desperate poverty added an impetus to increased political mobilization. New parties, such as the Bund and the Agudah, emerged on both the Left and the Right.[4] Yet on the whole, the majority of Jews experienced rapid acculturation to Polish society, language, and culture. Despite the reality of violence, political anti-Semitism, and anti-Jewish economic policies, Jews were not restricted in political organization or the development of their cultural life. However, hooligan violence, especially among university students, increased against Jews in the 1930s and stoked fears of further physical threats. In fact, Max Weinreich himself lost sight in one eye after being accosted one night by a group of students at Vilnius University in 1933.[5]

Although Weinreich began his scholarly career in Poland within the confines of fairly traditional linguistic and literary disciplines, the opportunity to attend the international seminar at Yale opened up a new realm of possibilities for his mission of Yiddish cultural advocacy, allowing him to address contemporary political concerns with his academic strengths. Beginning with the publication of the Yiddish-language academic journal *Yidishe filologye* (*Yiddish Philology*) in 1924, Weinreich began to gain a reputation as a linguist. During this period he also became acquainted with Dr. Edward Sapir, a prominent anthropologist and linguist in the United States and a native Yiddish speaker who had published several articles on Yiddish linguistics. Impressed by Weinreich, Sapir offered him the fellowship that would allow Weinreich to study with him at Yale for the international seminar. Titled "The Impact of Culture on Personality," the seminar was partially funded through the Rockefeller Foundation. Edward Sapir and his colleague John Dollard chose Weinreich as one of thirteen Rockefeller Foundation foreign research fellows in the social sciences selected to achieve a balance representing a variety of different countries, including Finland, Norway, Turkey, India, and Japan. They hoped that these scholars would, as representatives of differing cultural traditions, "combine the roles of informant and analyst, and the result would be a social science transcending the limitations of any one set of cultural assumptions."[6] The seminar proved distinctive in its use of Freudian theory within cultural anthropology and in its focus on psychoanalysis as a social scientific methodology.[7]

Weinreich was eager to work with Sapir, who continued to offer him scholarly advice and to develop public support for Weinreich's work at YIVO. The two remained close until Sapir's untimely death from heart failure in 1939. Nevertheless, Weinreich formed a long-term and life-changing intellectual relationship at Yale with Sapir's colleague John Dollard, who trained in sociology at the University of Chicago. Dollard encouraged Weinreich to delve into the psychological aspects of culture, especially the formation of the psyche of individuals within minority cultures. Dollard advocated the "Chicago methodology" of social science, which required in-depth personal interviews, life

histories, and ethnographic observations, particularly of immigrant neighbor-
hoods and communities. Dollard's focus on race and class in the seminar reflected his own research interests. The overlap between his teaching interests
for the Yale seminar and his own work is especially reflected in his 1937 book
Caste and Class in a Southern Town, a sociological study of race relations based on
analysis of economic and social stratification.[8] Weinreich later applied these
techniques in his work at YIVO, particularly by founding a series of autobiography contests that generated hundreds of pages of detailed information on
every aspect of the lives of young Polish Jews.[9]

While the seminar included instruction by Dollard that educated the fellows
on the peculiarities of the American racial system, the politics of race in America simultaneously played out in the contemporary media, and thus could not
have been far from Weinreich's notice. In November 1933, alongside reports
of the election of Franklin Delano Roosevelt to the White House, headlines
announced the new trial that the Supreme Court had ordered for the Scottsboro nine, a group of young black men accused of raping two white women
in Scottsboro, Alabama in March 1931. The Supreme Court had ruled that the
initial trial could be thrown out because the defendants' right of counsel had
been violated. Southern racists targeted the Jewish attorney hired for the retrial, Samuel Leibowitz, for defending the accused. Thus, just by reading the
newspapers or listening to the radio, Weinreich would have seen evidence of
the racial divisions in American society. Despite widespread racism and prejudice against them, Jews stood to gain access to privilege because of their whiteness, whereas blacks struggled for their lives within the political, economic,
and legal systems.

As Eric Goldstein notes, by the 1930s, Jews had been integrated into the
white power structure in ways still completely restricted for blacks. Yet, many
Jews saw the ultimate impossibility of achieving social acceptance as whites
while preserving a "distinctive minority sensibility" as Jews.[10] Despite the vast
economic hardships affecting the country at this time due to the Depression,
Jews were not victims of the same level of organized political marginalization
and economic discrimination in the United States that they were in Poland. Yet
they also lacked the great political and cultural mobilization that characterized
Jewish life in interwar Poland. The ability to blend in allowed them to survive
and thrive materially, but, as Weinreich would later note, the ability to escape
Jewishness amounted only to a myth detrimental to the construction of meaningful, long-term Jewish culture and identity in the United States.[11]

In December 1932, when the Yale seminar broke for Christmas vacation, Dollard and Sapir encouraged the seminar's fellows to undertake short-term projects dealing with specific aspects of American culture that could be contrasted
with their own cultures. Dollard most likely suggested Weinreich's specific
destination, the Tuskegee Institute. Founded in 1881, the Tuskegee Institute
originally hired the young Booker T. Washington to head its teachers college.

Washington widely promoted the program of vocational training he developed there. The students themselves constructed the school buildings, located on a former plantation, as a form of tuition payment. The school emphasized self-reliance and the importance of learning practical skills, especially trades. The institute encouraged its teachers to return to the plantation districts and not only to teach practical life skills such as improved farming techniques but also to add renewed inspiration to the intellectual, moral, and religious life of their constituency. The school grounds included a farm from which the students consumed the produce. This model of vocational education proved fertile for Weinreich's comparisons between the situations of American blacks and eastern European Jews.

Although Weinreich alone promoted Tuskegee among eastern European Jews, the American Jewish community had long been supporters of the college. As Hasia Diner notes, the Tuskegee Institute enjoyed strong support from American Jewish philanthropists. Julius Rosenwald, president of Sears, Roebuck, gave significantly to black education, as did other major Jewish figures, such as the banker Jacob Schiff. Diner writes that "Jews gave more money to Tuskegee than to any other black school," and many also served on its board of directors.[12] Jewish donors believed that blacks needed to develop the skills to make them integral to the southern economy. Thus, when Weinreich arrived in Tuskegee, he followed in the footsteps of many other Jewish community leaders. However, his agenda differed from the American Jewish philanthropic model because he saw that the college's model of self-sufficiency was directly applicable to the predicament of Jews in eastern Europe.

Not all black intellectuals and community leaders at the time fully embraced Tuskegee's educational model, however. One notable critic of the college was W. E. B. Du Bois (1868–1963), a Harvard-educated historian and sociologist raised in a historically free, land-owning black family in Massachusetts. A contemporary of Booker T. Washington, the two carried on a public dialogue over whether or not blacks should give up their struggle for equal rights in exchange for higher economic and educational standards. Du Bois differed from Washington by emphasizing the importance of scholarship, especially a classical, liberal arts education, over vocational training.

Although Weinreich championed Washington's model, his approach to the study of prejudice much more closely resembles Du Bois's own work. Although Weinreich does not address these parallels in his own work, it is probable that he read Du Bois at some point or discussed his ideas during the Yale seminar. Dollard and Du Bois were certainly familiar with each other's work, and Du Bois reviewed Dollard's 1937 book in the *North Georgia Review.*[13] In his 1903 book, *The Souls of Black Folk*, Du Bois introduced the concept of "double consciousness," as a way of explaining the identity conflicts experienced by young American blacks. Du Bois believed that African Americans struggled between "two warring ideals": the desires to be both black and American at the same time.[14] Yet he defined double consciousness not as a conflict of identity but as a conflict stemming from a lack of identity. Du Bois recounts the story of his own first encounter with prejudice, leading him to attempt to address the question, "How does it feel to be a problem?"

> Being a problem is a strange experience,—peculiar even for one who has never been anything else, save perhaps in babyhood and in Europe. It is in the early days of rollicking boyhood that the revelation first bursts upon one, all in a day, as it were. I remember well when the shadow swept across me. I was a little thing, away up in the hills of New England . . . in a wee wooden schoolhouse, something put it into the boys' and girls' heads to buy gorgeous visiting cards— ten cents a package—and exchange. The exchange was merry, till one girl, a tall newcomer, refused my card,—refused it peremptorily, with a glance. Then it dawned upon me with a certain suddenness that I was different from the others; or like, mayhap, in heart and life and longing, but shut out from their world by a vast veil.[15]

This narrative closely resembles the form that Weinreich's ethnographic notes would take from his conversations in Tuskegee. It parallels his formulation of the "shock of difference," when children all of sudden realize that they are perceived differently from how they perceive themselves. "Being a problem" is not simply the experience of prejudice but also a deeper reflection on belonging to more than one category of identity and struggling to maintain integrity and balance between the two. Du Bois notes that it was possible to rid himself of this experience while in Europe (he studied in Berlin in the 1890s); Weinreich's sojourn in the United States perhaps allowed him a similar sense of security and perspective on the problem of anti-Jewish prejudice in eastern Europe. Thus, the two men crossed paths intellectually, from their parallel yet vastly different set of historical contexts, yet do not seem to have addressed these similarities during their lifetimes.

One reason, perhaps, that Weinreich's reflections on the similarities and differences between American blacks and eastern European Jews did not lead to further social scientific discourse on the issue is that Weinreich never published a full account of his time in the South. This was perhaps because he found his visit so short that it could only serve as inspiration and encouragement for future analysis. He did not collect sufficient data for an extensive study of the possibilities the Tuskegee model could provide Polish Jews. However, he left behind in a notebook a series of vignettes that illuminate his experiences there, suggesting the origins of the parallels that he would later draw between Jewish and African American experiences. The notes he jotted down suggest his framing of the adolescent experiences of minorities, a topic he would cover extensively in his 1935 book *Der veg tsu undzer yugnt* (*The Way to Our Youth*). The book, a kind of social science manifesto, compiled large amounts of sociological data

on contemporary Jewish life, analyzed through Freudian and child development psychology. Largely written while Weinreich was at Yale, he considered
it the cornerstone to any future social scientific project on Yiddish-speaking
Jewry.

Like Du Bois, Weinreich was clearly drawn to personal narratives that explored the origins of individuals' discovery of their own sense of self and of the
revelation that, as a minority, they were different from their peers. One anecdote from the trip that he recorded in his notebook tells the story of an adolescent African American boy on the day he first discovered he was different from
his white playmates:

> At the sociology class of the high school I asked the students to tell me some-
> thing about the way they felt for the first time them [sic] being disadvantaged
> as compared with the whites. A boy from Pennsylvania told me that he was on
> very friendly terms with a white boy. When he was about 13 this friend invited
> him to a party. When they were to go to eat, the white boy's father called him
> upstairs and began talking to him, holding him there for a long time. When
> they went downstairs everybody was already through with the eating. Then the
> father sat down and ate with this Negro-guest. The boy could not understand
> what happened and afterward asked his friends. The answer was: "We don't care,
> but my father thought it wouldn't have been suitable for the white girls to eat
> together with a colored boy." (Unfortunately, I did not write about what the reac-
> tion of this Negro-boy was.)[16]

In this story, the formative moment for the boy occurred when he realized that
he merited different treatment from his peers because society put him in a
different category of being. Weinreich did not analyze this statement in his
notes, but he alluded to it later in *Der veg*, in his discussion of what happens
when a Jewish child first becomes aware that he belongs to a discriminated
against group. Weinreich emphasized the concept of the "shock of difference"
as a common experience among socially integrated adolescents who discover
themselves to be in a perceived minority by their peers in the dominant population. According to Weinreich, these minority youths face a double disadvan-
tage: they must experience the universal pubescent shock of first perceiving
themselves as individuals differentiated from society as a whole as well as the
shock that minorities experience when they understand that their own place
in society is fundamentally different from that of their peers in the majority
group. Weinreich interested himself most in this heightened sense of double
insecurity: he considered the first shock natural because of its universal psychological elements, whereas the second shock was unnatural because it was
caused by prejudice. Although reactions to this double shock could vary by
group, he claimed, most adolescents within minority groups would go through
a similar experience of the "shock of difference."[17]

Weinreich recorded another story of an adolescent boy coming to terms with his minority status. Although Weinreich hesitated to draw explicit parallels between this boy's perspective and his own, he clearly empathized with these experiences. Even more than that, however, he found them instructive. If this is how black children felt growing up, what kind of similarities and differences might he find in studying Jewish children? The answers to these questions formed the root of Weinreich's social science research agenda at YIVO in the 1930s.

In his notebook he wrote, "A boy of about 18 guided me for half an hour. I asked him what the purpose of his studies was. He told me he would like most to go to Berlin and to study history there."

"Why just to Berlin?" Weinreich asked him.

His response was because Berlin was the place his former teacher, Carter Woodson, the editor of the *Journal of Negro History*, had studied.[18]

Weinreich inquired if the boy had "any definite field of interest in history?"

The boy's answer was that "he would like to prove the theory that Negroes had come to this country long before Columbus."

Weinreich added, "It is a mere supposition now but he thinks that the archives may contain some material, or maybe archaeological evidence can be given." Weinreich challenged the boy, "Don't you think the Negroes' rights in this country are justified if you have been here for 300 years?"

The boy's answer was, "That's right, but for social purposes and for argument's sake it could be fine to prove that."[19]

Weinreich may have found a compelling parallel between the boy's expressed need to justify his group's existence in the United States and a similar feeling among Jews to justify their own presence in eastern Europe. He may also have found the boy's statement useful in that it showed how other minorities also saw scholarship as a way to insert their claim for belonging into a political and cultural debate over minority rights.

Weinreich's notes on his experiences in Tuskegee suggest that he found some analytic utility in mining ethnographic data on a broad spectrum of minority relations in the United States in order to compare these experiences with the Jewish experience in eastern Europe. In February 1933, near the end of his semester at Yale, Weinreich composed a summer research proposal addressed to both Sapir and Dollard:

> I want to devote my summer time to the subject which since long has been the main point of my interest, namely the culture and personality problems as they develop in minority groups. . . . My Christmas trip to the South, short as it was, it has given me not only much of insight into the Negro question but also more understanding of general personality problems than many a month of library studies could have done. Thus, I should like to work during summer in two other sections of America where minority groups are concentrated, namely in Canada and the South-West of the United States.[20]

After discussing the possibility of investigating French Canadian culture in Quebec, Weinreich concluded that he would rather choose a location where the minority population was not so numerous or dominant and would instead like to visit the Canadian province of Manitoba, in order to study the Doukhobor (a Russian-origin sect of Spiritual Christians) population there. He wrote, "From my studies at the university of St. Petersburg I happen to know fairly well the earlier history of this sect, and I feel the dissolution of this community must be of importance to a student of personality development in a minority exposed to an external cultural pressure." Furthermore, Weinreich added, he was interested in visiting the American Southwest, where he was "attracted by the problem of the Mexicans, and, in Texas, by the triangle Whites-Mexicans-Negroes." He hoped to learn more about a five-year study underway there investigating new educational methods for non–English-speaking populations. Weinreich suggested that this study would be useful as the basis for a comparison to be made by undertaking a parallel study with "a bi-national territory in eastern Europe, . . . where people have to strive with similar difficulties and several attempts to approach the problem have been made already."[21] While at Yale, Weinreich sought to build a collection of data for his own research, and he hoped that the American context would furnish him with the kind of material and comparative frameworks he could use to place Jewish—and specifically Yiddish—culture within the paradigm of minority/majority cultures, especially within the Polish context.

Despite his intimate acquaintance with the great material hardships that Jews experienced at that moment in eastern Europe, Weinreich was not interested in Jewish political mobilization as the basis for a Jewish survival strategy there. Because of his deep investment in the transformative power of language and culture, Weinreich eschewed strictly political forms of collectivization. Nevertheless, as a card-carrying Bundist also concerned by the ongoing battles for Jewish political rights in Poland of the 1930s, Weinreich believed that change must first come from internal transformations within the Jewish community. Jewish individuals, he argued, ought to address their own specific psychological needs but could be united in this endeavor through the common project of revitalizing Yiddish language and culture. Yiddish-speaking Polish Jewry could emulate the Tuskegee model by focusing on developing practical education and vocational training programs focused on the economic, as well as the interrelated cultural and psychological, needs of the community. With a self-supporting economic base, young Jews would have the confidence and the opportunity to pursue a more enriching cultural and educational life. In turn, this would help them develop as individuals and enable them to contribute to the larger Jewish community as future leaders and cultural actors.[22]

After a brief trip back to Vilna in 1933, Weinreich traveled to Vienna, where he spent several months studying child psychology with Charlotte Buhler and immersed himself in the psychoanalytic community there. He befriended

Siegfried Bernfeld, a proponent of both psychoanalysis and Jewish youth movements. According to Weinreich's son Gabriel, Bernfeld also served as Weinreich's analyst in several psychoanalytic sessions.[23] Weinreich then returned to Vilna, where he put the finishing touches on his book *Der veg*, began working on his Yiddish translation of Freud's "General Introduction to Psychoanalysis" (published by YIVO in 1937), and wrote a Yiddish pamphlet popularizing psychoanalysis. He then published a series of articles in New York's *Forverts* in 1936 on the occasion of Freud's eightieth birthday, arguing for the importance and relevance of Freud's theories for the general Jewish population. Thus, Weinreich laid the groundwork for a popularization and dissemination of Freudian theory to the general Yiddish-speaking public, in both Poland and the United States, in order to show that it had applicability to a *yid fun a gants yor*, an ordinary Jew with little formal higher education.

Weinreich further attempted to engage popular support for his project in the pages of *Yedies fun YIVO* (*News from YIVO*), the newsletter for friends and supporters of the institute. In the first issue of 1934, he published a programmatic statement explaining his new project of *yugnt-forshung* (youth research). He wished to amass a vast collection of data on eastern European Jewish youth in order to provide better material and educational resources for them. He appealed to his readers to send in materials to be analyzed and recorded. "The situation for Jewish youth has never been more complicated than it is today," he wrote.[24] With material conditions grim and the educational system losing its ability to cope, young Jews faced a set of life experiences completely different from that of their parents, making relations between the two groups difficult. Weinreich argued that the only way to remedy this situation was to fully understand it. He claimed this could be best accomplished by studying the problem scientifically, creating a large body of both practical and theoretical knowledge. To put his plan into action, Weinreich announced the second of the series of YIVO autobiography contests, hoping to reach Jewish youth from all over Europe. He encouraged the youth themselves to give their own voices to articulating the problems and experiences of their generation.[25]

Weinreich received the opportunity for his ideas to reach an even broader audience at the YIVO conference of 1935 in Vilna. He recounted his experience at the Tuskegee Institute and indicated how profoundly the students and teachers had influenced him by the example they set: "The Tuskegee Institute was a Negro primary school in a half-falling down house with a roof with holes in it; now it is an institute that itself is an entire settlement; a primary school, a middle school, and a college, with technical departments, with a teaching staff in this department alone numbering in the hundreds."[26] Weinreich described how the vocational training in Tuskegee meant that most people there were capable of raising chickens, laying water irrigation systems, and developing food production techniques and implied that YIVO sorely lacked this kind of practical education.

Weinreich argued for a vocational approach to acquiring skills as superior to the usual methods of intellectual self-improvement, such as debating: "Was Sholem Asch the greatest Yiddish writer?" Weinreich concluded, "There is no scrap of doubt as to which is the better method."[27] Clearly impressed by Tuskegee, Weinreich hoped to transport some of its ethos to YIVO and to implement scholarship that addressed the material concerns, and deprivations, of Polish Jews. Weinreich believed that vocational programs such as technical schools and farm colonies could substantially develop Jewish survival skills and economic opportunities, especially for Jewish youth. Through vocation-oriented programs such as youth movements and summer camps that fostered cultural literacy, Jewish youth could turn their own experiences of prejudice and hardship into a more tangible form of cultural citizenship.

Weinreich emphasized and developed these themes in his 1935 book, tying the need for education to the psychological process minority adolescents experienced as they matured. In *Der veg*, he argued that adolescence was the critical period when Jewish persons acquired the subjective knowledge of their own difference and that they belonged to a minority group. He defined this process of discovery as the "shock of difference." Weinreich believed that this was a universal experience among adolescent minorities and drew on his experiences in the South by way of comparison: "In one of the black universities in the south of the United States, in the end of 1932 I had the opportunity to acquaint myself with a collection of autobiographies of the students; in another black college I carried on a long conversation with the students and teachers. Not seldom did I find out, that the discovery of "racial" separateness for the black child came in the form of a shock."[28]

Weinreich believed that this "shock" of discovering one's difference, whether the difference was racial, ethnic, or cultural, marked the key psychological moment that needed to be understood in order to save young people from self-hatred and psychological fragmentation. Whether Jewish or black, Weinreich thought, adolescents needed to be taught that their own perceived sense of difference was something to embrace, rather than reject.

Although Weinreich believed he could learn much from the African American example, he was not immune to his own set of cultural prejudices. He worried that black culture might not be substantial enough to act as a unifying force, because blacks lacked a separate language and had lost much of their cultural and regional specificities. In *Der veg*, he claimed that the majority of blacks do not aspire to possess their own culture or civilization. Rather, he complained, their standard is that of "white America," and their common language of cultural expression is that of the dominant culture, English. He worried that when blacks become aware that "only blue eyes and smooth brown hair are the keys to the garden of Eden, they are met with surprise."[29] Considering that he could also be intensely critical of Jewish culture, particularly in the United States, Weinreich's attitude could perhaps be explained by the fact that he saw in black culture what he feared most about Jewish culture in both the United States and eastern Europe: the loss of the tangible aspects of minority identity, especially language, could help create a scenario in which minorities would be, in a sense, lulled into a false sense of their own whiteness, which could only break when outsiders pointed out to them signs of racial or cultural differences they themselves could not see.

Without distinctive, tangible aspects of difference to form the cornerstone of group pride, Weinreich hypothesized, minorities would be left only with the pain of being singled out as different. In his discussion of this phenomenon in his book, Weinreich recounted the story of one particular black girl, who, similar to Du Bois, was born into an economically advantaged family in New England and attended an integrated school. After answering a question in class correctly, she was praised by the teacher, only to have a blond classmate turn to her and whisper, "Nigger."[30] Weinreich argued that such shocking, hurtful adolescent experiences could only be mitigated if the persecuted adolescents had something to fall back on, something positive they could associate with their perceived difference, so that they could avoid internalizing the hatred of their tormentors.

In this vein, Weinreich attempted to explicate the notion that blacks who try hard to fit seamlessly into integrated environments are similar to the assimilated Jews of Warsaw who do not wish to acknowledge their own differences from the Polish majority. Weinreich wrote, "I do not wish to go too far into the analogies, but one must recognize that there is indeed a similarity between African Americans in the United States and the *varshever negers* [Warsaw Negroes, or assimilated Jews] as designated by the playwright Antoni Slonimski."[31] In other words, assimilated Jews accustomed to "passing" faced trauma, particularly in adolescence, when they experienced a moment that showed them that others regarded them not as they saw themselves but rather as representing negative aspects of the notion that they are indelibly, unalterably different.

In Warsaw, Weinreich claimed, perhaps more than in other European cities, one could find illustrations of his theme. The extent of this *negrizirung* (Weinreich's term for "blackening" or assimilation) of eastern European Jews, he noted, indicated that abuse and oppression not only affected Jewish material conditions and physical security but also left a deeply traumatic, long-lasting effect on the Jewish psyche. The whole life pattern of a person, he concluded, could depend on how early and in what way he comes to realize that he does not live in a world that wishes him well. After this moment, individuals must be aided in developing the tools to direct this sense of difference to their own internal development and psychological maturity, which can only come through embracing the tangible aspects of their difference: language and culture.[32]

Weinreich continued to develop his programs at YIVO through the late 1930s, especially by establishing the *aspirantur* (graduate) program for training graduate students and by running the 1939 autobiography contest. In September 1939, Weinreich traveled to Copenhagen to deliver a paper at a linguistics conference and thus was spared from the Russian occupation of Vilna. He managed to flee to the United States, along with his son Uriel, and was later able to bring over his wife and younger son, Gabriel.[33] Upon arrival, Weinreich immediately got back to work and tried to establish academic continuity with his projects in Poland. With Dollard's help, he began to apply, ultimately unsuccessfully, for major grants from the Rockefeller Foundation to carry out social scientific studies of Jewish youth in America.

Despite being largely rebuffed in his attempts to create a uniquely American Yiddish social science, Weinreich continued to believe in the importance of a Jewishly engaged social science. To a certain extent, he came to believe in its even greater importance in the American context, in which Jews had begun to lose so many of the benefits of culture, without fully being able to reap the rewards of Americanization. Like the *varshever negers,* Weinreich believed, American Jews had to develop psychological compensations for their minority status. Although they enjoyed the political and economic privileges of American life, they experienced a specific form of alienation as a result of being publicly distinguished by their Jewish difference. Without cultural and linguistic resources on which to draw, Weinreich complained, American Jews were unable to mature and to develop in a healthy manner, both as Jewish individuals and as a Jewish community.[34]

Weinreich continued with these themes, even five catastrophic years later, in 1945, in a commencement address he gave at Baltimore Hebrew College. The context of the immediate postwar was evident in the themes he drew out for his audience: Jews would never be able to completely evade being categorized or discriminated against as Jews by the outside world, he argued, and thus they should not try to escape their Jewishness—doing so will only harm them. Rather, they should embrace the positive content of their Jewishness by living a life characterized by Jewish culture and values. "No escape from common Jewish fate is possible even if it were desirable; so let us make the best of it," he concluded. In his notes for an earlier draft of this speech, Weinreich scribbled an old joke: "What's worse than finding a worm in your apple?" The answer, he writes, is "half a worm." This half worm, Weinreich, explains, is the result of the pernicious effects of denying one's own identity as a Jew, leaving one's Jewishness to be defined by outsiders, thus becoming something disgusting to the individuals themselves: "This unfinished assimilation, which robbed hundreds of thousands of Jews of all pleasures of Jewishness, and left them only the kernel . . . is the central problem of Jewish life in this country."[35] Weinreich did not include these notes, which he scribbled over, in the final drafts of any speeches he gave in English, perhaps worrying his remarks were too inflammatory for a non-Yiddish-speaking audience. Ultimately, Weinreich reasoned that if Jews continued to reject Jewishness while still being defined and categorized by others as Jews, they would break, unable to exist in one world or the other.

According to Weinreich, Jews needed Yiddish as a means to fully realize themselves as Jewish individuals who could integrate into a Jewish collective, thus compensating for their exclusion from mainstream society. This problem of Jewish difference, Weinreich believed, could only be resolved once American Jews came to acknowledge their unique status and acted both individually and collectively to recoup what they had lost. Like African Americans, they had to act decisively in turning away from the false offers of acceptance into a society that would always see them as somehow not quite equal. Rather, he hoped, they would develop the material and cultural resources that would allow the continued internal growth of a modern Yiddish culture.

Weinreich completed his masterwork, the four-volume *History of the Yiddish Language,* shortly before his death in 1969. The work combined a rigorous linguistic and phonological analysis of the origins and development of the Yiddish language with a historical and cultural analysis of Yiddish as a cultural system. Weinreich showed that the Yiddish language, like Jewish culture, did not develop in isolation; rather, it formed through constant contact with non-Jews, shaping a culture and language that consciously fused Jewish and non-Jewish elements into a holistic religious-cultural-linguistic system. Weinreich argued that the idea of Jewish life originating in externally imposed ghetto isolation during the medieval period amounted to nothing but a myth. Rather, Jews chose to segregate themselves from their European neighbors in order to protect their most precious asset, their distinctive way of life. Weinreich's scholarship from the early 1930s onward demonstrated a passion, perhaps even an obsession, with the idea of the wholeness of culture and of its power to transform historical reality. By analyzing the American context of racial difference and of black attempts to build a distinct society, Weinreich added another layer to his project of an engaged Yiddish social science.

Through exploring the contexts of cultures outside of his own, Weinreich broadened the scope of possibilities for Yiddish scholarship and for the continued creation of Yiddish culture. Despite the Nazis' destruction of eastern European Jewish civilization, Weinreich believed that Yiddish culture still lived. Most American Jews may not speak Yiddish, he concluded, but they still dream in Yiddish; it was still the "idiom of their collective unconscious."[36] In order to live out tangible, rather than abstract, Jewish lives, American Jews would have to find their way back to Yiddish to heal their psyches and to heal their collective culture. This idea of Yiddish as the foundation of modern Jewish culture, forged in Weinreich's social scientific encounter with American racism and black cultural life, continued to echo in his work throughout his lifetime. Its message of cultural renewal resonated in the postwar context and left a legacy for the institutionalization of Yiddish studies within and beyond the academy.

Notes

1. The institute was founded in 1881; its first president, Booker T. Washington (1865–1915), who was born into slavery, championed the idea of self-reliance: African Americans could learn practical skills such as construction, agricultural, and domestic work and could dignify labor as a meaningful task. The Tuskegee Institute became well known much later for its role in a controversy linked to the federal government's public health department. In 1932, the institute began its cosponsorship in a public health study run by the US Public Health Service on the progress of syphilis in a group of African American men. The participants did not know that they had syphilis and did not receive treatment. The study continued after 1947, when penicillin became a widely available and effective treatment. The study concluded after the story broke to the media in 1972. In 1996, President Bill Clinton formally apologized for the government's role in the experiment.

2. For a more complete biography of Weinreich, see Paul Glasser, "Max Weinreich," in *The YIVO Encyclopedia of Jews in Eastern Europe,* ed. Gershon David Hundert (New Haven: Yale University Press, 2008), 2:2014–16.

3. See C. Kuznitz, "The Origins of Yiddish Scholarship and the YIVO Institute for Jewish Research" (PhD diss., Stanford University, 2000).

4. Yisrael Gutman, "Polish Antisemitism between the Wars: An Overview," in *The Jews of Poland between Two World Wars,* ed. Yisrael Gutman et al. (Hanover, NH: University Press of New England, 1989), 97–108, 102.

5. For a complete account of this incident, and for other personal recollections of Max Weinreich, see his son's recently published autobiography. Gabriel Weinreich, *Confessions of a Jewish Priest: From Secular Jewish War Refugee to Physicist and Episcopal Clergyman* (Cleveland: Pilgrim Press, 2005).

6. Judith Irvine, *The Psychology of Culture: A Course of Lectures,* 2nd ed. (New York: Walter de Gruyter, 2002), 4.

7. Barbara Kirshenblatt-Gimblett provides a thorough description of the seminar and its aims in her article "Coming of Age in the Thirties: Max Weinreich, Edward Sapir, and Jewish Social Science," *YIVO Annual* 23 (1996): 1–103.

8. John Dollard, *Caste and Class in a Southern Town* (1937; Madison: University of Wisconsin Press, 1989).

9. For a complete history of the project and a selection of translated texts of the pre–World War II YIVO autobiography contests, see Jeffrey Shandler, ed., *Awakening Lives: Autobiographies of Jewish Youth in Poland before the Holocaust* (New Haven: Yale University Press, 2002). Daniel Soyer also includes a full discussion of the founding of the autobiography contests at YIVO in Poland in his article "Documenting Immigrant Lives at an Immigrant Institution: YIVO's Autobiography Contest of 1942," *Jewish Social Studies* 5, no. 3 (1999): 218–43.

10. Eric Goldstein, *The Price of Whiteness: Jews, Race, and American Identity* (Princeton: Princeton University Press, 2006), 164.

11. Note card, 1940s, Max Weinreich Papers (RG 584, folder 576b, YIVO archives).

12. Hasia Diner, *In the Almost Promised Land: American Jews and Blacks, 1915–1935* (1977; Baltimore: Johns Hopkins University Press, 1995), 168.

13. Du Bois reviewed Dollard's *Caste and Class in a Southern Town* in *North Georgia Review* 2 (winter 1937–1938): 9–10. David Levering Lewis calls Du Bois's review "calculatingly generous," as Du Bois ultimately recommends the book after criticizing Dollard's schematized use of caste as insufficiently focused on economics, slotting racial groups into timeless categories. Lewis, *W. E. B. Du Bois: The Fight for Equality and the American Century, 1919–1963* (New York: Henry Holt, 2000), 444.

14. W. E. Burghardt Du Bois, *The Souls of Black Folk: Essays and Sketches* (1903; New York: Bantam Classic, 1989), 3.

15. Ibid., 2.

16. Notebook entry, 1930s, Max Weinreich Papers (RG 584, folder 345, YIVO archives) (in English).

17. Max Weinreich, *Der veg tsu undzer yugnt: yesoydes, metodn, problemen fun yiddisher yugnt-forshung* [The Way to Our Youth: Foundations, Methods, and Problems of Jewish Youth Research] (Vilna: YIVO, 1935), 190-92.

18. Carter Woodson (1875-1950) is considered one of the first African Americans to stress the importance of scholarship on black history. In 1915, he founded the Association for the Study of Negro Life and History.

19. Notebook entry, 1930s, Max Weinreich Papers (RG 584, folder 345, YIVO archives) (in English).

20. Max Weinreich, letter to Drs. Sapir and Dollard, February 22, 1933, Max Weinreich Papers (RG 584, folder 345, YIVO archives) (in English).

21. Ibid.

22. For Weinreich's parallels with both Washington and Du Bois, see David Levering Lewis, *W. E. B. Du Bois: Biography of a Race, 1868-1919* (New York: Owl Books, 2004).

23. Dr. Gabriel Weinreich, personal interview, March 25, 2006, Ann Arbor, MI.

24. *Yedies fun YIVO* [News from YIVO], January-March 1934 (my translation).

25. Ibid.

26. *Der alveltlekher tsuzamenfor fun yidishn vinshaftlekhn institut: tsum 10-yorikn yoyvl fun YIVO; opgehaltn in Vilne fun 14tn bizn 19tn oygust 1935* [Proceedings of the World Convention of YIVO on Its Ten-Year Anniversary; held in Vilna, August 14-19, 1935] (Vilna: YIVO, 1936), 32-34 (my translation).

27. Ibid.

28. Weinreich, *Der veg tsu undzer yugnt*, 190-91 (my translation).

29. Ibid., 192 (my translation).

30. Ibid.

31. Ibid., 190-91. Weinreich is referring to Slonimski's 1928 play *Murzyn warszawski* [The Warsaw Negro]. Slonimski (1895-1976), a Jew born into a polonized family, cofounded the experimental literary group Skamander. His play *Murzyn warszawski* "satirized cultural snobbery as an engine of assimilation." Hundert, *YIVO Encyclopedia of Jews*, 2:1760.

32. Weinreich, *Der veg tsu undzer yugnt*, 192-94.

33. For more on this move, see Kalman Weiser's essay in this book.

34. Note card, 1940s, Max Weinreich Papers (RG 584, folder 576b, YIVO archives).

35. Ibid.

36. Dan Miron, "Between Science and Faith: Sixty Years of the YIVO Institute," *YIVO Annual of Jewish Social Science* 19 (1990): 1-17, 14.

COMING TO AMERICA

Max Weinreich and the Emergence of YIVO's American Center

KALMAN WEISER

In early October 1939, the Ampteyl (short for Amerikaner opteyl, or American Division) of YIVO released a pressing announcement. A month earlier the German-Soviet partition of Poland severed the contested multiethnic city of Vilna (Vilnius) from that country. The scant information available revealed that the institute remained intact despite Vilna's occupation by the Red Army. With the city's future uncertain, the Ampteyl announced that Vilna could no longer continue to serve, at least for the duration of the war, as the world center of YIVO (Yidisher visnshaftlekher institut, the Jewish [Social] Scientific Institute). The Ampteyl, YIVO's "main backbone and chief support," would assume YIVO's primary functions, including publications and acquisitions. Jews everywhere were urged to send materials intended for YIVO scholars and archives in Vilna instead to the Ampteyl's offices in lower Manhattan.[1]

Soon after this announcement appeared in the American Yiddish press, the Red Army's forty-day occupation of Vilna came to an unanticipated end. The Soviets transferred the city into Lithuanian hands and Vilnius, as it is known in Lithuanian, was made the new capital of the independent Lithuanian Republic in mid-October.[2] Although fears of the sovietization of the institute and the complete severing of Lithuanian Jewry from the West were allayed, at least for the time being, the future of YIVO-Vilna, like the fate of eastern European Jewry as a whole, remained a matter of profound angst. After having weathered the increasingly anti-Semitic climate of Poland in the late 1930s and survived a Soviet takeover without damage to its building or collections,[3] YIVO found itself under a new regime with an unpredictable attitude toward it. The war had effectively cut it off from its material and cultural base, the more than

3 million strong Jewish community of Poland. Much of YIVO's academic and administrative leadership was not located in Lithuania. In September the Soviets arrested the philologist and newspaper editor Zalmen Reyzen, a pillar of YIVO, along with other important Jewish political and cultural figures, for reasons then unclear.[4] As the only member of the prewar executive office possessing Lithuanian citizenship, the philologist Zelig Kalmanovitch begrudgingly accepted approval as the institute's curator by the new regime.

This situation led to a severe impairment of communications with the outside world. The staffs of YIVO's branches across the globe relied largely on correspondence arriving with delays of weeks and sometimes even months to construct an image of the situation. Inevitably, miscommunications and misunderstandings arose. The only reliable means of communication remained telegrams. However, their expense and brevity impeded conducting the full business of an intercontinental organization. From Copenhagen, the renowned scholar Max Weinreich, the institute's research director and guiding spirit, relayed news and information between colleagues in Kovno (Kaunas), Vilna, Paris, and New York City to help coordinate the activity of the institute.

Despite the murkiness of the picture emerging, YIVO's staff on both sides of the Atlantic sensed that a new era in Jewish history was dawning. Since the Nazi and Soviet invasions of Poland in September 1939, they acknowledged, Polish Jewry had experienced a veritable *khurbn*, a destruction of historic, if yet unknown, proportions.[5] The temporary administration of YIVO in Vilna, a mixture of old and newly co-opted members, found itself confronted with an existential dilemma. Should it continue and perhaps even expand its activities despite a paucity of material resources to meet the needs of the influx of refugees to Vilna and the native Lithuanian Jewish population, all starved for culture and activity in a time of despair and deprivation? Or should it suspend and perhaps even transfer its operations and select personnel, as the Amopteyl urged, to the distant safety of New York City?

Since YIVO conceived of itself as a global organization and of Yiddish as a language and culture without borders, such a move was arguably justified even before the war on demographic grounds alone. On the eve of World War II, more than 2 million Jews lived in New York City, a Jewish population dwarfing that of any other urban center in the world, including that of Warsaw, Europe's most numerous Jewish community (375,000 Jews in 1939).[6] America's nearly 5 million Jews, themselves largely immigrants from eastern Europe and their progeny, were relatively affluent and supported an eclectic array of Yiddish newspapers, theaters, schools, and other cultural institutions.[7]

On the other hand, such a decision would remove YIVO from the midst of its primary constituency, the Yiddish-speaking Jews whose "homeland" was noncommunist eastern Europe, and above all Poland. The decision to relocate from the beleaguered European capital of an imagined *Yiddishland* to its more secure province on the Hudson would not only affect the functioning of YIVO[8] but also send a message to world Jewry about the Vilna institute's confidence in its own future and that of the Jews of eastern Europe.

Historians typically locate an epoch-making shift in YIVO's trajectory sometime during the first year of World War II. They mention recognition of New York City as the new world center—the heart—of YIVO as the result of an uncontroversial, pragmatic reckoning necessitated either by January 1940, due to the conditions of war, or by October of that year because of the sovietization of the institute in Vilna.[9] Yet, the replacement of Vilna with New York, marking the beginning of the still unfolding "American period" in YIVO's history, was hardly an easy and uncontested decision. A close examination of institutional records and correspondence between YIVO's offices between October 1939 and June 1940, the period during which Vilna belonged to neutral, noncommunist Lithuania, reveals that the question of where YIVO's center lay—and, implicitly, its periphery and that of Yiddish culture as well as of world Jewry—aroused passions in Vilna, New York, and wherever else YIVO maintained branches. Discussions and debates among YIVO's staff point not only to institutional divides and rivalries played out across geography but also to anxiety over the future of the institute both in its own right and as a symbol of the continued relevance and perhaps even survival of eastern European Jewry, as a seismic shift in Jewish life was underway.

The Historiography of YIVO

Scholars divide the history of YIVO since its founding in 1925 into two main periods separated by World War II. In the first, post–World War I period, the fledgling institute came into existence in order to serve as a national university, language academy, and library for a stateless Yiddish-speaking Jewry at a time before Jewish studies was widely recognized in academia. Headquartered in Vilna, it had branches and support groups throughout the world. It found its primary constituency, however, among the impoverished Jewish masses of non-Soviet eastern Europe, especially in eastern Poland and the Baltic states, who eagerly contributed data and material for its collections and research. YIVO's mission was to apply the latest techniques in the social sciences to gather information about and study objectively their language (to whose standardization it made major contributions), history, psychology, economics, and culture. At the same time, it endeavored to disseminate its work through its publications and exhibitions both to the broader world and specifically to the objects of its study to improve eastern European Jews' present-day conditions and help them build a secularized, Yiddish-speaking future.

Without official state support, YIVO relied desperately on a combination of meager sources: grants from Polish municipalities and *kehilot* (state-recognized Jewish communities), private donations and contributions from individuals and Jewish organizations in Poland, and, above all, support from abroad, especially the United States. Nevertheless, it operated on a budget often on the verge of bankruptcy. At the beginning of the academic year 1938/39, it included fourteen professional and clerical workers on its staff. Sixteen students were enrolled in its *aspirantur*, the graduate-level program for training scholars under the guidance of senior staff. It also maintained a *proaspirantur* program to prepare students without university experience to enter the *aspirantur*.[10]

During the second, post–World War II, period of adjustment, rebuilding, and reorientation in the United States, the salvaged collections and surviving personnel of YIVO-Vilna fused with those of the Amopteyl to carry on the institute's academic-populist mission in New York. The most important of YIVO's branches outside its headquarters in Vilna, the Amopteyl was founded in late 1925, not coincidentally the same year as YIVO, under the guidance of historian Jacob Shatzky, himself a recent transplant from Poland. It had earned a positive reputation with its annual conference and the publication of a number of important scholarly works as well as the journals *Der pinkes* (*The Record Book*; 1927–1929) and *Yorbukh fun amopteyl* (*American Section Yearbook*; 1938–1939). Moreover, as historian Cecile Kuznitz notes, through its fundraising campaigns and solicitation of donations from organizations such as the American Joint Distribution Committee, "the section became crucial to YIVO's fundraising efforts, with American sources contributing as much as two-thirds of the institute's total budget."[11] By the outbreak of World War II, a majority of the members of YIVO's philological section—Yudl Mark, Judah Joffe, and Shmuel Niger—and one of its European founders—Jakob Lestschinsky, who headed, together with Elias Tcherikower, the economic-statistical section—resided in New York City.

Nonetheless, YIVO-Vilna and much of the Amopteyl's own staff saw the Amopteyl as playing an auxiliary role in the broader YIVO organization. In this way, it mirrored the image common among eastern European intellectuals of Jewish America as a culturally dependent (and culturally inferior) "colony" of eastern Europe despite its demographic, political, and financial weight.[12] It remained subservient to Vilna, the unofficial capital of secular Yiddish culture and the universally acknowledged center and home of YIVO. In Vilna, YIVO possessed a building of its own that housed the bulk of YIVO's staff and rich scholarly holdings. YIVO in Vilna received the loyal support of a public whose lives it aimed to study and enrich. In contrast, the Amopteyl was housed in comparatively small, drab quarters on Lafayette Street in a building it shared with HIAS and other Jewish organizations.[13] Even the work of the Amopteyl focused primarily on researching Jewish life in eastern Europe, not the United States, and on helping to support and maintain the center in Vilna. Symbolic of Vilna's centrality to YIVO's mission as a Yiddishist academic institution was the publication of *YIVO-bleter* (*YIVO Pages*), the institute's flagship journal, exclusively in Vilna.

The destruction of eastern European Jewry and the dynamic encounter with a massive American Jewish community little attuned to Yiddishist ideals obliged YIVO as an institution to reconsider its ideology, goals, and methods. In the post-WWII period, YIVO in New York City has continued work on behalf of and in Yiddish. This includes the training of scholars and the publication of new scholarship and important linguistic and cultural reference works. With the passage of time and generations, however, an "Americanized" YIVO has increasingly made "compromises" with English and revised its focus to reach a broader audience and remain relevant to both the Jewish and scholarly worlds.

The Centrality of Max Weinreich

No single figure was more crucial in linking these two periods in YIVO's history than Max Weinreich. Both literally and figuratively caught between Vilna and New York, Max Weinreich was a stateless refugee torn between his personal and professional commitments to the city where he and his colleagues had built YIVO and the haunting fear that YIVO's tentative future depended on the concentration of energies in the development of the American branch. He had left Vilna with his wife Regina and older son Uriel in August 1939 to speak about the history of Yiddish at an international linguistics conference in Brussels. Soon after the signing of the Hitler-Stalin nonaggression pact, Regina returned to Vilna at the behest of her mother, Stefania Szabad, who was caring for the Weinreich's younger son Gabriel and who presciently understood that Germany would now invade Poland with impunity. A more optimistic Max chose to remain, hoping to enjoy the sights of Copenhagen a bit longer and to continue on to the conference.[14] Consequently, Max and Uriel stayed in the Danish capital, separated from their family, when war erupted. The conference now cancelled, they hoped to return home, but with their passports effectively worthless and any travel difficult and fraught with danger, they had no choice but to wait. With their personal funds severely limited, they relied largely on support provided by the Amopteyl and the generosity of the local community of eastern European Jews in Copenhagen during a nearly six-month stay there. During this time, Max worked on a dictionary of the Yiddish literary language in addition to occupying himself with personal affairs and those of the institute. His thirteen-year-old son studied in a Danish high school, acquiring proficiency in the local language with remarkable speed.[15]

Writing to the Amopteyl after the transfer of Vilna into Lithuanian hands in October 1939, Weinreich expressed hope that YIVO would survive and even flourish under a regime more favorably inclined to Jewish culture than Poland's. As long as the Soviets did not intervene in Lithuania's domestic affairs, he wrote, "YIVO is saved, then my place is in Vilna." If not, "we must think about saving the collections and people by transporting them to America and ending the European period of YIVO's history."[16]

Naftali Feinerman, secretary of the Amopteyl, was less hopeful in his analysis. He confided in a letter to YIVO cofounder Tcherikower, who was in Paris at the time, that he feared Weinreich and Kalmanovitch, the institute's leading figures along with Zalmen Reyzen, would be lured by the siren song of Lithuanian control to return to Vilna. It would only be a matter of time, Feinerman predicted, before Stalin returned and sovietized Lithuania, endangering the independent operation and holdings of the institute.[17] As announced in its October 1939 press release, the Amopteyl endeavored to bring YIVO scholars working in neutral lands to the safety of the United States. Meetings of the Amopteyl explored the possibility of sending a delegate to help transport archival materials and rare items from Vilna to New York. It also considered obtaining a microfilm machine from the Rockefeller Foundation to photograph documents.[18] Tcherikower shared Feinerman's evaluation, and he hoped to make YIVO's Paris branch its European center. Tcherikower cautioned Feinerman, however, not to underestimate the profound psychological impact that the necessary transfer of materials and key people across the ocean would have on those who remained.[19]

The Amopteyl begged Max Weinreich to come with his wife and sons and stay in America, at least until after the summer of 1940. It promised to take care of his travel expenses and support him in New York. If he did not intend to head first to Vilna to take stock of the situation and settle matters there, Feinerman urged, he should come directly to America. Tirelessly appealing for aid from American consular authorities and academics, the Amopteyl would arrange for the necessary visas.[20] Regina and Gabriel Weinreich would necessarily travel independently from Vilna to join them.

America was not terra incognita for Weinreich. In 1924 he visited the country to raise funds for YIVO and to deliver lectures. With the support of the Rockefeller Foundation, he returned in 1932 to spend a year as a research fellow at Yale University's Institute of Human Relations. Having participated there in the Seminar on the Impact of Culture on Personality led by professors John Dollard and Edward Sapir, he had formed positive relationships with American colleagues and enjoyed their respect.[21] Still, the thought of leaving behind his friends and colleagues, as well as a city and, above all, the institute that meant so much to him—even if only temporarily—proved agonizing for Weinreich. He confided to Feinerman that he had delayed a visit to the American consulate to investigate the possibility of obtaining a tourist visa to the United States because "my heart is torn between the two possibilities: of going home and continuing to work as much as possible [there] and of coming to you and assuring, as much as can be foreseen, a life for my wife and children free of bombardments and protectors from the East."[22]

His wife Regina, an accomplished pedagogue from a prestigious Vilna family, expressed even more reluctance to leave for America. The Western democracies impressed her as "impotent rich gentlemen."[23] Ignorant of English, she was afraid of starting life anew, impoverished, "pitiful and helpless" in "capitalist" America. Moreover, she believed, America offered no real escape from ubiquitous racism and anti-Semitism.[24] Finally, she was consumed with guilt over the possibility of leaving behind her aged mother and less fortunate friends: "I absolutely can't imagine now any travel to America. I never wanted to go there. Nothing ever impressed me there. I am probably afraid of it. I can't overcome the feeling of guilt and the consciousness of having betrayed, which will oppress me, if we have to leave."[25] Intellectually, she wrote to Max, she accepted the necessity of leaving for America. Emotionally, however, she lacked the resolve.[26]

Max Weinreich privately expressed doubts about the continued viability of Vilna as YIVO's center and mulled over coming to America. He even initially requested that Feinerman keep secret this possibility.[27] Indeed, as soon as the Red Army left Vilna, he and Kalmanovitch, who remained in Kovno (Kaunas) during the first Soviet occupation of Lithuania (September–October 1939), sent dispatches proclaiming their intentions to return and resume work.[28] On November 7, Kalmanovitch publicly issued a statement rejecting the validity of a notice appearing in the Vilna daily *Ovntblat* (*Evening Paper*) under the title "YIVO Moves from Vilnius to New York." He blamed the newspaper for reprinting a statement, likely culled from the American press, that had lost its validity since Vilna had come under Lithuanian control.[29] In a letter to Feinerman, Weinreich reproached the Amopteyl for making unilateral decisions and declaring that YIVO had relocated to America. In doing so, wrote Weinreich, it inadvertently threatened to demoralize not just their colleagues in Vilna but even broader circles:

> You have become so detached in a few months that you have forgotten that YIVO is a small world *of its own* with a few tens of people, that around YIVO [there] is an organized society of a few hundred people and that Lithuania on the whole was more involved in the work of the institute than any other land (proportionally speaking) . . . here they had to establish themselves after the "kolebla" of September–October: receive the legal recognition from the government, raise at least some money in order to overcome the greatest want, to do at least part of the work that can be done. And they go around with the announcement from the Amopteyl that the center of YIVO has moved, carried to America. You will certainly understand that Kalmanovitch had to make a declaration.[30]

As Weinreich's letter to Feinerman was in transit, a letter from New York headed to Vilna. In his January 19, 1940, letter, Feinerman urged YIVO in Vilna to keep its activities to a necessary minimum, to finish only those projects it had undertaken before the war, and to catalog its holdings. Without direct consultation with Vilna but with Weinreich's encouragement,[31] he announced that publication of *YIVO-bleter* would continue in New York City until further notice because "the Jewish community in Poland is now destroyed; it is technically impossible to deliver *YIVO-bleter* to America. So, for whom will Vilna print them?"[32] It is notable that not only had YIVO activity not ceased in Vilna, but it also had, in fact, undergone expansion, particularly in the areas of research and teaching, despite now only receiving a fraction of the mail and periodicals it previously received.

In the evaluation of Yiddish author Joseph Opatoshu, active in the Amopteyl, recent events spelled the end of the Vilna period in YIVO's history and the beginning of an American era: "In Jewish history, such cases are already known when one center is destroyed and another arises in a different land."[33] Not all in America, however, shared Opatoshu's fatalistic conclusion or his optimism about the cultural potential resident in American Jewry. For many, including members of the Amopteyl, faith more than profound conviction fueled their support for New York City as YIVO's new world center. Despite rational arguments for concentrating Vilna's operations in America, Feinerman harbored doubts about the degree of enthusiasm with which Jews would support YIVO's academic mission, especially in time of war, in America. Writing to Tcherikower in Paris, whom the Amopteyl helped support with regular payments of thirty dollars per month, he worried that "the wide public is taken with the justified feeling of sympathy and will certainly give for shrouds for the dead and bread for the living. Will it also want to give for cultural matters, esp. for Jewish cultural institutions in America—God knows?"[34] Expanding the Amopteyl's activity, in addition to providing support to Vilna and YIVO colleagues elsewhere, also meant rising costs. YIVO colleagues in London, Paris, and Buenos Aires, he explained to Weinreich, all suggested that YIVO's center shift to America given the circumstances in Europe. But whereas they had all previously helped to support the Vilna center financially, they now asked America to send them money: "Our position is extremely difficult. Fund raising is monopolized in the USA by the Joint, the Zionist Organization, and the Jewish Workers' Committee."[35]

The question still loomed: would American Jewry, a relatively young settlement whose emotional maturity and identity as a national collective many eastern European Jewish intellectuals on both sides of the Atlantic deemed still underdeveloped, be suited for the task that stood before it?[36] Would it readily inherit the Vilna scholarly tradition, especially when its upwardly mobile youth were drawn to English rather than Yiddish and it demonstrated little interest in, and remained woefully ignorant of, the achievements of modern Jewish culture?[37] "The problem with our America," wrote the Yiddish *Forverts* in New York in March 1940, is not a lack of Judaica scholars but "is what is called here making 'a living,' and in the present time it diverts much time and causes much concern. It is, however, different in Vilna. There, they don't make a living. The means don't exist. . . . Therefore, they have more time and more patience for scholarly work. Our Americans can help them very much now with the work but it won't do for our Americans to try to become the heirs of Vilna."[38]

Ironically, the "blessings" of eastern European poverty compared favorably in this context with the "burdens" of professional and commercial opportunities in America.

Members of the Amopteyl executive office voiced similar concerns, prompting Jacob Shatzky to emphasize the need to prepare American Jewry psychologically to give money to YIVO not because it represented Vilna—that is, a metonym for the entire population of Jewish eastern Europe and its traditions—but because it represented modern Jewish scholarship. The vital importance of Jewish scholarship for collective survival and the need for self-reliance in this regard had to be impressed on American Jewry, which made a cause of donating to its less fortunate brethren in the old country more than it invested its finances and energies into developing a self-sustaining high culture on its own.[39]

The Yiddish American writer H. Leivick adamantly argued for the need of the Amopteyl to expand its functions in the case that Vilna disappeared. Its members, he wrote, must cease seeing themselves "only as helpers in America and not as independent builders." The need for the Amopteyl to rise to the occasion and act independently was hammered home by the linguist Judah Joffee, who opined, "The same people who complained yesterday of Vilna's hegemony, now complain that we can do nothing without it."[40] From Europe, Max Weinreich enjoined the Amopteyl to broaden its activities in order to ready itself for what lay ahead: "Now we must at least reckon with the possibility that for years to come, the few tens of our own people must stand at the fore posts. American Jews are not yet ready. We know that. But you, our people, must be ready to take over the [YIVO] mission."[41]

By bringing key personnel to the United States—including Weinreich, Kalmanovitch, and the young Czernowitz (Cernauti)-based linguistics aspirant Khayim Gininger—a "jewel of an institute" could be built with ten select people joining forces with the researchers already present in America.[42] As a show of his recognition of the importance of America as a Jewish center, Weinreich supported the publication, in coordination with Vilna, of an American edition of *YIVO-bleter* under a name that would indicate the journal's new, hopefully temporary, provenance. He also explained to Feinerman that he was in the midst of preparing a dictionary of literary Yiddish for use by those with competence in English as a second language (users would consult a word known to them in English in order to find its Yiddish equivalent). The choice of English rather than another language, such as Polish or Russian, as the auxiliary language emphasized that "the center of gravity (let us not decree for how long) has moved to you."[43] These publications would thus simultaneously point to the Amopteyl's continuity with YIVO-Vilna while emphasizing its independent identity and asserting its relevance.

Undeterred by the war, from January 6 to 8, 1940, the Amopteyl held its annual conference. In addition to the usual opening addresses, academic lectures, and expressions of sympathy and solidarity with the suffering Jews of eastern Europe in general and YIVO colleagues in Vilna in particular, the conference affirmed the Amopteyl's commitment to execute all duties that could not be performed by the center in Vilna, among them the coordination of activities with YIVO divisions throughout the world. Girding itself for its new role, the Amopteyl embarked on a program of expansion, including a research agenda addressing the unique history and culture of American Jewry. It announced having collected $3,000 in contributions from private individuals and organizations for activities in America.

The Amopteyl absorbed the independent Central Jewish Library and Press Archives, making its 5,000 square foot office no longer adequate. It also announced a plan to found a special commission for trade unions to collect materials and the necessary funds to publish a volume on the history of the Jewish workers' movement in the United States.[44] *Jews in Poland,* an anthology of articles by YIVO scholars originally intended to be edited and published in Vilna, was also in preparation and was expected to generate wide interest given the circumstances of the day. Following the conference, the Amopteyl announced, "It is possibly of the greatest importance to emphasize that the time has come for America, which has the largest and most secure Jewish community in the world, also to become the greatest Jewish cultural and academic center in the world."[45]

In confirmation of the Amopteyl's new importance, volume 15 (January–February 1940) of *YIVO-bleter,* a double issue edited by the executive office of the Amopteyl, appeared in New York City. The journal's name and design remained unchanged, but its cover announced under the title that the Amopteyl published it. The editors' preface explained that additional issues devoting significant attention to American themes (volume 15 contained only two articles about America) were to follow. Although assuring readers that this arose as a response to the "temporary weakening of publication activity in the Jewish Scientific Institute, whose center is in Vilna," it erroneously informed them that this decision had been made "with the agreement of the Vilna leadership."[46]

On the contrary, news of the publication caused great alarm, dismay, and indignation within the temporary administration in Vilna: "We have heard that a new issue of *YIVO-bleter* has appeared in America," Bundist educator Gershon Pludermakher lamented. "This is symptomatic—they probably think that YIVO-Vilna has gone under. The true milieu around the YIVO is in Vilna. The Yiddish movement is not faring well in America." Fellow educator Khayim Shloyme Kazhdan echoed these sentiments: "*YIVO-bleter* is the property and the symbol of the YIVO-Vilna. If it is published in America, that is [tantamount to] a slow liquidation and transfer to America."[47] From the perspective of most YIVO members in Vilna, not only was it unthinkable to declare New York YIVO's center, effectively announcing an end to the cultural and intellectual preeminence of eastern Europe in the Jewish world, but it was also wholly unwarranted, as Vilna's importance as the capital of Yiddish-speaking Jewry had only increased with the absorption of refugees, including YIVO scholars and activists, from Poland since September 1939.

With Vilna virtually the only escape route from Poland to the free world by late 1939, more than 14,000 Polish Jews, including members of political, cultural, and religious elites, gathered there between the outbreak of war and June 1940. The presence of so many refugees coupled with the absorption of tens of thousands of other Jews by Lithuania, most of them Yiddish speakers, actually made possible something of a cultural efflorescence in Vilna. Lithuanian Jewry had been isolated from its Polish brethren throughout most of the interwar period due to the absence of diplomatic relations between the two lands. Now it received these refugees generously and was eager to benefit from their creative and organizational talents.[48] The departure of the Soviets, who had banned the Yiddish press in Vilna and pursued individuals and organizations deemed dangerous to their interests,[49] opened—as Max Weinreich had hoped—new vistas for Jewish culture in a more tolerant Lithuania that posed no real impediments to YIVO's activities once the authorities legalized the institute. The state offered support to Jewish schools, and Lithuanian academic circles even evinced enthusiasm for Yiddish culture and YIVO.

From Copenhagen, Weinreich argued to Feinerman and the Amopteyl that conditions under independent Lithuanian rule could be far better for YIVO and Yiddish culture than in Poland, because in Lithuania "there is no assimilation." There, in contrast with Poland, where most Jewish children attended Polish-language state schools, state support for schools in Jewish languages existed throughout the interwar period. Consequently, Weinreich argued, Yiddish schools would continue to grow there and necessarily turn to YIVO for guidance on questions of language and pedagogy. This would justify the need for the *aspirantur* and *proaspirantur* programs, which prepared researchers, teachers, and social workers. Instead of losing a generation in the long struggle with the "the other side" (*sitre-akhre*), the demonic forces that Weinreich had earlier located in polonization, the dream of a self-sustaining, multigenerational intellectual and academic culture seemed possible in Lithuania. "If Vilna does not become a backroom of Russia, it can again become a mother-city in Israel—not only for Lithuanian Jews" but for Jews arriving from elsewhere, too, wrote Weinreich to Feinerman. It was of the utmost importance to prepare a new generation of scholars, both in Europe and America, within YIVO's path rather than to hope that scattered individuals would carry on with the institute's work in isolation and without the benefit of systematic academic training in Judaica, as was generally the case in eastern Europe in the years before the creation of YIVO.[50]

Within the temporary administration in Vilna, only Zelig Kalmanovitch openly rejected such optimism. Since his very return to Vilna, Kalmanovitch expressed grave doubts for the future of YIVO due to a lack of money and a loss of key personnel. He also had little confidence in Yiddishism, which he deemed an unviable ideology in an age of assimilation, and in eastern European Jewry itself.[51] Nonetheless, he remained willing to continue his work. His colleagues respected his commitment to YIVO despite condemning what they saw as his demoralizing negativity.[52] Without granting his accord to its content, Kalmanovitch sent a telegram on behalf of the executive office to the Ampteyl to halt the publication of *YIVO-bleter*. In it he denounced the possibility of dual sites of publication as a sign of disorganization. Personally, however, he argued before his Vilna colleagues that no reason existed not to publish in New York: two of the journal's editors, Lerer and Leshchinsky, already lived there, and two others, Weinreich and Tcherikower, were also not present in Vilna. New York could also more easily communicate with the rest of the world. Further, Vilna lacked the money to publish.[53]

In February 1940, Feinerman and Niger protested once again in the name of the Ampteyl against any changes in Vilna as long as the war continued and urged it to undertake no "work of a local character," namely courses "that can be met by a local institution and have nothing to do with the institute as a world center." They requested Vilna not to launch any new publications and to yield in the matter of *YIVO-bleter*, as the journal's appearance in New York, they claimed, had deeply impressed the American public. Without it, it would be difficult to raise money from Americans.[54] A letter sent the following month reiterated these objections concerning *YIVO-bleter*. By this time, the Ampteyl questioned whether Vilna was even receiving its letters. (Indeed, as reflected by YIVO-Vilna's internal date stamp, the letter, unbeknown to the Ampteyl, was actually received only in mid-May.) It concluded that it had better assessed the situation than Vilna and expressed its intention to publish a second double issue of *YIVO-bleter*:

> We strongly doubt whether you have even a concept [of] what would happen here if we do not publish an issue of *YIVO-bleter*. . . . We can imagine that we will have no one to whom to send it [if we wait] until it will be possible for you to publish an issue of *YIVO-bleter* and until it will reach our subscribers in America. True, publishing an issue of *YIVO-bleter* in New York costs much more than in Vilna; it is also true that the first issue was not technically overly successful but it is still better than nothing.[55]

At almost exactly the same time, in mid-March 1940, Max Weinreich arrived with his son Uriel aboard a Swedish ship in New York harbor after a twelve-day voyage from Copenhagen. Officially, his purpose lay in launching a fundraising and publicity campaign for YIVO while visiting America. He intended to return to Vilna after the summer.[56] His presence would also help to elucidate the situation of Vilna for the Amopteyl, with whom communication still remained difficult and on whose irregular remissions Vilna depended for survival. YIVO in Vilna would meanwhile take the necessary steps to procure Lithuanian citizenship for him.[57]

Reports from Kalmanovitch increased the incentive for Weinreich's return. In a departure from his customary pessimism, Kalmanovitch indicated with satisfaction that the situation in Vilna had largely stabilized thanks to the support of the Joint Distribution Committee, the Argentina YIVO, and fundraising and book sales in Lithuania. In his newest evaluation, YIVO served as an intellectual and cultural center more than ever, despite an alarming desperation for funds. The reading room and exhibitions were drawing record numbers of visitors from the local population, among them representatives of Lithuanian academia. Refugee scholars previously uninvolved in Jewish research now conducted research in their areas of specialization with Jewry as their subject of study. In some cases, they even demonstrated a new eagerness to learn Yiddish and Hebrew. A plan was made, although ultimately never realized, for volume 16 of *YIVO-bleter* to appear after the summer in Vilna.[58]

At a press conference in June, Kalmanovitch offered an overview of YIVO's activity of the past several months. This included the acquisition of folklore materials from Lithuania, Romania, Palestine, America, England, and elsewhere, including the archives of the Greditser (Grätz in Posnan) rebbe; a proposal for economic-statistical research on the Jews in Lithuania; the research activity of sixty researchers, among them tens of refugees and eleven *aspirantn*; the training of *proaspirantn* in Yiddish and Hebrew, Jewish history, literature, and folklore; the use of the institute by various private researchers; the publication of the sixth volume of a Yiddish translation of Simon Dubnow's *History of the Jewish People,* the first volume of Y. L. Cahan's collected folklore writings; the preparation of a volume of *Psikhologish-pedagogishe shriftn* (*Psychological-Pedagogical Writings*); the second edition of Max Weinreich's *Der veg tsu undzer yugnt* (*The Path to Our Youth*); and a monograph on the history of Hasidism. In the preceding four months, YIVO editions had been sold for Lt10,000 (about $1,000). Drawing on the expertise of its enlarged staff, YIVO also organized popular academic lectures about Yiddish grammar, Jewish history, Lithuanian Jewish history, and Jewish literature, folklore, and demography—each lecture drawing on average eighty listeners. The twenty-fifth anniversary of Y. L. Peretz's death was marked with ceremonies such as a radio program featuring Dubnow and Vilnius University's rector Professor Mykolas Biržiška. An exhibit dedicated to the writer drew more than 5,000 visitors.[59]

All of these efforts were crowned by the anticipated opening of a chair for Yiddish language and literature in the humanities faculty of Vilnius University, to be supported by the Jewish community, in the spring. Such a position was hardly conceivable while the same institution was the Polish Stefan Batory University. A referendum conducted via telegram among members of the philological section nominated Weinreich for the position in expectation of his return by the fall.[60]

Parallel to this celebration of the YIVO-Vilna's collective accomplishments, Shmuel Niger in New York reflected on the achievements of YIVO in America. Before YIVO, Jewish scholarship in America, as exemplified by the American Jewish Historical Society, focused on the "Judaism" of German and Sephardic Jewries. Privileging Judaism as a religious system rather than as a civilization with its own unique cultural forms in all aspects of life, it paid little attention to eastern European Jews and *Yidishkeyt*. Even the Amopteyl conducted no systematic work on American Jewry and sent materials about it to Vilna. "The possibility of Jewish scholarship in America was doubted just as for a long time there was no confidence in American Jewish literature. The 'true' writers were in the old home. The 'true' scholars were also there. There—and not here. A war had to erupt, the oldest and most rooted Jewish community in Europe had to experience a catastrophe for Jews in America to assume new duties, a great new responsibility." The last world war, Niger continued, had brought the "emancipation" of American Jewish scholarship. Scholarship in America was now forced "to stand on its own feet and to cease being merely an auxiliary agency for YIVO in Vilna."[61]

For a brief period YIVO indeed possessed two centers, each exceptionally productive and convinced of its preeminence (if only for the time being). This period, however, came to an end with the return of the Red Army to Vilna in mid-June 1940 and the annexation of Lithuania as the sixteenth Soviet Socialist Republic in August. Even before changes were made in YIVO, a despondent Kalmanovitch foresaw the worst: "The destruction of not just YIVO but of scholarship, civilization, autonomy." Accordingly, he encouraged Weinreich to develop the center in New York. Expecting the rapid sovietization of the institution and its decimation, he was pleasantly surprised that he was able to continue his function there and to communicate with colleagues in New York for weeks to come. Nonetheless, his optimism was very much guarded: "This is a good-bye letter," he wrote Weinreich, "if we cannot continue to correspond."[62] He vowed to Weinreich that he would continue working in YIVO and protect it as long as permitted.[63] By July 1940, Kalmanovitch was receptive to the Amopteyl's proposal to bring him to America. The necessary visa was obtained for him through the intervention of the Amopteyl, and YIVO offered him employment as a "lecturer in linguistics, esp. Arabic and Syriac, for $1,800 per year."[64] Yet for reasons unclear, Kalmanovitch never made the trip to the United States.[65]

The imposition of Soviet order meant that the plan for a Yiddish chair at Vilnius University would now be achieved with full state funding—the fulfillment of Yiddishist dreams impossible elsewhere. It also meant, of course, the eventual purging of YIVO of ideologically unsuitable elements. This resulted in the removal of most of its staff, including Kalmanovitch, who thereafter eked out a living as a copy editor.[66] Now exclusively a research institution, YIVO was integrated in January 1941 into the Scholarly Academy of the Soviet Lithuanian Republic. Soviet officials made Noah Prylucki, for whom Kalmanovitch (and also Weinreich) expressed contempt as both a scholar and a person, the director as well as the chair for Yiddish.[67] Tcherikower managed to come in the summer of 1940 to New York, adding another YIVO founder to the staff of the Amopteyl.[68]

By now, if not earlier, it was clear to Weinreich not only that Vilna could no longer serve as YIVO's center but also that YIVO as he had known it there had ceased to exist. Privately anxious about the welfare of his friends and his own family,[69] he expressed publicly his hope that from the ravages of war the Yiddish language—which he called the "official language" of Jewish life in polyglot Nazi ghettos—and culture would emerge only stronger, especially wherever eastern European Jews would migrate in large numbers.[70] He predicted that YIVO would play an essential role in rebuilding postwar Jewish life. The task of the Amopteyl was, according to him, to assume the mantle of YIVO-Vilna, to draw together the various threads of the organization across the world, and to attract new blood. Only then could YIVO do good work and thereby achieve the recognition for it and for Yiddish that it lacked in America. This meant reproducing the *aspirantur* in New York and attracting American-born scholars and scholars to whom Jewish research was previously foreign, as well as pursuing a research agenda that gave American topics their due. American Jewry had to be made to understand how important Yiddish and Jewish research were for its very existence. YIVO, Weinreich affirmed in the middle of World War II, had a crucial role to play in American Jewish life: "The world is today drenched with oppression but there will come a time when the world will be free again and the Jews in Europe together with it. Then YIVO will be needed again, so we must see to maintaining it. But America also needs an institution that researches Jewish life with the methods of modern social science. Let us roll up our sleeves and get to work."[71]

At a 1945 YIVO conference, Weinreich spoke of the urgent need for YIVO to serve as an institute of higher Yiddish studies that would bring semi-assimilated, English-speaking American Jewish youth closer to eastern European Jewish civilization. Providing an alternative to the equally uninspiring poles of immigrants, "Hester Street" and the de-ethnicized "Reform Temple," secular Yiddish culture and scholarship would help American-born youth gird themselves psychologically to overcome the stigma of Jewishness and develop a proud, modern Jewish identity that would embrace the cultural heritage of eastern Europe without rejecting its American identity.[72] In private letters to poet Avrom Sutskever, though, Weinreich expressed his great frustration with the pitiful state of Yiddish language and culture in America in comparison with eastern Europe and the prospects for YIVO in America. Refusing to succumb to pessimism, however, he wrote in these letters of his will to "Vilnaize" American Jewish life with the help of other former Vilna residents active in YIVO.[73]

Weinreich, like a number of his colleagues in Vilna and New York, expressed deep pessimism by the early 1940s over the future of YIVO and of Yiddish in America—a language in a "state of disintegration" in the mouths of American-born speakers unaccustomed to speaking it outside the home.[74] Nevertheless, he strongly believed in the importance of YIVO for American Jewry and of American Jewry for world Jewry. To be psychologically healthy and whole, he explained to his student, later the renowned literary scholar Dan Miron, not long before his death in 1969, American Jews must someday return to Yiddish, the "language of their collective unconscious." Only with the help of *Yidishe visnshaft*—Jewish social science in the YIVO tradition—could they grasp the "hidden parts of their national personality."[75] Hence, even if an English-speaking American Jewry had assumed preeminence in the Jewish diaspora, if not the Jewish world, it could never understand itself until it chose Yiddish and embraced its eastern European cultural legacy.

Weinreich's misplaced optimism—his decision to stay in Copenhagen rather than return immediately to Vilna—saved him and his family. Most of his colleagues who remained, returned, or took refuge in Vilna, including Kalmanovitch and Prylucki, were murdered at the hands of the Nazis and their accomplices. His refusal to accept American Jewry *as it was* has shaped the subsequent history of Yiddish studies as an academic field and of YIVO as an institution, helping make New York City a world center of Jewish research. New York City did not emerge as YIVO headquarters overnight, however, with Weinreich's arrival. Nor was the decision to make New York City the center universally accepted and embraced, either in Vilna or New York. As soon as war erupted, the Amopteyl began, with Weinreich's encouragement, preparing itself for a leadership role despite objections. The arrival of Weinreich and other refugee scholars helped to make the fulfillment of this role possible; the destruction of YIVO-Vilna made it a necessity if YIVO and its values were to have a future.

Notes

1. "Erklerung fun idishn-visnshaftlikhen institut vegen ihr vayterdiger tetigkeyt," *Forverts* October 2, 1939. Unless otherwise noted, all translations are mine.
2. Dov Levin, *The Lesser of Two Evils* (Philadelphia: Jewish Publication Society, 1995), 198-217.
3. Minutes of the meeting of YIVO's temporary administration (YTA), Vilna, December 9-10, 1939 (RG 1.1, box 3.1, folder 631, YIVO archives, New York City).
4. Dov Levin, "The Jews of Vilna under Soviet Rule, 19 September-28 October 1939," *Polin* 9 (1996): 107-36, 117; According to Yisroel Lempert, it was then believed in Vilna that Reyzen was arrested for writing an article critical of the Hitler-Stalin Pact in his newspaper *Unzer tog*. Yisroel Lempert, "Der goyrl fun yivo in historishn iberbrokh (1939-1941)," *YIVO-bleter*, n.s., 3 (1997): 9-42, 9.

5. Opening the December 9-10 meeting of YTA, Zelig Kalmanovitch lamented, "I consider it my duty to honor the memory of all those who have died in the current *khurbn* of Polish Jewry" (YTA minutes, Vilna, December 9-10, 1939), 1.

6. Leo Herskowitz et al., "New York City," in *The Encyclopaeida Judaica*, 2nd ed. (Detroit: Macmillan Reference, 2007), 15:212; Antony Polonsky, "Warsaw," in *The YIVO Encyclopedia of Jews in Eastern Europe*, ed. Gershon David Hundert (New Haven: Yale University Press, 2008), 2:2001.

7. As determined by the 1930 US census, the Jewish population of the United States was 4,770,647. H. S. Linfield, "Jewish Communities of the United States," in *American Jewish Year Book 1940-1941*, ed. American Jewish Committee (Philadelphia: Jewish Publication Society, 1941), 42:218.

8. On the term *Yiddishland*, see Cecile Kuznitz, "On the Jewish Street: Yiddish Culture and the Urban Landscape in Interwar Vilna," *Studies in Jewish Civilization* 9 (1998): 65-92.

9. Cecile Kuznitz provides the former date (p. 2090) in her overview of the institute's history in "YIVO," in *The YIVO Encyclopedia of Jews in Eastern Europe*, ed. Gershon D. Hundert (New Haven: Yale University Press, 2008), 2:2090-96. Zachary Baker offers the latter date (p. 225-26) in "Die Amerikanisierung der jiddischen Wissenschaft," *Judaica* 51, no. 4 (1995): 222-36. Both devote little attention to this transitional period. According to Lucy Dawidowicz's memoir, *From That Place and Time* (New York: Bantam Books, 1989), 207, New York became YIVO's headquarters in September 1940 because "The Vilna YIVO as I had known it no longer existed, though we heard that its physical facilities had remained intact." Dov Levin does not point to a specific month for this development but offers the most substantial scholarly treatment of this period in his article, "Tsvishn hamer un serp. Di geshikhte fun yidishn visnshaftlekhn institut in vilne unter der sovetisher memshole," *YIVO-bleter* 46 (1980): 78-97, 83-85. Despite its title, Lempert's "Der goryl fun yivo in historishn iberbrokh (1939-1941)," *YIVO-bleter*, n.s., 3 (1997): 9-42 treats almost exclusively the second Soviet period beginning in June 1940.

10. On the history of YIVO before World War II, see Cecile Esther Kuznitz, *The Origins of Jewish Scholarship and the YIVO Institute for Jewish Research* (PhD diss., Stanford University, 2000) as well as her overview of the institute in *The YIVO Encyclopedia*, 2:2090-96; Yankev Shatski, "Finf un tsvantsik yor yivo," in *Shatski-bukh*, ed. Y. Lifshits (New York: YIVO, 1958), 303-17; also, Dawidowicz, *From That Place and Time*. The figures for YIVO's staff and students for the academic year 1938/39 are taken from Dawidowicz, *From That Place and Time*, 78, 89.

11. Cecile Kuznitz, "YIVO Institute for Jewish Research in the United States," in *Encyclopedia of American Jewish History*, ed. Stephen H. Norwood and Eunice G. Pollack (Santa Barbara, CA: ABC-CLIO, 2008), 768-69.

12. See Nina Warnke, "Of Plays and Politics: Sholem Aleichem's First Visit to America," *YIVO Annual* 20 (1991): 239-76; Chone Shmeruke, "Sholem Aleichem and America," *YIVO Annual* 20 (1991): 211-38; Michael Brown, *The Israeli-American Connection* (Detroit: Wayne State University Press, 1996).

13. Dawidowicz, *From That Place and Time*, 212-13.

14. Max Weinreich, letter to Naftali Feinerman, August 24, 1939 (RG 584, folder 293b, YIVO archives); Gabriel Weinreich, *Confessions of a Jewish Priest: From Secular Jewish War Refugee to Physicist and Episcopal Clergyman* (Cleveland: Pilgrim Press, 2005), 35.

15. "D'r Vaynraykh brengt grus fun dem yidishn yishev in norvegye," *Der tog*, March 20, 1940; Feinerman, letter to Kalmanovitch, December 5, 1939 (RG 100A, box 24, YIVO archives). In late 1939 Weinreich, hardly a devout religious believer, wrote to Feinerman of the Amopteyl: "Personally, we are doing well. All are friendly to us. My son is going to a Danish school. In the beginning, they took him for a trial period of two weeks but now he is one of their own. They gave him textbooks and he is already writing assignments

in Danish, mastered it faster than I. If only my wife and other son could be gotten out of there, I would thank the master of the universe thrice daily" (undated fragment, RG 584, folder 293b, YIVO archives).

16. Weinreich, letter to Feinerman, October 14, 1939 (RG 584, folder 293b).
17. Feinerman, letter to Tcherikower, December 6, 1939 (RG 101 A, box 24, folder *tet*).
18. Meeting of Amopteyl executive office, December 28, 1939 (RG 1.1, box 33, folder 690).
19. Tcherikower, letter to Feinerman, November 15, 1939 (RG 101 A, box 24, folder *tet*).
20. Feinerman, letter to Weinreich, January 23, 1940 (RG 100A, box 28, folder M. Weinreich). See also the letter from the Rockefeller Foundation to Feinerman, November 20, 1939 (RG 584, box 81, folder 696).
21. "D'r Maks Vaynraykh kumt dinstik keyn Amerike," *Der tog*, March 17, 1940. For details on Weinreich's year at Yale, see Barbara Kirshenblatt-Gimblett, "Coming of Age in the Thirties: Max Weinreich, Edward Sapir, and Jewish Social Science," *YIVO Annual* 23 (1996): 1-103; See also Jennifer Young's essay in this book.
22. Weinreich, letter to Feinerman, November 14, 1939 (RG 584, box 293b).
23. Regina Weinreich, letter to Max Weinreich, December 2, 1940 (RG 584, box 71, folder 604).
24. Regina Weinreich, letter to Max Weinreich, December 3, 1940 (RG 584, box 71, folder 604).
25. Regina Weinreich, letter to Max Weinreich, December 2, 1940. According to Dawidowicz, she never forgave herself for leaving behind her mother (Dawidowicz, *From That Place and Time*, 217).
26. Regina Weinreich, letter to Max Weinreich, January 1, 1940 (RG 584, box 71, folder 604).
27. Weinreich, letter to Feinerman, December 22, 1939 (RG 100A, box 28, folder M. Weinreich); Feinerman, letter to Tcherikower, December 5, 1939 (RG 101 A, box 24, folder *tet*).
28. YTA minutes, Vilna, December 9-10, 1939, 5-6.
29. "Der yivo banayt zayn tetikeyt in vilne," November 7, 1939 (RG 1.1, box 32, folder VIII/672).
30. Weinreich, letter to Feinerman, December 24, 1939 (RG 100A, box 28, folder M. Weinreich).
31. Weinreich approved of issuing *YIVO-bleter* with a title indicating its origins, such as "*American YIVO-bleter*" (Weinreich, letter to Feinerman, n.d. [RG 584, folder 293b]). In a personal letter to Kalmanovitch in December 1939, Feinerman complained that he had received no news directly from Kalmanovitch or YIVO-Vilna and relied on Weinreich to transmit information. Further, he alerted Kalmanovitch to the Amopteyl's publication intentions: "What are your plans? What about *YIVO-bleter*? Meanwhile, we have prepared to print an issue of *YIVO-bleter* that will appear at the end of the month. For us it is clear that two issues of *YIVO-bleter* ought not to be published. If Vilna can publish *YIVO-bleter* and send them to America, we will, of course, stop further publication." Feinerman, letter to Kalmanovitch, December 5, 1939.
32. Feinerman, letter to YIVO-Vilna, January 19, 1940 (RG 1.1, box 31, folder 664).
33. Minutes of the Amopteyl executive office, September 9, 1939, p. 5 (RG 1.1, box 33, folder 690).
34. Feinerman, letter to Tcherikower, December 5, 1939. The Amopteyl sent regular payments for personal expenses to Kalmanovitch, his son in Palestine, and the *aspirant* Khayim Gininger in Czernowitz (Cernauti) in addition to Weinreich and Tcherikower.
35. Feinerman, letter to Weinreich, November 21, 1939 (RG 584, folder 293b).
36. YIVO scholar Jakob Lestschinksy expressed a common sentiment when, at the Amopteyl's conference in 1942, he observed that American immigrant "ghettos" served as a sort of "ingathering of the exiles." They united Jews of various backgrounds who were integrated to varying degrees into non-Jewish society in their native lands. For some

time, ghettos resisted waves of cultural assimilation. In the long run, however, they were not strong enough to generate a national culture to resist these powerful waves in America ("Toyznt mentshn bay erefenung fun konferents fun yidishn visnshaftlekhn institut," *Forverts*, January 11, 1942).

37. Characteristically, Max Weinreich was sensitive to Yiddish's status as an immigrant language threatened with being overrun with anglicisms or disappearing in the United States. He noted how even Jews whose dominant language was English spoke English in a manner reflecting Yiddish syntactical and other influences. M. Weinreich, "English un di imigrantn-shprakhn in Amerike," *YIVO-bleter* 3 (January–May, 1932), 79–85.

38. Editorial, "Yidishe interesn," *Forverts*, March 3, 1940.

39. On the ambivalent attitudes of immigrant Jews in America toward their home communities in eastern Europe, see Rebecca Kobrin, "The Shtetl by the Highway: The East European City in New York's Landsmanshaft Press, 1921–1939," *Prooftexts* 26, no. 1–2 (2006): 107–37; Daniel Soyer, "Transnationalism and Americanization in East European Jewish Immigrant Public Life," in *Imagining the American Jewish Community*, ed. Jack Wertheimer (Waltham, MA: Brandeis University Press, 2007), 47–66.

40. Meeting of Amopteyl, September 21, 1939 (RG 1.1, box 33, folder 690).

41. Weinreich, letter to Feinerman, September 25, 1939 (RG 584, folder 293b).

42. Weinreich, letter to Feinerman, October 30, 1939 (RG 584, folder 293b).

43. Weinreich, letter to Feinerman, September 25, 1939 (RG 584, folder 293b). The folder also contains the five-page plan for Weinreich's proposed dictionary.

44. "Yivo-konferents in nyu-york" (RG 1.1, box 32, folder VIII/672); "Yidishe interesn," *Forverts*, January 16, 1940.

45. "Yidishe interesn," *Forverts*, January 9, 1940.

46. "Fun der redaktsye," *YIVO-bleter* 15 (1940): 1–2.

47. YTA minutes, Vilna, January 27, 1940, pp. 23–24 (RG 1.1, box 3.1, folder 361).

48. See, for example, Moyshe Mandelman, "In freyd un leyd tsvishn litvishe yidn (fun 1938 biz 1940)," in *Lite* [Lithuania], ed. Mendel Sudarsky, Uriah Katzenelenbogen, and J. Kissin (New York: Jewish-Lithuanian Cultural Society, 1951), 1333–58.

49. On this period, see, Dov Levin, "The Jews of Vilna under Soviet Rule," *Polin* 9 (1996): 107–37.

50. Weinreich, letter to Feinerman, October 14, 1939 (RG 584, folder 293b). On issues of schooling and linguistic acculturation, see Gershon Bacon, "National Revival, Ongoing Acculturation—Jewish Education in Interwar Poland," *Jahrbuch des Simon-Dubnow-Instituts/Simon Dubnow Institute Yearbook* 1 (2002): 71–92.

51. Joshua Karlip, "At the Crossroads between War and Genocide: A Reassessment of Jewish Ideology in 1940," *Jewish Social Studies* 11, no. 2 (2005): 170–201.

52. See, for example, David Kaplan-Kaplansky's disapproval of Kalmanovitch as a candidate for the proposed chair for Yiddish at Vilnius University: "It's not possible for him to occupy the post because in my ears resound his talk about Jews not being a people and Yiddish not surviving." Session of YTA, March 10, 1940, p. 15 (RG 1.1, box 3.1, folder 631).

53. YTA minutes, January 27, 1940, 14–15.

54. Letter from Amopteyl to YIVO-Vilna, February 21, 1940 (RG 1.1, box 31, folder 664).

55. Letter from Amopteyl (Feinerman) to YIVO-Vilna, March 12, 1940 (RG 1.1, box 31, folder 663).

56. "D'r Maks Vaynraykh kumt dinstik keyn Amerike," *Dertog*, March 17, 1940; "D'r Vaynraykh brengt grus fun dem yidishn yishev in Norvegye," *Dertog*, March 20, 1940.

57. Kalmanovitch, letter to Weinreich, May 17, 1940 (RG 584, box 30, folder 293b).

58. Letter from YIVO-Vilna to Amopteyl, May 10, 1940 (RG 1.1, box 30, folder 664).

59. N. S., "A shitkl balans fun der arbet fun 'yivo,'" *Yidishe shtime* (Vilna, Lithuania), June 6, 1940; V., "Avire d'YIVO," *Vilner togblat*, June 7, 1940; "Profesorn fun vilner universitet oyf

der perets-oysshtelung yivo" (RG 584, box 30, folder 293); Mandelman, "In freyd un leyd tsvishn litvishe yidn," 1349.

60. On controversies surrounding the chair and Weinreich's nomination for it, see Kalman Weiser, "YIVO and the Chair for Yiddish at the University of Vilnius," *Polin* 24 (2012): 223-55.

61. Shmuel Niger, "Yidishe visnshaft antdekt Amerike," 1940 (RG 1.1, box 32, folder VIII/672).

62. Kalmanovitch, letter to Weinreich, June 17, 1940 (RG 584, box 30, folder 293b).

63. Kalmanovitch, letter to Weinreich, July 1, 1940 (RG 584, box 30, folder 293b).

64. Society of Friends of the Yiddish Scientific Institute (Feinerman), letter to Kalmano-vitch, July 29, 1940 (RG 1.1, box 31, folder 664).

65. "Awaiting passport transitvisa secured concerning steamticket will cable separately Kal-manovitch." Kalmanovitch, telegram to Amopteyl, September 15, 1940 (RG 1.1, box 31, folder 664).

66. Shmerke Kaczerginski, *Tsvishn hamer un serp. Tsu der geshikhte fun der likvidatsye fun der yidisher kultur in sovetn-Rusland* (Buenos Aires: Der emes, 1950), 28.

67. In November 1939, Kalmanovitch wrote to Feinerman expressing his concern that Noah Prylucki and his folkist "friends," namely David Kaplan-Kaplansky, would at-tempt to join the YIVO executive office. "Weinreich and I," he wrote, "are completely against this. He is a personal disgrace and unpleasant—a danger to the YIVO executive office. Our American friends are also dissatisfied with his work." Kalmanovitch, letter to Feinerman (Amopteyl), November 9, 1939 (RG 100A, box 24). He also attempted to block Prylucki's nomination as chair for Yiddish at Vilnius University. Kalmanovitch, letter to Weinreich, n.d. (RG 584, box 30, folder 293b). Weinreich expressed his low re-gard for Prylucki's editorship of *Yidish far ale* in a mordant review of the journal (Max Weinreich, "Zibn numern 'Yidish far ale,'" *Yidish far ale* 10 [December 1938]: 280-90).

68. Dawidowicz, *From That Place and Time*, 214.

69. Weinreich managed to obtain visas for his younger son and wife, who arrived in New York in January 1941 (Dawidowicz, *From That Place and Time*, 217).

70. Weinreich, "Vos vet zayn mit undzer yidisher shprakh nokh der itstiker milkhome?" *Forverts*, February 8, 1941.

71. Max Weinreich, "Der yidisher visnshaftlekher institut hot zikh 'bazetst' in Amerike biz di milkhome vet fariber," *Forverts*, January 11, 1942.

72. Weinreich, "Der yivo un di problemen fun undzer tsayt," *YIVO-bleter* 25, no. 1 (1945): 3-18.

73. Weinreich, letter to Avrom Sutskever, January 9, 1947, "Briv fun Maks Vaynraykh tsu Avrom Sutskever," *Di goldene keyt* 95/96 (1978): 171-203.

74. Weinreich, "Vegn englishe elementn in undzer kulturshprakh," *Yidishe shprakh* 1/2 (1941): 34.

75. Dan Miron, "Between Science and Faith: Sixty Years of the YIVO Institute," *YIVO Annual* 19 (1990): 14.

YIDDISH ENCOUNTERS HEBREW

Prelude

BARBARA MANN

I came to Yiddish, to YIVO, in order to fully get Hebrew. This was my story for years (first mistake[1]). As a student of modern Hebrew culture, I maintained, it was impossible, irresponsible, really, to fully enter into Hebrew literature without somehow encountering, accounting for, Yiddish along the way. This "accounting" included a recognition of the degree to which modern Hebrew literature emerged from a Yiddish-speaking-writing-thinking milieu and how many early modern Hebrew writers worked in both languages; it also entailed an appreciation of the full "polysystem" of modern Jewish culture broadly conceived and the specific matrix of modernism within which these authors operated. The main critical gesture still seems to me one of examining some sort of codependence, of admitting the relationship and beginning to unpack its import.

At some point I realized that the very act of studying Yiddish, of reading poems written in that language in the New York where I'd been born and raised, was itself a kind of memorial, more important, possibly, than studying the Hebrew-Israeli writing that—*meyle*—was being lived and breathed by millions every day (second mistake[2]). Midway through the summer program at YIVO, I called my father to ask about the only grandmother I'd known, who had died when I was ten. My teachers said I had a "natural" Litvish accent and I wanted to know why. Nana was from Romania. What had my young ears absorbed and retained, buried in some deep linguistic subconscious, now shocked back to life in the presence of real live Yiddish speakers. He picked up the bedroom phone. "Did Nana speak Yiddish around me when I was little?" I asked. "No," I heard him shrug and shake his head on the other end. From the downstairs phone my mother's voice cut him off: "We spoke it in the kitchen all the time."

Litvish. Romania. The kitchen. YIVO. Despite its putative reputation as a displaced language, and despite my own initial inclinations to the contrary, it turns out Yiddish is quite "placed" for me. Though wishing to "locate" Yiddish within Hebrew, or in relation to Hebrew, Yiddish's own narrative of place has stubbornly reasserted itself, even as—it must be said—the actual places in which Yiddish is spoken have themselves largely migrated and dispersed. If Ashkenaz was "home," how can we begin to theorize the various diasporic "Yiddishlands" that have emerged since the break, especially in relation to normative Jewish notions of homeland and exile? Ironically, when Yiddish moves out of Europe it remembers the *alte heym* in terms that evoke the enduring memory of Jerusalem and the temple: the *landslayt* (compatriots) may well be in exile (again) but the abiding object of their longing and nostalgia is not *Eretz Yisrael*, but the streets and grand public spaces of Lodz and Minsk, and the steppes and forests of the Ukraine.

The relation between geography and language has emerged as a central concern in Jewish studies in recent years, enabling us to see more clearly how the encounter between Yiddish and Hebrew evolved in spectacularly spatial terms: Zionism cast Hebrew as the hyperterritorialized language, possessing a special relationship to a privileged national space, and denigrated Yiddish for its diasporic and (therefore) "rootless" status. Yet even the personal anecdote offered above demonstrates not only how embedded Yiddish has been in particular places but also the degree to which it has also been constitutive of space; Yiddish, for its part, seemed to shrug off any notion of rootlessness per se and instead reveled in its mobility, its far-flung network of reference and intimacy precisely because it was NOT tied to a single space:

> From Vilna to Buenos Aires,
> From Tel Aviv to New York,
> The miracle of generations has spread—
> the kingdom of the Yiddish word.[3]

And yet Yiddish, as it traveled through the market squares, the train carriages, the *shtetl*, and beyond, often remained bound up with Hebrew and its liturgical domain. Some of the most consequential encounters between Yiddish and Hebrew are constituted through the practice of translation, a movement over, from one linguistic, cultural space to another. The seminal instance may be the *tsene u-rene*, the Yiddish rendition of the Hebrew Bible—"for women and men who are like women"—that moves out of the domain of "holy text" to near-folkloric vernacular. Hayyim Nachman Bialik's autotranslation of *Be'ir haha-reiga* (*In the City of Slaughter*) into *In shkhite shtot* is a keen example of how a quintessentially Yiddish space (the detailed parameters of the Jewish quarter, its courtyards, homes, attics, basement, cemetery, and sites of prayer and ritual) attains its place, so to speak, in Hebrew's tradition of remembering catastrophe.

The Hebrew poem is, of course, already a kind of "translation," in that the poet incorporated the Yiddish oral testimony of Kishinev's (Chişinạu's) survivors, and his own Yiddish notes, into the highly stylized prophetic cadences of revival age Hebrew.[4]

The essays included here elucidate the connection between Yiddish and Hebrew within disparate historical and geographic locales. Tracing the trajectory of Yiddish as a point of contention within the nineteenth-century Hebrew press to Israeli Yiddish poetry as a topic of contemporary scholarship draws our attention to the enormous symbolic weight still accorded the relationship between these two languages. Furthermore, to say that for the last century or so, Yiddish has been "in *goles*" is to begin to rethink the very terms and attributes of both diaspora *and* home and to interrogate those paradigms that would too narrowly place or situate cultural practice. Contemporary encounters with Yiddish are as likely to occur within the virtual arena of the web as they are in the kitchen, evidence that Yiddish continues to create new notions of home within the already-bustling and noisy arena of modern Jewish experience.

Notes

1. I was perpetuating (albeit in secular form) the adage about Yiddish being the *shifḥa* (handmaid) of Hebrew, deriving from Yiddish's functional usage in the cheder to explicate *ḥumash*.
2. The mourning of Yiddish became a veritable industry, as Jeffery Shandler has persuasively demonstrated, although all the while Yiddish was actually living, in some fashion, a "postvernacular" existence that was quite joyous, even irreverent.
3. Leon Feinberg, *Yidish: poeme* [Yiddish: A Poem] (unpublished, 1950), 1. Cited in Jeffrey Shandler, *Adventures in Yiddishland: Postvernacular Language and Culture* (Berkeley: University of California Press, 2005), 42.
4. The Hebrew poem appeared in 1903. The Yiddish was first published in a collection of Bialik's poems called *Fun tsar un tsarn* (Odessa, Ukraine: Farlag kadima, 1906). For an extended discussion of the poem's cultural politics—then and now—see the special issue of *Prooftexts* 25 (winter/spring 2005):1-2.

A MISTRESS, A NANNY, OR A MAIDSERVANT

Discourse on Yiddish in Fin de Siècle Hebrew Newspapers in Eastern Europe

ELA BAUER

In March 1889, shortly after the publication of *Der hoyz fraynd* (*The House Friend*) by Mordkhe Spektor in Warsaw and *Di yidishe folks-bibliotek* (*The Jewish People's Library*) by Sholem Aleichem (Shalom Rabinovitz) in Kiev, a columnist in *Hatzefira*, Naftali Herz Nenmanowitz,[1] wrote, "What is *zhargon*? a plain ordinary Jew asked when he found on my desk such new *zhargon* books as *Di yidishe folks-bibliotek* by Sholem Aleichem and *Der hoyz fraynd* by Mr. Spektor. Did you not know [I answered], that *zhargon* is the spoken language among the Jews in our country? A Jewish language? this person wondered. What do you know? For 40 years already I've been speaking it and didn't know I was speaking *zhargon*."[2]

When Nenmanowitz penned this column, the Jewish spoken language stood at a crossroads. Until the late nineteenth century, most literature written in Yiddish, at that time known as *zhargon*, was designed for washerwomen and cooks.[3] However, it had begun to branch into modern literature that included various genres and held high aesthetic standards. The turning point occurred at a time when many Jewish intellectuals in eastern Europe considered this spoken language a low tongue devoid of grammar or any other rules. For many Jewish intellectuals Yiddish comprised a slang in which no moral philosophy or any other kind of serious thinking could be written.[4] Hence attempts by the founders of *Di yidishe folks-bibliotek*, *Der hoyz fraynd*, and *Di yidishe bibliotek* in the Russian Empire and in Congress Poland to legitimize the Jewish *zhargon* reflected a struggle among Jewish intellectuals themselves regarding the profile of modern Jewish literature.

This discussion on the new Yiddish literature in the last decade of the nineteenth century occurred in several private and public arenas. A central stage for this debate was the European Hebrew newspapers of the time, although the

issues addressed were far from new. As Nancy Sinkoff has shown in her book
on Mendel Lefin, at the end of the eighteenth century, following the decision
of Lefin to translate the Bible into Yiddish, a polemic over the language question had developed.[5] Indeed, Lefin's recognition that the enlightened leadership could use Yiddish in order to reach a wider, mass audience is impressive
for its insight and prescience.[6] Nevertheless, Lefin's vision remained limited:
he only suggested translating the Bible into Yiddish, whereas different Jewish
intellectuals at the end of the nineteenth century created modern, unique, and
even secular literature in Yiddish with high aesthetic standards, thus reaching far beyond the basic goal of Yiddish translations aimed at the Jewish
masses. Furthermore, the earlier polemic over Yiddish did not take place in
a public sphere such as the eastern European Hebrew press; instead, the debate took place through correspondences between Mendel Lefin and other east
European maskilim. Thus, the echoes of the first polemic over the language
question remained in relatively limited circles. By contrast, the polemic that
took place in the eastern European Hebrew press in the late nineteenth century had a broader reach and therefore increased the cultural impact of that
discourse.

This essay will examine the triangular discourse on the role of Yiddish that
played out in the pages of *Hatzefira*, *Hamelitz*, and *Hamagid* from 1889—the
year the first volume of *Di yidishe folks-bibliotek* was published—until 1894.[7]
These first five years mark the simultaneous beginning of the publication of
different Yiddish periodicals and almanacs in different eastern European cities. This phenomenon suggests a rethinking of the growth and diversification
of Yiddish literature and also the way in which Jewish intelligentsia in various
Jewish eastern European cultural centers referred to the Jewish masses.

These three Hebrew European newspapers represented local Jewish culture in Congress Poland (*Hatzefira*), in the Russian Empire and the Pale of
Settlement (*Hamelitz*), and in the Hapsburg Empire (*Hamagid*). Each reflected
changes in the attitude of the Jewish elites to the masses in their respective
geocultural spheres. As Y. L. Peretz wrote to Sholem Aleichem in 1888, a huge
difference existed between Polish and Russian Jewry regarding the language
question.[8]

In addition, the intellectual status of each newspaper affected differences
in their positions vis-à-vis Yiddish. In the last decades of the nineteenth century, *Hatzefira* remained the leading European Jewish newspaper. Discussions
in its pages throughout the 1880s and 1890s were indeed open and varied, but
Hatzefira also attempted to preserve its own hegemony. As a result, Nahum Sokolow and other permanent editors and contributors, including Nenmanowitz
(Hanetz), participated vigorously in this language discussion. With their read-
erships in decline, *Hamagid* and *Hamelitz* occupied a different position concerning the language issues: neither the editors nor the central writers of these
newspapers were directly involved in the debate.

Those who shaped the discourse on the role of Yiddish in the pages of Hebrew newspapers represented a new Jewish secular elite different from the generation that emerged during the start of the Haskalah. Intellectuals such as Sokolow and Sholem Aleichem had not faced the struggles of previous maskilim
in that their attempts to acquire non-Jewish education involved no struggle
with their families or with Jewish traditional surroundings, as the previous
generation of eastern European maskilim had experienced. Many of the intellectuals of this later generation grew up in families that already had a maskilic
orientation; therefore, they were exposed from an early age to secular and non-
Jewish reading material.[9] This generational discrepancy also reflects the tremendous demographic, economic, and social developments of the last decades
of the nineteenth century: Jewish traditional life underwent many changes,
including the decline of its own influence within Jewish society. New political
movements arose and reorganized Jewish life along with the rapidly urbaniz-
ing population.[10] Thus the struggle between the maskilim and Orthodox circles
lessened in intensity amid the backdrop of the transformation of Jewish life in
eastern Europe.

Several of these intellectuals even expressed an awareness of the differences
between themselves and their enlightened predecessors.[11] They developed new
attitudes that sometimes included disapproving of the previous maskilic ideology. Several of these new Jewish intellectuals pointed out that they were closer
to the rest of the Jewish society, and not as alienated. Others emphasized their
practical approach and how it influenced the new generation in terms of what
kind of non-Jewish and secular education they should acquire.[12]

Indeed, these intellectuals saw themselves as leaders with the power to influence Jewish public opinion and the new modern Jewish culture. Whereas the
previous generation of maskilim created an exclusive culture, the new generation's cultural output reached broader social circles. This generation made the
elite maskilic attitude accessible to mass Jewish culture by bringing Yiddish to
the fore of this discussion in the public sphere.[13]

Building on Jurgen Habermas's seminal work, *Strukturwandel der Öffentlichkeit*, the formation of the eastern European Jewish public sphere in the second
half of the nineteenth century included public debates that helped form public
opinion, and this process occurred through various social and cultural institutions such as political and social clubs, literary salons, public assemblies, pubs,
coffeehouses, and public gardens.[14] As a result of Russian policy in Congress
Poland after the failed Polish uprising in 1863, which prohibited the establishment of new public institutions and affected internal Jewish developments in
Congress Poland and the Russian Empire, Jewish periodicals played a central
role in the formation of an eastern European Jewish sphere. It is difficult—in
fact, nearly impossible—to describe the social, political, and cultural Jewish life
of eastern Europe without considering the contribution of Jewish periodicals,
since a significant part of the political, social, cultural, and intellectual activi-

ties of Jewish society took place through these channels.[15] Most, if not all, of those engaged with the various editorial boards of the leading Jewish periodicals in the second half of the nineteenth century believed that the first task of these publications entailed not only reporting but also establishing an arena in which the central ideological and intellectual debates could take place.[16] As a result, most if not all of the Jewish public intellectual debates occurred within the pages of these central Hebrew newspapers. Hebrew newspapers of the second half of the nineteenth century included discussions on the essence and tasks of modern Jewish education, religious reforms, the duties of religious leaders, and, most significantly for our purposes here, the role of Yiddish in Jewish life.

By the last decades of the nineteenth century, no single ideological commitment to either Hebrew or Yiddish existed yet among eastern European Jewish readers, who read several different Jewish periodicals in various Jewish and non-Jewish languages. Nevertheless, the majority of the Jewish readers at that time read Hebrew, whereas only a relatively small number of Jewish readers read periodicals in non-Jewish languages.[17] Until the beginning of the twentieth century, the imperial Russian authority refused to license the publication of newspapers in Yiddish either in Russia or in Congress Poland because the Russian authorities feared that Yiddish newspapers would spread provocative ideas.[18] Consequently, the first Yiddish periodicals published in the region in the 1880s and 1890s looked more like literary anthologies. An alternative sphere for hosting Jewish public intellectual discussions about Yiddish in Yiddish had yet to emerge, and many of the participants did not possess the ability to write in Russian or Polish. In addition, Jewish intellectuals interested in developing the new Yiddish literature had not yet chosen Yiddish as their exclusive writing language; many Jewish writers were at that time dual-language writers, and others, such as Sokolow, Nenmanowitz, Peretz, and Shmuel Frug even wrote in three languages. Therefore, the intellectual debate about *zhargon* had to be conducted in Hebrew and in the European Hebrew newspapers.

Hamagid, the first European Hebrew weekly, appeared first in Lyck near the Prussian-Russian border in 1856, and it remained a weekly throughout its entire lifespan (1856-1903). Until 1890 *Hamagid* published in Prussia to evade Russian censorship, although Russian-Jewish readers comprised its principal intended audience. In its last years it published first in Berlin and then in Crakow.[19] *Hamagid* also appealed to Jews in the Hapsburg Empire and in particular to Galician Jewry. Even before it began to publish in Cracow, *Hamagid* reported regularly on Galician communities. From a relatively early period *Hamagid*'s leanings were strongly national, and in the early 1880s this tendency translated into strong support for Ḥibat Tzion (the proto-Zionist organization), whereas in the late 1890s the weekly energetically supported the Zionist movement.

The public debate about *zhargon* also occurred in the Hebrew newspaper *Hamelitz*, the first Hebrew weekly to appear in czarist Russia. In 1886 it became a daily newspaper and remained so until its last issue in 1904.[20] Its founder and chief editor for most of that time was Aleksander Zederbaum. As an editor of a Hebrew periodical, Zederbaum believed that the one task of *Hamelitz* was to develop the Hebrew language and its literature as national assets.[21] From the early 1880s until its final issue, the newspaper and Zederbaum staunchly supported the new Jewish national association Ḥovevei Tzion and the Zionist movement that emerged later.

Hatzefira also played a role in this debate. Founded in Warsaw in 1862 by Hayim Zelig Slonimski, *Hatzefira* originally sought to develop popular scientific writing in Hebrew. In the 1880s, a young journalist named Nahum Sokolow undertook key changes in the periodical's content and turned *Hatzefira* into the most important Hebrew periodical in eastern Europe. Nevertheless, its identification with Jewish national organizations began relatively late, after the first Zionist Congress in 1897. Notably, *Hatzefira*'s two editors held different views on the renewed Hebrew language. Slonimski's pragmatic approach viewed Hebrew as the language many Jews could read. He showed his lack of interest in nurturing the language per se when he told his readers that he would not publish belles lettres of any kind. Sokolow, on the other hand, believed that Hebrew was part of the Jewish national heritage; by writing in Hebrew in *Hatzefira* and other literary frameworks, he and other writers would nurture the Hebrew language.[22]

The discussion regarding the new *zhargon* literature in *Hatzefira* and *Hamelitz* opened at the beginning of 1889 with two articles by two relatively unknown writers. *Hatzefira* ran an article by Elhanan Kalmannsohn,[23] whereas *Hamelitz* published a piece by Elhanan Leib Lewinsky.[24] Kalmannsohn and Lewinsky held similar views in which they criticized different *zhargon* publications that had recently appeared. Nevertheless, Kalmannsohn's article related not to the publication of any specific *zhargon* periodical but rather to the broad context of that new cultural phenomenon, the rise of *zhargon* literature. Lewinsky's criticism, by contrast, aimed at a specific target: Sholem Aleichem's *Di yidishe folks-bibliotek*.

As many scholars have already indicated, the appearance of *Di yidishe folks-bibliotek* constituted a milestone in the development of Yiddish literature.[25] In this seminal work Sholem Aleichem declared his mission to change *zhargon* literature into a literature with aesthetic values. As shown in a letter to his friend Yehoshu'a Hana Ravnitsky (Bar Kazin), "You are talking about the significance of our *zhargon*, you admire it and see it as the people's language, but what about the literature? There is no literature in *zhargon*."[26] In his article in *Hatzefira*, Kalmannsohn argued that although books in Jewish *zhargon* had already existed for a fairly long period, *zhargon* literature was a new phenomenon; he remained undecided on whether the Jewish literary public should welcome or mourn this occurrence. According to Kalmannsohn only Hebrew could serve as the eternal language, whereas *zhargon* fulfilled a temporary need; eventually, all of Jewish society would speak different non-Jewish languages.[27] He believed the new *zhargon* literature should include books to improve the Jewish reader's taste, and he suggested that instead of developing original *zhargon* literature, it would be more useful to translate the Bible, non-Jewish literary classics, and science books into Yiddish.[28] Ultimately, Kalmannsohn firmly distinguished between what he perceived as elite Hebrew literature and Yiddish (*zhargon*) literature.

Writing in *Hamelitz*, Lewinsky also took upon himself the task of protecting the hegemony of Hebrew. However, whereas Kalmannsohn's article presented a moderate tone appropriate to the overall tendency of *Hatzefira*, Lewinsky took a more direct approach. Using a reference to Proverbs 30:21–23 as his opening, he wrote, "For three things the earth is disquieted, and for four which it cannot bear: a servant when he reigneth and a fool when he is filled with meat; an odious woman when she is married, and an handmaid that is heir to her mistress." With this biblical text as his prelude, Lewinsky undertook a sharply toned article that outlined his attitude toward the new *zhargon* literature's status. Ironically, from the responses published from March until June 1889 in *Hamelitz*, it seems that the biblical quotation bothered *Hamelitz* writers more than the article.[29]

In this article Lewinsky also argued that the revival of *zhargon* comprised an artificial process and that there was no need to protect a language that lacked past and future grammar rules.[30] For him, protecting the eternal language that made the Jewish people a nation provided a more essential task. He even suggested that the revival of the Jewish *zhargon* might be the result of Sholem Aleichem's decision to pay Hebrew writers well if they agreed to use it. In his vivid formulation the maskilim were falling from the top of a mountain, and as they descended they wrote in Yiddish, the language of *Tsene-rene* (go forth and look), old maids, and the fish market.[31] Lewinsky ended the first part of his article with a plea to other Hebrew writers to help him in the mission of protecting the Hebrew language.[32] Although he had weighed in on this subject earlier, this particular *Hamelitz* article on *zhargon* and those that followed on Hebrew literature and language in 1889 formed Lewinsky's reputation as a Hebrew writer.

Although Kalmannsohn's article in *Hatzefira* preceded Lewinsky's article, it received few responses, whereas Lewinsky's commentary provoked a wide discussion. It seems that many Jewish intellectuals involved with *Hamelitz* could not agree with Lewinsky's attempt to attack Sholem Aleichem and *Di yidishe folks-bibliotek*. In addition, Sholem Aleichem could not ignore this attack, for despite Lewinsky's relatively marginal literary position at the time, the renowned author needed to respond to any kind of criticism that could adversely affect his agenda.[33]

In his response to Lewinsky's article, Sholem Aleichem presented his involvement in the new *zhargon* literature as one project among assorted Jewish national activities.[34] He argued that he and others promoting the new *zhargon* literature did not deny the existence of the Jewish people as a nation but rather believed that Jewish national literature should not be written exclusively in Hebrew; in other words, it had to have broader appeal. All the Jewish people understood *zhargon*, whereas few understood Hebrew.[35] In this rebuttal Sholem Aleichem referred to many of the arguments that Lewinsky raised, including the claim that Sholem Aleichem paid the writers of *Di yidishe folks-bibliotek*. Nevertheless, the significance in Sholem Aleichem's response lies in his vision of the new *zhargon* literature as forming a national language. He believed that Jewish literature should be written to broad audiences and that Jewish writers should take the needs of the Jewish masses into consideration. This, he argued, entailed writing in the language they used, *zhargon*. Hence in 1889, a relatively early moment in the discussion being mapped here, Sholem Aleichem had already made a connection between national language and literature.[36]

Beyond responding to Lewinsky's arguments, Sholem Aleichem wished to present himself to the readers of *Hamelitz* as a leading figure in the new process of changing *zhargon* literature. However, wary of appearing too eager to cement his status, he responded to only one article. Thus at Sholem Aleichem's request, other Jewish intellectuals, such as his close friends and colleagues Yehoshua Ravnitski and Zvi Sakamarawski, replied to Lewinswky's other articles.[37] Whereas Lewinsky and Sholem Aleichem mainly emphasized the pros and cons of upgrading the *zhargon,* and the power balance between Hebrew and the Jewish spoken language, Ravnitski sought to emphasize the value of *zhargon* literature to the Russian-Jewish masses. Although he agreed that in several European Jewish environments the use of *zhargon* had ceased, this was not the case in Russia.[38] Ravnitski admitted that Jewish literature in *zhargon* had a doubtful reputation in terms of its writing style and themes, but thanks to the attempts of several Jewish writers, this literature stood at the precipice of change. Using common phraseology of the time, he argued that it was going to remove its muddy clothes, clean up its wretched appearance, and adopt a new, more attractive look. The new writers beginning to write in *zhargon* understood its power, and they knew that it could provide the people with what they truly needed—not merely "novels for housemaids."[39] Returning to Lewinsky's opening quotation, Ravnitski argued that the new *zhargon* literature would not challenge the hegemony of Hebrew; rather than take the place of the mistress, the handmaid would remain near her.[40]

In a subsequent article published a few months later, Ravnitski stressed that the Jewish spoken language was the people's language and that writers who chose to write in *zhargon* should not think of the benefits to the language but rather of the benefits to the Jewish people.[41] Hence what had initially begun in *Hamelitz* as criticism of Sholem Aleichem's *Di yidishe folks-bibliotek* developed into a wider discussion questioning the nature of the national Jewish language and how it could serve the Jewish people.[42] Whereas writers like Lewinsky believed that the national literature of the Jewish people should be written solely in Hebrew,[43] Sholem Aleichem and Ravnitski argued that the new *zhargon* literature also formed a national literature.[44]

Lewinsky's approach changed in his last article in *Hamelitz* in 1889.[45] Rather than condemning writing in *zhargon*, he suggested that if Sholem Aleichem and others wanted to change the literary taste of the Jewish masses, they should translate non-Jewish books into *zhargon*. Sparking much controversy, he even recommended that *zhargon* sponsors begin by translating Jules Verne.[46]

Only a few months later, Aharon Kaminka published a long series of articles in *Hatzefira* titled, "Warning to Labor Letters" ("Azhara lemikhtevei amal"),[47] with the title based on Isaiah 10:1: "Woe unto them that decree unrighteous decrees, and write grievousness which they have prescribed." "Labor Letters" referred to rulings by writers working with the judges who rendered miscarriages of justice. Kaminka's participation in this discussion proved unique, because unlike the others engaged in the language debate, his intellectual and literary activities took place in the western European spheres of Berlin, Vienna, and Paris.[48] Perhaps Kaminka's distance from eastern Europe, where Yiddish was more of a lingua franca than in western Europe, gave him a different perspective on the elevation of *zhargon* into a national language. In these *Hatzefira* articles Kaminka left no doubt regarding his attitude toward *zhargon*: he questioned how the "filthy" *zhargon* fit for the dirt served as the national language.[49] He argued that only the language of the synagogue, Hebrew, could serve as the language of the Jewish people and that even popular literature should appear only in that language.[50] In this series of articles Kaminka refrained from challenging the attempts of those he called *zhargonistim* to improve the Jewish masses, but he expressed his deep rejection of *zhargon* in Jewish life: "I despise the *zhargon*. The *zhargon* nauseates me. It attacks the spiritual forces of the people and corrupts their spirit."[51]

At this point *Hatzefira*'s coeditor Sokolow stepped in, although this was not the first time that the pivotal writer had weighed in on the debate.[52] Sokolow accepted the negative arguments concerning the Jewish *zhargon*, but he could not ignore its living literary development, therefore entitling Sholem Aleichem to nurture the new writing. Nevertheless, he told his readers, Jews had an obligation to preserve and develop Hebrew literature and had no similar obligation regarding literature in *zhargon*. That literature could exist as long as its secondary importance to Hebrew remained clear, and it should be used primarily as an instrument for promoting more important goals.[53]

In fact, Kaminka's approach aligned with the attitude of Polish-Jewish intellectuals in Warsaw. He argued that Jewish life had room only for two languages: Polish or another non-Jewish language and Hebrew. In his view, *zhargon* could not become a recognized language.[54] In several articles that appeared in the 1870s in *Izraelita*, a Jewish periodical in Polish, different writers worried about the danger of *zhargon* and how it delayed the progress of the Jewish masses.[55]

However, one can observe a change by the 1890s, when *Izraelita* began translating Yiddish literature.[56] The development of modern Yiddish literature began to gain the approval of leading Jewish intellectuals in Warsaw, including Sokolow.[57] It seems that Kaminka, at that time living in western Europe, remained unaware of this change and that other members of *Hatzefira*'s editorial board did not share Sokolow's attitude. Hanetz, for example, wrote a weekly column presenting a different ideological stance.

Hanetz's involvement with *zhargon* began in the 1860s, when he worked on the *Varshover yudishe zeitung*, a periodical for Polish Jewry. He and his colleagues had a different agenda from that of Peretz and Spektor in the last two decades of the nineteenth century. *Zeitung*'s editor, Hillel Glatstern, used Yiddish as a means of connecting with those who could read no other language.[58] Apparently Nenmanowitz shared this view, which possibly led him to translate Ludwik Łazarz Zamenhof's textbook for studying Esperanto from Polish into Yiddish in 1888. He also wrote several guidebooks for Yiddish readers learning Polish, Russian, and German. In 1886 Sokolow offered him a position with *Hatzefira* shortly after he moved to Warsaw and needed a job, suggesting that his decision to write in *Hatzefira* could be understood as economically motivated. However, a close look at Hanetz's *Hatzefira* columns from 1887 to 1896 suggests that ideology also motivated his decision to write in Hebrew. The Jews inherited Yiddish, he wrote, from a nation that hates Jews. With that he argued that the Jewish intelligentsia could use Yiddish to advance and educate the Jewish people, but under no conditions would Yiddish, the servant, stand on equal ground with Hebrew, the mistress.[59]

Hanetz used several such images borrowed from Lewinsky to depict *zhargon*'s low position. He tempered his comments by writing that *zhargon* should nevertheless play a functional role to improve and educate the low strata of Jewish society, without harming Hebrew as a result.[60] Perhaps as a result *Hatzefira* refrained from supporting the periodicals of Mordkhe Spektor and Peretz in the same way that *Hamelitz* showed its support for Sholem Aleichem and his literary project, even though *Hatzefira* disapproved of other *zhargon* periodicals, in particular those published by Spektor and Peretz in Congress Poland as well as other *zhargon* writers who were not engaged with *Hamelitz*.[61]

Although Sholem Aleichem praised Spektor and his periodical, he did not show similar support for Peretz and his literary project. When the serial *Yidishe bibliotek* began to appear, Sholem Aleichem even accused Peretz of taking the name from his own anthology *Di yidishe folks-bibliotek*.[62] Sholem Aleichem represented Russian Jewry, with *Hamelitz* as their Hebrew newspaper. Peretz, however, identified with Polish Jewry and with Warsaw, at the time a new eastern European Jewish cultural and literary center that posed a challenge to cities such as Odessa. It seems that *Hamelitz* supported Sholem Aleichem's position on Peretz, as seen in a July 1894 article on the dispute.[63] What began as an almost conventional attack on *zhargon* literature soon developed into direct and broader criticism of Peretz, including *Haḥetz*, the Hebrew periodical he edited and published that year.[64]

Hatzefira took a different approach, directing criticism not at specific *zhargon* publications but at the whole phenomenon of the new *zhargon* literature. Indeed, when the first volume of *Yidishe bibliotek* appeared, *Hatzefira* barely referred to it. This approach differed from that of the *Hamelitz* writers. Only in 1892 did Peretz and *Yidishe bibliotek* earn a reference in *Hatzefira* and a growing legitimacy in the local Jewish literary community, perhaps in part owing to his growing reputation in Warsaw, his home since the late 1880s.[65] However, the local Jewish intelligentsia granted only limited legitimacy to writing in *zhargon*, deeming its only respectable aim as educating the masses and improving their cultural and intellectual worldview. Yiddish literature could not, from this perspective, be measured with any aesthetic value; only Hebrew could fill that role for the Jewish people.

In fact, several *Hatzefira* writers engaged with the renewal of Hebrew with the aim of taking the holy literary language into the streets for everyday use.[66] Hence, in Warsaw, and in the pages of *Hatzefira*, the discourse on *zhargon* and the discussion about the legitimacy of spoken Hebrew and of popular literature in Hebrew comprised a distinct discourse whose common theme was the legitimacy of a popular, nontraditional Jewish culture. These discussions manifested in actions such as the establishment, in the early 1890s, of an association called Safah brurah (Clear Language), whose members met every Shabbat afternoon in the Nalevki Street synagogue and listened to lectures delivered in Hebrew. Prominent Jewish intellectuals such as Peretz, Hanetz, Sokolow, and others from different intellectual circles of Warsaw took part.[67] At about this time, the young writer and publisher Ben-Avigdor began to create a penny book series in Hebrew. Whereas Peretz and his circle tried to confer legitimacy on the *zhargon* and write belles lettres in Yiddish, Ben-Avigdor made the first attempt to write for the masses about the masses in Hebrew, with a story that later became famous on Leah the fish peddler in the market.[68]

As the analysis thus far has demonstrated, examining the development of newspaper discourse helps to highlight crucial differences between the two geocultural centers that comprised the bases of each respective publication. *Hamelitz* was published in Saint Petersburg, at that time not a leading Jewish literary center. Sokolow and *Hatzefira*, however, emerged from Warsaw, which in the 1880s had developed into the most important center of Jewish literature and culture in eastern Europe.[69]

Whereas the *Hamelitz* writers who participated in discussions on the new Yiddish writing tried to present this material as literature that belonged both to national and popular traditions, *Hatzefira* writers such as Nenmanowitz wondered about the link between the new Yiddish periodicals and the Jewish masses.[70] All those interested in improving the *zhargon*, argued Nenmanowitz, were in fact the readers of the Hebrew papers (*Hamelitz, Hatzefira*, and *Hamagid*), whereas the Jewish readers of the lower strata, to whom the new *zhargon* periodicals were aimed, did not read them.[71] The periodicals of Sholem Aleichem and Spektor, wrote Nenmanowitz, included many high quality literary works, but he doubted whether these works offered any benefit to the Jewish masses. He believed that one small, low-cost booklet published in Odessa, *Di kleyne yidishe bibliotek,* benefited the Jewish masses much more than these two periodicals.[72] Hence, akin to Lewinsky's claim that the Jewish masses would benefit most from translations of non-Jewish literature into Yiddish, Nenmanowitz supported the view of Yiddish literature as a pedagogical tool for improving the Jewish masses. However, he condemned what to him looked like an attempt to create high literature in Yiddish.[73]

Hamagid was directed more or less toward the same readers as the two other Hebrew European newspapers, yet it acted under different political and cultural conditions than *Hamelitz* and *Hatzefira.* Moreover, several of the writers in *Hamagid* who covered the new *zhargon* literature came from Galicia. Indeed, until World War I Galicia was part of the Austrian Empire, yet this area played a leading role in the formation of Polish political and cultural life. Nationalized Galician cities such as Lwów (Lviv, or Lemberg) provided an alternative for those interested in the creation of the modern Polish nation.[74]

Thus *Hamagid* contained both digressions from and overlap with the positions of the other newspapers. Although *Hamelitz* and *Hatzefira* all but ignored Mordkhe Spektor's annual *Der hoyz fraynd, Hamagid* wrote that the annual demonstrated the great potential of *zhargon* literature for changing and supporting the masses.[75] However, as in *Hatzefira,* the main writers in *Hamagid* also referred to *zhargon* from the perspective of the Jewish masses; therefore, they argued that Yiddish possessed agency and could act as a tool to bring modernity to traditional Jewish circles.

In a series of articles in *Hamagid* titled, "Whose Fault Is It?" Mordechai Ehernpreis, a principal participant in this discourse who grew up in Lwów (Lviv), focused on the ways in which the Poles in Galicia nurtured their language. He believed that Jewish society in Galicia and in other eastern European areas should learn from the Polish case and turn the language of the people into a national language. He therefore made a connection between writing for the people in the people's language and not only in a Jewish context.[76]

> When assimilationist tendencies among Poles grew and enlightened, educated people read only French and despised their own language, the writer Karashwski decided to write day and night. Every year he published dozens of books in Polish until the Poles rejected books in French and returned to their language and literature with a great deal of love. Fifty years later, Polish literature was almost at the zenith of its development. Our writers, on the other hand, knew only how to complain to the Jewish readers like people who sit and wait for the readers to come to them and beg for books. When someone like Ben-Avigdor

in Warsaw tried to develop penny books, he was much criticized, as if scientific translations were meant only for doctors and we the common people had no right to deal with scientific literature. Most Jewish writers did not understand the needs of the people and had no knowledge of European education.[77]

In the early 1890s, Ehernpreis mainly concerned himself with fostering written *zhargon* for propagandistic purposes and directed it at Jewish readers who read no other language. He also intended for his works to be read by enlightened circles.[78] He felt *zhargon* could be useful to members of progressive Jewish circles who distanced themselves from Judaism.[79] With *zhargon*, the intelligentsia could address enlightened circles and persuade them to take part in Jewish public affairs.[80] Ehernpreis and his colleagues in Galicia believed they could use *zhargon* even though they had no interest in nurturing the language per se. This can be seen in a letter that Ehernpreis wrote to Ben-Avigdor in Warsaw: "You already know our viewpoint regarding jargon. We do not deal with it for the purpose of its revival, but for our masses who do not yet understand Hebrew. We have an obligation to get close to them, to influence them in any way we can."[81]

He and his friends knew of the *zhargon* publications printed in the Russian Empire by Sholem Aleichem and Y. L. Peretz. Ehernpreis even employed the same terminology Lewinsky used in his first article in *Hamelitz*, writing that *zhargon* literature was the handmaid to "our literature" (i.e., Hebrew literature). He criticized the attempts of Sholem Aleichem and others to upgrade *zhargon* to a level that most of the Jewish public failed to understand.[82] Yet Ehernpreis's innovation lay in his idea that programmatic use of Yiddish could change not only the masses but other strata within Jewish society as well. Ultimately, he argued, it could bring the masses closer to the non-Jewish world and the progressive circle closer to the Jewish world.

Viewing the triangular discussion in *Hamelitz*, *Hatzefira*, and *Hamagid* from the perspective of geocultural history yields certain key insights. For *Hamagid* and *Hatzefira* in the 1890s, improving *zhargon* and its literature was not a goal in and of itself. Rather, *zhargon* served as a tool. In *Hamagid* Ehernpreis and his colleagues expressed their hopes that by writing in *zhargon*, national circles would be able to influence traditional Jewish masses in Galicia to support their Jewish national activity. They knew that a political movement could not confine itself to the elite but rather required a wide basis of support. For different writers who wrote in *Hamagid* and *Hatzefira* at the beginning of the 1890s, such as Nenmanowitz, Sokolow, and Ehernpreis, *zhargon* served only a temporary role, as a vehicle for greater aims. Meanwhile, Sholem Aleichem and others who wrote in *Hamelitz* believed that *zhargon* could fulfill long-term goals beyond low culture. They wanted to create a new Yiddish belles lettres with artistic standards, and at the same time they believed that this new Yiddish literature should comprise a national literature for the people. The various intellectuals who participated in this vigorous discourse pondered these issues and debated whether the readers of the new *zhargon* literature would be the lower layers of the Jewish society or the elite. The editorial boards of *Hamelitz, Hatzefira,* and *Hamagid* approached these issues differently, and those distinctions may be attributed to the particulars of the political, cultural, and social environments from which they wrote.

In particular, their different approaches mirrored the local Russian and Polish interpretation regarding the task of literature in national and social life. Although Auguste Comte, Henry Thomas Buckle, Herbert Spencer, and Charles Darwin were read in both places, local intellectual circles drew different inspiration from their ideas. In both places writers and journalists agreed that literature had a utilitarian function. Yet in Polish areas different members of the Polish intelligentsia understood that the obligation of the national literature lay in assisting the Polish people with the preservation of collective memory and the creation of a national Polish culture. Therefore Polish literature tended more toward nationalism. On the other hand, Russian literature was supposed to help spur the development of new radicalism in universalist directions.[83]

Additionally, Polish and Russian intellectual groups held different positions regarding the societal role of the masses. Polish leaders believed industrialization would bring independence to Poland; thus, the economic basis of the masses had to change. Therefore, the Polish intelligentsia dedicated themselves to attempting to educate the Polish masses through special adult educational programs and by publishing a special series of popular science books and translations of classic literature. In Russia the attitude was markedly different: the peasantry (the *muzhik*) was seen as the bearer of social reform. Young intellectuals were supposed to abandon universities, head to the village, and explain to peasants why they should become revolutionaries; intellectuals should settle in the village and learn from the peasants, instead of trying to teach them.

Drawing on the philosophical influence of their environment, Jewish writers in Warsaw such as Nenmanowitz and Kalmannsohn approved of the notion of translating non-Jewish literature into Yiddish and publishing popular science books in Yiddish, but on the other hand they did not believe that the Jewish masses would derive any benefit from high literature and belles lettres in Yiddish. In Galicia, Ehernpreis relied on the Polish concept of "work at the foundations" (*parca u podstaw*), which among other things meant working for all layers of Jewish society; he understood that the new Yiddish literature could change not only the masses but also other strata within Jewish society.

In Congress Poland and Galicia various Jewish intellectuals became aware of the power of *zhargon* not only as a method of propaganda but also as a means to self-improvement for the masses via the language they spoke and understood the most. This new viewpoint on *zhargon* by different members of the Jewish intelligentsia amounted to their own interpretation of the growth of new social and political forces that had begun to be active on the Polish street during the

last decades of the nineteenth century. These included mass movements and
the democratization of cultural and political processes related to the masses.
In contrast, Jewish Russian writers were influenced by the development of the
new Russian radical wing in the 1880s and 1890s, and they believed that the
Jewish masses should have a distinct modern high literature.

In *Hatzefira* this tendency manifested in the argument that *zhargon* was en-
gendering a new Jewish culture that could reduce the holy characteristics of
traditional Jewish culture and expand its boundaries, while also increasing the
secular characteristics of the new Jewish culture.[84] Some Jewish intellectuals
wanted to take *zhargon* out of the hands of the cook in the kitchen and move it
to the living room.[85] Yet at the same time, these Jewish intellectuals wanted to
take Hebrew, the lofty literary language, and move it to the streets. These writers therefore worked on behalf of Yiddish to integrate it with work on behalf
of Hebrew, and as such this approach was influenced by the Polish concept of
"work at the foundations."

The tenor of the discussions that took place in *Hamelitz* proved more provocative; after all, *Hamelitz* and its first editor, Aleksander Zederbaum, acted
more radically than other Hebrew editors and newspapers. The contributors
to the discussion in *Hamelitz* presented different attitudes regarding Jewish
intellectuals and their relationship to the Jewish masses. Although they wrote
about the obligation to consider the needs and the rights of the masses, including the obligation to give the Jewish masses access to a variety of reading
material in their own language, they also argued that the new *zhargon* literature stood by itself as an aesthetic literature with artistic standards. In addition,
Sholem Aleichem and others who debated in the pages of *Hamelitz* wanted to
develop a similarity between national Jewish literature and literature for the
people.

Those who addressed the future of Yiddish in *Hatzefira* and *Hamagid* argued
that Jewish political and national movements could use Yiddish in order to
explain their ideological positions and promote their goals. For example, the
local Ḥovevei Tzion organization in Warsaw published a call for the best Jewish writers in the "Jewish spoken language," even without referring to it as a
Jewish national literature. In this announcement, they declared a competition
for writing a book in Yiddish with the aims of raising support for Jewish settle-
ments in the Holy Land and presenting both the life of the Hebrew farmers in
Palestine and the life of "our brothers," the peddlers, merchants, and bartend-
ers in the diaspora. The book had to be written according to aesthetic conventions and without too much philosophizing.[86]

When Mordkhe Spektor, Sholem Aleichem, and Y. L. Peretz began to publish
their periodicals, Jewish intellectuals associated with different Hebrew periodicals disputed not only the role of Yiddish in Jewish life but also the legitimacy of Jewish popular culture. However, soon after this initial period of dis-

pute, most agreed that Yiddish amounted to more than merely *zhargon:* it was a language that had a literature with artistic standards. Furthermore, many of the external obstacles of only a decade before no longer existed. For example, in January 1903, the Russian governmental restrictions on the Yiddish press relaxed, and by the beginning of the twentieth century, a new competitor to the Hebrew press emerged.[87] The new Yiddish press offered to the Jewish public in eastern Europe a new style of newspaper. In this contest the Hebrew press lost, for Yiddish newspapers soon became what we may call the mass media for much of the Jewish world in the subsequent decades. Yet the birth of this press came alongside early Hebrew periodicals, through which both languages took fateful turns.

In the 1890s none of those who debated language issues in the three Hebrew European newspapers surveyed here believed that the new Yiddish literature should be disconnected from Hebrew literature. Sholem Aleichem and other writers did not demand exclusivity of any language (Hebrew or Yiddish). In fact, Sholem Aleichem believed that Hebrew and Yiddish integrated into one unit, observing that the two languages were not rivals.[88] However, the idea that Hebrew and Yiddish literatures could coexist within the framework of Jewish cultural nationalism remained short lived; within a decade the two literatures had already moved toward an institutional and ideological divorce.[89] Hence, what has been described as the language war (*riv ha-leshonot*) actually began several years later, at the dawn of the twentieth century, and in particular after the Czernowitz (Cernauti) conference in the summer of 1908.[90]

Notes

1. Nenmanowitz signed the column with the acronym of his name, Hanetz, which in Hebrew means "hawk."
2. Hanetz, "Berosh homyot" [Top Crowded], *Hatzefira*, March 3/15, 1889. Dates in periodicals published in the Russian Empire follow both the Western and Russian Orthodox calendars and are cited here in that order. One can see that the phrase that Nenmanowitz used here has similarities with Molière's well-known quotation in the play *The Would-Be Gentleman* (*Le Bourgeois Gentilhomme*): "For forty years already I've been speaking in prose without knowing it."
3. As Dan Miron has written, "At the end of the nineteenth century the word Yiddish which was meant to describe the Jewish language that was used in eastern Europe was not in use yet. This language was called *Yidish-daytsh* (Judeo-German) and later (until the time of Sholem Aleichem and Peretz) *Zhargon*." Miron, *A Traveler Disguised: A Study in the Rise of Modern Yiddish Fiction in the Nineteenth Century* (New York: Schocken Books, 1973), 47. David Fishman identifies this process as "the transformation of jargon into Yiddish." Fishman, *The Rise of Modern Yiddish Culture* (Pittsburgh: University of Pittsburgh Press, 2005), 1.
4. Alexander Guterman, "Tzmiḥat hazramim haḥadashim baḥevra hayehudit bePolin kefi shemishtakefet bekitvei ha'itonut hayehudit bein hashanim 1861-1881" (PhD diss., Hebrew University, 1983), 214.

5. Nancy Sinkoff, *Out of the Shtetl: Making Jews Modern in the Polish Borderlands* (Providence, RI: Brown Judaic Studies: 2004), 172.

6. Ibid., 169.

7. Getzel Kressel, "A historish palemik vagen der yiddish literature," *Di goldene keyt* 20 (1954): 338-58. It is important to note that in this article Kressel did not mention discussions in *Hatzefira* and *Hamagid*.

8. Y. L. Peretz, "Letter to Sholem Aleichem, 4 July 1888," *Moznayim*, 1929, 15. In this letter Peretz explained the differences between his approach and Sholem Aleichem's in terms of how they envisioned the themes of the new *zhargon* literature. Peretz argued that the new *zhargon* literature should include science books and useful literature and not necessarily original high literature, as Sholem Aleichem argued. In addition, he wrote, "I do not understand why you, sir, want to write about the life of the Jewish people and you do not think it is important that the Jewish people should also learn about the life of the people we live with." Information on literary polemics between Polish and Russian maskilim can be found in Shmuel Finer, *Haskala vehistoria: toldoteha shel hakarat avar yehudit modernit* (Jerusalem: The Zalman Shazar Center, 1995), 368-74; and Ela Bauer, *Between Poles and Jews: The Development of Nahum Sokolow's Political Thought* (Jerusalem: Magnes Press, 2005), 43-50. The difference between Polish Jews and Russian Jewish regarding the language question is discussed later in this essay.

9. Sholem Aleichem's father exposed his son to ideas of the Haskalah and read him secular books. In addition, Sholem Aleichem attended a local Russian secondary school. Lewinsky's father gave him an intensive Talmudic education, but at the same time Lewinsky had the opportunity to read maskilic literature. Through tutors, Peretz learned a variety of languages, including Hebrew, German, Russian, and Polish before his arrival in Warsaw, where he became a successful Jewish writer and lawyer. Nahum Sokolow's grandfather, a well-known Torah scholar adept in many works of philosophy, introduced the young Sokolow to nonreligious books. Also, Sokolow's father ran a lending library that included secular books, providing the young Sokolow with more exposure to non-Jewish reading material.

10. Israel Bartal, "Teguvot lamoderna bemizraḥ Europa," in *Tziyonot vedat*, ed. Shmuel Almog, Jehuda Reinharz, and Anita Shapira (Jerusalem: The Zalman Shazar Center, 2004), 21-33, 25.

11. This self-consciousness of the new generation can be seen, for example, in Reuven Breinin, "Ezrat sofrim utzu etza," *Hamelitz*, March 11/23, 1888; Nahum Sokolow, "Tziyonim," *Hatzefira*, April 25/May 7, 1901.

12. Samuel Leib Citron, "Ezrat sofrim et la'asot," *Hamelitz*, March 17/29, 1891; Breinin, "Ezrat sofrim utzu etza." See also Abraham Kotik, *Dos lebn fun a yidishn inteligent* (New York: Toibenslag, 1925), 88.

13. Shmuel Feiner, "Keyonek hanoshek shedei emo, post haskalah beketz hame'ah ha-19," *Alpayim* 21 (2000): 63-75. In this article Feiner defines the end of the nineteenth century as the post-Haskalah era.

14. Jurgen Habermas, *Strukturwandel der Öffentlichkeit* (Berlin: Nevwied, 1974). See also Ela Bauer, "From the Salons to the Street: The Development of a Jewish Public Sphere in Warsaw at the End of the 19th Century," *Jahrbuch des Simon-Dubnow-Instituts/Simon Dubnow Institute Yearbook* 7 (2008): 143-59.

15. Ehud Luz, *Makbilim Nifgashim* [Parallels Collide] (Tel Aviv: Am Oved, 1985), 27-29.

16. For more about the role of Jewish periodicals in eastern European Jewish life during the second half of the nineteenth century, see Ela Bauer, "Dialogue or Monologue? The Relationship between Jewish and Polish Journalists in Warsaw at the End of the 19th Century," *Polin* 22 (2009): 332-34.

17. Sarah Abrevaya Stein, *Making Jews Modern: The Yiddish and Ladino Press in the Russian and Ottoman Empires* (Bloomington: Indiana University Press, 2004), 26-27.

18. Ibid.

19. Menucha Gilboa, *Leksikon ha'itonut ha'ivrit bame'ot ha-18 veha-19* (Jerusalem: Bialik Institute, 1992), 117-35, 25.

20. For more information on *Hamelitz*, see, for example, Avner Holtzman, "*Hamelitz*," in *The YIVO Encyclopedia of Jews in Eastern Europe*, ed. Gershon David Hundert (New Haven: Yale University Press, 2008), 1:1149-50; Alexander Orbach, *New Voices of Russian Jewry: A Study of the Russian-Jewish Press of Odessa in the Era of the Great Reforms, 1860-1871* (Leiden, Netherlands: Brill, 1980).

21. Aleksander Zederbaum, "Sholo sholo panu derekh," *Hamelitz*, October 13/15, 1860.

22. See the opening article of the first issue of *Hatzefira*, January 18/February 4, 1862; See also note 2 on the citation of dates in periodicals published in the Russian Empire and Bauer, *Between Poles and Jews*.

23. Elhanan Kalmannsohn, "Lesifrut jargonit," *Hatzefira*, December 26, 1888/January 7, 1889-January 11/23, 1889.

24. Elhanan Leib Lewinsky, "Ezrat sofrim: sfat ever vesafah yehudit meduberet," *Hamelitz*, March 10/22-March 12/24, 1889. For more on Lewinsky, see Avner Holtzman, "Lewinsky Elhanan Leib," *The YIVO Encyclopedia of Jews in Eastern Europe*, 1:1028.

25. See, for example, Dan Miron, *A Traveler Disguised*.

26. Sholem Aleichem, "Letter to Ravnitski, June 5, 1887," in *Briefe fun Sholem Aleichem*, ed. Abraham Lis (Tel Aviv: Beit Sholem Aleichem, 1995), 163.

27. Elhanan Kalmannsohn, "Lesifrut jargonit."

28. *Hatzefira*, January 11/23, 1889.

29. Following is a chronological list of the writers (with their articles) who took part in the discussion in *Hamelitz* in 1889: Elhanan Leib Lewinsky, "Ezrat sofrim: sfat ever vesafah yehudit meduberet"; Sholem Aleichem, "Ezrat sofrim: leshe'elat hasafah," April 14/26; Yehoshua Hana Ravnitski, "Ezrat sofrim, hayesh tzorekh besifrut jargonit?" May 3/15-5/17; Lewinsky, "Ḥayei olam veḥayei sha'ah," May 12/24-15/27; Lewinsky, "Joḥanan hasandlar lefanim ve'ata, leharḥavat hajargon," May 23/June 4; Yehudah Leib Gamzu, "Teshuvah kahalakhah," June 2/14; Ravnitski, "Od bezkhut safrut ha'am," June 15/27-16/28, June 19/July 1; Zvi Sakamarawski, "Ezrat sofrim, e'eneh af ani ḥelki," June 19/July 1; Lewinsky, "Ezrat sofrim hamartze'a vehasifrut," June 25/July 7.

30. Lewinsky, "Ezrat sofrim: sfat ever vesafah yehudit meduberet," *Hamelitz*, March 21/24, 1889.

31. Ibid.

32. Lewinsky, "Ezrat sofrim: sfat ever vesafah yehudit meduberet," *Hamelitz*, March 10/22, 1889.

33. See Dan Miron, *Sholem Aleichem, pirkei massa* (Gamat-Gan: Massada, 1970), 16-18. In this book Miron describes Sholem Aleichem's attempts to control all areas of Jewish *zhargon* literature and to arrange the hierarchy of the new *zhargon* literature. In this hierarchy Mendele Mokher Seforim (Sholem Yankev Abramovitsh) was the grandfather, and Sholem Aleichem the grandson.

34. Sholem Aleichem, "Ezrat sofrim: Leshe'elat hasafah."

35. This ruling that all the Jewish people understood *zhargon* may raise some questions; we can assume that Sholem Aleichem did not believe that all the Jews in the world understood Yiddish. Hence, either he referred to any kind of Jewish jargon (and not necessarily only Yiddish), such as Ladino, or he meant all the Jews in his world, meaning eastern Europe.

36. In Hebrew the connection is quite clear because the phrase *sifrut am* may be understood as "national literature" and "the literature of the people."

37. We know that Sholem Aleichem asked different Jewish intellectuals to respond to Lewinsky's articles from an undated letter to Ravnitski published in Abraham Lis, *Briefe fun Sholem Aleichem*, 237, and from letter to Yehuda Gamzo of April 25, 237. As Sakamarawski

explains in his article "Ezrat sofrim, e'aneh af ani ḥelki," in 1888, Heinrich Graetz re-fused him permission to translate *Geschichte der Juden* into *zhargon*. After the refusal was made public, many Jews complained about Graetz's attitude.

38. In the first part of "Hayesh tzorekh," Ravnitski mentioned an episode related to the Rus-sian-Jewish scholar Zvi Sakamarawski (see previous note), regarding Graetz's refusal to have *Geschichte der Juden* translated into *zhargon*. Ravnitski wrote that, indeed, the use of *zhargon* had stopped in Graetz's surroundings. This, however, was not the case in the Russian Empire.

39. Ravnitski, "Ezrat sofrim, hayesh tzorekh besifrut jargonit?"

40. Ibid.

41. Ravnitski, "Od bezkhut sifrut ha'am," *Hamelitz*, June 16/28, 1889.

42. Ravnitski used the term "national Jewish language" (*safah le'umit*), not "language of the people" (*sfat ha'am*).

43. Lewinsky, "Ḥayei olam veḥayei sha'ah," *Hamelitz*, May 12/24, 1889.

44. Sholem Aleichem, "Ezrat sofrim, le'she'elat ha-safah," *Hamelitz*, April 14/26, 1889.

45. Lewinsky, "Ezrat sofrim hamartze'a vehasifrut," *Hamelitz*, June 25/July 7, 1889.

46. Ibid. Lewinsky's choice of Jules Verne is not surprising, considering that in 1892 Lewin-sky published a utopian tale of the Jewish State to arise in 2040.

47. The series was published in *Hatzefira* May 29/June 10; June 1/13; June 2/14; June 6/18-June 9/21; June 8/20; and June 16/28, 1889.

48. For more information on Kaminka, see Nahum Sokolow, *Sefer hazikaron lesofrei Yisra'el* (Warsaw: Meir Yechiel Halter, 1888), 98.

49. Kaminka, "Azhara lemikhtevei amal," *Hatzefira*, May 29/June 10, 1889.

50. *Hatzefira*, June 5/17, 1889.

51. *Hatzefira*, June 4/16, 1889.

52. Bauer, *Between Poles and Jews*, 103–4.

53. Nahum Sokolow, "Yakar umezulzal," *Hatzefira*, June 16/28, 1889.

54. Jacob Shatzky, *Gheshikhte fun yidn in varshe* (New York: YIVO Institute for Jewish Re-search, 1953), 3:272–75; Israel Bartal, "Medu leshoniyut leḥad leshoniyut le'umit," *Shvut* 15 (1992): 183–93.

55. See, e.g., "Pogadanki," *Izraelita*, April 20/May 2, 1877; Adolf Jacob Cohn, "O zargonie zy-dowskim," *Izraelita*, May 22/June 1, 1879.

56. For one translation among many, see Y. L. Peretz, "Wenus i Sulamita humoreska," *Izra-elita*, February 8/20, 1891.

57. Jacob Kirszrot and Israel Leon Grosglik (a former Hasid and the community secretary) agreed to support Peretz's new literary project financially. Jacob Shatzky, "Peretz stud-ies," *YIVO-bleter* 28 (1946): 66–76.

58. Marian Fuks, *Prasa żydowska w Warszawie 1823–1939* (Warsaw: Państwowe Wydawnictwo Naukowe, 1979).

59. Hanetz, "Berosh homiyut," *Hatzefira*, March 3/15, May 4/16, November 19/December 1, 1889; March 2/14, 1890; March 1/13, May 4/16, May 15/27, 1892.

60. Hanetz, "Berosh homiyut," *Hatzefira*, March 4/16, 1889; May 4/16, 1892.

61. *Hamelitz* editor Aleksander Zederbaum did not take part in the discussion on the *zhar-gon* in his newspaper, owing at least in part to his strong involvement in the devel-opment of Yiddish periodicals in the Russian Empire. In 1862 Zederbaum began to publish the weekly *Kol mevaser*, Russia's first Yiddish newspaper, initially as a supple-ment to *Hamelitz*. In 1869, *Kol mevaser* became an independent weekly and appeared in this form until 1872. A decade later, Zederbaum became involved with another Yid-dish weekly, *Dos yidishes folksblatt*, published until 1887. Perhaps personal reasons also prevented him from taking part in this discussion. In the later 1880s the precarious financial situation of *Hamelitz* led Zederbaum to expend much effort on attempts to improve it.

62. See Sholem Aleichem's January 5, 1894 letter to Spektor in Lis, *Briefe fun Sholem Aleichem*, 281 and Miron, *Sholem Aleichem, Perkei Massa*, 18.

63. Anonymous, "Ezrat sofrim, nitba'eim la'egel ve notnim," *Hamelitz*, July 12/24, 15/27, 1894. Among those who wrote about the personal and literary relationship are Nahman Meisel, *Sefer Y. L. Peretz* (Tel Aviv: Sefriat Hapoalim, 1960) and B. Garin, "Varsha und Odess, Perez on zayne erste critices," *YIVO-bleter* 28 (1946): 548-52.

64. The periodical had only one issue with a literary supplement.

65. See, for example, B. Garin, "Varsha und Odess," *YIVO-bleter* 28, no. 1 (1946): 548-52.

66. See, for example, *Hatzefira*, June 1/13 and 3/15, 1890.

67. *Hatzefira*, March 8/20 and March 27/April 8, 1890 report on the activities of this organization. Also the memoirs published in *Hatzefira* on March 2/8, 1917 describe a lecture Peretz gave at one such meeting.

68. Ben-Avigdor, *Merehov hayehudim: tmunot, tziyurim vesipurim merehov hayehudim* (Warsaw: Thushiea, 1891).

69. On these reasons and others, see Dan Miron, *Bodedim bemo'adam* (Tel Aviv: Am Oved, 1987).

70. Naftali Herz Nenmanowitz (Hanetz), "Berosh homyot," *Hatzefira*, March 3/15, 1889.

71. Ibid. See the opening quotation of this article.

72. What Nenmanowitz refers to here is the development of Jewish penny books in the early 1890s. Following their publication by Ben-Avigdor, a new public discussion arose on whether Jewish penny literature should be in Hebrew or in *zhargon*.

73. In fact, Nenmanowitz presented a view here similar to the one that Peretz presented in his letter to Sholem Aleichem on July 4, 1888. See note 8. On another, later polemic on high culture in Yiddish, see Kenneth Moss, "Jewish Culture between Renaissance and Decadence," *Jewish Social Studies* 8, no. 1 (2001): 153-93.

74. Harald Binder, "Making and Defending a Polish Town: Lwów (Lemberg) 1848-1914," *Austrian History Yearbook* 34 (January 2003): 57-81.

75. *Hamagid*, March 28, 1889.

76. M. Ehernpreis, "Bemi Ha'asham," *Hamagid*, February 4-18, 1892.

77. *Hamagid*, February 18, 1892.

78. *Hamagid*, April 5, 1894.

79. M. Ehernpreis, "Stam Siha," *Kantschik* 1, no. 1 (1890): 21.

80. *Hamagid*, April 5, 1894.

81. Ehernpreis, letter to Gnazim Institute for the Research of History of the Hebrew Literature in the *New Era*, December 22, 1895 (File no. 29107/1/157, Gnazim archives).

82. Ehernpreis, "Letikun hasifrut hajargonit," *Hamagid*, March 15, 1894.

83. For more on this issue, see Richard Pipes, *Russia under the Old Regime* (London: Weidenfeld and Nicolson, 1995), 278-80 and Jerzy Jedlick, *Cywilizacji polacy poterrebbują* (Warsaw: Panstowe Wydawn Nauk, 2002).

84. See, for example, *Hatzefira*, June 1/13 and 3/15, 1890.

85. The association of *zhargon* with the cook in the kitchen is taken from Gershon Levin's book *Peretz a Bosel Zikhroynes* (Warsaw: Yehudia, 1919), 3-4. Levin wrote, "I became familiar with jargon literature as a child in the kitchen of my family house. In the other rooms of my house we read different kinds of literatures. My sister read books in Polish and Russian. My brother-in-law read only books in Russian and my father read Hebrew. Perl the cook read Yiddish folktales and sometimes the stories of Mendele Mokher Seforim.... I did not understand anything from the books she read; however I understood that besides the important books in Hebrew, there are other books that respectable people did not read. When I was ten years old my father brought home a folktales book in Yiddish. The fact that my father bought this book convinced me that it was an important book. It was the first folktales book that the rest of my family members read not in the kitchen but in other rooms of my family house."

86. "Davar el tovei hasofrim besafah yehudit meduberet," *Hatzefira*, March 19/31, 1890. This announcement was also published in *Hamelitz*.

87. In January 1903, *Der fraynd* began to be published in the Russian Empire.

88. Getzel Kressel, "A historish palemik vagen der yiddish literatur."

89. Moss, "Jewish Culture," 174.

90. Fishman, *Rise of Modern Yiddish Culture*, 19-21; Yechiel Szeintuch, "Ve'idat Tzernovitch," *Khulyot* 6 (2000): 255-84.

CHOOSING YIDDISH IN ISRAEL

Yung Yisroel between Home and Exile,
the Center and the Margins

SHACHAR PINSKER

On May 24, 1978, when the Yiddish poet Rukhl Fishman received the Itzik Manger Prize for Yiddish Literature in Tel Aviv, she noted in her acceptance address, "Before Itzik Manger undertook to settle in Israel, he wrote: *Kh'hob zikh yorn gevalgert in der fremd / itst for ikh zikh valgern in der heym*" (For Years I have been homeless among strangers / Now I go off to be homeless in my own home).[1] Manger, said Fishman, "referred to his own fate and to the fate of his poetry. But that is virtually the fate of the Yiddish language in Israel. It is homeless in its own home." And yet, in the same breath, Fishman continued, "I choose to write Yiddish in Israel, in Kibbutz Beit-Alfa."[2] Thus, Fishman forcefully posed the question Is a Yiddish poet like herself, living on a kibbutz and writing about Israeli reality, an Israeli poet? Or does she perhaps only become, partially, an Israeli writer when her friend Aryeh Aharoni, who lived in the same kibbutz as she and worked for the publishing house Sifriat Poalim, translates her poetry and publishes it in Hebrew?[3]

Fishman's address clearly raises some important issues beyond her own predicament. In the second half of the twentieth century, modernization, migration, and the Holocaust drastically transformed and displaced Yiddish language, literature, and culture. The newly established State of Israel also displaced Yiddish, even as it served as a site for the displacement of Yiddish-speaking immigrants in the postwar period. Among these immigrants, many Yiddish writers, such as the renowned poet Itzik Manger, found new homes in Israel. Manger traveled extensively to and around Israel in the late 1950s and 1960s and resided there just before his death in 1969. Rukhl Fishman immigrated in 1954 at the age of nineteen. She served as an active member of the literary group Yung Yisroel and wrote Yiddish poetry until her premature death in 1984.

Yet, what was the status of Yiddish in Israel then, and more specifically, what role did Yiddish play in Israeli literature and culture during the formative years of the state from the 1950s to the 1970s? Was Yiddish "homeless in its own home" as Fishman asserted in her speech? Perhaps the very fact that Meyer Vaisgal (fundraiser for the Weizmann Institute of Science in Israel), along with Zalman Shazar, the third president of Israel, established the Manger Prize for Yiddish Literature in 1968 as well as the fact that some of Manger's works were hugely popular (albeit mostly in Hebrew translation) point to a slightly different picture?[4]

The Fishman/Manger anecdote constitutes only one of many examples of the complex question of the place and role of Yiddish in Israel, which proves difficult to answer for at least two interrelated reasons: First, since there is no doubt that the pre-state Yishuv and the young State of Israel neglected and sometimes forcefully rejected Yiddish, this topic elicits strong emotional, psychological, and ideological reactions.[5] Second, scholars have, until recently, almost totally neglected the place of Yiddish within Israeli literature and culture. For a long time, scholars either chose not to touch the issue or believed it did not warrant serious study. The prevalent notion among scholars of Jewish and Israeli literature and culture suggested that in the post-Holocaust period—with the notable exception of Avrom Sutskever, whom many consider "the last Great Yiddish Poet" (to use Ruth Wisse's expression)[6]—nothing significant emerged in Yiddish in Israel. In recent years, a pronounced change appears to have occurred, mainly in Israeli academia, and a movement toward probing the place of Yiddish language, literature, and culture in Israel has begun to emerge.

Even early research on Yiddish in Israel pointed to the derisive attention the language and its cultural output received. In what remains a pioneering and very important survey of Yiddish in Israel, written in 1973, Joshua and David Fishman (who are, not incidentally, the brother and nephew, respectively, of Rukhl Fishman, living and working in New York City), wrote,

> The Yiddish book, particularly the serious book . . . still strikes many . . . as an oddity. Yiddish is most firmly established as a vernacular . . . and as such, its association with radio, theatre, and even daily press is not hard to fathom. . . . However, books of modern Yiddish poetry, novels, dramas, short stories, essays, literary criticism . . . have rarely reached beyond a very small and select circle of aficionados anywhere in the Jewish world. . . . The Yiddish book market and literary scene are hardly known to Israelis outside of specialized circles. Thus, the Yiddish writer and Yiddish literature must cope with studied neglect and opposition. . . . "High Yiddish," the Yiddish of literature of the highest quality and worldwide repute . . . is rejected both cognitively and affectively. "Low Yiddish" is shrugged off with a wry smile.[7]

Writing twenty-one years later, Dan Miron chose to ignore or to put aside the question of "high literature" and stressed the exploitation of what was perceived as the "low" and comic Yiddish in Israel: "One of the implicit assumptions of young Israeli culture was that that the Yiddish which the east-European immigrants brought with them is a comic 'funny' language. Saying something in Yiddish in the right circumstances—always in public—would be funny almost independently of its content. This very 'fact' was exploited by many actors, comedians and other people who needed a kind of 'comic relief.'"[8]

In the same year, 2004, Rachel Rojanski, an Israeli historian who studies the policy on and official attitudes toward Yiddish in the early years of the State of Israel, claimed almost the opposite of Miron:

> Israel's attitude towards Yiddish culture in the 1950s can be summed up as follows: as long as there were sporadic popular attempts to revive Yiddish as a daily language, to present it as one of the languages of the Jewish people, and to bring it back into the Israeli street, the establishment rejected it, even fought against it. However, at the same time, the state's policy makers favored the creation of a kind of small island of Yiddish culture, as a positive feature of the past, to be preserved, nurtured, and developed, in the central state of the people, not in its Diaspora. . . . A high culture in Yiddish developed, while a popular culture in Yiddish was relegated to the sidelines.[9]

In reading these studies, we find conflicting accounts of the status of Yiddish in Israel. In the following pages, I engage these tensions not by examining the attitudes toward Yiddish by the government, policy makers, and other organizations and figures of political and cultural importance but by focusing on the activity, reception, and unexpected impact of an understudied Yiddish literary group, Yung Yisroel, during the 1950s and 1960s. This examination of Yung Yisroel—and in particular the journal and the book series they published, the literary texts they produced, the ways in which they were received and understood, and the impact (or lack thereof) they made—proves that this group's output cut through the heart of what it meant to "choose Yiddish" in Israel.

Due to the lack of comprehensive research of this group, many important questions still surround Yung Yisroel, which consisted of refugees and immigrants situated within an emerging social and cultural backdrop indifferent or even hostile to their activities.[10] The motivations behind the establishment of this group in 1951 are not entirely clear, and no singular artistic, social, or ideological platform bound them together. It is also uncertain why the group ceased its collective activity by the end of the 1950s and whether they or others considered it a success or failure. Nevertheless, the group and its activity raise other important questions: Did the writers of Yung Yisroel see themselves as part of Israeli culture-in-formation or as part of an international Yiddish culture? Who comprised their readers, and where were they located? How did the Yiddish and Israeli Hebrew literary worlds perceive them? How did their literary texts interact with "Israeli" elements and with elements of east European

Jewish culture? Finally, what does the story of Yung Yisroel teach us about the place of Yiddish in Israeli literature and culture, then and today?

The story of Yung Yisroel begins around 1948, when a number of Yiddish writers (or aspiring writers) immigrated to the young State of Israel. They arrived as refugees, survivors of the Holocaust who ended up in displaced persons camps in countries such as Germany, Italy, and Cyprus. A few immigrated to Israel from other Yiddish centers such as North America and Australia. Some settled on kibbutzim, whereas others found homes in cities such as Tel Aviv and Haifa. The core group included the poets Moshe Yungman, Rivka Basman, Avrom Rinzler, H. Binyomin (better known as Binyamin Hrushovsky, and, later, Harshav), Moshe Gurin, and Rukhl Fishman (who joined the group when she immigrated in 1954) and the fiction writers Zvi Eizenman, Yossl Birshtein, Avrom Karpinovitsh, and Shlomo Vorzoger. Other new immigrant Yiddish writers such as Mordkhe Lifshits, Mendel Mann, Leib Rokhman, Malasha Mali, and the older poet Yankev Fridman refrained from partaking of the group's meetings and activities but associated themselves in a number of ways. The poet Avrom Sutskever acted as a mentor to the group. Even though he had migrated to Israel just a mere few years earlier and was not much older than some of them, Sutskever belonged to a different literary generation because he was already an eminent Yiddish poet before he migrated. Sutskever also established in 1949 the quarterly *Di goldene keyt*, which served as one of the world's leading Yiddish literary journals of the postwar period.[11]

The evocative name Yung Yisroel signified the "youth" and newness of the group, its desire to be part of the newly forming Israeli culture, and its links to the modernist Yiddish literary movements that blossomed throughout the first half of the twentieth century in Europe and America. These groups often called themselves "young" (Di yunge, Yung Yidish, Yung Vilne, and others) and sometimes also "wild" (for example, Di khaliastre, "The Gang"). In the case of Yung Yisroel, the members were in fact young (the average age was twenty-six) and truly novice. Only four members of the group had their first books (of poetry) published by the time of their immigration: Moshe Yungman's *Hinerplet* (*A Nightmare*, Rome, 1947), H. Binyomin's *Shtoybn* (*Dusts*, Munich, 1948), Shlomo Vorzoger's *Zayn* (*To Be*, 1948), and Yossl Birshiten's *Unter fremde himlen* (*Under Alien Skies*, Melbourne, 1949). All the other writers began their literary careers in Israel, and even those who published before made drastic changes in their writing after their immigration.

For example, Birshtein, Eizenman, and Vorzoger switched almost immediately after their immigration from poetry to prose fiction. The style and themes in the work of other writers (H. Binyomin, Yungman, Rinzler) changed dramatically. Most noticeably, their writing began to reflect Israeli life, landscape, and language as well as to respond to the challenges of writing Yiddish in Israel.

Some members of the group published their Yiddish poems and stories almost immediately after their arrival in Israel in venues such as *Nayvelt* (*New World*), a Yiddish weekly newspaper published by the left-wing party Poale Zion (which was generally more supportive of Yiddish from the outset) between 1934 and 1955.[12] However, the first collective publication took place in 1951 in a special section of *Di goldene keyt* titled "Fun der yunger yidisher literatur in Yisroel" ("From the Young Yiddish Literature in Israel") with poems by H. Binyomin, Rivka Basman, Avrom Rinzler, Moshe Yungman, Yossl Birshtein, and Shlomo Vorzoger and short stories by Zvi Eizenman.[13]

Following an inaugural meeting at Kibbutz Yagur, where Zvi Eizenman lived, in October 1951, the core members of the group emerged. In this original meeting (which became a tradition for a number of years), some attendees gave addresses and the group also used the occasion to ponder and debate its path. When the group published again in *Di goldene keyt* (1952), it used the name Yung Yisroel.[14] It took the group two more years to edit and produce its own journal—*Yung Yisroel: literatur, kunst, kritik* (*Yung Yisroel: Literature, Art, Criticism*). The journal, like the group itself, took many cues from earlier modernist Yiddish groups and their publications. An editorial committee collectively edited it, with the poet Avrom Rizler serving as editor in chief. The first volume (1954) included poetry and prose, critical and programmatic essays by members of the group, and artwork by Yossl Bergner (sketches for illustrations of Kafka's texts) and Ya'akov Shteiner (reproductions of sculptures).

This combination of art and literature is an example of the ways *Yung Yisroel* followed the model set by the great modernist Yiddish journals in Europe and

Meeting of Yung Yisroel in Kibbutz Yagur, 1956. *Right to left*: Avrom Rinzler, Rukhl Fishman, Avrom Karpinovitz, Yossl Birshtein, Avrom Sutskever, Rivka Basman, Moshe Gurin, Moshe Yungman, Zvi Eizenman, Shlomo Vorzoger. Courtesy of Rivka Basman.

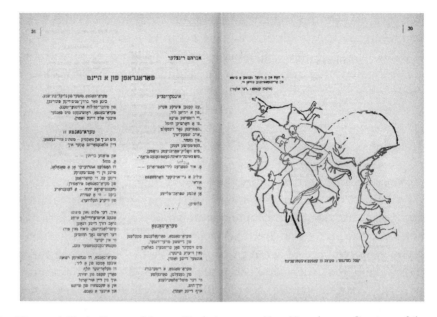

Yossl Bergner's illustrations and Avrom Rinzler's poems, *Yung Yisroel*, 1954. Courtesy of the Jewish National Library of Israel.

America, to which major artists regularly contributed works. In a Yiddish journal such as *Albatross* (1922–1923), the integration of poetic, essayistic, artistic, and typographic values was achieved by the juxtaposition of the literature of the Di khaliastre group (Uri Zvi Greenberg, Peretz Markish, Melekh Ravitch, and others) with the artwork of Henryk Berlewi and Mark Schwartz. As Avidov Lipsker has observed, the journal marked "a milestone in the integration of poetic, publicist, graphic and typographic values."[15] In the journal *Yung Yisroel*, one can find Bergner's illustrations for Kafka's novel *The Castle* side by side with Avrom Rinzler's cycle of poems *Paragrafn fun a haynt* (*Paragraphs from a-Today*). The combination and juxtaposition of literature, art, and criticism created new and unexpected links suggesting a modernistic whole bigger than its parts. Bergner's illustrations of Kafka's novel, as seen on ‹page 000›, for example, suddenly seem to comment on Rinzel's avant-garde poems and vice versa.

Two more volumes of the journal appeared, in 1956 and in 1957, and both featured works by members of the group and writers associated with it. According to the correspondence between Zvi Eizenman, Avrom Rinzler, and Rukhl Fishman, some members of Yung Yisroel intensively attempted to publish a special fourth volume of the journal in 1958, coinciding with the tenth anniversary of the State of Israel, but the plan failed to materialize.[16] In fact, within a couple of years after the publication of the third volume of the journal in 1957, the journal, and the group itself, had more or less dissipated. No single decisive reason exists for the gradual dissolution of the group. In the extensive correspondence among members of the group and in interviews I conducted with some of them more recently, they mention many different reasons, including tiredness and loss of energy for the journal and the annual meetings. Personal and ideological tensions also existed among members of the group (such as between the modernist and more conservative authors). The strong force of Hebrew and the lack of interest in their activities and generally in "high" Yiddish literature in Israel of the 1950s also caused some members of the group to choose new directions.[17] Beyond all these specific reasons, we must also remember that similar modernists groups—working in Yiddish, Hebrew, and many other languages—often lasted for only a few years, and their collective activities, more often than not, were transient.

After 1959, some of the writers of Yung Yisroel continued to write Yiddish literature and publish in other Yiddish publications for many years, whereas others switched gradually to Hebrew or to academic ventures. A few, notably the managing editor of the journal, Avrom Rinzler, ceased publishing literary works almost altogether. Still, a vital afterlife to the activity of the group existed in the form of a book series with the title *Yung Yisroel,* in which members of the group published their creative work. All in all, between 1954 and 1966 seven books of poetry and fiction were published under this imprint by Moshe Yungman, Zvi Eizenman, Yossl Birshtein, Rivka Basman, Avrom Karpinovitsh, Rukhl Fishman, and Moshe Gurin.[18]

In spite of the many differences between the mentality and the literary tendencies and styles of its members, evident in all of their writing is the synthesis of the traditions of Yiddish literature in Europe and America and the new Israeli reality. Because most members of the group were survivors of the Holocaust, albeit with different experiences among them, and east European in origin, they tried to use Yiddish as a bridge across time and space, connecting the tradition of Yiddish with the new environment. At the same time, the group of Yung Yisroel was also distinctively Israeli. This synthesis manifested in areas of plots and narrative, characters, diction, images, the representation of landscape, and the ways in which they transformed Yiddish literary language.

In stories and poems of Yung Yisroel writers, we find the Israeli kibbutz with its sensual "sun over everything" (Fishman and Basman), as well as the sheep and its pastors (Birshtein's "Khonen the Pastor"), the *ma'abara* or "transit camp" (in stories by Eizenman and Birshtein), and the scorching hot desert of Sodom and the Negev (H. Binyomin, Karpinovitsh, and Rinzler). We find Arabs and Bedouins (Birshtein's "Between the Olive Trees" and Eizenman's "The Woman from the Mountain") and Jewish immigrants from Yemen (Eizenman's "A Courtyard in Jaffa"), Morocco (Yungman's cycle of poems *Moroccan Motifs*) and every corner of eastern, central, and western Europe and beyond. At the same time, figures and motifs from the Ashkenazi distant and close Jewish past

Cover of Rukhl Fishman's *Zun iber Altz*. Illustration by Dani Karavan (Tel Aviv: Y. L. Peretz Publishing House, 1962). Dani Karavan is a recipient of the Israel Prize (1977) and one of Israel's most important artists. He was a member of Kibbutz Hare'l until 1955.

appear within the Israeli landscape, and vice versa. Thus, for example, in "A mayse vegn Nisim fun Har-Tov" ("A Story about Nissim from Har-Tov") by Zvi Eizenman, a Sephardic man riding a donkey visits the narrator in his Warsaw courtyard. In this story, the use of the fantastic and Yiddish folk motifs enables the narrator to create an effective fusion of the world of Jewish Warsaw with the fluid, even chaotic reality of the Israeli "transit camp" world in the late 1940s and 1950s.[19]

Through implicit and indirect references, the Holocaust stands as an omnipresent dark "shadow" in almost every text of *Yung Yisroel*. This is especially pronounced in the fantastic stories of Zvi Eizenman, for example in "Der karshnboym" ("The Cherry Tree"), in which the narrator describes a nightmare about the destruction of a friend from his youth, and characters move from a courtyard in Warsaw to an Israeli town.[20] The destruction of European Jewry in the Holocaust also appears in subtle ways in the poetry of Moshe Yungman, Moshe Gurin, and Rivka Basman. In the poem "Nit-hige" Basman's speaker, living in an Israeli kibbutz, spends her nights without sleep because guests come from *umetland* (the land of gloom):

> Comes walking the little shepherd
> with burned lambs,
> comes the white little goat/brick
> abashed from cradles.[21]

Beyond these thematic commonalities, unmistakably eclectic qualities exist in the literary output of Yung Yisroel, a result of the poetic differences between the members of the group. One may detect a conscious attempt not to pose a unified poetic dogma to which the group must adhere. This aspect harks back to the group's establishment. In his unpublished speech, given during the founding meeting of the group in 1951, Sutskever emphasized that the group should not have "any collective ideological and conceptual underpinning, but an artistic pluralism; they should do what is good and has a special appeal to a young literary group."[22] It is important to remember that Sutskever served as a *sandek*—a respected "godfather" and mentor of the group, and he could not and probably did not want to dictate its literary and artistic direction.

However, two distinct fundamental poetic and ideological trends existed within the group. For the sake of simplicity, I call them the "conservatives" and the "modernists." Avrom Karpinovitsh's prose and some of Zvi Eizenman's stories perpetuated the conservative tendency, as with the poetry of Moshe Yungman, Rivka Basman, Moshe Gurin, and Shlomo Vorzoger. In contradistinction, the modernist trends appear in the poetry of H. Binyomin, Avrom Rinzler, Rukhl Fishman and the prose fiction of Yossl Birshtein. Both poetic trends may be seen both in their implicit poetics (in their poetry and prose) and in their explicit poetics (articles, manifestos, speeches, etc.).[23]

In 1954, founding Yung Yisroel member Moshe Yungman published a programmatic essay, titled "Shtrikhn" ("Lines") in the first volume of the journal *Yung Yisroel*. In this essay Yungman meditated on some artistic and poetic issues, but his main preoccupation concerned the predicament of young Yiddish writers in their new land and what he called the *shotn* ("the shadows") that these writers carry with them. Yungman suggested that instead of ignoring these traumatic experiences, Yiddish writers should engage them and try to communicate them. Indeed, for Yungman, the task of the Yiddish writer is to connect with the people:

> Real art is bounded to its spiritual and physical environment, and it gives it expression. Real art stands at the service of the people (folk), in its dynamic aspect....We should focus on spiritual proximity rather than on linguistic divisions. This proximity is the bridge that binds people and unites them. In this spiritual proximity there is a new truth for Yiddish literature; especially in the last generation, when it grows in the shadow and sprouts between the falling walls, attempting to reach the light.[24]

This description, full of pathos, represents not only Yungman's style but also a certain tendency within the group, which saw itself as attempting to find light within the shadows and to connect with what Yungman called a "nation that is not yet a nation, but *erev rov fun shvotim* [a multitude of tribes]."[25] Yungman was not oblivious to the marginality of Yiddish in Israel, but he retained a belief in the power of art and in the ability of young Yiddish writers to create bridges and to grow "sprouts between the falling walls." This is something Yungman expressed in his essay/manifesto as well as in the poetry he wrote and published in the 1950s and 1960s.

Avrom Rinzler and Yossl Birshtein opposed this point of view and presented their own poetic and ideological positions in a very different style in the form of essays and manifestos. Rinzler's two-part essay "Randn" ("Margins") was published in the second volume of *Yung Yisroel* (1956); the first part was titled "Vortshaft" ("Wordiness"), and the second "Freud und Besht in Beys-Dagon" ("Freud and the Ba'al-Shem-Tov in Beit Dagan"). The essay should be read as a manifesto in the tradition of the great modernist Yiddish manifestos of the first half of the twentieth century. Its argumentative style and combative rhetoric (its call for a new approach and a rejection of conventions), the use of extravagant imagery and neologism, and the fusion of the poetic and the essayistic are all characteristic of modernist manifestoes from the Russian and Italian futurist manifestos to the expressionist and Inzikhist manifestos in Yiddish:[26]

> We must not erect a vacuum-barrier, but a clear and sharp distinction ... between Yiddish language and literature. What we need in order to preserve the breath of our language is not anymore a matter that concerns the writer. The further development of our literature is not dependent on any cultural-political preconceptions or preconditions. No neo-national conceptions will affect its continuation. For us, language and literature must start to exist as two independent and separate territories. Yiddish literature doesn't need to be involved with the campaign for a better social position for its language, which goes together with a language-politics of renaissance. This will only slow down the development of literature itself and at the same time will cause it to spread

its energies thin, with very problematic results. The metaphysics of miraculous language revival will give nothing and will not enrich the functional expression of our literature.[27]

Curiously, this text not only follows the iconoclastic tradition of modernist manifestos of the avant-garde but it also anticipates—in its attention to the difference between Yiddish as a vernacular and Yiddish as a literary, poetic language—recent developments in the field of Yiddish studies such as the divorce of ideology from the use of the language and its cultural production. In its imagery of "territorial" elements of language and literature it also anticipates postmodernist theories such as Gilles Deleuze and Felix Guattari's theory of "minor literature" and the deterritorialization of literature.[28] "If we need a living vocabulary," writes Rinzler, "we can find it in the written word (*vortshrift*), which can be the bastion of our literary language." He declares that there must be "a sharp turn of one hundred and eighty degrees from our old embittered conceptions, and [we must] smash the archaic frames of the *loshn-mame-koydesh*." The consequences of such a "pogrom," claims Rinzler, are the creation of "a free territory for a functional literature. We must be prepared to sacrifice the full inventory of emotional complexes ... but our great concern should be to establish a better future prospect for our Yiddish literature."[29]

This radical and controversial perspective—with its original and iconoclastic and yet functional use of highly loaded terms such as "pogrom" and a neologism *loshn-mame-koydesh* (a fusion of the two designations *loshn-koydesh* for Hebrew and *mameloshn* for Yiddish)—seems surprising for a Yiddish writer during the 1950s. In fact, this manifesto and its language and images served as a natural extension of Rinzler's avant-garde poetry, which constantly sought to redefine, on a conceptual level, the relations between Yiddish as a *folkshprakh* and Yiddish as a language of experimental modernist poetry. It also represents a profound, albeit extreme response to what Rinzler identified, as early as 1956, as a growing gap between Yiddish as a vernacular and the rise of what Jeffery Shandler has recently called "postvernacular" literature and culture.[30]

Yossl Birshtein, Rinzler's friend and collaborator in the group, dealt with some of the same poetic issues and with the implications of choosing Yiddish in Israel. Birshtein did this implicitly in his short stories and in his novel *Oyf shmole trotuarn* (*On Narrow Paths*), the first and only novel in Yiddish about life on the kibbutz.[31] Birshtein also dealt with these poetic and ideological questions explicitly in an address titled "A yidisher shrayber in kibbutz," which he gave at the founding meeting of Yung Yisroel in 1951. He spoke about his experience of writing Yiddish in an Israeli kibbutz. Birshtein opened his address with the following words: "On the first day when I arrived at the Kibbutz, I received a letter from an old Yiddish poet. The letter said: You live in a Kibbutz now, *farges nisht dort az du bist a yidisher dikhter* [do not forget there, that you are a Jewish/Yiddish poet/writer]." What the Yiddish poet said in his letter reminded Birshtein of his father's warning when he emigrated from Poland to Australia as a young lad: *zolt nisht fargesn in dem goyishn land, az du bist a yid* (do not forget in the foreign land that that you are a Jew).[32]

The very title of Birshtein's address, "A yiddisher shrayber in kibbutz," reflects the anomalous predicament in which he and other Yiddish writers found themselves in Israel in 1951. In the essay, he suggests the Yiddish writer who writes in the distinctly Israeli paradigm of Zionist-socialist culture should carry on as if in the diaspora, namely, surround himself with Yiddish books and create a spiritual atmosphere in which Yiddish will not be forgotten. However, in Israel, for the first time, Birshtein wrote of the need to justify his writing Yiddish literature and of his desire not to apologize for it: "Such justifications [for writing Yiddish] as that 'Yiddish is a means of keeping the treasures of the Diaspora' ... [or] the thought that 'because my ancestors spoke Yiddish, I have to continue it,' are all nice sentiments, but they won't be successful if Yiddish will not flourish in this land and in my life here."[33] Birshtein attempts to articulate a position that accepts "art for art's sake" as suggested by Rinzler, but as part of a self-conscious approach to writing in a minor language. He does not offer a clear-cut solution but exhibits an acute awareness of the complex predicament of Yiddish writings in Israel.

A few years later, Birshtein wrote another essay-cum-manifesto titled "Aspektn" ("Aspects"), which was published in the second volume of *Yung Yisroel* in 1956. In this essay, Birshtein analyzes Rinzler's "difficult" conceptual poetry, at least in part as an implicit means to further his own arguments and his views of the modernist elements in *Yung Yisroel* as totally different and unique in the landscape of post-Holocaust Yiddish literature, which according to David Roskies is built on two pillars: utopian faith and collective lamentation.[34] In this essay Birshtein writes,

> Our Yiddish poetry suffers from too many familiar moods that have lost, a
> long time ago, their personal quality and became a collective property. In just
> the same way, there are familiar overused rhymes—poetic and prosaic, that the
> inept writer and the one who becomes inept can emulate too easily. These familiar
> moods, emotions and poetic devices appear in almost all the poetry that
> was published in Yiddish ... after the War. It is enough that a writer ... should
> make mention of "six million," and right away he sees himself walking onto the
> stage and—the world becomes full of malice, everybody is bad, the hatred is big
> but he, his own heart, is full of love and pity, only that no one understands him.
> And mumble, he mumbles to himself and speaks; he speaks directly to God,
> and all—
>
> —with drawn-out rhymes,
> with *Tsene-rene* paced stresses.—[35]

A mere decade after the end of World War II, Birshtein already opposed the invocation of the "six million," which according to him had already become an "overused mood," and found it parallel to overused "rhymes"—poetic and prosaic. At the same time, Birshtein sharply identified the problem of this modernist, forward-looking endeavor. "Rinzler's poems," writes Birshtein (and here also he uses Rinzler as an extreme example among Yung Yisroel), "are not good for journals whose readers are sixty or seventy years old. His poetry and his path is a new one, and therefore he requires the attention of new and young readers that have all the advantages and disadvantages of youthfulness." However, he adds, "Dos iz nishto; nisht do un nisht umetum" (this is not to be found; here or anywhere).[36]

The reception of *Yung Yisroel* suggests Birshtein's accuracy in his observation. To be sure, readers, writers, and critics from all around the Yiddish world gave *Yung Yisroel* a great deal of attention. Almost every major and minor Yiddish journal and newspaper in the United States, Canada, Argentina, Australia, and France covered the group and its activities. When the journal *Yung Yisroel* was published, great Yiddish writers and critics such as Shmuel Niger, Yankev Glatshteyn, Aaron Leyeles, Itzik Manger, David Pinski, Nokhum Borukh Minkov, and Melekh Ravitch wrote and published reviews of it.[37]

Itzik Manger's review of the first volume of the group's journal, published in *Der veker* May 1, 1955, captures a common element in the reception of the group and its literary output in the Yiddish world outside Israel. Manger complemented the group members for having *erd unter di fis* (the earth beneath their feet).[38] Most critics, including Manger, celebrated the writers' ability to connect the tradition of Yiddish with Israeli life and reality and with the physical and social landscape of the country.[39] However, most significantly, Yiddish modernist luminaries such as Glatshteyn, Leyeles, and Minkov curiously highlighted the conservative elements of the group and were reluctant, sometimes even hostile, to the modernist tendencies of Birshtein, Binyomin, Fishman, and Rinzler.

For example, in a review from March 1956, Glatshteyn wrote, "Neither Rinzler, nor his colleagues in Yung Yisroel can spit in the well of the 'loshn-mame-koydesh.' Rinzler's pure art-production doesn't give him such a license. The *vort-shrift* as the only future for our language is an excuse for the writer to exempt himself from the struggle for a better social position for Yiddish." "The pogrom, my dear Rinzler," wrote Glatshteyn in direct response to Rinzler's essay quoted above, "even if it works well in individual poems, *kon nokh nit shnaydn keyn kunst kupon* [does not allow you to take advantage of it]."[40]

Ironically, Glatshteyn—who along with his fellow Inzikhistn was the direct inspiration for the modernist works of H. Binyomin, Rinzler, Birshtein, and Fishman—was one of the very few figures around the world who could read these manifestos seriously and understand them. But writing in the post-Holocaust period and concerned as he was with the future of Yiddish language

and culture, he rejected them. As is well known, Glatshteyn himself transformed his poetic form and content in response to the Holocaust, eschewing
many of the modernist tones he had once heralded, and expressed the need to
write a poetry of consolation and mourning, giving voice to the millions who
could no longer speak, in a language they would themselves have used.[41] Thus,
although he clearly identified the inventiveness and originality in the poetry
of Rinzler, Binyomin, and Fishman, as well as the stories of Birshtein, he could
not tolerate the ideological aspects of this Israeli-modernist Yiddish literature.

Thus, in America and Europe Yung Yisroel received a great deal of attention, though not always positive. In Israel, however, the group and its activities
barely received any mention outside small Yiddish-Israeli newspapers such
as *Letste nayes*. Apart from a couple of announcements about their meetings
in Kibbutz Yagur (in the Israeli-labor-oriented paper *Davar*), a short review
of their journal in a newspaper for new immigrants (*Omer*), and an extremely
negative review (in *Al hamishmar*), nothing appeared about Yung Yisroel in the
Israeli Hebrew press of the 1950s and 1960s.[42]

Despite the relative silence of Israeli Hebrew literary circles and press about
Yung Yisroel, its members, publications, and literary activities, I would like to
suggest, as I have shown in other studies, that the group did have an impact on
Israeli literature and culture, though it was never acknowledged at the time.[43]
Given the heterogenic nature of the literary group, different areas of influence
exist following both the conservative and modernist threads. The more conservative literature of Yung Yisroel was remarkable in 1950s and 1960s Israel—
especially in the subtle ways it dealt with the Holocaust and the devastation of
the Jews of eastern Europe. During the first two decades of Israel's existence,
few literary works sought to actualize the human experiences of the Holocaust
by transmuting them into a poetic discourse that would make them emotionally and intellectually accessible.[44] Yung Yisroel and Yiddish writers associated
with them represented a clear departure from this, prefiguring developments
that occurred in Israel in the writings of prominent Israeli authors such as
Aharon Appelfeld and Yitzhak Orpaz (Averbuch).[45] Appelfeld's essays on Leib
Rochman (published in Yiddish in *Di goldene keyt*), Yankev Glatshteyn, Aaron
Zeitlin, and Yiddish-Soviet writers indicate how preoccupied he was with pre-
and post-Holocaust Yiddish literature in Israel, the Soviet Union, and America
as well as the importance of Yiddish in his own Hebrew writings.[46]

The impact of the modernists in Yung Yisroel on canonic Israeli literature
was no less important, but it was also hidden and unacknowledged. The modernist poetry and essays-cum-manifestos of Rinzler, Birshtein, Binyomin, and
Fishman influenced what many consider the most important Hebrew literary group in Israeli of the 1950s—the group known as Likrat (Forward), whose
most famous members included the poets Natan Zach, Yehuda Amichai, Moshe
Dor, and Aryeh Sivan. The interaction between the two groups occurred mainly
through H. Binyomin (Binyamin Hrushovsky), who served as a literary and

cultural "double agent" because he actively belonged to both the Yiddish and Hebrew groups of young Israeli poets. In spite of the huge differences between the two groups, they shared a common source of inspiration—the American and European modernist Yiddish poetry of the 1920s and 1930s.[47] A similar trend of influence, mutual interaction, and cross-fertilization occurred in the 1960s and 1970s when another "double agent," Yossl Birshtein—who became a bilingual writer in this period—wrote some of the most path-breaking texts in Hebrew prose fiction.

As a result of these interactions, Yiddish—and specifically the writers and work associated with Yung Yisroel—affected and was at the root of some highly significant changes in Israeli literature from the 1950s onward. But since Yiddish was deemed as, to use Yael Chaver's expression, "the language that must be forgotten," this influence remains hidden, and so far unacknowledged. Yiddish might have been extremely marginal, or even "homeless" in Israel, as Rukhl Fishman put it. However, Yiddish was also a potent force, a kind of secret but effective "double agent" in Israeli literature and culture. Even if this was *not* its intention, Yung Yisroel, in fact, served as an important bridge for the literature and culture of young Israel into the present.

Notes

I would like to thank the Fishman family and Stanford University Special Collections for allowing me to look at documents from Rukhl Fishman's archive and Zvi Eizenman and the Gnazim Institute in Tel Aviv for the use of Eizenman's archive. Unless otherwise noted, all translations from Yiddish and Hebrew are mine.

1. Itzik Manger, *Lid un balade* (New York: Itzik Manger Komitet, 1952), 486-87. The translation is by Seymour Levitan. This highly ambiguous poem has been translated into Hebrew and English in many different ways. Leonard Wolf translated the famous first line as follows: "For years I wallowed among strangers / Now I'm going home to wallow there." Itzik Manger, *The World According to Itzik: Selected Poetry and Prose* (New Haven: Yale University Press, 2002), 106.

2. Rukhl Fishman, "Etlekhe verter bay der farteylung funem Manger prayz" (speech given May 24, 1978), in Rukhl Fishman Papers, 1940-1990 (collection no. Mo778, Department of Special Collections and University Archives, Stanford University).

3. After the publication of Fishman's first and second books in Yiddish *Zun iber alts* [Sun on Everything] (Tel Aviv: Farlag Y. L. Peretz, 1962) and *Derner nokhn regn* (1966), she made an effort to publish her poems in Hebrew translation. First she published the bilingual volume *Shamayim ba'esev*, trans. Aryeh Aharoni (Tel Aviv: Alef, 1968), which presented a selection of poetry from 1954-1968. Her third book, *Vilde tsig/Iza Pziza* (Jerusalem: Kiryat Sefer, 1976), was published in a bilingual Hebrew-Yiddish edition.

4. The many Hebrew translations of Manger's poetry into Hebrew include Itzik Manger, *Shir, balada, sipur*, trans. Shimshon Meltzer (Tel Aviv: Farlag Y. L. Peretz, 1962); Manger, *Shirim uvaladot*, trans. Binyamin Tene (Ramat-Gan, Israel: Al Hamishmar, 1968); Manger, *Levana aduma al gag makhsif*, trans. Mordekhai Amitai (Tel Aviv: Ha-menorah, 1975); Manger, *Mivhar shirim*, trans. Natan Yonatan (Jerusalem: Keter, 1986); Manger, *Mishirei tavas hazahav*, trans. Ya'akov Orland (Jerusalem: Carmel, 1995); and Manger, *Tzror shirim uvaladot*, trans. Me'ir Avni (Kibbutz Shamir, Israel: Me'ir Avni, 1999). Manger reached something of celebrity status in Israel with the stunning success of the dramatic ad-

aptation of his *Megile lider* (*Megillah Poems*), produced and performed by the Burshtein family in Jaffa in 1965-1966. On the reception of Manger's work in Israel and on the Manger Prize and the history of its establishment, see Naomi Brenner, "Itzik in Israel: Itzik Manger's Yiddish in Hebrew Translation," *Prooftexts* 28, no. 1 (2008): 53-84.

5. For an excellent study of Yiddish literature during the pre-state Yishuv period, see Yael Chaver, *What Must Be Forgotten: The Survival of Yiddish Writing in Zionist Palestine* (Syracuse, NY: Syracuse University Press, 2004). My study is an attempt to continue the work of Chaver into the Israeli period.

6. Ruth Wisse, "The Last Great Yiddish Poet?" *Commentary* 76, no. 5 (1983): 41-48.

7. Joshua Fishman and David Fishman, "Yiddish in Israel: The Press, Radio, Theatre, and Book Publishing," *Yiddish* 1, no. 2 (1973): 4-23, 11.

8. Dan Miron, "Hem tzoḥakim, ani bokhe," *Ha'aretz Literary Supplement*, July 16, 2004. Reprinted in Miron, *Hatzad ha'afel bitzḥoko shel Shalom Aleichem* (Tel Aviv: Am Oved, 2004), 9-15, 9.

9. Rachel Rojanski, "The Status of Yiddish in Israel 1948-1958: An Overview," in *Yiddish after the Holocaust*, ed. Joseph Sherman (Oxford: Boulevard Books, 2004), 46-60, 59. See also Rojanski, "The Struggle for a Yiddish Repertoire Theatre in Israel 1950-1952," *Israel Affairs* 15, no. 1 (2009): 4-27.

10. The only attempts to describe and analyze certain elements of Yung Yisroel are an unfinished essay by David Roskies, "Di shrayber grupe Yung Yisroel," *Yugntruf* 28-29 (September 1973): 7-12, 33; *Yugntruf* 33 (July 1975): 7-8, 24; *Yugntruf* 34 (February 1976): 4-7, 12 and Moshe Yungman, "Draysik yor *Yung Yisroel*," *Di goldene keyt* 108 (1982): 59-66. Except for these two essays, there has been, to date, no comprehensive study of the group. My own discussion represents an initial stage of my extensive archival research of published and unpublished materials, literary and critical texts by the group and about the group, the correspondence among the members of the groups and between them and key figures in Israel and around the world, and interviews I have conducted with members of the group.

11. Although *Di goldene keyt* was published in Tel Aviv with support from the Histadrut (General Federation of Labor in Israel), it cannot be considered an "Israeli Yiddish journal" because it is a forum for Yiddish writers around the world and was read by Yiddish readers from all over the world. The journal revolved mainly around the charismatic personality of Avrom Sutskever, its editor.

12. Poems by Zvi Eizenman, Avrom Rinzler, Shlomo Vorzoger, and Moshe Yungman and stories by Avrom Krpinovitch were published in *Nayvelt* between 1948 and 1950. On Poale Zion, see Henry Shebrnik, "The Left Poalei Zion in Inter-War Poland," in *Yiddish and the Left*, ed. Gennady Estraikh and Mikhail Krutikov (Oxford: Legenda, 2001), 24-55.

13. *Di goldene keyt* 7 (1951): 150-80.

14. *Di goldene keyt* 13 (1952): 192-227. Additional writers in this publication included Moshe Gurin and Mordkhe Lifshits.

15. See Avidov Lipsker, "The Albatrosses of Young Yiddish Poetry: An Idea and Its Visual Realization in Uri Zvi Greenberg's *Albatross*," *Prooftexts* 15, no. 1 (1995): 89-109.

16. See the correspondence between Zvi Eizenman and Rukhl Fishman in Fishman's collections at Stanford University and in Eizenman's collection in the Gnazim Archive at Tel Aviv. The inability to produce the 1958 volume was one indication of the end of the journal and the dissipation of the group itself.

17. Financial difficulties were not a concern because although Yung Yisroel did not receive any support from any organization or individual in Israel, the journal was financially supported by Americans such as Max Holtzman and others.

18. Moshe Yungman, *In shotn fun molad* [In the Shadow of the Moon] (Paris: Goldene pave farlag, 1954); Zvi Eizenman, *Di ban* [The Train] (Tel Aviv: Ahdut, 1956); Yossl Birshtein,

Oyf shmole trotuaren [In Narrow Paths] (Tel Aviv: Farlag Y. L. Peretz, 1958); Rivka Basman, *Toybn baym brunem* [Doves by the Well] (Tel Aviv: Farlag Y. L. Peretz, 1959); Avrom Karpinovitsh, *Der veg kayn Sdom* [The Road to Sodom] (Tel Aviv: Farlag Y. L. Peretz, 1959); Rukhl Fishman, *Zun iber alts*; Moshe Gurin, *Di grine brik* [The Green Bridge] (Tel Aviv: Farlag Y. L. Peretz, 1966).

19. Zvi Eizenman, "A mayse vegn Nisim fun Har-Tov," *Yung Yisroel* 2 (1956): 14-16. See also the reflections of Eizenman on representing Israeli reality in Yiddish in his essay "Problemen fun a yiddish shreyber baym moln di Israel virklekhkayt," *Undzer Vort*, November 27, 1978.

20. See Zvi Eizenman, "Der karshnboym," *Yung Yisroel* 2 (1956): 14-19. For more on this, see Roskies, "Di shrayber grupe Yung Yisroel" and Shachar Pinsker, "That Yiddish Has Spoken to Me: Yiddish in Early Israeli Literature," *Poetics Today* (forthcoming).

21. Rivka Basman, *Toybn baym brunem*, 16.

22. Quoted in Yungman, "Draysik yor *Yung Yisroel*," 62.

23. David Roskies claims that the group failed to produce any revolutionary collective manifestos in the manner typical of literary Yiddish groups such as the Inzikhistn, Di yunge, and Yung Vilne. This leads him to argue that the group possessed no literary, cultural, or ideological platform. Although it is true that Yung Yisroel refrained from publishing a collective manifesto, members of the group held strong poetic, cultural, and ideological opinions that they did not hesitate to express in manifesto-like essays. Roskies, "Yung Yisroel," *Yugntruf* 28-29 (September 1973), 7-12, 8.

24. Moyshe Yungman, "Shtrikhn," *Yung Yisroel* 1 (1954): 35-36.

25. Ibid.

26. For an excellent and comprehensive presentation of these manifestos, see Benjamin Harshav, *Manifestim shel modernism* (Jerusalem: Carmel, 2001). See also Janet Lyon, *Manifestos: Provocations of the Modern* (Ithaca: Cornell University Press, 1999).

27. Avrom Rinzler, "Randen," *Yung Yisroel* 2 (1956): 58-60.

28. Gilles Deleuze and Felix Guattari, *Kafka: Toward a Minor Literature*, trans. Dina Pollan (Minneapolis: University of Minnesota Press, 1986).

29. Rinzler, "Randen," 58-60.

30. Jeffery Shandler, *Adventures in Yiddishland: Postvernacular Language and Culture* (Berkeley: University of California Press, 2005).

31. Yossl Birshtein, *Oyf Shmole Trotuarn* (Tel Aviv: Farlag Y. L. Peretz, 1958). On Birshtein's novel and Yiddish work in the 1950s and 1960s, see Avraham Novershtern, "The Multicolored Patchwork on the Coat of a Prince: On Yossl Birstein's Work," *Modern Hebrew Literature* 8-9 (1992): 56-59; David Roskies, *A Bridge of Longing: The Lost Art of Yiddish Storytelling* (Cambridge: Harvard University Press, 1995), 329-47; Shachar Pinsker, "The Bilingual Project of Yossl Birshtein and the Role of Yiddish in Israeli Literature and Culture" (forthcoming).

32. Yossl Birshtein, "A yiddisher shrayber in kibbutz," *Yung Yisroel* 1 (1954): 31.

33. *Yung Yisrael* 2 (1956): 57.

34. Roskies, *Bridge of Longing*, 332.

35. Avrom Rinzler, "Inscription," *Yung Yisroel* 2 (1956): 54-57.

36. Ibid.

37. Shmuel Niger, *Der tog*, January 1952, *Der tog* 1955; David Pinski, *Der tog*, November 1952; Nokhum Borukh Minkov, *Der tog*, December 1952; Yankev Glatshteyn, *Yidisher Kemfer*, November 15, 1952, February 11, 1955, March 9, 1956; A. Leyeles, *Tog morgen jurnal*, January, February, April, and August 1955, August 1956; Itzik Manger, "Yung Yisroel," *Der Veker*, May 1, 1955; Melech Ravich, *Freye Areberter Shtime*, September 1955.

38. Manger, "Yung Yisroel," 21.

39. For more on the reception of *Yung Yisroel*, see Yitzhak Korn, "Yiddish in medines Yisroel," *Bay Zich* 20 (1982): 22-27.

40. Yankev Glatshteyn, "Kistererisher neitralism zu yidish," *Yidisher Kemfer*, March 9, 1956.

41. Anita Norich describes Glatshteyn's poetic and ideological stance after the Holocaust as "an ambivalent farewell." Norich, *Discovering Exile: Yiddish and Jewish American Culture during the Holocaust* (Stanford: Stanford University Press, 2007), 42–73.

42. See "Sofrey Yung Israel bekinusam," *Davar*, November 4, 1952; Y. Ch. Biltsky, "Shirat Yung Yisroel," *Al hamishmar*, October 9, 1957; "Yung Israel," *Omer*, November 1, 1957.

43. Pinsker, "That Yiddish Has Spoken"; Pinsker, "The Bilingual Project of Yossl Birshtein."

44. Much has been written on this subject. See, for example, Gershon Shaked, "Facing the Nightmare; Israeli Literature on the Holocaust," in *The Nazi Concentration Camps: Structure and Aims, the Image of the Prisoner, the Jews in the Camps*, ed. Israel Gutman and A. Saf (Jerusalem: Kernermann, 1984), 683–96; Yael Feldman, "Whose Story Is It Anyway: Ideology and Psychology in the Representation of the Shoah in Israeli Literature," in *Probing the Limits of Representation*, ed. Saul Friedlander (Cambridge: Harvard University Press, 1992), 223–40.

45. On Appelfeld and Yiddish, see Shachar Pinsker, "Harakevet hadoheret Pnima," *Mikan* 5 (January 2005): 77–88; and Zelda Kahan-Newman, "Yiddish Haunts: The Yiddish Underpinnings of Appelfeld's 'Laylah ve'od laylah,'" *Mikan* 5 (January 2005): 81–90.

46. Aharon Appelfeld, "Hasho'a besifrut yiddish bivrit hamo'etzot," *Yediot yad va-shem* 14 (1957): 13, 16; Appelfeld, "Yiḥuda shel shirat Aaron Zeitlin," *Gazit* 18 (1960): 5–8, 97–98; Appelfeld (signed Aharon Appel), "Bema'agal ha'ashlaya: al hagutu hasifrutit shel Ya'akov Glatshteyn," *Gazit* 7–12 (1960): 170–73; Appelfeld, "Yedid Nefesh," *Di goldene keyt* 99 (1979): 15–20.

47. See Chana Kronfeld, "'*Likrat*': Towards A New Poetics and Politics of 'the Statehood Generation'" (unpublished manuscript, 2007).

HEBREW REMEMBERS YIDDISH

Avot Yeshurun's Poetics of Translation

ADRIANA X. JACOBS

A few days after his death, the *New York Times* published a short obituary in honor of the Israeli poet Avot Yeshurun (1904–1992).[1] The laconic headline "Poet in Unusual Idiom" accurately summed up a career that spanned most of twentieth century modern Hebrew and Israeli writing, one that encompassed and articulated the various subjects, themes, questions, and polemics that preoccupied modern Hebrew poetry throughout the twentieth century, particularly with regard to language politics.[2] Like many writers of his generation, Yeshurun was not a native Hebrew speaker, and his poetry, like theirs, maps not only the linguistic shifts and transformations that occurred within modern Hebrew itself but also the long-standing tension between a "revived" Hebrew vernacular and native, diasporic languages, Yiddish in particular. The *Times* characterization of Yeshurun as "an Israeli poet who wove Arabic and Yiddish idiom [*sic*] into a unique and influential form of Hebrew verse" understates the extent to which Yeshurun constantly challenged and subverted Israel's ethos of monolingualism and rejection of the diaspora (*shlilat hagalut*) by developing a radically experimental and multilingual poetics.

Multilingualism was one of the more prominent features of Yeshurun's earliest work.[3] "Balada shel Miryam hamagdalit uvnah halavan" ("The Ballad of Mary Magdalene and Her White Son"), one of his first major Hebrew poems, featured Yiddish, Russian, and Polish words in Hebrew transliteration.[4] A quotation from the Gospel of John, which Yeshurun included in Hebrew translation, added a layer of Greek. In this period, however, multilingual writing in modern Hebrew was hardly exceptional. Many of the canonical writers who emerged in the pre-state period and would later become major national poetic figures—poets like Avraham Shlonsky, Natan Alterman, and Leah Goldberg—

frequently incorporated foreign words, to varying degrees, in their own texts, which were discernibly influenced by their native (predominantly western European and Russian) literary cultures. In fact, the linguistic acrobatics that Yeshurun performed in his poems—e.g., multilingualism, neologism, formal hybridity—also characterized Yiddish modernism of the early twentieth century, so arguably a Yiddish poetics or poetic sensibility shaped his very approach to writing Hebrew.[5] What distinguished Yeshurun was the extent to which he engaged in these practices, resulting in what some early critics regarded as a "deformation" (more pronounced over time) of the Hebrew language.[6] Yeshurun was also one of the few poets who, to quote Michael Gluzman, "declined to participate in the systematic erasure of the past, making the return of the repressed past the leitmotif of his poetic oeuvre."[7] Indeed, Yeshurun sensed early on that Hebrew literature's fixation on creating an autochthonous national literary culture in Hebrew risked cultural amnesia, and he sought to redress this danger through hybrid and multilingual writing practices, even when doing so increasingly put him at odds with Israeli readers and the Israeli literary establishment.[8]

Yeshurun's early poems, including the 1942 collection *Al ḥakhmot drakhim* (*On the Wisdom of Roads*), were largely invested in acknowledging and articulating Palestine's multilingual landscape, and in this context, Yiddish emerged as one of many languages that Yeshurun employed to challenge the hegemony of Hebrew.[9] After the Holocaust and the emergence of the State of Israel, an intensified sense of loss, guilt, and betrayal shaped the poet's use of Yiddish and motivated its increased visibility in his poems. His later work not only thematized the desire to recover, remember, and repair Yiddish but also enacted the tensions and ruptures that had come to characterize the Hebrew-Yiddish relation in his own broken, fragmented, and hybrid poetic language. To this end, Yeshurun not only employed his more overt multilingual strategies but also relied increasingly on translation, and specifically the translation of Yiddish into Hebrew. In the poet's own words: "'From my mother I brought a word into Hebrew,' I wrote once. Everyone brings a word from his mother ... to the world, to literature."[10] Although referring broadly to the influence of the past on present writing, Yeshurun's comments implicate Israeli literature's entangled relationship with its diasporic past, one further complicated by the fact that Hebrew was not the native language of many of its early writers. For writers like Yeshurun, bringing the mother tongue into Hebrew involved, and even required, an act of translation, and in many cases, the "mother's word" was in Yiddish.

Following the work of scholars like Michael Gluzman, Lilach Lachman, and Yochai Oppenheimer, my reading of Yeshurun focuses on his translations of Yiddish words and phrases into Hebrew and interrogates how these instances of translation further inform the relation between memory and writing that preoccupied Yeshurun throughout his literary career.[11] Although breakage, or *shevirut*, became the cornerstone of Yeshurun's poetics, Hebrew translations of Yiddish (as well as other languages) in Yeshurun's work arguably served a prosthetic function. In several contexts, which my reading will explore, Yeshurun described modern Hebrew as a body disabled by hegemonic monolingualism and the rejection of the past, but to the extent that translation marked the absence of Yiddish in his work—and even could be construed as a form of replacement—it also served a constructive and reconstructive function. For Yeshurun, translation offered Yiddish a form of textual afterlife that also undermined the national desire for the normalization of Hebrew monolingualism.[12]

In *Prosthesis*, the literary theorist and translator David Wills observes that "the writing of prosthesis . . . is inevitably caught in a complex play of displacements; prosthesis being about nothing if not placement, displacement, replacement, standing, dislodging, substituting, setting, amputating, supplementing."[13] Likewise, the movements of Yiddish in Yeshurun's Hebrew, particularly in Hebrew translation, articulate a "complex play of displacements" that marks, as well as creates, sites of rupture and repair. In the process, Hebrew is resized in order to engage with and give space to Yiddish (as well as other languages), creating a new Hebrew "body" that better accommodates its immigrant "baggage."[14] In this respect, to quote Wills, "translation is precisely such a prosthetic economy, a matter of making things fit."[15] But precisely how (and how precisely) Hebrew translation "fits" Yiddish in Yeshurun's Hebrew poems, and what meanings and relations emerge when it attempts to do so, motivates my reading of his work, particularly the poems of the 1964 collection *Shloshim amud shel Avot Yeshurun* (*Thirty Pages of Avot Yeshurun*). In this cycle of thirty poems, Yeshurun incorporates Hebrew translations of private Yiddish letters in ways that alternately camouflage and reveal their presence. In these instances, as in many others in Yeshurun's work, the translation of Yiddish becomes "a catalyst for irrepressible transformations" in and of the Hebrew text.[16]

In an intimate 1982 interview with his daughter Helit Yeshurun, Yeshurun discussed the relation between his Hebrew writing and Yiddish, his native language, as a constant and complicated negotiation between absence and presence: "My Hebrew is a person who lives here, in the land, right now. . . . It's not Hebrew, it's Yiddish, Polish, and it's also Hebrew, everything that I accumulated on the way. The Yiddish element is missing for me. There is a hole in the soul because of the fact that I don't write in Yiddish, because I have no Yiddish. This is fulfilled in all sorts of bits of words and expressions, markings, signs, in order to relax that demand of the missing expression."[17]

Although Yeshurun articulates in this passage a binary between "present" and "living" Hebrew and absent Yiddish, a closer reading of his comments suggests that the relationship between the two languages is less dichotomous and antagonistic. For Yeshurun, Hebrew—or rather, "his" Hebrew—is not a monolithic language, rather it is an amalgamation of other languages, notably Yiddish. At the same time, the poet acknowledges the absence of Yiddish as a persistent "hole in the soul" of his Hebrew (and modern Hebrew in general) that the act of writing both addresses and attempts to repair. The "bits of words and expressions, markings, signs" that replace absent Yiddish in Yeshurun's Hebrew poems account for their radical linguistic heterogeneity and experimentalism. Years of attempting to "relax that demand" of Yiddish, as well as other repressed and suppressed languages, resulted in a way of writing in Hebrew that ultimately made these tensions and fissures more visible, insistent, and extreme. This way of writing, on the other hand, was also prosthetic. The "bits" of language that Yeshurun employs attempt to impart a new integrity to Hebrew, but like a prosthetic limb that can be removed, replaced, and changed, they do not guarantee its stability, nor can they ameliorate the phantom pain that the absent element leaves behind. The demand may be relaxed but it is still missing.

Born Yechiel Perlmutter in 1904 and raised in a devoutly Hasidic home in Krasnystaw, Poland, Yeshurun emigrated in 1925 against his family's wishes to Palestine, where he worked as a land laborer and night watchman for many years.[18] The poems that he wrote in this period culminated in the 1942 collection *Al ḥakhmot drakhim*. Most of the Perlmutter family perished in the Holocaust, including Yeshurun's mother, a loss that haunted the poet's subsequent work. Following the death of his family, he did not resume publishing his work until the 1961 collection *Re'em*.[19] During that period, he officially changed his name to Avot Yeshurun, which in Hebrew translates as "the fathers are watching us" or "the Fathers of Israel."[20] Although he would later adopt an ostensibly masculine, paternalistic Hebraic name, Yeshurun was very attached to his mother, who came from a family of rabbinic scholars; it was primarily through her influence that he became interested in literature and languages at an early age. Indeed, a maternal, as well as Yiddish, association underlies the very name "Avot Yeshurun":

> I said to myself: remember your childhood: Maybe I could come up with something from my childhood. I remembered my mother singing beautiful lullabies to my brothers in her beautiful voice. Once, she bent over the cradle and sang to the youngest one in Yiddish and Ukrainian. But the children wouldn't fall asleep, and my mother stopped singing and instead called out excitedly, "*tatelekh, tatelekh.*" And then the child understood that she wasn't going to sing and he went to sleep himself. From this I took the name Avot.[21]

In a cogent reading of this anecdote, Naomi Seidman observes that "the disappearance of the diminutive in the move to Hebrew might signal the process of replacing a Yiddish childhood with a Hebrew adulthood, but it might also be a clever concealment of the continuing existence of the Yiddish boy."[22] Following Seidman's observation, one could also claim that *tatelekh* (little fathers) functions as a metonym for the Yiddish language itself. Though concealed in translation, the Yiddish mother tongue, or *mameloshn*, nevertheless remains present in the new, masculine national culture and language. Indeed, it is the translation of the Yiddish endearment into Hebrew that allows its survival. But in the story, as was the case of Yiddish in Israel, the mother's song is cut off and this severance or breakage also underlies the Hebrew name.

The loss and recovery of the mother tongue are the prevailing themes of Yeshurun's 1964 collection, *Shloshim amud shel Avot Yeshurun*, which comprises poems that attempt to reconstruct an epistolary exchange between the poet and his family, particularly his mother Rikl.[23] Yeshurun's letters from his family, and his failure to respond to many of them, are a major motif in his work, and in this collection Yeshurun's terse quotations, excerpts, and Hebrew translations of their Yiddish missives underscore the emotional, geographical, and temporal ruptures that underlie this correspondence. The poems—as letters—attempt to repair what is ultimately an irrevocably broken connection, but at the same time articulate its broken quality.

As Benjamin Harshav and Helit Yeshurun observe in their notes to the poems, the relation between mourning and writing is invoked in the very title: *shloshim* refers not only to the number of poems in the cycle but also to the thirty days of mourning that follow burial in Jewish tradition. The first poems describe this "burial" of the mother's letters in the poet's desk, mixed with other letters and papers and "put to the side" (Poem 5). Instead of writing letters home, the son writes poems (in Hebrew) on the very desk that contains these letters, in a sense, writing on the grave of Yiddish. These scenes conflate the abandonment of the family and the Yiddish mother tongue in favor of Hebrew writing, as well as the turn to poetry as a form of writing back to the past:

> *Yom yavo ve'ish lo yikra mikhtavim shel imi.*
> *Yesh li mehem ḥavilah.*
> *Lo shel mi*
> *velo milah.*

> *Yom yavo ve'ish lo yikaḥ otam layad.*
> *Yesh mehem tzror vehoter.*
> *Yomru: neyar pisat*
> *velo yoter.*

> *Bayom hahu avi'em el me'arat bar-kokhva*
> *leha'alotam ba'avak. Ha'olam hakodem*
> *lo yaḥkor bah*
> *sfat em.*

The day will come and no one will read my mother's letters.
I have a pack of them.

No one's
no one word.

The day will come and no one will take them by the hand.
There's a bundle of them and more.
They will say: paper scrap
and nothing more.

On that day I will take them to Bar Kokhva's cave
to send them into the dust. The ancient world
will not search there
mother tongue.

The line "The day will come and no one will read my mother's letters," which
opens the first poem in the cycle, encapsulates the fundamental irony of these
poems. For the mother's letters, though unread in their native language—the
Yiddish "mother tongue" (*sfat em*)—are being read, actually continuously re-
read, through the Hebrew poems. As the cycle progresses, the mother's voice is
further uncovered, indeed exhumed, but the fragmentary and grammatically
disjointed quotations that comprise her voice underscore the incompleteness
and impossibility of repair. One could also draw an analogy between the image
of the "paper scraps" that opens these poems and the Jewish practice of *keri'ah*,
the rending of garments by mourners before burial. The tear not only marks the
state of mourning but also serves as an open wound (usually located over the
heart if the deceased is a parent). Repairing the torn garment is also prohibited.
In Yeshurun's cycle, the mother's letters are broken apart but never returned to
a state of wholeness. At the same time, quotation and translation work together
to grant the "mother tongue" a degree of mobility that it does not have in its
original, native state. Through quotation and translation, the language of the
letters is both displaced and replaced in contexts that ultimately expand its
range of meaning.

Bundles of letters from the Bar Kokhva period were discovered in 1960 and
1961 during an archaeological expedition led by the famed Israeli archaeologist Yigael Yadin,[24] an event that Yeshurun uses as a framework for the burial
of the mother's letters. The juxtaposition of the mother's letters and the letters
discovered in the Cave of Letters situates the burial of the mother tongue in the
ongoing discourse of recovery and memory in Israeli culture, but it is one that
privileges Hebrew over Yiddish. Whereas the Bar Kokhva letters further legitimized the territorial continuity of Hebrew, the Yiddish letters that the speaker
plans to bury in the caves represent a deterritorialized history that "no one will
search for."

The rejection of Yiddish in Israel, in this regard, can be understood as a
form of burial. As the Old World of the diaspora is increasingly cut off and
communication between the family members breaks down, the letters grow

shorter, their exchange infrequent. As the cycle progresses, the letters slowly turn into postcards and then into telegrams, but the very shape of the poems also suggests this breakdown. Each stanza begins with a long line that begins to taper off—in most of the poems, each stanza consists of four lines with 5-4-3-2 words respectively—visually demonstrating the increasing compression and breakdown of language into "paper scraps." The final lines of the first poem's three stanzas—"no one word" (*velo milah*), "and nothing more" (*velo yoter*), and "mother tongue" (*sfat em*)—emphasize this move toward absence and silence in relation to Yiddish, the mother tongue that can only be recalled in a fragmented Hebrew.[25]

Later, though the speaker professes a desire to forget the mother's letters, he gathers up the pieces of paper and files them "one by one ... even the stamps." This attempt to put the letters in order sparks an ambivalent temptation to read them—"read or don't read"—but ultimately the speaker determines that "there is interest even / in the letters of the dead" (Poem 5), a line that also refers back to the historical interest in the Bar Kokhva letters. The Hebrew *inyan* can also refer to the content of the letters, suggesting that "letters of the dead" have something to say. As the speaker bides his time, the voices of the dead begin to insist on a response. In Poem 7, this demand takes the form of a letter from home urging the son to write back:

> *Kibalti mikhtavkhem uvo aneh aneh.*
> *Ad nose hapost bigvurato*
> *over hatal eynayim.*
> *Aneh aneh.*
>
> *Aniti bemikhtav uvo yafim lekane*
> *atzei shitim va'azei shamuti.*
> *Ani hayiti me'aneh.*
> *Aneh aneh.*
>
> *Eyn li babayt milah tovah.*
> *Bemikhtavkha eyn zekher li.*
> *Keha'et avar hashemesh.*
> *Aneh aneh.*
>
> I received your (*pl*) letter and in it Answer Answer
> Until the postman in his glory
> dew passes over eyes.
> Answer Answer.
>
> I replied with a letter and in it beautiful things to envy
> acacia and shamouti orange trees.[26]

I would torture.
Answer Answer.

I have no good word from home.
In your letter there's no mention (*memory*) of me.
Just now the sun passed over.
Answer Answer.[27]

Yeshurun's biographer Eda Zoritte notes that many letters from Rikl Perlmutter included the exhortation "Write! Write!"[28] In this poem, the command to write becomes *aneh*, Hebrew for "reply," a verb that also shares a root with the verbs "to torture" and "to sing." In this case, the decision to translate a word that was most likely written in Yiddish into Hebrew creates a more expansive series of associations. In this poem, the son's failure to write back to the mother is perceived by the parent (or rather, imagined by the surviving child) as an affliction, but at the same time, the association with "singing" that the root *ayn-nun-he* carries further elaborates the idea of poetry as a form of response. The poem replies belatedly to these letters.

These associations continue to develop in the second stanza of Poem 18, which opens with the question *She'ei mizeh matayhu pa'am erekha?* (For where at what time will I see you again?). As Harshav and Helit Yeshurun point out, this is one of several lines from family letters that reappears in other poems.[29] The translation of this question into Hebrew also serves as a mode of transport that, unlike the direct quotations from the Yiddish that Yeshurun also practiced, allows the poet to vary the original language of the quotation to "make it fit," as Wills observes, in a variety of ways in the Hebrew text. The movement of this line from one poem to another creates a relation between these poems, generating a family tree of texts for which the original Yiddish material serves as an unstable, shifting root. The poem "Zikhronot hem bayt" ("Memories Are a House"), which appeared in the 1990 collection *Adon menuḥah* (*Master of Rest*), emerges, particularly in its final three stanzas, as a companion text to the poems of *Shloshim amud* through this kind of movement:

> *Eyneni makhḥish, she'adam hamagi'a legil,*
> *eyno yakhol lekavot*
> *she'eleh shemehem yatza yisardu*
> *od ḥayim imo, kefi shekatvah li*
>
> *Imi pa'am be'aḥad mimikhtavey*
> *hadimdumim shelah. Midimdumey mikhtaveyah*
> *begoraliyot enosh: vekhi matayhu*
> *yekholim hen. Halo eyn sikui lirot otkha.*

Ufa'am bemikhtav nidaḥ venishkaḥ:
"Layla tov lekha, Yeḥiel alter leben. Naflah alai tardemah.
Aḥazu bi ḥevlei shenah. Kh'bin
shleyferik gevorn." Ne'emar bemikhtav shelo korim. Shelo karu.

I do not deny that a man who reaches a certain age
can no longer hope
that those from whom he came will remain
still alive with him, as my mother once

Wrote to me in one of the letters
of her twilight. From the fadings of her letters
into the fatedness of man: but when can they.
After all there's no chance of seeing you.

And once, in a discarded and forgotten letter:
"Good night, Yehiel *alter lebn.* Slumber has descended upon me.
I am caught in the throes of sleep. *Khbin*
shleyferik gevorn." Said in a letter that nobody reads, that nobody read.[30]

The question in Poem 18 of *Shloshim amud* reappears in this poem in the last two lines of the second stanza of the above excerpt. In "Memories Are a House," the question "For where at what time will I see you again?" is broken apart and reconstructed as a statement of fact, "but when can they. / After all there's no chance of seeing you." It becomes its own reply. This is one example of how translation not only mediates between the past and present in Yeshurun's work but also creates new frames of reference in the process. A close reader of Yeshurun's work may recognize the origin of this line, but its placement, or rather "displacement," in this poem conflates the voices of son and mother.[31]

Whereas the poems of *Shloshim amud* do not quote Yiddish directly, the poem "Zikhronot hem bayt" juxtaposes translations of Yiddish and Yiddish quotation (directly or in Hebrew translation).[32] Because Hebrew and Yiddish share an alphabet, the presence of Yiddish in this poem is perhaps less intrusive when compared to the appearance of other alphabets—Cyrillic, for example—in Yeshurun's work.[33] Nevertheless, the appearance of Yiddish in this line is not seamless. Although the Hebrew and Yiddish clauses balance each other metrically, creating a fluid line, a Hebrew reader would immediately grasp the linguistic shift. Closer scrutiny of the language Yeshurun employs reveals the significant word play and even translation occurring in the Yiddish. The phrase "Yehiel alter lebn" could be read as "Yehiel, dear eldest (son/brother)" or "Yehiel, long life (to you)," the latter also a translation of the name Yehiel (may G-d live).

Yeshurun's placement of the Yiddish *khbin shleyferik gevorn* (I've become sleepy) also involves elaborate maneuvers of quotation and translation. Two Hebrew translations of the line *khbin shleyferik gevorn* preface the Yiddish: *naflah alai tardemah* (deep sleep fell over me) and *ahazu bi ḥevlei shenah* (the cords of sleep grasped me), both idiomatic phrases for "going to sleep." In the translations into Hebrew, the relation between sleep and death is further intensified. In Hebrew, *tardemah*, meaning "deep sleep," also refers to the period of dormancy between fall and spring. In the second translation, the expression *ḥevlei shenah*—literally the "cords of sleep"—imagines sleep/death as an aggressor, locking the mother in its grip.[34]

Ḥevlei shenah also recalls the expressions *ḥevlei ledah* (labor pains) and *ḥevlei lashon* (inarticulateness; literally, language pains), the latter also the title of a seminal essay by the Hebrew poet Hayyim Nachman Bialik. In "Language Pangs" (1905), Bialik argues in favor of a vital and dynamic approach to writing and speaking in Hebrew that resists the constraints of "normative rules," which strip language of its vitality, revealing "the dry bones of its philological skeleton."[35] The translation of *shleyferik* into *ḥevlei shenah* reveals a possible intertextual relation between this poem and Bialik's essay that further elaborates a relation between memory, language, and writing.

The very title of the poem also underscores these relations. In Hebrew, *bayt* is both "house" and "home," a crucial distinction in the context of Yeshurun's work, which resisted Zionism's demand to replace the home of the past with the Israeli national home. The speaker's memories encompass a personal and private space that "houses" him and his dead, but *bayt* also means stanza, highlighting the correlation between memory and writing that pervades Yeshurun's work. As in *Shloshim amud,* the speaker of "Zikhronot hem bayt" constructs the poem as a space of constant mourning and recollection, where the letter "that nobody read" is continuously recalled and even partially revived. Bringing, that is translating, the mother's Yiddish into the Hebrew poem offers the mother tongue "a better semblance of afterlife."[36] At the same time, as Yeshurun explained in the interview cited earlier, Hebrew is continuously made present and alive in his work by the other languages, particularly Yiddish, that shape its expression, by the memories to which these other languages are tethered.

Although the process of creating a modern Hebrew vernacular in the late nineteenth century required weeding out its Yiddish and diasporic influences, the vast corpus of Yiddish vernacular texts provided a vital foundation for Hebrew.[37] Indeed, the translation of Yiddish texts into Hebrew in the late nineteenth century proved instrumental in creating a modern Hebrew vernacular. For example, loan translations and adaptations of Yiddish words and phrases frequently crept into Hebrew writing of the early twentieth century.[38] Even when Hebrew successfully asserted its hegemony over Yiddish, Yiddish remained for many new immigrants a language inextricably tied to personal histories and memories.[39] In his autobiography *Haḥalom veshivro* (*The Shattered Dream*), the Hebraicist Eliezer Ben-Yehuda (1858-1922), a major figure in the revival of vernacular Hebrew, describes the persistence of Yiddish and other diasporic languages as follows:

> I must confess once more: sometimes, when my mind is submerged in thoughts, especially of days past, of childhood and youth, and it releases itself momentarily, without my sensing it, from the Hebrew yoke that I have mounted on it by force for so many years—I suddenly realize that for a moment I was thinking not in Hebrew; rather, from under my thinking in Hebrew words, a few foreign words, in Yiddish (*ashkenazit*) and also in Russian and French floated to the surface! And then I realize that Hebrew isn't a mother tongue even for me, for my first words were not in Hebrew. I didn't suckle the sounds of this language with my mother's breast milk, and my ears did not hear them when my mother rested me in my cradle, and so I feel that despite my love for the Hebrew language, I certainly can't claim that same predisposition for loving the language that someone who has heard it spoken from birth can, someone who spoke his first words in [that language].[40]

That Ben-Yehuda is often credited with the revival of modern Hebrew as a spoken language makes this admission even more remarkable. In this passage, it is Hebrew, and not a diasporic language, that is characterized as a burden ("the Hebrew yoke"), forcibly submerging other languages. Ben-Yehuda's choice of words describes the speaker of Hebrew as a slave or servant to the language, and it is only during a respite from the effort of "thinking in Hebrew words" that these other languages surface like divers from a wreck. For Ben-Yehuda, as for Yeshurun, the native tongue not only carries strong maternal associations—in fact, the authors employ similar images of infancy in making this connection—but also represents a state of able-bodiedness that the Hebrew yoke compromises. The image of free-floating "foreign words" illustrates a state of fluency in these languages that contrasts sharply with the exertion of speaking in Hebrew.

Challenging Hebrew's hegemony and the way it actively suppressed personal memories, thereby creating fragmented identities, became a major preoccupation for Yeshurun. The rupture with the past results in and is articulated by linguistic breakages that are manifested in Yeshurun's work as an increasing disregard for conventional syntax, grammar, orthography, and monolingualism, thereby creating a poetic language that becomes even *more* unstable and idiosyncratic with time. The visibility and prominence that Yeshurun gave to Yiddish and other languages in his work resisted the decidedly pro-Hebrew, monolingual ethos that determined literary canonicity in the pre-state period. However, as Oppenheimer notes, not only would many of the Yiddish words and expressions that Yeshurun employed have been intelligible to many of his readers, but also many of these words and expressions had already found their way, either verbatim or via translation, into modern Hebrew.[41]

Nevertheless, the Yishuv's ambivalence toward Yiddish, a language that remained in daily use despite its erasure in official histories of the period, created and marked, to borrow terms from Homi Bhabha, a "liminal space" or "in-between" zone. In her study of Yiddish culture in the Yishuv, Yael Chaver refers to these sites as "the location of a vigorous, though unacknowledged Yiddish culture that expressed itself in a rich array of unique literary work."[42] Although Chaver focuses her study on Yiddish writers in Palestine, she acknowledges Hebrew writers, such as Esther Raab and Yeshurun, who developed poetic languages arguably destabilized by the "continued presence" of earlier native languages, Yiddish among them.[43] In other words, sites of tension between Yiddish and Hebrew, and the subsequent marginalization and negation of the Yiddish language in the Yishuv, created a rupture that was ultimately productive, a wound from which new writing emerged.

In 1964, Aharon Megged, the editor of the journal *Massa*, invited a number of writers to submit recollections of their first creative work for publication in a special issue. Yeshurun's contribution, a poetic prose piece titled "Ad henah vesham nishar" ("Hither and There It Remained"), reveals that Yeshurun's first poem was, in fact, a Yiddish poem lost during the Second World War:[44]

> *Yom eḥad ḥibarti shir arokh beyidish: "Di nevue in gezang." Nevi'im mitnabim beshirah vezimrah. Naflah eyni al kufsat hakarton hamerushelet veḥasrat hamikhseh shel savi, bah netunim be'irbuviyah ḥozim shel ribit, shel mekhirah ushe'ar neyarot—vehashir nivla imahem. Hashir nishar sham.*

> One day I strung together a long poem in Yiddish: "Di nevue in gezang." Prophets prophecy in poetry and song. My eye fell on a ragged, lidless cardboard box belonging to my grandfather, inside of it a muddle of interest and sales receipts, and remainder of papers—and the poem was swallowed up with them. The poem remained there.[45]

In the Hebrew original, Yeshurun first provides the name of the poem in Yiddish and follows it with a nonliteral Hebrew translation. The Yiddish line *di nevue in gezang* translates literally as "prophecy in singing," whereas Yeshurun's Hebrew translation, *nevi'im mitnabim beshirah vezimrah*, translates as "prophets prophecy in poetry and song." The poem, like the letters of *Shloshim amud*, is packed away with other scraps of paper, which are later left behind.[46] Although the poem highlights the displacement of the Yiddish poem, it also gestures to the relation between Hebrew and Yiddish in the poet's own upbringing. The poem "Tovland" ("Goodland," a pun on *Altneuland*), written in 1975, makes reference to *Mikra'ei Ziyon* (*Readings of Zion*), a series of pamphlets of Hebrew poetry that were part of Yeshurun's Hebrew language instruction as a youth.[47]

The poems in these pamphlets spanned a long tradition of Hebrew poetry, beginning with the poetry of Al-Andalus. According to Zoritte, the Yiddish translations that accompanied these poems revealed "the beauty of Yiddish" to the poet and inspired his own writing in the language.[48] "Before I returned to Hebrew, I returned to Yiddish," the poet writes in "Tovland." In this context, the poem "Di nevue in gezang" represents the poet's participation in and commemoration of Yiddish as a language of high culture.[49] Zoritte speculates that the grandfather's "cardboard box" may represent the disregard with which this writing is treated. "The [poet's] spiritual roots, connected to his mother's side of the family, were hidden in a kind of disorderly and impious material greenhouse that characterized his paternal grandfather's home," she observes.[50] The cardboard box, in this regard, corresponds to the cave, desk, and briefcases in *Shloshim amud* that bury the "scraps" of the mother tongue. It is only later, when the box is discovered and reopened, like the letters filed away in *Shloshim amud*, that a scrap of the poem resurfaces.

In the stanza that immediately follows this passage, Yeshurun recounts an incident concerning a Jewish National Fund stamp that he and his younger brother coveted, an event that he references in other poems.[51] In his version, Yeshurun steals the stamp in the middle of the night and by doing so instigates a tug-of-war, each brother conspiring to steal the stamp from the other.[52] For the poet, a relation emerges between this stamp and the Yiddish poem:

> *Yom ehad ahi hatza'ir hehezik bul keren kayemet leyisra'el. Bahashai balaylah lekahtiv ani. Baboker heheziro elayv. Bahashai balaylah lekahtiv ani. Velakahnu vehehezarnu velakahnu vehehezarnu pe'amim harbeh, velo amarnu davar.*
>
> *Yom ehad aliti le'eretz-yisra'el.*
> *Habul nishar sham.*
>
> *Katavti habayta shivhei ha'aretz.*
> *Hashir nishar sham.*

One day my younger brother took hold of a Jewish National Fund stamp. At night I secretly took it. In the morning it returned to him. Secretly at night I took it. And we took and returned and took and returned many times, and didn't say a word.

One day I immigrated to the Land of Israel.
The stamp remained there.

I wrote homeward in praise of the land.
The poem remained there.[53]

The episode with the stamp dramatizes the tension between native and adopted homelands, a tension that is played out over the lost Yiddish poem and the *keren kayemet leyisra'el,* Jewish National Fund, stamp that can only belong to one brother. But the tug-of-war between Yechiel and his brother represents not only the struggle between *sham*—the land over there, the diaspora—and Eretz Yisra'el, but also the vexed relation between Yiddish and Hebrew in the Yishuv. In fact, the conflation of the Yiddish poem and the Jewish National Fund stamp—which Yeshurun underscores in their mutual "remain[ing] there"—invites this comparison. Rather than share the riches of the stamp, the promises of renewal that it offers, the brothers instigate numerous betrayals on its behalf. We do not know who ultimately comes into full and final possession of the stamp, but we learn that the poet's immigration to Palestine renders the stamp useless in some way. For what need does he have of the bucolic images of the land featured on many of these stamps now that he is there, *ba'aretz,* in the land? But one could also read the stamp as a ticket or passage for the poet's literal and poetic *aliyah,* the price of translation. The Yiddish poem, like the stamp, is a loss that has to be incurred, the price that the poet must pay, in order to write Hebrew poems. Yet, although it appears to be irrevocably exchanged, the expression *nishar sham* leaves open the possibility of retrieval.

The movements of Yiddish in Yeshurun's Hebrew mimic the stealthy tug-of-war between the two brothers. The challenge of finding sites of concealment in a home they both know intimately creates dramatic ruptures, provoking a linguistic back-and-forth between Hebrew and Yiddish that often results in the increasing hybridity and heterogeneity of Yeshurun's Hebrew. The fissures and repairs that occur at their sites of contact continuously generate poetic language itself. Lachman has observed that "however urgent and all-encompassing breakage may have been for Yeshurun, retrospectively it can be reinterpreted as a struggle for construction."[54] This is the paradox of breakage that the English words "hole" and "whole" cleverly articulate.

To the extent that breakage and reconstruction come to define the Hebrew and Yiddish relation in Yeshurun's work, they are also fundamental to the way Yeshurun thought about poetic language in general. In a 1974 essay titled "Shnei nofim" ("Two Landscapes"), Yeshurun explicitly describes the relation between writing and breakage as a productive one. "For a writer," he writes, "language is like a child's toy. Language is in the hand of the creator—he doesn't feel it until he breaks it; when he throws it down—he hears the voice of language, the language that is his."[55]

In the prevailing discourse of the early twentieth-century language war (*milḥemet haleshonot*), Yiddish was often cast as a disease, a weakness, a burden holding back the possibility of a new, revolutionary national life.[56] However, as far as Yeshurun was concerned, the absence of Yiddish also disabled Hebrew. Through the strategies of breakage—translation among them—by which Yeshurun paradoxically reconstructs the Hebrew poem, a visible or concealed Yiddish surfaces and attempts to reintegrate the Hebrew poetic text. In the process, translation also creates and marks sites of linguistic discomfort or phantom pain, as in the case of the grammatically convoluted line "for where at what time will I see you again?" and its permutations. But ultimately, translation serves for Yeshurun as a crucial mode of retrieval, albeit one that is fragmentary. In and through translation, the stamp and the lost Yiddish poem, as well as the mother's letters "that no one will read," reemerge in the space of the Hebrew poem—and in the highly personal Hebrew of scraps and remnants that the poet reconstructs, the Hebrew that is his, Yiddish is continuously remembered.

Notes

I would like to thank Alan Astro for organizing the Modern Language Association session Foregrounding Yiddish, in which an earlier version of this essay was presented (December 2006). Unless otherwise noted, all translations from Yiddish and Hebrew are my own.

1. Obituary of Avot Yeshurun, *New York Times*, February 24, 1992, national edition.
2. Yeshurun began to publish his Hebrew poems in various journals in the early 1930s. His published collections include the following: *Al ḥakhmot drakhim* (*On the Wisdom of Roads*, 1942), *Re'em* (1961), *Shloshim amud shel Avot Yeshurun* (*Thirty Pages of Avot Yeshurun*, 1964), *Zeh shem hasefer* (*This Is the Name of the Book*, 1970), *Hashever hasuri afrikani* (*The Syrian-African Rift*, 1974), *Kapela kolot* (*A Cappella Voices*, 1977), *Sha'ar kenisah, sha'ar yetziyah* (*Entrance Gate, Exit Gate*, 1981), *Homograf* (*Homograph*, 1985), *Adon menuḥah* (*Master of Rest*, 1990), and the posthumous collection *Eyn li akhshav* (*I Have No Now*, 1992).
3. In many poems, for example, Yeshurun would graft foreign words into the Hebrew text with varying degrees of visibility, alternating between Hebrew transliteration and transcription in the foreign alphabet. Another common multilingual strategy in Yeshurun's poetry was the creation of portmanteaus from the fusion of other languages (e.g., Yiddish, Polish, and Arabic) with Hebrew. Cf. Theodor W. Adorno, "On the Use of Foreign Words," in *Notes to Literature,* ed. Rolf Tiedmann, trans. Shierry Weber Nicholsen (New York: Columbia University Press, 1992), 2:286-91.
4. Published in 1937 in the periodical *Davar.* Avot Yeshurun, *Kol shirav* [Collected Poems] (Tel Aviv: Hakibbutz Hameuhad, 1995), 1:7-13.
5. Chana Kronfeld, *On the Margins of Modernism: Decentering Literary Dynamics* (Berkeley: University of California Press, 1993), 13. Benjamin Harshav cites the Yiddish and Hebrew poet Uri Zvi Greenberg as one of two major "evolutionary lines" in the development of Hebrew modernism in the 1920s: "When Grinberg suddenly left Europe for Erez Yisra'el in 1924 and resumed writing in Hebrew, he brought Whitmanesque rhythms, Futurist metaphors, Expressionist rhetoric, and the syntax of a spoken language saturated with political, journalistic, and 'International' diction from Yiddish to Hebrew poetry, which did not permit these elements before." Harshav, *The Meaning of Yiddish* (Stanford: Stanford University Press, 1990), 145. Yael Chaver briefly addresses Greenberg's "linguistic ambivalence" in later years in her study of Yiddish culture in Palestine. Chaver, *What Must Be Forgotten: The Survival of Yiddish in Zionist Palestine* (Syracuse, NY: Syracuse University Press, 2004), 111-13. Michael Gluzman also acknowledges the tense friendship between the poets in his reading of Yeshurun's "Pesaḥ al kukhim."

Gluzman, *The Politics of Canonicity: Lines of Resistance in Modernist Hebrew Poetry* (Stanford: Stanford University Press, 2003), 164.

6. The 1942 collection *Al hakhmot drakhim* was the most conventionally prosodic of Yeshurun's works. In a foreword to his translations of Yeshurun, the poet Harold Schimmel characterized Yeshurun's break with the conventions of early twentieth-century modern Hebrew prosody as a multilingual act: "The quatrain spills, opens, takes in prose, dialogue, grows asymmetrical—top-heavy, or sagging. It is undermined, extended. . . . As do the city's signs and billboards, newspapers and libraries and theaters, speak in all languages (the waiter speaks seven, the laundress speaks five), so does Yeshurun's quatrain." Schimmel, "Translator's Foreword," in *The Syrian-African and Other Poems* (Philadelphia: Jewish Publication Society, 1980), xi-xxi, xv. In a review of *Adon menuhah* (*Master of Rest*, 1990), the writer Batya Gur remarked with regard to Yeshurun's reception, "It had taken thirty years . . . to crack the wall that isolated [Yeshurun] from his generation." The critic Dan Miron responded that the marginal reception of Yeshurun was a "banal folktale." According to Miron, Yeshurun's contemporaries admired his "linguistic deformation" (*deformatzyah leshonit*), as evidenced by Yeshurun's publication history. Other critics weighed in with their own assessments of Yeshurun's reception. The critic and translator Shimon Sandbank, in particular, disagreed with Miron. For a full discussion of this episode, see Eda Zoritte, *Shirat hapere he'atzil: biografyah shel hameshorer Avot Yeshurun* [The Song of the Noble Savage: A Biography of the Poet Avot Yeshurun] (Tel Aviv: Hakibbutz Hameuhad, 1996), 254-55.

7. Gluzman, *Politics of Canonicity*, 143.

8. Yeshurun spoke very candidly about his relationship with his literary contemporaries, particularly Natan Alterman, in a 1982 interview with his daughter, the editor and translator Helit Yeshurun. Helit Yeshurun, "Ani holekh el hakol: re'ayon im Avot Yeshurun" [I Walk Toward Everything: Interview with Avot Yeshurun]. *Hadarim* 3 (1982): 92-109, 93-94.

9. According to Benjamin Harshav, the Yiddish *hokhmes*—"clever insights, anecdotes (of the roads)"—underlie the title of Yeshurun's first book *Al hakhmot drakhim*. Some later editions of this work, as well as scholarly and bibliographic sources, substitute the more grammatical and Hebraic *hokhmat* for *hakhmot* (Benjamin Harshav, e-mail message to author, October 12, 2009).

10. Yeshurun, "Ani holekh el hakol," 94.

11. Michael Gluzman, "The Return of the Politically Repressed: Avot Yeshurun's 'Passover on Caves,'" in *The Politics of Canonicity: Lines of Resistance in Modernist Hebrew Poetry* (Stanford: Stanford University Press, 2003), 141-72; Lilach Lachman, "'I Manured the Land with My Mother's Letters': Avot Yeshurun and the Question of the Avant-Garde," *Poetics Today* 21, no. 1 (2000): 61-93; Yochai Oppenheimer, *Tnu li ledaber kemo she'ani: Shirat Avot Yeshurun* [Let Me Speak As I Am: The Poetry of Avot Yeshurun] (Tel Aviv: Hakibbutz Hameuhad, 1997).

12. Cf. Walter Benjamin, "The Task of the Translator," in *Walter Benjamin: Selected Writings*, vol. 1, 1913-1926, ed. Marcus Bullock and Michael W. Jennings, trans. Harry Zohn (Cambridge: The Belknap Press of Harvard University Press, 2004), 253-63.

13. David Wills, *Prosthesis* (Stanford: Stanford University Press, 1995), 9.

14. See the poem "Pekla'ot" [Packages, from the Yiddish *peklakh*, "bundle"], which appeared in the 1974 collection *Hashever hasuri afrikani* [The Syrian-African Rift]. Avot Yeshurun, *Kol shirav* [Collected Poems] (Tel Aviv: Hakibbutz Hameuhad, 1997), 2:33-41.

15. Wills, *Prosthesis*, 309.

16. Johannes Göransson and Joyelle McSweeney, "Manifesto of the Disabled Text," http://exoskeleton-johannes.blogspot.com/2008/06/manifesto-of-disabled-text.html. A print version of this essay was also published in *New Ohio Review* 3 (2008): 94-98.

17. Helit Yeshurun, "Ani holekh el hakol," 98-99.

18. For a full biography of the poet, see Zoritte, *Hapere he'atzil*.

19. The title *Re'em* is one of many portmanteaus in Yeshurun's poetic vocabulary. The title's possible associations and meanings include "wild ox," "look at them," and "thunder." Yeshurun, *Kol shirav*, 1:286.

20. Isaiah 44:1-2.

21. Translation by Naomi Seidman. Seidman, *A Marriage Made in Heaven: The Sexual Politics of Hebrew and Yiddish* (Berkeley: University of California Press, 1997), 119. Seidman takes this account from Hayyim Nagid's 1974 interview with Yeshurun, published in *Yediyot Ahronot*. It was a story that Yeshurun often related, "one of the more vital images in his memory," according to his biographer Eda Zoritte. Zoritte, *Hapere he'atzil*, 16.

22. Seidman, *A Marriage Made in Heaven*, 119.

23. According to Harshav and Helit Yeshurun, "The poems were written between March 1, 1962 (the month of Adar) and May 15, 1963. The number thirty, as in thirty days of mourning, was determined from the onset. Six poems open the cycle, twenty epistolary poems that are shaped by letters that [Yeshurun] received from his family, and four closing poems." Yeshurun, *Kol shirav*, 1:299.

24. In 1960-1961, the renowned Israeli archaeologist Yigael Yadin led an expedition around Wadi Murabba'at in the Judean desert that uncovered several letters written by Simon Bar Kokhva, most of which were related to orders addressed to his supporters. The letters were written in Hebrew, Aramaic, and Greek. Yigael Yadin, *Bar-Kokhba: The Rediscovery of the Legendary Hero of the Last Jewish Revolt against Imperial Rome* (New York: Random House, 1971); Yael Zerubavel, *Recovered Roots: Collective Memory and the Making of Israeli National Tradition* (Chicago: The University of Chicago Press, 1995).

25. According to Harshav and Helit Yeshurun, Yeshurun devised this pattern before writing the poems. Yeshurun, *Kol shirav*, 1:299.

26. The shamouti orange, more commonly known as the "Jaffa orange," is a sweet, almost seedless variety of orange that was cultivated in Jaffa, Palestine in the mid-nineteenth century and became a popular export. Cf. Carol Bardenstein, "Threads of Memory in Discourses of Rootedness: Of Trees, Oranges and Prickly-Pear Cactus in Palestine/Israel," *Edebiyât: A Journal of Middle Eastern Literatures* 8 (1998): 1-36.

27. Yeshurun, *Kol shirav*, 1:187. The third line of the second stanza—*Ani hayiti me'aneh*—translates literally as "I would torture" ("I would sing" is another possibility) but also may be a nonstandard conjugation for the verb "answer."

28. Zoritte, *Shirat hapere he'atzil*, 90.

29. See Avot Yeshurun, "Habalada shel Berl Shloser," in *Kol Shirav*, 2:152-54; Yeshurun, "Ma shenoge'a," *Kol Shirav*, 2:161-62; Yeshurun, "Zikhronot hem bayt," in *Kol Shirav* (Tel Aviv: Hakibbutz Hameuhad, 2001), 4:130-31.

30. Avot Yeshurun, *Kol shirav*, 4:130-31; Avot Yeshurun, "Memories Are a House," trans. Leon Wieseltier, *Poetry* 192, no. 1 (2008): 49. In Hebrew, the word *dimdum* can mean both "fading" and "twilight" (*dimdumim*).

31. See Lilach Lachman's reading of Yeshurun's "Poem on the Guilt" and her provocative analysis of the way Yeshurun overlaps personal and collective histories. "The frames unfold through displacements of memory rather than through chronological linking; space is organized through leaps from one frame to another, presenting time as an aberrant movement." Lachman, "I Manured the Land," 70.

32. In the English translation by Leon Wieseltier, which I have excerpted above, the Yiddish text is italicized. I have modified Wieseltier's transliteration of "shleyferik," which he renders as "shlayferig."

33. See the poem "Spasiba zyemlya" ("Thank You, Land"), which appeared in the 1985 collection *Homograf*. Yeshurun, *Kol shirav* (Tel Aviv: Hakibbutz Hameuhad, 2001) 3:167.

34. The expression *ḥevlei shenah* appears in the opening of the "Bedtime Shema" ("Kri'at shema al hamitah").

35. Hayyim Nahman Bialik, "Ḥevlei lashon" [Language Pangs], in *Kol kitvei H. N. Bialik* (Tel Aviv: Dvir, 1953), 185-90. For a more extensive analysis of this essay see Kronfeld, *On the Margins of Modernism*, 83-92.

36. Joseph Brodsky, "In a Room and a Half," in *Less Than One: Selected Essays* (New York: Farrar Straus Giroux, 1986), 447-501, 461.

37. When the writer Mendele Mokher Seforim wanted to use the plural "potatoes," he created *bulbusin*, a combination of the Latin *bulbus* and the Yiddish *bulbes* to which he gave an Aramaic plural ending. Later, this word was replaced with *tapuḥei adamah*, literally "apple of the earth," which is currently in use in Israel. However, as Harshav notes, *tapuḥei adamah* is in turn a calque of the French *pomme de terre*. But the advantage of *tapuḥei adamah* over *bulbusin* is that it does not sound like Yiddish. For a full account of this transmission, see Benjamin Harshav, *Language in Time of Revolution* (Berkeley: University of California Press, 1993), 83.

38. Chaver provides several examples of Yiddish loan translations in the works of Shmuel Yosef Agnon and Yosef Hayyim Brenner. Chaver, *What Must Be Forgotten*, 29-31.

39. Cf. Rachel Katznelson, "Language Insomnia" [Nedudei lashon], trans. Barbara Harshav, *Language in Time of Revolution*, 183-94, 187.

40. Eliezer Ben-Yehuda, *Haḥalom veshivro* [The Shattered Dream] (Jerusalem: Mossad Bialik, 1978), http://benyehuda.org/by/index.html. In translating this quotation, I also would like to acknowledge T. Muroaka's translation of Ben-Yehuda's biography, *A Dream Come True*, ed. George Mandel (Boulder, CO: Westview Press, 1993).

41. Oppenheimer, *Tnu li ledaber kemo she'ani*, 139-40.

42. Chaver, *What Must Be Forgotten*, 44. Though a number of scholars have turned their attention to the Yishuv's "language wars" and rejection of Yiddish, Chaver's research is deeply invested in exploring the ways Yiddish literary culture not only survived but even thrived in a national culture that, at least on the surface, repudiated multilingualism in general and Hebrew-Yiddish bilingualism in particular.

43. Chaver, *What Must Be Forgotten*, 28-29. For a fuller discussion of Raab's multilingualism and its relation to her poetry, see my article "Paris or Jerusalem? The Multilingualism of Esther Raab," *Prooftexts* 26 (2006): 6-28 (published as Adriana X. Tatum). The influence of Yiddish and Yiddish modernism on Yeshurun's work is also discussed at length in Gluzman, "The Return of the Politically Repressed" and Oppenheimer, *Tnu li ledaber kemo she'ani: Shirat Avot Yeshurun*.

44. Yeshurun, *Kol shirav*, 1:213-16.

45. Ibid., 215.

46. Zoritte suggests that they may have been recovered at some point. Zoritte, *Hapere he'atzil*, 28.

47. Yeshurun, *Kol shirav*, 2:169; Zoritte, *Hapere he'atzil*, 28.

48. Zoritte, *Hapere he'atzil*, 28. For example, Poem 28 in *Shloshim amud shel Avot Yeshurun*, which arguably reflects on this past writing in Yiddish, contains an allusion to the poem "Dror yikra," a *piyyut* authored by the ninth-century Andalusian poet Dunash Ben Labrat. Yeshurun, *Kol shirav*, 1:208.

49. The poem "Shnei netzaḥim" ("Two Eternities") in *Sha'ar kenisah sha'ar yetziah* also makes reference to this poem: "Studying *lataynish*, writing, [for] the first / time in my life, a song 'Di nevue in gezang' / in Yiddish." Yeshurun, *Kol shirav*, 3:72-73.

50. Zoritte, *Hapere he'atzil*, 28.

51. The brother in the poem may be Israel Mordechai Perlmutter, who was a year younger than Yechiel and also emigrated to Palestine. The two brothers were the only surviving members of their family. According to Yeshurun's niece Chaya Meroz, their political differences provoked an estrangement that lasted for many years. (See "Avot Yeshurun," *Shireshet*, accessed June 22, 2012, http://www.snunit.k12.il/shireshet/tel_avot .htm.) The brothers later reconciled, an episode that Yeshurun recounted in his

poem "Al eleh ani atuf," which appeared in the posthumous *Eyn li akhshav*: "Many years my brother is here in this country / he didn't come to me. Until I was lying in an isolation ward. / He came. I had the chance to say to him: / Didn't we have once *imali, abali*" (Yeshurun, *Kol shirav*, 4:210). In the version that Yeshurun related to Zoritte, instead of the Hebrew *imali* (mommy) and *abali* (daddy)—words that employ the Yiddish-inspired, though old-fashioned, modern Hebrew diminutive suffix *-li*— Yeshurun uses the Yiddish *mameshi* and *tateshi* (Zoritte, *Hapere he'atzil*, 257).

52. This event is also the subject of the poem "Eynbul" ("Stampless"), which appeared in the same collection. Yeshurun, *Kol shirav*, 1:219.

53. Yeshurun, *Kol shirav*, 1:215.

54. Lachman, "I Manured the Land," 83–84.

55. This essay appears in the collection *Hashever hasuri afrikani* (*The Syrian-African Rift*) in a section titled "Prozah devarim kolshehem." Yeshurun, *Kol shirav*, 2:126–30.

56. Rachel Katznelson also addresses the "revolutionary" aspect of Hebrew in her essay "Language Insomnia": "The essential thing was that, even though Yiddish is a living language, the language of the people and of democracy, there is a trend of thought, which for us was revolutionary, that expresses itself in Hebrew; whereas Yiddish literature is ruled by narrow-mindedness, mostly inert and reactionary in our eyes and, at best—only a weak echo of what was revealed in Hebrew" (Katznelson, "Language Insomnia," 185).

HEAR AND NOW

Prelude

ARI Y. KELMAN

Too often, we focus on oral culture to the neglect of aural culture. What about the sound of Yiddish? Often what makes a language "dead" or "alive" (or perhaps, as we say in Yiddish, *goyses*) is whether or not people *speak* it. But what about listeners? What about people who can and do listen in multiple languages even if they do not speak them? Anyone who has ever learned a language knows that it is easier to understand a language than it is to speak it—and listening is certainly less fraught with the anxieties of accent and performance. But when measuring "fluency" or even "competence," aurality often takes a distant second place behind orality.

It is the exact inverse of how we encounter much of what we aurally know. Listening, as something different from simply hearing, implies an active engagement with sonic phenomena. It implies, perhaps, a conscious engagement with sound; we hear things all day long, but how often do we actually listen? At the very least, listening takes attention—at most, cognition. We learn how to listen, how to attend to sonic phenomena in ways that parallel how we learn to read, speak, watch movies, shop, attend museums, and pray.

Listening is a cultural practice. How one listens to music is different from how one listens to his or her grandmother. And how Anglophone Jews listen to Yiddish is different from how they listen to English.

Stories about immigrant families often feature the language gap between parents and children. Early twentieth-century Jewish immigrant parents frequently spoke Yiddish and understood English, whereas their American-born or American-raised children spoke English and understood their parents' Yiddish. Not quite bilingual, members of these families—and their broader communities—did a lot of listening in languages that they did not necessarily speak either comfortably or well.

For many American Jews, listening to Yiddish has maintained a particularly powerful resonance that has little to do with understanding it and nothing to do with speaking it. This resonance is not concerned with grammar and vocabulary; rather, it centers more on one's ability to garner a broader cultural meaning from the language. Sociologist Herbert Ganz captured this phenomenon in an essay on comedian and bandleader Mickey Katz, whom he observed "is comprehensible even to the younger Jews who do not understand Yiddish, and can achieve a comic effect largely because of the incongruity between American material and a more or less Yiddish language."[1] In order to comprehend Katz, younger audiences had only to listen.

Most of us read more than we write, watch more movies than we make, see more art than we create, worship more often from the pew than the podium, and (hopefully) listen more than we speak. Most of our engagement in culture comes as consumers (though I use that word advisedly), and I am advocating here that we attend a bit more to how we consume culture aurally.

In the postvernacular Yiddish world, listening is perhaps the premier cultural practice of people involved in Yiddish culture, particularly those who do not live in the Yiddish-speaking enclaves of Brooklyn and Jerusalem. All of the subjects of the essays that follow are involved in Yiddish culture via their ears; their songs and words sound right or better or correct or authentic *in Yiddish*. And their choices of Yiddish—loan words, vintage cantorial recordings, and songs—echo a variety of aural orientations to the language that do not, on their own, speak to fluency.

Sarah Bunin Benor's respondents choose, on some level, to pepper their speech with Yiddish words because they signify Jewishness whether or not speakers can translate their own words precisely. Asya Vaisman's interviews with Hasidic women reveal that they sing certain songs in Yiddish because of the language's imagined connection to the old country. Finally, as Shayn Smulyan suggests, SoCalled chooses his samples because they sound good or right or work for his music. In each of these three cases, it is a relationship to the sound of the language, not its precise vocabulary, grammar, or utility, that speaks loudest.

But each speech act is accompanied by a listening act that helps give it meaning, context, and currency. Benor's respondents speak to people who understand their Yiddish interpolations, Vaisman's Hasidic women sing only among other women whose experiences and local knowledges are shaped by the larger structures of gender politics, and SoCalled approaches bins of old records as a listener and a consumer of records.

Each act of speech or song discussed in these essays relies on a community within which that speech is meaningful. And thus, although the three essays focus on acts of articulation (speaking, singing, and remixing), they share a commitment to the aural culture of Yiddish, especially when they take it for granted. Sonically speaking (is there any other way?), the sounds under discussion here are only important if they encounter ears. And, yes, that means that if nobody hears a tree fall in a forest, it does not speak Yiddish.

To speak of Jewish culture is also to speak of Jewish communities, and for the majority of Jews in the world, to choose to speak Yiddish in the twenty-first century means engaging a particular kind of audiocultural construction. And although younger Jews interpolate Yiddish terms in their everyday speech, Hasidic women sing, and SoCalled replays records, they're all playing to audiences and communities for whom the resonances, echoes and overtones of their choices of Yiddish resonate louder than speech alone.

Notes

1. Herbert Ganz, "The 'Yinglish' Music of Mickey Katz," *American Quarterly* 5, no. 3 (1953): 213-18. See also Josh Kun's introduction to *Papa, Play for Me: The Autobiography of Mickey Katz*, by Mickey Katz (Middletown, CT: Wesleyan University Press, 2002), xiii-xlix, the reissued autobiography of Mickey Katz. For a provocative account of how Katz's acoustic contributions fit in to broader notions of music, ethnicity, and race, see Josh Kun, *Audiotopias: Music, Race and America* (Berkeley: University of California Press, 2005).

ECHOES OF YIDDISH IN THE SPEECH OF TWENTY-FIRST-CENTURY AMERICAN JEWS

SARAH BUNIN BENOR

Introduction

From the *Shtender* (desk/lectern) of the Kluggerebbie:

As a bona fide member of the global Jewish conspiracy to make the world a better place, I hereby testify to the wisdom exhibited herewith by the author. With a deft pen and a happy heart, she has distilled the deepest soul, the *kishkes* [intestines] of the Jewish people, into a remarkable work that would have made her *bubbie* [grandma] so proud and full of *nachas* [pride] if it were not for those Nazi bastards who took her to the next world.[1]

So begins Lisa Alcalay Klug's 2008 book *Cool Jew*. In this faux rabbinic *haskama* (letter of approval), Yiddish serves as a hook to pull the reader into a vision of "cool" Jewishness. Klug's use of Yiddish words represents not an isolated instance but a widespread phenomenon among contemporary American Jews. In the twenty-first century, young American Jews are using Yiddish-influenced English to indicate facets of their ethnic and religious selves, even when their parents and grandparents do not.

Today most descendents of Yiddish-speaking immigrants in the United States have little knowledge of their ancestors' *mameloshn* (mother tongue). Small pockets exist where Yiddish is still spoken as an everyday language, both in *Haredi*/Black Hat Orthodox communities[2] and among a few hundred other Jews dedicated to keeping Yiddish alive. Yet, for most American Jews, Yiddish is a "postvernacular language," a source of nostalgia, crystallized in the form of jokes, *tshatshkes* (keepsakes), refrigerator magnets, and festivals.[3] As part of this change in vernacularity, Yiddish has left its mark on the English speech and writing of American Jews, as well as Americans more generally, in the form of Yiddish-origin words, phrases, and grammatical constructions.[4] In this essay, I investigate some of these echoes of Yiddish among English-speaking American Jews.[5]

Based on a large-scale online survey, I found that some Yiddish influences are making a comeback, that is, they are used more by younger people further removed from the generation of immigration. Even Jews who report that none of their ancestors who immigrated to the United States spoke Yiddish (10 percent of respondents, including descendents of speakers of German, Russian, Ladino, (Judeo-)Arabic, Farsi, and other languages) use many of the Yiddish influences. Two overlapping groups of American Jews seem to draw on Yiddish as a form of identification: those who emphasize their religious distinctiveness and those who emphasize their ethnic (and often secular) distinctiveness. Yiddish is connected culturally and emotionally to the Jewish collective memory of a recent eastern European past that includes robust strains of both religiosity and secularism. Whether contemporary American Jews consciously draw on these links or simply use words they associate with friends or relatives, it is useful to analyze the relationships between past and present and between language and identity.

The quantitative data in this essay come from an Internet survey about the use of Yiddish-origin words (known in linguistics as "loanwords") and other elements of language that I conducted with sociologist Steven M. Cohen in 2008.[6] We disseminated the survey to Jews and non-Jews using snowball sampling and yielded more than 40,000 responses. In this essay, I analyze a sample of 26,429 respondents who self-identify as Jews, were born and live in the United States, and spoke only English as children (not including languages learned in school). For comparison, I also look at a sample of 4,874 respondents who do not identify as Jews or as having Jewish heritage. Although the sample is by no means random and therefore does not constitute an accurate representation of Americans or American Jewry overall,[7] it allows comparison across subgroups. We can compare the reported use of Yiddish-influenced English among people of different ages, ancestral origins, and levels of Jewish engagement. In addition, the survey left spaces for individuals to write comments, and I offer qualitative analysis of some of these. I also present qualitative data on the use of Yiddishisms by young Jews in film, online, and in other venues.

Proficiency in Spoken Yiddish

According to the survey, a small percentage of American-born Jews are proficient enough to carry on a full conversation in Yiddish. The survey asked, "How much spoken Yiddish do you know?" In age groups under 65, less than 2 percent of respondents answered, "I'm fluent or proficient." For those aged

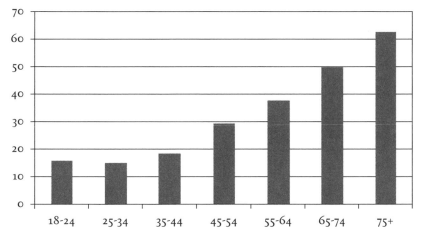

Percentage of survey respondents who report at least some Yiddish knowledge by age.

65–74, this number increases only to 3 percent, and for those over 75, to 8 percent. When we look at those who say they are "fluent or proficient" or "understand some," we see a sharply decreasing pattern: younger respondents are less likely to report Yiddish proficiency. A majority of the respondents in all groups under 65 years of age reported that they understand "only a few words" or "none."

The decreasing age pattern and the low Yiddish proficiency across the board come as no surprise. The sample includes only Jews born in America, and, for the most part, the younger they are, the further removed they are from the generation of immigration.[8] As we might expect, the self-reports of Yiddish proficiency are almost identical for generation and age. For the most part, immigrants did not speak Yiddish to their American-born children. This comment, from a second-generation survey respondent, sums up a common situation: "As with many people of my generation ([baby] boomers), my parents kept Yiddish as a 'secret language' when they did not want us to know what they were talking about." Among those who did speak Yiddish to their children, many preferred that their children speak English in an effort to integrate culturally and economically into American society. A respondent from Minnesota writes, "I understood everything my grandparents said to me, as we lived with them, but they wanted me to speak back in English: '*Red tzu mir in ainglish.*' Therefore I don't speak Yiddish well, but *ich farshtait* [sic]."

Use of Loanwords According to Age

Based on this pattern of decreasing language proficiency, we would also expect the use of Yiddish loanwords within English to decrease in the younger generations. And several words do:

TABLE 1. Yiddish words used less by younger Jews: % who report using them according to age

Yiddish word	Age (and approximate N)*						
	18–24 (1,160)	25–34 (2,857)	35–44 (2,779)	45–54 (5,228)	55–64 (7,550)	65–74 (4,490)	75+ (1,731)
mensch (good person)	83	86	90	95	96	96	95
maven (expert)	33	48	61	75	84	88	89
nachas (pride)	43	50	59	72	79	82	84
macher (big shot)	31	47	56	71	77	80	79
heimish (homey)	20	33	45	60	68	76	78
nu (well, let's go)	44	51	55	65	72	76	76
bashert (predestined match)	46	61	60	63	70	75	76
takeh (really)	9	8	10	17	25	37	48

*N represents the total number of people in each age group who answered the question. To save space, I only present approximate N's for each group (although each question had slightly different numbers of respondents, the numbers were very close).

TABLE 2. Yiddish words used more by younger Jews: % who report using them according to age

Yiddish word	Age						
	18–24	25–34	35–44	45–54	55–64	65–74	75+
shul (synagogue)	64	64	60	59	52	44	43
good Shabbos (Sabbath greeting)	50	49	44	42	40	36	32
bentsh (bless, say Grace After Meals)	43	43	35	33	31	31	33
drash (sermon)	28	28	25	24	19	15	9
leyn (read Torah)	26	27	22	18	14	11	8

However, we also see an unexpected result: some Yiddish-origin words are *more* common among younger respondents (see table 2). In addition, we see several Yiddish-influenced grammatical constructions that follow the same pattern (see table 3).

This surprising result can be explained by two separate phenomena: (1) Yiddishisms spreading to non-Jews and (2) Yiddishisms increasing in the religious domain. We find that non-Jews use "enough already" and "money, shmoney" in large numbers; in fact, a slightly higher percentage of non-Jews than Jews report using them. These two phrases of Yiddish origin have clearly become part of the American English language. Their greater use by younger Jews parallels their greater use by younger non-Jews. These phrases offer evidence of

TABLE 3. Yiddish constructions used more by younger Jews: % who report using them according to age

	Age						
Yiddish Construction	*18–24*	*25–34*	*35–44*	*45–54*	*55–64*	*65–74*	*75+*
Enough <u>already</u> (cf. Yid. *genug shoyn*)	85	86	89	85	81	74	67
Money, <u>shm</u>oney (cf. Yid. *gelt, shmelt*)	48	42	33	23	22	19	18
Are you coming <u>to us</u> for dinner? (vs. to our place; cf. Yid. *tsu undz*)	39	41	36	38	36	29	21
She's staying <u>by us</u> (vs. at our house; cf. Yid. *bay undz*)	30	29	26	27	24	16	8
She has <u>what</u> to say (vs. something; cf. Yid. *vos tsu zogn*)	16	16	15	14	11	9	7
What do we <u>learn out</u> from this? (vs. learn; cf. Yid. *oplernen**)	14	10	8	8	7	6	4

*There are several phrasal verbs used by Jews in English with influences from Yiddish, including "answer up" (counter, retort, cf. Yid. *opentfern*), "bring down" (cite, mention, declare to future generations based on past wisdom, cf. Yid. *aropbrengen*), and "give over" (impart, cf. Yid. *ibergebn*). The cognate of "learn out," *lern oys*, exists in Yiddish but with a different meaning: "learn completely." The English cognate phrase for *lern op* would be *learn up*, but this is not used, likely because of its perfective aspect. The "out" in "learn out" implies "derivation."

American Jews' integration into American society: their immigrant language has influenced the local language. We also see this phenomenon in the words "klutz," "shpiel," and "shmutz," which are used by large numbers of Jews and non-Jews and do not exhibit as clear trends according to age.

The majority of the words and phrases in tables 2 and 3 may be accounted for due to their use in religious spheres. Although these constructions can be used in many types of conversations, they are most commonly used in religious contexts. More religious American Jews use the Yiddish-influenced "by" and "to" (with syntax and pragmatics similar to Yiddish *bay* and *tsu*) in discussions of Sabbath meal plans, and Yiddish-influenced phrasal verbs like "learn out," "bring down," and "tell over" are common in the domain of traditional text study. The increasing use of these words and phrases in the younger generations relates to the growing importance of religious activities among many younger American Jews. Along with distinct practices in religious, social, culinary, and other spheres, young Jews use influences from Yiddish (and Hebrew) to index their belonging to Jewishly engaged communities. This is certainly the case for *ba'alei teshuva*, non-Orthodox Jews who become Orthodox,[9] but it can also be seen among Reform, Conservative, and other Jews who have increased their religious engagement.

Factors in the Use of Yiddishisms

Thanks to statistical analysis, we can determine whether age/generation plays a role on its own or merely seems to play a role because of its interaction with other factors. Steven M. Cohen and I conducted two separate regressions with scales built on the basis of highly correlated dependent variables (Pearson correlations greater than 0.5). The Beta values in Tables 4 and 5 represent the predictive power of each variable when all of the other variables are held constant: the higher the numbers, the greater the independent effect of the variable on that scale. For example, Table 4 indicates that not handling money on Shabbat and attending services frequently have much stronger independent effects on the use of *leyn, drash,* and *bentsh* than being Orthodox or having Yiddish-speaking ancestors. Except where "not significant" (N.S.) is indicated, all values are significant at the $p \leq .01$ value.

TABLE 4. Regression analysis for a scale combining *leyn, drash,* and *bentsh*

	Beta values: Standardized coefficients
Does Not Handle Money on Shabbat	.246
Attends Services More than Monthly	.234
Minyan Member	.163
Spent 10+ Months in Israel	.127
Jewish College Group	.086
Attended Jewish Day School or Yeshiva	.076
Almost All Friends Jewishly Engaged	.048
Orthodox	.048
Jewish Summer Camp	.040
Jewish Youth Group	.039
Ancestral Language: Yiddish	.025
Age, Generation	N.S.
Adjusted *R*-square*	.455

*The adjusted *R*-square value tells us the extent to which all of the independent variables, taken together, can accurately predict the linguistic scale. In a perfect model, *R*-square would be 1. From this we learn that the *leyn-drash-bentsh* scale is much better predicted by these independent variables than the "by us—to us" scale.

TABLE 5. Regression analysis for a scale combining "by us" and "to us"

	Beta values: Standardized coefficients
Does Not Handle Money on Shabbat	.117
Orthodox	.113
Ancestral Language: Yiddish	.071
Attended Jewish Day School or Yeshiva	.063
Spent 10+ Months in Israel	.043
Age, Generation	−.038
Minyan Member	.032
Almost All Friends Jewishly Engaged	.027
Attends Services More than Monthly	.019
Jewish College Group	N.S.
Jewish Summer Camp	N.S.
Jewish Youth Group	N.S.
Adjusted *R*-square	.089

Most strikingly, these regression analyses indicate that the **age-generation** variable has much less impact on the use of these words and constructions than other factors. In fact, age-generation is not even a significant predictor in the *leyn-drash-bentsh* scale, and it has only a minute effect on the "by us— to us" scale. In the latter, the small negative value indicates that Jews who are younger and further removed from the generation of immigration are slightly more likely than their elders to use these Yiddish constructions, keeping all other factors constant. If age and generation have so little impact, what causes the seeming age pattern? One explanation is sampling error: it is possible that the nonrandom sample includes an overrepresentation of religiously engaged young people and that in the actual population young Jews are less likely than their elders to use Yiddishisms. However, several other factors may play a role in the seeming age pattern.

Young Jews are more likely than their elders to have participated in **childhood Jewish education**, both formal (especially Jewish day school attendance) and informal (youth groups, overnight summer camps), due to an increase in these forms of Jewish socialization over the past several decades. Attending Jewish day school or yeshiva does have an independent effect on both scales, whereas other childhood Jewish socialization experiences have little or no effect.

Another factor is **Jewish socialization experiences during early adulthood**: participation in college Jewish groups and yearlong programs in Israel. These opportunities for Jewish engagement have also increased in the past few decades, and those who have taken part in them use more of the religiously oriented Yiddish words and phrases (as well as Hebrew and Aramaic words).

TABLE 6. Percentage of frequent *shul* goers who use *leyn,* according to age and denomination

Age	Reform (Total: 1,674)	Conservative (Total: 2,538)	Orthodox (Total: 1,435)
18–24	17	44	87
25–34	30	67	83
35–44	23	61	86
45–54	17	52	83
55–64	12	45	80
65–74	9	39	73
75+	6	24	50

Jewish college group participation has no effect on "by us—to us," but it has a strong effect on *leyn-drash-bentsh.* This is not surprising, as Jews involved in college Jewish groups may have frequent opportunities to discuss reading Torah, sermonizing, and saying Grace After Meals.

When we look at patterns according to denomination and age, we see evidence of the importance of young adult socialization experiences. For many of the words, the age trend is bucked by the youngest group among non-Orthodox Jews. That is, younger Jews use the words more than older Jews, but those under twenty-five use them less. An example is *leyn* (see table 6).

This dip may be evidence of a transition among many young Jews in colleges with high concentrations of observant Jews (such as Columbia, Harvard, Brandeis University, University of Pennsylvania, University of Maryland, and State University of New York-Binghamton) and in Israel, where many Jewishly engaged American Jews spend a year before, during, or after college, studying in universities and yeshivot. Many Jews in these densely Jewish environments become more Jewishly observant and knowledgeable and, I would argue, more linguistically distinct. For example, a high school student who is a leader of her Conservative youth group might talk about "synagogue," "services," and *Birkat hamazon* (or *Birkat* for short, i.e., "Grace After Meals"). While participating in Jewish religious life at Brandeis for four years and studying for a year at Pardes in Jerusalem, she may replace those terms with *shul, davening,* and *bentshing* in her in-group conversations. The dip in the youngest group's use of Yiddish words among non-Orthodox Jews[10] can be explained by the fact that fewer of them have spent a year in Israel and completed college.

Although these institutionally based Jewish socialization experiences are important in the use of Yiddish words among young Jews, their predictive power is much less than current social networks, as we see in the next several factors. The survey asked, "Of your close friends who are Jewish, how many are highly engaged in Jewish life?" When we look at those who report "all or almost all," we see that **having Jewishly engaged friends** has a moderate effect on *leyn-drash-bentsh* and a weak effect on the constructions. **Synagogue attendance and participation in a minyan** have a very strong effect on *leyn-drash-bentsh* and a weaker effect on the constructions. This is not surprising, as these words refer to concepts that frequent synagogue goers—and especially those who participate in the service (common in minyan settings)—need to discuss.

The most important factor in both scales is **Shabbat observance**. The survey asked respondents whether they refrain from handling money on Shabbat. The responses show a strong trend for younger people to observe Shabbat in this way more than their elders, both among those who identify as Orthodox and those who do not. Why would the use of Yiddish words correlate with not shopping on Saturdays? Although the survey did not ask how often Jews host or attend Shabbat meals, we can assume that Jews who observe at least some Shabbat prohibitions are likely to share many Friday night dinners and Saturday afternoon lunches with like-minded Jews. Essentially, these Jews spend half of each weekend interacting with other observant Jews. In these intensive periods of interaction, these Jews are likely to hear, use, and spread Yiddishisms.

Finally, whether a person **identifies as Orthodox** has a strong effect on their use of "by us—to us" and a moderate effect on *leyn-drash-bentsh*. As I explain elsewhere, Yiddish-influenced English is so important in Orthodox communities, that *ba'alei teshuva*—Jews who become Orthodox—often incorporate it into their speech.[11] This is related to the dense and multiplex social networks common among Orthodox Jews, as well as their greater exposure to people who speak Yiddish.

Clearly adult social networks and Jewish activities are important in the use and spread of Yiddishisms. Some of the survey comments offer further evidence for this. One woman says, "In the past fifteen years here, I have made some close Jewish friends, and joined a temple, so some Jewish phrasing/Yiddish intonations have actually become stronger!" Another says, "As a result of being in a Jewish book club I've learned more Yiddish or Hebrew-derived words." Conversely, one person says her speech has become "less Yiddish" because she now has fewer Jewish friends.

In addition to these factors that have a moderate to strong correlation with age (these religious activities are more common among younger than older Jews), we see an effect of **Yiddish ancestry**. We asked respondents what language(s) their immigrant ancestors spoke. Those who checked "Yiddish" are somewhat more likely to use "by us" and "to us," but this variable has very little effect on *leyn-drash-bentsh*. In fact, the respondents whose ancestors spoke Ladino or Arabic/Judeo-Arabic are *more* likely to use all of these words and constructions, probably related to these respondents' greater religiosity. The independent effect of Yiddish ancestry on "by us" and "to us" may be due to the 773 respondents who are converts to Judaism. Most of these Jews do not have Yiddish-speaking ancestry, and they are slightly less likely to use "by us" and "to us" (but more likely to use *drash* and *leyn*). Perhaps some converts feel comfortable incorporating Yiddish loanwords into their vocabulary but less comfortable using nonstandard English grammar.[12]

Why Yiddish?

It is not surprising that many young Jews—with their greater participation in religious activities and densely Jewish social networks (as children and adults)—speak more distinctly from the general population than their elders, especially in religious spheres. What is surprising is that Yiddish plays a role in the distinctness of their language. Why would religiously engaged Jews prefer a word brought to this country by their great-grandparents over one from their holy tongue?

Certainly Hebrew and Aramaic play a major role in Jewish linguistic distinctiveness. When we look at words of textual Hebrew/Aramaic origin, including those that also exist in Yiddish (*has v'shalom, davka, kal vahomer, l'hathila, lav davka*), we see similar age trends, which are also related to religiosity (see table 7). Clearly, textual Hebrew and Aramaic (as well as Israeli Hebrew) are important sources of loanwords among religiously oriented Jews. Why are words from Yiddish also important?

One possible explanation is brevity: some of these Yiddish words and constructions are shorter than their English and Hebrew counterparts. Why say "read Torah" when you can save two syllables with *leyn*? Why say "at our house" when you can simply say "by us"? Why say "Grace After Meals" or *Birkat Hamazon* when you can just say *bentsh*? The desire to say more with less may play a role in the spread of these words: it makes sense that those who refer to these

TABLE 7. Hebrew/Aramaic words used more by younger Jews: % who report using them according to age

Hebrew/Aramaic word	Age						
	18–24	25–34	35–44	45–54	55–64	65–74	75+
has v'shalom (God forbid)	28	26	19	16	13	12	12
davka (particularly)	24	27	23	20	15	13	12
kal vahomer (all the more so)	17	17	11	8	5	3	2
l'khathila (before the fact)	13	12	8	6	4	3	3
mo'adim l'simha (times of gladness)	12	13	12	9	7	6	6
hameyvin yavin (those in the know will understand)	7	8	6	5	4	2	1
lav davka (not necessarily)	7	6	4	4	3	2	1

concepts more frequently (religiously engaged Jews) would prefer the shorter words.

However, I would also argue that a major factor behind the spread of Yiddishisms is an increasing desire among religiously engaged Jews to distinguish themselves from non-Jews and from Jews who are less religiously engaged. The increasing role of Yiddish (in addition to Hebrew) in that process of distinction likely represents a trickle-down effect from Yiddish-speaking Orthodox Jews. When Jews become more religiously observant—in an Orthodox or non-Orthodox milieu—they often look to the more religiously observant for cultural norms, including the use of Carlebach melodies, the celebration of the end of Shabbat with a *melave malkah,* and the use of Yiddish words and constructions. These practices often spread from Orthodox Jews to non-Orthodox Jews. More specifically, Yiddishisms likely spread from Yiddish-speaking Black Hat Orthodox Jews to non–Yiddish-speaking Black Hat Orthodox Jews to Modern Orthodox Jews to non-Orthodox Jews.

This transmission likely happens through overlapping social networks. For the most part, non-Orthodox Jews have little contact with Yiddish-speaking Black Hat Orthodox Jews (with the exception of *Chabad* emissaries), but many non-Orthodox Jews who are highly engaged in Jewish life have contact with Modern Orthodox Jews, especially in university settings.[13] Many Modern Orthodox Jews have contact with those further to the right on the continuum of Orthodoxy. In fact, sociologist Samuel Heilman attributes the "slide to the right" within contemporary Orthodox circles partly to the preponderance of *Haredi* teachers in Modern Orthodox schools.[14] These overlapping social networks help spread Yiddishisms and other distinctive practices. The increasing use of Yiddish among religiously oriented non-Orthodox Jews, I posit, stems from a trend started by Black Hat Jews.

By talking about a *drash* rather than a "sermon" or inviting friends to eat "by them" rather than "at their place," Jews can—consciously or subconsciously—align themselves with some Jews and distinguish themselves from others. Through language, they can indicate to other Jews their level of religious observance. However, the increasing use of Yiddish loanwords is not merely a remnant of Jews becoming more observant. Linguistic features have spread past religious circles to people who have contact with them and beyond. Even Jews who have not altered their level of religiosity use *shul* increasingly where they once used "synagogue" and *leyn* where they once used "read Torah." An example is a baby boomer who grew up in California attending Conservative services regularly and now rarely attends services. She wrote in the comments section of the survey, "When I was growing up, I called it Temple. When my children went to a day school, I called it synagogue. I now call it *shul.* I am not sure why." The reason, I would argue, is that *shul* is gradually replacing "synagogue" and "temple" in Jewish American English.

A few decades ago, "synagogues" were generally Conservative, "temples" were generally Reform (except in California, where they were also Conservative), and *shuls* were generally Orthodox.[15] Today these associations continue to some extent. As the survey data show, Reform Jews are much more likely than others to use "temple." Conservative, Reconstructionist, Renewal, and Orthodox Jews tend to use "synagogue" when speaking to non-Jews and Jews who are not engaged in religious life and *shul* to Jews who are engaged in religious life. For some, *shul* still has the connotation of a small room where elderly Orthodox Jews *daven*.[16] However, many American Jewish newspapers now use *shul* as a generic word for Jewish house of worship, where they once used "synagogue" or "temple." Even many non-Jews use the word *shul*.

An example of these trends can be seen in an article in the Los Angeles *Jewish Journal*.[17] The article uses both "synagogue" and *shul* to refer to a Persian synagogue that had been vandalized. It also quotes Los Angeles Mayor Antonio Villaraigosa, who is not Jewish but has strong ties to the Jewish community: "A shul represents more than just a place of prayer or worship. It represents a place where faith binds a community." If a Mexican American politician and the Anglo-Jewish press use this Yiddish word in an unmarked way to refer to a Persian house of worship, it seems clear that *shul* has made inroads to replacing "synagogue" and "temple." In fact, my informal observations of Persian and other non-Ashkenazi Jews in Los Angeles suggest that *shul* is a common way for observant English-speaking Jews to refer to "synagogue."

More generally, the survey offers quantitative evidence for American Jews' increasing use of loanwords—both Hebrew and Yiddish. The survey asked, "In the past 10-15 years, would you say that the number of Yiddish-derived and Hebrew-derived words you use within English speech has increased, decreased, or remained the same?"[18] The results were striking (see table 8).

More than half of all Jewish respondents report that their use of Hebrew- and Yiddish-derived words has increased. We even see increases among many people who currently attend religious services the same amount as or less than

TABLE 8. Percentage of Jewish respondents (*N* = 26,429) who report changes in their use of Yiddish and Hebrew loanwords

	Percentage
Increased a lot	17
Increased a little	34
Remained about the same	39
Decreased a little	5
Decreased a lot	2
Not sure	3

they did as a child. The replacement of English and Hebrew words with Yiddish ones may originate among Orthodox Jews and spread to non-Orthodox Jews who are becoming more religious. Through overlapping social networks, it spreads to other American Jews and beyond.

Other Areas of Yiddish Influence among Young American Jews

Outside of the religious sphere, young people use Yiddish words and phrases selectively in a number of domains, including references to older Jews and cultural products targeted toward hip, urban Jews. Young people use Yiddish when discussing or alluding to grandparents and other older Jews, even if their own grandparents did not speak Yiddish to them. I found some examples of this phenomenon in a *Yizkor* (memorial) booklet compiled by members of a young Jewish congregation in Los Angeles in memory of their loved ones who had passed away. The writers (mostly aged 25–45) used Yiddish words when discussing their grandparents (sometimes referred to as Zeide or Bubby) or parents, even if they might not use those words in their everyday lives. Sometimes they marked these words with quotation marks or italics, and sometimes they overtly attributed them to an older Jew. For the most part, it is clear that the writers are connecting these Yiddish phrases with the loved ones they are memorializing (translations are mine):

> "Children were your joy! Would that you could see them today!!! You would really 'ickle challish,' [*ikh'l khaleshn* (I'll faint)] and be jumping for joy!"
> "Her unconditional love was boundless, demonstrated through her devotion to biting our feet or admiring our shaina punums [beautiful faces]."
> "No matter how thrifty, he never refused when my grandmother told him to give his kindela [*kinderlekh* (kids)] some money."
> "His constant need to clean around the house with his infamous shmata [rag]"
> "I ... try to live a life that would make her kvell [express pride and joy]."
> "I can almost hear her voice as I write this, '*You had to do it at an egalitarian service? Feh* [yuck].'"

A similar example comes from an e-mail sent to a listserv of Jewish leaders by a Reconstructionist rabbi in his thirties: "Well, live long enough and you see everything. As my late zayde would have said, *S'iz a meshugene velt* [it's a crazy world]." He knows enough Yiddish to write this sentence, but he considers it far enough removed from his regular speech to attribute it to his late zayde, even though the e-mail had nothing to do with his grandfather.

In addition to using Yiddish when discussing grandparents fondly, some young Jews use Yiddish when joking about older Jews. A contributor to a blog discussion about our survey commented, "They don't distinguish between Yiddish you use because it's Yiddish you use, and Yiddish you use because you are making fun of old Jews. *Schmuck* is in the former. *Feh! It's a shandeh to the goyyim!* is in the latter." Although this distinction might not always be completely clear in practice, it is important to realize that some Yiddishisms are used in a joking or marked way.

Surely it is not only younger Jews who mark Yiddishisms as foreign to them; middle-aged Jews also do so, sometimes attributing speech to parents rather than grandparents. An example comes from a Jewish studies scholar in his fifties. When I e-mailed him an update, including news that I was expecting a baby, he responded, "Congratulations on all those glorious developments in your life, in particular the one for which my mother would say, 'In ah gute shooh [in a good hour].'" In other circumstances, this man might say, "b'sha'a tova," the Hebrew translation of this Yiddish phrase, which is more common among non-Orthodox American Jews; however, he chose to use the Yiddish phrase (perhaps because he is aware of my interest in Yiddish and my research on Orthodox Jews) and to mark it as foreign to him. We see another example in the speech of Joseph Lieberman, Democratic vice-presidential candidate in the 2000 election. Lieberman rarely uses Yiddishisms in public settings. But in a 2000 televised interview, when asked about the problem that Inauguration 2001 was to fall on Saturday, he responded, "Well, as my mother would say . . . 'Sweetheart, we should have such a problem.'" By using this Yiddish-influenced construction, he indexed his ancestral connection to Yiddish, and by attributing it to his mother, he marked it as unusual in his speech. When Jews several generations removed from Yiddish cite their parents or grandparents in this way, they are able to accomplish two contradictory tasks simultaneously: demonstrate their affinity for Yiddish and distance themselves from it.

Another example of the associations of Yiddish with older Jews can be seen in the names chosen for two political projects related to older Jews: Operation Bubbe (2004) and The Great Schlep (2008). Both of these initiatives, spearheaded by Mik Moore and others, encouraged young Jews to travel to Florida, a swing state, to convince their grandparents and other elderly Jews to vote Democratic in the presidential elections. By using Yiddish words in their titles, the organizers emphasized not only that these initiatives were geared toward (young) Jews but also that they had to do with elderly Jews.

In a sense, these initiatives commodify Yiddish by using it to advertise or sell their products. This is a common practice in *Heeb Magazine*, a quarterly geared toward "Jewish young adults and their friends, ages 18–34, who are searching for a connection between their heritage and their secular daily lives."[19] *Heeb* advertisers use Yiddish to sell products, including T-shirts and books. For example, an ad for Michael Wex's books about Yiddish, *Just Say Nu* and *Born to Kvetch*, uses these quotes:

"This is not your bubbe's—or Leo Rosten's—Yiddish."

"More than just a dictionary. Wex's parents must be kvelling."

"If you haven't already, get off your tukhes and get BORN TO KVETCH."[20]

Although this book is also marketed toward older Jews, the appearance of Yiddishisms such as *bubbe*, *kvell*, and *tukhes* in an ad in *Heeb Magazine* indicates an assumption that young Jews will recognize and appreciate them enough to buy the book. *Heeb Magazine* also uses Yiddish to sell itself, such as in recurring section names within the magazine:

"The Whole Megillah" [a partial translation of *di gantse megile*]

"Nosh Pit" [a section about food, based on "mosh pit"]

"Urban Kvetch" [likely based on the short-lived New York delivery service "UrbanFetch"]

In "Heebster" culture, Yiddishisms seem to mark young, urban, hip Jewishness. Another example of Heebster Yiddish comes from twenty-nine-year-old Jonathan Kesselman's 2003 movie *The Hebrew Hammer*, a satire of 1970s "blaxploitation" films. The Jewish characters use Yiddish words like *shlep* and *bubbele* and Yiddish-influenced constructions like "eat by us," "you want I should talk dirty to you?" and "you may have what to brag about." They also Judaify words by replacing /h/, /k/, and even /r/ with the "kh" sound, including "The 'khood," "Khebrew," "Khadillac," and "khemove" (remove). These exaggerated Yiddishisms contribute to the movie's over-the-top, self-consciously Jewish satire and connect the film to a broader American Jewish culture and an emerging American Jewish youth culture.

We see a similar phenomenon in the book *Cool Jew*, cited at the beginning of this essay. This humorous book represents Jewish ethnicity, culture, and religiosity as cool by combining information on holidays, life cycle events, kabbalah, and history with top ten lists, diagrams, and hip hop imagery. Filled with Yiddishisms (as well as Hebrew and a smattering of Ladino, in line with the multicultural trend), *Cool Jew* includes religiously oriented words such as *shul*, *frum*, and *shlogn kapores*, and other Yiddish terms such as *gornisht*, *shmear*, and *yidishe kopf*. This book even features a chapter titled "Heebster Spoken Here" and a recurring sidebar called "FYI: For the Yiddish Impaired."

Yiddishisms appear ubiquitously in the book's publicity website (**bold** is mine):

DA LOVE FEST in LA was awesome. The TAILGATE at Jewish Heritage Night was **da bim bom** . . . If by chance, *Cool Jew* isn't yet slated to come to you, **as they say in Chinese, don't vorry**. Click on contact and drop Lisa a line. We've got street teams taking shape across North America, so **G-d Villing**, it's only a matter of time before your vision takes shape in your beachside getaway, provincial hamlet and downtown loft! **So nu, vhat are you waiting for?**[21]

Similar to the book itself, this excerpt combines general American English with hip hop language ("da bomb") and Judaifies it with loanwords ("bim bom" and "nu"), religious Jewish writing conventions ("G-d" for God), and Yiddish pronunciations of English ("vorry," "villing," "vhat"), all in an attempt to make Judaism attractive to young Jews, or perhaps also to demonstrate to older generations that Jewishness is hip. This book demonstrates the intersection between the "Heebster" world and the religious world: the writer taps into cultural practices of American youth to try to "sell" religious engagement to young Jews. And Yiddish clearly plays a major role in that enterprise.

As we see with T-shirts, mugs, oy-oys (Yiddish yo-yos) and other merchandise that displays Yiddish, this commodification of a language is only possible in a postvernacular era.[22] The fact that these films, magazines, and books are created by and for young, hip Jews and not just the children and grandchildren of immigrants suggests the ongoing strength of Yiddish as a symbol of Jewish ethnicity and religiosity in America.

Sociohistorical Factors

Why are young people using more Yiddish in the sphere of religious engagement *and* in the sphere of popular culture? What is it about this historical moment that is conducive to this linguistic change? There are a few factors. We are now about one century removed from the mass wave of Yiddish-speaking immigration. Jews feel comfortable enough in the United States to go back to some of the religious and cultural traditions of their grandparents and great-grandparents.[23] In addition, historical events have affected Jewish self-expression.[24] Since the 1960s, American ethnic groups have been more willing to express their distinctness through discourse and cultural practices. We see an example of this in Joshua Fishman's analysis of United States census data from the middle of the century.[25]

Although a wave of Yiddish-speaking immigrants arrived between 1940 and 1960, the number of people who claimed Yiddish as a mother tongue dropped significantly. And although very little Yiddish-speaking immigration occurred between 1960 and 1970, the number of people who claimed Yiddish as a mother

TABLE 9. People who claimed Yiddish as their mother tongue in the US Census

Census year	Number of people who claimed Yiddish
1940	1,751,100
1960	964,410
1970	1,593,990

tongue increased significantly. This increase, which can also be seen in Italian, Norwegian, and other languages spoken by turn-of-the-century immigrants and their descendents, reflects changing attitudes toward ethnic distinctiveness in the 1960s. For all languages, including Yiddish, this trend subsided to some extent in the 1970s—most likely due to the aging population of immigrants and their children and the tendency for mother tongue claiming to ebb and flow. Nonetheless I would argue that the spirit of ethnic distinctiveness has remained a part of the American cultural landscape and currently may be on a rising tide. Just as it was increasingly acceptable in 1970 for middle-aged Jews to tell a census interviewer that Yiddish was their mother tongue, it is increasingly acceptable today for Jewish young adults to pepper their English with Yiddish words and phrases, both in religious and nonreligious spheres.

Conclusion

The path of Yiddish influences on Jewish American English has hit a fork. On the one hand, we see decreased use of words such as *bashert* and *heimish*. On the other hand, we see increased use of religiously oriented Yiddishisms such as *shul, leyn,* and "by us," and we see the use of Yiddishisms in new media connected to a Jewish hipster youth scene. This fork in the road is unexpected, given the general trajectory of Yiddish in America (outside of Black Hat communities). But it might be explained by the growing importance of religious observance and Jewish cultural distinctiveness among young American Jews. Young Jews of various communities are tapping into the rich well of Yiddish (along with Hebrew) not only to indicate that they are Jewish but also to align themselves with certain types of Jews.

What lies ahead on this road? Although social scientists are not in the business of prognostication, I do think we can expect more and more Jews to incorporate some religious-based Yiddishisms into their English speech. Currently, many rabbinical students at the Los Angeles campus of Hebrew Union College—Jewish Institute of Religion (the Reform movement's training institution, where I teach) say *daven* for "pray" but "read Torah" rather than *leyn*. Given the current trends, I predict that in twenty years Reform leaders will say *leyn*. To quote Isaac Bashevis Singer's Nobel Prize acceptance speech, "Yiddish has not yet said its last word." That last word may be generations away, if it ever comes. Even if it does, the echoes of Yiddish may continue to reverberate among American Jews.

Notes

Thanks to Steven M. Cohen for his help with the quantitative analysis in this essay, and thanks to the editors of this volume for including me and for giving me valuable comments. Unless otherwise noted, all translations are mine.

1. Lisa Alcalay Klug, *Cool Jew: The Ultimate Guide for Every Member of the Tribe* (Kansas City, MO: Andrews McMeel, 2008), xv.

2. Ayala Fader, "Learning Faith: Language Socialization in a Hasidic Community," *Language in Society* 35, no. 2 (2006): 207–29; Fader, "Reclaiming Sacred Sparks: Linguistic Syncretism and Gendered Language Shift among Hasidic Jews in New York," *Journal of Linguistic Anthropology* 17, no. 1 (2007): 1–22; Miriam Isaacs, "Haredi, Haymish and Frim: Yiddish Vitality and Language Choice in a Transnational, Multilingual Community," *International Journal of the Sociology of Language* 138 (1999): 9–30.

3. Jeffrey Shandler, *Adventures in Yiddishland: Postvernacular Language and Culture* (Berkeley: University of California Press, 2005).

4. Leo Rosten, *The Joys of Yiddish* (New York: McGraw-Hill, 1968); Sol Steinmetz, *Yiddish and English: A Century of Yiddish in America* (Tuscaloosa: University of Alabama Press, 1986); David Gold, "On Jewish English in the United States," *Jewish Language Review* 6 (1986): 121–35; Gene Bluestein, *Anglish/Yinglish: Yiddish in American Life and Literature* (Lincoln: University of Nebraska Press, 1998); Chaim Weiser, *Frumspeak: The First Dictionary of Yeshivish* (Northvale, NJ: Jason Aronson, 1995); Sarah Benor, "Yavnish: A Linguistic Analysis of Columbia's Orthodox Jewish Community," *'Iggrot ha'Ari: Columbia University Student Journal of Jewish Scholarship* 1, no. 2 (1998): 8–50; Benor, "Loan Words in the English of Modern Orthodox Jews: Yiddish or Hebrew?" in *Proceedings of the Berkeley Linguistic Society's 25th Annual Meeting, 1999*, ed. Steve S. Chang, Lily Liaw, and Josef Ruppenhofer (Berkeley, CA: Berkeley Linguistic Society, 2000), 287–98; Sarah Bunin Benor, *Becoming Frum: How Newcomers Learn the Language and Culture of Orthodox Judaism* (Piscataway, NJ: Rutgers University Press, 2012); Cynthia Bernstein, "Lexical Features of Jewish English in the Southern United States," in *Language Variety in the South III: Historical and Contemporary Perspectives*, ed. Michael D. Picone and Catherine Evans Davies (Tuscaloosa: University of Alabama Press, forthcoming). As I explain in my studies of Orthodox Jews in America (Benor, "Yavnish"; Benor, *Becoming Frum*), Yiddish influences include not only loanwords and constructions but also intonation, discourse patterns, and phonological features, especially in the Ashkenazic-influenced pronunciation of Hebrew words. In addition, many Yiddish loanwords exhibit changes in usage. For example, in Yiddish *shlep* (carry) is transitive, but in English it can be both transitive ("I shlepped my laptop here for nothing?") and intransitive ("I shlepped all the way to Queens for this?"). And Yiddish-origin nouns tend to be pluralized with English plurals (*shuls* vs. *shuln*, *mentshes* vs. *mentshn*).

5. For a discussion of non-Jews' use of Yiddish loanwords as well as Jews' use of Hebrew loanwords and other distinctive linguistic features, see Sarah Bunin Benor and Steven M. Cohen, "Talking Jewish: The 'Ethnic English' of American Jews," in *Ethnicity and Beyond: Theories and Dilemmas of Jewish Group Demarcation*, vol. 25 of *Studies in Contemporary Jewry*, ed. Eli Lederhendler (Oxford: Oxford University Press, 2011), 62–78.

6. For details, see Benor and Cohen, "Talking Jewish." The survey also includes questions about words and phrases from Israeli Hebrew and textual Hebrew and Aramaic. These linguistic features are central to American Jews' distinctiveness from non-Jews and from each other. For example, Jews who have spent time in and feel strongly connected to Israel are more likely to use Israeli Hebrew words such as *yofi* (nice) and *balagan* (mess, bedlam). And Jews who are engaged in religious life and learning are more likely to use textual Hebrew and Aramaic words such as *kal vahomer* (all the more so) and *davka* (specifically). Although some of these words are discussed (see Table 7), this essay focuses on the Yiddish words and constructions within Jewish American English.

7. Compared to the 2001 National Jewish Population Survey (NJPS), the current sample is somewhat skewed toward Jews engaged in religious life (62 percent of Jews report being members of a synagogue, compared with 46 percent of respondents to the NJPS long-form questionnaire) and toward Jews with Jewish social networks (80 percent of Jews re-

port that half or more of their close friends are Jewish, compared with 52 percent of all NJPS respondents). In addition, the survey sample probably includes a disproportionate number of people who have an interest in and knowledge of Yiddish, as they were more likely to receive the e-mail invitation and participate. In fact, some respondents who studied Yiddish in *shule* (childhood supplementary school with a Yiddishist bent) or in college commented that they are probably "unusual" or "not typical." We can assume that the actual population of North American Jews has somewhat less proficiency in Yiddish and less use of the loanwords discussed below.

8. Age and generation from immigration are highly correlated in the survey sample. Among respondents with Yiddish-speaking ancestors (90 percent of the sample), a correlation test for age and number of parents and grandparents born in the United States or Canada is highly significant (p = .000; Pearson correlation = -0.564).
9. Benor, *Becoming Frum*.
10. Orthodox Jews tend to spend an extra year in Israel immediately after high school.
11. Benor, *Becoming Frum*.
12. We also see this trend among some *ba'alei teshuva* (see Benor, *Becoming Frum*).
13. In fact, the boundary between Modern Orthodox and Conservative Jews is porous, as some Jews who identify as Orthodox experiment with gender egalitarianism and some non-Orthodox Jews participate in Orthodox communities.
14. Samuel Heilman, *Sliding to the Right: The Contest for the Future of American Jewish Orthodoxy* (Berkeley: University of California Press, 2006).
15. See David Kaufman, *Shul with a Pool: The "Synagogue-Center" in American Jewish History* (Lebanon, NH: Brandeis University Press, 1999).
16. For example, see Frank Chapper, "My grandfather's shul," *Washington Jewish Week*, July 10, 2008. Also, one survey respondent, who grew up going to Reform "temples" in a number of US cities, commented, "'Shul' was what we said to the grandparents so they'd understand where we were headed that evening."
17. Adam Wills, "Mayor Carries Torah to Vandalized Tarzana Synagogue," *Jewish Journal*, July 10, 2006.
18. We did not separate Yiddish and Hebrew in this question, because often loanwords derive from both Hebrew and Yiddish (see Benor, "Loan Words"). Although some people may be referring to words derived only from Israeli Hebrew and not from Yiddish, we can assume that at least some respondents are referring to Yiddish words.
19. *Heeb Magazine*, accessed January 2009, http://heebmagazine.com. Parts of this section come from Erin Mason, "The Use of American Jewish Language in Jewish Magazines" (term paper, Hebrew Union College, Jewish Institute of Religion, 2008).
20. *Heeb Magazine* 18 (fall 2008): 2.
21. Lisa Alcalay Klug, "The Ultimate Guide for Every Member of the Tribe," accessed September 2008, http://eventscooljewbook.blogspot.com/2008/08/announcing-2008-2009-cool-jew-book-tour.html.
22. Shandler, *Adventures in Yiddishland*.
23. Marcus Lee Hansen, *The Immigrant in American History* (New York: Harper and Row, 1964).
24. Marc Dollinger, "Jewish Identities in 20th-Century America," *Contemporary Jewry* 24, no. 1 (2003): 9–28.
25. Joshua A. Fishman, "Mother-Tongue Claiming in the United States since 1960: Trends and Correlates," in *The Rise and Fall of the Ethnic Revival: Perspectives on Language and Ethnicity*, ed. Joshua A. Fishman, Michael H. Gertner, Esther G. Lowy, and William G. Milán (New York: Mouton de Gruyter, 1985), 107–94.

"HOLD ON TIGHTLY TO TRADITION"

Generational Differences in Yiddish Song Repertoires among Contemporary Hasidic Women

ESTER-BASYA (ASYA) VAISMAN

Mame:	Mother:
Alts vos du host tsugezen–	Everything that you witnessed
Un mitgelebt inderheym	And experienced at home
Zolstu nokhmakhn–	You should emulate
Punkt un daytlekh leman hashem!	Exactly and precisely for the sake of God!
Vayl di ale gute zakhn shtamen	Because all good things originate,
Geyarshnt fun dayn mames mamen	Are inherited from your mother's mother,
Un zi mistame, oykh fun ir mame . . .	And she, probably, also from her mother . . .
Loz zikh kholile gornisht beygn	Don't, God forbid, let anything sway you
Keyn hor zolstu nisht avekneygn	Not a hair should you move away
Vayl mesoyre halt dayn yidishkayt!	Because tradition maintains your Jewishness!
Ester:	Esther:
[Soten] kumt ober azoy klug un–	But [Satan] comes so smart and
Kintslekh vi a fraynt	Clever like a friend
Zogt mir du kenst nisht vi–	Says to me you can't do
Di bobes ales ton haynt . . .	Everything today like the grandmothers . . .

"Mesoyre lid" (Tradition Song)[1]

The main message conveyed by "Mesoyre lid"—the critical importance of adhering to "tradition"—is hardly surprising given its provenance: the song comes from the Tosh Hasidic community based near Montreal. The emphasis placed on tradition, or on what is perceived as tradition, by contemporary Hasidim is apparent in many facets of their lives: they make an effort to dress, cook, pray, and speak in the manner of their ancestors. After the Holocaust and the relocation of the centers of Hasidic life to America and other countries, these features of Jewish life in eastern Europe were canonized and acquired a new importance due to the destruction of the *alte heym* (old home).[2] The very fact that "Mesoyre lid" is in Yiddish—the language spoken historically by Hasidim in eastern Europe—attests to the importance placed on retaining and reinstituting the imagined ancestral way of life in reconstructed communities.

Yet "Mesoyre lid" presents an irony not immediately obvious to the outside observer. A Hasidic woman wrote the song within the past forty years for use in Hasidic girls' schools and summer camps.[3] The "mothers' mothers" of the girls for whom the song was written clearly never sang "Mesoyre lid," just as they never sang the vast majority of the songs in the repertoire of contemporary Hasidic women and girls. This present-day repertoire consists primarily of songs written by Hasidim in the past fifty years, whereas the Yiddish songs that the "mothers' mothers" did sing have, for the most part, not been transmitted to following generations. Even the styles and genres of the current female song repertoire differ from the types of songs sung in previous generations. This reality contrasts with the song culture of men, which, although constantly expanding with new pieces written regularly, finds its continued foundation in the *nigun* tradition of eastern Europe.

I discovered "Mesoyre lid" in a song booklet that I collected in Williamsburg, New York, while doing fieldwork for my dissertation on the Yiddish songs and singing practices of contemporary Hasidic women. *Kol B'Isha*, a Jewish religious regulation on a woman's voice, prevents Hasidic women from publicly performing or commercially recording songs, as the law stipulates that their voices may be sensually attractive to men.[4] Thus, whereas Hasidic men's music has been collected, published, and analyzed to an extent, virtually no research exists outside of the community on the enormous repertoire of the Hasidic women's songs.[5] Due to the insular nature of Yiddish-speaking Hasidic communities, information on this subject may be obtained only through fieldwork, which consists of identifying the Yiddish-speaking informants, approaching women directly, and conducting interviews.

In the course of four years of ethnographic fieldwork for this project in Brooklyn, Jerusalem, Rehovot, London, and Antwerp, I established contact with my informants—Hasidic women from the Satmar, Bobov, Puppa, Vizhnits, Tosh, Belz, and other communities—in several ways.[6] In some cases, I approached individual women on the street and asked, in Yiddish, if they knew any Yiddish songs and if they had time to meet in order to discuss and sing these songs. My ability to speak Yiddish often sparked the woman's curiosity sufficiently for her to agree to a later meeting. Once contact with one woman was established, it became easier to interview her family members. On occasion, the woman introduced me to her neighbors or friends, but often, especially in the Satmar community, women refused, claiming that no one else in the community would agree to be interviewed. In other cases, I established contact through common acquaintances. I also visited several Hasidic girls' schools and observed school performances and rehearsals, graduations, and classes in which teachers taught songs.

This essay examines why Hasidic women's songs, unlike men's songs and unlike most other Hasidic cultural characteristics, represent a new phenomenon in post-Holocaust Hasidic life. It describes the contemporary repertoire of women and girls, discusses the origin of this repertoire, and explains how and why it developed, replacing the songs that Hasidic women sang in previous generations. The essay presents ethnographic data about the singing practices of women who grew up before the changes took place in the community and offers suggestions for the striking generational differences in female song repertoire.

"I learned most of the songs in school," said Esty Kahan, a twenty-six-year-old Puppa[7] woman from Boro Park, when I asked her how she knew the songs that she sang for me during an interview.[8] In fact, the vast majority of interviewed women under the age of fifty, from every Hasidic group and geographical community, listed school, summer camp, and tapes as the three main sources from which they learned songs. Almost no one mentioned learning songs from home or from her mother or other relatives during the open-ended portion of the question. Only after I specifically asked, "Did you learn any songs from home or from your parents?" would some of the women assent that they learned some songs from their mothers. Even then, the woman typically said that she either does not remember or does not sing her mother's songs and that songs that her mother and grandmother sang were "More like children type, more rhymes, like lullabies, not so much real, real songs."[9]

The songs learned at school and camp typically consist of original Yiddish lyrics written by Hasidic teachers, principals, camp counselors, or students set to borrowed melodies. Melodies are taken from a variety of sources: from wordless or *loshn koydesh* (a combination of biblical Hebrew and Aramaic) *nigunim* and *zmires*—traditional songs from the men's repertoire (learned by women and girls in synagogue, or from male relatives or commercial recordings); from Hasidic pop recordings of songs in *loshn koydesh* or English recorded by male artists for a primarily female audience; and from non-Hasidic and even non-Jewish songs (usually learned by girls from demo tunes preprogrammed into the Yamaha or Casio keyboards that they sometimes use for musical accompaniment or from unmarked, unattributed cassettes that are passed around from girl to girl).

A twenty-five-year-old Tosh[10] teacher, Suri Gold, described how she created a song for one of her classes: "[This is] a song I wrote myself. I made it for my class for before *davening* [prayer]. I took a tune of the "Yerushalayim" song, a song that I remember singing as a kid, [and wrote new words]."[11] Occasionally, depending on the financial resources available to the school or camp, a semiprofessional woman from the community may be hired to write theme-appropriate songs or melodies for an especially large-scale performance. Hasidic girls today sing not only in classes in school but also during performances, which are very common in girls' schools and summer camps. Examples of musical performance opportunities include an eighth-grade graduation when girls move on to high school; plays in camps that girls prepare for the end of the summer, when their female relatives come to pick them up; and fundraising events and performances for charity, for which students and teachers write new songs.

These school and camp songs are primarily religiously didactic, intended to shape a girl's understanding of faith and her role in the Hasidic community.[12] The songs always have an instructive element, in that they teach the importance of the values of modesty, caring for the husband and the children, lighting the Sabbath candles, and placing one's faith in God, all of which reinforce the schools' mission and the greater concept of the woman's role in Hasidic society. As noted by sociolinguist Miriam Isaacs, teachers use the songs as a tool to achieve the religious, moral, and ethical goals that the Hasidic communities seek to foster. Educators use songs extensively in girls' education particularly, and singing never occurs purely for entertainment: "Girls are taught many songs throughout their schooling, and music is a central educational tool, enhancing rote memorization."[13] Anthropologist Ayala Fader points out that "Yiddish literacy lessons and texts . . . always include a moral message . . . even the picture books for very young children."[14] This kind of instruction has led to younger women's perception that "good" and "interesting" songs must have a *pshat* or a moral.[15]

In a number of occasions throughout my interviews, women described songs without a moral in a derisive manner. Dvoyre Horowitz, a twenty-four-year-old Satmar[16] interviewee, sang a song about a mother asking her children to send her a letter, and she said she never understood this song because it has no *pshat*. She said that people sing it with a lot of feeling, but without the *pshat* it is not a very interesting song.[17] Similarly, a twenty-two-year-old Bobov[18] woman, Rokhi Davidson, sang a children's song about the holiday of Purim, which focused more on rhyming words than on having a meaning, and she said, "We learned this song in second grade. It's weird because it has no *pshat*."[19] The Tosh informant, Suri Gold, reinforced this idea of a song requiring a moral level of meaning: "This is [a song by] Yomtov Ehrlich.[20] His songs are really great because he's always bringing out a lesson in his songs. It's not just *abi a song* [any old song]."[21] The moral messages that appear in the "good" songs include the importance of trust in God, observing the commandments, and honoring one's parents, particularly the mother.

The practice of using songs as educational tools and as religiously enriching entertainment arose with the development of Hasidic schools for girls, which occurred only in the latter half of the twentieth century. Traditionally, law and custom exempted Jewish women from religious study, without forbidding such study.[22] Thus, whereas boys in Ashkenazi communities in the early modern period attended religious school, girls often received no formal education. The situation changed in the nineteenth century, when education became normative for both boys and girls, with girls attending secular schools in greater numbers as a result of either state policy or local custom, which privileged religious education for men. As girls learned the local vernaculars (such as Russian, Polish, German, or English), their Yiddish and Jewish knowledge rapidly declined.

In reaction to the loss of tradition that was looming on the horizon if the girls were to stay in the non-Jewish schools, Sarah Schenirer founded the Beys Yakov Jewish women's school movement in Poland in 1917. The movement spread throughout Europe, Palestine, and the United States. The schools taught Hebrew, Torah, and Rashi's commentary, among other subjects. Yiddish language learning was not equally stressed in all Beys Yakov schools, and schools outside of Europe particularly deemphasized its instruction.[23]

In the second half of the twentieth century, the state of affairs regarding girls' schools in Hasidic communities varied according to local conditions. Fader notes that when Hasidic centers shifted to the United States after the Holocaust, "very few Hasidic leaders initially built private parochial schools for girls although these were immediately established for Hasidic boys."[24] Parents consequently had to send their daughters to the existing Orthodox Jewish schools for girls such as Beys Yakov, where the languages of instruction remained English and Hebrew, and as a result, the Hasidic girls did not formally gain Yiddish literacy.

When religious stringency increased in the second half of the twentieth century among Hasidic communities in reaction to the changes wrought by modernization, migration, assimilation, and the trauma of the Holocaust, changes arrived in girls' education. By the 1970s, a number of Hasidic leaders began establishing girls' schools, which offered Yiddish language instruction while also conducting morning classes in Yiddish.[25] The late establishment of specifically Hasidic girls' schools caused several generations of Jewish women in some communities to grow up with limited Yiddish proficiency.

Indeed, within the large Bobov community, which constitutes the majority in the neighborhood of Boro Park, New York, Hasidic girls today are more fluent in Yiddish than their mothers and some of their grandmothers, many of whom attended school before the establishment of the Hasidic educational system for girls. In Williamsburg, however, where the Satmar community predominates, Yiddish education for girls began almost immediately after the Holocaust; in fact, Satmar communities had established girls' schools even shortly before the war in Hungary.[26] Among ultra-Orthodox communities in Israel, a shift toward stricter education for girls, which included a move toward incorporating Yiddish, happened between the 1950s and 1970s.[27]

The establishment of Hasidic girls' schools thus had the dual effect of creating an institutionalized venue for female singing and motivating the development of a new body of specifically educational Yiddish songs for women. Because of *Kol B'Isha*, women's involvement in singing was significantly more in the private sphere before the founding of these schools. As Suri Gold explained, "Even if [songs by women] existed before, it was so private, no one would know. How do we know now? Because we have copying machines and tapes. Back then, there was no such thing. So if you had a *nign* [tune], that you made yourself, you sang it with your child, your daughter, and that's it. It wouldn't become famous."[28] Without the schools, in which teachers distribute photocopied lyric sheets of songs that Hasidic women and girls write, women's songs could not become widely known. It is therefore useful to examine what women did sing before the school and summer camp songs came into existence and why those songs are not part of the contemporary repertoire, if the Hasidic communities encourage girls to "emulate exactly and precisely" what they "witnessed and experienced at home," as "Mesoyre lid" indicates.

Since Hasidic women in eastern Europe could not propagate any religious songs that they created, it seems that no specifically *Hasidic* popular women's songs existed. This situation contrasts with that of men's song repertoire, which generally consists of a continued tradition of *zmires* (traditional songs often based on medieval poetry by rabbis and sages) and *nigunim* (songs based on vocables or on a repeating line from a classical Jewish text), usually composed by rebbes and other important spiritual and religious figures. Because there is no parallel restriction on men's voices, men often attended large gatherings at a rebbe's table (*tish*), which involved a great deal of singing and where everyone could learn a common repertoire of songs. Whereas men's songs were thus often attributable to a particular Hasidic court, before the creation of Hasidic girls' schools, the songs that women did sing and listen to were primarily popular secular Yiddish songs, including theater, art, and folk songs all from outside the Hasidic community.

In many of my interviews, older women in their late fifties and sixties, particularly those born in eastern Europe, spoke of having listened to "Jewish radio" in their youth, owning popular Yiddish tapes or records, or even sometimes having gone to the theater, all activities now strictly forbidden in their Hasidic communities. For example, a fifty-five-year-old Ger[29] woman living in Jerusalem, Khane Feldman, admitted to having an entire library of CDs and tapes of Chava Alberstein (a popular female Israeli Hebrew and Yiddish singer and songwriter), Dzhigan and Schumacher (a duo of Polish Yiddish comedians), Mike Bursteyn (a secular Yiddish singer), and many other secular recordings.[30] To have a tape of a woman singing in a modern Hasidic home suggests an extremely unusual situation due to the danger of a man in the family accidentally hearing it. When asked why she thinks it acceptable to listen to secular recordings, she replied, "But it comes from Yiddish! It comes from Jews."

A Bobov woman in her late fifties, Khave Bernstein, who lives in Boro Park, expressed a similar sentiment. She said that when she was young, she used to listen to "Jewish radio" and records, where she learned such songs as "Mayn shtetele belz."[31] She noted, however, that it is not acceptable to listen to "*goyishe* [non-Jewish] tapes. It's not good to listen to *goyishe* music because it doesn't come from a clean place."[32] She thought that Yiddish songs, in contrast, even "modern" Yiddish songs and secular Yiddish songs, are acceptable because "if they were Jewish, it's okay." She noted very vehemently, however, that her children never listen to this kind of music, and when she turns on the radio in her children's home, they ask her to turn it off. She remarked that she is happy that her children are "more Hasidish" than she is.[33]

In a Satmar family, the mother knew many theater songs and Yiddish secular songs because she had heard them on the radio at her aunt's house. The mother, who was in her late fifties, had no concerns about singing these songs. Her daughters, who were in their mid-twenties and early thirties, knew the songs because they had grown up hearing them from their mother. The daughters said, however, that they would never sing these songs among themselves or to their children, because the songs did not originate in the Hasidic community.[34]

The young Tosh woman, Suri Gold, similarly described the song repertoire of her grandmother's generation:

> The songs that the women used to sing long ago were more like ... the common songs ... that were on the records, not the Hasidic *nigunim*. More like that modern type, I don't know what I would call them, my grandmother [knows] the names. There were popular ones that people sang, but they were not Hasidic. The first Hasidic ones were Yomtov Ehrlich. And when I was little, Yomtov Ehrlich was popular, but it was very long songs, and my mother wouldn't sing such a long song to me. These shorter songs came out much later.... The songs that were public were more modern songs, like "A brivele der mamen," right?[35] And these songs ... people heard them on the Yiddish radio, but it was more modern, it wasn't ... Hasidic. Hasidic there's no radio, Hasidic there's no records, Hasidic was sung by the rebbe's *tish* (table). Women began to write [popular Hasidic] songs a little later.[36]

Due to the increased religious stringency that occurred in Hasidic communities post–World War II, the second- and third-generation American and Israeli Hasidic granddaughters were not interested in adopting these secular Yiddish songs. In fact, none of the interviewed women in their twenties and thirties owned any tapes of secular music. They also never listen to the radio, and they have certainly never attended the theater.

In many interviews, I asked women whether they have heard "Afn pripet-shik" ("On the Heating Stove"), an extremely popular song in prewar eastern Europe by the non-Hasidic songwriter Mark Warshawsky.[37] One young Bobov woman in Boro Park, Rokhi Davidson, said that the first time she heard "Afn pripetshik" was on a visit to a nursing home when she was a child.[38] She never heard it at home or in school, but she said, "In nursing homes we hear this [song] a lot." Davidson asserted that she would sing this song, an unusual reply for a young woman among those canvassed for this project. Her willingness probably results from her origins in the Bobov Hasidic group, which is more lenient than some other groups, such as Satmar. When asked why other young women do not usually sing this song, she said that she thinks the reason for the taboo is the song's former use in theaters, which are considered objectionable. She did not know the author of "Afn pripetshik," and after being told his name and that he was not an observant Jew, she theorized that people probably do not sing the song because the author was not observant. Davidson nevertheless said that she sings it because "the words are kosher."[39]

A young Satmar woman in Williamsburg, Blumi Zilberstein, noted that she knows "Afn pripetshik" but "the kids don't sing it, the parents sing it. It's a common song but only the elderly know it."[40] Suri Gold agreed, "It's not so commonly sung today. It's like one of those old, old melodies. But being that it's from Europe and it sort of reminds [one] of Europe, they'll sing it, because it has a certain *tam* [taste] of Europe."[41] The sanctioned singing of non-Hasidic songs in the context of nostalgia for Europe is a remarkable phenomenon and will be addressed further.

After hearing some of the words of "Bay mir bistu sheyn" ("I Think That You're Beautiful," a very popular secular Yiddish song by Sholem Secunda), Rokhi Davidson recognized the song and said, "I don't think there is anything else that I would know from that world. Maybe my mother would know, but I wouldn't have access to these songs; it's not something I would really be exposed to."[42] When I asked Blumi Zilberstein about "Tum balalaika" (a folk song popular in Russia), she said, "I've heard it, but it's not part of the Hasidishe songs." The only reason she heard it was that her mother had a neighbor who was not very religious, and she used to sing "Tum balalaika" frequently.[43] In a more extreme case, when I asked a young Satmar woman in Williamsburg, Dvoyre Horowitz, if she learned songs from her mother or grandmother, she replied, "You want to hear old songs? They exist, but I don't know them."[44]

The rejection of secular songs came about by the particular interaction, in the minds of younger Hasidic women, of nostalgia and religious stringency. After the destruction of traditional Jewish life in eastern Europe during the Holocaust, the transplanted Hasidic communities romanticized and idealized that life. Because of this nostalgia for the *alte heym*, the Jews in the new communities perceived the people of the old country to be inherently more righteous, a righteousness to which the descendants aspired. This phenomenon is discussed extensively in historical and sociological literature; the analyses most relevant to the present project appear in works by Ayala Fader and Menachem Friedman.[45]

At the same time, the break in continuity created a need for and facilitated a reinterpretation of Judaism in a stricter sense, closer to the "books" than to "tradition," as discussed in detail in the works of Haym Soloveitchik and Menachem Friedman, among others.[46] Friedman theorizes that with the disintegration of traditional Judaism, ultra-Orthodoxy (or Haredi Judaism) developed to counter the trend of bending Jewish law to adapt to modernity. Haredi Judaism emphasized fulfilling "halakhah as it stands, without consideration."[47] This approach constituted a deviation from the established practice of Judaism, as it required a stricter interpretation of rules than had been previously observed.

Friedman goes on to argue that the Holocaust and the migrations associated with it created the conditions that enabled the spread of ultra-Orthodoxy. Because of the break in the personal relationships that had formed the traditional community, the living tradition could not be transmitted directly from generation to generation as it previously had been. This rupture "naturally created a sense of a lack of confidence, the remedy for which was found in the strengthening of the attachment to the tradition of the book, written halakhah."[48] The transplanted Hasidim lost touch with the customs and songs of the past and had to recreate them in the new country,[49] and in an effort to live up to the imagined righteousness of the martyred ancestors, the new customs ended up being stricter than the old.

This irony of an imagined idealized past combined with an increased insularism against the influences of the modern world caused a marked break with the popular Yiddish culture that had been fairly accessible to previous generations. The stricter descendants deemed the popular songs sung by their grandmothers, such as "Sheyn vi di levone," "Abi gezunt,"[50] and "Vu iz dos gesele,"[51] as no longer "kosher." Based on my observations, in the eyes of contemporary Hasidic women the perceived inherent higher spiritual and religious level of old-country women justified their secular repertoire. Newer generations believed that exposure to the lenient outside world could not contaminate the righteous women of the past. The new generations, however, considering themselves "less moral," have demonstrated an avoidance of the outside influences that secular songs threatened to impose. In their place, they developed a new repertoire of didactic religious songs intended to elevate the spirituality of women today to the aspired level of their grandmothers.

Hasidic girls' schools enforce this shift to increased religiosity by specifically proscribing singing the popular songs of previous generations, except in designated special contexts, and encouraging learning the new, didactic repertoire. As ethnographer George Kranzler observes, "A central feature of Hasidic education is the rejection of the values, conduct and trends of the outside world, many of which are seen to contradict or violate the spirit or laws of the Torah and the Hasidic tradition."[52] Knowing the pedagogic power of music, educators censor and ban songs that come from outside the Hasidic community, deeming them carriers of countertraditional values. To protect younger generations from unwanted influences, they disseminate only culturally sanctioned, usually culturally internal sources.[53]

Indeed, many of the popular Yiddish theater and folk songs that previous generations have sung contain themes entirely incongruous with contemporary Hasidic norms, including romantic love and political agendas incompatible with Hasidism (socialism and secular Zionism, for instance).[54] Intriguingly, the interdiction often holds true even for songs from the outside with harmless content, which seemingly could not negatively influence the sheltered listener in any way, songs such as "Yankele,"[55] "Undzer nigndl," and "Fraytik af der nakht."[56] The explanation lies in the contemporary Hasidic belief that an author's religious outlook is conveyed through any product of his or her creative expression, but particularly through music, even if it is not overtly expressed in the composition itself. To escape the potentially negative influence of an objectionable background, Hasidic educators avoid using any works by non-religious authors.[57] Since most young Hasidim equate Jews who are not strictly observant with non-Jews, being Jewish alone does not sanction an author's inclusion into the permissible category.[58] In one of the interviews for this project, Suri Gold, who lives in Boro Park, expressed her understanding of the prohibition:

> Music could affect you; if you're listening to music from a *goy* [non-Jew], even if it's a beautiful song, it can affect you, because it has influence on your soul. We don't want a *goy* to have influence on the *neshome* [soul], right? Even though he might be a good person, but we still don't want a *goy* to have an effect on us. The same with nonreligious Jews. Just like you wouldn't trust a nonreligious Jew on something you would eat, a *hekhsher* [kosher certification], with food, you wouldn't trust a nonreligious Jew with music.[59]

Thus, in both America and Israel, schools reject using Yiddish songs and texts written by non-Hasidic Jews, even in cases in which their curriculum is in need of supplementary materials. Writing of Boro Park, Fader notes, "There is a huge secular Yiddish literature, which I have not seen read in homes or schools. This can be considered one more form of censorship which Hasidim engage in to create clear and stark contrasts between gentile and Jewish, secular and religious."[60] Bryna Bogoch depicts a similar situation with Hasidic schools in Israel, which, although in grave need of learning materials, believe that "none of the classic Yiddish literary texts are ... appropriate for these schools, because even if the content is innocuous, no material written by non-Haredi writers is permitted."[61]

A chapter from a recently published book of interviews with Hasidic women educators in Israel elaborates on both the issue of songs with no *pshat* and the issue of innocuous songs from non-Hasidic sources, linking the two:

> Moreinu HaGaon HaRav Nissim Karelitz, *shlita*, was asked if it is permitted to sing a song that is *reik mitochen* (has no substantial content) and has nothing *posul* (forbidden) in it. Is this in the realm of *moshav leitzim* (a gathering of scoffers)?[62] HaGaon, HaRav Nissim, *shlita*, answered that for boys this is certainly *moshav leitzim*. For girls, even if it isn't *moshav leitzim*, it is nevertheless not from our *mekoros* (sources), our *chareidi* sources. If it's not from our *mekoros*, then it is certainly not for us. We want to emphasize the point that writers must be *chareidim* (meticulously Torah observant Jews) with pure *hashkofos* [perspectives]. What we bring to the students must be full of *yiras Shomayim* [fear of heaven].[63]

In addition, Hasidic educators consider the towns and cities of eastern Europe to have posed less of a threat than outside influences today, particularly large urban centers in America.[64] Although immodest literature and culture certainly existed in sizable quantities in the *alte heym*, they remained less prevalent and provocative than today. In the eyes of contemporary Hasidim, the increasingly suggestive nature of popular culture calls for ever greater measures of protection.

Although the division of songs into permissible and no longer permissible by younger generations seems rather fixed today, I discovered several remarkable exceptions in the course of my research. Upon hearing four preadolescent Satmar girls sing a series of popular secular Yiddish songs, including "Mayn yidishe mame,"[65] "Mayn shtetele belz," "Yomele Yomele,"[66] and "Papirosn,"[67] I asked their mother, Leye Levinson, if she knew the origins of these songs. She responded, "They are songs still from Europe."[68] She explained that the girls learned these songs in a choir that was organized to sing at a party for grandmothers and great-grandmothers. All of the girls dressed up in headscarves and flowery dresses reminiscent of early eastern European popular fashions. They pretended to be in the old country, and they sang old-country songs in an effort to make their grandmothers and great-grandmothers happy. Leye Levinson disclosed the controversy that erupted as the girls prepared for the party: some parents were very upset, claiming that the girls should not be learning and singing these non-Hasidic songs. The performance took place, however, because the old-country context ultimately legitimized the otherwise unacceptable songs.

I also discovered that the singing of non-Hasidic songs occurs in cases when Hasidic women are unaware that the songs come from an outside source. One song that is very popular among Hasidic women and children is "Oy khanike";

although the melody is indeed based on a Hasidic *nign*, the non-Hasidic Vilna-born Mordkhe Rivesman (1868–1924) wrote the lyrics.[69] All of the women interviewed, however, thought that the song (music and lyrics) had Hasidic origins and noted that it is thus totally accepted in the community. According to Suri Gold, "A lot of these songs are old, old songs from Europe, and people have no idea who was composing these songs. Now that it's so embedded into the community, and every kindergartener sings it, I don't know if they would take it out. I don't know if they realize the severity of it. Today, if someone would make such a song, no matter how pretty it is, they wouldn't take it in."[70]

The genre of songs about the Holocaust represents another unacknowledged exception to the avoidance of Yiddish non-Hasidic songs. This genre includes several songs from outside the community. For instance, a number of Hasidic women of various ages have sung or mentioned in interviews the Holocaust-themed song "In a litvish derfl" ("In a Lithuanian Village"), which also appears in many pamphlets of collected school and camp songs. Yet what is never acknowledged on the photocopied lyric sheets, or verbally by the women, is that the song was written by Khane Kheytin-Weinstein (1925–), a non-Hasidic woman from Šiauliai (Shavl), Lithuania.[71] The song tells the story of a mother who has to give up her young son to a non-Jewish home during the Holocaust so that he will survive. The Hasidic version of the song varies somewhat from the original. There are some minor technical changes—the rhyming words were changed to rhyme in the Hasidic Hungarian/Polish Yiddish dialect, several stanzas were cut, and the order of some lines reversed. The most striking difference, however, appears at the end of the third stanza. In the original, nonreligious version of the song by Kheytin-Weinstein, the mother says to the child, "Not another Yiddish word, not another Yiddish song, for you are no longer a Jew." Such a statement is clearly not permissible in the Hasidic world, so the Hasidic version consistently reads, "Not another Yiddish word, not another Yiddish song, but remember in your heart that you are a Jew!" Hasidim believe that one of the primary responsibilities of a mother is conveying to her children the value of maintaining Jewish identity even in the most difficult circumstances; by changing the song to conform to their convictions, the Hasidic women were able to render the song "kosher."[72]

The mother character in "Mesoyre lid" strives to communicate this same value to her daughter when she instructs Ester to "hold on tightly to tradition." When the young heroine expresses fear of Satan convincing her that "you can't do everything today like the grandmothers," she unwittingly encapsulates the paradoxical interaction of Hasidism with modernity, particularly as it relates to female singing. Many factors have conspired to create a generational chasm in the female song tradition. The establishment of Hasidic girls' schools in the second half of the twentieth century brought about the creation of a religiously didactic repertoire of songs intended to both teach girls about their role in the Hasidic community and provide them with entertainment approved by community leaders. These new songs comprise the repertoire of contemporary women and girls under the age of fifty, replacing the secular Yiddish theater, art, and folk songs that were sung in previous generations. A shift toward heightened insularity and religiosity that occurred in the mid-twentieth century rendered the old songs unacceptable and created an opportunity for the development of new traditions in an old language.

These new traditions are blossoming as the granddaughters of thirty years ago are becoming today's grandmothers and witnessing the proliferation of the songs of their youth. Certain songs created and sung by women have been growing in popularity, traveling across continents and between Hasidic groups. Those songs that appear in multiple booklets at summer camps, across communities tend to be of higher quality, having been filtered through the school and camp systems that generate dozens of songs every year, in every class. Because the dynamic repertoire is constantly developing, a richer, more refined body of songs is growing in these communities. One can already see the formation of a canon of Hasidic women's songs. As an example, the songs of Shifra Laven, author of "Mesoyre lid," have appeared on a recently produced CD from 2009, "Dos yidishe trer," performed by men and boys.[73] This relatively new tradition represents a renewed confirmation of the viability of Yiddish within the Hasidic lifestyle.

Notes

1. Excerpt from song by Shifra K. Laven, a Hasidic female school teacher in Tosh, Quebec. This and all subsequent translations into English are mine, unless otherwise indicated.
2. The majority of Hasidic immigrants arrived in America and other countries after the Holocaust. See, for example, Jerome Mintz, *Hasidic People: A Place in the New World* (Cambridge: Harvard University Press, 1992) and Israel Rubin, *Satmar: Two Generations of an Urban Island* (New York: Peter Lang, 1997).
3. Dvoyre Horowitz, interviewed by Ester-Basya Vaisman, March 2007. Following convention, the names of all informants have been changed for confidentiality.
4. The *Kol B'Isha* prohibition can be traced to the Babylonian Talmud, *Berachot* 24a, which states, "A woman's voice is *ervah* (an erotic stimulus), as it is written, 'For your voice is pleasing and your appearance attractive' (Song of Songs 2:14)." This line has been interpreted to mean that a woman's voice could lead a man to engage in impure thoughts and possibly actions, and thus it is prohibited to him; it is generally accepted that this prohibition applies only to a woman's singing voice, and not to her speaking voice. *Kol B'Isha* usually does not apply to a woman's immediate relatives, such as her husband, brother, father, and son, except when the man is praying or when the woman is menstruating, though in Hasidic circles there are restrictions even on family members.
5. The studies most relevant to this essay include Mark Kligman, "The Media and the Message: The Recorded Music of Brooklyn's Orthodox Jews," *Jewish Folklore and Ethnology Review* 16, no. 1 (1994): 9-11; Mark Kligman, "On the Creators and Consumers of Orthodox Popular Music in Brooklyn," *YIVO Annual of Jewish Social Science* 23 (1996): 259-93; and Velvel Pasternak, *Songs of the Chassidim: An Anthology* (New York: Bloch Publishing, 1970-1971). Two significant works on Lubavitch women's music do exist— Ellen Koskoff, *Music in Lubavitcher Life* (Chicago: University of Illinois Press, 2001) and

Ruth Rosenfelder, "Hidden Voices: Women's Music in London's Lubavitch and Satmar Hasidic Communities" (PhD diss., City University, 2003)—but my research concerns non-Lubavitch Hasidic women, as explained later. My work also differs significantly from Ruth Rosenfelder's in that she analyzes women's song only in London Hasidic communities, whereas I conducted research in the United States, Israel, and Belgium, as well.

6. My research excludes Lubavitch Hasidim, because this group differs significantly from the other Hasidic groups. An important aspect of Lubavitch philosophy is *kiruv* (outreach to nonreligious Jews). Because of outreach activities, Lubavitch Hasidim engage in much more contact with the world outside their community, and a much higher percentage of this community's members come from non-Hasidic families. As a result, Yiddish is not the primary language of Lubavitch Hasidim, and their music is much more heavily influenced by non-Hasidic sources.

7. Puppa is a Hungarian Hasidic group currently based primarily in Williamsburg, New York, with smaller communities in other locales in the United States, Europe, and Israel.

8. Esty Kahan, interviewed by Ester-Basya Vaisman, March 2007.

9. Suri Gold, interviewed by Ester-Basya Vaisman, April 2007.

10. The Tosh Hasidic dynasty traces its roots to Hungary. Today it is based in the town Kiryas Tosh, near Montreal in Canada.

11. Gold, 2007. The "Yerushalayim" song that she is referring to is a song with a new Yiddish text about the destruction of the temple, set to a melody that comes from Tisha B'Av liturgy; the original text is in biblical Hebrew.

12. In his article on the women of Williamsburg, George Kranzler writes, "The schools reenforce and deepen the zeal, religious fervor, and faith that the youngsters absorb in their homes and experience in the daily lifestyle of the community. . . . Girls follow a curriculum that emphasizes the inculcation of faith and the will to live up to the rigorous standards of the community. Character formation, moral and ethical conduct, and uncompromising adherence to religious laws and Hasidic customs are prime goals of this program." Kranzler, "The Women of Williamsburg: A Contemporary Hasidic Community in Brooklyn, New York," in *Ethnic Women: A Multiple Status Reality*, ed. V. Demos (Dix Hills, NY: General Hall, 1994), 69–81, 73.

13. Miriam Isaacs, "Creativity in Contemporary Hasidic Yiddish," in *Yiddish Language and Culture Then and Now—Proceedings of the Ninth Annual Symposium*, ed. L. J. Greenspoon (Omaha, NE: Creighton University Press, 1998), 165–88, 172–74.

14. Ayala Fader, *Mitzvah Girls: Bringing Up the Next Generation of Hasidic Jews in Brooklyn* (Princeton: Princeton University Press, 2009), 129.

15. Although the word *pshat* literally means "simple" and is used in contexts of Torah study to describe the apparent or intended meaning of a text, among contemporary Hasidic women the word has come to signify a *deeper* meaning, or the moral lesson of a song.

16. Satmar Hasidim trace their roots to Hungary and are considered to be one of the most insular Hasidic groups. The largest Satmar community today is in Williamsburg, New York. For more on Satmar Hasidim, see George Kranzler, *Hasidic Williamsburg: A Contemporary American Hasidic Community* (Northvale, NJ: Jason Aronson, 1995); Rubin, *Satmar*; and Solomon Poll, *The Hasidic Community of Williamsburg: A Study in the Sociology of Religion* (New York: Schocken, 1962).

17. Horowitz, 2007.

18. Bobov Hasidim originate from southern Poland. The biggest Bobov community today is in Boro Park, New York. For more on Bobov Hasidim, see Mark Kamen, *Growing Up Hasidic: Education and Socialization in the Bobover Hasidic Community* (New York: AMS Press, 1985) and Janet Belcove, "A Quest for Wholeness: The Hasidim of Boro Park" (PhD diss., Cornell University, 1989).

19. Rokhi Davidson, interviewed by Ester-Basya Vaisman, August 2005.

20. Yomtov Ehrlich, a Stoliner Hasid, was an extremely prolific singer and songwriter whose moralistic songs are still very popular among Hasidic women, despite the growing trendiness of pop-style musicians such as Michoel Schnitzler and Mordechai ben David.

21. Gold, 2007.

22. For a brief history of Jewish girls' education, see Tamar El-Or, *Educated and Ignorant: Ultraorthodox Jewish Women and Their World* (Boulder, CO: Lynne Rienner Publishers, 1994), 66–69.

23. Fader, *Mitzvah Girls*, 123.

24. Ibid., 122.

25. Ibid., 123.

26. Ibid., 119, 131.

27. El-Or, *Educated and Ignorant*, 69.

28. Gold, 2007.

29. The Ger Hasidic group was one of the largest Hasidic groups in Poland before the Holocaust. Today most Ger Hasidim reside in Jerusalem and Bnei Brak in Israel.

30. Khane Feldman, interviewed by Ester-Basya Vaisman, January 2005.

31. "Mayn shtetele belz" ("My Town Belz") is a song of the American Yiddish theater written by composer Alexander Olshanetsky (1892–1944) and lyricist Jacob Jacobs (1890–1977) for the 1932 play *Dos Lid fun Geto*. In a very nostalgic tone, the song describes the narrator's childhood in the town of Belz, where he played with other boys by the river. See Anna Shternshis's and Shayn Smulyan's essays in this book for different contemporary approaches to this song.

32. Khave Bernstein, interviewed by Ester-Basya Vaisman, November 2007.

33. Among the more insular Hasidic groups, it is very uncommon to find a radio in the home. Other groups are more lenient on the subject, and sometimes a radio is present because it comes as part of a stereo system that is used to play Hasidic tapes and CDs.

34. A Satmar family, interviewed by Ester-Basya Vaisman, August 2005, Williamsburg.

35. "A brivele der mamen" ("A Letter to Mother") is considered to be "the most famous Yiddish mother song.... [It is] about trans-Atlantic separation; it speaks from the viewpoint of a mother in Europe imploring her emigrant child to write home." Mark Slobin, *Tenement Songs: The Popular Music of the Jewish Immigrants* (Urbana: University of Illinois Press, 1996), 124. The song was written in 1908 by songwriter and singer Solomon Smulewitz (Sol Small) (1868–1943), who was born in Pinsk (Russia, now Belarus) and immigrated to the United States in 1889. He was one of the most prolific Yiddish composers at the turn of twentieth century and left behind songs and song lyrics on diverse subjects.

36. Gold, 2007.

37. James Loeffler notes that even by 1900, this song "had spread so far and wide in the Pale of Settlement as to be quickly folklorized and refashioned as [an] anonymous, orally transmitted song." See James Benjamin Loeffler, "'The Most Musical Nation': Jews, Culture and Nationalism in the Late Russian Empire" (PhD diss., Columbia University, 2006), 115. For more on this topic, see David Roskies, "Ideologies of the Yiddish Folk Song in the Old Country and the New," *Jewish Book Annual* 50 (1992): 143–66 and Roskies, *A Bridge of Longing: The Lost Art of Yiddish Storytelling* (Cambridge: Harvard University Press, 1995).

38. Davidson, 2005.

39. The song is about the importance of a Jewish education. The first stanza reads, "A fire burns on the heating stove, and the room is warm; a rabbi teaches small children the *alefbeys* [Hebrew alphabet]. Look, children, remember, dear ones, what you learn here; say it again and yet again: *komets alef: o.*"

40. Blumi Zilberstein, interviewed by Ester-Basya Vaisman, November 2004.

41. Gold, 2007.

42. Davidson, 2005.

43. Zilberstein, 2004.

44. Horowitz, 2007.

45. Fader, *Mitzvah Girls*, 121-25; Menachem Friedman, "Life Tradition and Book Tradition in the Development of ultra-Orthodox Judaism," in *Judaism Viewed from within and from Without*, ed. H. Goldberg (Albany: State University of New York Press, 1987), 235-56, 246. Friedman writes, "Among those elements desirous of reconstructing that which had been, [there was] a clear-cut tendency to see the society that was as having been composed of righteous people, a society in which daily life and the tradition of the book were in full harmony with each other." Fader describes how this trend is expressed among women in the Bobov Hasidic community of Boro Park. She notes that "although the women I worked with often drew on biblical narratives to comment on the contemporary world, the most nostalgia was inspired by the more recent past, prewar eastern Europe" (122). She depicts two events that involved "nostalgically remembering life in the *alte haym*": a Chinese auction with the theme "Once upon a *Shtetl*" and *alte haym* day at a girls' summer camp. The participants in these events, characteristically, imagine that the eastern European Hasidic women being imitated were at a higher religious level than the Hasidic women today. Thus, "the challenge for Hasidic women in contemporary Brooklyn is to return to the higher religiosity of their foremothers" (161). Fader's transliteration (*alte haym* rather than *alte heym*) corresponds to the Polish Yiddish pronunciation of the word by her informants, Bobov Hasidic women. The Bobov Hasidim originate from Poland and thus speak that dialect.

46. Haym Soloveitchik, "Rupture and Reconstruction: The Transformation of Contemporary Orthodoxy," *Tradition: The Journal of Orthodox Jewish Thought* 28, no. 4 (1994): 64-130; Friedman, "Life Tradition and Book Tradition," 235-56.

47. Friedman, "Life Tradition and Book Tradition," 240.

48. Ibid., 244-46.

49. Hasidic communities exist today in New York, Montreal, Jerusalem, Bnei Brak, Antwerp, London, Vienna, and other cities and towns.

50. "Sheyn vi di levone" ("Beautiful Like the Moon") and "Abi gezunt" ("As Long as You're Healthy") are songs from the Second Avenue Yiddish musical theater world in New York City, both extremely popular in the early mid-twentieth century and still sung today. Joseph Rumshinsky (1881-1956) and Abraham Ellstein (1907-1963) are the composers, and Chaim Tauber (1901-1972) and Molly Picon (1898-1992) the lyricists. The songs were published as individual sheet music and known outside the theater in the United States and eastern Europe. "Sheyn vi di levone" is a love song that exalts the beauty of the narrator's beloved, and "Abi gezunt" proclaims that in order to be happy, one does not need wealth or riches, only good health.

51. "Vu iz dos gesele" ("Where Is the Street") is a folksong first published in 1912 by Y. L. Cahan in his *Yidishe folkslider mit melodiyes* [Yiddish Folksongs with Melodies] (New York: International Library Publishing, 1912), with the lyrics, "Where is the street? Where is the house? Where is the girl that I love?"

52. Kranzler, "The Women of Williamsburg," 73.

53. See Isaacs, "Creativity in Contemporary Hasidic Yiddish," 169-70, and Ayala Fader, "Literacy, Bilingualism and Gender in a Hasidic Community," *Linguistics and Education* 12, no. 3 (2001): 261-83. Fader writes, "Especially in children's socialization contexts, secular texts are monitored and controlled by parents, rabbis, and teachers" (262).

54. Fader confirms, "Caregivers . . . fear that *goyishe mases* (gentile stories) will introduce representations of inappropriate females, which might include romantic relationships and/or express certain kinds of knowledge" (Fader, "Literacy, Bilingualism and Gender," 272).

55. "Yankele," by Mordechai Gebirtig (1877–1942), is a song in which a mother rocks her son to sleep, expressing the hope that he will become a Torah scholar and bridegroom, even if it is at the expense of her tears. Although there is a recently written song by K. Kroys (a Hasidic female teacher) with very similar lyrics, "Rivkes lid," "Yankele" is never sung in Hasidic communities. Mordechai Gebirtig, a poet, songwriter, and carpenter born in Cracow, Poland, was a member of the Jewish Social Democratic Party and was not a Hasid.

56. "Undzer nigndl" ("Our Tune") and "Fraytik af der nakht" ("Friday Night") are both songs by Nachum Sternheim (1879–194?), poet and songwriter born in Rzeszow, Poland. "Undzer nigndl" tells a story of a tune that was sung by all the family members—the mother, father, grandmother, and grandfather—with happiness, luck, and blessing when they were children, and it continues to resound to this day. "Fraytik af der nakht" relates the narrator's memories of a typical Sabbath in his childhood, when the father sang *zmires* with his eight children and tested his son on his knowledge of *Gemora*, while the grandmother read from the *Tsene urene*, a book of Yiddish stories from the Torah for women. Despite their religious themes and content, Sternheim's songs would not be accepted in contemporary Hasidic communities, because although the author grew up in a Hasidic family, he later became a committed Zionist who often spoke and wrote disparagingly of the anti-Zionist Hasidim.

57. Ayala Fader's findings confirm this observation: "Nonreligious texts ... [are] thought to have the potential to corrupt or elevate a person ... [and] Hasidic ideologies of literacy emphasize the importance of the outlook of authors ... rather than the language of the text" (Fader, "Literacy, Bilingualism and Gender," 262, 279).

58. Fader has found in her research that "Hasidic women caregivers rarely invoked the complex range of Jewish difference that constitutes Judaism. ... Rather, they drew on the 'black-and-white' distinction between Jews and Gentiles, which is inherently less problematic to explain to children." Ayala Fader, "Learning Faith: Language Socialization in a Hasidic Community," *Language in Society* 35, no. 2 (2006): 207–29, 212.

59. Gold, 2007.

60. Fader, "Literacy, Bilingualism and Gender," 278.

61. Bryna Bogoch, "Gender, Literacy, and Religiosity: Dimensions of Yiddish Education in Israeli Government-Supported Schools," *International Journal of the Sociology of Language* 138 (1999): 123–60, 136.

62. *Moshav leitzim*, a concept found in *Thilim* (Psalms) 1:1 has been interpreted to signify an unproductive activity, one not related to Torah learning or performing commandments. Among many other sources, *Shulchan Aruch Hilchos Shabbos* 307:16 states that non-Jewish literature is prohibited under *moshav leitzim*.

63. B. C. Glaberson, *Educating Our Daughters, Why?: Extraordinary Interviews with Women Educators* (Jerusalem: Feldheim Publishers, 2006), 147.

64. Lewis Glinert, personal communication, December 2007.

65. "Mayn yidishe mame" ("My Jewish Mother") was written by Jack Yellen (1892–1991) in 1925 in the United States. An instant hit popularized by Sophie Tucker, the song describes a mother as a valuable gift from God and declares the importance of appreciating one's mother for her unconditional love.

66. "Yomele yomele" is a folksong from eastern Europe in which a mother tries to find out what it is her daughter wants, eventually learning that it is a husband.

67. "Papirosn" ("Cigarettes") was written by the actor Herman Yablokoff (1903–1981) in Kovno (Kaunas), Lithuania after World War I. It was popularized and subsequently folklorized in America when Yablokoff moved to New York and played the song on his radio show. The song is the lament of a poor orphan who is forced to sell cigarettes in the rain to avoid dying of hunger. See Anna Shternshis's essay in this book for a reading of this song in Soviet and post-Soviet culture.

68. Leye Levinson, interviewed by Ester-Basya Vaisman, April 2007.

69. "Oy khanike" was first published in 1912 in a collection of the Society for Jewish Folk Music in St. Petersburg. See Loeffler, "The Most Musical Nation," 235. The first stanza reads, "Chanukah, oh Chanukah, a beautiful holiday; a happy, joyous one, there is no other like it. Every night we play dreidel; we eat boiling hot latkes. Faster, children, light the Chanukah candles! Say *al hanisim* [a traditional Chanukah prayer], thank God for the miracles, and come quickly to dance in a circle."

70. Gold, 2007.

71. Miriam Isaacs's research yielded an analogous instance: "The most notable exception to the rule of avoiding secular and especially Jewish secular texts was the use of a poem by the Israeli poet, Avrom Sutskever, in a Hasidic girls' school in a class on the Yiddish language, and the Holocaust in particular. Notably, the poet's name was not mentioned but a written copy of the poem with questions and notes on meanings of words was included." Isaacs, "Creativity in Contemporary Hasidic Yiddish," 170. The lack of author attribution is not surprising—unless the author was a rebbe or another important spiritual or religious figure, a name is almost never associated with songs or poems used in school and camp.

72. It was impossible to determine who exactly authored the revisions to the lyrics, as authorship is very rarely attributed in the Hasidic communities for women's songs. However, all versions of the song that I found were consistent in incorporating these changes. The altered song was probably spread both within and throughout Hasidic communities via photocopied lyric sheets distributed in summer camps.

73. In recent years, it has become increasingly common to find recordings of songs written by Hasidic female authors performed by men and boys. The primary intended audience for these edifying recordings is women and children, though men also listen to them occasionally. Notably, female authors are inclined to use only their first initial and last name in liner notes, purposefully making it difficult to determine the gender of the author.

THE SOCALLED PAST

Sampling Yiddish in Hip-Hop

SHAYN E. SMULYAN

"You know what I'm saying. It's like they put it there like eighty years ago so that we could use it now." Commenting on a short instrumental riff from an old Yiddish record, Montreal-based musician SoCalled[1] begins an interview as such. He continues,

> I found this album because I was looking for samples to make beats, because I make hip hop stuff for rappers. So, I was looking for sounds to sample, and I would just buy all the crap I could find, whatever in the garbage, in Salvation Armies, in people's basements, in garage sales kind of stuff. . . . So, I found all that, and it's a treasure. But, I found it because I was looking for samples, things to sample, little noises that I could put into my magic machine and chop up with other sounds from other sources.[2]

This brief comment epitomizes SoCalled's compositional approach of recombining discarded sounds in new forms. To the average listener of traditional Yiddish music, sampling sounds off of eighty-year-old records and mixing them with other samples and electronic beats might seem novel, possibly even gimmicky, but to anyone familiar with hip-hop, this approach is a standard method of music making. Sampling short musical phrases from old recordings and using them to make beats is a well-established compositional technique of hip-hop. Artists and fans consider this kind of sampling foundational to the genre's history and development, and it signifies an unquestionably authentic hip-hop practice, in spite of its recent decline due to the threat of copyright infringement suits and expensive licensing fees.[3] As such, SoCalled's use of samples and his emphasis on that aspect of his music position him in the mainstream of authenticated hip-hop practice even if the most notable and noted sources for his samples—Yiddish records from the first half of the twentieth century—differ from those of most hip-hop producers with respect to the age and cultural origins of the material. In SoCalled's words, "Hip-hop is the overarching umbrella," although he incorporates Yiddish musical influences into his work.[4]

A thirty-something musician, visual artist, and performing magician, So-Called lives in Montreal and regularly tours Europe, North America, and even, recently, China, playing his Yiddish-infused hip-hop. Born in Ottawa and raised just north of the city in the small town of Chelsea, Quebec, SoCalled became interested in hip-hop as a teenager, and through early experimentation making beats, he found old, discarded Yiddish records and heard in them a storehouse of break beats and other musical samples to weave into his unique brand of hip-hop songs. In the intervening years, he has collaborated with major figures in the hip-hop, funk, and klezmer/Yiddish music scenes, most notably klezmer clarinetist David Krakauer and funk trombonist Fred Wesley. SoCalled has gained a sizable mainstream following in Europe, particularly in France, whereas his North American audiences occupy more of a niche market, often heavily drawing from Jewish communities.[5] SoCalled signed with the Jewish not-for-profit record label JDUB in 2005, and they have since released two of his albums. For its part, JDUB promotes a roster of young, hip musicians who make "music that is Jewish as defined by the artists creating it."[6] SoCalled remains one of their headliners, even though he has expressed ambivalence about the mainly Jewish audience this affords him within the United States and Canada.[7]

Although SoCalled's primary musical identities come from hip-hop, as producer, songwriter, and DJ,[8] elements of his music also work to create hip-hop that signifies some level of Jewishness to his mostly Jewish North American audiences[9]: the sampled Yiddish musical material; other musical references to klezmer (melodies, rhythms, modes, instrumentation); incorporation of Yiddish words, phrases, or whole lyrics; album and song titles that refer to Jewish themes[10]; his collaboration with Yiddish singers and klezmer musicians; his affiliation with JDUB records; and his personal narrative as an artist finding his own musical and cultural roots. Likewise, the popular press and Jewish music communities in North America tend to portray SoCalled as primarily a maker of Jewish music breathing new life into Yiddish using hip-hop to add some novel color or modernized style.[11] These representations, however, disregard not only how SoCalled understands his music and his artistic persona but also the structure and history of hip-hop sampling. Within this discrepancy between production and reception—the identity of the artist and the identification of the audience—lies fertile ground for exploring SoCalled's use of Yiddish in his hip-hop music making.

Although it might be tempting to analyze SoCalled's music and his musical persona as a simple dichotomy, divvying up the Yiddish elements on one side and the hip-hop elements on the other and positioning them in tension or in tandem, SoCalled's Yiddish-infused hip-hop and his own discourse about his music force us beyond such a dualistic and compartmentalized reading.[12] Hip-hop and Yiddish elements are certainly both at play in SoCalled's music, but they function very differently. Hip-hop is the overarching structural, social, and aesthetic framework, into which Yiddish material is artfully inserted according to the aesthetic, technical, and social conventions of hip-hop. Both have something to say, but one could say that Yiddish speaks on hip-hop's terms or, conversely, that the hip-hop structure serves as a vehicle for the Yiddish voice. I argue that not only is SoCalled's hip-hop an expressive medium for Yiddish sounds, language, and voices, but it also, through the mechanism of sampling, brings a Yiddish past into the present in ways consistent with normative hip-hop practice. Through this specific form of evocation, SoCalled's music is simultaneously nostalgic and romantic while also intentionally critical of nostalgia and romanticization. Further, SoCalled's hip-hop serves as a tool to interpret, critique, and make meaning of both the nostalgicized Yiddish past and even offers a critical take on the contemporary use of Yiddish (his and others') as it relates to this imagined past.

In this essay I intend to explore these ideas about hip-hop and the Yiddish past by means of an ethnographically informed, interpretive reading of two of SoCalled's recent compositions from his 2007 album *Ghettoblaster*. I will pay particular attention to the way that musical samples[13] mediate between two simultaneous, but not necessarily competing, notions of authenticity: hip-hop and Yiddish. Following musicologists Joanna Demers and Abigail Wood, I suggest that in SoCalled's hip-hop, the sampled musical material, the sensibilities of its original historical period, and the meanings of that period translated into the present day by the listener are all legible in the final composition and that composition serves as a critical commentary on them. It should be noted that the ethnographic present for this essay is 2007 at the time of *Ghettoblaster*'s release. SoCalled's musical goals and composition style have evolved and changed since then and in all likelihood will continue to develop well into the future.[14]

My foray into SoCalled's work is part of a larger, more traditionally ethnographic, project on the strategies and techniques of contemporary musicians working with (or in) the Yiddish language. Therefore I approach this material with particular attention to the ways that Yiddish hip-hop intersects with these broader strategies and techniques that enable Yiddish to be performed for audiences that do not understand the language. These strategies include, but are not limited to, translation, oral or textual interpretation, musical virtuosity, dance, gesture, costumes, props, and visual performance. SoCalled employs a variety of these techniques in his performance career—through song choices, album packaging and promotional materials, performance gestures and between-song patter, and even the occasional magic trick in the middle of a set. My focus here, however, represents a further strategy: the use of old Yiddish samples within hip-hop, a musical genre that so forcefully calls to mind the modern and contemporary with its technologically mediated sounds. Framing SoCalled's contributions to contemporary Yiddish music in this light allows the application of some of the same ideas to the work of artists creatively using Yiddish musical or textual elements within other overtly modern genres such as punk, rock, jazz, and reggae, even without the direct technological mediation of sampling.[15] In addition to the relevance to the world of Yiddish and even Jewish music more broadly, an affinity also exists between Yiddish hip-hop and other global hip-hops, which use an explicitly African American expressive form to perform, invoke, and critique non-African American identities and their own pasts.[16]

By making prolific use of samples as the foundation of his songs, SoCalled works firmly within the boundaries of authentic hip-hop practice as defined by artists, fans, and scholars of the genre. Moreover, SoCalled's musical career evidences other elements of hip-hop authenticity as well: in compositional structure and use of certain musical idioms or conventions of hip-hop,[17] in an attitude of musical expansiveness, in affinity networks of other hip-hop artists, and in invoking the past musically to critically comment on the present. According to Schloss, hip-hop authenticity depends not on the race or ethnicity of the artist but on certain aesthetic conventions, social processes, and an expressive purism focused on getting "the right sound."[18] SoCalled demonstrates this privileging of "the sound" through the sheer volume and diversity of his sampling. He casts a broad musical net to achieve the right sound—even if that means using funk, Latin, or Asian samples as well as Yiddish—and often points this out when pigeonholed by others as a Yiddish or klezmer musician.[19] In a recent interview, he explained, "I'm pretty democratic about sampling. I love to take from high culture, low culture. I love to take from any era, any instruments."[20] "Digging in the crates" to find the next fresh or innovative sound remains a primary creative and symbolic activity among hip-hop producers, an activity in which SoCalled clearly partakes. Furthermore, SoCalled's collaboration with a diverse array of other musicians, including DJs and rappers, demonstrates the kind of musical sociality that remains integral to the culture of hip-hop production.[21] When asked about his relationships with other hip-hop artists, he replied, "I think they see me as a bit of a freak, but they also love it ... even at the beginning when I started making beats, using Jewish sounds, using Yiddish samples, and I would just play it for rappers and they would 'get it' and start rapping. So, that works pretty well. And DJs [also 'get it']. I'm pals with a lot of hip hop-y people and they think what I do is cool. It's taking it somewhere."[22]

In spite of his frequent billing as a "Yiddish rapper" in the popular press[23] and among some members of the Yiddish music community, SoCalled rarely raps in Yiddish and has never written an original rap in Yiddish. Although he does not "speak" Yiddish in a fluent, vernacular sense, SoCalled does engage with it constantly. He understands the Yiddish lyrics that he sings, and on occasion pulls out a Yiddish/English dictionary for reference.[24] By rapping almost entirely in English and not in Yiddish, SoCalled demonstrates his belief that rapping should properly come from a place as authentic to self-experience as possible.[25] Separate from his hip-hop career, as Josh Dolgin rather than SoCalled, he performs as a singer and interpreter of Yiddish songs with various klezmer bands. However, he draws a distinction between Yiddish singing and rapping: "And frankly, the more I perform, the more I want to perform in a language I understand. So, in a way I sing in Yiddish because I couldn't help it, that's what got me into making music, and now I'm learning more and more Yiddish. And I do, I rap a song in Yiddish, and I think it's a little silly to do that. Because I do not speak Yiddish, and I think rap should be in a language that you actually speak."[26]

The one song that he does rap in Yiddish, breaking his own rule, is his rendition of the popular Yiddish theater song "Ikh bin a border bay mayn vayb" ("I'm a Boarder at My Wife's"). In it, he raps the Yiddish lyrics to the verses and sings the title line to the chorus with its original melody. He has indicated that his initial performance and subsequent development of this piece (which he has performed for several years but only recently released on a studio recording) was a capitulation to the audience expectations that he rap in Yiddish.[27] Although SoCalled admits that this rap treatment of "Ikh bin a border bay mayn vayb" is at one level a gimmick or novelty, his arrangement, composition, and production of it on the recording reveals a level of self-reflexive commentary on this very gimmick.

"Ikh bin a border bay mayn vayb" opens with a thirty-second outtake exchange from the recording studio between SoCalled, the recording engineer, and nonagenarian Jewish lounge pianist Irving Fields, famous for his Jewish-inflected Latin jazz numbers of the 1940s and 1950s, including "Bagels and Bongos" and "Miami Beach Rhumba." SoCalled asks the engineer for a time check, and it becomes apparent that Fields thought they had been rehearsing when in fact the recording session was already underway: "I thought this is rehearsal. I did that once with RCA/Victor. I said 'when the hell are we doing the session?' He says 'it's over.' That's good, alright." The inclusion of Fields's voice with its New York Jewish accent and references to his long musical career invokes an older Yiddish musical authenticity, and the entire use of the spoken "outtake" makes the act and site of musical production explicit, an established aesthetic convention of contemporary hip-hop.

The "music proper" begins with a funk bass line and a sample of one bar of klezmer drummer Elaine Hoffman-Watts's unmistakable *freylekh*[28] beat, which elides into electronic drum beats. SoCalled raps the verses in Yiddish and sings the title/chorus line in the original 1920s melody, which is then answered by a sample of a female voice singing in English, "Young man, single man." A short melodic motive shared between a trumpet and a synthesizer also echoes the

original theatrical arrangement from which SoCalled borrows, though over
a complex layering of electronic and vocal beats, sparse electric guitar, whis-
tling, and chords on the synthesizer. Approximately halfway through the piece,
after the second chorus section, SoCalled breaks into a wholly different kind
of rap, not from the original theater tune's lyrics but of his own composition,
with the notable addition of sampled Hasidic-style singing on the vocables
"ya-ba-bay-bay-bay."

> *Eyn, tsvey, dray, fir* [one, two, three, four]
> *Eyn*—drop your feet, clap, *patsh* [clap] your hands, bring that
> *Tsvey*—to the left, *patsh*, know the tune, sing that
> *Dray*—gonna ya-ba-ba-ba-ba, stop that
> *Fir*—to the right, snap, careful gonna drop that
> Beat.

In contrast to the rapped lyrics of the original tune in their English-inflected
Yiddish, this brief section uses a Yiddish-inflected English, with Yiddish elements likely to be understood by those with even a very cursory familiarity
with the language.[29] The counting and the calls to bodily movement bring an
element of liveness (the live performance context) into the studio recording,
using long-standing conventions of hip-hop meant to reference and encourage dancing on the part of the listeners. The "ya-ba-ba-ba-ba" in the third line
mirrors the vocables of the sampled Hasidic-style singing in the background
and presents an innovative juxtaposition of hip-hop and Jewish elements, both
musical and linguistic. The rhythm of the rapping mirrors the structure of the
freylekh beat, with the stressed beats in each line creating a 3+3+2 structure: *eyn*,
clap, bring; *tsvey*, *patsh*, sing; etc.

"Ikh bin a border bay mayn vayb" ends with a pointed parallelism and reference back to its beginning. SoCalled announces, "And I'm out" proceeding to
another lengthy "outtake" by Irving Fields layered over the song's now persistent beats making the circumstances of the song's studio production apparent
once again. "Now turn over the fucking tape. Not you, you degenerates. Turn
over the tape. . . . Let's start from the beginning. Okay, start from the beginning
on the back side. You understand, shmuck?" Field's voice is calm and conversational, in contrast to the language he is using, which allows listeners to ponder
the circumstances that elicited such a reaction from Fields. Was he relating
another story from his earlier years recording for RCA/Victor? Playing a joke
on SoCalled and the engineer? Perhaps even performing a scripted speech in
the style of an outtake?[30] Whatever the previous context of Field's speech, its
place in the final composition frames the musical piece with references to contemporary hip-hop practice, which often utilizes seemingly unrelated exegetic
speech samples in addition to studio outtakes. It also utilizes Field's own au-

thenticating history as a seasoned musician and a voice of the Yiddish musical past, and it forces the listener to attend to one of the sites of the song's technological production—the recording studio.

The most obvious and significant Yiddish samples in "Ikh bin a border bay mayn vayb" are the previously mentioned klezmer drum beat played by Hoffman-Watts and the Hasidic-style singing. These, along with the short repeated melodic motive—the hook from the original theater tune—manage to reference three major domains of early twentieth-century Yiddish music making: instrumental dance music (known today as klezmer) played at weddings and other celebrations; the popular songs of the Yiddish theater; and music associated with religious practice, in this case paraliturgical vocable tunes known as *nigunim*. As with the relationship between mainstream hip-hop and 1970s soul music, SoCalled's use of samples and musical quotations in "Ikh bin a border bay mayn vayb" imports the sensibilities of that earlier era. But, as a self-consciously performed "gimmick" (rapping the Yiddish lyrics of an already supposedly frivolous pop tune), he only implies the kind of critical reflection on those sensibilities more explicit elsewhere in his repertoire. For instance, on the track "(Alt. Shul) Kale Bazetsn" he uses the first line of "Ikh bin a border bay mayn vayb," "Ikh bin shoyn vider singl, punkt 'zoy vi a yingl" (I'm single again, just like a boy), in a much more explicitly interpretive and critical context. The line ends a rap that criticizes the institution and ritual of marriage as outdated and heteronormative.[31]

The actual Yiddish linguistic content of "Ikh bin a border bay mayn vayb" remains largely irrelevant to SoCalled's hip-hop treatment of it, except as it relates to the repeated line "young man, single man."[32] The original "Ikh bin a border bay mayn vayb" is a comic number by Yiddish theater composer Rubin Doctor and famously performed and recorded by Aaron Lebedeff. The song is sung from the first-person perspective of a man whose wife, upon their separation, convinces him to live with her as a boarder. It unmistakably references the boarder-landlady relationship particular to the immigrant era, a theme addressed in various aspects of this popular culture. The language of the song is an idiomatic theatrical Yiddish with obvious English borrowings, like "boarder" and "moving." None of this appears especially evident to the monolingual Anglophone audience from SoCalled's arrangement. The "young man, single man" phrase stands out as a translation of or hint at the original lyrics, and it is ambiguous enough that the listener might interpret it in any number of ways unrelated to the Yiddish context of the song.

However, as Jeffery Shandler's work attests, the meanings conveyed by Yiddish in what he calls the "postvernacular mode" go far beyond the literal meanings of any given text. In any utterance or instance of postvernacular speech, the language's aesthetic or cultural significations become more vital than its mimetic or linguistic significations; therefore, "every utterance is enveloped in a performative aura, freighted with significance as a speech act quite apart from the meaning of whatever words are spoken."[33] Indirectly, musical sounds—in this case the characteristic timbres, modes, vocables, and ornaments of traditional Yiddish music—may signify the same array of meta-meanings as the postvernacular performed language. Therefore, both the lyrics in SoCalled's compositions and his use of samples of Yiddish and klezmer recordings represent prime examples of postvernacular performance. They enable another layer of meaning in which the Yiddish (words or music) convey a sense of Jewishness—particularly a prewar, seemingly authentic Jewishness—without detracting from the authenticity of hip-hop practice at the level of compositional process.

The ability of musical samples to signify distant places and times and bring them into the present is the means by which hip-hop compositional practice meets Yiddish musical and cultural material, affirming both. Samples from Yiddish songs, instrumental klezmer music, cantorial pieces, and other Jewish musical references in SoCalled's work function to signify Jewishness in a vague, general sense to a listener unfamiliar with the references, just as mainstream American hip-hop samples register simply as black or African American to listeners unfamiliar with the nuances of funk, Motown, or older hip-hop. But for the in-group listener, and for SoCalled himself, the samples from Yiddish songs and other Jewish sonic material signify particular Jewish places, times, and sentiments—real or imagined—with a heightened importance of Ashkenazi cultural history. They invoke an accumulated sensibility of both real and imagined pasts when Yiddish culture thrived, when in SoCalled's words, "People lived culture."[34] Through SoCalled's imagining and perhaps intentional oversimplification of these pasts, his music makes feelings of cultural (linguistic, musical, historical) loss and disjuncture emotionally resonant and present for his listeners and himself, whether or not they fully understand or have experienced firsthand the past he evokes.

SoCalled's use of samples acts as sonic signifiers of a culturally significant or idealized past and of his particular relationship with Yiddish music. He considers Yiddish part of his cultural heritage and feels a sense of loss that the language and the music no longer exist in many everyday, unselfconscious, "lived" contexts.[35] By bringing Yiddish into hip-hop he reintroduces the language and its culture into these everyday, vernacular contexts using a common hip-hop practice of bringing the past into the present through samples. As Joanna Demers has shown, much of normative African American hip-hop engages in a similar process of signification. For example, hip-hop samples taken from blaxploitation film music self-consciously reference and reinterpret music of the 1970s, a period with heightened cultural and political significance for African American culture.[36] Hip-hop that references and samples from popular music and films of the 1970s invokes the sensibility of that era and simultaneously criticizes it, thereby also bringing the past into the present.[37]

SoCalled's approach to using Yiddish samples is not, therefore, something unique he developed in order to make a Yiddish hip-hop hybrid but, rather, the normative practice for all sample-based hip-hop. As with Demers's examples, SoCalled's music references and engages with an era of heightened cultural and political significance: Jewish North America from the turn of the twentieth century through the early 1940s, when Jewish immigrants created popular Jewish culture in the United States particularly and expanded it with the second generation, much of it in Yiddish. This immigrant era links the legacy of Yiddish expressive culture back to Europe, where Yiddish cultural life began and continued during this period. SoCalled draws musical inspiration, samples, and lyrical themes from this period when Yiddish theater and music publishing industries thrived, providing a stage for performing artists such as Aaron Lebedeff and Moishe Oysher.[38]

Not coincidentally for the purpose of sampling, sound recording technology became widely available at that point as well. Radios and phonographs soared in popularity and the record companies mined all kinds of "ethnic" talent to create records for the burgeoning market of immigrant consumers.[39] In turn, the founders of the klezmer revival of the 1970s and 1980s used those early recordings of Jewish instrumental tunes as models to learn repertory, technique, and musical style.[40] Between, for example, synagogue music popularized by Oysher, the songs of Lebedeff's Yiddish stage, and the instrumental dance music repertory of the klezmorim, Jewish music from the early part of the twentieth century makes a wide breadth of material and meanings available for referencing, appropriation, and interpretation through contemporary musical sampling.

The samples (Yiddish and non-Yiddish alike) that SoCalled uses come from both old records and live sounds that he collects on a portable recorder.

> That's the miracle of this type of music making. 'Cause you get the real sound. I could play that [with acoustic instruments]. ... I could also get an orchestra to play it, but that's not the point. I could also write something else ... and that's cool, and I do that too, but the whole point of it is that you find these sounds and when you hear them you can hear the context, you hear where it was recorded, it has so much, it comes from a place, it's not just a melody, it's real, what is it, it's magic. And to mix those magic moments together you create something new out of that, but it has all these echoes of the past in it.[41]

This quote, then, reveals at least some of the motivation behind SoCalled's use of samples in his process of making music, akin to the audible echoes of the past invoked in hip-hop practice generally. In SoCalled's music, "the past" that is echoed and interpreted through samples includes the immigrant era of early twentieth-century Jewish North America in which the sampled recordings were produced and, by extension, the European Jewish homelands nostalgically referenced and invoked by those recordings. This is a period with continuing significance for contemporary Yiddish culture, just as the 1970s audible in normative African American hip-hop sampling continues to bear significance for contemporary African American cultural production.

Another example of Yiddish hip-hop commenting on and interpreting the past can be found in *HipHopKhasene*, a concept album themed around traditional Jewish wedding rituals that SoCalled made in collaboration with violinist, composer, and DJ Sophie Solomon. Subtly mocking while simultaneously embracing nostalgia, it critiques the relevance of traditional wedding rituals while appropriating pieces of those very rituals. Abigail Wood emphasizes the ability of the hip-hop in *HipHopKhasene* to comment on contemporary Yiddish culture, particularly the culture of Yiddish music revivalists.[42] The compositional strategy of importing sensibilities and meanings from past eras suggests that Yiddish and hip-hop authenticities do not conflict or compete in SoCalled's music. The former is used in the service of the latter, and they occupy separate but intersecting domains of *content* (the Yiddish musical elements), on the one hand, and *process* (the hip-hop compositional techniques), on the other.

As Wood has noted, the ability for critique, parody, and deconstruction only flows in one direction—from hip-hop to Yiddish, and not the other way around.[43] Why is it that hip-hop can comment on Yiddish culture, but Yiddish (or any of the other musical and cultural elements that are combined with hip-hop around the world) conversely cannot seem to function as a commentary on hip-hop culture? I believe this apparent asymmetry is a function of the process/content split. In addition to being a culture, a music genre, and a movement, hip-hop can be understood as a compositional process. This process, through the use of samples, allows musical content from any cultural or historical source to be brought into the present and interpreted. The overarching framework (hip-hop) can more readily be used to comment on the pieces slotted within it (sampled Yiddish material) than those pieces can comment on the framework.

Because hip-hop has the capacity, through the fundamental process of sampling, to incorporate any number of musical and cultural sources while still adhering to the social and musical norms of authentic hip-hop, SoCalled's work with Yiddish is akin to any other non–African American hip-hop. This is not to say that Yiddish (or any other non-black American) content cannot expand the bounds of hip-hop culture at large by extending its pool of sonic resources or the cultures and eras it engages with, but within any given song the direction of interpretation or critique flows from hip-hop to Yiddish. This kind of critique, which invokes the past into the present and demonstrates an ambivalent nostalgia, will be more clearly illustrated in the reading of a second of SoCalled's songs, "(Rock the) Belz."

"(Rock the) Belz" provides a contrastive example to "Ikh bin a border bay mayn vayb," also from the same album. The title is a reference to and pun on "Rock the Bells," the iconic 1985 rap single by LL Cool J, or the annual hip-hop festival of the same name. This kind of clever display of in-group knowledge is another way SoCalled performs hip-hop authenticity, yet it is also an interpretation of "Mayn shtetele Belz." Like "Ikh bin a border bay mayn vayb," this piece also presents a version of a classic Yiddish American popular song with its hip-hop arrangement providing both contemporary relevance and a self-reflexive critique. In this case, the main theme is very common to contemporary uses of Yiddish culture: nostalgia, with all its imprecision, ambiguity, and sentiment.[44] As with the Irving Field's sampled speech in "Ikh bin a border bay mayn vayb," "(Rock the) Belz" brings in the literal voice of authenticity in the form of an older, audibly Jewish, male, Theodore Bikel, who sings both the Yiddish lyrics to "Mayn shtetele Belz" and speaks a translation and commentary on the song. The track opens with Bikel's speaking voice—very deep and audibly accented[45]—giving a highly poetic and idealistic account of why he sings "Jewish songs," his phrases punctuated here and there by an out-of-context shout or laugh mixed in by SoCalled. Bikel sings the verse and chorus to "Mayn shtetele Belz" with their original melodies in his slightly theatrical vocal style (recognizable from his many appearances as Tevye in *Fiddler on the Roof*), and SoCalled introduces electronic beats and sampled shouts right before Bikel comes in with the chorus.

Even more so than "Ikh bin a border bay mayn vayb," "(Rock the) Belz" invokes a hip-hop authenticity at the level of compositional process and musical sociality, particularly through the presence of two other voices on the track besides Bikel's, those of SoCalled rapping in English and Sans Pression, a Congolese-Canadian musician from Montreal, rapping in French. The sonic presence of the French rapping in combination with the English section affirms SoCalled's emphasis on the diversity of his neighborhood community and music scene in Montreal, and the inclusion of languages other than Yiddish reflects his belief that hip-hop serves as a vehicle to communicate universally, not just to one's own ethnic or racial group.[46] French rapping juxtaposed with Yiddish samples may also be heard as evoking the history of tensions between French Canadian and Jewish communities in Montreal, yet another layer of the Jewish, in this case Canadian, past of the early twentieth century.

Although "(Rock the) Belz" communicates to a broader audience by incorporating languages other than Yiddish, it also reflects on SoCalled's own explicit expression of self. His English rap speaks to his personal history and thereby adds a layer of commentary to the nostalgia for the original "Mayn shtetele Belz" as put forth by Bikel's voice in the piece. SoCalled nostalgically recounts scenes from his small-town Canadian childhood, while Bikel sings and speaks of nostalgia for a vanished east European Jewish town. SoCalled raps,

Yeah, everybody's talking about the good old days.
Every Friday night, we're stayin' up too late
Can't get a ride from mom so you make the whole crew wait
Bonfire, pool party, pd days, and spring break
Runnin' through the forest, jumpin' in the lake
We were spoiled, upper middle-class, livin' a life of ease
Worse case scenario, yo, we're skinnin' our knees
I think today if I could I would run back
But it's never the same when you try to come back.

And Bikel's commentary follows:

> Some of the songs are songs of nostalgia, for a world that existed, for a world
> that no longer is accessible, or no longer even is on the map anymore. Belz is a
> little town, *shtetl* like they used to call, and the person [the song's "I"] recalls the
> days that he spent there as a boy and he remembers going to the pond with the
> other boys, throwing stones into the pond. But now the roof is leaky, there are
> no panes in the window, and everything seems gone, but what is still there is
> the memory.

The dense and complexly layered texture of the piece brings the Yiddish past
into the present more directly than does "Ikh bin a border bay mayn vayb."
Similarly, the hip-hop production and arrangement offers commentary on
the themes of the original song. The vast differences between the two sites of
nostalgia—middle-class Canada and the vanished east European *shtetl*—are audible in the sonic differences between Bikel's singing and SoCalled's rapping.
They express a self-reflexive ambivalence toward the whole sensibility of nostalgia, which in turn may be read as a metacommentary on the larger project
of working with old Yiddish sound materials in the first place. "It's never the
same when you try to come back" applies equally to the original song's protagonist pining for the *shtetl* of his youth, SoCalled's invoking of Yiddish American
culture of the early twentieth century, and his own small-town Canadian childhood. Likewise, Sans Pression's rapping in French touches on the same themes
of ambivalent nostalgia and memories of one's personal and cultural history,
resisting the idea that the past is an idealized "good old days."[47]

He talks about the ravages of genocide, poverty, and AIDS in his native
Congo but asserts that he cannot forget where he comes from. SoCalled's nostalgia for his privileged youth stands in contrast to the pining for the now an-
nihilated *shtetl* of Belz and the stark conditions that Sans Pression describes
in the Congo. His claim of "worse case scenario, yo, we're skinnin' our knees"
in juxtaposition with the "Belz" lyrics and the French rap may be read as an
ironic commentary on the process of romanticizing the past as the "good old
days." It may also stand as an ambivalent self-critique of his use of old Yiddish

songs that do just that kind of romanticizing from the comfort of his privileged, middle-class position. By extension, SoCalled critiques not only his own penchant for nostalgia but also the ease with which assimilated North American Jews as a whole tend toward a romanticization of their individual and collective pasts.[48] This simultaneous utilization of the past in the form of sampled sounds and the resistance to the past in the form of oversimplified "good old days" is a theme that runs throughout the *Ghettoblaster* album. For instance, the song titled "These Are the Good Old Days" illustrates the absurd and almost bitter side of nostalgia by applying it to the hyperconsumerist, hypertechnological present day.

The two songs that I have discussed at length from that album stand at extremes ends of the spectrum when it comes to the literal significance of Yiddish within them. For the average non–Yiddish-speaking listener, the Yiddish lyrics in SoCalled's "Ikh bin a border bay mayn vayb" have almost no bearing on the meaning of the song as a whole. Like the original 1920s version, it could be heard as simply a fun, catchy, and dance-oriented piece of music. However, "(Rock the) Belz," with its English and French commentary and translation, conveys the sentiment and themes of the Yiddish lyrics with a slower, more introspective musical accompaniment. Other songs on *Ghettoblaster* fall somewhere in between, with different musical and textual techniques to explicate the Yiddish text or not.[49]

SoCalled's relationship with Yiddish as a language remains complicated, ambivalent, and continually evolving. On the one hand, he acknowledges that part of his inspiration to make music all together comes from Yiddish music, and particularly songs with Yiddish lyrics. On the other hand, he feels that singing in Yiddish would be too insular and culturally inward looking, as he wants his music to reach broad audiences.[50] Yet judging from his expressed view that we are all living in a state of cultural loss and displacement, when he says, "I think rap should be in a language that you actually speak," "actually speak[ing]" suggests not only a literal mastery of the language, but also "living in" a language or having full experiences in the culture from which that language emerges, something that SoCalled feels he does not do, no matter how much he engages with Yiddish texts and Yiddish records.[51] His ambivalence toward using or claiming Yiddish is also a product of his belief that hip-hop, and rap in particular, should be an expression of personal experiences.[52] SoCalled links this expression of self to how he began sampling from Yiddish records: "And then it struck me that I should represent myself, who I am, in this music making, so instead of sampling black music all the time or salsa music, or all these musics that people already know are funky and that have been accepted as such, I could start to reference my own culture, even though it wasn't my own culture at all, I didn't grow up with Yiddish at all."[53]

By this reasoning, if the authentic representation of self is seen as the primary agenda of hip-hop, samples of Yiddish music effect this representation, even though SoCalled only ambivalently or tentatively takes ownership of Yiddish. He nonetheless engages in a process of self-representation through it, and the universalizing processes of hip-hop seems, for SoCalled, to temper the in-group insularity of the Yiddish elements in the music.

The question of Yiddish-infused hip-hop's ability to speak to expansive rather than bounded groups of people can be further contextualized. Part of SoCalled's understanding of the relationship between hip-hop/rap and identity may be traced to his sociocultural location as a Canadian, and particularly as a resident of Montreal. Canadian hip-hop, like most global hip-hops, is appropriated for particular political and artistic agendas, particularly in expressing various kinds of localized, minority identities.[54] Though the hip-hop industry in Canada is oriented toward the United States, the social landscape of hip-hop in Canada is drastically different for reasons of geography, race, and class.[55] So-Called is rooted in and identifies strongly with Montreal and he emphasizes its ethnic-linguistic and ideological diversity as influential to his music making.[56] The particulars of Quebec hip-hop style inform his compositional choices, all of which can be heard in the two songs that I have discussed at length: multiple languages in each piece, the use of rhythms from French rap, refrains sung in a soul style, a tendency to have emerged from the suburbs and moved to the city, and a celebration of Montreal as multicultural and musically hybrid.[57]

SoCalled's choice to live in Montreal and his expressed pride in the cultural diversity of his neighborhood place him firmly within the norms of Quebec hip-hop culture, in spite of any potential insularity that using Yiddish samples brings to his music. Montreal's particular history of racial, religious, linguistic, and ethnic tensions surely also informs the reception of his work and his place in the local hip-hop scene, but SoCalled does not overtly emphasize them in relation to his own music making there. Montreal also has a uniquely vibrant history of Yiddish culture, where, in Ira Robinson's words, "Yiddish organizations appeared first and bloomed in the brightest of colours,"[58] making it a particularly fitting place as the twenty-first-century home of Yiddish hip-hop.[59]

Furthermore, because hip-hop in Canada is not overwhelmingly associated with one or another ethnic group, the idea of Yiddish hip-hop is less shocking or gimmicky than it might seem in the United States, where hip-hop is much more closely associated with the African American experience. In Canada, Yiddish represents an additional element in an already multicultural hip-hop, and SoCalled likewise claims that his use of Yiddish samples adds a previously unknown musical element to the hip-hop repertoire that can enrich and enhance the musical resources of the greater hip-hop community.[60] Conversely, klezmer musicians and Yiddish singers who collaborate with him remark on how hip-hop, through SoCalled's musical contributions, can enrich and enliven Yiddish music at large. If, in fact, as Tony Mitchell suggests, we must look outside the United States for innovation and creativity among localized and syncretic hip-hop communities,[61] perhaps the use of Yiddish samples in a hip-hop compositional process—merging the expressive force of two major global diasporas along the way—will place SoCalled's music in the midst of a new cutting edge.

Scholarly and popular sources alike speculate on the special relationship between Jewish and African American musics historically.[62] If there is a particular affinity between Jews and hip-hop, similar perhaps to the affinity between Jews and jazz as an African American expressive form,[63] then another layer of analysis is called for in making sense of hip-hop that employs Yiddish. Hip-hop does not cease to be a thoroughly African American music, no matter what cultural materials are inserted into the expansive framework of sampling, no matter how thoroughly a non-African American hip-hop artist conforms to the conventions of hip-hop musicality and sociality, and no matter whose sonic and cultural pasts are invoked. This is as true for SoCalled's hip-hop as any other, but given the long-standing relationship between Jews and African American music, it is perhaps fitting that hip-hop is the medium that makes Jewish pasts meaningful in and for the present and that hip-hop is where Jewish sensibilities of cultural loss are negotiated and Jewish nostalgia is both utilized and critiqued.

The so-called past, with all its nostalgia and ambivalence, will surely continue to play a role in Jewish life and Jewish music, and Jewish artists' engagements with these imagined and real histories will continue to find expression in new cultural forms. Hip-hop, as it continues to become a globalized and glocalized genre, affords the opportunity to interpret and reinterpret these pasts to a diverse array of local communities, and these communities in turn bring innovation and substance to hip-hop music and culture.[64] In spite of his concerns about insularity, and even as he addresses such powerful sentiments for Jewish audiences as nostalgia, longing, and anxieties over culture loss, SoCalled operates in a widening, universalizing milieu. Following his lead, we can productively reframe the conventional thinking about Yiddish hip-hop and other contemporary Yiddish musics, placing them in wider contexts that have relevance beyond just the Jewish community or Jewish scholarship. SoCalled's own expressed sentiments and his music both encourage a refreshing antiexceptionalism, in which hip-hop is hip-hop, no matter whose samples it uses and no matter whose past it reimagines and critiques.

Notes

1. In personal encounters, as a teacher in music workshops, and in non-hip-hop performance contexts, SoCalled uses his given name, Josh Dolgin; but with regard to his hip-hop music, his preference is to be referred to as SoCalled. As the scope of this essay is exclusively his hip-hop material and for the sake of consistency, I use SoCalled throughout.
2. Garry Beitel, "SoCalled and Sampling" (interview with SoCalled, 2007), accessed August 12, 2009, http://youtube.com/watch?v=nNwW-r33R1Y.
3. Wayne Marshall, "Giving Up Hip-Hop's Firstborn: A Quest for the Real after the Death of Sampling," *Callaloo* 29, no. 3 (2006): 1–25; Joseph Glenn Schloss, *Making Beats: The*

Art of Sample-Based Hip-Hop (Hanover, NH: Wesleyan University Press, 2004), 63–65. Schloss notes that unlike some other musical discourses around sampling and authenticity, hip-hop's primary concern is aesthetic rather than technical or identity driven.

4. SoCalled, interviewed by Shayn E. Smulyan, December 24, 2008. This stands in contrast to other artists, such as Psoy Korolenko and Efim Chorny, who work primarily within the Yiddish/klezmer idiom and occasionally rap in Yiddish but employ no other conventions of hip-hop.

5. SoCalled, December 24, 2008. "Mainstream" in this instance is indicated by radio airplay and venue size.

6. JDUB Records, "About JDUB," accessed August 12, 2009, http://jdubrecords.org/customPage.php?id=146.

7. SoCalled, interviewed by Shayn E. Smulyan, June 2006.

8. SoCalled, interviewed by staff, interns, and Shayn E. Smulyan, the National Yiddish Book Center, July 2006.

9. These points, as with this essay as a whole, only apply to SoCalled's career in the United States and Canada. His reception in Europe, particularly France, is much more broadly popular and less coded as Jewish. SoCalled, June 2006.

10. His albums to date, for instance, are called *The SoCalled Seder* (2005), *HipHopKhasene* (2003), and *Ghettoblaster* (2007). *Ghettoblaster* makes use of a well-worn pun on "ghetto" as simultaneously referencing impoverished, largely black, inner-city communities and the Jewish ghettos of eastern Europe. Moreover, the use of "ghettoblaster" referring to the large, portable radio and cassette players that were popular in the 1980s marks SoCalled as someone engaged with hip-hop culture and its history.

11. See, for example, Alexandra J. Wall, "Klezmer Gets a Jolt of Yo from Hip-Hop Canadian," *The Jewish News Weekly of Northern California*, http://www.jewishsf.com/content/2-0-/module/displaystory/story_id/21727/format/html/displaystory.html and Caitlin Crockard, "Hip Hop, Oy Vey!" *The Ottawa Citizen*, November, 2, 2005, accessed June 22, 2012, http://www.canada.com/ottawa/ottawacitizen/news/arts/story.html?id=547280f5-233c-429d-acbd-f261aab2aa6b.

12. I purposely avoid the term "fusion" as a descriptor of this kind of hip-hop. I believe it is misleading, because it implies equal, parallel, and symmetrical contributions from both (or all) musical-cultural elements.

13. Joseph Schloss defines sampling: "The digital recording and manipulation of sound that forms the foundation of hip-hop production. . . . In order to sample, there must be something to sample *from*. For sample-based hip-hop producers, the source is usually vinyl records." Schloss, *Making Beats*, 79.

14. SoCalled, December 24, 2008.

15. For instance, the work of Golem, the Klezmatics, Marilyn Lerner and David Wall, and King Django.

16. Tony Mitchell, "Introduction," in *Global Noise: Rap and Hip-Hop outside the USA*, ed. Tony Mitchell (Hanover, NH: Wesleyan University Press, 2001), 1–39.

17. These include nonmusical samples and extramusical sounds from the recording process, break beats, and the importation of "liveness" into recorded songs by addressing the listener directly.

18. Schloss, *Making Beats*, 10, 64.

19. Beitel, "SoCalled and Sampling"; SoCalled, June 2006, December 24, 2008.

20. SoCalled, December 24, 2008.

21. Schloss, *Making Beats*.

22. SoCalled, December 24, 2008.

23. For example, Gaby Alter, "A Musical Coat of Many Colors," *Hadassah Magazine* 87, no. 2 (2005), accessed June 12, 2012, http://www.hadassahmagazine.org/site/c.twI6LmN7IzF/b.5768613/k.C738/October_2005_Vol_87_No_2.htm.

24. Personal observation of the author, KlezKamp Yiddish Folk Arts Program, December 2008. Like many people who currently engage with Yiddish scholars, artists, and cultural activists alike, SoCalled's primary sources are textual (books, sheet music, even recordings) rather than spoken vernacular language. So, to say that he does not "speak" Yiddish is potentially misleading in the context of secular Yiddish culture. However, with regard to hip-hop and rapping and his opinion that rap should be in the vernacular, it remains a salient point.

25. SoCalled, interviewed by Shayn E. Smulyan, July 2006.

26. SoCalled, interviewed by Shayn E. Smulyan, June 5, 2007.

27. Ibid.

28. A fast-paced klezmer dance rhythm (3+3+2 or long+long+short), which in Hoffman-Watts's usage is indistinguishable from the *bulgar,* arguably the most stereotypically klezmer-sounding beat.

29. That SoCalled has some working knowledge of Yiddish without being a fluent speaker puts him in a particularly good position to utilize the occasional Yiddish loanword in English without overwhelming his listeners. Depending on the subject position of any given audience member, these insertions may be taken as clever wordplay, an appeal to insider status, or nonsensical cultural color.

30. SoCalled confirmed that the whole exchange really did occur in the studio unscripted as part of the same conversation that the song's opening outtake comes from, though this is not necessarily apparent to the listener. SoCalled, December 24, 2008.

31. For instance, "It's a fucked up institution, economic solution to socialize absolution. Hype the hetero norms. Yo, it's just ancient psychic residuals, but folks are sentimental and they'll always need their rituals. As a concept it's dated, *ketuba* outmoded and faded. Power politic-ing, nepotism, cheapest way to get related. . . . We're all so happy for you. It's just not my thingl, *Ikh bin shoyn vider singl punkt azoy vi a yingl.*"

32. This disjuncture between the words and the musical elements represents an intentional aesthetic move by SoCalled. In the making of *Ghettoblaster,* he set out to prove that unlikely combinations of musical materials could be starkly juxtaposed in ways that made for catchy and provocative songs. SoCalled, December 24, 2008.

33. Jeffery Shandler, "Postvernacular Yiddish: Language as a Performance Art," *The Drama Review* 48, no. 1 (2004): 19-43, 20.

34. SoCalled, December 24, 2008.

35. Ibid.

36. Joanna Demers, "Sampling the 1970s in Hip-Hop," *Popular Music* 22 (January 2003): 41-56.

37. Ibid.

38. SoCalled has named Lebedeff and Oysher as particularly influential. Lebedeff was a popular, comic singer of the Yiddish theater in the 1920s and 1930s, whose style and repertoire continue to be influential in the klezmer revival scene. Oysher was a cantor turned popular entertainer, recording artist, and Yiddish film star of the same era, whose voice was particularly well esteemed and whose repertoire ranged from elaborate *khazones* (cantorial pieces derived from the liturgy) to jazzy pop tunes.

39. See, for example, Ari Y. Kelman, *Station Identification: A Cultural History of Yiddish Radio in the United States* (Berkeley: University of California Press, 2009) and Henrey Sapoznik, *Klezmer: Jewish Music from Old World to Our World* (New York: Schirmer Trade Books, 2006).

40. Much of the contemporary klezmer scene has since shifted its focus toward traditional European styles and sources for inspiration and toward learning repertoire aurally, from living tradition bearers, rather than from recordings. SoCalled's reliance on old recordings for samples sets him apart from the European influence somewhat (though it comes through in other ways, such as the studio recording he does or collaboration

with klezmer musicians who employ such styles) and roots him in the American context, if only by virtue of where and when the old records were made.

41. Beitel, "SoCalled and Sampling."

42. Abigail Wood, "(De)constructing Yiddishland: Solomon and SoCalled's HipHop-Khasene," *Ethnomusicology Forum* 16, no. 2 (2007): 243–70. Wood's reading of the album as critique and commentary shows that, although his music is not divorced from regular hip-hop practice (where critique and commentary by means of historical disjuncture is the norm), it also offers a significant contribution to Yiddish expressive culture.

43. Ibid.

44. Mark Slobin, *Tenement Songs: The Popular Music of the Jewish Immigrants* (Urbana: University of Illinois Press, 1982), 58–59; Svetlana Boym, *The Future of Nostalgia* (New York: Basic Books, 2001), xiii–xvi.

45. Bikel is originally from Austria, has lived in several countries, and is a classically trained actor. In this context, to my ear, his accent sounds generically European but not strongly identifiable with any particular country or language. The speech sample used in the beginning of "(Rock the) Belz" sounds clearly preplanned and declamatory, in contrast to his speech used later in the song, which is more conversational in style.

46. SoCalled, June 5 2007. This is also in keeping with Russell Potter's claim that, in spite of anxieties about appropriation, hip-hop "is music about 'where I'm from,' and as such proposes a new kind of universality." Russell A. Potter, *Spectacular Vernaculars: Hip Hop and the Politics of Postmodernism* (Albany: State University of New York Press, 1995), 146.

47. Many thanks to Alegria and Victor Barclay for their help with the French translation.

48. Barbara Kirshenblatt-Gimblett, "Imagining Europe: The Popular Arts of American Jewish Ethnography," in *Divergent Jewish Cultures: Israel and America*, ed. Deborah Dash Moore and S. Ilan Troen (New Haven: Yale University Press, 2001), 155–91.

49. Of the ten tracks on *Ghettoblaster* with lyrics (excluding an instrumental piano piece and two songs based on a wordless, sung melody), four include Yiddish lyrics, whereas others make use of Yiddish/klezmer samples, breakbeats, melodies, and rhythms in various degrees. This represents a departure from his previous work on *HipHopkhasene* and *The SoCalled Seder* and is indicative of SoCalled's more recent goal of writing catchy pop songs that can reach a widespread audience.

50. SoCalled, June 5, 2007.

51. SoCalled, December 24, 2008.

52. SoCalled's more individual approach to hip-hop's power to represent personal experience differs from Tricia Rose's sociological interpretation of African American hip-hop as representing the collective experience of black Americans. For instance, she suggests, "Rap's stories continue to articulate the shifting terms of black marginality in contemporary American culture" (Rose, *Black Noise: Rap Music and Black Culture in Contemporary America* [Hanover, NH: Wesleyan University Press, 1994], 2–3). Yet both positions firmly place hip-hop as the expression of lived experience. There is a tension between individual and collective representations in SoCalled's hip-hop as well, wherein the Yiddish past he invokes is a collective one, but his voice as inheritor and interpreter of that past is that of an individual.

53. Beitel, "SoCalled and Sampling."

54. Mitchell, "Introduction," 2, 32.

55. According to Roger Chamberland, hip-hop in Canada was first adopted by white, middle-class youth, rather than impoverished youth of color who were hip-hop's first innovators and audience in the United States. Chamberland attributes this difference to patterns of Canadian socioeconomic geography. Roger Chamberland, "Rap in Canada: Bilingual and Multicultural," *Global Noise*, 302–26, 309. For a contrastive example of

subcultural hip-hop in Canada, see Adam Krims, *Rap Music and the Poetics of Identity* (Cambridge: Cambridge University Press, 2000).

56. SoCalled, June 5, 2007.

57. Chamberland, "Rap in Canada," 319–20.

58. Ira Robinson, Pierre Anctil, and Mervin Butovsky, eds., *An Everyday Miracle: Yiddish Culture in Montreal* (Montreal: Véhicule Press, 1990), 17.

59. See also Rebecca Margolis, *Jewish Roots, Canadian Soil: Yiddish Culture in Montreal, 1905–45* (Kingston-Montreal: McGill-Queen's University Press, 2011); and Margolis's essay in this volume.

60. SoCalled, July 2006, December 24, 2008.

61. Mitchell, "Introduction," 3.

62. See, for example, Jeffrey Melnick, *A Right to Sing the Blues: African Americans, Jews, and American Popular Song* (Cambridge: Harvard University Press, 1999); Michael Paul Rogin, *Blackface, White Noise: Jewish Immigrants in the Hollywood Melting Pot* (Berkeley: University of California Press, 1996); Schloss, *Making Beats*; Jason Tanz, "Assimilation and Its Discontents: Why Jews Love Hip-Hop (and Try So Hard to Befriend Black People)," July 17, 2007, accessed June 22, 2012, http://www.jewcy.com/feature/2007-07-17/assimilation_and_its_discontents.

63. Melnick, *Right to Sing the Blues*; dNa, "Too Sense Sunday: The Jew in Hip-Hop," December 2, 2007, http://halfricanrevolution.blogspot.com/2007/12/too-sense-sunday-jew-in-hip-hop.html.

64. Tony Mitchell suggests that localized and syncretic hip-hop outside of the United States is the major place one can find "a sense of innovation, surprise, and musical substance in hip hop culture and rap music." Mitchell, "Introduction," 3.

EPILOGUE

JEREMY DAUBER

The remarkable collection of essays that constitute *Choosing Yiddish*—wide in range, surprising in argument—suggests a series of thoughts and, perhaps, concerns to the reader familiar with the field of Yiddish studies and that of Jewish studies, its close and partially—though only partially—encompassing cousin.

A first, comforting, observation regards the works'—and their authors'—assured sense of Yiddish studies' confirmed place within the academy. Looking at the essays' rich and informative scholarly footnotes, one notices the high number of seminal and recent works in the field of Yiddish studies published by mainstream university presses and the articles on the topics cited from leading humanities journals. Such confidence stems in part from a phenomenon related to the expansion of Jewish studies more generally, transcending the traditional dominance of Jewish history and philosophy, as well as the changing foci of attention within the humanities. And Yiddish studies—in its role of providing attention to the voices of the understudied, whether that be women's, those of popular history and culture or those of the less attended aspects of elite performance—has increasingly served as a complementary corrective to the crucial but at times overly grand narratives set by the pathbreakers in the field. Many of this book's essays, for example, take on a central tenet of the American Jewish historiographical story, and convincingly shake it at its foundations. Indeed, the authors all seem to be sharing in the same excitement that animated the founders of modern Yiddish scholarship almost a century ago—not just cultural autonomy or Nationalist sentiment or aesthetic pride but also the scholar's excitement in *getting the story right*, in uncovering or unlocking or explaining something that did not make sense before or—even more thrilling—that did make sense but was wrong, truthy (to use a more contemporary locution), but not true.

This corrective importance gets to an inherent (though fruitful) blurriness at the heart of Yiddish studies: its methodological interdisciplinarity or, perhaps, its multidisciplinarity. That is, many of these essays fruitfully cross boundaries to make their points: they are smart historical scholarship combined with acute literary analysis combined with sociological insight, and the works benefit from these approaches. It is worth noting, though, that if the essays' methodologies are newly forward looking, their concerns—and certainly their categories of concern—are much less so. The scholars who founded YIVO might not have envisioned scholars taking on Yiddish studies in universities across the United States (though the brace of nuanced essays in this volume on Weinreich and YIVO show us that it may not have been as inconceivable as once supposed). And one can only imagine their perspective on the resurgence of Yiddish activity in twenty-first-century Germany, more than a half-century after the defeat of the movement that murdered so many of their scholars and readers and forced their relocation, or on the complex resolution of the great language war between Hebraists and Yiddishists in a State of Israel. But they certainly *could* have predicted the kinds of topics that have attracted twenty-first-century scholarly attention: Yiddish writing as a response to apocalypse; the effects of urban life on Yiddish culture; high and low culture in Yiddish, and folk art, like music, particularly with respect to the interplay between Jewish and non-Jewish culture; the nature of American Yiddish life, and the relationship between Yiddish and Hebrew. It is not difficult to imagine articles on any of these topics appearing in the first series of *YIVO-bleter*. This is, of course, only another way of saying that the best scholarship is attuned to the concerns of the subject studied.

Still, the nature of the disciplinary departmental structure of most universities means that, methodologically speaking, fidelity must be sworn primarily to one particular approach. It is a sign of the shift in the field that only one or two of the pieces could be firmly located in the first, classic home for Yiddish studies in the American academy, which was linguistics. In my reading, most of the essays here would belong more firmly in faculty publications listed by history or comparative literature departments. This may, at times of economic stress, lead to problems: outside of departments specifically dedicated to Jewish studies, with humanities under assault by the force of narrowly defined utilitarian thinking, will there be room to choose Yiddish? With this in mind, then, where will Yiddish studies, gaining its power (as Anita Norich eloquently suggests) from the tension of being central and not-central, locate itself in a university structure that barely has room for what it considers to be essential?

Jeffrey Shandler—a touchstone author for many of the contributors to this book, and rightly so—has convincingly argued for the robustness of a postvernacular model of Yiddish, with its own dignity and merit, and just as that sort of Yiddish increasingly permeates American Jewish culture on new terms, it may be that Yiddish studies, as a mode rather than a specific corpus or core area of study, will be a crucial part of many scholars' work and a valued part of others'. Such postvernacular scholarship, to coin an awkward phrase, might end up choosing and using Yiddish in ways very different from those in previous decades—so much so, in fact, that the ideologizing resonances inherently associated with "choosing" become entirely vitiated and that studying Yiddish in many subfields becomes simply de rigueur, as French and German often are in certain areas of graduate studies to this day. Whether one views this as victory, defeat, or something other probably says a good deal about the individual's perspective on the term "Yiddish studies" itself.

Overall, however, for those who choose their topics of study, or objects of aesthetic appreciation, or matters of interest, the chosen, multifaceted item is invariably viewed both as the sum of its varying parts and as a complete item. Which is to say that for true, responsible, rigorous scholars like the ones whose work is represented here, the choice to choose Yiddish is inseparable from a multitude of other choices—but, on the evidence of the works here, a choice that will have increasingly significant impact in the years and decades to come.

CONTRIBUTORS

ELA BAUER is the chair of the Department of Communication and Film at the Seminar Ha-Kibbutzim College in Tel Aviv. In addition, she teaches in the Jewish History Department at Haifa University and is the academic coordinator of the Posen Research Forum at Haifa University. Her academic interests include the history and culture of Polish Jewry and the history of the Jewish press.

SARAH BUNIN BENOR is an associate professor of contemporary Jewish studies at Hebrew Union College, Jewish Institute of Religion (Los Angeles). She received her PhD in linguistics from Stanford University in 2004, and she writes and teaches about Jewish language, culture, and community. She is the author of *Becoming Frum: How Newcomers Learn the Language and Culture of Orthodox Judaism* (Rutgers University Press, 2012).

JEREMY DAUBER is the Atran Associate Professor of Yiddish Language, Literature, and Culture at Columbia University, where he directs its Institute for Israel and Jewish Studies. He is the coeditor of *Prooftexts: A Journal of Jewish Literary History*. His most recent book, *In the Demon's Bedroom: Yiddish Literature and the Early Modern*, was published in 2010 by Yale University Press.

HASIA DINER is the Paul S. and Sylvia Steinberg Professor of American Jewish History, a professor of Hebrew and Judaic studies and history, and the director of the Goldstein-Goren Center for American Jewish History at New York University. Her most recent book, *We Remember with Reverence and Love: American Jews and the Myth of Silence after the Holocaust, 1945–1962* (New York University

Press, 2009), won the 2010 National Jewish Book Award in the category of American Jewish studies. Her past titles include *The Jews of the United States: 1654–2000* (University of California Press, 2004), *Hungering for America: Italian, Irish, and Jewish Foodways in the Age of Migration* (Harvard University Press, 2001), and *Lower East Side Memories: The Jewish Place in America* (Princeton University Press, 2000).

GENNADY ESTRAIKH is an associate professor of Yiddish studies in the Skirball Department of Hebrew and Judaic Studies at New York University. His most recent books are *Yiddish in Weimar Berlin: At the Crossroads of Diaspora Politics and Culture* (Legenda, 2010), *Yiddish and the Cold War* (Legenda, 2008), and *In Harness: Yiddish Writers' Romance with Communism* (Syracuse University Press, 2005).

JORDAN FINKIN is the Weinstock Visiting Lecturer on Jewish Studies at Harvard University. Specializing in modern and modernist Hebrew and Yiddish literature, his research has appeared in a number of venues, including *The Jewish Quarterly Review*, *Prooftexts*, and *Modernism/Modernity*. His book, *A Rhetorical Conversation: Jewish Discourse in Modern Yiddish Literature* (Pennsylvania State University Press, 2010), recently appeared, and he is currently at work on a book about the use of time and space in modernist Jewish literature.

SHIRI GOREN is a senior lector in modern Hebrew at Yale University. Her areas of specialization include modern Hebrew literature, Israeli culture, Yiddish literature, the novel, and film theory. She received her PhD from New York University in 2011 and is currently working on the monograph *Creative Resistance: Literary Interventions in the Israeli-Palestinian Conflict*, which explores how violence affects real and imagined spaces in Israel of recent years. Goren's latest article, on Israeli author Gabriela Avigur-Rotem, appears in the anthology *Narratives of Dissent: War in Contemporary Israeli Arts and Culture*, edited by Rachel S. Harris and Ranen Omer-Sherman (Wayne State University Press, 2012).

DARA HORN received her PhD in comparative literature from Harvard University in 2006, where she studied Hebrew and Yiddish. Her first novel, *In the Image* (W. W. Norton, 2003), received a National Jewish Book Award, the Edward Lewis Wallant Award, and the Reform Judaism Fiction Prize. Her second novel, *The World to Come* (W. W. Norton, 2006), received the 2006 National Jewish Book Award for Fiction and the 2007 Harold U. Ribalow Prize, was selected as an editors' choice in the *New York Times Book Review* and as one of the Best Books of 2006 by *The San Francisco Chronicle*, and has been translated into eleven languages. Her most recent novel, *All Other Nights* (W. W. Norton, 2009), was selected as an editors' choice in the *New York Times Book Review*.

ADRIANA X. JACOBS is currently an American Council of Learned Societies New Faculty Fellow at Yale University in the Department of Comparative Literature and the Program in Judaic Studies. Her areas of specialization include modern Hebrew and Israeli poetry, translation studies, and comparative poetics. At present, she is working on a book manuscript that examines how translation practices and politics have shaped modern Hebrew and Israeli poetry. Her articles, reviews, and translations have appeared in several academic and literary publications, including *Prooftexts: A Journal of Jewish Literary History*, *Metamorphoses*, and *Zeek: A Jewish Journal of Thought and Culture*.

ARI Y. KELMAN is the Jim Joseph Professor of Education and Jewish Studies at Stanford University, where he is also an affiliate of the Taube Center for Jewish Studies and the American Studies Program. He is the author of *Station Identification: A Cultural History of Yiddish Radio* (University of California Press, 2009) and the editor of *Is Diss a System? A Milt Gross Comic Reader* (New York University Press, 2009). He is also the coauthor of *Transforming Synagogues from Functional to Visionary* (The Alban Institute, 2010). Together with Steven M. Cohen, he has coauthored numerous influential studies of contemporary Jewish identity and culture.

BARBARA KIRSHENBLATT-GIMBLETT is university professor and professor of performance studies at New York University. She is currently leading the Core Exhibition Planning Team for the Museum of the History of Polish Jews on the site of the former Warsaw ghetto. Her previous books include *They Called Me Mayer July: Painted Memories of Jewish Life in Poland before the Holocaust* (with Mayer Kirshenblatt; University of California Press, 2007) and *Image before My Eyes: A Photographic History of Jewish Life in Poland, 1864-1939* (with Lucjan Dobroszycki; Schocken, 1994).

REBECCA KOBRIN is the Russell and Bettina Knapp Assistant Professor of American Jewish History at Columbia University. Her book, *Jewish Bialystok and Its Diaspora* (Indiana University Press, 2010), was a finalist in the National Jewish Book Award and earned her the Sandra and Fred Rose Young Historian's Award from the Center for Jewish History. She is currently working on a book concerning failed Jewish immigrant bankers and is the editor of two forthcoming collections, *Chosen Capital: The Jewish Encounter with American Capitalism, 1850-1950* (Rutgers University Press, 2012) and *Purchasing Power: The Economic Dimensions of the Jewish Past* (University of Pennsylvania Press, 2013).

JOSH LAMBERT is the academic director of the National Yiddish Book Center and a visiting assistant professor of English at the University of Massachusetts, Amherst. In 2009, he received his PhD from the University of Michigan. He is the author of *American Jewish Fiction: A JPS Guide* (Jewish Publication Society, 2009) and a contributing editor to *Tablet*. His essays have appeared or are forthcoming in *Cinema Journal, Contemporary Literature, Modernism/Modernity,* and *The Jewish Graphic Novel.* He is currently working on a book titled *Unclean Lips: Obscenity, Jews, and American Literature.*

BARBARA MANN is an associate professor of Jewish literature and serves as the Simon H. Fabian Chair in Hebrew Literature at the Jewish Theological Seminary. Her areas of expertise include Israeli and Jewish literature, cultural studies, modern poetry, urban studies, literary modernism, and the fine arts. Dr. Mann is currently writing a book about conceptions of space and place in modern Jewish studies. She is the author of *A Place in History: Modernism, Tel Aviv and the Creation of Jewish Urban Space* (Stanford University Press, 2005) in addition to numerous scholarly articles. She is coeditor-in-chief of *Prooftexts: A Journal of Jewish Literary History.*

REBECCA MARGOLIS is an associate professor at the University of Ottawa's Vered Jewish Canadian Studies Program. She is the author of *Jewish Roots, Canadian Soil: Yiddish Culture in Montreal, 1905-1945* (McGill-Queens University Press, 2011). She is currently working on a study of how Canadians responded to the Holocaust within as well as outside the Yiddish milieu.

TONY MICHELS is the George L. Mosse Associate Professor of American Jewish History at the University of Wisconsin, Madison. He is author of *A Fire in Their Hearts: Yiddish Socialists in New York* (Harvard University Press, 2005) and editor of *Jewish Radicals: A Documentary History* (NYU Press, forthcoming in 2012).

ANITA NORICH, a professor of English and Judaic studies at the University of Michigan, teaches, lectures, and publishes on a range of topics concerning Yiddish language and literature, modern Jewish culture, Jewish American literature, and Holocaust literature. She is the author of *Discovering Exile: Yiddish and Jewish American Literature in America during the Holocaust* (Stanford University Press, 2007) and *The Homeless Imagination in the Fiction of Israel Joshua Singer* (Indiana University Press, 1991). She coedited *Jewish Literatures and Cultures: Context and Intertext* (Brown University, 2008) and *Gender and Text in Modern Hebrew and Yiddish Literature* (Harvard University Press, 1992).

SHACHAR PINSKER is an associate professor of Hebrew literature and culture at the University of Michigan. He is the author of *Literary Passports: The Making of Modernist Hebrew Fiction in Europe* (Stanford University Press, 2010) and the coeditor of *Hebrew, Gender, and Modernity* (University of Maryland Press, 2007). He has published articles and chapters dealing with Hebrew, Jewish, and Israeli literature and culture. He is currently working on a book titled *To Write in a*

Silent Language: Yiddish as a Double-Agent in Israeli Literature and Culture and a book on urban cafés and modern Jewish culture.

EDWARD PORTNOY received his PhD from the Jewish Theological Seminary, where he completed a dissertation on cartoons of the Yiddish press. He also holds an MA in Yiddish studies from Columbia, having written on artists/writers Zuni Maud and Yosl Cutler. His articles on Jewish popular culture phenomena have appeared in *The Drama Review, Polin,* and *The International Journal of Comic Art.* In addition to speaking on Jewish popular culture throughout Europe and North America, he has consulted on museum exhibits at the Museum of the City of New York, the Musée d'Art et d'Histoire du Judaïsme in Paris, and the Joods Historisch Museum in Amsterdam.

HANNAH S. PRESSMAN is a PhD candidate in modern Hebrew literature at New York University, where she received her MPhil in Jewish studies as well as the Advanced Certificate in poetics and theory. She served as the 2007–2008 Hazel D. Cole Fellow in Jewish Studies at the University of Washington, where she is now an affiliate instructor for the Stroum Jewish Studies Program.

LARA RABINOVITCH received her PhD in modern Jewish history from New York University in 2012. She is working on a book project about "Little Rumania" and the origin of pastrami in early twentieth-century New York. As managing editor for two years, she helped launch McGill University's *CuiZine: The Journal of Canadian Food Cultures/Revue des cultures culinaires au Canada* in 2008.

JEFFREY SHANDLER is a professor of Jewish studies at Rutgers University. He received a PhD in Yiddish studies from Columbia University. His most recent books include *Jews, God, and Videotape: Religion and Media in America* (New York University Press, 2009) and *Adventures in Yiddishland: Postvernacular Language and Culture* (University of California Press, 2005). He is also coauthor and coeditor of *Entertaining America: Jews, Movies, and Broadcasting* (Princeton University Press, 2003) and translator of *Emil and Karl,* a Holocaust novel for young readers by Yankev Glatshteyn (Roaring Brook Press, 2006).

ANNA SHTERNSHIS is the Al and Malka Green Associate Professor in Yiddish Language and Literature at the University of Toronto. She is the author of *Soviet and Kosher: Jewish Popular Culture in the Soviet Union, 1923–1939* (Indiana University Press, 2006) and a number of articles on Soviet and post-Soviet-Jewish popular culture in, for example, *The Journal of Jewish Identities* and *Jewish Social Studies.*

SHAYN E. SMULYAN is a PhD candidate in ethnomusicology at Brown University. Smulyan studies the performance practices and communicative strategies of contemporary Yiddish singers.

ZEHAVIT STERN is the Haase Fellow in Eastern European Jewish Civilization at the University of Oxford. In 2011, she received her PhD in Jewish Studies from the University of California, Berkeley, and the Graduate Theological Union, and her dissertation was titled "From Jester to Gesture: Eastern European Jewish Culture and the Re-imagination of Folk Performance." She also holds an MA in Yiddish culture from the Hebrew University, where she examined Yiddish film melodrama.

ESTER-BASYA (ASYA) VAISMAN is currently a visiting scholar working on the Archives of Historical and Ethnographic Yiddish Memories project at Indiana University. After receiving her PhD in Yiddish language and culture from Harvard in 2009, she spent a year at the University of Washington in Seattle as the Hazel D. Cole Postdoctoral Fellow. She has published articles on the singing practices of contemporary Hasidic women, Yiddish folksongs, and the history of Yiddish theater in the Soviet Union.

KALMAN WEISER is the Silber Family Professor of Modern Jewish Studies at York University. He is the coeditor of *Czernowitz at 100: The First Yiddish Language Conference in Historical Perspective* (Lexington Books, 2010) and the author of *Jewish People, Yiddish Nation: Noah Prylucki and the Folkists in Poland* (University of Toronto Press, 2011).

JENNIFER YOUNG was in 2011-12 the Dr. Sophie Bookhalter Graduate Research Fellow at the Center for Jewish History in New York. She is completing a dissertation at New York University on American Jewish communists and the politics of ethnic culture from 1930-56. She also works as an educator and researcher for the Lower East Side Tenement Museum.

GERBEN ZAAGSMA studies modern history and Yiddish studies and holds a PhD from the European University Institute in Florence, Italy (2008). He has also published work on the digital humanities and is particularly interested in the methodological implications of using new technologies in historical research and writing. He currently works at the Huygens Institute for the History of the Netherlands in The Hague.

INDEX

Moyshe Kulbak - Yiddish Novel
The Zelmenyaners'